TARNISHED VICTORY

BOOKS BY WILLIAM MARVEL

The First New Hampshire Battery, 1861–1865

*Race of the Soil: The Ninth New Hampshire
Regiment in the Civil War*

The Battle of the Crater (Petersburg Campaign)
(cowritten with Michael Cavanaugh)

Burnside

*The Battles for Saltville:
Southwest Virginia in the Civil War*

Andersonville: The Last Depot

*The Alabama and the Kearsarge:
The Sailor's Civil War*

A Place Called Appomattox

The Monitor Chronicles: One Sailor's Account
(editor)

Lee's Last Retreat: The Flight to Appomattox

Mr. Lincoln Goes to War

Lincoln's Darkest Year: The War in 1862

*The Great Task Remaining:
The Third Year of Lincoln's War*

Tarnished Victory: Finishing Lincoln's War

TARNISHED VICTORY

Finishing Lincoln's War

William Marvel

Houghton Mifflin Harcourt
BOSTON • NEW YORK
2011

For information about permission to reproduce selections from this book,
write to Permissions, Houghton Mifflin Harcourt Publishing Company,
215 Park Avenue South, New York, New York 10003.

www.hmhbooks.com

Library of Congress Cataloging-in-Publication Data
Marvel, William.
Tarnished victory : finishing Lincoln's war / William Marvel.
p. cm.
ISBN 978-0-547-42806-2
1. United States — History — Civil War, 1861–1865 — Campaigns.
2. Lincoln, Abraham, 1809–1865 — Military leadership.
I. Title.
E470.M38 2011
973.7′3 — dc22   2011009156

Book design by Melissa Lotfy

Maps by Catherine Schneider

PRINTED IN THE UNITED STATES OF AMERICA

DOC 10 9 8 7 6 5 4 3 2 1

To the camaraderie of two boys
who fended off many a Yankee charge
from behind South Conway's stone walls
in that memorable summer of 1961

Contents

List of Illustrations and Maps

All illustrations courtesy of the Library of Congress unless otherwise credited.

MAPS
All maps are by Catherine Schneider.

Preface

Writing late in April of 1864 to his mother, back in Confederate Texas, Major Thomas Goree reminded her, "God has certainly blessed our armies this year. Whenever we have met the enemy . . . the victory has been ours, with apparently very little effort on our part." He listed seven states where Southern arms could claim recent triumphs. Of the actions he alluded to, only the repulse of forty thousand Union soldiers on Louisiana's Red River involved what would have been considered significant fighting and casualties as the fourth year of the Civil War began, but Goree assured his mother that all his comrades in Robert E. Lee's army shared his "great confidence" that peace and independence would soon be theirs.[1] Wishful thinking and exaggerated accounts of minor exploits helped to maintain or restore such confidence for many loyal Confederate citizens and soldiers that spring, but even without such artificial stimuli a genuine conviction survived in the seceded states that the battle would ultimately be won. A comprehensive examination of the military situation, or the condition of Southern agricultural and industrial systems, might have fractured the foundations of that faith, but such examinations were not readily conducted, and in any case faith often persists in the face of the most contradictory evidence.

Despite signal Union victories at Gettysburg, Vicksburg, and Chattanooga in the second half of 1863, Confederate confidence still leaned heavily on the expectation of defeating Union armies in the field. Major Goree had seen more of the winning side of the war, even during a season in the Western theater, where rebel armies routinely failed, and experience allowed him to imagine that General Lee could save the new nation by destroying a Union army roughly twice the size of his own. That dream

dissipated through the spring and summer of 1864, as the principal armies in Virginia and Georgia fell steadily backward under the pressure of
greater numbers and Ulysses Grant's coordinated grand strategy, losing
both the tactical initiative and more soldiers than they could ever replace.
Thereafter, rebel hopes lay more in endurance than in military prowess,
with much emphasis on the 1864 presidential election.

North and South, the campaign to unseat Abraham Lincoln was
viewed with equal exaggeration as an expression of the Northern people's
readiness to give up the fight. On that assumption, ardent Confederates
hoped he would be cast from office, and with a war for the national des-
tiny in the balance President Lincoln came much closer to that fate than
his ten-point margin of the popular vote seemed to suggest. It was a
measure of dissatisfaction with the administration's war, or wartime policies, that Lincoln's Democratic opponent, George McClellan, won enough
popular votes to have secured a majority of the electoral college, had they
been distributed a little differently. When Lincoln survived the election,
stubborn advocates of Southern independence could cling only to the
prospect of holding out until the next one, in 1868, but a surprising number of rebels in and out of uniform embraced that daunting determination.

Belief in both Confederate military capacity and Southern obstinacy
flourished in the loyal states, too, as the great armies heaved from their
winter's slumber and swarmed toward each other for a fourth bloody year.
As firm a supporter of forcible reunion as the affluent New Yorker George
Templeton Strong sensed a perilous degree of impatience with the economic and human cost of a war that multitudes considered unwinnable,
or not worth pursuing. Writing in the wake of the Union disasters hailed
by Major Goree, Strong feared overwhelming public outrage at anything
short of quick and complete success on the battlefield. While the progress
of the spring campaigns did not constitute decisive success, it did post-
pone any crescendo of complaint, but when the war bogged down at midsummer the cry for peace again rose high and clear above the fray. Defeat,
through frustration and discouragement, seemed possible until near the
very end. Yankee soldiers and newspapers described increasingly numerous signs of imminent Confederate collapse after the November election,
but the administration's friends had been retailing similar observations
for three years, crippling the credibility of such claims, and many in the
North doubted that the South could ever be beaten. While Union cavalry
and William Sherman's relentless infantry pushed the remnants of rebel
armies all over the rest of the map, Lee's ragged divisions kept those
doubts alive by occasionally trouncing Grant's troops in Virginia, embar-

rassing the vain and aggressive Phil Sheridan as late as ten days prior to the surrender at Appomattox.[2]

Defeatism attracts a particular opprobrium in wartime, as though anything less than a willingness to fight to the death amounts to treason, but by the spring of 1864 some of the most loyal supporters of Lincoln and his war began to show subtle evidence of the ennui that long contests inevitably breed. The politically supportive father of one conscientious soldier applauded tales of widespread reenlistment among the Union army's veterans, but he revealed a disposition to avoid any more sacrifices of his own, if possible: he urged his own son not to sign up for another term, and to accept a discharge before his first enlistment expired, if the opportunity offered. The wife of one of the most senior generals in the U.S. Army wondered what good could possibly come of all the bloodletting. Ten days before Major Goree wrote his optimistic view of Confederate prospects, the commanding general of the Army of the Potomac admitted to his wife that he sometimes felt "very despondent" about the war ever ending, or of coming out of it alive. That April, even President Lincoln seemed to recognize that the war had become a liability, for which he sought to escape political responsibility.[3]

The intensity of the exhilaration, dejection, and uncertainty felt by those who witnessed the worst of all American conflicts is often diminished in the telling, and especially in those stage-by-stage analyses that usually follow a predictable if spasmodic pattern of gradual Union dominance. A chronological perspective affords a better view of the degree of pessimism and opposition that infected the Northern population, as well as a better understanding of why it existed. This book concludes a four-volume history of the Civil War that began with *Mr. Lincoln Goes to War*, each volume of which encompasses a thirteen-month segment, beginning just before South Carolina militia fired the first shot at the *Star of the West* and ending with the Grand Review, a few days after the war's final volley had been delivered in faraway Texas.

Most multivolume histories of the war have tended to emphasize the more attractive elements of the story — commemorating the abundant heroism, celebrating the restoration of the Union, and hailing the eradication of slavery. Those works frequently overlook that much of the heroism was wasted by military ineptitude and political perfidy; they usually ignore that the restored Union was no longer a voluntary community, and forget that the war did not really eradicate human bondage. Although none of those historians do, or could, deny the tragedy of the conflict, neither do any allow it to cloud the overall theme of glorious triumph. Yet it would be difficult to imagine a more inefficient and undesirable path to the original goal of reunion, or to the subsequent aim of emancipation. Because the leaders of that period chose to address their differences with the sword, it is now impossible to know with any certainty whether, sometime between the Civil War of the 1860s and the civil rights struggle of the 1960s, those issues might not have been resolved more satisfactorily, less acrimoniously, and without resort to such an orgy of violence. Neither, however, can it be confidently claimed — although many seem to believe as much — that the actors of that day took the best, or only, courses available to them.

Intolerant nationalism made it dangerous to speak against going to war in the days following Fort Sumter, and that necessarily muted the volume of opposition to coercion, but a vocal minority of Northerners nevertheless denounced Lincoln's decision to fight. On May 4, 1861, while militia and volunteers gathered in Washington in response to the first call for troops, the *Democratic Standard* of Concord, New Hampshire, warned its readers that the country was diving headlong into something much worse than anyone anticipated. "When our land is filled with widows and orphans," wrote the editor, "and our homes [are] draped in mourning as they will be in two short years, and we then find our brothers of the same race still unconquered, all will be for peace." Those prophetic words went unheeded, but not unpunished, and three months later the office of the *Democratic Standard* was destroyed by a Unionist mob led by some of the state's returning ninety-day heroes.[4] The prudent scoffed at the common belief in a quick triumph over supposedly halfhearted rebels, warning that victory would require vast armies and years of bloody struggle. Some added that, even if Union forces prevailed in such a cataclysm, it would take decades of military occupation to reconcile Southerners to reunion by force, and in fact the additional postwar demands for immediate emancipation and black suffrage made that prediction especially accurate. As so often happens, the determination to win the peace fell far short of the enthusiasm for going to war, and the victors finally settled for a sullen reunion only by sacrificing the freedmen to a reconstructed version of slavery.

PART I

LIKE SNOWS THE CAMPS
ON SOUTHERN HILLS

1

Inscription Rude in Virginia's Woods

❦ OLD YANKEES WOULD remember the spring of 1864 as a phenomenal sugaring season. In the Androscoggin Valley of western Maine, Edgar Powers tapped the trunks of 118 maples on March 9, and by April 8 he had boiled down 379 pounds of sugar and syrup, despite one cold week when no sap ran. April 11 brought a heavy, wet snowstorm that covered most of New England, and more fell in the third week of the month. New Englanders believed that snow would prolong the run, and indeed farmers in southern New Hampshire were still sugaring off past the middle of April. On the upper reaches of Vermont's West River it was nearly May before they began taking down their buckets.[1]

Two thousand miles to the west, where the Missouri River found its source in the shadows of the Bitterroot Mountains, the scattered residents of what would soon become Montana Territory also saw unseasonable cold and late snow. They, too, had had a profitable season, however, and many of the miners were preparing to cross over the Rockies on the long road back to civilization as soon as the weather broke, taking their accumulated gold where it could buy so much more than in the costly boomtowns of Virginia City and Bannack. Others turned their sights several hundred miles north, to the Kootenai country of Idaho, where men were rumored to be sifting as much as six pounds of gold a day from their claims. Such riches lured migrants up the big river by the hundreds. Down in the lower corner of Dakota Territory, entrepreneurs worked hard to assure that the Missouri remained the dominant route to the gold fields; scoffing at the notion of a long road over the prairie from Saint Paul, they lobbied the government for a string of forts to protect the pilgrims who would buy their last load of supplies from Yankton merchants.

Three thousand mounted volunteers from Iowa, Minnesota, and the territories gathered at Sioux City that spring to satisfy those constituents, and Brigadier General Alfred Sully came up from Saint Louis to lead them against the Sioux in and beyond the Black Hills.[2]

This Sully, a West Point graduate and the son of a renowned portrait painter, had come out to the Indian country after a contretemps in the East the previous spring, in which his superiors disliked his handling of a mutiny. He had served in the West before, but most of the troopers in his new brigade had not, and had never dreamed that they would. The vast majority of them had enlisted under the expectation (which some newspapermen mistook for a desire) that they would go south to fight the Confederate army or occupy captured territory in the Southern states. Low water kept the expedition on the Iowa side of the river weeks longer than anyone had anticipated; by the time Sully started into Dakota Territory at the end of spring, he was fielding reports of raids by the "warlike Uncpapas," who were so brazen as to demand compensation for the buffalo and timber taken from their lands to feed white settlers and Missouri River steamboat furnaces. When he finally passed Fort Pierre, Sully found the Hunkpapas and other Sioux holding ominous tribal conventicles.[3]

The labors and tribulations of Sully's command escaped the notice of the rest of the country, except for those few with an immediate relative in the gold fields or the frontier army. From New England to the Continental Divide and beyond, the Southern rebellion occupied most people's minds to one degree or another that sodden spring. On the upper Missouri the war with the Confederates posed a more hypothetical interest, for so many men from that sparsely settled expanse had volunteered to fight Indians that no draft ever intruded on the territories. That — and the hope for government troops to encourage the emigrant trade their way — may have contributed to the fervent editorial support that Abraham Lincoln and his war enjoyed in that region. More evidence of dissent surfaced from the Mississippi eastward, where men as old as forty-five stood a good chance of being forced into the contest, and even those who brayed loudest for aggressive war often strove to stay clear of the fighting themselves.[4]

"*I do not want to go,*" insisted Judson Bemis, a Saint Louis physician who very much wanted to see the Confederacy crushed, and who had made so much money the previous year that his income tax assessment alone exceeded three times the annual pay of a Union soldier.[5] He could afford the price of a substitute or commutation if he were drafted, but those of less means than the doctor often cherished less ardor for the war than he, and had to devise other methods of avoiding service. The young men in one Ohio family simply scattered, keeping a step ahead of the enrollment officers or evading them completely. "I shant go if there is any Honest way of getting Out of it," one of them informed his father, and constant travel seemed as honest a method as any: he drifted across Iowa and into Nebraska, while one of his brothers fled to Canada West.[6]

Conscription now worked its way inexorably from the White House to the family parlor. President Lincoln issued a call for troops in the hundreds of thousands, and the provost marshal general apportioned the magic figure among the states, according to population. The state's quota was further divided among the congressional districts, each of which had its own district provost marshal, who calculated how many men each city and town owed the government. Some corners of the country still harbored plenty of men old enough or young enough to join the army, but most regions had bitten deeply into that cohort, and many had already recruited everyone who was willing. A scarcity of farm hands impeded the planting of corn north of the Ohio, and an imminent draft threatened to take the few able men who would have remained to make the harvest.[7]

In February the president had called for half a million more troops, who were to be drafted if they failed to come voluntarily. Just as that call came due, in the middle of March, he issued a supplementary order for another two hundred thousand, but at the same time he extended the deadline to April 15, and eventually to May 1. That initiated another round of frantic public meetings that were intended either to attract recruits through patriotic allure or raise money to pique more mercenary spirits. Those rallies persisted until each town's draft quota was met, or until the draft lottery was actually held, after which most municipalities turned their fundraising energies toward finding willing substitutes for those citizens whose names had been drawn. Apprehension predominated among the men who were left as the first of May approached, and afterward a pervasive sadness settled over some communities because so many had been selected, but at this stage of the war barely one drafted man out of twenty-five ever submitted to actual service: the rest either were exempted, paid commutation, or hired substitutes. Most who could not escape by physical disability or economic hardship chose to pay the $300 commutation fee, which freed them from service unless and until they were drafted again, but thousands paid substantially more to hire three-year substitutes, who protected their principals from conscription for the length of their enlistments even if they died or deserted.[8]

Even with a clear majority of civilians shrinking from military service, recruiting still satisfied much of the president's spring appeal. Tens of thousands of veterans kept their old regiments alive by reenlisting, and entirely new military organizations were springing to life from Maine to Nebraska — for Lincoln's War Department, unlike the one in Richmond, always relied heavily on the politically attractive but militarily inefficient habit of raising fresh regiments from scratch. A $300 federal bounty, an additional $100 bounty for veterans, and offers of several hundred dollars per man from towns and cities went a long way toward replenishing some of the depleted old regiments as well as filling new ones. Edgar Powers considered enlisting that spring, while he boiled maple syrup on his father's farm. He was about to turn twenty-one, and such generous bounties had been spoken of that the notion caught his fancy, so he wrote to an acquaintance who might know of a good opportunity. Maine was still trying to fill up two new regiments of infantry, but the corner of Oxford County where Powers lived was a hard place to make the land pay, and fat bounties had allowed most nearby towns to secure all their required volunteers already. Once a town completed its quota the residents' immediate danger of being drafted disappeared, and so did those alluring local bounties, so young Powers lost interest accordingly. Elisha Cowan, another Maine bachelor who had migrated to Minnesota, anticipated that he would be drafted anyway, so rather than miss out on the volunteer's windfall he enlisted for the federal bounty and a municipal offer of $140, going directly to guerrilla country in Arkansas.[9]

Chauncey Hill had also come to Minnesota from the East. He had just married a girl barely eighteen years old, the daughter of other westering pilgrims, but the promise of a cash stake persuaded him to volunteer late in the winter. Before he left for Fort Snelling he and his beloved Sarah had their photograph taken together, but so dismal did the impending separation leave them that when the plates were developed she complained that they both looked "mad." She begged him to come home one more time before he started down the Mississippi to his regiment, but so frequently did recruits slip away with their bounty money that such furloughs were seldom granted anymore; the last she saw of him was an imperfect ambrotype he sent her from the fort, showing his beard spilling out over his new uniform. When he boarded the steamboat for Saint Louis to join his regiment, neither he nor she yet knew that he had left her with child.[10]

Since the beginning of the war, military pay and growing enlistment bounties had appealed to men strapped for cash, luring the unemployed and the unemployable: grey-haired privates who had completed their sixth decades were not unknown in the Union army, for their labor could seldom bring them as much as their willingness to wear a uniform. The pecuniary considerations also amplified the attraction for teenaged boys who saw glory and adventure in the engravings of the illustrated newspapers. Acute poverty struck the family of Henry Van Deusen, of Farmington, Wisconsin, when he fell gravely ill, and his frail young son,

Edward, solved that problem by enlisting in one of the new regiments in camp at Madison. Before his regiment departed for Washington, at the end of April, Edward was able to give his parents more money than his father and siblings would earn all year, even with only a portion of his federal bounty.[11]

The younger the boy, the more plaintively he begged to enlist, and the army had begun taking them as young as sixteen, with consent. The accumulated bounties seemed to offer profound wealth to those lads, who little understood the cost of living — with or without wartime inflation. They often bartered that windfall for parental permission, and sometimes for the additional aid of perjury, in the case of a son who was only fourteen or fifteen. By the third year of fighting, the War Department had established specific rules for accepting soldiers under eighteen, and by the fourth year those rules were being stiffened, although recruiters were paying less heed to them than ever.[12]

The youngest recruits suffered the acute shortsightedness of youth, usually failing to consider the progress of the war, and whether their sacrifice might be wasted: for that matter, most of them regarded it as less of a sacrifice than as a grand opportunity. No such myopia affected adults who read the newspapers, like Dr. Bemis in Saint Louis, whose admitted disappointment with the prosecution of the war may have contributed to his unwillingness to participate in an endeavor he endorsed so heartily. George Templeton Strong, a comfortably situated New York City lawyer near the upper limits of draft age, never had to fear conscription, because of his wealth; neither did he ever even consider the possibility of volunteering for military service, as much as he hoped for success in the field, and his disdain may also have resulted from oscillating confidence in the triumph of Union arms. To the exasperation of the soldiers who would pay the price for either victory or defeat, such parlor patriots as Bemis and Strong wailed privately for some decisive action by the armies, and newspaper editors made those plaints public.[13]

In the offices at Washington and in tents at the headquarters of the various armies, clerks transcribed the orders that would provide that action. Reenlisted veterans returned from their furloughs, and men who had secured comfortable details or beds in army hospitals were sent back to their regiments. New regiments, full of men who had felt the chill of conscription and the thrill of bounty money, came down in fresh blue uniforms from New England, Indiana, and Wisconsin to report for duty in Washington, Nashville, and New Orleans. Troops who had spent more than two years on the South Carolina coast boarded transports for Fort Monroe, to bolster Union forces in Tidewater Virginia, where military mandarins had decided to shift their focus.[14]

Certain soldiers tried to take themselves out of the way of these grand, ominous movements. It was frowned upon for an officer to resign on the eve of a campaign, but some did: the colonel of the 10th Vermont submitted his resignation — right on the heels of one of his captains — just as his regiment prepared to take the field against the enemy. Men who had enlisted in the first days of the war champed and clamored for their discharges when the War Department cited technicalities to hold them beyond the three years they had agreed to serve, and they earned the sympathy of such exalted figures as Major General George Meade, who commanded the Army of the Potomac.[15]

Most of the men in the camps merely observed the omens of impending violence with varying admixtures of dread and resignation. Soldiers from the northern fringes of New England and the Great Lakes relished the deliciously early greening of the hills and blooming of the orchards, but that gift of the lower latitudes was tempered by portentous orders and events in their various armies. Itinerant photographers improvised camp studios for procrastinating recruits who wanted to send home what might be the last, or only, portraits their families would ever have of them. In the waning days of April came the orders to turn in overcoats (and dress coats, in those armies that maintained the pretense of fancy parades), which left men in the valleys of the Rapidan and Tennessee Rivers shivering through chilly spring nights. Sutlers packed up the overpriced merchandise in their mobile general stores and pointed their wagons toward the safety of the rear. Hordes of troops pressed forward from their camps near Washington and Chattanooga to reach the armies at the front.[16]

Regimental quartermasters requisitioned new clothing to ready their commands for the field, charging the cost to the accounts of the men whose wardrobes had been declared unserviceable. Official judgments on the condition of their uniforms infuriated some in the ranks who had to pay for the decision, and indignation soared in the two regiments of United States Sharpshooters with the Army of the Potomac. These units had come into the army wearing conspicuous forest-green uniforms with black broadcloth stripes and dark gutta-percha insignia, rather than the bright gold and brass of the regulations. Over more than two years of active service most of the men had found it necessary to replace their clothing, one garment at a time, and the Quartermaster Department offered only dark-blue coats and sky-blue trousers, but a majority of the celebrated marksmen may have been perfectly content to blend in with the rest of the army, rather than draw the concentrated enemy fire that their fame warranted. Bits and pieces of the original green wool still speckled the sharpshooters' formations, however, and the regimental commanders hoped to impress the generals with a consistent, unique appearance for the division reviews that spring. Most of the officers had maintained their green wardrobes at considerable cost, so the enlisted men were all forced to shed their blue replacements and buy expensive, special-order green outfits.[17]

The compulsory replacement of passable garments was not the only indignity imposed on the two sharpshooter regiments that spring. Both of them belonged to the Third Corps, and that was one of two old corps that disappeared as General Meade reorganized the Army of the Potomac. Especially in the Eastern armies, corps designation provided a more important part of Civil War soldiers' identity than any other level of military unit except their regiment. For nearly a year the caps and flags in the Potomac army had borne distinctive symbols for each corps: for the Third Corps it had been a lozenge, and many resented having to exchange it for the badge of a rival corps. General orders insisted that they wear the new emblems (although they were allowed to keep their old ones as well), but several officers from the old Third devised an imaginative means of expressing their dissatisfaction while still complying with the orders. Once reassigned to the Second Corps, at least half a dozen officers sewed its flannel trefoil badge on the seat of their pants. The Second Corps judge advocate subjected them all to court-martial, but a staff officer in the Second Corps sarcastically congratulated the disgruntled officers for wearing their badges on the portion of their anatomy that was always closest to the enemy.[18]

With the consolidation of corps and a reshuffling of commanders, Meade reduced his army to three powerful wings led by three proven major generals. He gave the Second Corps back to its former commander, Winfield Hancock, who was just recovering from a troublesome Gettysburg wound, and shifted Gouverneur Warren from the Second Corps to the Fifth Corps, while John Sedgwick held on to the Sixth Corps, which he had led for more than a year. These all lay along the left bank of the Rapidan River, facing well-fortified heights on the right bank occupied by Robert E. Lee's Army of Northern Virginia. Behind Meade, Ambrose Burnside's huge Ninth Corps worked its way up the Orange & Alexandria Railroad to cooperate in the latest spring offensive, bringing Union manpower in that sector to twice that of Lee.

Five hundred miles to the south and west, William T. Sherman readied a similar host below Chattanooga for operations against Joseph E. Johnston's Army of Tennessee. Johnston had spent the winter in northwestern Georgia, just across the state line, and Sherman gathered three different armies against him, also amounting to nearly twice the number of troops Johnston could put in line. The largest of the three was the Army of the Cumberland, under the loyal Virginian George H. Thomas, who had already moved his troops down to Ringgold, Georgia, by late April. James B. McPherson, newly assigned to the smaller Army of the Tennessee, followed Thomas from northeastern Alabama, while John Schofield came down from Knoxville with the single remaining corps in the Army of the Ohio.[19]

Sherman's vast command also saw some consolidation that eliminated old corps. The previous autumn the War Department had uprooted the Eleventh and Twelfth Corps from Virginia and sent them to Chattanooga under Joseph Hooker. For the sake of efficiency Sherman melded the two of them into a single new entity, the Twentieth Corps, and gave that command to Hooker. Perhaps because neither of the old corps had won much fame under its former badge and banners, and neither survived to excite the jealousy of the other, the amalgamation seemed to go more smoothly than the one in Virginia.[20]

With the ascension of Ulysses S. Grant, now lieutenant general and general in chief, all the Union forces in Virginia and Georgia would move simultaneously against their immediate opponents. From his headquarters at Fort Monroe, on the tip of the James River Peninsula, cross-eyed Ben Butler organized what he would call the Army of the James for a strike at Richmond from the southeast while Meade and Burnside bore down from the north. At the same time, in the new state of West Virginia, Franz Sigel prepared to lead a division south, up the Shenandoah Valley, while George Crook would leave from Charleston with an infantry division, aiming for the Virginia & Tennessee Railroad below the New River. Crook also diverted a cavalry division under William Averell to strike the same road farther down the line. These five concerted attacks within Virginia would make it difficult for Lee to shift enough troops to resist them all, and coordinated offensives in both major theaters would prevent Lee and Johnston from sending reinforcements from one department to the other.[21]

Even after distributing twice as many troops as the Confederates could present in any region, the War Department at Washington could still depend on generous reserves. The big forts surrounding the capital bulged with well-fed, superbly equipped heavy-artillery regiments, each of which could muster eighteen hundred men at full complement, rather than the thousand or so of a new infantry regiment. These bandbox soldiers still retained their brass shoulder scales and white gloves, and in comparison to their comrades in Sherman's and Meade's armies they had had it very easy for the past one, two, or nearly three years. Their version of hardship involved drilling in the rain, which required them to clean their rifles. Heavy-artillerymen could almost always depend on abundant free time for swimming, reading, visiting around the countryside, writing letters, or engaging in philosophical discussions with comrades or correspondents. One New Yorker at Fort Lyon, near Alexandria, assured his mother that "this is a pleasant place and we have a good time here." Fear of conscription had swollen one Pennsylvania heavy-artillery regiment far beyond its allotted maximum with potential draftees seeking the least objectionable duty, but to their consternation the surplus men had been organized into a makeshift infantry regiment for service with Burnside near the front.[22]

To further augment Grant's numerical superiority, Secretary of War Edwin M. Stanton cannibalized military posts in the northern tier of states, sending down nearly three thousand heavy-artillerymen and U.S. Regulars from New York City alone. Unwelcome orders uprooted nearly a dozen more independent companies of heavy artillery from garrisons near their homes on the coast of Massachusetts, where they had fully expected to run out the war in relative ease and comfort. Come May, those disappointed tenderfeet began pouring into fortifications around the outskirts of Washington, or plodding on even farther south, to join the field armies and learn the privations of an active campaign.[23]

The draft quotas of October, February, and March all came due in April, and they totaled seven hundred thousand men. On paper that figure was reduced by more than 40 percent because some states had already exceeded their quotas on previous calls, and because thousands of men had paid the $300 commutation fee to be excused from service. Just over four hundred thousand men were ultimately required after those credits had been applied, and generous, draft-driven bounties had prompted nearly half a million potential draftees to enlist before their names were drawn. That produced a significant surplus, but the draft was held before all the credits had been counted, and 13,296 men were still pressed into the service, while nearly 35,000 more were forced to hire substitutes. Due primarily to commutation and the insistence on credit for extra volunteers from earlier quotas, the levies from all the recruiting and drafting barely kept pace with attrition.[24]

The two-to-one battlefield superiority against Confederate field forces still did not quite promise the prompt, irresistible suppression that President Lincoln had always hoped for. Plead as the administration might for more soldiers, though, the pool of men who could be induced to commit themselves to three years of deadly strife had been all but exhausted. Local authorities and state governors understood that the most emphatic threat of conscription now would merely impel vigorous male citizens to renew their entreaties for others to enlist, while fundraising would resume for bounty money that might give those pleas substance. A little adventure flavored by theoretical proximity to the battlefield was just the thing a young Victorian dandy wanted to round out his social persona, but the thought of three years' absence from home, family, or business made the hand hesitate to take the pen — as did the increasing odds against surviving such long exposure to gunpowder and pestilence.

During earlier crises in this conflict, state governors had often tried to convince the War Department that they could more easily supply volunteers for thirty, sixty, or ninety days, or for six months, than for three years, and in moments of panic the administration had often accepted those short-term troops. Ninety-day regiments had begun the war, and another small army of them had been called out, at considerable expense but to no strategic purpose, in the spring of 1862. The most notorious experiment with abbreviated enlistments had put nearly ninety thousand infantrymen into uniform in the late summer and fall of 1862 — nominally for nine months, although administrative complications had detained some of them closer to a year. Many of the nine-month men saw combat, mostly in the resounding defeats at Fredericksburg and Chancellorsville, but they spent much of their service in winter quarters, suffering severely from disease. Then they headed home just as they had begun to learn their new trade, adding to the pension rolls without making any tangible contribution to the course of the war.[25]

Despite those lessons, the spring campaigns of 1864 in Virginia and Georgia had not yet begun (and one on Louisiana's Red River had just come to an inglorious end) when the governors of Ohio, Indiana, Illinois, Iowa, and Wisconsin offered the president tens of thousands of raw recruits for a hundred days' duty. Doubting their constituencies could much longer sustain the administration's manpower demands, they evidently hoped to bolster the national forces for a decisive blow that would end the rebellion instantly, and toward that end the five governors promised to raise their corps of summer soldiers within twenty days from the date Lincoln accepted their proposal. Perhaps having learned something from earlier failures, they also suggested posting the new men in forts, to free more seasoned garrisons for the field armies. The president asked his war minister for an opinion, and Stanton passed it on to General Grant, who bore the dim Regular Army view of short enlistments, but six weeks into his tenure as general in chief he, too, considered the chance to field an overwhelming force. If their numbers were not to be deducted from the quotas of three-year men, he replied, then let them come. Once assured of his general's approbation, Lincoln approved the plan.[26]

In some places the hundred-day regiments developed as volunteer organizations always had, with entrepreneurial recruiters advertising for men in the hope of attracting enough followers to secure commissions. Within days of the president's approval, aspiring captains hosted patriotic rallies at their town houses and meeting halls, bringing forth a surprising number of recruits without offering a dollar in bounties. Most of those who came forward were young or middle-aged men who had never served under arms before and never intended to do so again. For the more prosperous, it may have seemed the greatest contribution they could afford to make, considering the demands of their businesses. Many doubtless hoped to dispel suspicions of cowardice or disloyalty with a season of presumably monotonous duty at some isolated post, and a hundred-day lark appealed to some harried parents whose young sons pleaded for permission to enlist. Boys who had just or not quite turned sixteen, and students little older than that, joined in such numbers that women's auxiliary groups adopted entire regiments of adolescents as their own pampered pets, to the vexation of forgotten veterans.[27]

"I suppose all those 100 day men think they are doing great things," groused an Iowa captain, "and will take a great deal of credit to themselves for being willing to go for 100 days with the understanding that they will not be placed where there is any danger of their seeing a rebel!" The captain supposed that he and his comrades should probably appreciate even so timid a gesture of assistance, but he admitted that "we despise the whole crew for not being willing to go to war in earnest, if they go at all."[28]

John Brough, the governor of Ohio, escaped the uncertainty of recruiting. He had only to call out the Ohio National Guard, which had been recruited under state auspices the year before. Clerks, shopkeepers, and students by the hundreds had filled those militia regiments, and one from Cleveland struck Senator Ben Wade's niece as downright aristocratic. Many a merchant found the timing exasperatingly inconvenient against recent investments: a few offered ample compensation for substitutes to serve their hundred-day tour, only to have to pay out several hundred dollars more for another substitute, almost immediately, when their names came up again in the federal draft. State and national conscription denuded whole neighborhoods of young men that spring, and a girl near Cincinnati reported to her brother, in Sherman's army, that "even the exquisite 'Awnderson' has had to try it." Most of the Ohio militiamen had been led to believe they would never have to serve outside their state: they regretted being called for duty at all, but their annoyance turned to dismay when, soon afterward, orders came for duty in Tennessee, Virginia, or Washington. Learning of the thwarted "stayathomes" through letters, veterans at the front groaned in mock sympathy, meanwhile cursing at the generous enlistment incentives they themselves had missed.[29]

By the time the first of the hundred-day men had boarded trains bound east or south, the real soldiers under Burnside, Butler, Meade, and Sherman had all heard their marching orders read at morning or evening parade. Most had spent their last night in winter quarters and had written home to offer last-minute financial instructions, advice on why a son or younger brother should not enlist under any circumstances, or nostalgic recollections of leisure hours at home. Myriad letters scribbled on the eve of the spring campaign bore a hint of nevermore, conveyed as an impotent belief in divine will or in unconscious reflection of personal dread, and many of the recipients of those letters would soon find the foreboding tone vindicated by another envelope addressed in a strange hand.[30]

It was at Martinsburg, West Virginia, that some now-nameless Union soldier took the first step in Grant's coordinated campaign to end the rebellion. Franz Sigel, who had been appointed to the grade of major general largely because of his influence among Saint Louis Germans, rather than for any obvious military talent, started his Army of West Virginia up the Shenandoah Valley on April 29, leading a six-mile column of cavalry and infantry on a seven-mile march to Bunker Hill over the smooth, dry Valley Pike. The sun shone brightly on this mild inaugural jaunt, and the leading brigades enjoyed a full day's rest among a riot of flowers and blossoming fruit trees before pressing on to Winchester on the first of May. Thousands of men in dusty blue uniforms tramped or rode through there that day and the next, camping a mile south of town. Quartermasters sought warehouses where they could stockpile supplies for either a lengthy occupation or an invasion of the valley. Residents of both political persuasions (and there were many of each, sometimes within the same immediate family) wondered whether Sigel would stay or move on, and their curiosity assumed a touch of anxiety when, early on the first morning after his arrival, flames consumed a big Winchester storehouse.[31]

Deeper into West Virginia, William Averell left Charleston on May 1, taking seven regiments of West Virginia, Ohio, and Pennsylvania cavalry and carrying orders to destroy the extensive salt distilleries at Saltville, in southwest Virginia. The next day, George Crook marched from the Kanawha River on a parallel route to the east with six thousand infantry from the same three states. Crook intended to strike the Virginia & Tennessee Railroad and destroy the massive railroad bridge over the gorge of the New River: he directed Averell to start working his way up the same railroad after smashing things at the saltworks, tearing up the tracks and burning the depots all the way up to Dublin, where they would combine for further antics in Confederate Virginia.[32]

Ben Butler was already in motion. On the last day of April he sent an expedition up the York River to reconnoiter and feint toward Richmond from the east. That detachment landed at West Point, and on May 2 a New York regiment ventured ten miles up the peninsula between the

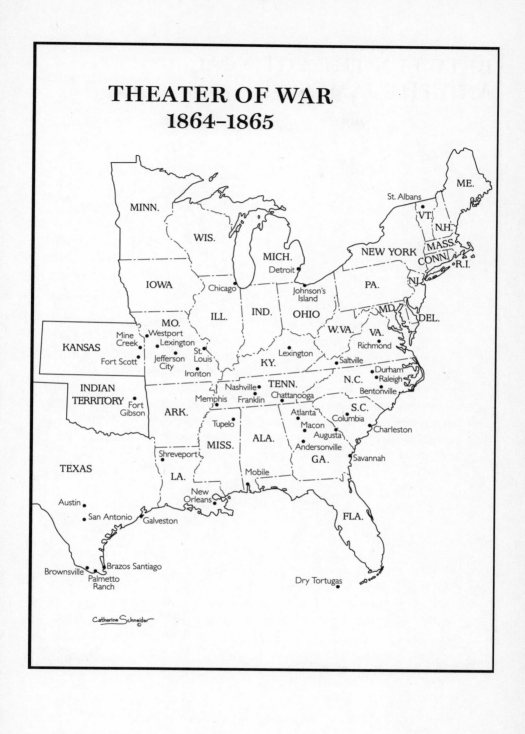

THEATER OF WAR
1864–1865

MINN.

WIS.

MICH.
Detroit

IOWA

Chicago

ILL.

IND.

OHIO

Johnson's
Island

MO.
Westport
Mine Creek
Lexington
St. Louis
Jefferson City
Ironton
Fort Scott

KANSAS

INDIAN
TERRITORY
Fort Gibson

ARK.

KY.
Lexington

Nashville
Memphis Franklin
Chattanooga

TENN.

Tupelo

MISS.

Shreveport

ALA.

LA.

Mobile

New Orleans

TEXAS

Austin
San Antonio
Galveston

Brownsville
Palmetto Ranch
Brazos Santiago

Dry Tortugas

FLA.

GA.
Savannah
Andersonville
Macon
Augusta
Atlanta

S.C.
Columbia
Charleston

N.C.
Durham
Raleigh
Bentonville

VA.
Richmond
Saltville

W.VA.

MD.
DEL.

PA.

NEW YORK

ME.

St. Albans

VT.
N.H.
MASS.
CONN.
R.I.
N.J.

Catherine Schneider ©

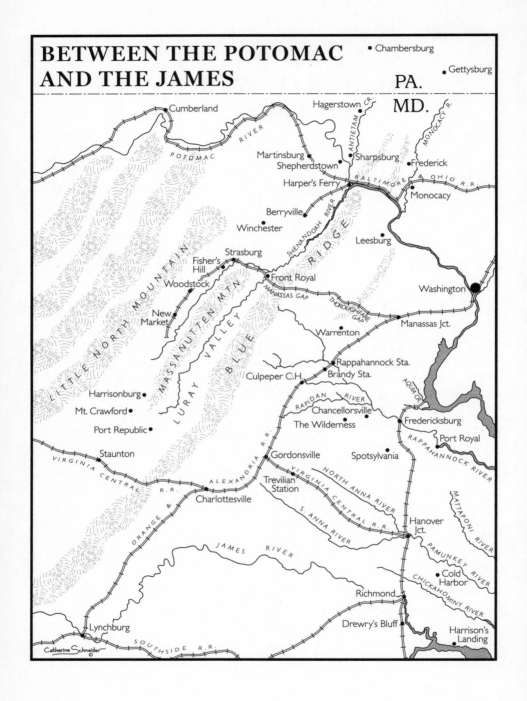

BETWEEN THE POTOMAC AND THE JAMES

PA.
MD.

Chambersburg

Gettysburg

Cumberland

Hagerstown

POTOMAC RIVER

Martinsburg
Shepherdstown

Sharpsburg

Frederick

ANTIETAM CR.

MONOCACY R.

BALTIMORE & OHIO R.R.

Harper's Ferry

Monocacy

Berryville

Winchester

SHENANDOAH RIVER

Leesburg

BLUE RIDGE

Strasburg

Fisher's Hill

Woodstock

Front Royal

MANASSAS GAP

New Market

LITTLE NORTH MOUNTAIN

MASSANUTTEN MTN.

LURAY VALLEY

Washington

THOROUGHFARE GAP

Warrenton

Manassas Jct.

Harrisonburg

Mt. Crawford

Port Republic

Culpeper C.H.

Rappahannock Sta.

Brandy Sta.

RAPIDAN RIVER

Chancellorsville

The Wilderness

AQUIA CR.

Fredericksburg

Port Royal

RAPPAHANNOCK RIVER

Staunton

VIRGINIA CENTRAL R.R.

ALEXANDRIA R.R.

Gordonsville

Spotsylvania

NORTH ANNA RIVER

Trevilian Station

VIRGINIA CENTRAL R.R.

Charlottesville

ORANGE &

S. ANNA RIVER

Hanover Jct.

MATTAPONI RIVER

JAMES RIVER

PAMUNKEY RIVER

Cold Harbor

CHICKAHOMINY RIVER

Richmond

Lynchburg

SOUTHSIDE R.R.

Drewry's Bluff

Harrison's Landing

Catherine Schneider ©

Pamunkey and Mattaponi Rivers, in the direction of White House Landing. White House had been George McClellan's supply base for his campaign against Richmond two years before, and this little excursion naturally caused some consternation in the Confederate capital. While rebels fretted over that diversionary force, Butler called it back down the York River, boarded his whole army on transports, and steamed up the James River, to stab at Richmond from below.[33]

On the afternoon of May 2 a torrential thunderstorm descended on Meade's army, running behind a violent gale. As afternoon turned to evening the tempest struck with one of "the most terrific whirlwinds" one witness had ever seen, and then the rain came pounding in behind it. The various corps commanders in the Army of the Potomac had just received orders that the army would move against the enemy early on May 4, and the turbulent skies seemed to portend the ferocity of the coming campaign.[34]

Those orders were read to most of the troops at the evening parade the next day, initiating more of those didactic letters cautioning against undue distress over any lapse in correspondence. General Meade wrote his own wife that night, beseeching her to remain calm. "Do not fret," he implored, "but be cheerful, and go about and do just as if nothing was going on, and above all things don't anticipate evil; it will come time enough." Captain Orville Bixby, who had helped raise a company for the 2nd Vermont in the first weeks of the war and had served at the front ever since, had also left a carking wife and a little boy at home in Royalton. He had sent her some money in a letter that had never arrived, and he knew she would be inquiring about it regularly, so he instructed her that "you mustnt think it strange if you do not hear from me again for some time." Like the general commanding, he expected to be kept busy every moment once they set out, but he reminded her that it would only be a few weeks before he came home to her for good.[35]

The 2nd Vermont had participated in fifteen major battles since 1861, and most of those who had been with the regiment from the beginning did not intend to see it through to the finish; of 147 men who had reenlisted in the regiment, at least 10 had used their reenlistment furloughs as a path to desertion, taking much of their reenlistment bounty with them. Corporal William Stow, from the tiny village of Calais, north of Montpelier, assured his mother that he would be coming home when the original men were mustered out in June. "Three long years I have bin surrounded with the trim sentinels of death," he explained, "& I want to get out of it."[36]

The campaign would essentially reprise General Meade's Mine Run plan of the previous November, in which Meade slipped around Lee's right flank on the lower fords of the Rapidan. On that occasion, a slow-moving Third Corps had given the Confederates an extra day to prepare an intimidating defensive line on high ground that easily compensated for the two-to-one odds they faced, and Meade had judiciously withdrawn to his side of the river. This time, Meade proposed dashing across in nearly the same spot and driving farther south before swinging to the west. That would nullify the danger of Lee's November fortifications, and force him to come out and fight in the open, where Meade could better apply his numerical advantage.[37]

At Mine Run Lee had been without his chief subordinate, James Longstreet, whom he had loaned (along with two of Longstreet's divisions) to the Army of Tennessee in September of 1863. "Old Pete" and his two divisions were back now, waiting at Gordonsville to reinforce either of Lee's flanks as needed, but those returned troops would not reduce the odds for Lee, at least in terms of numbers. Longstreet's nine brigades had lost heavily during their service in Georgia and Tennessee, and they were offset by the twenty thousand Yankees under Burnside, who waited just behind Meade's hundred thousand. Lee would still be able to field barely half as many bayonets as his adversaries.[38]

This plan, which Meade submitted to General Grant, should have doomed the Army of Northern Virginia. Lee had previously survived against similar odds, most notably at Antietam, twenty months before, but there he had faced George McClellan, who was always handicapped by the misunderstanding that Lee outnumbered him. The main Union disadvantage this time was that Grant's presence discouraged Meade from exercising complete discretion in the use of his own army, while Burnside's corps took all orders directly from Grant. The general in chief intended to travel with the Army of the Potomac, and (as Meade predicted) that would diminish Meade's public and historical prominence in the subsequent fighting. Worse still, such close oversight would soon lead to intense frustration for Meade, and trouble for the campaign.[39]

That trouble began in the Wilderness. Hardwood in the region below the Rapidan had been stripped to provide charcoal for iron-smelting furnaces in the vicinity, leaving dozens of square miles of slash, underbrush, and a dense second-growth tangle. Even where mature trees flourished, scrub pine and briars covered the forest floor, and few decent roads traversed this brake. Joseph Hooker had come to grief there exactly one year before, when Lee caught him at Chancellorsville, but Meade hoped to navigate the forest on the first day's march and camp beyond it by nightfall, in position to strike Lee from behind before he could react.

Union cavalry went to work late on May 3, guarding all the houses along the river to prevent their occupants from alerting Confederate pickets that the Yankees were coming. At midnight the infantry and artillery began tearing down their camps; by 2:00 A.M. the first of them started to move, but others waited until daybreak to fall in and follow. At daylight engineers started assembling a pontoon bridge on the Rapidan at Ely's Ford, and the last plank had hardly been laid when the vanguard of Winfield Hancock's Second Corps started thundering across. Several miles upstream, at Germanna Ford, another detachment of engineers had already completed a pair of bridges over the river for the Fifth and Sixth Corps, and between those spans they built another for the supply train at Culpeper Ford.[40]

The general staff of the Army of the Potomac crossed at Germanna Ford just after midmorning. An aide stood on the heights above the ford for a long while, mesmerized by the endless line of troops below him, treading at the route-step over the swaying bridges, four abreast; not until evening did Meade's last man land on the right bank. The engineers started dismantling one of the bridges, leaving the other for Burnside's four divisions, which were still guarding the Orange & Alexandria Railroad from Manassas Junction to Rappahannock Station. The nearest of Burnside's infantry had spent the night fifteen miles away, and the farthest — Edward Ferrero's division of U.S. Colored Troops — awoke more than thirty miles from Germanna Ford. On Grant's orders most of them started for the Rapidan late in the afternoon, making forced marches into the night.[41]

Burnside might have been better employed farther up the Rapidan, as a threat to Lee's left flank. That should theoretically have induced the rebel chief to leave even more troops than he did at the upper fords when he reacted to Meade's crossing, but military theory did not always apply to so bold a character as Robert E. Lee. For his part, though, Meade seemed just as happy to have Burnside come over with him. If Lee hit them with everything he had, Meade reasoned, it would only make the inevitable Union victory all the more complete.[42]

Cavalry led the way through the Wilderness, scooping up only one roving rebel before emerging on open ground by midafternoon, but darkness caught the infantry and the guns still deep in the wood. Warren's Fifth Corps and Sedgwick's Sixth camped around a decrepit old stage stop called Wilderness Tavern and all the way back to the river on the Germanna Ford Road, while the Second Corps settled in at Chancellorsville. Hancock's troops stretched their picket line down the Orange Plank Road to connect with Warren, over the battlefield of the previous May, where the Eleventh Corps had been utterly surprised and driven blindly through the forest. The Army of the Potomac had crept away in defeat that time, leaving many of its dead behind in that eerie weald, and when Hancock's men bedded down that night many of them could see the skulls of unburied Union soldiers grinning at them from the peripheries of their campfires.[43]

This pause in the Wilderness foiled Meade's plan for getting behind the enemy and cutting him off from his base. With no threat left across the Rapidan, Lee could divert both the corps that had held that line, and he responded much faster than he had in November, when Meade approached Mine Run. For his part, Meade was moving more slowly than he had in November. Apparently the plan to flank Lee by racing far around his old Mine Run line had been abandoned, or postponed, for the orders that went out for the morning directed the three Union corps to sidle together in a front facing generally west, with their right at Wilderness Tavern. The all-but-impenetrable forest would still hide them, and there they would wait until Burnside came up.[44]

The rebels arrived first. Meade's three corps had only begun to ease toward the positions he had assigned them when, just after breakfast on Thursday, Warren's advance ran into resistance on the Orange Turnpike, a couple of miles beyond Wilderness Tavern. By 8:00 A.M. rebel cavalry appeared on the Orange Plank Road, which ran parallel to the turnpike two miles to the south. Lee was sending Richard Ewell's corps in on the turnpike, and A. P. Hill's on the plank road. While Ewell confronted the division on Warren's right, Hill drove toward — and ultimately past — Warren's unsupported left. Sedgwick, still on the road from the ford, marched Horatio Wright's division down a farm track to brace Warren's right on the turnpike, and directed George Getty's on a roundabout route behind Warren to reach his unprotected left, on the plank road. Hancock had marched miles south from Chancellorsville, well below Warren's left, and when Meade comprehended the size of the force in front of his army he sent for Hancock to come back on the run, but until the Second Corps arrived Warren had to contend with two-thirds of Lee's whole army.[45]

Lee meant to stall Meade in the Wilderness, where he could hardly maneuver his larger army, until James Longstreet came up from Gordonsville. Longstreet's two divisions of Deep South rebels would arrive on a third, roughly parallel route known as the Catharpin Road, below the fighting and, ideally, behind Meade's left flank. The surprise might stun the Yankees as badly as Stonewall Jackson had the year before, and in the dense vegetation the battlefront would be narrow enough that the Confederates would only have to contend with a portion of the enemy at one time. The limited visibility also saved Lee the added affliction of Meade's superior artillery.

After using up the morning arranging his own and borrowed troops, Warren spent the early afternoon hammering at Ewell, and being hammered by him, while two divisions of A. P. Hill's corps slid past Warren's left and came nearly to the Brock Road, behind Warren's line. Getty's Sixth Corps division met them there just in time to keep them from getting behind Warren, but Ewell's pressure had bent the center of Warren's line back half a mile by the middle of the afternoon.[46]

The head of the Second Corps had begun to arrive near the junction of the Brock Road and the Orange Plank Road, but it was Getty's division that first tried to clear the intersection, and it was the Vermont regiments of Lewis Grant's brigade that went in at the head of Getty's attack. In the thick foliage they blundered head-on into a line of Southern infantry lying behind a slight fold in the ground that offered them almost complete protection. Rippling volleys felled Vermonters by the hundreds (the front line "melted like wax," said a soldier in the second line), but the survivors threw themselves to the ground and returned as rapid a fire as they could, rolling on their backs to reload rather than stand up under that leaden hailstorm. Here, as elsewhere in the Wilderness, the musket decided the entire contest: most who thought about it realized that they never heard a single piece of artillery. Captain Bixby, who two evenings before had urged his wife not to worry if he failed to write for a while, went down early in the fight with a bullet through his head, and by nightfall he was dead. The 2nd had but one captain left when the sun set; both its colonel and lieutenant colonel had been fatally wounded, and a field officer from the 3rd Vermont had to take command. Dozens of others in the 2nd Vermont who would have started home in another forty days were killed on the spot, including Corporal Stow, still surrounded by those "trim sentinels of death."[47]

The shooting sputtered out in the darkness, while Longstreet raced to Lee's aid and Burnside hurried to Meade's. Men on both sides settled in for a chilly night's sleep without blankets, and Grant planned an overwhelming attack for the morning, but his dispositions required his troops to take their positions in the darkness. Burnside in particular had to arrange his divisions in the pitch dark of a new moon, over terrain that confused everyone sufficiently in the daylight.[48]

When day dawned on May 6, Sedgwick hurled a division at Ewell's breastworks along the Orange Turnpike, without success. Meanwhile, Hancock started a motley Union assault down either side of the plank road from the Brock Road intersection. He concentrated five mostly fresh Union divisions from all three of Meade's corps against two of A. P. Hill's divisions, both of which had been heavily engaged the previous day. The rebels held their ground until the longer Union line overlapped theirs on both ends, at which they started falling back, and the Confederate front had nearly collapsed when the head of Longstreet's corps came trotting up and stopped the Union advance cold. Hancock organized another assault soon afterward, but Longstreet sidled a makeshift division toward Hancock's left and launched a flank attack that struck the end of Hancock's line obliquely, driving him all the way back to the Brock Road; rebels spilled right into half-finished Union breastworks at some points.[49] A great many of the greenest recruits in Hancock's line stood fast, while quite a few of the veterans fled, and especially those with only days or weeks to serve. A stampede of blue-clad stragglers came streaming out of the thick woods — "hundreds and thousands" of them, thought Meade's surly provost marshal — and they joined other fugitives on the far side of the Brock Road who had been lurking there since their regiments first went into action, the day before.[50]

Like Stonewall Jackson, though, Longstreet fell seriously wounded when his own men accidentally fired on him, and there the Confederate tide began to ebb. Burnside finally thrust two divisions at Longstreet's flank, but he went in alone and soon came out on the run. Some of his infantry seized the rebel rifle pits long enough to send back a flock of Southerners in grimy grey, only to find other grey uniforms loping around behind them, and when Burnside's troops fell back they left at least as many of their own comrades in enemy hands.[51] The blazing musketry ignited the tinder-dry carpet of leaves and twigs, and the flames spread quickly; Yankees back at Wilderness Tavern presumed the rebels had set the woods afire on purpose, to discourage further attack.[52] Toward sunset Confederates lunged at Sedgwick, on the northern extremity of the Union line, capturing a couple of brigadiers and starting another panic, but that was soon repaired. When dark fell again, Warren still occupied about the same position he had held on the morning of May 5, and the Brock Road was still in Union hands.[53]

Wounded men had begun trickling to the rear on Thursday morning; they formed a steady stream by afternoon, and a torrent on Friday. Surgeons established hospitals near Wilderness Tavern, where musicians-turned-nurses fashioned saplings and brush into shaded bowers where the wounded could lie while awaiting treatment. The Second Corps hospital alone took in about four thousand patients by Friday evening. Initially they were to be sent back across the Rapidan to the Orange & Alexandria Railroad, but then they were directed to Fredericksburg, fifteen miles to the east. Wagons and ambulances jounced them over the turnpike, with an endless parade of walking wounded shambling alongside.[54] The smoldering vegetation of the Wilderness claimed many who would never be found, who had fallen dead or dying, unseen by messmates who wondered at their fate.[55]

Surgeons and civilian nurses started pouring into Fredericksburg. Wives hurried down to attend wounded husbands, or to sit with them as they died. Arabella Barlow, the young wife of Brigadier General Francis Barlow of the Second Corps, came to don an apron and help. Returns showed twelve thousand wounded in the Army of the Potomac and Burnside's corps, with over three thousand more missing, and total Union casualties approached eighteen thousand. A Quaker woman who had served as a nurse with Meade's army since Gettysburg reached Fredericksburg with the first wave of medical personnel; she had made many friends in the Second Corps over the winter at Brandy Station, and her heart sank as she heard, one after the other, that they had been killed.[56]

Lee's army lay behind its entrenchments on the third morning, challenging the Federals to try it again. The game had ended that way at Mine Run, five months before, with Lee eagerly awaiting an attack behind imposing works, but Meade had not taken the bait on that bitterly cold day: with his supplies running low, he had returned to his own side of the Rapidan. After Fredericksburg and Chancellorsville, too, the Army of the Potomac had retreated to lick its wounds. Had the same thing happened a fourth time, Northern morale might not have borne it, but this time Grant opted to turn south, toward Richmond. By the afternoon of May 8 residents of Boston could hear newsboys barking that Grant was driving the enemy.[57]

The Brock Road led to Spotsylvania Court House, ten winding miles southeast of the Wilderness battlefield. There the ground remained heavily wooded, but with more conventional hardwood forests and more frequent clearings. The two armies sidestepped in that direction, but Confederates won the race over longer and worse roads, so Lee was able to throw five divisions across Grant's path at Laurel Hill, a couple of miles above Spotsylvania. Warren and Sedgwick attacked them there on the evening of May 8, but failed to dislodge them. Both sides brought up more troops the next day, and the Confederates perfected their fieldworks while the skirmishers sputtered at each other, incidentally killing John Sedgwick. On May 10, at the opposite end of Grant's army, a stray bullet also killed Brigadier General Thomas Stevenson, one of Burnside's better division commanders, as he and his staff sought relief from the broiling sun under a tree.[58]

East of Laurel Hill the rebel entrenchments formed a loop that suggested the shape of a mule shoe, and it invited attack. On the afternoon of May 10, Horatio Wright, Sedgwick's successor at the head of the Sixth Corps, threw the equivalent of an entire division in picked regiments at it. He massed the men in close ranks, launching them from woods that would screen them until they were nearly upon the enemy, and they broke through fairly easily, but counterattacks sent them sprinting back the way they had come.[59]

Rain soaked the combatants and their battlefield for most of the next two days, but before dawn on May 12 Meade arranged a more ambitious version of Wright's massed attack. He formed the entire Second Corps in close columns in the sodden oak woods half a mile north of the Mule Shoe, while Grant ordered Burnside to bring his infantry against the eastern face. In the darkness Hancock's troops surged quietly forward, flushing the rebel skirmishers and boiling over the fortifications behind them. They caught the worn-out defenders asleep and captured most of a division, along with the division commander and a brigadier. Hancock's spearhead drove hundreds of yards past the breastworks, to the very base of the Mule Shoe, before meeting serious resistance. Burnside struck later than Hancock, overrunning the rebel works at one point only to be thrown back with considerable loss. Lee hurled every available man at the rupture, recovering all the lost ground that morning, but a desperate struggle ensued. The Sixth Corps joined the fray on Hancock's right, and the contest for the entrenchments continued at point-blank range from first light until well into the night, in periodic downpours. Only a few feet of logs and earth separated the antagonists across much of the front, and men swathed in mud fired into each other's faces. Casualties literally accumulated in heaps, especially on the Confederate side of the works, where the dead — and often the wounded — rolled into the trenches only to have others fall in on top of them. So long did intense musketry concentrate on the same narrow crescent that it felled whole trees, including one more than a foot in diameter.[60]

While their infantry held the enemy at bay, Confederate engineers and pioneers extemporized a new line across the heel of the Mule Shoe, and the next day Lee stepped back to that new, stronger perimeter. All that blood had bought the Union forces barely a hundred acres of useless ground.

Grant's sanguinary stalemate below the Rapidan offered the best tidings from Virginia. Union armies had penetrated elsewhere, but their principal success lay in requiring the Confederates to keep their forces scattered. Just as the fighting began in the Wilderness, Ben Butler landed the Tenth and Eighteenth Corps at Bermuda Hundred — a broad triangle between the James and Appomattox Rivers and, more to the point, between Richmond and the crucial railroad center at Petersburg. Butler began stabbing at the Richmond & Petersburg Railroad, and there he met the first resistance. His corps were commanded by two worthy engineers, William F. Smith ("Baldy," to his friends) and Quincy Gillmore, who counseled Butler to avoid the fortified approaches to the railroad and seize Petersburg from an undefended quarter by bridging the Appomattox. The imperious Butler peremptorily refused, advising the two West Pointers

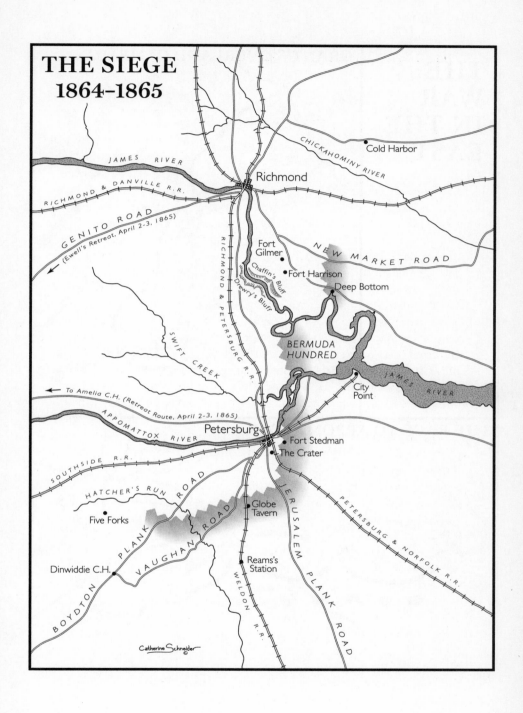

THE SIEGE
1864–1865

JAMES RIVER

Cold Harbor

CHICKAHOMINY RIVER

RICHMOND & DANVILLE R.R.

Richmond

GENITO ROAD
(Ewell's Retreat, April 2-3, 1865)

Fort
Gilmer

NEW MARKET ROAD

Chaffin's Bluff

Fort Harrison

Drewry's Bluff

Deep Bottom

RICHMOND & PETERSBURG R.R.

BERMUDA
HUNDRED

SWIFT CREEK

JAMES RIVER

To Amelia C.H. (Retreat Route, April 2-3, 1865)

City
Point

APPOMATTOX RIVER

Petersburg

Fort Stedman

The Crater

SOUTHSIDE R.R.

HATCHER'S RUN

PLANK ROAD

JERUSALEM PLANK ROAD

PETERSBURG & NORFOLK R.R.

VAUGHAN ROAD

Globe
Tavern

Five Forks

Dinwiddie C.H.

BOYDTON PLANK ROAD

Reams's
Station

WELDON R.R.

Catherine Schneider ©

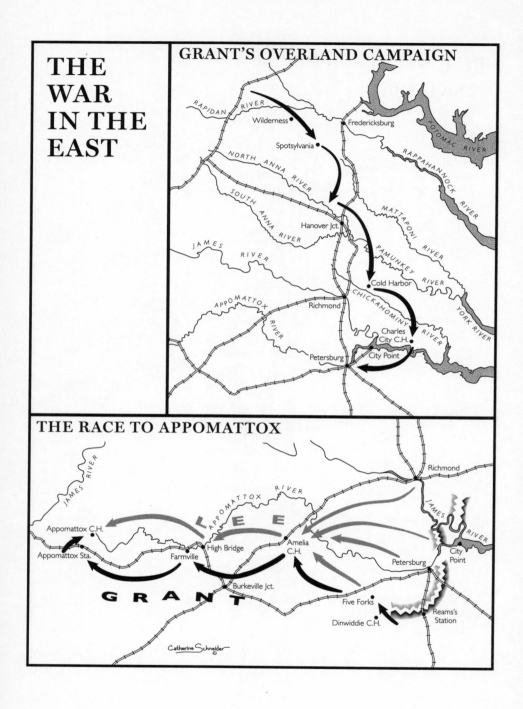

THE WAR IN THE EAST

GRANT'S OVERLAND CAMPAIGN

RAPIDAN RIVER

Wilderness

Fredericksburg

POTOMAC RIVER

Spotsylvania

NORTH ANNA RIVER

RAPPAHANNOCK RIVER

SOUTH ANNA RIVER

MATTAPONI RIVER

Hanover Jct.

PAMUNKEY RIVER

JAMES RIVER

Cold Harbor

CHICKAHOMINY RIVER

Richmond

APPOMATTOX RIVER

YORK RIVER

Charles City C.H.

Petersburg

City Point

THE RACE TO APPOMATTOX

JAMES RIVER

Richmond

APPOMATTOX RIVER

L E E

JAMES RIVER

Appomattox C.H.

High Bridge

Amelia C.H.

City Point

Appomattox Sta.

Farmville

Petersburg

G R A N T

Burkeville Jct.

Five Forks

Reams's Station

Dinwiddie C.H.

Catherine Schneider ©

that he had already sent cavalry toward Petersburg to cut the railroads there. Two of his cavalry brigades did burn a couple of railroad bridges and threaten Petersburg briefly, but when those horsemen returned they brought word that large numbers of Confederates were approaching Petersburg from the south. Pierre G. T. Beauregard was bringing up half a dozen brigades from the Carolinas, which Grant's grand strategy had ignored, and that closed the opening Smith and Gillmore had detected. Efforts to crack the Confederate line along the railroad came to naught. A few days later Butler took his infantry north, to sever more railroads below Richmond, but the rebels thrashed him severely under cover of a dense fog on May 16. The enemy "out Generalled" Butler, admitted a Cape Cod Yankee: they took hundreds of prisoners, including a pair of brigade commanders. When Butler retreated to his original lines, his Army of the James was effectively barred from interceding again between Richmond and its lifeline to Petersburg.[61]

Back in Washington, Chief of Staff Henry Halleck secretly criticized President Lincoln for appointing lawyers and politicians like Butler to high command. It was — Halleck informed a prominent New York correspondent — as predictably disastrous to turn such men into generals as it would be to fill the Supreme Court with soldiers.[62]

Phil Sheridan, whom Grant had brought east to command Meade's cavalry, left the main army on the morning of May 9 to raise havoc behind Lee. He took three divisions in a column more than a dozen miles long. Late that first night, George Custer's brigade crossed the North Anna River and seized Beaver Dam Station, on the Virginia Central Railroad, burning the depot and ninety railroad cars containing enough commissary stores to feed Lee's army for a week, besides repatriating several hundred captured Federals; at least those were the accomplishments Custer claimed. On May 11, Sheridan — West Point, Class of 1853 — made straight for Richmond, coming in from the north on the Brook Turnpike, and J. E. B. Stuart — West Point, '54 — met him at Yellow Tavern. So desperate was Stuart to save his capital that he joined the fight with drawn revolver and went down with a bullet in the belly. Sheridan probed the city's inner defenses a little more the next day, retiring finally to the old Peninsula battlefields downriver, with his troopers and mounts alike physically drained and famished.[63]

Rough roads over rugged terrain brought George Crook and William Averell to their respective destinations in southwestern Virginia by the second week of May, but when Averell heard exaggerated estimates of Confederate troops at Saltville he gave up on his main target and turned for the Virginia & Tennessee Railroad. At Cloyd's Mountain on May 9 Crook sent the badly outnumbered rebel defenders flying toward Dublin, on the railroad, and the next day he chased them up the railroad to the bridge over the New River gorge, where they rallied on the far side until Crook's artillery persuaded them to withdraw. Crook's men burned the towering bridge, but then he started for home: at the telegraph office in Dublin he had found erroneous dispatches reporting that Grant had been repulsed, and that would have allowed Lee to hurry reinforcements down by rail. Crook moved as quickly as his men could march, but rain hampered him from the start, burying his wagons to their beds on the primitive, bottomless roads. Quartermasters dumped piles of baggage along the way, even throwing away the men's knapsacks, and food ran out in a countryside that held little for man or beast. Averell's retreating troopers joined him on May 15: after a brush with John Hunt Morgan's cavalry, Averell had ridden for the railroad, where he burned some machine shops and the Christiansburg depot before turning for safety himself over muddy mountain tracks so narrow his men had to lead their horses. Not until May 19 did the reunited column reach its old campsite in West Virginia.[64]

What little Crook and Averell did accomplish reflected the wisdom of Grant's coordinated pressure, for southwest Virginia had been stripped of most of its defenders to meet Franz Sigel, who was pushing up from Winchester with a division each of infantry and cavalry, amounting to as many as eight or nine thousand Yankees altogether. Unaware that Crook had returned to West Virginia, Sigel expected to join him in the valley, and Robert E. Lee suspected Sigel was preparing to strike the Army of Northern Virginia from behind, through one of the Blue Ridge gaps. To avert that danger he called on Major General John C. Breckinridge, former vice president of the United States and now commander of the Department of Western Virginia. Turning his back on Crook and Averell, Breckinridge sent every man he dared down toward Staunton — two small infantry brigades along with the cavalry he already had in the lower valley — and then he followed them himself. He even mobilized the cadet corps of the Virginia Military Institute, which added another infantry battalion to his ranks.[65]

Breckinridge met Sigel outside New Market in a driving rainstorm on May 15. Sigel led more of both infantry and cavalry, but Breckinridge instantly took the offensive. With their shrill yell eight regiments of his rebels drove four brigades of Federals over a mile, then shot it out with them for hours in the downpour before the entire Confederate line surged forward, cadets and all, and swept the invaders from the field. Sigel ran about babbling in German while his command disintegrated. Believing themselves overpowered by a much larger force, rather than by a smaller one, the fugitives dropped knapsacks, blanket rolls, and rifles in their haste to get away: they crossed the swollen Shenandoah River, burned the bridge behind them, and kept on running. A dismal parade of dejected stragglers and wounded passed through Winchester three days later, testifying to the severity of their defeat. In his report, General Sigel doubled the number of Confederate troops to justify his disaster.[66]

While the various columns moved into Virginia, William Sherman's three armies assembled in the rippling, timbered terrain of northwest Georgia, settling into a broad arc around Joe Johnston's Dalton encampments and trimming for battle. Like their comrades along the Rapidan, they culled their possessions of all but the most essential clothing and comforts, and the quartermasters pared down the wagon trains. The night of May 5, George Thomas's Army of the Cumberland bivouacked around Ringgold, where thousands of men burned up their last candles on the eve of the campaign, scratching off letters. That common epistolary impulse set each little shelter aglow, suggesting an impromptu illumination. Appreciating the sheer romance of the scene on the eve of another perilous campaign, other men lighted their candles, too, spreading the sentimental effect through the sprawling camps.[67]

The campaign began the next morning, banishing any further wistful reflections. Johnston's Army of Tennessee, upwards of fifty thousand strong, defended a rugged, steep slope known as Rocky Face Ridge. Most of Sherman's troops had camped out of sight behind Taylor's Ridge, one more geographical undulation to the west. McPherson struck south with his twenty-four-thousand-man Army of the Tennessee, in a wide arc around Johnston's left toward Snake Creek Gap, on the road to Resaca: that little town sat right behind Johnston on the railroad to Atlanta, and if it fell he would be trapped, with no other source of supply. Thomas, with more than sixty thousand, crossed Taylor's Ridge to threaten Johnston directly, while Schofield's Army of the Ohio hovered to the north, on Johnston's right flank, with another thirteen thousand.[68]

In earlier commands Johnston had demonstrated a preference for the Fabian retreat when he was outnumbered — falling slowly backward while fighting defensive battles that theoretically exhausted his enemy and forced him to depend on an attenuated, vulnerable line of supply. Logically, he would have to pursue a similar strategy against Sherman, but Atlanta lay only a hundred miles away, and the threat to Resaca would require him to yield one-fifth of that distance at the very outset.

At first Johnston remained ignorant of McPherson's movement to Snake Creek Gap, deploying all his infantry along Rocky Face Ridge and using cavalry to guard his flanks. Thomas occupied Johnston's attention in front with convincing demonstrations on May 7 and 8, sending his infantry swarming up precipitous Rocky Face Ridge, where they had to claw their way up by holding on to bushes and saplings. That ambitious diversion killed and maimed hundreds of men, but the next day Sherman hurled all his scattered elements in for what he supposed would be the kill. Schofield pushed down from the north, McPherson lunged at Resaca, and Thomas's army kept up a sharp fire against Rocky Face, all to no avail.[69] Johnston had finally directed one brigade of infantry to hold Resaca, where he had already prepared some forts and fieldworks, and McPherson so magnified the size of that brigade that he withdrew back to Snake Creek Gap. Sherman decided to force matters, leaving a single corps above Dalton as a decoy while he moved everyone else down to join McPherson. Johnston eventually detected that ploy, too, and he had no choice but to abandon his winter-long position to save his rail line.[70]

When he reached Resaca, Johnston put the rest of the army in the entrenchments, which lay behind a creek parallel to the railroad; the Oostanaula River protected him on the left. Sherman played the same game again here, though, and it was just what Grant had begun doing to Lee. He attacked Johnston behind his works, pressing him in front and flank, all the while bridging the Oostanaula to leapfrog around him again and cut him off from Atlanta. Johnston held his ground on May 14, and even considered a counterattack, but that night he learned of the new threat to his flank and prepared for another withdrawal. All day May 15 he defended Resaca against steady pressure while his pioneers fashioned their own bridge. The Yankees had some embarrassing moments: one Pennsylvania regiment with less than two weeks to serve broke shamelessly for the rear when confronted with a volley after dark. Johnston expected Sherman to lose enough old troops by the expiration of their terms to weaken him for a decisive attack, but he saw no such opportunity at Resaca. In the early morning darkness of May 16 Johnston spirited his army across the river, looking for another promising spot to make a stand. He found none until he reached Cassville, barely fifty miles from Atlanta.[71]

The Yankees crept forward under the next day's blazing sun, encountering no enemy but the dead and dying — at least one of whom asked them to put him out of his misery. Then they resumed the dusty roads south, tramping after the elusive Johnston through what had, until a generation before, been the heart of the Cherokee homeland. The harried Confederates plodded mile after mile in search of an advantageous position, prompting an Ohio private to wonder whether they would ever make a stand.[72]

Only the two principal armies could boast much success. Outside Virginia and Georgia, active operations had ground to a halt or deteriorated into

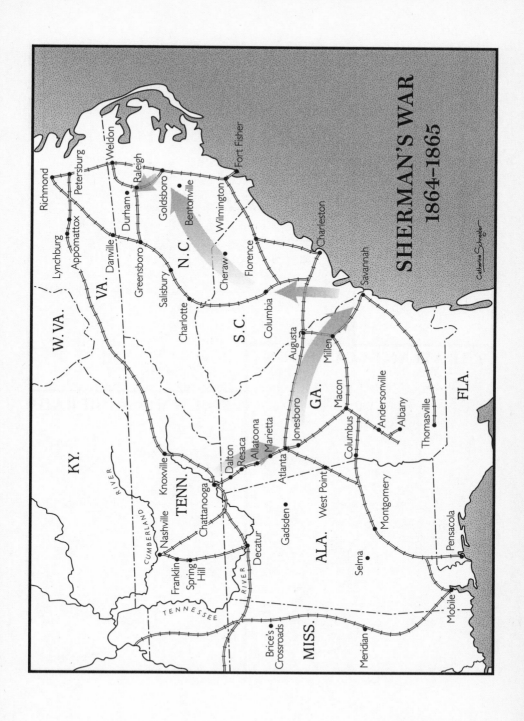

SHERMAN'S WAR
1864–1865

Catherine Schneider

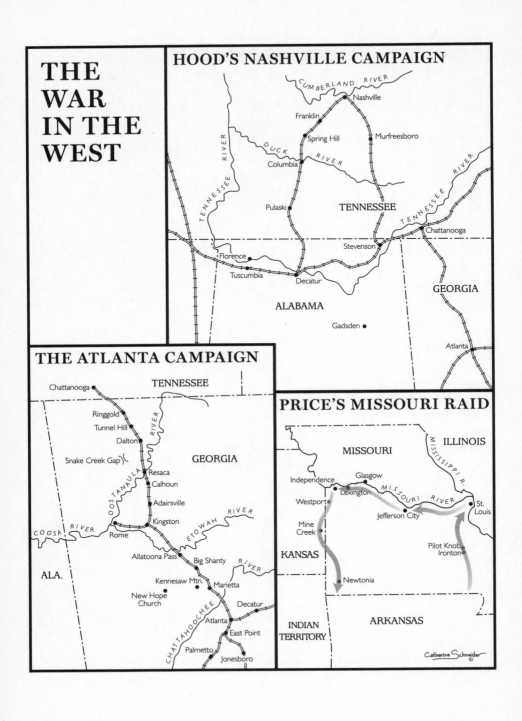

THE WAR IN THE WEST

HOOD'S NASHVILLE CAMPAIGN

CUMBERLAND RIVER

Nashville
Franklin
Spring Hill
Murfreesboro
Columbia
DUCK RIVER
TENNESSEE RIVER
Pulaski
TENNESSEE
Chattanooga
Stevenson
TENNESSEE RIVER
Florence
Tuscumbia
Decatur
GEORGIA
ALABAMA
Gadsden ●
Atlanta

THE ATLANTA CAMPAIGN

Chattanooga
TENNESSEE
Ringgold
Tunnel Hill
Dalton
Snake Creek Gap
GEORGIA
OOSTANULA RIVER
Resaca
Calhoun
Adairsville
Kingston
ETOWAH RIVER
COOSA RIVER
Rome
Allatoona Pass
Big Shanty
RIVER
ALA.
Kennesaw Mtn.
Marietta
New Hope Church
Decatur
Atlanta
East Point
CHATTAHOOCHEE
Palmetto
Jonesboro

PRICE'S MISSOURI RAID

MISSOURI
ILLINOIS
MISSISSIPPI R.
Independence
Glasgow
Lexington
Westport
MISSOURI RIVER
St. Louis
Jefferson City
Mine Creek
KANSAS
Pilot Knob
Ironton
Newtonia
INDIAN TERRITORY
ARKANSAS

Catherine Schneider ©

farce. With most of their complement drained to reinforce the Virginia armies, coastal garrisons in North Carolina felt outnumbered and cynical; they fell into such torpor that a Connecticut Yankee thought his comrades might relish the diversion of a hundred-mile march into enemy territory. In South Carolina, an amphibious Federal convoy left Hilton Head for a raid on the Charleston & Savannah Railroad, but came to an inglorious end on the Ashepoo River, where the steamers ran aground. The troops had to wade ashore in neck-deep water and stand around shivering all night, soaking wet, while Confederate field artillery shelled their boats. One of the transports could not be freed, and rebel gunners riddled her until the crew abandoned ship, first setting it ablaze to keep it from falling into enemy hands and leaving nearly a hundred cavalry mounts aboard to die in the flames. The rest of the flotilla slunk back to Hilton Head.[73]

West of the Chattahoochee River, Union fortunes fared even worse. General Grant had hoped to begin operations against Mobile, Alabama — partly to close that port to further blockade running, but also to relieve the pressure against Sherman as he approached Atlanta. The Mobile campaign had originally been meant for Major General Nathaniel Banks, commander in the Department of the Gulf, but early in the spring Banks left his New Orleans headquarters to march up the Red River with a substantial army, including thousands of troops borrowed from Sherman and thousands more cooperating from the Department of Arkansas, besides a powerful naval escort. By the middle of April Banks had been defeated and demoralized by a Southern force half the size of his own, but low water on the river had slowed his flight; he was still retreating to New Orleans after Joe Johnston abandoned Resaca. The pointless foray had mortified and discouraged everyone in Banks's department, and spoiled the plans for Mobile, allowing Confederate troops there to reinforce Johnston: the first division from Mobile had reached the Army of Tennessee in time to help defend Resaca. The Union column from Arkansas scampered all the way back to Little Rock, and its commander seemed content to remain there in safety, emphasizing the brilliance of his retreat. The absence of Sherman's borrowed divisions had freed Confederate cavalryman Nathan Bedford Forrest to raid at will through west Tennessee and Kentucky. West of the Mississippi River, rebel horsemen also undertook the only organized offensive operations, by either army, for ten weeks after Banks first turned his back on his weaker opponent. From Saint Louis to Santa Fe, no action more deadly than a skirmish disturbed the plains until summer.[74]

That strategic inertia throughout most of the embattled South reflected the concentrated efforts in Virginia and Georgia. To create the

massive armies on the main fronts, the two pairs of opposing army commanders had siphoned troops from every available source. Seventeen
days into his offensive against Lee, Grant had lost thirty-six thousand
men — fully 30 percent of those who had crossed the Rapidan with him.
Union soldiers as far west as central Missouri began to worry that they
might be called upon to make up for those devastating losses, and they
had cause to worry, for Grant would eventually strip troops from as far
away as Louisiana to replenish his armies in Virginia. On the day of
grisly battle around the Mule Shoe, Grant wired for ten thousand of the
best infantry around Washington, and the next day Halleck forwarded
ten thousand replacements consisting of infantry, cavalry and mounted
rifles (some on horseback and some dismounted), and heavy-artillerymen
armed as infantry. He arranged for another seventeen thousand reinforcements to Meade and Butler over the next few days, drawing most of
them from the garrisons of forts around Washington and Baltimore, with
heavy artillery predominating.[75]

The 3rd Delaware had enjoyed safe and sedentary duty in upper Maryland for more than a year and a half; when the order came to leave, it fell
with the weight of a death sentence. The quartermaster of the regiment, a
semiliterate beneficiary of his family's political influence, sent his brother
what amounted to his will, with power of attorney and instructions for the
care of his wife and children. At least one cavalryman at the remount
camp near Washington balked at taking a musket to serve as infantry,
swearing that he and his comrades would mutiny before they would let
the government send them down to Grant to be butchered, but for all the
bluster a "foot battalion" of several hundred disgruntled cavaliers boarded
steamers for Belle Plain, to guard swarms of rebel prisoners. Even some
idle gunners from field artillery batteries found themselves converted to
infantry, and others bridled at the mere idea of it.[76]

It was the heavy-artillerymen who took the news hardest. Two regiments of them (and a regiment of dismounted cavalry) had begun the
campaign with Burnside's corps, while most had stayed behind to protect
the capital, beyond earshot of the ominous rumble below the Rapidan.
Few of them had ever faced an extended march with all their belongings
squeezed into a single knapsack, and for their first field campaign they
disposed of extravagant wardrobes with an air of resigned trepidation.
Bravado alone must have accounted for the rare burst of enthusiasm
claimed by a New York lieutenant, who assured his family that his regiment left Washington in a merry mood at the prospect of quenching
an alleged "thirst for excitement."[77] Thirteen hundred of those "heavies"
would lie dead or wounded within four days after reaching the front lines,
and most of them were thinking about just such prospects — rather than

any thirst for excitement — when they bid farewell to their soft bunks and cozy barracks.[78]

Some veteran infantry regiments had come out of the Wilderness with barely a hundred men in the ranks, and a week into the fighting at Spotsylvania many of the new regiments had shrunk below three hundred. Two days after the bloodbath at the Mule Shoe, the first heavy-artillery reinforcements reached the front in their bright blue uniforms, with each regiment bigger than most brigades in Meade's army. The 1st Vermont Heavy Artillery was nearly two years old, but, thanks to recent recruits seeking soft duty, it reached the front seventeen hundred strong: the three battalions were divided for independent service, but each of them still dwarfed any infantry regiment in the field.[79]

General Meade sprinkled nine of those regiments through his army during his second week at Spotsylvania. His provost marshal, whose duties included corralling and returning anyone who parted ways with his regiment, grumbled that the ersatz infantrymen straggled badly. The veterans tended to laugh at the vast formations of well-dressed neophytes, offering boisterous predictions that they would run at the first sign of danger.[80] The artillerymen seemed concerned about that possibility themselves: the sergeant major of the 1st Vermont Heavy Artillery felt confident of the original men, who had initially enlisted as infantry, but he worried that new men who had chosen the heavy artillery for comfort and security would bolt under fire. An infantry captain elicited a common emotion among the transmogrified heavy-artillerymen when he met an officer perilously close to the front lines with scarlet trim on his uniform: the captain inquired the stranger's unit, and the unhappy fellow spat back that he belonged to the "14th Heavy Artillery, caliber 58, bayonets on the end!"[81]

Then, on May 19, most of those fresh heavy-artillerymen passed their first test with Lee's veterans. Richard Ewell ventured out of his works to investigate Grant's latest attempt to flank the Confederate right, and that afternoon he stumbled across the main road to Fredericksburg, catching Meade in the flank. The Yankees thought Ewell was trying to sever their supply line, and promptly counterattacked with two nearby brigades of heavy artillery from New York, Massachusetts, and Maine. Seven bulging regiments of them pushed off in some confusion, firing once or twice into each other, but their dense ranks blunted the rebels' advance and drove them to cover. In the process they lost a good tenth of those they took into the fight. The commander of the Fifth Corps artillery brigade thought they had suffered half those casualties because their officers didn't know their business, but that evening the victorious heavies seemed perfectly satisfied with the cost of their newfound confidence. Everyone knew that most of them had chosen their branch of service to avoid combat, but no one made any more remarks about how well they might stand fire.[82]

The casualties since the beginning of the campaign exceeded anything the oldest soldiers among them had ever seen. "Our losses have been frightful," General Meade admitted to his wife; "I do not like to estimate them." On May 14, after ten days of fighting and before the heavy artillery started to come in, one of Grant's staff officers did estimate them, concluding that Meade could field fewer than half as many effective troops as he did on May 4. At General Warren's headquarters they calculated that only twelve thousand men remained with the Fifth Corps out of the original twenty-seven thousand.[83]

"The slaughter has been terrible," reported a lieutenant just arrived at Belle Plain, where entire trains passed regularly, filled with wounded. A first sergeant in the 121st New York counted two officers and thirty-seven enlisted men in his company on May 4, but by May 13 he was the ranking man: the two officers had both been killed, and there were only a dozen privates left standing. A New Hampshire lieutenant reported more than half of his company killed and wounded after ten days in the maelstrom, while his brigade of three old regiments and three new ones had been whittled down from twenty-four hundred to nine hundred.[84]

Webster Brown, a young private from East Baldwin, Maine, had foreseen such unwonted butchery as much as a month previously, betting that it would be a lucky man who suffered a light wound early in the campaign, but such luck did not fall to him: late in May a messmate sent word home that Brown was missing, with optimistic speculation that he might have been wounded or captured, but strangers had already buried him. A Vermont lieutenant with the heavy artillery offered his wife dubious comfort with the information that a wound would send him to Washington, where she could join him during his recovery, and he did soon suffer a slight one, but it failed to remove him from the front; five weeks afterward, he and most of his battalion were "gobbled up" and landed in Confederate prisons.[85]

Company commanders had traditionally borne the duty of writing those painful letters to next of kin, but the need had grown so frequent that sergeants assumed some of the burden. The tragedies of neighbors had trained civilians to anticipate bad news after a week or so without letters, and to allay domestic apprehension soldiers with access to plenty of paper sent flurries of notes to their families every couple of days. That habit flourished among the generals and their various staffs. Men in the ranks could seldom match the volume of those assurances, for stationery came more precious to them, and whenever they stopped moving they generally fell asleep, but even with bullets zipping over their rifle pits many a man sharpened his pencil stub and hunched over a flat surface to send a few words home. Often he had no idea where he was, and his only news entailed the names or numbers of the dead and wounded, which tended to defeat the comforting purpose of the letter: one Vermonter advised his wife not to "borrow trouble" over his safety, then told her of the man who had been shot dead right behind him, the night before. Still, those few scrawled sentences smudged with red clay told the recipients that their son, brother, husband, or father was still in the land of the living — or at least that he had been alive a few days before.[86]

Grant and his staff had endured weeks on end of less deadly sieges at Vicksburg and Chattanooga, but never had the Virginia armies grappled so closely for so long. The ceaseless peril and toil had begun to wear on everyone. After Spotsylvania one Massachusetts lieutenant tallied four killed out of his regiment's twenty-eight officers, of whom another thirteen had been seriously wounded, and two of the remaining eleven had been winged. Oliver Wendell Holmes Jr. tried to portray the horror of it all for his father, explaining that "nearly every Regimental off[icer] I knew or cared for is dead or wounded." It was Holmes's diary, though, that inadvertently revealed the surprisingly demoralizing effects of neglected hygiene and nutrition when he recorded, two weeks into the campaign, how miraculously a bath, a meal, and a drink had rejuvenated him. Amid all the death and mutilation, one of Burnside's staff officers complained worst about how dirty he was: with their baggage train miles away, they had been sleeping without tents, and he had not changed his shirt in nine days. "Everyone is played out," confessed a major on Gouverneur Warren's staff, "including your humble servant," and he implied that General Warren had grown quite testy, as well.[87] A lieutenant on division staff duty in Burnside's corps remarked on Saturday, May 14, that the campaign was already "using us up very fast, especially in spirits." The following Wednesday, after his division had made another futile assault against Lee's fieldworks, Brigadier General Francis Barlow apprised his mother that after fifteen consecutive days the fighting had become "rather tedious," and two days later he showed less restraint in confiding to his brother that "I long for this damn campaign to be over."[88]

His own persistence and his opponent's aggressiveness had cost Grant more men by May 21 than Sherman would lose all spring and summer, and his long casualty lists had cost more than mere strength and morale. One of Meade's corps commanders had been killed, and one of Burnside's division commanders; another division commander had been wounded, and in Grant's four corps nineteen brigade commanders had been put out of action, including two in the Ninth Corps who had fallen out with sunstroke on the march to join the fighting. The death, disabling, or capture of each of those officers had initiated an upward shuffle as less experienced men moved up to fill the void, often depriving regiments of good colonels to supply a mediocre brigadier.[89]

Nowhere, probably, did the drain of command talent show more conspicuously than in Burnside's first division, after Tom Stevenson was drilled through the head by a chance shot on May 10. His death left the division to Colonel Daniel Leasure of the 100th Pennsylvania, who seemed well regarded in his regiment, and one of Stevenson's staff officers thought him quite satisfactory as a brigade commander, but that good opinion changed the moment Leasure assumed command of the division. Burnside may have felt the same, because he quickly replaced Leasure and dropped him back to his brigade. Leasure may have reached his limit in both capacity and courage: during the assault on the Mule Shoe, Colonel Leasure could not be found, and the lieutenant colonel of the 21st Massachusetts had to take control of the brigade through that grueling day's work. Two days later, Leasure relinquished command altogether and retreated to a sickbed. The first division ultimately went to James Ledlie, who had twice been appointed a brigadier general without winning Senate approval. His own staff officers later came to conclude that Ledlie was "useless or worse" in a fight, but Ambrose Burnside's patience allowed Ledlie to command his division long enough to account for some of the more renowned failures and fiascoes in the Ninth Corps.[90]

More common, and sometimes more debilitating, was the disintegration of lower-level command structures, with captains of dubious merit assuming control over veteran regiments, and sergeants moving up to direct their companies. The colonel of the 9th New Hampshire had pleaded illness as the campaign commenced, decamping until the year's fighting was over, and the lieutenant colonel and major were both shot through the thigh on May 12. The senior captain went down with his death wound a few days later, leaving Captain Daniel Buswell in charge, but Buswell immediately pronounced himself sick and asked stretcher-bearers to carry him to the rear while the regiment marched past him to the front. After that, the other company officers refused to recognize his authority, and Buswell quietly gave way to a still-more-junior captain, who took to the bottle and to highhanded abuse of his subordinates as soon as he was installed.[91]

The rise of such dross to leadership vacancies and the relentless struggle in the burnt-umber Virginia mud had ground the confidence and courage out of many men that brutal spring. Four steamboats reached the docks at Washington on May 11 with every deck covered in wounded, including four generals, but about a hundred men and one officer who disembarked with them could show no blood. These were merely the ones who had been caught, and rumor had it that the transports had carried nearly as many malingerers as wounded: officers seen loafing in hotel lobbies soon afterward were thought to have arrived on those boats. Detectives had been arresting the occasional deserter or innocent transient for months past, but after this discovery armed patrols started circulating around the capital, collaring stray soldiers wholesale. Thereafter, surgeons were sent aboard the transports at the dock to inspect each wounded man before allowing him to go ashore.[92]

Wilbur Dubois, of the 20th Michigan, worked a more common variation of that scheme. He spent most of the spring campaign in his division hospital, playing up a bruise and then, when the bruise faded, staying on to tend the wounded until a surgeon ordered him back to his regiment. He dodged out of the next fight by helping wounded men to the rear, one after the other, and lingering at the hospital until the fighting was over. Dubois wrote to an accommodating uncle that he suffered from a vague, debilitating weakness, whereupon the uncle, a Michigan congressman, inquired of his nephew's health in a letter to the boy's division commander, Orlando Willcox. Willcox, himself a Michigan native and resident, took the hint and assigned Dubois to hospital duty until his resourceful uncle could wheedle a commission for him. A Massachusetts lieutenant made unflattering remarks about a fellow officer who also milked a mere scratch at the division hospital, while more seriously wounded comrades returned to duty voluntarily.[93]

Other stragglers hovered right on the fringes of the army in the field, having vanished in the chaos of combat in dense forests, without even the excuse of the hospital ploy. Wilbur Fisk, the 2nd Vermont's correspondent for the *Green Mountain Freeman,* confessed to his readership that he had slipped to the rear in the Wilderness — though he may have absconded a day earlier, and remained absent longer, than he admitted — and as the army moved away from Spotsylvania he dropped out again. For the next week he lagged behind repeatedly, either alone or in the company of other "coffee boilers." In his diary Fisk blamed sickness, fatigue, and hunger for his failure to keep up with comrades who faced the same difficulties, but in the *Freeman* he emphasized the confusion of a night march. Neither the overpowering fatigue that he cited nor the perpetual occupation that he described prevented him from composing a long letter for the newspaper during that same week.[94]

Rumors of widespread cowardice among army officers spread homeward, and indeed the unrelenting stress gradually produced an irresistible weakness in the knees that respected no rank. However, an officer's duty in battle often required him to stand behind his men, encouraging them or shoving them back into line if they started to bolt, and that breastwork of standing bodies may have posed an additional temptation to those whose commissions did not make them any less human than the shellshocked privates they shouldered back into line. Punishments for dishonorable behavior tended to be more lenient among officers than those meted out to enlisted men, consisting often of nothing more than the demand for a resignation, but there was always the occasional unfortunate who found himself used to set an example. A second lieutenant who ducked one of Grant's fights and fled to the rear had his insignia and buttons stripped from his coat before a guard detail escorted him back to his regiment with his hands tied behind his back. As the 31st U.S. Colored Troops went into action for the first time the major of that regiment sought shelter in an ambulance, and when a surgeon refused to send him to the rear for treatment he tried to resign. A court-martial sentenced him to three years on Dry Tortugas, but first he had to suffer the public indignity of having his uniform stripped and his sword broken by one of his own sergeants.[95] The colonel of the 32nd Maine, whom a veteran officer said "does not amount to much," stayed home until the end of May, purportedly with dysentery, but even when he returned to duty he allowed his young lieutenant colonel to lead the regiment into battle — while the major of the 32nd bore the secret nickname "John Gilpin," perhaps because of a tendency to lose control and run.[96]

General officers were not immune. Joshua Owen, a rakish brigadier in the Second Corps, began showing the white feather at Spotsylvania, but the charge of misconduct before the enemy bore the less opprobrious phrasing of "disobedience of orders," and he was mustered out without a fuss. Brigadier General Lysander Cutler, formerly of the renowned Iron Brigade, bore a long and honorable battlefield record, with the scars to show for it, but his subordinates still thought him more timid than he talked; after the dreadful spring and summer of 1864 he asked to be reassigned to a peaceful post well in the rear, and it was done.[97] A captain in the Iron Brigade may have been thinking of Cutler when, while trying to explain to his wife why he felt he could not leave his men even after his three years had expired, he wrote that there were already too many officers "trying to Shuffle out Ass backwards and every other way."[98]

Butler's army on Bermuda Hundred saw a proportionate measure of that phenomenon. After a week of frequent fighting there, a New York sergeant noticed that his officers hid behind trees while they waved their troops to the attack, and a private in the 3rd New Hampshire reported that his own captain and the regimental commander had developed the same practice, as had many of the rest of the officers in his regiment, and in others. Two captains in the 4th New Hampshire underwent the formal insignia-stripping and drumming-out for retiring their skirmish lines without orders, but one of them later won reinstatement, eventually taking command of the regiment. Officers in the 3rd New York who wanted out of the service in the middle of the summer campaign tried to have their regiment consolidated with a newer regiment, which would have left them subject to discharge as supernumeraries; when that scheme failed, five of the lieutenants tried to resign, but their resignations were rejected in favor of summary dismissals on the charge of "resigning in the face of the enemy."[99]

There seemed to be less of that sort of thing under Sherman's command, for all the wavering of that Pennsylvania regiment at Resaca. The campaign in Georgia involved more maneuvering, and by the time Sherman had pushed Johnston halfway to Atlanta he had fought only one significant battle. Besides, the three armies under Thomas, McPherson, and Schofield were all dominated by Westerners from rural communities, who enjoyed none of the personal anonymity that tinged city life and abetted any inclination toward shameful conduct. They were men whose neighbors paid attention to how they performed, for whom the dread of a bad reputation may have helped them to better resist the perfectly natural — and even sensible — impulse to turn tail at the threat of death or mutilation. The teeming cities of the Eastern Seaboard offered less of that influence, and they also provided multitudes of mercenary substitutes and volunteers with tenuous devotion to the nationalistic ideal that drove the war, who often put little stock in the traditional concept of honor anyway. Still, the subordination of reputation to personal safety was not unknown among Sherman's officers, but they, too, also preferred more acceptable avenues of escape, like the hospital ruse. A New York captain whose regiment was getting chewed up in Georgia tarried all summer in Chattanooga on a plea of illness: he wrote his father just after one of Sherman's costlier battles that he was "some better" — just not well enough to go to the front. He was unable to go home on a furlough because that would require a surgeon's certificate that he was disabled, which he wasn't, so he planned to hang on at Chattanooga until autumn, when the fighting would presumably be over and he stood some chance of having a resignation accepted.[100]

Even when Sherman's officers showed more obvious symptoms of uncontrollable fear, it generally provoked less notice than in Virginia. Henry Kennett, the colonel of the 79th Ohio, never commanded his regiment in a battle after Resaca, and when he offered his resignation in July his men clearly understood that "he don't like to smell the powder." Officers who tried to resign in Virginia that summer were often court-martialed and dismissed in disgrace, like the five New York lieutenants in Butler's army, but the men of the 79th were happy just to be rid of Colonel Kennett, and apparently so was General Sherman.[101]

One weakness that proved fairly prevalent among officers ended up costing more than the understandable fear of shot and shell. A fondness for alcohol, or a dependence on it, appears to have been the most frequent cause of misfeasance, and often it produced especially lethal consequences. General Ledlie, who had never seen any large-scale fighting before wearing a star on his shoulder, seemed unable to face either hostile fire or the responsibilities of battlefield command without priming himself liberally. In the Army of the Potomac he would come to epitomize the cost of inebriation in the commissioned grades, but a florid face and fuzzy mind could be found between shoulder straps on almost any battlefield. In the Army of the James a Connecticut captain followed his company into one engagement too drunk to stand without holding on to something solid, and a lieutenant colonel from New York found himself in arrest for having taken too much aboard while he was in command of his brigade picket line. A disastrous campaign into Mississippi that spring would begin with the commanding general drinking himself blind the night before he started, while his principal division commander appeared on the first day's march so intoxicated that he fell on his face and had to be supported by his staff officers. The two of them continued to imbibe along the way, and a quarter of the men who started out with them ended the brief campaign either dead or in Confederate prisons. Sometimes the soldier's worst enemy was the man who led him into battle.[102]

2

The Mouldering Coat and
Cuddled-up Skeleton

⋘ THE WAR DEPARTMENT telegraph conveyed both good news and bad from the front, with the bad news usually disguised as periodic demands for medical supplies and reinforcements. Observers of an optimistic turn could, and did, greet the reports from the two principal theaters as evidence of looming triumph. Sherman seemed to gain twenty miles a week, driving Johnston's disheartened divisions ever closer to Atlanta, and Grant wired frequent descriptions of what sounded like a Confederate army at the last ditch, steadily losing prisoners, guns, and ground. "All the prospect of this campaign is splendid beyond our hopes," wrote forty-four-year-old George Templeton Strong, from his luxuriously appointed Gramercy Park brownstone. "But will it last?"[1]

Forty-year-old Edward F. Hall, a private in Butler's army at Bermuda Hundred, felt less hopeful about the chances of success, at least within the foreseeable future, but his opinion may have been colored by his uneasiness about being captured or killed just as his enlistment expired. No such worries afflicted Second Lieutenant Rufus Kinsley, down on Ship Island, Mississippi, but he shared Hall's contempt for civilian speculation about how soon the war could be won, and he seemed to predict a long struggle yet. Tench Tilghman, the grandson and namesake of one of George Washington's staff officers, agreed with the two soldiers: the old Marylander evidently clung to the Union, albeit with the common discontent of the conservative, but two of his sons had taken commissions in the Confederate army, and one of them had already gone to his grave. Writing to console a New York friend who had just lost his daughter, Tilghman interpreted the murderous conflict as expiation for the sins of the nation, but he doubted the scale had been balanced and expected that the worst was yet to come.[2]

Women seemed less able to tolerate the human toll of the war, and more inclined to question whether it was worth so many lives. Death came to almost every community that spring, and sometimes in flurries. The sight of yet another family that had just gone into mourning — or several families, simultaneously — moved mothers, wives, and young girls to write long, sad letters, often to friends or relatives in the army, some of whom might have found those missives depressing or politically insinuating. Tend as they might toward the lugubrious prose of their era, women expressed a sincere compassion for those who had lost loved ones, while men seemed better able to deflect or repress such sympathy, or to withstand it — including men in uniform who had seen much death themselves. Their pity for the bereaved, and their solicitude for the endangered, may have given women greater strength to resist emotional patriotic appeals that proved more successful among their menfolk. Reading newspaper accounts of the cataclysmic struggle, even Ben Butler's wife could doubt the wisdom of it.[3]

"How anyone can deliberately make up their minds to go I cannot understand," a young Maine woman finally confided to her fiancé, who did not go. Like many men who opposed the war, she supposed that there would be much less enthusiasm for continuing it if every man had to serve.[4]

Men who did doubt the merits of the conflict usually voiced objections more political in nature, but some also shared the distaff sensitivity to brutality and destruction, like Nathaniel Hawthorne, of Concord, Massachusetts. That teller of New England tales reflected the instincts of his old friend Franklin Pierce: the former president would only have advised taking up the sword against the seceded states if they first made an attack on the remaining states, or on Washington. Pierce scorned reunion by force as impractical, and Hawthorne appeared to agree with him. In the spring of 1862 Hawthorne had taken a trip to Washington and Hampton Roads to visit the forts, the generals, and the president, and he had written a humorous article about the journey that hinted subtly at his underlying disapproval of the war effort; the pro-administration *Atlantic Monthly* would not publish the unexpurgated version, and even after Hawthorne deleted some irreverent vignettes of the high and the mighty the editors felt constrained to ameliorate his captious remarks with mild chastisement of their own. Hawthorne and Pierce tolerated that censorious atmosphere with poor grace for another year, until Pierce exploded at a Fourth of July Democratic rally in 1863, excoriating Lincoln for the constitutional infringements he had deemed necessary to prosecute a war that Pierce did not believe in.[5]

That outburst led the administration's many friends to brand Pierce with the accusation of treason they were wont to cast at any who questioned their aims. The seeming apostasy of a former president required particularly vehement defamation, and Pierce's antebellum friendship with Jefferson Davis fueled widespread insinuations that he was working in league with the Confederates. Hawthorne stood by Pierce, dedicating his last book to him against the advice and wishes of his publisher. By the time Grant's spring offensive began, Hawthorne was sinking fast into his final illness, but he was still troubled by the sectional conflict, and the collector of internal revenue was pestering him for the new tax on his income, which had been imposed to pay for the war he despised. In an effort to restore the ailing writer's health, Pierce escorted him on one last excursion through the White Mountains.[6]

No train had yet penetrated the highlands, and the pair proceeded by stagecoach, alighting at the sprawling Pemigewasset House in Plymouth on the afternoon of May 18, 1864. The two illustrious travelers retired early, as Hawthorne had felt weak all day, and Pierce looked in on him each time he woke up during the night. A couple of hours before dawn he noticed that Hawthorne had not moved since about midnight, and a single touch revealed that the body was already cold.[7]

Seven hundred miles away lay the gory breastworks at Spotsylvania, where tired, frightened men rested in the mud from their latest efforts to kill one another, but in the mountains the war seemed a mere fantasy. At the Pemigewasset House more interest may still have lingered in the elopement of one of its managers, two seasons before, with a married lady who had lodged there while the leaves turned, and with a local legislator who had run away with the daughter of a neighbor. "Were the war between the Crim-Tartars and the Hottentots we this way could not apparently care less about it," confessed a Bostonian sojourning on his brother's farm in central New Hampshire, and much of the population did seem quite capable of ignoring all the exciting news from Virginia and Georgia. The third week in May concluded the longest and deadliest spell of continuous fighting that Union forces had ever known, but it seemed to escape the attention of some who recorded their every thought and activity. One young lady in rural Connecticut spent that week painting her room and writing her customarily gossipy letters to friends, in which she almost never mentioned the unpleasant events to the south, or anyone connected with them. An eighteen-year-old girl from a comfortably fixed New Hampshire family passed her time that spring entertaining young admirers, including some of the Granite State governor's sons — none of whom ever served in uniform. When men started killing each other wholesale in Spotsylvania County, she returned to her finishing school in Boston, and although she hobnobbed there with a former lieutenant from a Brahmin nine-month regiment, no talk of soldiers or war seemed to intrude upon their conversations. With one of her classmates she went to the theater each Sunday, seeing *The Lady of Lyons* on May 14 and *The Marble Hearts* on the twenty-first, both of which included "that blessed J. Wilks Booth." Her detailed diary entries seldom so much as alluded to the great national drama that spring, or for the rest of the year.[8]

The executive usurpations and infringements that Franklin Pierce had denounced seldom troubled those who took no notice of the strife, for they had no occasion to comment on public affairs and therefore seldom risked the ire of the government. In addition, if through some accident they or one of theirs should become the victim of overweening federal authorities, they could usually call upon influential friends for relief. A woman whose brother was mistakenly arrested as a deserter while passing through New York had to invest enormous time and effort to have him released, and had she not been acquainted with her state's military agent in that city her brother might have languished in unjustified confinement for quite a while longer.[9]

Those who dared to disagree had better cause to fear the government they censured, for no critic seemed too exalted to arrest, and if Mr. Lincoln rose above the vindictive or partisan abuse of executive authority, his secretary of war did not. Ex-president Pierce might well have anticipated arrest for his Independence Day expression of independence. Democratic congressional and gubernatorial candidates had been jailed for campaign statements that the War Department now prosecuted as sedition, and Charles Stone, a very capable general of conservative mien, had been notoriously persecuted by Edwin Stanton and the clique of Radical Republicans whose favor Stanton clandestinely cultivated. Stanton had arbitrarily cast Stone into prison for half the year of 1862, and just as arbitrarily he relieved Stone of duty and mustered him out of the volunteer service as the campaign season of 1864 began, essentially demoting him to his Regular Army rank of colonel.[10]

Samuel Barlow, a prominent New York critic of the administration, had been alerted at the vernal equinox that Stanton's detectives viewed him and other Democrats as "fit subjects for summary acts," and that information evidently had some foundation. When the *New York World* and the *Journal of Commerce* unwittingly published a fraudulent presidential proclamation that portrayed the war as an endless and escalating calamity, the authorities called first on Barlow. The bogus decree echoed the antique phrasing of other formal pronouncements from Lincoln's desk, declaring a day of fasting, humiliation, and prayer based on "the situation in Virginia, the disaster at Red River, the delay at Charleston, and the general state of the country." Worst of all, perhaps, was the addition of another call for four hundred thousand more recruits, to be raised by "an immediate and peremptory draft."[11]

Professing to issue that levy "with a heavy heart, but with undiminished confidence in our cause," the document reeked of ill-disguised desperation, but its most alarming aspect lay in the threat of a massive draft, apparently without the opportunity for drafted men to avail themselves of either commutation or substitution. That possibility terrified those hundreds of thousands of eligible citizens who thought themselves insulated from service by their wealth or savings. Even if it had not seemed suspiciously defeatist, the forgery contradicted the federal conscription law, most obviously by mistaking the lower limit of draft age as eighteen, rather than twenty, and hours after it appeared the War Department telegrapher in New York inquired whether it was genuine. Both newspapers that carried the proclamation had been flaying the administration for its excesses for most of the war, which led Lincoln partisans to instantly identify it as the work of "Copperheads" — a term originally coined to vilify antiwar Democrats, which Republicans eventually modified to smear any Democrats who failed to wholeheartedly embrace Republican doctrine. George Templeton Strong wrote that this "act of moral high treason" was immediately ascribed to Barlow, who was directed to the headquarters of Major General John Dix, along with the two publishers. The newspaper offices were both seized by armed squads of soldiers under direct orders from President Lincoln, who characterized the spurious publication as "treasonable," and asserted that it was "designed to give aid and comfort to the enemies of the United States," for which he intended to consign the suspects to another of the military commissions with which the government had superseded the legally constituted courts. Stanton also ordered the arrest of employees from an implicated telegraph company in New York and other cities.[12]

General Dix undertook an investigation, but Stanton reproved him for doing so, insisting that he let the military commission conduct any inquiry. That would have condemned the arrested parties to weeks or months in Fort Lafayette — which, considering his treatment of General Stone, may have been Stanton's purpose. Given the propensity for such commissions to convict on the flimsiest evidence, more serious consequences could have followed. To the discomfiture of the impulsive secretary of war, though, Dix had already extracted a confession from a reporter for the firmly pro-administration *New York Times*, who had exploited the delivery system of the Associated Press to lend the fraud authenticity. Only by the accident of their press schedules did other New York papers fail to publish it, and a copy went aboard a transatlantic steamer, for telegraphic distribution at Queenstown. The ruse had been intended to cause enough public discouragement to send the price of gold skyrocketing, allowing for a hasty and substantial profit, and gold did soar before the corrections appeared. The reporter went to Fort Lafayette instead of Barlow and the Democratic newspapermen, whom Stanton ordered released with a lecture to go forth and err no more. Post office inspectors apparently used the incident as an excuse to start opening most of Barlow's mail, and they were still doing so more than a week after he had been exonerated. Having lost its attraction as an example of Copperhead treachery, however, the fraud merited no further attention from the War Department, and the admitted perpetrator of what Stanton had called "a great national crime" was eventually released without trial.[13]

A few weeks later Lincoln personally ordered the arrest of a United States senator. John Carlile, of West Virginia, invited a Saint Louis man to come to Washington to confer with him, purportedly about extracting cotton from Confederate territory, as General Banks had once hoped to do during the Red River campaign. Missouri was full of men with very confused allegiances: Union troops had attacked the state legislature and militia even though the state never seceded, causing many Missourians to consider themselves the loyalists as they fought Federals whom they saw as renegades. Carlile's visitor was one such Missourian, but he had apparently retired to his home and given up the fight. He still maintained Confederate connections that he said he was going to use to get the cotton, but he was arrested as a spy anyway, and when told of the case the president ordered Carlile taken into custody as well.[14]

Devoted as he was to the Union, Carlile took a conservative view of the Constitution, dissenting from much of the Radical Republican agenda. Peremptory handling of men like him improved Lincoln's image among the Radicals, and at that moment he may have thought it best to court that faction a little. Lincoln had but nine months left in his first term, and only five before the presidential election. He faced no real challenge for the Republican nomination, but his chances of winning reelection depended upon several other factors: the progress of the war probably bore the most weight, but it mattered a great deal whom the Democrats chose to run, and it was even more important that no third-party candidate run who might appeal to Republicans.

Writing on the occasion of Ulysses Grant's promotion to general in chief, a prominent Pennsylvania Republican confided to Radical congressman Thaddeus Stevens that Lincoln's "errors" might lose him the election against the right Democrat. He supposed that Grant would be the only Democrat who could beat the president, if he ran, and he questioned whether Grant could be restrained from accepting a nomination. If not, he wondered, could Lincoln's nomination be quashed? Grant's wife seemed to allay any apprehension of a challenge before the Republican convention, telling an assistant secretary of the Treasury Department privately that her husband "would not think for one moment" of running for president.[15]

If that were the case, Republicans supposed that the Democrats would select George McClellan, who retained the regard of not only Northern Democrats but of most of the soldiers, at least in the Army of the Potomac. Radicals had pegged him as the man to beat more than a year before, so they had done their best to stigmatize him and everyone associated with him. The Radicals' single greatest weapon in Washington, the Joint Committee on the Conduct of the War, had produced a report the previous year that threw all the blame on McClellan for his army's failures while he commanded it, and a court-martial initiated and presided over by Radical-friendly generals had dismissed McClellan's closest subordinate from the army for disobedience of orders in a degree approaching treason. McClellan countered with his own official report, doctoring it to flatter himself, and he asked permission to have it printed, but for a time Stanton hesitated to authorize government publication of a rebuttal to the joint committee with which he was so friendly. Eventually he permitted a truncated version, and McClellan supplemented that with a private edition.[16]

Whomever the Democrats chose, Lincoln faced a more formidable threat from a Republican schism, and Radical Republicans seemed the likeliest to bolt. The previous December the president had announced an amnesty proclamation and a provision for the seceded states to form their own loyal governments, requiring only that enough citizens accept the offer to equal at least 10 percent of each state's 1860 voters. It was an extremely generous invitation back into the Union, allowing the penitent provinces even to decide the ultimate legality of slavery within their borders — although they had to recognize the freedom of those slaves who had actually been released by his Emancipation Proclamation. The Radicals had balked at that, insisting instead on universal abolition as a prerequisite of reunion. Senator Ben Wade and his House colleague Henry Winter Davis of Maryland collaborated on a bill to wrest control of the issue from the president, demanding that the amnesty and the recognition of new state governments include the precondition of constitutional amendments banning slavery. Conservatives, including firm Democrats, defended Lincoln's more lenient policy because it would be less likely to repel wavering Confederates. Congressman Samuel Cox of Ohio, a leading Democrat, rebuked Winter Davis for proposing to force "the freed ne-gro into the very nostrils of the southern man," but the House had passed the Wade-Davis Bill on the same evening that the Army of the Potomac crossed the Rapidan.[17]

The Radicals' long and divisive fight to control Reconstruction had be-gun, and the president who had nearly played the part of their agent for two years began to resist. Since the early days of the administration, aboli-tionists had looked fondly on Salmon P. Chase, the secretary of the treas-ury, who had never softened his early antislavery convictions. The tension between the president's Reconstruction plan and the Radicals' alternative brought Chase back to mind as a rival candidate, which gratified the proud and ambitious secretary no end. A Chase proponent had raised the only real objection to the president in the first state caucus to endorse Lincoln for reelection. In early March, though, Chase had taken himself out of consideration in favor of Lincoln, citing a lack of support rather than any abatement in his desire. A few days after announcing his with-drawal he claimed that he was merely *trying* to avoid any presidential ambitions — snidely remarking that he could probably take better care of the treasury as president, with the help of a secretary, than he could as secretary without the help of a president. His early champions heeded his public assertion more than his private equivocation, and Chase's hopes ended there.[18]

Others proposed Ben Butler, a former Democrat whose transition to the Radical perspective had come with all the excessive fervor of a reli-gious convert and all the opportunism that characterized Butler's entire existence. Some of Lincoln's own public supporters reportedly whispered their secret preference for that cockeyed, sly little general, but his name went nowhere. Most dissatisfied Republicans, who consisted almost en-tirely of Radicals frustrated by Lincoln's deliberation on the matter of race, flocked to John Charles Frémont, who had carried the standard for the party in its first national election, in 1856. Like McClellan, Frémont had been an unemployed major general since his last failed campaign, in 1862, but unlike McClellan he had shown no hesitation on emancipation. As the commander of U.S. forces in Missouri, in 1861, he had been up-braided by Lincoln for unilaterally proclaiming freedom for all the slaves in the department who belonged to "secessionists" — however one might identify such a person in a place like Missouri. While the larger Republi-can Party operated under a nominal, one-sided alliance known as the Union Party, a splinter convention of Radicals met in Cleveland and nom-inated Frémont, who could be expected to siphon enough votes away from the Union candidate to change the outcome of a close election.[19]

The Union Party convention met in Baltimore a few days later. Delegates haggled more over the continuation or replacement of Lincoln's cabinet members than over any other potential nominee for president: a cabal of Missouri Radicals pressed for the expulsion of Postmaster General Montgomery Blair and, to a lesser degree, Attorney General Edward Bates, but Lincoln himself came away with a unanimous endorsement. There still remained the serious problem presented by Frémont, however, as well as the more difficult task of winning the war.[20]

In his most recent address to Congress the president had highlighted the military successes against the Confederacy, noting that Union forces had conquered vast domains in the seceded states, dividing them in two by opening the Mississippi. "Tennessee and Arkansas have been substantially cleared of insurgent control," he said, concluding that "the crisis which threatened to divide the friends of the Union is past." The optimistic took heart from his observations, and often repeated them to the cynical, as did a frequent correspondent of Mr. Barlow's, but Barlow responded with bitter amusement. John Morgan's latest raid caused Barlow to point out that Kentucky was "overrun" by rebels, while most of Missouri was "given over to the reptiles of the Earth," and Arkansas was only held by the stranded garrison at Little Rock, surrounded by hostile territory. The entire army under Banks had been "destroyed," Barlow claimed, and United States forces controlled none of Texas beyond the range of the navy's biggest gunboats. Far from being open, the Mississippi remained perilous, and the early conquest of North Carolina had been abandoned, while Sherman's army risked being cut off so far from its base of supplies. Grant, meanwhile, was butchering "the bravest and best troops God ever gave a nation." Even if Grant succeeded in taking Richmond, Barlow argued, the fight would simply proceed into North Carolina. The same strategic situation could produce either hope and cheer or anguish and despair, depending on which ingredient one emphasized.[21]

General Sherman shared Barlow's concern for his increasingly protracted and vulnerable line of communications. Joe Johnston also appreciated the opportunity that Sherman's long umbilical offered for harassing or even crippling his powerful opponent. That, after all, formed a fundamental principle of the Fabian retreat, but an effective blow against that artery required Sherman to penetrate a little deeper: first came aggressive resistance, and from his new position at Cassville Johnston coordinated one attack, collecting two-thirds of his troops to strike half of Sherman's bifurcated army on May 19. Courtesy of Nathaniel Banks's disastrous digression from Mobile, Johnston had been reinforced with Lieutenant General Leonidas Polk's corps, from the Gulf: with Polk's and John Bell Hood's corps he would have wielded almost equal numbers against the isolated Yankees, but Hood botched the plan when he allowed himself to be distracted by erroneous reports of a threat to his rear. That chance lost, the inept Polk and the reputedly aggressive Hood convinced Johnston that their position at Cassville was untenable. Reluctantly abandoning a stronghold from which he had hoped to repel an assault by Sherman, Johnston marched across the Etowah River on May 20, inadvertently leaving a wagon bridge for the use of Sherman's army.[22]

The troops traveling with Sherman suffered far fewer casualties than those under Grant, but the constant proximity to the enemy was new in this theater, and daily fighting brought early comments suggesting the onset of the syndrome that a later generation would call battle fatigue. The endless danger may have been at least as taxing as the occasional battle or loss of friends: more than one man found it unusual enough to warrant special mention that comrades were wounded half a mile behind the lines, while relaxing in presumed safety. Those three Union armies nevertheless rolled steadily toward Atlanta in high verve, tramping through country deserted by its apprehensive inhabitants. Ignorant of the accidents and arguments that led Johnston to relinquish so much ground, the invaders believed that they were "putting down the rebellion in earnest," and that victory lay only days or weeks ahead.[23]

By now Johnston thought the time had come to work on Sherman's supply line, and he dispatched the greater part of his cavalry for that purpose under Joseph Wheeler, who circled around the broad enemy front. On May 24 Wheeler fell on a wagon train near Cassville, scattering the Union horsemen who rode with it and capturing or burning the entire train, besides taking prisoners, horses, and mules. He also cut the railroad before hurrying back with his booty, but such damage caused little more than inconvenience for the Federals. The track was easily repaired, and the lost supplies created only passing discomfort for even a portion of so large an army. That very successful raid failed to delay Sherman's advance a moment; it would have required more comprehensive or persistent pressure to divert his attention.[24]

Below the Etowah, Johnston gathered his forces around the railroad at Allatoona, but Sherman slipped west, to Johnston's left, before crossing the river into a dense, lightly populated wilderness and striking toward the town of Dallas. The Confederates quickly followed, preparing log breastworks for a couple of miles on either side of New Hope Church. On May 25 Joe Hooker's corps pushed an unusually pliant rebel line back up rising ground to the ridge where those trenches lay waiting, and there, finally, Johnston enjoyed the sight of Union infantry sacrificing itself in frontal assaults against his fortified line. The Yankees held what they had gained after darkness fell, and in a cold rain they started building their own works. The rest of Sherman's army came up to begin flailing away with shovels, and there everyone remained for the next week, alternately digging at the clay or ducking a sporadic fire that seemed never to wane and often erupted in roaring, flashing volleys in the middle of the night. Another dash at Johnston's line on the twenty-seventh gained as little as Hooker's had, and cost Sherman nearly as many men. Confederates came out of their own works with their peculiar falsetto yell on the afternoon of May 28, hoping to hit Sherman while he was pulling back, but he had not yet withdrawn and their alacrity cost them a bloody repulse, in turn. Casualties mounted steadily that week, especially for Sherman, who had to carry his wounded back over the river to the railroad. About five trains a day brought rations from Chattanooga, and as the armies closed to shorter range those rail cars started filling up with wounded for the return trip, and with the occasional privileged corpse in a metallic coffin.[25]

Not until the first of June did Sherman swing around Johnston's flank again, rather than make another attempt at those ominous breastworks. He shifted his line gradually eastward, toward the railroad at Acworth, until Johnston could no longer stretch his front to match and had to withdraw again. This time he entrenched himself above Big Shanty, but Sherman worked his way toward him by a siege approach, extending his trenches rather than battering his men against solid earthworks. Behind him, Sherman's engineers started building a new railroad bridge over the Etowah to improve his connection with Chattanooga. In a week punctuated by unseasonable cold, saturating rain, and the slow, steady loss of men to sharpshooters and respiratory ailments, Sherman maneuvered Johnston back a short distance to a range of hills near Marietta, the tallest peak of which the Cherokees had named Kennesaw. Once again Johnston burrowed in and waited, with only twenty miles of road and the Chattahoochee River remaining between him and Atlanta.[26]

Beset as he was, Johnston could hardly detach enough manpower to effectively interrupt Sherman's communications, but others made the attempt from hundreds of miles away. As May turned to June, John Hunt Morgan — the Kentucky cavalier who had so easily diverted William Averell from Saltville in early May — burst out of southwestern Virginia into Kentucky through Pound Gap in what seems to have been both an official mission and an effort at personal expiation. He intended to cut the railroads in central Kentucky, and especially the line from Louisville to Nashville, which carried much of Sherman's supplies. Morgan may have been calculating that an accomplishment of that magnitude could restore his tattered military dossier: the previous year, he had flagrantly and foolishly exceeded his instructions on another Kentucky raid by crossing into Indiana and Ohio, where he and most of his command were captured. After a spectacular escape early in the winter, Morgan drew the assignment of defending the dismal border country of Virginia and Tennessee, where he seemed to champ impatiently for a little excitement, and his latest gambol into Kentucky represented his alternative to a rejected proposal for a raid on Nashville. Well over two thousand men followed him out of Virginia. Morgan hoped, as usual, to expand his ranks with recruits from his native state, and he would not have been alone in supposing that he would have good hunting among residents outraged at the absorption of Kentucky slaves into the Union army.[27]

Morgan ranged deep into the state, reaching the outskirts of Mount Sterling on June 7. His troopers galloped into town at daylight the next morning, subduing its garrison within a couple of hours, after which they began plundering the stores and houses. At least two men associated with the general's staff robbed the local bank of tens of thousands of dollars in greenbacks. Morgan rode on toward Lexington with one brigade, leaving behind the rest of his command, which was surprised by Union cavalry the next morning and routed with the loss of several hundred men. Reuniting with his retreating forces, Morgan pressed on to Lexington and to Cynthiana, which he seized with little effort on June 11, capturing a large garrison composed principally of two regiments of hundred-day men who were less than thirty days into their term. He plunged the Bluegrass into a frenzy that carried as far as the national capital, where President Lincoln worried that recruiting excesses among Kentucky slaves had alienated white citizens, but the day after Morgan took Cynthiana a combined force of Union cavalry and infantry charged his camp and all but destroyed his division, shooting or capturing as many as seven hundred and dispersing the rest. The remnant of one brigade swam the Licking River and fled south, making its way back to Virginia by circling south of Lexington and returning with only two hundred men still in the saddle. Morgan led the survivors of the other brigade straight up the Licking, abandoning his prisoners and crossing out of Kentucky a week later with a few hundred more. Those were the Confederates with whom Samuel Barlow had said Kentucky was "overrun."[28]

Sherman concerned himself little about Morgan. Other and better Southern cavalrymen looked covetously on the long rail lines that fed Sherman's army. The Louisville & Nashville Railroad covered nearly two hundred miles between the Ohio and Cumberland Rivers, while the Nashville & Chattanooga wound about a hundred and fifty more, by way of Stevenson, Alabama, and Sherman had pushed Johnston nearly a hundred miles below Chattanooga. No other roads could serve him, especially below Nashville, and the threat to this lifeline that he feared most took the shape of a tall Tennessean named Nathan Bedford Forrest. Early in the spring Forrest had ridden roughshod over western Kentucky and west Tennessee with a few brigades of cavalry, trying to draw troops from Sherman's main body below Chattanooga, and Sherman had anticipated before he even started after Johnston that Forrest would try to sever the rail lines to and from Nashville, to stymie his campaign into Georgia. Late in April Cadwallader Washburn, the Union commander in west Tennessee, sent three thousand cavalry and two thousand infantry out under Brigadier General Samuel Sturgis to try to catch Forrest, but Sturgis ran out of forage and returned less than ten days later, having succeeded only in chasing Forrest to Tupelo, Mississippi.[29]

Washburn had to accumulate a larger force if he hoped to corner Forrest and finish him off, but he had to act quickly, too, for he had word that Forrest left for Alabama on May 23, to operate against the railroad. In fact Forrest intended to make such a raid, but he lingered at Tupelo through the end of the month, by which time he was just preparing to leave on a railroad-wrecking expedition into middle Tennessee. Troops that Sherman had loaned to Nathaniel Banks started coming back to Memphis from the Red River campaign late in May, but of the first eighteen hundred to disembark from the transports only eight hundred could still be considered fit and equipped for the field. "As good luck would have it," wrote Washburn, the 9th Minnesota arrived on May 31 from Missouri, where it had spent the winter in scattered garrisons, and at the last moment he added the six hundred men of that regiment to the force, which finally totaled thirty-three hundred cavalry, five thousand infantry, and sixteen guns.[30]

The 9th Minnesota included recruit Chauncey Hill, who had said goodbye to his wife at Fort Snelling not quite three months before. He had joined his company at Warrensburg, in troubled Johnson County, Missouri, which had been home to many of William Quantrill's Southern-leaning guerrillas. Four companies of the Minnesota regiment had been sent to Warrensburg late that winter, to quell guerrilla depredations, but in mid-May the whole regiment started concentrating at Saint Louis for service "at the front," which for them lay down the Mississippi River. By the time Private Hill boarded the boat for Memphis, his wife had surely apprised him that she was pregnant.[31]

Forrest's camp at Tupelo sat alongside the Mobile & Ohio Railroad, which crossed the Memphis & Charleston Railroad at Corinth, Mississippi, before continuing on into Tennessee. The Mobile & Ohio served nearly the entire length of Mississippi, and the commander of the Confederacy's Department of Alabama, Mississippi, and East Louisiana, Stephen D. Lee, desperately wished to keep it in running order. Solicitation for his own supply corridor left Lee a little reluctant to release Forrest even to tear up Sherman's communications, but at last he ordered Forrest to take three thousand men into Alabama and Tennessee to do what damage he could. Forrest led the vanguard out of Tupelo on June 1, the same day that Washburn's expedition departed from Memphis. Forrest rode northeast, aiming to cross the Tennessee River at Muscle Shoals, Alabama, but he had not reached that river when a courier overtook him with word of the strong Yankee column headed their way from Memphis.[32]

Under the impression that his superiors wished it, Washburn assigned General Sturgis to lead his second foray after Forrest, and Sturgis may have assumed command with a crippling hangover. He only received his orders the day that the troops left Memphis, on June 1, and that evening a Wisconsin colonel saw the general stumbling down the stairs of the Gayoso House, giggling foolishly as he slammed the hotel register shut and brandished it like a club at a black servant. Another officer evidently tried to lead Sturgis out to the street to hail a hansom, but when they reached the sidewalk Sturgis — who had just returned from a visit to his wife and children — threw his arm around a passing woman who seemed not altogether offended, for she allowed him to keep his hold while Sturgis's companion tried to hoist the general into the cab. Given Sturgis's renowned appetite for alcohol, he may have doctored himself with a hair of the dog as he chased after his new command on the morning train. Colonel William McMillen, who took charge of all three brigades of Sturgis's infantry contingent by virtue of seniority alone, was also priming himself for the campaign as the expedition set out. When the troops climbed out of the cars, thirty-five miles from Memphis, McMillen fell on his face and had to be helped to stand up. Plenty of officers and enlisted men saw him in that condition, and those who had accompanied McMillen and Sturgis in the operations of early May entertained creditable opinions of neither. Sturgis, the story ran, was drunk most of the time.[33]

From the railroad the column marched southeast on June 2. Because of the inaccurate reports that Forrest was already well on his way to interfere with Sherman's rail line, Washburn had supposed that he was too late to forestall that damage, but he hoped to destroy the Mobile & Ohio all the way from Corinth to Meridian. Confederate intelligence inadvertently worked against Confederate interests, though, for the Memphis spies who alerted Stephen Lee to the departure of Sturgis's force conveyed the information quickly enough to bring Forrest galloping back. Had another day or two elapsed, Forrest would already have crossed beyond recall, north of the Tennessee River, where he would probably have wrought a great deal more harm to Sherman than Sturgis could have inflicted on Lee.[34]

Their route lay through country that Chauncey Hill thought "poor &

wild." Occasional plantations relieved the monotony, but most of them had fallen into neglect through three years of war; Hill's agricultural eye assessed the majority of the region as "running to waste." Oppressive heat had settled on north Mississippi by June, often building to long and violent cloudbursts. Heavy showers or steady rain tormented Sturgis for at least a good part of eight consecutive days, soaking his men and their every possession while the cavalry, infantry, and their wagons churned the yellow roads into a thick soup. The wagon teams suffered worst of all, straining against the clutching mud at every step, and Sturgis found forage as scarce as he had in May. Washburn had supplied him with only twenty days of provisions for his troops, and they had been out nine days when the main body camped fourteen miles beyond Ripley, on June 9.[35]

June 10 dawned hot and humid, and that heat intensified as the day progressed. Both Sturgis and McMillen each began the day with a bracer of whiskey. Soon after daylight the cavalry, amounting to ten regiments in two brigades, left camp under Brigadier General Benjamin Grierson. The mounted division took the road to Guntown, where the railroad lay. McMillen's three brigades of infantry trailed after them, an hour and a half behind. A brigade of four Illinois regiments led, followed by five regiments from Ohio, Indiana, Illinois, and the 9th Minnesota. Two regiments of U.S. Colored Troops from Alabama, Tennessee, and north Mississippi brought up the rear, guarding the wagon train: some of their former masters may have been riding with Forrest, who led cavalry from all three of those states.[36]

Forrest was farther up the railroad, expecting Sturgis to strike there, but during the night he had learned that the enemy was camped on the road to Guntown and he moved out with part of his command before dawn, taking a route that met the Guntown Road at a place called Brice's Crossroads. Grierson was moving slowly, but Forrest had nearly twice as much ground to cover, and the first mounted Federals passed through the crossroads at midmorning. Forrest had sent a small detachment ahead that met them there and delayed them until the general came up with his leading brigade. That brigade consisted mostly of mounted infantry, armed with long-range rifles, and he dismounted those men to fight on foot. The Union cavalry all carried carbines, so they could barely reach the Confederates who were picking them off, and most of those carbines were breechloaders, with hundreds of repeaters, so they quickly fired up all their ammunition. After a couple of hours of heavy skirmishing, the Yankees had been driven back almost to the intersection. Playing a close game, Forrest held back until the last of his four scattered brigades had all come in. He had only fifteen regiments to Sturgis's twenty-one, and most of them were not nearly as full as Sturgis's, but he fought the Union cavalry to a frazzle first and handled the infantry later. Those foot soldiers came panting up early in the afternoon, with men dropping from sunstroke, and Grierson slowly extricated his horsemen, most of whom were running out of cartridges.[37]

While the white infantry deployed, Forrest peeled off a regiment to turn their left flank and a few companies to threaten their right. Confederates reported none of the sunstroke or heat exhaustion that afflicted the Northern troops, although most of Forrest's men fought much longer than any of Sturgis's. By late afternoon the Union infantry shrank back to a tight arc around the crossroads, and after an ominous lull Forrest started to close his snare, pressing his dazed and weary enemies on both flanks until they started to crumble. Steadied by another drink or two, Sturgis tried to relieve the last of his beleaguered cavalry with part of a fresh infantry regiment, only to have both horse and foot come tumbling back over him, followed by what he characterized as an "avalanche" of fugitives from front, left, and right, many of them throwing away cartridge boxes and rifles. A Tennessee regiment on Forrest's extreme right tried to cut off their retreat between the crossroads and Tishomingo Creek, but one of Sturgis's brigade commanders stalled it with an Ohio regiment and a couple of companies from the 55th Colored Troops. Portions of the 9th Minnesota and the 114th Illinois joined them on rising ground near the creek, checking the rebel tide momentarily, but Confederate artillery converged on that courageous fragment and soon drove it away. With nothing more to stop him, Forrest came on fast and hard, and as the day's light faded Sturgis's expedition rushed back the way it had come, in profound confusion. One brigade of Grierson's cavalry formed across the road to try to halt the flight, without much success; his other brigade rode all the way back to the Stubbs plantation, nine miles from Brice's Crossroads, to form another new line on high ground there. Forrest pursued them into the night, overrunning their wagon train, all their ordnance wagons, and all their artillery. So many abandoned vehicles filled the road that he had to leave his own artillery behind and follow with mounted men alone in what became a running fight fifty miles long. Most of Sturgis's survivors finally scattered into the woods, and Forrest gave up the chase.[38]

On the way back, Forrest spread his command out and swept several hundred cowering Northern soldiers out of their hiding places. At a cost of fewer than 500 casualties, his inventory of trophies included all 16 pieces of Sturgis's artillery, with its caissons, limbers, and several hundred rounds of case shot, shell, and canister; 1,500 rifles and carbines; 300,000 rounds of small-arms ammunition; 192 wagons and ambulances; 184 horses and mules; 1,618 prisoners, and a pair of flags. Sturgis had lost 2,168 men, altogether, and he left almost all his wounded on the field or on the retreat: a quarter of those who had departed from Memphis under his command did not return. The colonel of the 9th Minnesota reported that his regiment went into action with 665 officers and men, of whom 7 had been killed: he counted another 272 as missing, of whom he knew that 20 were wounded, and most of those had probably been lost at the last stand on the knoll near Tishomingo Creek. Chauncey Hill, the recruit from Winona County, shuffled off among the dejected prisoners herded south along the railroad they had planned to destroy, and a week after the battle he and his comrades waited at Mobile for transfer to Americus, Georgia, where their captors told them they would find an "exchange camp."[39]

The spectacular battle sparked widespread comment about heavy drinking among general officers. Sturgis had been beaten nearly as badly as a general could be, and by a force barely half the size of his own, causing at least some of his men to suspect him of treachery; an Iowa soldier told his relatives that "any old Farmer" could have handled the troops better than Sturgis did. A board of inquiry looked into it, and found abundant evidence that Sturgis and McMillen were prone to overindulgence, but General Sherman put much of the blame on Forrest's legendary ferocity. He described the rebel cavalryman as "the very devil," and promised to send another expedition to hunt him "to the death, if it cost 10,000 lives and breaks the Treasury." In passing down the orders to meet that promise, Sherman directed that those who pursued Forrest should lay waste to the countryside where he operated, so as to weaken his support among the inhabitants.[40]

What no one seemed to comprehend, at the time, was that in spite of himself Sturgis had distracted Forrest from his designs on Sherman's communications, and had done so at a much lower price than Sherman had set for the job. Forrest's intricate information network from Memphis, his antebellum home, apprised him well ahead of time about the preparations to send yet another expedition against him, and that kept him at Tupelo all the longer, planning for the destruction of that latest enemy.[41]

Had it not been for Sturgis's abbreviated jaunt into Mississippi, Sherman might not have been able to devote as much of his attention to Johnston's army as he did. He worried constantly about the integrity of his supply line, remarking at Big Shanty that he wished he could build up a new supply depot closer to his position below the Etowah, but the Western & Atlantic Railroad already carried as much freight as it could just to bring his armies their daily bread and bullets. Few other supplies came down the line save provisions and ammunition: men who had to sleep, work, march, and fight in the same clothing were beginning to find the fabric wearing thin and their cuffs ragged, and they wrote home for new boots or for luxuries like stationery. There was plenty of standing grain to feed the animals, but the civilian population had largely decamped, taking whatever edible livestock Johnston's commissaries had not requisitioned. Six weeks of strenuous campaigning on regular or shortened rations had left few of Sherman's men with much surplus meat on their frames, and putting the tracks out of commission for a week would have produced painful hunger among them; more serious damage should have left them starving. Johnston repeatedly asked Richmond to order a cavalry raid against Sherman's rear from Stephen Lee's department, but that availed him only a feeble effort toward the Western & Atlantic by Gideon Pillow, one of the Confederacy's worst political generals, who never even reached the railroad.[42]

The heavy rains that had plagued Sturgis for the first nine days of June also drenched the armies in Georgia, continuing with little respite until the twenty-first. Deep mud hindered the advance, but Union skirmishers and sappers still crept or shoveled their way forward, accompanied by the bass throbbing of artillery when visibility allowed. Johnston had perched his troops on three mountaintops that presented an inverted V to the foe: Pine Mountain formed the point, while his left flank rested on Lost Mountain and his right on Brushy Mountain, beyond the railroad. The rain abated briefly on June 14 after two days of incessant downpour, and Union gunners started pounding Pine Mountain, where Johnston was beginning to realize that he was vulnerable at the apex of his line. A shell plowed through General Polk from side to side as he, Johnston, and William Hardee reconnoitered there, nearly cutting him in half. Union signalmen had deciphered the key to Confederate semaphore, and they learned of Polk's death that day as the flags waggled between the three peaks of Johnston's line.[43]

The next morning, not a Confederate remained on Pine Mountain. Johnston had withdrawn from that protruding position, and on June 16 Federals swarmed up Lost Mountain, inching ever closer. Two nights later, in another torrent that muffled the sounds of trace chains and clanking equipment, Johnston withdrew again, falling back a mile or two to a tighter perimeter anchored on Kennesaw Mountain, where rifle pits had been etched into an arduous slope and the peak had been studded with artillery. On the morning of June 19 Sherman informed Washington that Johnston had abandoned his last position before the Chattahoochee, but within half an hour his skirmishers had discovered Johnston's new line, still short of Marietta, and Sherman had to retract his claim — adding, by way of excuse, that the persistent rain hampered every movement.[44]

Kennesaw gave the rebels a panoramic view of the Union approach, and with the reappearance of the sun their advance resumed its former pace. Using his greater strength in the traditional way, Sherman extended his right flank to the south, forcing Johnston to stretch his smaller force as well. John Schofield took the extreme right on a direct road to Marietta, with Hooker's corps beside him, and as they pushed ahead on June 22 Hood launched his own attack against them. Bugles blew, the rebel yell rang from the forest, and a broad front of brown and grey burst out of the woodline in front of Hooker, only to be driven back time after time. The opponents finally raised new breastworks right there, and their contest dissipated into sporadic exchanges, but the vigor of Hood's attack suggested to Sherman that Johnston had weakened his front elsewhere.[45]

His dependence on the railroad dissuaded Sherman from reaching any farther around Johnston's left, so only a frontal assault would allow him to keep the initiative. Supposing the Kennesaw line had a soft spot somewhere, he instructed James McPherson, George Thomas, and Schofield to reconnoiter and prepare their troops for a simultaneous attack to begin at 8:00 A.M. on Monday, June 27, with each of them aiming for a particular weak spot. The rains had ceased, and the weekend weather turned sweltering. Dawn of June 27 brought the promise of more stifling heat, and at the appointed hour Union artillery opened with a roar. McPherson's skirmishers loped toward the rifle pits at the base of Kennesaw, at the northern extremity of the ten-mile front, while his main attack struck for a well-defended gap a mile or more to the south, between the lower elevation of Kennesaw and little Pigeon Hill. A couple of miles south of that, Thomas hurled numerous brigades toward a low ridge, the southern end of which would ever afterward bear the name of its Confederate defender, Benjamin Cheatham. Down on Sherman's distant right, Schofield only feigned attacks all day, belching shells at Johnston's flank and throwing out a skirmish line every now and then. That kept Hood from reinforcing Cheatham's Hill, where one segment of Thomas's column broke through the abatis and multiple rows of palings to scramble briefly over the top of the entrenchments. Cheatham's Tennesseans ultimately closed that breach, fighting at such close range that they killed an unusual number of the men they shot, and after a brutal hand-to-hand struggle they drove the survivors back on their supports. Finding retreat more dangerous than running for cover, the Federals started digging in under the muzzles of the rebel rifles. McPherson had no better luck on his end, and the day ended in a heavy toll for this campaign, with more than two thousand casualties on Sherman's rolls, including two brigadiers in Thomas's Army of the Cumberland. Johnston had lost only a few hundred, but at least on Thomas's front the Yankees lay within sprinting distance of those imposing breastworks, which they might seize by a nighttime rush as Hancock had carried the Mule Shoe, in May.[46]

From the shadow of Kennesaw Mountain most of the soldiers in blue could plainly hear the trains coming up from Atlanta to bring supplies and occasional reinforcements for Johnston's army. The governor of Georgia had provided a division of militia that one of Sherman's scouts reported as twenty thousand strong, although it really came closer to three thousand, but it was detachments from the Army of Northern Virginia that the Yankees feared most. Troops under Sherman who had previously faced Lee in Virginia judged that Confederates in the West did not fight with the same determination as those in the East. Sherman kept moving to prevent Johnston from sending men to Lee, and he operated in the faith that Grant was doing the same for him.[47]

His losses at Kennesaw paled alongside the casualties in Virginia, but with only one fragile rail line that barely met his daily needs Sherman concluded that he could not replenish his ranks fast enough to absorb the daunting losses that Grant incurred. So he reverted to his standard maneuver: extending his lines on either side until Johnston grew too nervous to remain. That point came on July 2, and during the night the Army of Tennessee vanished once again. For another week Johnston stalled his nemesis on the north side of the Chattahoochee, backing right up to the river itself against all the dictates of military science, but when Sherman crossed troops above him and below, he had no choice but to make his way across the river on July 9 and march for the suburbs of Atlanta. Every time he took a backward step, Johnston's army hemorrhaged more demoralized stragglers. The Fifteenth Corps alone found hundreds of them loitering between Kennesaw Mountain and Marietta, ready to surrender. Dejected Confederates from Kentucky, North Carolina, and Tennessee explained that they had no intention of going past the Chattahoochee to defend Atlanta if the Confederacy was going to abandon their own homes, and many seemed convinced that Johnston's army would desert en masse if he gave up Atlanta, too.[48]

Back in Virginia, Grant's progress had reflected Sherman's almost precisely, except for churning out such astounding casualties. Grant had pulled away from the deadlock at Spotsylvania, finally, and started south again, with Lee racing ahead of him to prepare a greeting at the next geographical barrier. Lee built new works in the shape of a wedge on the southern bank of the North Anna River: the tip of the angle faced Ox Ford and his left ran back to a secure terminus at another substantial stream, while his right passed before Hanover Junction and ended at a downstream loop of the North Anna. Hancock's corps crossed below, on Lee's right, while the Fifth and Sixth Corps bridged the river at Jericho Mills, upstream, to Lee's left; Burnside approached the river directly opposite the angle in Lee's line. General Grant misunderstood that Lee was still in retreat, instead of solidifying an enviable position between the isolated halves of the Army of the Potomac, so when Burnside complained that the enemy was too strong for him to cross at Ox Ford, Grant brusquely insisted that he get his men over somehow. Burnside split his corps to do it: he put his second division across on the left, downstream, with Hancock, and sent his first division over a ford upstream, which placed it right in front of Lee's entrenched infantry but beyond easy supporting distance of the Fifth and Sixth Corps. The first brigade commander to cross there was none other than the bibulous James Ledlie — who, with what one of his colonels considered a snootful, threw his fifteen hundred men against A. P. Hill's entire Confederate corps, only to have them come reeling back in a confused mass, badly bloodied. As many a Federal officer recognized, the terrain and the troop positions offered an ideal opportunity for defeating the Yankees in detail, with a river at their backs: Lee might have severely punished Grant's mistake by holding off one of his isolated wings with a detachment and using most of his army to drive the other wing into the river. Luck fell to the Union, though, for Lee came down with an acute illness that all but disabled him for a few days, robbing his army of the command spirit and the expertise required for so bold a gamble.[49]

At the North Anna Grant finally assigned the Ninth Corps to the Army of the Potomac, putting Burnside under Meade, but the change essentially reduced Meade to the position of an executive officer: Grant issued far more detailed operational orders than he might have from a desk in Washington, and Meade carried them out with little of the discretion that Sherman exercised. Realizing the strength of Lee's position, if not the jeopardy of his own, Grant decided to disengage and vault around Lee's right flank once again. The commander of Fifth Corps artillery wondered if that single tactic was the only one Grant knew, or if he was merely so obstinate that he would attempt no other: three times he had tried to strike points below Lee's right flank, and three times Lee had been sitting there, waiting for him, when he arrived.[50]

Based on the condition and attitudes of the prisoners they were taking, Grant optimistically reported that Lee's army was "really whipped." As in Georgia, every step southward brought deserters trickling into Union lines, but the drain amounted to much less than in Johnston's army. Lee's veterans were, however, coming to appreciate the advantage of meeting Union attacks from behind fieldworks, especially with their depleted ranks, and Grant would soon find his own men faltering when he asked them to carry manned fortifications.[51]

Meade's army — or Grant's army, as it had become — pulled back to the north side of the river for a roundabout march through country thickly littered with dead horses from recent cavalry operations. Union troopers had stripped the farms that lay in their path, and as the infantry swept through they broadened the scope of the plunder, now that they had stretched their supply line so far that rations were beginning to fall short. The North and South Anna Rivers met to form the Pamunkey, and the Army of the Potomac crossed it on a pontoon bridge, miles downstream from the confluence. Veterans of McClellan's army recognized the south bank as the outer fringe of their domain during the Peninsula campaign, and every mile raised another reminiscence. Union soldiers had shown better respect for private property in those early days under McClellan, so the region had never seen widespread despoliation, and plantations that had suffered from the occupation had had nearly two years to recover. The men under Grant showed less restraint: the veterans among them tended to feel less sympathy for Southern civilians, and less fear of reproach from their superiors, while the recruits had never known the era of civilized war. A relative cornucopia of food and fence rails began disappearing into Yankee bellies and campfires.[52] A spirit of vandalism frightened the civilian inhabitants even more. Union soldiers chopped furniture and pianos into kindling for the sheer joy of destruction, or smashed gigantic mirrors and ripped open feather beds, and such fiendish behavior ignited a particular terror when black troops began to imitate it. During one incursion along the James River, the previous May, a brigade of U.S. Colored Troops from Butler's army had already ransacked the manor houses of several Tidewater plantation families — destroying the library of former president John Tyler, along with all the furnishings. Then a soldier in one of Burnside's black regiments struck the deepest chord of fear when he attempted to force himself on a young white woman at New Kent Court House.[53]

The end of May brought the Army of the Potomac back to the threshold of Richmond. Below the Pamunkey they crossed Totopotomoy Creek and fanned out to a place called Cold Harbor — nine miles, in a beeline, from Jefferson Davis's bedroom — and finally to the marshy bottoms along the fabled Chickahominy River. Grant moved his supply base from the Rappahannock River down to White House Landing, where McClellan had had his base on the Pamunkey. He also summoned reinforcements from Butler's lines at Bermuda Hundred: Baldy Smith arrived at White House on May 30, with four divisions from his own Eighteenth Corps and the Tenth Corps, all of which he estimated as sixteen thousand strong. Lee also picked up a few thousand from the Shenandoah Valley and from Beauregard, at Petersburg, but he could collect nowhere near the eighty thousand he was presumed by Stanton's War Department to have under his command, besides a reserve force of militia.[54]

With those he did have at hand, Lee once again beat his opponent to the field, and for several days the armies jockeyed about, at and above Cold Harbor, sparking skirmishes that would have been considered full-scale battles in the early days of the war. Then Grant grew impatient with his goal so near, as Sherman had at Kennesaw Mountain, and he, too, tried to crack his antagonist's lines with an all-out frontal assault.[55]

The ball opened at daylight on June 3 in front of Cold Harbor, a furlong or two from the scene of Lee's costly triumph at Gaines's Mill, nearly two years before. On that day in 1862, as the new commander of the Army of Northern Virginia, Lee had been the aggressor and the victor, flinging one brigade after another at the Union lines until they began to waver. By this day in 1864 attrition had forced him to husband his strength, and his three corps stood behind solid works to receive the attack. At the southern end of the battle front Hancock's Second Corps made a rush like the one that overran the Mule Shoe, and one division actually spilled into the Confederate works, but a counterattack drove them out in short order. Wright led the Sixth Corps into a gale of musketry and canister on Hancock's right, and Smith's Eighteenth Corps went in to the right of the Sixth, but the attack bogged down short of Lee's works and the long blue lines sank to the ground, seeking shelter from the sheeting volleys of lead and iron. From what meager protection they could find, the Yankees opened a feeble return fire, and there they lay for hours, some of them as close as forty yards from those blazing entrenchments. Thousands of them had already fallen: the 8th New York Heavy Artillery alone lost more than five hundred men that morning. Retreat would only have subjected them to further decimation, besides starting an inevitable panic, so late in the morning Meade sent out an order to dig in and hold the ground gained. In the afternoon Lee tried an attack of his own on the far end of the line, but he found Union breastworks as strong there as his own had proven elsewhere.[56]

Cold Harbor descended into a trench fight from that moment. Wounded Federals lay for days between the works, under a broiling sun. Constant picket fire and occasional volleys prevented most rescue attempts, and in desperation some Vermonters threw a rope over their rifle pits to a man who had been shot through one arm and both legs; he held the rope with his good arm while they dragged him back to safety. Three days later the stench had grown so odious that the generals finally swallowed their pride and asked for a truce to bury the dead, and for a few hours the sniping gave way to cheerful camaraderie between rebels and Yankees, but when the white flags came down they resumed their best efforts to kill each other. Sharpshooters, random shells, and occasional sorties bred an atmosphere of perpetual and universal nervous tension even for those far behind the lines, for the belligerents lay so close to one another that no one felt safe. Cooks well to the rear found themselves ducking solid shot; detailed men arranging shady quarters for their officers fell to stray bullets, and sudden dashes against inviting flanks or inattentive picket lines made prisoners of men relaxing in presumed security with their latest mail delivery.[57]

This feral monotony took even more out of the troops than the brutal cycle of battle that had typified Grant's campaign thus far. Tough veterans started hinting at the additional stress only days into their first taste of siege warfare — damning the holes in which they lived around the clock, reviewing the cavalcade of friends who had gone under the sod, counting the weeks (five, for most of them) since they had been spared the sound of gunfire, and trying to describe an overpowering sense of melancholy and doom. "The fighting becomes more terrible every day," wrote an officer who had seen Antietam, Fredericksburg, and the worst of Spotsylvania; "in fact I am almost bewildered with the sights and sounds of war."[58]

Not far from the contending armies lay the skeletal remains of Union soldiers killed at Gaines's Mill, still clothed in their rotting uniforms, and the trees there still bore the scars of old battles. Among such scenes, men who had seen this landscape before inevitably began to compare the generalship of Ulysses Grant to that of George McClellan. Peninsula veterans then serving as far away as Sherman's army had something to say about it, and even those who were new to the Chickahominy watershed finally appreciated the difficulties it had posed for McClellan. Colonel Charles Wainwright, of New York, fumed at the praise heaped on Grant for having his troops butchered in front of Lee's works, yet the press and the administration had hounded and cursed Little Mac when, according to Wainwright, McClellan was making better progress. Grant had begun his campaign with a much greater numerical superiority than McClellan, Wainwright noted, and McClellan had inflicted heavier casualties than he suffered, while Grant had lost far more than Lee. A battle-weary staff officer at Fifth Corps headquarters nevertheless defended Grant, asserting that whittling at the enemy's strength was the very point, and Grant's allusion to the legend of the Kilkenny cats confirmed as much: the Kilkenny cats reputedly fought until there was nothing left but their tails, and on the way down to Cold Harbor Grant had remarked that his army had the longer tail. That comment circulated through the upper echelons and disgusted Wainwright, who saw no genius in a man whose only talent was to supply the most troops for slaughter. He predicted that morale would soon evaporate unless Grant pursued more inspired tactics, and a Confederate general had already remarked that the Army of the Potomac seemed a little more timid on the attack than it had in earlier campaigns.[59]

Troops just joining Grant, especially those under Butler, showed much admiration for the lieutenant general's tenacity, and a Ninth Corps captain asserted that in the Army of the Potomac "we all believe in Grant," but his assumption of unanimity was mistaken.[60] It did not escape the notice of many who had survived the campaign from the Rapidan (or the notice of Lincoln's secretary of the navy, for that matter) that just reaching the outskirts of Richmond had cost Grant more than twice as many men in five weeks as McClellan had lost during all five months of his Peninsula campaign. An Ohio sergeant detected a certain disdain for Grant among his comrades, blaming it specifically on his apparent indifference to stunning casualties, and in his newspaper column Wilbur Fisk regretted Grant's evident policy of attrition, confessing a preference for "some prodigious display of strategy." McClellan's reliance on the shovel had brought him public ridicule, administrative badgering, and ultimately executive recall, but now his approach struck many a soldier as a lot more prudent than brute force. McClellan partisans emphasized that Grant also enjoyed unlimited discretion where McClellan had been fettered and foiled, and the old battlegrounds seemed to imbue the veterans of the Army of the Potomac with an ardent nostalgia for the general who had brought it to life.[61]

For the next week that army labored day and night on its earthworks, building bastions for the guns and transforming rifle pits into formal, connected trenches. Grant was not the type to settle for a siege if he could help it, though: exercising the free hand that no other general had been allowed, he decided to move his entire army south of the James River, to try seizing the rail center at Petersburg that Butler had left unmolested in May. The maneuver uncovered Washington, which (as the soldiers again noted) the president and the War Department had never permitted McClellan to do, but perhaps Abraham Lincoln had learned something in three years of war.[62]

Butler had again tried to take Petersburg, sending Quincy Gillmore by the old route from Bermuda Hundred while a cavalry column came at the city from the south, but both efforts failed, so Grant decided to take the place in yet another flank movement around Lee's right. First he sent the Eighteenth Corps back to White House Landing, to board steamers and seize Petersburg ahead of the rest of the army, and on the night of June 12 he started peeling one division after another from before Lee. That night regimental bands played evening serenades and the bugles sounded retreat as usual, but the men had shouldered their knapsacks and were making for the Chickahominy bridges, downstream, and then for Charles City Court House, on the banks of the James. The Fifth Corps led the march, followed by the Second Corps, while the Sixth and Ninth took a different road. Reinforced picket lines and a few "reliable regiments" stayed behind to hold the enemy's attention until the morning of the thirteenth, and only then did Confederate pickets creep forward and find Grant's long array of fortifications perfectly empty.[63]

For once, Grant had caught Lee napping. Down at Petersburg, General Beauregard had predicted the flank movement to the James three days before Grant even issued his orders for it, but the Confederate high command seemed distracted by other activity north and west of Richmond. Grant had sent Phil Sheridan on another raid with most of his cavalry, directing him toward Charlottesville with instructions to destroy the Virginia Central Railroad. At the same time David Hunter, an aging, ambitious, but not particularly adroit major general, had taken over Franz Sigel's New Market refugees and turned them back up the Shenandoah Valley to Staunton, smashing and scattering a much smaller Confederate force that tried to step in his way. General Crook joined him there with the troops he had led into southwest Virginia, including Averell's cavalry, and after raiding Staunton's tobacco warehouses this substantial little army pushed on to Lexington before light resistance. There Hunter burned both the Virginia Military Institute and the home of Virginia's governor, in retribution for the cadets' participation in the defense of the valley and the governor's appeal for the citizens to help repel the invader. Grant had hoped that Sheridan and Hunter would also meet, somewhere around Charlottesville, and after they tore up the railroads Grant wanted them to come east and join him, but Sheridan ran into trouble at Trevilian Station, on the Virginia Central, well before Charlottesville. Wade Hampton's rebel horsemen caught him there on June 11, and although Sheridan outnumbered him significantly Hampton gave him such a drubbing that he abandoned his mission and ran for home the long way, circling back to the relic-littered battlefields of Spotsylvania County before turning south again.[64]

Had Sheridan returned to Cold Harbor the way he came, he would have run right into Stonewall Jackson's old corps — or what was left of it. After his vandalism in Lexington, David Hunter had veered up over the Blue Ridge toward Lynchburg. That posed a direct threat to the technical left flank of the Army of Northern Virginia, and Lee wanted it eliminated immediately, so he detached Richard Ewell's attenuated corps and sent it west under Jubal Early, meanwhile retiring Ewell from the field to command the Richmond defenses. Early marched his men on foot to Charlottesville, where they boarded cars on the Orange & Alexandria Railroad and started arriving in Lynchburg on June 17. John C. Breckinridge had resumed command of the remnants of his valley army and arranged a tight perimeter around the city. Reinforcements kept rolling in to the Lynchburg depot through the eighteenth, but Hunter held the numerical edge all day. He may still have had more troops at hand after the last of Early's units came in from Charlottesville, but he doubted it, and during the night Hunter slunk away, leaving behind his worst-wounded men and shooting his worn-out horses in his haste to escape. Early chased him for days, sweeping up his stragglers and nipping at his heels; the pursuit continued for sixty miles, all the way to Salem, where Early lashed out again and took all of Hunter's artillery. Could he have brought the Yankees to bay one last time Early might have finished them, but Hunter drove his men mercilessly, striking for the Allegheny Mountains and the Kanawha River rather than turning back down the valley whence he had come. Rations ran short again, as they had for Crook and Averell in May: some went four or five days without food, and the famished, footsore raiders only found provisions when they reached Gauley Bridge, on the ninth day of their flight.[65]

Grant's army, meanwhile, had gathered at the James River landings below the confluence of the Appomattox, near where McClellan had fortified his army after the Seven Days battles. Country boys who had never seen anything more majestic than the Merrimack or the Wabash stood on the bluffs over the James to gape at the broad, tidal river, which struck an Indiana cavalryman with the thrill he imagined De Soto must have felt when he first glimpsed the Mississippi. Men of all ranks took off their dusty clothing for a refreshing swim as engineers began stringing together the longest pontoon bridge they had ever built (a Vermont musician counted 102 pontoon boats, sixteen feet apart), steadying it with anchored steamboats here and there. Until that was ready, a fleet of ferryboats started shuttling the Second Corps over the river: most of Hancock's men had landed at Windmill Point by sunrise of June 15, but General Butler was supposed to send him three days' rations from his stores at Bermuda Hundred, and Hancock waited in vain for the provisions until late in the morning, when he finally stepped off without them.[66]

That same morning, at 4:00, Baldy Smith started his own troops for Petersburg from a point opposite Bermuda Hundred, at least a dozen miles closer than Hancock. The head of his column had reached the City Point Road, about halfway to Petersburg, when a battery opened up from a nearby hilltop, dropping shells in the road with enough precision to bring everything to a halt. Finally three black regiments from the leading division fanned out to confront that threat, backed up by three others; when the gunners found their range the colonel of the 22nd U.S. Colored

Troops ordered a charge, and his men loped four hundred yards up that broad, grassy slope, driving out the gunners and their cavalry supports and opening the road again by nine o'clock.[67] Around noon Smith's skirmishers came within sight of the northeastern extremity of the ten-mile circuit of fortifications that protected the city below the Appomattox, but he spent most of the remaining daylight placing his troops, and it was well into the evening before he launched an attack on a protruding salient by the Jordan house, on the City Point Railroad. He sprang forward after 7:00 P.M., with the division of Colored Troops on his left and a white one on his right. A single skirmish line led the way, rather than the dense ranks that might have made such good targets for the Confederate artillery. They bounded over a stump-studded, freshly plowed field, ignoring the shot and shell that slanted across their ranks, and in a matter of minutes they were swarming over the works, seizing guns and driving the rebels back toward the city. They pushed a little beyond the captured crescent of forts in the gathering dusk, then fell to digging in with their bayonets and bare hands.[68] The surgeon of the 22nd crowed that his regiment "fought like tigers," and most of the white troops who saw it seemed to agree.[69]

As impressive as their maiden battle was, the Colored Troops' charge would have failed had Beauregard not had to fight so pitifully shorthanded. He repeatedly telegraphed to Richmond that his force was too small to hold both Petersburg and the Bermuda Hundred line, and all day June 15 he could fill his prodigious works at Petersburg with only one infantry brigade, two little regiments of cavalry, and a gaggle of militia. Not until well after dark did a few brigades of reinforcements begin to arrive from Lee's army; had Smith pressed on he would likely have beaten those reinforcements into the city, for his three divisions should have made short work of the retreating rebel brigade, but he had done all he was going to do that day. Men in the ranks took note of how lightly the defenses had been manned, but when Hancock's first division came panting in after a hot and dusty march, around 6:30 that evening, Smith deployed them to solidify his gains, rather than using them to take more. It was a mistake costly enough to hound Smith the rest of his life, and he wasted no time trying to place the blame elsewhere.[70]

That afternoon Butler's signalmen from Bermuda Hundred had reported clouds of dust raised by columns of infantry and long caravans of wheeled vehicles trundling toward the south side of the James, so it seemed certain (not to mention logical) that Lee's army was on the way — although, in fact, Lee still doubted whether Grant's whole army was crossing the James, and withheld most of his troops. If Smith failed to take Petersburg under the bright gibbous moon of June 15, Grant believed the place would be well defended thereafter, and he wanted to bring up all his own troops before going in for the kill. The morning of June 16 therefore passed with most of the opposing forces plodding steadily toward the embattled city on forced marches through choking dust and heat. On their road from the riverbank, Union stragglers burned the occasional house or barn along the way, having learned the delights of that amusement at Charles City Court House, while waiting to cross the river.[71]

While Beauregard's skirmishers kept an eye on that thickening band of blue uniforms, their comrades behind them traded their rifles for shovels and flailed at the red earth on the far side of what the Yankees were calling Harrison's Creek, two miles from downtown Petersburg. Up at Bermuda Hundred, Butler found the enemy lines empty where Beauregard had pulled his troops out to defend Petersburg, so he threw a few thousand men forward to destroy the railroad, but some of those rebels hurrying down from Richmond paused long enough to drive them back to their old works. Meade arrived before Petersburg late in the afternoon, and on Grant's instructions he directed Hancock to make another dash that advanced his lines a little, but Beauregard's heavily outnumbered Confederates opened up from those fresh new works beyond the creek, and as the daylight turned to darkness most of Hancock's men scrambled back to their own lines.[72]

At daybreak on Friday, June 17, Robert Potter's division of Burnside's corps stormed out of the ravine cut by Harrison's Creek, surging over the crest and running right against the new Confederate trenches near the Shand house. Barlow's division of the Second Corps went in alongside, on the hill where the Hare house stood. Those who made the assault had feared the worst: one officer anticipated something like the charge of the Light Brigade at Balaklava, but such anxiety was misplaced for once. Taken completely by surprise, the somnolent rebels surrendered by the hundreds, and those who fled left behind a battery of guns and enough weapons to arm a brigade. James Ledlie was supposed to bring the first division to Potter's support, but he didn't, and later he gave vague excuses about it that General Burnside seemed to believe. Burnside's third division, under Orlando Willcox, met worse luck than Potter: when he finally charged, Willcox lost nearly half the men in one brigade. Ledlie's division went in at last to take over for Willcox, but when one of Ledlie's colonels came back to see about his neglected requests for ammunition he found his general asleep on the ground; that colonel and another regimental commander independently concluded that Ledlie was dead drunk on the field — for at least the second time in a month. After dark a furious counterattack drove Ledlie's division out of the captured works and sent it racing back to its original rifle pits.[73]

Again Beauregard established a new line of fortifications, this time behind Taylor's Creek, closer to the city, while his bone-weary infantry held back the tide of blue. Until late on June 17 Lee would send him no more fresh troops, for he still questioned where Grant's army had gone; Lee retained much of his own army before Bermuda Hundred, keeping Butler away from the line of the railroad, and on the north bank of the James, in case Grant reappeared there. Only at 10:00 P.M. did he relent, and begin moving every spare man down to Petersburg, posthaste.[74]

The dawn of June 18 showed that Beauregard had abandoned his second line of works and fallen back to the new ones along Taylor's Creek. Meade had planned another assault like that of the previous morning, with Burnside advancing again with the Second Corps on his right and the Fifth on his left, but as the leading division of each corps splashed once more through the headwaters and ravines around Harrison's Creek they met no picket fire. They climbed the hill, and mounted the silent breastworks where they had fought the night before, in which the dead lay thick and mingled, blue and grey. From there they rolled across the fields beyond, and into a band of woods, about a mile from where they had begun. In those woods they met the enemy's skirmishers and started driving them into the open fields on the far side, where they could see the cut of the Norfolk & Petersburg Railroad, the brushy banks of Taylor's Creek, and beyond that the new (and already substantial) Confederate trenches, just filling up with two fresh divisions from the Army of Northern Virginia. Willcox's division carried the railroad cut, but started taking enfilading fire from the left and right. Samuel Crawford's Fifth Corps division moved up on the left, but Francis Barlow hung back on the right with his division of the Second Corps, so Potter came up from behind Willcox to stiffen his right. The generals discussed another simultaneous, impromptu charge, but Barlow wanted orders before he took such a chance.[75]

The spires of Petersburg taunted them from behind the Confederate defenders, about a mile away, but the firing slackened for two or three hours while the corps and division commanders tried to coordinate their movements before those frowning fortifications. So long did the lull last that men sat down in the ranks and wrote letters. Captain Frederic Howes, of the 1st Maine Heavy Artillery, seated himself midway between the abandoned Confederate position behind him and the occupied Confederate position in front of him to assure his wife that he was well. "God has been very good to me," he told her. Men had been killed and wounded all around him, but he had always been spared.[76]

By the middle of the afternoon George Meade grew so frustrated with all the dithering that he ordered each corps commander to go in as soon as he could mount an assault, regardless of whether adjoining divisions were prepared. The various corps complied with that astonishing requirement, dutifully battering themselves against those fresh earthworks, but those lines were too full of determined Southern marksmen now, and too well abetted by artillery. Many a Union soldier declined even to follow his regiment over the last rise, or ravine, between him and the enemy, especially after getting a glimpse of Beauregard's fortifications. "The very sight of a bank of fresh earth brings them to a dead halt," observed Colonel Wainwright, of the Fifth Corps artillery. Meade recognized as much himself, blaming the heavy casualties on hesitation and timidity. The best any of his troops could do was brave the storm of canister and musketry until they came as close as they dared to the blazing line, and take the best cover they could find. Willcox plowed forward to within a hundred yards, and Potter ventured a little closer, where their men flattened themselves on the ground and waited for dark. Once the sun had set, they started to scratch up some protection for themselves, intending to hold even the most inconvenient and dangerous of the ground they had taken.[77]

Meade's petulance sent hundreds of men to their deaths, and nowhere did the fatal impact of his temperamental order fall heavier than on the 1st Maine Heavy Artillery, in the Second Corps. Hancock was ailing from his old wound that day, and David Birney had assumed temporary command. In his desperation to satisfy the commanding general's impatient demands, Birney ordered a charge toward a concave portion of the new Confederate line where a dense crossfire assured the destruction of any assailants. The 1st Maine occupied the entire first line, still mustering some nine hundred men after having lost five hundred on May 18 at Spotsylvania. The heavies went in gamely enough, but they never had a chance; barely a third of them came back unwounded, and in the few minutes their charge lasted they earned the dubious honor of losing more men in a single engagement than any other regiment during the Civil War. A chaplain working at the division hospital remarked that "a pile of loyal Maine arms and legs is the token of what the day's work has been."[78]

Captain Howes, who had been so grateful for divine protection, failed to come back with the remnants of his regiment. A bullet punctured his chest as he led his company in the charge, and he staggered to the rear for medical treatment. On the way he weakened, stopped to rest beneath a tree, and never rose again.[79]

The 1st Maine was originally recruited as the 18th Maine, for the infantry, but had been converted to heavy artillery a few months after it was mustered in. That conversion required an additional eight hundred re-

cruits who enlisted specifically as heavy artillery, and the ranks had remained nearly full with subsequent volunteers who preferred that branch
to being conscripted into the infantry. It was customary, and usually fairly
accurate, to suppose that the men in the heavy artillery had enlisted
for the purpose of avoiding battle and long marches; soldiers from private to major general acknowledged it, like the New Hampshireman who
observed that the heavies who had been consigned to the Army of the
Potomac all seemed to look "rather sour" at their misfortune. Heavy-
artillerymen seemed even more despondent over coming to the front than
the horrified hundred-day men, whole brigades of whom also ended up
before Petersburg, contrary to all expectation.[80] Although the original
members from the 18th Maine could not be suspected of timid motivation, and despite the regiment's devastating combat losses, the 1st Maine
reflected a curious tendency that ran through that entire branch of the
service: for some reason, commissioned officers in the heavy artillery
seemed to enjoy noticeably better odds of survival than their counterparts
in the infantry, cavalry, or light artillery, even when their regiments were
sent into the front lines.

In those states that provided any heavy artillery, only 4.21 percent
of the heavy-artillerymen who died of wounds were officers. The corresponding figure for infantry was 5.61 percent, and for the cavalry 6.06
percent, even though the ratio of company officers to enlisted men was
slightly higher in the heavy artillery than in the infantry. The 1st Maine
left 423 men dead or dying on its various battlefields, of whom 23, or 5.44
percent, were officers, but Maine's infantry regiments lost 172 officers out
of 2,633 killed, or 6.53 percent, and of the 184 Maine cavalrymen who fell,
17 were officers, for a ratio of 9.24 percent. More revealing, perhaps, is the
difference between regiments that were converted to heavy artillery and
those that were raised from the start for that service: in those that began
as infantry, with men who expected rough duty, the proportion of officers
who died on the battlefield was 4.81 percent, but in those where every
man joined for the comfort and safety of the forts, officer mortality plum-
meted to 3.36 percent. The officers in heavy-artillery regiments enlisted
with the same variety of expectations as their men, and under fire officers could more easily hang back and hide than the enlisted men could.
That phenomenon became notorious in some regiments, and the statistics would suggest that heavy-artillery officers may have been a little more
prone to the practice.[81]

Popular as it was to associate skulking with untried recruits, and especially with the bounty men, that habit became at least as prevalent among
the veterans as Grant's pugnacity promised to consume every man under
his command, and that was especially so among those whose enlistment

had nearly run out. The traditional standards of martial ardor had deteriorated irreparably in the armies around Petersburg by late June, and the heavy-artilleryman's proclivity for avoiding danger made much more sense to those who had clawed their way within easy rifle range of Lee's works. As they settled into more permanent digs they noticed that life had to be lived at the crouch, if one was to avoid a bullet through the brain, and no imputation of shame accompanied the awkward postures of trench life; there was, after all, no glory in being shot dead while sauntering back to the rear for water, or a call of nature.[82]

The tense respite that followed the last assault gave the opportunity for reflection on the losses of their forty-five-day running fight, and the leisure for calculation imposed an insidious gloom among the survivors. A drummer boy in an Indiana regiment told his father that they had lost nearly all of their best men, and a sixteen-year-old private in a new company of Ohio sharpshooters informed his sister that only twenty-seven remained of the one hundred neophytes who had boarded the train with him in Cleveland three months before. Reading of the casualties in the newspapers, and of the comrades whose death her brother recounted in letters, a Connecticut girl began to doubt that the war would ever end until everyone had been killed: as the ghastly carnival dragged on into the summer without pause or tangible progress, that morbid speculation matured into a stygian probability to the men under Grant. After the Petersburg assaults a Massachusetts captain in the Fifth Corps mentioned, when he had but ten weeks left to serve, that "everybody that was good for much" had been killed or crippled for life. Winfield Hancock's best division commander described all the marching and fighting they had done in the past five weeks, none of which had seemed to accomplish much, and he confessed that "things do not look very bright." About the same time, a Pennsylvania sergeant lamented that "the ones that escape today fall tomorrow," and Major Washington Roebling, a staff officer with General Warren, fully concurred. "This business of getting killed is a mere question of time," Roebling confided to his fiancée, who was Warren's sister; "it will happen to all of us sooner or later if the war keeps on."[83]

Under Grant, the war would surely "keep on." The second day after the last bloody bashing in the suburbs of Petersburg, Grant urged Meade to start encircling the city, to cut it off from all supply. He suggested sending James Wilson and the cavalry deep into Virginia, to cripple the railroad connection with western North Carolina, while simultaneously reaching around Petersburg with infantry as far as it would stretch. Under Grant's prodding, Meade thought he might seize the two remaining railroads into Petersburg over the course of two days, although in reality Grant would not be able to do that for nine more months. Wilson set off on June 22, crossing the Weldon Railroad at Reams's Station and planning to come back in five days to a city that had been completely invested.[84]

With the loan of a corps from Butler's army, Meade shuffled his own troops south, and then west. Warren's Fifth Corps had spread out as far as the Jerusalem Plank Road, and on the night of June 21 Meade started pushing both Hancock and Horatio Wright's Sixth Corps beyond that, to the Petersburg & Weldon Railroad. Robert E. Lee sent A. P. Hill to reprove them, and on the evening of June 23 Hill burst toward them near the railroad, striking at the junction between Hancock's corps and Wright's. The old Vermont Brigade held that point, sorely depleted of veterans from the Wilderness and Spotsylvania, but well padded with three bulging battalions of the 1st Vermont Heavy Artillery. The Vermonters gave way to the onslaught sooner than some witnesses thought commendable, and Confederate infantry curled around behind them, sifting hundreds of prisoners from the milling mass of what had been a firing line.[85]

Wilson burned a few bridges and tore up some tracks, but he was severely chastened along the way by rebel horsemen and by one ragtag collection of militia, convalescents, and civilians. On his return he nearly rode straight into the hands of Confederate cavalry at Reams's Station, which he had supposed would be firmly in Union control by that time; then rebel infantry came up in force. An expedition went out from Meade's army to rescue him, but to no avail: Wilson had to abandon all his impedimenta and run for it from pursuing rebels, darting two dozen miles south in desperation before swinging east and north again, twenty miles wide of Petersburg. He lost touch with part of his command, which had to find its own way back, and early in July he brought his main body to the banks of the James River. Recuperating at City Point, a spent Indiana sergeant who had warned his parents that his regiment was bound on a raid wrote to assure them that it had indeed gone, but he admitted that "we didn't all come back." Wilson had lost more than one-fifth of the five thousand troopers he took with him, besides all his guns and wagons.[86]

Far from surrounding Petersburg, which Wilson had been told he would do, Grant had fallen back on a partial, creeping siege of the rail center at Petersburg and, by extension, the city of Richmond.[87] His simultaneous campaigns had prevented the enemy from using interior lines for significant reinforcement of critical points, but that success lacked conspicuous visibility. Grant had caused Lee enormous casualties, but at much greater cost to himself: McClellan, Joe Hooker, and Meade had made far better bargains in that respect in the Seven Days, at Chancellorsville, and at Gettysburg. Most Northerners comprehended the appalling casualties, but few suspected (and none knew for certain) that Lee's losses would prevent him from resuming the initiative against the Army of the Potomac. The steady geographical progress in both theaters had made Grant the man of the hour so far as the administration was concerned, but others perceived that he had merely restored the strategic situation President Lincoln and Radical Republicans had found so intolerable two years before, and had squandered seventy-five thousand troops to accomplish even that much. Optimists in the Army of the Potomac wrote of taking Petersburg by Independence Day, and declared that the army enjoyed high spirits, but plenty of soldiers in the trenches outside Petersburg wondered whether their cause had gained anything in the twenty-two months since McClellan had been ordered to bring his army back from the gates of Richmond. "I fail to see what damn great things Grant has done more than George B done before him," wrote a seasoned gunner in a Massachusetts battery, who resented that McClellan "was cursed and reviled by the very men that now pretend to say that Grant is working wonders."[88]

3

From Their Graves in the Trenches

⋘ THE GRIM IMPLICATIONS of Grant's game of mutual attrition troubled the civilian population as well as the soldiers whose lives paid the ante of his wager. The price of gold gauged the public's belief in the government, and therefore in the war: the higher the price climbed, the less faith it reflected, and gold had been rising steadily with the mounting casualties of May and June. On June 17 a false report swept New York City that Petersburg had been taken, and the administration's friends in that town gloated for a few hours over what they presumed was the prelude to Richmond's fall, but even one of the vigorous gloaters had to admit the next morning that he had been too quick to "cackle." The bursting of that rumor only gave all the more credence to the naysayers, who doubted that the Confederacy could ever be conquered. On June 21, after the news sank in along Wall Street that the Army of the Potomac was resorting to another siege before Richmond, gold finally hit the 200 mark — meaning that greenbacks had dropped to half the value of gold dollars. Congress had just reacted to the spring inflation with a new law discouraging further speculation in gold, but that created a black market that sent the price soaring. The stock market stopped trading in it, and heartbreaking columns of casualty lists pushed the daily gold report from its customary spot on the back page, but by June 22 gold was selling at 230 where it could be had, and from there it climbed well past 250 before the hint of a decline, bringing the worth of paper currency below forty cents on the dollar. Feeling pinched between the escalating congressional appropriations to maintain the war and the growing shortfall in the treasury, Salmon Chase submitted his resignation, and that did nothing at all to restore confidence.[1]

The financial pages held little attraction for the women who tried to support their families while their husbands served in the ranks. Probably in response to the latest crest of inflation, Congress passed an army pay raise on June 20, authorizing an increase in the pay of a private soldier from $13 a month to $16. Sergeants earned only a two-dollar jump, from $18 to $20, and officers were not included at all, so the intent was obviously to save the poorest families from outright penury. Although it added a few million dollars a month to the cost of the war, the bill offered little help to the soldiers' families, for the $16 a private received after June of 1864 still represented only $6.40 in 1861 dollars. Provisions to augment the bland army rations had grown almost out of reach for the enlisted man: around the camps, a bushel of onions cost a third of a month's pay. Food was nearly as high at home, and other necessities were often higher still. Calico, for the mother who could make her daughter's dresses, cost thirty-five cents a yard, and cotton cloth was seventy-five. "I cant get for four dollars what I could get for one the summer you went away," grieved a New Hampshire woman whose husband had enlisted in 1862. A volunteer nurse at Armory Square Hospital in Washington found victuals so dear that she and the woman she boarded with never felt adequately nourished, especially with her labors in the ward. A moderately wealthy Philadelphian who wanted to build a new summer cottage gasped when told that it would cost $10,500, because every material had doubled or trebled in price.[2]

A Louisville newspaper asserted late in May that the paper currency printed by the Continental Congress — the very name of which became a synonym for worthlessness — had depreciated only 10 percent by the end of its third year, while Secretary Chase's greenbacks were barely two years old when they had lost 60 percent of their value. Rural Easterners who heard of the gold coin circulating in Nevada and California drooled in envy, having access only to the shrinking paper dollars that some would call "Lincoln skins." Fears circulated that the government might even repudiate its bonds, unnerving the father of Jay Cooke, who had overseen Mr. Chase's bond sales. The elder Cooke asked his son to liquidate all his U.S. securities for him as quickly as he could, and with as little loss as possible.[3]

So thoroughly had the army depleted the civilian labor force that high wages and plentiful work awaited most men who enjoyed both good health and some form of draft exemption. Much of the slack was taken up by women, both in industry and agriculture. Single women might easily find factory jobs, particularly in the production of war materials ranging from wool cloth to ammunition, but soldiers' wives could often only resort to piecework at home, knitting or sewing shoe uppers, and women frequently took over the field work on their own farms. While the Army of the Potomac hurled itself against Beauregard's entrenchments, a Maine newspaperman saw a young lady getting her own hay in from fields along the Kennebec River, and she appeared to have become as adept at it as any man. Railroad hands in Cincinnati felt secure enough to strike for higher wages that spring; farm laborers in Michigan demanded as much as eight dollars a week; teamsters could get fifty dollars a month in government employ. Schoolteachers were drawing the phenomenal sum of a hundred dollars a month in far-off California, but that brought no relief for the woman with a husband in uniform.[4]

Like a spendthrift living beyond his means, the treasury was always so short of cash that government bursars tried to put off paying any creditors who could be stalled, and the nation's soldiers represented the preponderance of that type of creditor. Most soldiers waited six months or more without seeing a paymaster, especially if they were in the field, so by the time they finally received a couple of months' back pay it was worth considerably less than when it had first come due. In the meantime they had often had to borrow against what the government already owed them, paying 6 percent interest because of Uncle Sam's tightfistedness toward the loyal troops. The practice caused widespread inconvenience and outright want among soldiers' families, including those of the upper ranks.[5] While Sherman was backing Joe Johnston's army toward Marietta, Brigadier General John Geary had to counsel his wife about borrowing money for a household expense, as he had not been paid since the previous winter. Mrs. Geary's crisis, which involved the purchase of some furniture, seemed frivolous alongside the dilemmas faced by women who could not afford clothing for themselves or their children, or food staples, or fuel for cooking and heating. The problem of withheld pay had afflicted the families of volunteers since the very beginning of the war, and galloping inflation only aggravated it during the fourth year of the conflict. Some of the most pitiful appeals from destitute wives came in the final days of their husbands' enlistments, when landlords threatened eviction over arrearages in the rent, perennial hunger had deteriorated into actual malnutrition, wardrobes had frayed beyond further patching, every source of borrowing had been exhausted, and every marketable item had been sold — including the family dog, in one case.[6]

When the soldiers weren't subjected to deliberate delay by their own government, they were often victimized by the inefficiency of its bureaucracy. Orra Bailey, of the 7th Connecticut, went unpaid for seven months from the date of his enlistment in 1862 because the treasury was postponing payment to most troops for lack of funds. Early in 1864 he was transferred to the Veteran Reserve Corps after a long illness, but he explained to his wife in June that the paymaster could not find his descriptive list, which served as individual identification in the age before routine personnel photographs. At the end of July the chief clerk in the pay department rebuffed him with the remark that he knew no soldier by the name of Orra Bailey in the United States Army, causing Bailey to wonder how they could hold him in the service if that were true. After another eight months without pay he wrote to the president in desperation, and that finally budged the bound machine.[7] Four months before he was killed in battle, and long after he had last been paid, Massachusetts soldier Eugene Hadley was refused further pay because of some inconsistency in his descriptive list — the wrong height, or hair color, perhaps — and he had to appeal to his state agent to track the matter down. As slowly as the wheels of government turned, the dirt had probably already been shoveled over Hadley's face before anyone corrected the mistake, and then his pay would have been withheld a little longer for the reconciliation of his accounts.[8]

Recruits who had enlisted during or since the winter usually had some bounty money to fall back on, either from the federal government or from the communities where they had allowed their enlistments to be credited against the draft quota, and there were still towns or states that paid monthly stipends to the dependents of volunteers. With apparent frequency, trouble developed with either the bounties or the family supplement, and sometimes that trouble was never resolved. A Canadian who enlisted in a Massachusetts heavy-artillery regiment did so not only for the pay and the bounty, but also for a promised state subsidy of twelve dollars a month for his wife and children. Six months after he reached his regiment his wife still could not draw the supplement, and he supposed it was because she didn't live in the United States. So badly did she need the money that he suggested she move to Massachusetts for a month or so, to "Yankeefy" herself, but in the end the state appears to have welshed on her allowance. Massachusetts also reneged on the subsidies due its own state residents, however, to the indignation of men who never would have enlisted without the promise of that money. A middle-aged Connecticut man with poor prospects resorted to the army to support his wife and mother, and they were to receive six dollars a month besides his bounty, but both the bounty and the supplement came to grief when he went to the hospital with an intestinal ailment and was falsely reported as a deserter. The deficiencies in his account persisted at least until a few months before he died.[9]

Even when the money did come regularly, which was seldom, it was never enough. That often sparked the entrepreneurial spirit, making speculators out of any soldiers who could save up a few dollars. In a more sedentary camp a few messmates might pool their resources to buy a barrel of apples, or potatoes, selling them singly in addition to improving their own diets. The artificer of a Wisconsin field battery started a newspaper and stationery business: he drew slightly better pay than a private, and he had the convenience of the battery wagon for safe and dry storage of his stock, even on the march, where he naturally found the most demand. In barely a year he made well over $1,000, with which he paid off a mortgage on his house, supported his motherless daughters, and banked several hundred dollars before selling his accumulated inventory toward the end of his term for another $700. A Connecticut musician collected enough capital to buy the bounty drafts of new recruits at discounted rates, sending them to his wife, and when those drafts came due she collected the full face value. Few showed that much initiative, though, and fewer could accumulate the capital. Commissioned officers had to supply their own food and a servant, leaving the more junior of them little to send home. Lieutenants might engage in small speculative ventures to earn their board, but it was only the field officers and the generals who could afford to risk large sums, and most of them put their money out at interest to banks and trusted friends, or gravitated toward the safer but still comfortable profits of treasury bonds. The occasional colonel, brigadier, or department commander would invest heavily, and sometimes illegally, in an attempt to make a killing.[10]

Now and then an enlisted man might find his duties sufficiently undemanding to take an extra job. One frugal Vermonter who had enlisted at the upper extremity of the army's age limits earned extra money to send home by taking in washing for his comrades, and others periodically worked as store clerks for their regimental sutlers. Hometown newspapers might pay a few dollars for regular contributions by soldiers at the front, and one inveterate schemer wheedled $150 a year out of the *Chicago Tribune* for that service; eventually he surreptitiously syndicated his letters, peddling them simultaneously to different newspapers. That same wheeler-dealer secured a detail as clerk in the quartermaster's department, where he conspired with his immediate superior to collect a civilian salary for his work, on top of his monthly army pay, besides filching provisions from the government stores to trade for his room and board in a private house. When that lucrative arrangement ended, he hired out as a stenographer for courts-martial and other military tribunals.[11]

All that additional income stopped the moment a soldier died, and when calculating his final pay the army deducted not only any sutler's debt and excess clothing issue but the remaining fraction of salary for the month in which the soldier died. His widow or a dependent parent might apply for a pension of eight dollars a month, plus a pittance for each child under the age of sixteen, but the application usually took several months to process — or years, if any questions arose. Even worse economic straits awaited the family whose supporting male fell into enemy hands. He could no longer earn any supplementary income, and if he could not stand at roll call with his company at the end of each two-month mustering period, even because he languished in a Southern prison, then neither he nor his dependents could draw his pay. That was the situation faced by Sarah Hill when Chauncey's letter of June 17 arrived in the little hamlet of Saratoga, Minnesota, explaining that Bedford Forrest had captured him at Brice's Crossroads. Sarah was barely eighteen years old and at least four months pregnant with her first child, but she would have to worry about a husband who would be unable to correspond with her at the same time that she must learn how to survive the coming months with only the dwindling remains of his enlistment bounty for support.[12]

Tens of thousands of prisoners' wives faced that same dual terror in the spring and summer of 1864. Two years before, Confederate and Union negotiators had established a cartel for the regular exchange of prisoners that assured prompt release for those taken in battle: captured men would be delivered to either Vicksburg, Mississippi, or Aiken's Landing, on the James River, where they were formally exchanged, officer for officer and man for man; any surplus prisoners were paroled, promising to fight no more until an equivalent enemy prisoner had been identified for their exchange. That agreement had fallen apart in the summer of 1863.

First, disputes arose over what constituted a legitimate parole. Confederates had captured entire large garrisons in the autumn of 1862, paroling them right where they stood, without delivering them to the specified exchange points: that had allowed rebel armies in Tennessee and Virginia to carry on their campaigns without diminishing their armies with sizable guard details. Edwin Stanton declared such paroles null and void on July 3, 1863, probably without realizing that Ulysses Grant had decided to do precisely the same thing with nearly thirty thousand Confederates whom he captured at Vicksburg. Grant might have argued that he did deliver his prisoners to the Vicksburg exchange point, since he had captured that very city, but in fact he was freeing them on parole for his own convenience — both to continue offensive operations and to avoid tying up the river transports that carried all his supplies. Stanton's decision to invalidate such paroles introduced immense confusion to the calculation of exchanges, since it made it difficult to determine how many legitimate prisoners each side could count, and within ten weeks Confederate authorities announced that they had exchanged thousands of the Vicksburg garrison on the basis of prisoners whom they had delivered and paroles they had collected from captured Yankees. Apparently because of the newfound disagreement about the number of valid paroles, Stanton's War Department disallowed those exchanges, and insisted that Richmond was forcing those Confederates back into the ranks against the provisions of the cartel. Then, in accordance with Stanton's disavowal of paroles issued in the field, the Confederate exchange agent deemed the entire rebel garrison of Port Hudson, Louisiana, free to return to duty, since Nathaniel Banks had also paroled them on the spot, instead of delivering them for exchange.[13]

Stanton appointed Ethan Allen Hitchcock, an aging major general, to investigate and negotiate that dispute, but — as though determined that exchanges should not resume — Stanton shifted the focus of complaint to the Confederate refusal to include black prisoners. Jefferson Davis had long since decreed that captured U.S. Colored Troops, whether enlisted men or white commissioned officers, would be prosecuted under the state laws regarding servile insurrection, and Stanton must have realized that the race issue posed an insurmountable obstacle to a nation founded to preserve black slavery and white supremacy. Late in November, 1863, Hitchcock reported that the Richmond government had cheated on the exchange, and had effectively abrogated the cartel through President Davis's proclamation. Stanton had the report published, and let it stand as his reason for suspending further exchanges.[14]

From his duty station in South Carolina, Brigadier General John Hatch devised a practical solution to that impasse, proposing the creation of a "reserve" class of Southern prisoners who would be withheld from exchange in numbers sufficient to match the black prisoners in Confederate hands. That class could be filled out with the sons of patrician families, Hatch suggested, while the rest of their comrades and all the white Union prisoners might regain the benefits of exchange. His idea won no support from superiors who seemed uninterested in finding a solution, and the principle of racial equality among prisoners remained the Lincoln administration's excuse for refusing a general exchange until near the end of the conflict, in spite of the terrible consequences of lengthy imprisonment. In the summer of 1864 General Grant admitted that he opposed further exchanges in any case, even knowing all the sufferings of Union prisoners, because it weakened Southern forces. The acknowledgment of that provocative ulterior motive may not have become public until his letter was published, thirty-five years later.[15]

A few influential citizens on either side arranged special exchanges for their sons, but the breakdown of the cartel assured that most prisoners would languish in enemy hands indefinitely. Each government soon faced a burgeoning population of captives, and each scrambled to find places to hold them. That proved a little easier across the North, where many states had provided their troops with accommodations since the opening days of the war, and erstwhile training camps became the favorite solution for the War Department's commissary general of prisoners, Colonel William Hoffman. Camp Douglas, in Chicago, had been the first to make that metamorphosis when Forts Henry and Donelson surrendered, early in 1862. When Stanton announced his revocation of field paroles, the United States held only 6,053 prisoners of war in a dozen different locations, some of which housed fewer than a score. Four months later, there were 26,519 prisoners, and 35,549 prisoners filled twenty-three different Union pens at the end of 1863. Mortality alone kept their number from increasing again the next month.[16]

By July of 1864, men captured at Gettysburg had been held a year, and fifty thousand prisoners jammed the federal facilities. Fort Delaware, a masonry bastion on a tiny island in the middle of the Delaware River, housed more than nine thousand prisoners; nearly fifteen thousand more lived on a sand spit at Point Lookout, Maryland, where the Potomac River pours into Chesapeake Bay, and over eight thousand filled spartan barracks on Rock Island, in the Mississippi River. Camp Douglas and other state training rendezvous at Camp Morton, Indiana, and Camp Chase, Ohio, all swarmed with thousands of prisoners. Johnson's Island, in Lake Erie, held twenty-three hundred Confederate officers. Overcrowding began to pose problems of supply, sanitation, and security, and at the beginning of July carloads of prisoners from Point Lookout started north for a new prison at Elmira, New York. Contractors had walled off an eight-acre stockade within the old training camp there, where many of Grant's wounded were also being cared for and a corral of deserters had been confined. The garrison consisted of a battalion of partially disabled soldiers in the light-blue uniforms of the Invalid Corps (the unfortunate name of which had lately been changed to the Veteran Reserve Corps); these "condemned Yankees" greeted the first two thousand prisoners early in the month. Through July more trainloads of them arrived periodically, and one collided with a coal train in northern Pennsylvania, killing dozens of guards and prisoners. By the end of the month the eight-acre enclosure had received nearly half of the ten thousand prisoners Colonel Hoffman had intended for it. The balance arrived in August, and by September they were dying off at the rate of more than a dozen a day.[17]

Similar burdens befell the Confederacy. Camp Ford, far away in the Trans-Mississippi Department at Tyler, Texas, collected 831 Union prisoners from the beginning of 1863 until the end of September. The suspension of exchange trapped them there through the winter, and in the spring of 1864 they were joined by another 3,696, most of whom were taken during the Red River campaign. Several smaller prisons accounted for a few hundred captives apiece, and two or three thousand always lingered around Richmond, but until the latter part of July most of the Union prisoners east of the Mississippi were eventually transferred to a new prison in Sumter County, Georgia, fifty miles southwest of Macon.[18] There, at Anderson Station on the Southwestern Railroad, the Confederate government had built a fifteen-foot-tall stockade from native pine logs for the containment of their unwilling guests. The post was officially known as Camp Sumter, but everyone at the prison called it Andersonville. A stream traversed the stockade, providing drinking water upstream, bathing facilities farther down, and current for an open sewer at the downstream extremity. When the first prisoners arrived, in February, they found the climate there a welcome relief from the cold quarters they had occupied on the James River, but by July the broiling Georgia sun beat directly down on them, for their captors had filled the prison without building barracks. Until some open sheds went up in August, prisoners had to provide their own cover in the form of tents, blankets, overcoats, or board shanties. Twenty-five thousand men lodged inside that sixteen-acre pen on the last day of June, with hundreds more lying in the hospital outside, but the next day the commandant opened up a ten-acre extension that eased the crowding considerably. For a short while, the Union prisoners at Andersonville enjoyed more space per man than their Confederate counterparts at Elmira, and already an officer from Andersonville had gone to Alabama seeking a site for spreading the prisoners out farther still, but nine thousand more arrived over the next six weeks: even with mortality of fifty to one hundred per day, the population of Andersonville reached thirty-three thousand with the morning roll call of August 9.[19]

For all the crowding and exposure, the worst curse at Andersonville was the diet. So many of the prisoners had already been confined for months without adequate vegetables when they arrived at the stockade that scurvy coursed the camp by the height of summer, either bringing men down by itself or contributing to other debilities. The camp sutler brought in a few vegetables for sale to the minority who still had money, but the intense heat prohibited the transportation of a regular, adequate supply. The rations consisted primarily of meat, rice, and bread — especially cornbread, baked from unbolted meal. The cornbread usually came in satisfactory portions: numerous prisoners indicated as much at the time, before politics and pension applications gave them incentives for exaggeration, but the sheer invariability of that staple came to offend the palates of all but the hungriest men. That was especially true among those who began to turn sick, and the rough granules of ground-in cob irritated intestines softened by scurvy or other nutritive deficiencies, causing ulcers and aggravating the common bowel complaints. Food gave camp administrators the most persuasive means of controlling so immense a prison, and Captain Henry Wirz, the commandant of the stockade, sometimes kept the commissary wagons outside the walls until the prisoners had complied with some disciplinary demand. At least once or twice he withheld the daily issue until the ensuing day, inflicting acute suffering despite allowing double rations on the morrow.[20]

Wirz withheld rations on June 29 to accomplish something the inmates appreciated beyond measure. A gang, or a coalition of gangs, had gathered early in the history of the prison, infesting one bank of the stockade stream near the south gate, where they maintained fairly commodious quarters. From that den they had sallied forth repeatedly to rob other prisoners of their possessions, generally at night, and they developed the habit of beating those who resisted. Their alliance made them formidable, for most of their fellow prisoners had only a few friends if any at all, and most were weakened by months of poor and paltry victuals. The "raiders," as everyone soon called the bandits, kept their strength by feeding well at the expense of their victims. Their depredations escalated in May, after thousands of well-equipped, cash-flush prisoners arrived from the captured garrison of Plymouth, North Carolina, and each new contingent brought fresh booty in the form of clothing, money, and valuables. Success made the raiders bolder still, and as June waned they went too far. The night of June 28 echoed with the howls of the robbed and beaten, but on June 29 a squad of thugs attacked a young man in broad daylight: he put up a stout, single-handed fight, and when they finally pinned him and stripped him of every valuable on his person he staggered to the gate and called for Captain Wirz. The furious boy's battered face corroborated his story, and Wirz sent a guard detail into the stockade with fixed bayonets. The commissary had been distributing rations, but Wirz announced in his thick Swiss German accent that no more food would come inside the prison until all the raiders had been brought out, and his guard detail soon had the enthusiastic assistance of vigilantes who helped identify the culprits and flush them out of their warrens. The sweep continued into the next day, when the ration wagons finally reentered the gate.[21]

With permission from the post commander, the prisoners tried the raiders themselves, complete with jury, prosecutor, and defense attorney. Six were found guilty of killing (or otherwise causing the deaths of) their own comrades, and those six were promptly condemned to hang. More than a week passed before Richmond authorities approved the sentences, but on the lowery afternoon of July 11 Wirz himself, mounted on a white horse, led a guard procession into the stockade with the six doomed raiders, turned them over to an impromptu force of prisoner-police armed with clubs, and left them to their fate. He had already provided lumber for a gallows, and as the condemned men were led to it one of the burlier of them broke through the cordon and fled toward the muddy banks of the creek until a Connecticut man tackled him and wrestled him back to dry ground. In a few moments the six mounted the narrow scaffold, babbled a few last words, and swung into eternity when the prop was knocked from beneath them. Willie Collins, the biggest of them, broke his rope and dropped to the ground, but with the help of the new camp policemen he was soon restored to the scaffold and pushed off with a stronger tether. Half an hour later, it was all over.[22]

That concluded the reign of terror, but not the misery of the long imprisonment. The rations remained invariable, unpalatable, and sometimes insufficient — early reports of which prompted Edwin Stanton to initiate a retaliatory reduction of 20 percent in the sustenance given to captured Confederates. Most inhabitants of the stockade lacked real shelter, at least from the violent storms of a humid Southern summer; mud and excrement mixed indistinguishably along the banks of the creek, despite Wirz's efforts to contain the sinks, and the filth spread through the camp on sodden, rotting shoes. Local spectators and inmates alike looked with disgust on the milling masses of grimy, verminous ragamuffins, whom the prisoners themselves characterized as "hogs," or "rotten sheep." Just after he was cast inside, a Vermont cavalryman recorded that his innumerable new comrades hardly looked human, and that was only three months after the first prisoner had stumbled into the enclosure.[23]

The first few minutes inside the gate left most men stunned and hopeless. For many, depression became a worse enemy than either the raiders or the rebel guards — who, by summer, consisted mainly of Georgia Reserves who were too young, too old, too lame, or too well connected to be conscripted for field service. Malnutrition, monotony, inactivity, the prevalence of death and disease, and the increasing conviction that relief would never come bore inexorably on the spirits of even those who sought their last refuge in the hope of divine protection. Confident rumors of imminent parole or exchange rose and fell like flocks of starlings, and the collapse of each tantalizing prophecy left the most credulous in worse spirits than before. After the third week of July the solution of suicide occurred to many of the despairing multitude, and several attempted it, with occasional success. Some tried to cut their throats or strangle themselves on makeshift, miniature gibbets. At least one despondent soul ducked under the scantling "dead line" that surrounded the interior of the stockade, inviting the guard to obey his standing orders to shoot anyone who intruded on that forbidden zone, but the guard refused.[24]

A score or so of prisoners who inadvertently infringed on the dead line saw less mercy from the sentries. Because of the crowding, blasts of buck-and-ball that were directed at guilty offenders sometimes injured or killed innocent bystanders, like the Pennsylvania cavalryman who died on July 27 at the upper end of the stockade stream, while fetching water. A flock of horrified hundred-day men had just entered the prison: it may have been one of them who reached too far beneath the dead line, prompting a guard from the Georgia Reserves to fire at him and hit the wrong man, who was carried out to the hospital with part of his head blown away. Every week or two another victim would serve as an example to reinforce that rule, and about a dozen men died to preserve the integrity of the dead line; similar regulations governed the officers' prison at Macon, Georgia, where at least one Union lieutenant was killed.[25] The next summer a military prosecutor would vastly exaggerate the number of prisoners who were shot at Andersonville's dead line, and try to cast the practice as an example of Confederate inhumanity, but the same or similar boundaries were enforced just as fatally in Northern prisons, and even in Union training camps.[26]

At Andersonville and at other prisons in the South, the chance of being shot dead added but little terror to the growing probability of demise through slower and more gruesome means, for doubt spread that release would ever come save through death. Cavalcades of fresh prisoners spilled through the gate almost daily, carrying the latest secondhand information about the exchange debate and the War Department's stubborn refusal to budge on the matter of black prisoners. Men whose terms of service had expired still shuffled about inside the "bull pen," as the inmates were calling the compound, and some had died after their enlistments had expired: the collapse of the exchange cartel had left some nine-month men in prison nearly a year after they would have been mustered out.[27] Another year or two of confinement therefore seemed entirely possible: if that happened, and if the midsummer mortality rate persisted, not a man of them would survive to see freedom. Men in tattered blue uniform fragments had begun as early as spring to show bitter animosity toward their own government for abandoning them to such an end over a political principle, and in July those sentiments circulated with the virulence of an epidemic.[28] The same spirit would eventually infect the officers in their own separate prisons, where conditions were never so primitive.[29] Stump speakers inside the stockade drew wide audiences with the argument that no government deserved allegiance if it would so heartlessly turn its back on those who had been captured in its service. The most generous critics supposed that their leaders in Washington probably had no idea of the desperate conditions in Confederate prisons. The administration might condemn the return of captured black soldiers to slavery, but the Andersonville prisoners compared that fate favorably to their own circumstances. Random speeches evolved into a convention of the indignant and disaffected, with the sergeants who commanded the various camp detachments selecting a committee that formulated a presidential petition from the destitute thousands who paid the price for their administration's scruples. A few prisoners were released on parole to deliver the petition, along with a similar appeal from Union officers held at Charleston, and once he was back inside his own lines one of those paroled emissaries embellished his tale with lurid descriptions of deliberate, fiendish cruelty, perhaps to better persuade his government to relieve the suffering of the comrades he had left behind.[30]

Little happened in secret at Andersonville, and Chauncey Hill witnessed all the events of that memorable summer. He and the rest of Bedford Forrest's prisoners from Brice's Crossroads had all come in by Sunday, June 19, just in time to see the tail end of a cold, rainy week to match the nine-day deluge that had followed them on the march into Mississippi. On that same Sunday, back on the edge of Winona County, Minnesota, his wife, Sarah, sat down with pen and paper to convey her worry over having gone more than two weeks without a letter from him. Through the wife of another soldier she learned that Chauncey's regiment had left Memphis to chase down Forrest, taking only limited rations, and had not been heard from since. She evidently attributed his silence to that mission, but because of the information about short rations she feared that something might have happened to the expedition. She still addressed the letter to his regiment, at Memphis, but his surviving officers evidently returned it to her, doubtless with the information that he was missing; by the time that reply made its way back up the Mississippi River she probably had his June 17 note from Mobile, consoling her with the news that he was well treated and was bound for an "exchange camp" in Georgia.[31]

Like anyone who approached the stockade, Private Hill would have smelled the foul aroma of the place before he could see the interior from the hilltop by Wirz's office. With that first glimpse he must have abandoned any optimistic illusions about Andersonville as a mere way station on the road to repatriation, and as he walked through the gate with his assigned detachment he, like all before him, would have recoiled at the sea of wretched wraiths teeming in such fetid squalor. He would have fifty-nine days in the bullpen to consider the consequences of the enlistment he had undertaken less than four months before. He could calculate the proceeds of his bounty, the extent of his debts, and the balance — if any — on which Sarah could subsist until his return. During those long, lean days when the raiders were taken out, tried, and hanged, he doubtless wondered how large his wife had grown with their first child, and whether it would be a boy or a girl. He may well have shared the rage of the other prisoners as they denounced their government for such insensitivity to their plight. When Union cavalry disrupted the rail lines that supplied Andersonville, late in July, Hill suffered short rations along with everyone else, and when hundreds of Yankee cavalrymen who had hoped to liberate the prisoners came into the stockade themselves, he could mourn with the rest.[32]

The sharply granular cornmeal and the abundant filth eventually provoked the same ailment in Chauncey Hill that afflicted so many others, and he started making frequent trips to the alfresco sinks at the lower end of the creek. Dysentery thinned his frame, and, like others whom it had drained, he may have resorted to a little pit in the vicinity of his own shelter. When torrential afternoon downpours flooded the camp during the second week of August he may have been one of those who had grown too weak to do more than lie in the mud. Sometime in the wee hours of August 17, while a comrade slept beside him unaware, Hill quietly gave up the ghost. The next day a work detail laid him in a trench north of the prison, snugly packed against his neighbors on either side. A clerk recorded the number 6,064 beside his name in the death register, for he was the 6,064th Yankee buried at Andersonville, besides the six raiders, and the cemetery was not yet half filled. Sarah Hill did not know she was a widow until months later, when one of her husband's comrades reached home and sent her the details of Chauncey's final hours.[33]

For those who knew the ordeal that awaited Union prisoners at Camp Sumter, it might have been possible to conclude that a soldier was more fortunate to be wounded than captured, but that assessment would have found little support from anyone following the Army of the Potomac. Far more than Sherman's campaign in Georgia, the bloodletting in Virginia had produced a collective agony that defied description.

After the Wilderness and the inaugural clashes at Spotsylvania, a veteran from New Hampshire wrote that not even the hardened soldier could watch the long, dolorous caravans of ambulances lurching toward Fredericksburg without shuddering. Then came the chaotic, daylong fracas in the rain at the Mule Shoe, on May 12, which sent thousands more to hospitals that had already been filled to capacity. John Wilcox, an eighteen-year-old veteran of two years' fighting, was shot through the leg on the skirmish line of Burnside's front that morning and was carried back to his division field hospital, where he found his major and lieutenant colonel both suffering from leg wounds like his. They lay all day in the rain, but in the evening an anxious order for evacuation reached the chief surgeon and he started transporting his patients to Fredericksburg, putting the officers in the first ambulances. Young Wilcox and most of the enlisted men waited through the night, expecting to be captured, and it was not until the afternoon of May 15 that ambulance drivers loaded him and two other men into the back of one of those springless contraptions for the jarring, painful journey over roads so rough and muddy that a boy from backwoods Maine considered their condition "shocking." Only when their ambulance reached the hill overlooking Fredericksburg, the following day, did someone offer Wilcox some coffee and hardtack. There they lingered the rest of the day, perhaps waiting for someone to find room for them, but near dark their conveyance lumbered into town and delivered them to one of the Georgian brick homes that Union artillery had not destroyed in 1862.[34]

So much of the army's transportation carried supplies and ammunition to the front that food ran short in Fredericksburg: most of the doctors and nurses were subsisting on crackers and tea themselves. The first thing Wilcox noted about his lodging was the meager fare served by the medical attendants, who were all strangers. His two field officers had preceded him into the city by the privilege of their rank. The major, George Chandler, had a brother who was the speaker of New Hampshire's legislature, and that brother was married to the governor's daughter, so it was not long before the Granite State's two Republican congressmen sent an agent to look after him. The governor, meanwhile, dispatched some envoys from the Christian Commission to establish a separate hospital for his state's soldiers, and by nightfall of May 17 Private Wilcox, the two officers, and a clamoring throng of other wounded New Hampshiremen occupied the home of Fredericksburg's mayor. Major Chandler and the lieutenant colonel shared the same bed, each with his wounded leg on the outside for easier dressing, and meals soon became a little more prompt and plentiful. Cornelia Hancock, a young Quaker woman who had served as a nurse in the vast tent hospital at Gettysburg, found far more wounded in Fredericksburg, and she thought it the more heart-rending of the two scenes, despite the amenity of dry houses. On some quest she glanced into a dank storehouse behind the house where she was working, only to open the door on a score of men who had not been seen since their ambulances had dumped them there, a full day previously. "O, God!" she exclaimed, in a note to her sister, "such suffering it never entered the mind of man or woman to think of."[35]

A soldier who had stopped in Fredericksburg on his way to the front explained to a young lady at home that there were not half a dozen houses in the city that had not been converted to hospitals, and all the front yards had been churned into cemeteries. The groans of the wounded filled the streets, he told her, and it was impossible to amble a hundred yards without meeting someone who had lost an arm or a leg — and there he excused himself for offending her feminine eye with the word "leg," aside from the mention of amputation. It was the same outside town. A signalman from the Sixth Corps found every house and barn full of wounded when he ran an errand that way, but he saw that they were being shipped off as quickly as they could be moved. A civilian at Aquia Creek Landing, where Fredericksburg's railroad met the Potomac, gaped in amazement at the hordes of wounded brought there on the cars.[36]

The Christian Commission and the Sanitary Commission, organizations analogous to the later Salvation Army and Red Cross, swooped down on Fredericksburg as it became the focal point for the human refuse of Grant's stubborn strategy. Edward Bartlett, a young neighbor of Ralph Waldo Emerson, Henry Thoreau, and the Alcotts, had served in two socially prominent, short-term Massachusetts regiments earlier in the war; by the spring of 1864 he had gone back to clerking, but when fighting started below the Rapidan he came to Fredericksburg to dress wounds for a while under the auspices of the Sanitary Commission. He congratulated himself that the organization performed great work there, by feeding and caring for the sick and wounded when no one else did: "The wounded men believe in two things," he wrote, "Genl Grant and the Sanitary Commission," and the national treasurer of the agency concurred. "We are working hard to support Grant's army," recorded George Templeton Strong, "spending $650 per day on river transportation, manning 50 to 60 wagons, and employing 150 to 200 relief agents, and twice as many teamsters, servants, and contrabands."[37]

The commander of the 10th Vermont regiment also praised the Sanitary Commission when he suffered a minor wound, directing his wife to donate ten dollars to the organization on the claim that he had enjoyed at least twice that much in benefits from it. Most soldiers seemed to contradict that colonel, however, and more than one called either the Sanitary Commission or the Christian Commission "a complete humbug," or even "a miserable humbug." The edible delicacies that came down to the armies were mostly "gobbled up by officers and Docts," complained one captain, and a field officer in the 17th Vermont confirmed that some agents of the Sanitary Commission diverted food and supplies for themselves and for favorites among the officers, particularly in the medical departments. The diary of one dainty Christian Commission volunteer who spent barely three weeks at the front alternately recorded his tasty meals and teas among the officers and his utter exhaustion at having to walk a few miles to distribute tracts, although two young contrabands carried the books for him.[38]

A lot of dedicated women nevertheless gave their time and talents to the Sanitary Commission, putting up little packages called "comfort bags," containing plain but precious items for personal hygiene, like toothbrushes, or tasty treats, like preserves, with an occasional generic letter thrown in by the woman who filled it, for the soldier who might like to cultivate a platonic correspondence. A Massachusetts man urged his wife to have her friends add a cube of chewing tobacco, to satisfy the more common nicotine addiction of that era. On the requisition of a chaplain or surgeon, the keeper of a Sanitary Commission storehouse at the front would supply underwear, towels, handkerchiefs, canned meat or fruit, condensed milk, ink, stationery, and the noxious weed, and once that shipment left the agent's hands it depended on that chaplain or surgeon how much of it reached the intended recipients. A significant proportion of surviving letters from Civil War soldiers bear the letterhead of the Sanitary Commission, particularly among those written from hospitals or parole camps, but soldiers so seldom mentioned receiving other Sanitary Commission goods, and so often remarked bitterly on senior officers hogging them, as to suggest ubiquitous, unpunished pilferage. Individual agents attended to their duties more conscientiously, and would sometimes go far out of their way to accommodate a soldier or his family, securing furloughs for the sick and wounded or arranging for the recovery of bodies from the battlefield. The Christian Commission occasionally assisted with the sick and wounded, but its mission leaned more toward saving souls and supplying religious arguments for the human cost of the war effort. When regimental chaplains failed to perform — and they failed to perform quite often — the Christian Commission would step in, holding religious meetings and handing out testaments, leaving most of the troops' unsatisfied physical wants to the care of the Sanitary Commission.[39]

As Grant pushed closer to Richmond he had to carry his wounded with him until he could open another supply base. Men who had been injured at the North Anna followed their comrades to Cold Harbor, whence they were shuttled to White House Landing and carried north by steamers. Arabella Barlow, the wife of General Barlow, came down to White House with Miss Hancock, and they worked under the perpetual roar of artillery for a solid week before catching up with the streams of wounded. After the most recent crop of mutilated bodies had been taken aboard steamers, Miss Hancock informed her mother that the only patient in her plantation-house hospital was an "embalmed Lieutenant," who lay on the porch waiting for delivery to his next of kin. At such moments when she had the leisure to think, she had no praise for the engineers of all the destruction. She may have judged the morality of the war itself with the influence of her Quaker faith, however much she admired its goals, but she also scorned the murderous strategy of the new general, who wore Lee's army down at a cost of two men for one. She who had dressed so many wounds and seen so much death could only note — as had many soldiers — that Grant's brute force had not brought the army as close to Richmond as McClellan had done, at far less cost, two years before.[40]

The lightly wounded remained on duty, or stayed in their quarters until they recovered. One artilleryman who fell into the sights of a sharpshooter had rolled his woolen and rubber blankets into a horse collar and slung it over one shoulder, so the bullet that was meant to kill him lost all its momentum in the layered fabric and on the tableware in his haversack; the bullet failed even to penetrate his clothing, instead leaving a huge black bruise on his hip that lamed him for days, but he refused to be counted among the wounded and never reported to the surgeon. William Henry, the lieutenant colonel of the 10th Vermont who wrote so flatteringly of the Sanitary Commission, had the last two phalanges of his right index finger smashed by a bullet at Cold Harbor, and his regimental surgeon lopped the wreckage from the stump that day. To the colonel's surprise, he was not even allowed a brief furlough while the throbbing lasted. For the next few weeks he just lounged around the hospital, feasting on Sanitary Commission supplies and chatting with his regimental surgeon, who traced the wounded hand on a piece of paper for the edification of Mrs. Henry.[41]

For most, the field hospital and the base hospital served only as way stations on the painful journey to long-term care. At first, the next destination was Washington, where the public lands had been speckled with military hospitals, including some semipermanent wooden structures in the pavilion pattern, with long wards radiating from a central hub. Grant's campaign prompted the medical department to increase the number of its hospital beds by nearly half that spring, to a total of more than 120,000 nationwide, and the surgeon general confided to a former senator that 30,000 were not enough to accommodate the casualties of the Virginia campaign alone. The first of the wounded from the Wilderness appeared at the docks in Washington Monday evening, May 9, and by Friday at least eight thousand of them had landed. Ambulances carted them to any number of hospitals, like Harewood, Armory Square, Douglas, Lincoln, or Carver, and the teams were kept at it so long without rest or nourishment that horses dropped in the traces on the streets of the capital and died, leaving the wounded passengers to walk or wait for a replacement.[42]

Walt Whitman, another hospital volunteer with Quaker antecedents, spent most of his time at Armory Square Hospital, which he described as having more residents than some fairly prominent New England villages. The population kept growing, too, with so many coming in from the Army of the Potomac that the wardmasters gave up their accounting for a time. Washington's hospitals were soon overflowing, and those who could stand to travel went back to the rail depot for transit farther north, to Hicks, Jarvis, and Patterson Park Hospital, in Baltimore, to St. John's College or the Naval Academy, at Annapolis, to Mower General Hospital at Chestnut Hill, outside Philadelphia, or to Portsmouth Grove, in Rhode Island; New York Harbor provided several havens for the wounded. The distribution of those who could be moved left the worst cases to linger in Washington, where they contributed to a higher rate of mortality and therefore a greater degree of strain on those who cared for them. Sarah Low, the twenty-year-old niece of Senator John P. Hale, had come down from New Hampshire to nurse at Armory Square. She explained to her mother that once a ward filled up it was painful enough to watch half a dozen of those patients carried out to their graves, but since the last swarms arrived after Cold Harbor and Petersburg some wards at Armory Square had lost more than a score.[43]

The first thing that Whitman noted was how many of that first influx bore only the slightest wounds. That was the same wave that had brought the uninjured skulkers, too, and there may have been a connection, for an attendant at Chestnut Hill detected a disproportionate number of wounds to the hand, consisting mainly of mangled or missing fingers. The ubiquitous use of earthworks accounted for much of that, since a man standing behind breastworks or lying behind a little rifle pit still had to expose one hand to ram the bullet down the barrel of his rifle, but blowing off a finger or two had been a favorite escape for the faint-hearted since the earliest battles. One Connecticut captain charged that at least two neighbors of his from the same company went home with self-inflicted wounds within two weeks that June, and both of them were veterans of nearly three years' service. The prevalence of that practice may have led to the restriction that kept Colonel Henry from a furlough when he lost his finger.[44]

The minority of seriously wounded demanded most of the time, strength, and emotional stamina of the staff. Infected and gangrenous injuries smelled like carrion, reported one detailed orderly, and he went about his duties barely able to stifle his gagging. Whitman devoted most of his time to sitting with the wounded, reading to them, writing letters for them, or tending to their comfort. Flies filled the hospitals, and the summer of 1864 seemed warmer than usual in the humid, marshy capital district, so Whitman would spend hours just fanning a dying boy. Until the end of May he paid particular attention to Charles Cutler, whom he supposed to be only seventeen years old, although Cutler had spent more than two years in the army. The boy had been gut-shot in the heavy artillery's baptism of fire at Spotsylvania, and spent his last days suffering with a hopeless case of peritonitis while the grizzled poet fanned him and mopped his brow. Whitman visited often with a legless Ohio lad until he, too, died, and he tried to spend time with all he could, but with two hundred of the army's worst cases in Armory Square his rounds took an insidious toll. More than a third of those he saw had endured a major amputation, he told his mother, adding that "it is enough to melt the heart of a stone." Whitman fell ill for a time, and Miss Low collapsed under the strain, as well, retiring for a week's rest late in June.[45]

Certain wounds, like those penetrating the peritoneal cavity, almost always ended fatally, and the futility of treating them aroused conflicting emotions in those who dressed such injuries. Miss Low concluded that everyone seriously wounded in the knee died, whether the leg was amputated or not, perhaps because that complicated joint defied thorough cleansing. She noticed in particular one captain who had been shot through the knee in a fight north of the James: his wife had come down to Washington to help care for him, but Miss Low wrote him off as a dead man. A study of shot fractures of the knee joint proved her more right than wrong, for over 60 percent of those whose leg was not amputated did die, as did about 54 percent of those who suffered amputation above the knee. The higher up the leg the doctors cut, the less chance the patient had of surviving: amputations at the hip proved fatal more than 83 percent of the time.[46]

With so many patients, some of whom were carried in horribly mutilated, wardmasters and surgeons at the general hospitals tended to delay the discharge of patients who had recovered from whatever brought them to the hospital. If a man had the use of both arms and legs and had enough strength to move around and carry things, it was in the interest of the hospital to keep him there as an informal orderly. That was usually fine with the soldier, despite the sometimes nauseating nature of the work, for even long hours of light duty indoors were preferable to service in the field for anyone who had already had a taste of it, especially if he had been much under fire. It was the safe spot that an influential man might solicit for a boy he wanted to keep from harm, and the sinecure that the scurrilous brother of a state governor would demand as his fraternal due, or that a wily veteran might finagle for himself. George Morgan, who had gone to the Chestnut Hill hospital from Burnside's corps that spring, sick, had gotten well enough to help with the wounded when they started coming in, and he considered his position a "nice place." To his intense chagrin, it all came to an end in July, when urgent orders instructed him

— and every other able-bodied man at that facility — to report to his regiment as soon as possible.[47]

The occasion that parted Morgan from his cozy assignment arose from David Hunter's failed campaign against Lynchburg and his flight into West Virginia, which left the Shenandoah Valley wide open. Twice before had Confederate excursions down that corridor thrown Washington into a panic, distracting Union troops and administration attention from the campaign against Richmond, and Jubal Early had brought with him General Lee's hope that he could sweep northward after neutralizing Hunter. While Hunter worried his divisions into the Alleghenies in ravenous retreat, Early turned his own troops toward Staunton. A week later he had reached the lower valley, where he met the hapless Franz Sigel.[48]

Sigel had been reduced to the command of a reserve division, nominally under the orders of the fugitive Hunter, but for this emergency he was on his own. Several thousand troops guarded the Baltimore & Ohio Railroad, but most of them consisted of hundred-day regiments of Ohio National Guardsmen, strewn by companies from central Maryland to the Ohio River. For independent operations Sigel could call on fewer than five thousand troops, nearly a third of them dismounted cavalry. He had failed miserably against Breckinridge and a smaller, hodgepodge army at New Market, and the appearance of a corps of seasoned Confederate veterans more than twice the number of his own command quelled any combative impulse that remained to him. Sigel's cavalry backed away from Early's at Winchester on the morning of July 2, and refugees reported the rebel infantry not far behind. When Early spread out the next morning to advance on Sigel's headquarters at Martinsburg, Sigel gathered all the men he could and scampered to Harper's Ferry, where, on the evening of the Fourth of July, he immediately retreated across the Potomac and took position on towering Maryland Heights. There he expected to be trapped by attacks from the front and rear, and so he would have been had Early considered Sigel's force worth capturing. Instead, Early crossed his army into Maryland over fords at Williamsport and Shepherdstown, each of which had provided the Army of Northern Virginia a narrow avenue for escape after other raids. Ignoring Sigel altogether, Early hurried his divisions over South Mountain through gaps still littered with souvenirs of the desperate Confederate rear-guard fight of 1862. With the reminder of that valiant incident from the heyday of Lee's army, the lean survivors of Stonewall Jackson's corps descended the steep eastern face of that long ridge, bearing down on Frederick City and the Monocacy River. Already the government functionaries in Washington were beginning to sweat, if only from the uncertainty left by Sigel's timid deportment, and nervous reports drifted from the War Department to the hospitals to the streets that Early was bringing thirty thousand men, or thirty-five, forty, or fifty thousand.[49]

That was the end of Sigel's career in the field. Another officer took over for him, and General Grant ordered troops up from the Army of the Potomac to defend the capital. Edwin Stanton, ever frantic at the thought of any Confederate incursion, demanded the immediate muster and deployment of Pennsylvania's recruits for the hundred-day service, and called on the governor of New York for his state militia in response to the threat. Once again, soldiers at the front snickered at the cowardice of citizens in Maryland and nearby Pennsylvania, who seemed unwilling to rally to the defense of their homes, as scores of old men and boys in Petersburg had done, a month before, to fend off a raid by Yankee cavalry. A general with Sherman supposed that "a thousand old maids with broomsticks" should have been able to stop Early.[50]

Waiting at the Monocacy was Major General Lew Wallace, whose department began at the river's edge. Wallace took position a couple of miles from Frederick on the eastern bank of the river, on high ground that looked down on a plain that the enemy would have to cross. At first, he had only the equivalent of a strong brigade consisting mostly of Maryland and Ohio troops, the majority of whom were hundred-day men. On Friday, July 8, two brigades from the Sixth Corps reached him by rail via Baltimore, bringing his command to about six thousand of all arms. The bright, warm morning of July 9 seemed peaceful enough, with some farmers hauling in their shocks of wheat on the plain, but then Early arrayed his main body directly across the river from Wallace's position and opened with his artillery. John B. Gordon's division, the largest one Early had, sought a ford downstream and — dry weather having left all the fords very low — Gordon soon found a route that put him on Wallace's left flank. The two Sixth Corps brigades held that wing, though, and they clung to their position from late morning until midafternoon, bolstered by many of Wallace's own troops, taken from his right. The numbers would have been about equal on that front, and Gordon's initial assaults were driven back with heavy loss, but eventually he swung the remains of the old Stonewall Brigade around to strike flat against Wallace's flank while the rest of his division advanced from the front, and that persuaded Wallace to call it a day. Gordon cut him off from the Washington Pike, and those Yankees who ran fast enough covered the extra distance to the Baltimore Pike, which they followed in feverish haste into the night and all the next day, but hundreds of them threw down their rifles and bolted into the woods, or just raised their hands. The flocks of prisoners included a sizable number of those hundred-day men: while their comrades turned for home with a lifetime to polish the story of their single day of danger, those unfortunate hundreds made their way to Andersonville, where dozens of them would lay their bones.[51]

After encouraging Wallace's retreat for a couple of miles, Early let him go, detaching only a few hundred cavalry to prod him along and wreak enough havoc to confuse and confound any pursuers. The next day the preponderance of the Southern forces turned toward Washington, where Sigel's threefold exaggeration of Confederate numbers had won a semblance of confirmation from reports by the soundly whipped Wallace. The rebel cavalry on Wallace's trail frightened Baltimore and then cut the telegraph line between there and Washington. Both cities girded for an attack, mobilizing the clerks and hospital orderlies of the Veteran Reserve Corps as well as arming able-bodied civilians from the government departments and the Navy Yard. Drums beat throughout the capital all day July 10, drawing mixed crowds of soldiers and curious, nervous citizens into the streets. Secretary Stanton called on the Navy Department for gunboats to patrol the deeper tributaries of Chesapeake Bay. As far away as Wilmington, Delaware, the city bells rang to bring out the militia, which repaired to the du Pont family's gunpowder mill and the key bridges around the city to fend off chimerical rebel bands.[52]

Navy secretary Gideon Welles tried to pry information from his colleague in the War Department, but Edwin Stanton seemed not to know anything; only the president offered him an assessment of the enemy's movements, and a surprisingly accurate one at that. Once Early's lean columns started raising dust clouds on the perimeter of the capital, Welles found Stanton suddenly "quiet, subdued, and apparently oppressed," in stark contradiction to his customary agitation at such times — and to his evident alarm of a day or two previously. A visitor who disliked Stanton less than Welles did thought the war minister felt perfectly secure, but that was after reinforcements began landing at the docks: before that help started coming in, Stanton showed his usual trepidation. He fretted disproportionately over a report that President Lincoln's carriage had been followed by a horseman wearing a strange uniform, who did not belong to the regular escort, and he advised special vigilance by the president's guard that night, on the ride out to the Lincoln family's summer residence at the Soldiers' Home. Stanton had some cause to worry about assassination attempts, if only from a shared sense of guilt: late the previous winter a cavalry raid on Richmond had ended in the death of Colonel Ulric Dahlgren and the discovery of his handwritten orders to find and kill Jefferson Davis, along with his cabinet officers. Despite official disavowal by Union authorities, that incident had at least introduced the concept of political murder, and diluted the air of opprobrium that surrounded it. It had not reconciled professional soldiers to the tactic, however, and even if an agent from Early's command had infiltrated the city with that intention he would hardly have adopted so conspicuous a disguise as the alien military attire Stanton had mentioned. The credence Stanton accorded that report typified his eternally suspicious nature, especially under the strain of enemy bayonets outside the seat of government, but the reflexivity of the secretary's fright did not preclude the possibility of secret Confederate activity.[53]

In fact, Robert E. Lee had entertained some faint hope of accompanying Early's raid with clandestine operations. With or without Early's support, he suggested the plan of ferrying a regiment or two across the mouth of the Potomac to free the Confederate prisoners at Point Lookout. Lee wrote President Davis on the subject at a time when Point Lookout held more than fourteen thousand prisoners — the most of any Union prison — and they were guarded by U.S. Colored Troops, whose effectiveness Lee doubted. He proposed that the liberated prisoners could arm themselves with rifles and artillery seized from the post, while the cavalrymen among them could mount themselves "on the march," and they all might then skirt Washington to the upper fords of the Potomac before Grant could send enough troops to stop them. That ambitious plot never reached fruition, failing ultimately from the loose lips of Confederate States Navy gossips, after which Union prison-keepers started moving the Point Lookout prisoners to Elmira. Lee's letter to his president also alluded to a plan proposed by George P. Kane, the former police marshal of Baltimore. Kane had harbored ill-disguised sympathy with states' rights and secession from the commencement of the war, but after Union soldiers threw him in prison for seventeen months he became an active enemy of the United States. Once released, he migrated to Canada, but by the summer of 1864 he had run the blockade into the Confederacy, lodging in Richmond as a self-appointed organizer of expatriate Marylanders. He had evidently presented the Davis administration with some plan to recruit soldiers or operatives while Early lingered north of the Potomac, but whatever the proposal entailed General Lee gave it little chance of success, and no obvious activity attributable to Marshal Kane attended that raid into Maryland.[54]

With barely ten thousand effectives left in the field, Jubal Early knew that he could never hope to seize Washington long enough to do more than burn a few buildings. Even if the imposing ring of forts around the city held only convalescents, militia, and civilians, they would likely have delayed him long enough for reinforcements to arrive, and he also had to consider all the Union forces he had already defeated, but not destroyed. Lew Wallace still had a few thousand men at Baltimore, and Sigel's command had survived intact, under a better general, while David Hunter's vagabonds from the Lynchburg campaign were making the circuitous trek east by way of Parkersburg, on the Baltimore & Ohio Railroad. The best Early could hope for was the satisfaction of creating consternation in the enemy's homeland, and he accomplished that much with the men at hand. His roving cavalry stopped a train from Baltimore, momentarily seizing Major General William Franklin, and his infantry tore up miles of tracks just beyond the outskirts of Washington. Confederates seemed to be everywhere. A former senator from Illinois had returned to Washington to find it under "a state of siege," with rebel soldiers lurking on the fringes of the capital.[55]

Civilians in and around Washington heard drums beating the long roll all afternoon on Sunday, July 10, and again from an early hour Monday morning, hailing the soldiers and militia into formation with their weapons. Mobilized government clerks boarded horse cars with their muskets and accoutrements to join the defense as Early brought his infantry down Seventh Street, north of the city, and marched inside the District of Columbia. His skirmishers fanned out within sight of Fort Stevens and Fort DeRussy and started popping away at the powder-blue uniforms of the Veteran Reserves, who opposed them from the cover of the private homes they had commandeered. Union pickets burned a few houses that would have offered similar havens for Confederate sharpshooters, and warned nearby residents to pack their belongings in case their homes had to be sacrificed as well. Just over the hill behind Fort Stevens lay the Soldiers' Home, and Abraham Lincoln's summer bedroom.[56]

Early allowed his men to rest after their marathon march in the stifling heat, and he soon determined that the solid line of works would cost him too much to carry, if he could do it at all with his ten thousand. He presented a bold front, both to cow the city's defenders and to blunt any reconnaissance that might reveal his actual strength. Again the population spilled into the streets to learn what neither the newspapers nor the government seemed able to tell them, grilling anyone who had been out to the forts, and an open carriage went that way with the president and Mr. Stanton, for all to see. Everyone, including the Confederates, knew that the other two divisions of the Sixth Corps were on their way up from City Point, but the first of them only reached Washington that evening, disembarking in the gathering dusk and gliding up Seventh Street at a rapid route-step by the dim glow of the city gaslights. More arrived early on Tuesday morning, and the rest had come in by midafternoon; soldiers cried out for "greenbacks" as they passed the Treasury Building on their way to protect a government that had long let them go unpaid. A Maine boy who seemed awed by the capital's architecture surmised that the buildings were more worthy of defense than

President Lincoln himself, "for we have got some don't think but little of him."[57]

Braver now, curious citizens mounted horses or carriages and started up to see the anticipated fight. Mobs of sightseers were soon milling around in their white dusters on the heights overlooking Early's position, aggravating the soldiers and the citizens who had taken up arms to defend the city: while those perfectly healthy civilians ambled about and gawked, the disabled veterans in light blue a few hundred yards below them gritted their teeth under those deadly orders to hold "at all hazards" until enough of the Sixth Corps came up to relieve them. Troops had already marched through the city in sufficient numbers that calm returned in many quarters: at noon the president sat at his desk in the White House, routinely signing commissions, and afterward he held his regular cabinet meeting. Over at the Smithsonian, the commissioner of public buildings made a speech to an assemblage of schoolchildren that undoubtedly occupied their attention less effectively than the occasional boom of artillery an hour's brisk walk away. Later in the day Gideon Welles left his office at the Navy Department to take a look, and Senator Ben Wade joined him as he wandered right into Fort Stevens; they gravitated toward the fighting side of the earthwork, and there sat the president, taking some shade with his back braced against the parapet. Shells soared overhead occasionally, and picket fire crackled all day long a few hundred yards farther out on Seventh Street. Finally, toward evening, a division of the Sixth Corps sauntered out to drive Early's skirmishers in, but his main line stood its ground and even counterattacked, holding on until darkness fell. In the morning the rebels were all gone, headed back the way they had come with a long wagon train filled with provisions and plunder. The home of Postmaster General Montgomery Blair, just outside the district, stood engulfed in flames as the red banners disappeared. On the rebels' departure, a Vermont veteran observed that they had come closer to Washington in five days than any Union army had come to Richmond in three years.[58]

A fortnight previously, General Grant had ordered the Nineteenth Corps from Louisiana with the intention of expanding his operations around Petersburg and Richmond. William Franklin represented the vanguard of that corps when Confederate cavalry plucked him from the train outside Baltimore. The first of Franklin's infantry arrived off Fort Monroe on the morning of July 12, while Early still demonstrated outside Washington, and instead of bringing it up the James, Grant sent it up Chesapeake Bay in the wake of the Sixth Corps convoy. Those boats started unloading at the capital the next afternoon.[59]

By then the pursuit had begun. On Wednesday morning Horatio

Wright sent his Vermont Brigade out to scour the suddenly quiet fields, groves, and neighborhoods where the intruders had camped, but they found only a few dozen stragglers, a few score of wounded, and some dead bodies. That afternoon the Sixth Corps (minus the battered division with Lew Wallace) started on the chase, and when the lead regiments of the Nineteenth Corps landed at Washington they hurried out the same roads. Wright promised Mr. Stanton that he would press on "to the limits of the endurance of the men," but that endurance lasted only until about 7:30 in the evening, and the head of his column camped barely eight miles beyond the district boundaries. Early had the start of him by several hours, and in spite of all the livestock and loaded wagons he was bringing away he widened that lead with long strides into the night. He hastened across the Potomac and was resting at Leesburg the next day long before Union cavalry appeared at Poolesville, a few miles on the Maryland side of the river. Yankee soldiers sitting around their campfires at Poolesville that night already entertained fears that their prey would escape, judging perhaps by their moderate march of only eighteen miles that day. Almost taking his leisure, Early waited until the next morning to put his divisions in a single column bound west, over the Blue Ridge and into the Shenandoah Valley. Not until a day and a half later did Sixth Corps infantry wade into Virginia at White's Ford and occupy Leesburg, chasing away Early's rear guard. Wright followed over the mountains when he heard that Early was waiting for him again on the far side of the Shenandoah River, but there he loitered for a couple of days, first thinking of a flank movement one way, then trying one in the other direction, and when that failed he finally made ready to bull his way across right under Early's guns, only to find that the Confederates had decamped again. Supposing the raiders were hightailing it up the valley to Lee's army, Wright turned everyone around and headed back to Washington.[60]

The condemnation and recriminations began even before Wright called the hunt to an end. Benjamin French, the commissioner of public buildings who had lectured schoolchildren at the Smithsonian to the echo of artillery, dropped in at the White House to lecture Abraham Lincoln a couple of days later. When the president revealed his doubt that Early would be caught, and then implied that he was resigned to that failure, French predicted that public disgust over that costly, humiliating episode might reach sufficient intensity to decide the election that lay only seventeen weeks ahead. At a cabinet meeting on July 15 the old attorney general, Edward Bates, ranted about the apparent imbecility in the War Department, taking particular aim at Henry Halleck. Edwin Stanton had stepped out of the meeting, and was not present to defend either his department or the former general in chief: Halleck's role had been reduced to passing on the orders of Ulysses Grant, and he seemed much more comfortable without the command responsibility that he had always tried to avoid anyway, so perhaps Bates resented Halleck's failure to take the initiative and manage the defense and pursuit directly. Gideon Welles shared the attorney general's exasperation (they were both readers of the hypercritical *National Intelligencer*), and he thought the president disingenuous when he seemed to credit Halleck's claim that Early had fielded a lot more troops than he did. As Welles left the cabinet meeting he bumped into the War Department solicitor, who also threw all the blame on Halleck, leading Welles to suppose that Stanton would do likewise. In fact Stanton seemed to blame everyone else — he disparaged Hunter, Sigel, and Wallace to one visitor — but the president worried less about the blame than he did about the political embarrassment, and the confidence the raid had cost his administration. He admitted to an old friend that it had left him "in the dumps."[61]

At least one Union officer looked on the raid as a blessing. Writing from Bermuda Hundred, a surgeon with the 22nd Colored Troops suggested that having a rebel army sweep through Maryland was just the thing "to keep the North up to fighting pitch." The same expectation troubled two fairly prominent Confederates just a few miles away, in Richmond: both the chief of ordnance and the head of the Bureau of War concurred that Early's depredations would do great harm to the resurgent peace movement in the North, and lend the Lincoln administration more support for waging war to the finish, regardless of how many lives it cost or how high the price of gold rose.[62]

It was the same argument that Clement Vallandigham had made a year before. Exiled into the Confederacy for criticizing the Lincoln administration while running for governor of Ohio, Vallandigham had strongly advised Confederate officials against any invasion of Northern territory. At that time General Lee was already starting from the Rappahannock on the march that would take him to Gettysburg. Just before leaving the Confederacy for Canada, Vallandigham assured his involuntary hosts that any incursion into Maryland or Pennsylvania would only hamstring Northern opponents of the war: not only would it transfer the moral distinction of bravely defending an invaded homeland from the Confederate army to the Union army, but the threat it posed would surely revive the dying will to extinguish the new nation below the Potomac. Vallandigham had been right in 1863, and the same logic may have applied in 1864, for all of Mr. Lincoln's gloom.[63]

General Sherman's three armies lay fairly quiet along the Chattahoochee until after the middle of July, waiting for engineers to finish a new bridge over the river. His men relaxed in camp for a change, feasted on black-berries, and scooped up butternuts (both the edible and political varie-ties) as the days turned unbearably hot and humid. The only complaint seemed to be the irregularity of their mail: letters from home probably followed second only to food in importance to soldiers in any theater, but to Sherman the second priority for his long rail line was ammunition, so the mailbags often gave way to ordnance supplies, and the troops some-times wondered if their families had forgotten them. Almost as an aside, Sherman ordered the destruction of a textile mill at Roswell, which had produced many a Confederate uniform. The mill employed hundreds of girls and young women, whom the Yankee soldiers imagined found them much better dressed and better looking than the Confederates who had just retreated across the river. That flattering impression probably evapo-rated when Sherman decided to treat the women as virtual prisoners of war, ordering them relocated to Indiana.[64]

Joe Johnston used those few quiet days to plan a ferocious reception for Sherman on the Atlanta side of Peachtree Creek, a mere three miles above the city. With thousands of Georgia militia holding the substantial fortifications around Atlanta, Johnston could at least enjoy the illusion of security there while he deployed what was left of his army. He calculated that he was down to barely fifty thousand men, which would require him to defeat Sherman in detail if he was to defeat him at all, and when Sherman detached James McPherson's Army of the Tennessee on a wide flanking movement, Johnston saw the opportunity he had been wait-ing for. George Thomas and John Schofield crossed the Chattahoochee July 17 on what some of their men supposed was the final drive to the "doomed" city; Johnston prepared to hit them hard once they came over Peachtree Creek, but in faraway Richmond Jefferson Davis had other plans. Davis and Johnston had never gotten on since the beginning of the war, and Johnston's strategy of retreat had aggravated the Confederate president's personal dislike for the general. Additionally, Davis seems to have been prodded by the Iago of his inner circle, Braxton Bragg, whose badly defeated army Johnston had taken over. Bragg had been snooping around the Army of Tennessee on Davis's behalf, and he offered a luke-warm report on Johnston's demeanor that prompted Davis to remove Johnston on the eve of the battle that Johnston's entire retreat had antici-pated. Davis gave the command to General Hood, who bore a reputation for aggressiveness, but who was himself responsible for wasting one of the more promising offensive opportunities of the campaign: Hood had spoiled Johnston's planned attack before Cassville, and had then argued successfully for retreat. With uncharacteristic self-sacrifice Hood suggested that Davis not change commanders with the battle for Atlanta so close at hand, but the Confederate president insisted on the substitution and Hood took the command with the vigor he knew was expected of him, rather than with the discretion that might have borne better fruits.[65]

As Thomas crossed Peachtree Creek with the largest of Sherman's columns, Hood pulled his army out of Johnston's extensive earthworks for the attack his predecessor had planned. He concentrated Hardee's corps and Alexander Stewart's — formerly Polk's — on the left, against Thomas, while Ben Cheatham, reluctantly serving as interim commander of Hood's old corps, entrenched on the Confederate right to hold off both Schofield and McPherson. Hood seemed to misunderstand the dimensions of the battlefield, however, and that led him to order some last-minute changes in his deployment that delayed the attack for hours. When it finally did come, it struck Thomas hard enough, but he managed to repel the Confederates at every point until dark fell. Hood had to recall his battered divisions, and instead of using them to man the commanding fortifications Johnston had constructed before the creek, he withdrew them all the way to the perimeter of Atlanta itself. When Sherman saw those daunting works empty, he thought the enemy had abandoned Atlanta altogether, for he knew Johnston would have tried to lure him into an attack on any position that strong, and he did not yet surmise that he was facing the rash strategies of a new opponent.[66]

While Thomas's men buried the dead in the sweltering heat and then clambered over the empty works below Peachtree Creek, McPherson moved in from Decatur along the Georgia Railroad, and one division of the Seventeenth Corps seized Bald Hill, a lofty prominence east of Atlanta from which artillery could reach the city. Hood sent William Hardee's corps and Joe Wheeler's cavalry on a roundabout path south of Atlanta, east, and then north, to try to roll up Sherman's left flank, recover the hilltop, and destroy McPherson's army. With little sleep and much fighting since the morning of the twentieth, Hardee's troops made a spirited attack from the south on July 22, carrying much of McPherson's line and killing McPherson himself when he rode out to reconnoiter. Cheatham threw Hood's corps against the same sector from the west, but because of the distance between him and Hardee their coordination suffered. Outnumbered Yankees around Bald Hill put up a prodigious fight, sometimes repelling one of Hardee's attacks from one side of their breastworks and then hopping to the other side to defend themselves against Cheatham. John A. Logan, an amateur soldier at the beginning of the war, took temporary command of McPherson's army and crafted a new flank for it by hinging his left on Bald Hill and "refusing" it, in military terms — that is, swinging it back to face the onslaught. All afternoon and into the evening Cheatham and Hardee pounded at the Union left, taking guns and hundreds of prisoners, and Wheeler's cavalry swept in to the right of Hardee, stabbing at the massive wagon train on the road from Decatur, but it was all for nothing. The fierce assaults cost Hood heavily as Union artillery, including a fusillade of guns from Schofield's front, mowed his men down in swaths. When Hood drew back into the city that night, Hardee's corps — once the most dependable in the army — had been badly weakened: Hardee had lost about twice as many casualties as he had inflicted. The battle that was supposed to have driven Sherman back across the Chattahoochee in confusion had accomplished nothing except to increase the numerical odds against the Confederates.[67]

Atlanta's importance lay in its manufacturing facilities and the rail lines that converged there. Four basic railroads fed the city. The Western & Atlantic, down which Sherman had come, ran north. The Georgia Railroad, to Augusta, still fell within the control of the late McPherson's troops after the brutal fighting of July 22. The other two, which led to Montgomery and to various corners of south Georgia, intersected at East Point, five miles south of Atlanta's defensive perimeter, and came into the city as a single line. This corridor became Sherman's next target.

First he tried cavalry raids. Giving George Stoneman and Edward McCook several thousand horsemen apiece, he sent Stoneman on a clockwise circuit around Atlanta while McCook followed a counterclockwise route. The two columns were meant to meet on July 28 at Lovejoy's Station, below East Point, and destroy as much of the Macon & Western Railroad as they could; they were also to combine against Joe Wheeler's cavalry. Stoneman wanted to ride on from there to Macon and Andersonville, to release the inmates of the officers' and enlisted men's prisons, and Sherman gave his assent, but Stoneman took that as license to ignore all his other orders, and in his lust for the credit of delivering thirty thousand prisoners he swung forty miles wide of Lovejoy's, leaving McCook to fend for himself. When Stoneman turned toward Macon, Wheeler detached a brigade to chase him and went after McCook with the balance of his command. A little brigade of Confederate infantry happened across McCook's path, slowing him just enough that Wheeler was able to overtake him, and in the ensuing melee he captured a thousand of McCook's troopers and sent the others racing for safety. Georgia militia stopped Stoneman just outside Macon, and when Wheeler's single detached brigade attacked Stoneman's four brigades the Yankees wheeled and ran; Stoneman himself made a last stand with a little Indiana brigade to cover the retreat of the rest of his command, losing about a third of the Indiana troopers in the process. Ultimately, early in August, he did make it into the Macon officers' prison, and hundreds of his men reached Andersonville as well, but not in the triumphal fashion any of them had intended.[68]

Appointing one-armed Oliver Otis Howard as McPherson's permanent replacement, Sherman tried to do with infantry what his cavalry had failed to accomplish. He marched the Army of the Tennessee from his left flank, east of Atlanta, most of the way around the city past his right. Howard crossed the tracks of the Western & Atlantic, from Chattanooga, and was heading south toward East Point when rebels sallied out from the city to stop him at Ezra Church, less than three miles from downtown Atlanta. Lieutenant General Stephen D. Lee, lately Bedford Forrest's department commander, had come into Atlanta to take over Hood's corps, and he joined Stewart in another fierce but fruitless expenditure of lives and ordnance. For several hours on July 28, Lee and Stewart charged Union soldiers who had already entrenched within sight of Atlanta's church steeples, losing at least five or six men for every Yankee who fell. Stewart went down wounded, and Hardee rushed out to take over the field, but he declined to renew the contest. The next day, the normally aggressive Hood warned Hardee that ammunition was running very low, and urged him to conserve it. He might also have observed that troops were running low, for in less than ten days he had consumed one-third of the army he had inherited from Johnston. If Hood could not acknowledge the error of his methods, though, Jefferson Davis could. The reports of Hood's serial defeats moved even so intransigent a soul as the Confederate president to a change of heart, and he advised Hood to desist from his debilitating assaults and defend his entrenchments, letting Sherman batter himself against them, instead of the reverse. In essence, Davis instructed Hood to do just as Johnston would likely have done, had he never been removed.[69]

For most of the men in both armies, the fight for Atlanta descended into pure siege warfare from that point. Embankments as ambitious as main-line breastworks protected even the picket posts, and Yankee pioneers hacked away at a circumferential road behind the expanding arc of their entrenchments, for ease of supply and troop movement. The spade dominated daily life, and Union soldiers who had made the long march from Dalton grumbled at having to live half underground for week after week. Dirt became a constant companion, and with few rivers and no rain, clothing became grimy and uncomfortable; an Iowa soldier confessed that for nearly sixteen weeks since the campaign began he had not been out of his clothes day or night, except for the few minutes it took to change them every now and then. No more did the two armies meet in epic combat. As before Petersburg, sharpshooters made life dangerous for the careless, and uncomfortable for the rest, with their frequent reminders to crouch low in the pits. Rebel gunners periodically sent a long-range round whistling overhead from one of their siege guns, but mostly they conserved ammunition, while Union artillerymen kept up a slow, steady barrage that occasionally ignited a home or a warehouse, bringing the echoes of fire bells and shrieking to the ears of Yankee pickets.[70] Belligerence abated under prolonged contact, though, and before long the infantrymen of one side or the other would propose an informal truce. That would bring everyone out of the dank, steaming trenches to stretch out, lie in whatever shade they could find, and chat with their opposite numbers. Three vocalists established a glee club in one regiment to relieve the monotony, writing home for new music to serenade their fellows (and presumably their foes) during the lulls.[71]

The ultimate doom of Atlanta seemed assured, but the most important question was how long it could hold out. As much as Sherman might now outnumber Hood after the savage contests of late July, he did not have enough men to completely encircle the city, and on the single rail line from Chattanooga he would not have been able to transport enough provisions to feed that many reinforcements even if they had been available to him. He had cut the eastern and northern lines that supplied Atlanta, and he interrupted the two southern lines by dint of cavalry raids, but not until he could stretch his forces far enough to seize and hold the East Point umbilical would Atlanta be his. That left both Atlanta and Petersburg as glaringly unfulfilled hopes for Northern citizens whose patience was wearing thin, and with a presidential election hanging in the balance it mattered a great deal by mid-August whether those two cities could hold out for another ninety days. At least one veteran with Sherman seemed to understand that the voters at home had no means of confirming the ultimate triumph that his direct observation led him to expect, and for that matter he admitted that his own hopes had not been met. The public up North had, after all, been persuaded too many times already to support one last, decisive offensive for them to put much faith in what appeared to be twin stalemates, and even the most stubbornly sanguine civilian could not deny the existence of a widespread, weary pessimism.[72]

Horace Greeley, editor of the *New York Tribune*, had involved himself in what he believed to be an effort to negotiate a peace settlement with Confederate emissaries in Canada, and he urged President Lincoln to hear them out, adding that Lincoln's rebuff of Confederate vice president Alexander Stephens as a "peace-maker" the previous summer had cost much support for the war. Stephens had actually been coming to iron out the prisoner-of-war cartel rather than discuss peace, but the real purpose of his mission had been unknown in the North, and the refusal to see him gave the impression that Lincoln was not interested in peace. He responded eagerly and earnestly to Greeley, offering safe conduct to any emissary of Jefferson Davis who carried a proposal for peace that entailed both reunion and "the abandonment of slavery." So ready was Lincoln to talk that he sent his own secretary to hand-deliver Greeley's reply, and part of the correspondence was published in late July to quell the suspicion that the administration was opposed to peace. In the end there was no such proposal, for Davis would never have entertained either prerequisite, and a majority of Confederate citizens would probably have rejected emancipation at that point, and perhaps reunion as well, but as exalted a soldier as George Meade thought they might have considered both if Lincoln would allow for gradual abolition. Meade was certain, though, that the entire South would never submit to immediate emancipation "until our military successes have been greater than they have hitherto been, or than they now seem likely to be."[73]

An opportunity for greater military success lay before — or rather beneath — the Army of the Potomac even as General Meade assessed the benefits it might bring. The last of the June 18 assaults on Beauregard's new Petersburg line had brought Ambrose Burnside's Ninth Corps within a hundred yards of the Confederate works. That proximity inspired Henry Pleasants, a mining engineer in command of the 48th Pennsylvania, to propose digging a tunnel from his trenches to the Confederate fort opposite his position, under which he said he could pack enough gunpowder to blow it to pieces. He won permission to start digging, and he made steady progress, overcoming one impediment after another — including a lack of material support from anyone above General Burnside. Finally his superiors started to take his mine seriously, thinking of it as the foundation for a grand assault that should deliver Petersburg into their hands. A project so lengthy and extensive invited discovery, primarily from the careless conveyance of information, and that came in abundance. Deserters may have taken the story straight across the lines, but indirect leaks also came daily from loyal Union soldiers. Letters went home from men high and low in rank who mentioned the construction of the mine, described its location down to the corps, division, or brigade front, estimated when it would be ready, and guessed at the date of its probable detonation. The Confederates got wind of it, and easily deduced that it had to lie along the closely juxtaposed lines of Burnside's corps, but no countermine ever detected the shaft. A Maine lieutenant sent home a detailed map of the fort they intended to destroy, including a diagram of the mine and magazines. Richmond newspapers evidently predicted the explosion, and a New England newspaper quoted one of those predictions, but by the end of July Colonel Pleasants had finished tunneling more than five hundred feet to reach the fort and had dug lateral galleries the length of it, packing them with tons of powder.[74]

The poor support that Pleasants recalled may have originated in the strained relations between Burnside and the high command of the Army of the Potomac. His failure as the commander of that army eighteen months before had left him with many critics in it, and he had not been getting along with the irascible, abusive George Meade in particular. Colonel Wainwright, of the Fifth Corps artillery, noted that Burnside's mine was "generally much laughed at" by Meade, his corps commanders, and his engineers. Meade gave it nominal support, but his provost marshal, Marsena Patrick, concluded that Meade had grown so antagonistic toward Burnside that he would never be able to back up his battle plan with much vigor.[75]

Patrick appears to have been correct, for on the very eve of the planned movement Meade admitted that he held out little hope for success in what General Grant and everyone else seemed to think of as the most promising plan of the entire war. At the last moment Meade vetoed Burnside's plan, which anticipated using Edward Ferrero's division of untried black regiments to spearhead the infantry assault once the fort had been destroyed. Much racial prejudice still permeated the army, and some white soldiers reacted bitterly to the reminder that black troops had played a prominent part in the initial drive against Petersburg. Even some sophisticated senior officers viewed Burnside as a "nigger man" for his advocacy on their behalf, and that may have created the impression that he sought an opportunity to showcase their effectiveness. When Meade first told Burnside to substitute a white division, he claimed that his objections were based on the black division's lack of experience, but Burnside argued so fervently for them that Meade agreed to take the matter to Grant. The lieutenant general seemed to believe that Ferrero's men were capable of pulling it off, but Meade changed his tactic when he saw Grant about it, overlooking their inexperience and contending, instead, that they could be a political liability: if the battle turned to disaster, Meade said, he and Grant would be condemned for having sacrificed Ferrero's innocents. That won Grant over, and he sustained Meade's veto, so a few hours before his troops were to start moving into position Burnside had to switch divisions. He made the egregious error of choosing the replacement division by lot, which threw the job into the tremulous, incapable hands of James Ledlie, and Burnside knew too little of his subordinate's personal failings to correct that misfortune.[76]

If Meade lacked wholehearted enthusiasm for the plan, Grant put everything behind it. He pulled thousands of Butler's troops out of Bermuda Hundred to support Burnside's assault, and drew the cavalry and Hancock's Second Corps from his Petersburg lines to threaten Richmond from Deep Bottom, north of the James. That caught Robert E. Lee's attention, and he stripped Petersburg of some of his best infantry divisions to confront Hancock, including one from right in front of Burnside. "We ought to be able to walk in," thought General Patrick, even with his pessimism about Meade.[77]

Burnside had also intended an intricate little maneuver for the leading division, involving the deployment of a regiment or two that would wheel to the right and left, sweeping up the Confederate lines to suppress the inevitable flanking fire and to widen the breach. Meade made him drop that part of the plan, too, in favor of a simple rush through the rubble, over all the rebel works, to the crest of the hill by Blandford Cemetery, overlooking Petersburg. That was probably just as well, given the difficult terrain that the explosion would create, and if the rest of the army followed the Ninth Corps those trenches would be emptied of rebels anyway.[78]

As soon as dark settled on July 29, the battalions began to march in the persistent, suffocating heat. Three brigades from Butler's army came up behind Burnside, whose divisions shuffled into place for their part in the drama. Colonel Pleasants lighted his fuse soon after 3:00 A.M. on July 30, but an hour later nothing had happened. At last one of his lieutenants and a sergeant volunteered to go in and investigate; that intrepid pair found that the fuse — mere scraps that Pleasants had been forced to knot together — had burned out at a splice, so they reignited it and scurried out of the tunnel. A few minutes later the earth began to tremble for a radius of at least a mile. A Wisconsin officer way down along the line of the Fifth Corps was shaken awake in his bombproof by vibrations stronger than any earthquake, and he stumbled outside in time to see the fort go up. It started to rise slowly in the dim grey light, as though levitating at first, but then crumbling and mixing as it was lifted higher. Men, guns, and earth blended into what a Wisconsin captain thought looked like "a vast column of muddy water" that some thought reached one, two, or three hundred feet in the air (others gauged it at more like fifty or sixty feet), and the astounding sight signaled the simultaneous eruption of Union artillery and musketry all along that sector.[79]

The debris, including at least a few dead, wounded, or stunned Confederate soldiers, rained down as far away as the trenches where Burnside's men lay waiting for the order to charge, leaving a yawning crater well over a hundred feet long, fifty feet wide, and more than twenty feet deep. It took the shape of a gigantic washbasin, noted a Massachusetts man in Ledlie's division. Heavy-artillerymen dominated the first brigade of that division to leap to the attack; the second brigade, composed mainly of Massachusetts men, went in under Brigadier General William Bartlett, who had already lost a leg earlier in the war and stumped along on a cork replacement. Ledlie himself remained behind, as was his timid custom, and with nothing more to do he repaired to a bombproof to solicit a little rum from a surgeon, perhaps in lieu of breakfast. His men poured right into what they would forever remember as the Crater — those who survived to carry away any memory at all — and stood as though awestruck by the residue of the explosion. Dead men, dying men, and half-buried men lay all about, sometimes with a wiggling head or arm visible to indicate that they were alive, or with their legs kicking in the air. The men who were supposed to lead the way into Petersburg instead put down their weapons and started clawing at the clay with their hands to disentomb the survivors.[80]

Robert Potter's division had formed on Ledlie's right, and Simon Griffin's brigade swept over its works north of the Crater. Part of Bartlett's brigade clambered over the far side of the Crater, dropping into the second line of rebel trenches behind it, and Griffin's men slid in alongside them. There they dallied, though, with no one to tell them what to do, while Confederate reinforcements rushed to plug the gap. Orlando Willcox's division was supposed to follow Ledlie's, but most of Ledlie's men were still milling about in the Crater, and as Willcox's men shoved ahead they had to crowd in with the others, almost shoulder to shoulder, or squeeze into the main Confederate trenches south of the Crater. Impatience brewed behind the lines, where Grant and Meade were watching, and Meade repeatedly prodded Burnside, who sent order after order to the front to push forward. Artillery and infantry soon began playing on the flanks of those Yankees around the Crater, and finally Burnside ordered in Ferrero's division of nine black regiments. Like his friend Ledlie, whom he later joined for stimulants in the bombproof, Ferrero sent his division in without bothering to accompany it. His men went into the cauldron gamely enough, but they only worsened the crowding in the captured works, and when some of them emerged on the far side to resume the advance toward Cemetery Hill they were badly disorganized. Resistance was growing steadily, and the sight of black soldiers only seemed to enrage the Southrons. Eventually enough Confederate troops arrived to drive the foremost Union wave onto Ferrero's front, and in a second counterattack the rebels flung themselves into those mingled black and white ranks with a savage fury. Sensing what was in store for them, most of the blacks who survived the first onslaught turned and ran wide-eyed, disrupting what little organization remained among the troops behind them and carrying their terror to the rest of the corps. They were, said a Massachusetts captain, "excellent to charge, [but] not worth a straw to resist," and he was one of many who described the black troops running "like sheep." Officers flailed at them with their swords, to no avail.[81]

Some of Ferrero's men complained that their officers abandoned them, and at least one white soldier who protested that he was no "Negro Lover" corroborated that a shameful number of their officers headed for the rear once the fighting grew intense; he reported perfectly healthy lieutenants and captains on their way to the rear, lending their arms or shoulders to sick or wounded fellow officers, and called it "a disgrace to our army." A captain in the 27th U.S. Colored Troops mentioned another captain by name whom he said "ran away." One of Burnside's staff officers observed that the "loss in officers was terribly disproportionate," adding that they "were cut down while rallying the men," but that was much less true among the Colored Troops than in the rest of the corps. Ferrero's black brigades suffered far more casualties than any of Burnside's other three divisions, which some took as evidence that they must have put up a good fight, but the proportion of commissioned officers among the casualties in that division was the smallest in the corps. Measured against the number of their enlisted men who were killed and wounded, those wearing shoulder straps in Burnside's white divisions suffered at nearly twice the rate of their counterparts in Ferrero's division.[82]

For some hours the motley, jumbled fragments of the four divisions clung to the ruined fort and to shrinking lengths of the captured trenches on either side, while a mob of wounded and terrified men accumulated in the bowl of the Crater. The sun blazed down on them, temperatures soared, and men passed out from heat exhaustion, while mortars started dropping shells right in among them. No troops moved up to their support on either side save the borrowed division from the Army of the James. Meade, whom General Patrick had predicted would lend the operation no vigorous assistance, finally ordered Burnside to call it off and bring everyone back. That was easier said than done, with the embattled corps and its old lines separated by an open plain that was now completely covered by a crossfire of rebel canister and bullets. At last Burnside and his brigadiers in the Crater arranged a plan for the Union artillery to unleash a new barrage while the troops remaining in the Crater rushed, en masse, back to safety. Just as that plan was being passed from man to man in the tangled throng at the front, a rebel brigade sprinted into sight over the brow of a ravine with bayonets leveled, pounding straight for the Crater. They numbered only a few hundred, against several times that many Union soldiers, but the rebels hurtled forward with a solid line, firm discipline, and singular purpose. A few indomitable Yankees kicked footholds in the lip of the pit and maintained a feeble defense, but the rest surged out the other side of the captured works and swarmed across the field as Confederate artillery and infantry dropped them by scores. The Confederates leaped among those who were left behind — shooting, stabbing, and clubbing until the last standing Federal had thrown down his arms to surrender, and even then they continued to vent their fury on their black prisoners.[83]

The haggard survivors who tumbled back into their own works wore traces of their ordeal on their uniforms, almost all of which were splattered with gore. Some officers, like Brigadier General Simon Griffin, were covered with blood, brains, and chunks of former comrades who were torn apart by the mortar shells that exploded in the Crater; even General Burnside's written order to evacuate the place, endorsed by several brigadiers and carried back by Griffin, bore a little gob of flesh on one of its folded sides. Only skeletons of the old regiments — and even the new ones — rallied behind their first line of trenches. Some four thousand men had disappeared from Burnside's corps. Griffin's brigade, consisting mainly of northern New Englanders, suffered particularly: the 11th New Hampshire could mount only sixty-eight fit for duty ten days later, and the 9th New Hampshire mustered even fewer; the 31st Maine, which had come to the army that spring with nearly a thousand men, was down to seventy-three; the equally new 17th Vermont could raise only sixty men after the battle. Recruits and the return of sick and detailed soldiers would eventually double or triple those figures, but immediately after the disaster of July 30 Griffin could barely find five hundred men in his entire brigade. A couple of weeks before, one of his colonels had observed that after receiving his new brigadier's star Griffin had begun putting on airs "quite noticeably," but the sight of his emaciated brigade evidently moved him to tears, and when his brigade bandsmen tried to cheer him up with a serenade that evening he came snarling out of his tent to chase them away. So distraught was the general, and so few men did he have left to command, that he went home on leave the second day after the battle.[84]

One of Burnside's staff noticed that the useless slaughter produced scowls and curses throughout the camps of the Ninth Corps. Frustration and anger festered into a deep, dismal sadness, especially after Lee allowed the Yankees to bury their dead and recover their wounded. Meade tried to avoid the traditional acknowledgment of defeat inherent in an official request for truce, so no one could reach the wounded until two days after the cataclysm. Most of those who might have survived their injuries had perished under the scorching sun, with neither shade nor water for up to forty-five hours. The bodies had bloated and blackened beyond individual recognition, and the stench had grown intolerable. As the grave-diggers separated the putrefied bodies in blue uniforms from those in grey, butternut, and brown, some very well-dressed Confederate officers chatted amiably with the Yankees, promising that the South would never be beaten. One soldier jumped up on the works as the bottom of the Crater became a mass grave, shouting to friends and enemies alike, "Let's all go home," as though convinced of the futility of taking the war any further.[85]

"We are down in the mouth," admitted one of Ledlie's staff officers, who apologized in his next few letters for his despondency; he seemed dejected over the apparent fruitlessness of the campaign against Petersburg, which he thought his army would never be able to capture. That atmosphere of hopeless, wasted effort only worsened when tongues started wagging about Ledlie and Ferrero begging drinks from the safety of a bombproof while their men entered the cauldron; unfounded rumors distorted that report to include several generals, and later encompassed many of the officers as a whole. Others thought jealousy had caused a lack of cooperation.[86] The idea that such valor and opportunity could be squandered by the vices, incompetence, or envy of a few may have triggered a strange malaise that seemed to grip the Union troops before Petersburg and Richmond early in August. A Connecticut soldier in the Eighteenth Corps disabused his mother of the myth that the army was in good spirits, let alone as feisty as the newspapers claimed, and a brigade staff officer in the Tenth Corps blamed the intense heat for "a certain apathy & indifference" that had taken hold of him. Returning to his regiment from a furlough the day after the fight, a young officer in Griffin's brigade depicted his comrades as "despondent & disheartened," naively attributing it to the lack of patriotism at home rather than to the cycle of danger, horror, and defeat. An aide to General Meade described the entire army as indifferent to the contest because of the repeated, bloody failures, while one of Grant's senior staff officers described "gloom and despondency" so pervasive that it seemed to paralyze everyone in the army. "My faith in the Army of the Potomac is gone," wrote a captain on Grant's staff — "gone."[87]

Men who had been six weeks in the trenches may have offered some corroboration for the diagnosis of indifference in the days after the mayhem at the Crater. Like the opposing forces before Atlanta, the pickets in the Virginia siege started to initiate local, informal truces, in which neither side bothered the other. Two days after the last of the dead had been buried, the two lines of earthworks facing each other below Petersburg sprouted miles of little white flags fashioned from handkerchiefs knotted on sticks, or bayonets. The front grew so quiet that a Union officer came up from headquarters to see about it, and only on his orders did that portion of the Army of the Potomac reluctantly and languidly resume the shooting war.[88]

Chauncey and Sarah
Hill at the time of
his enlistment in
the 9th Minnesota,
February, 1864.

The Wilderness battlefield: Confederate entrenchments on the
Orange Plank Road.

Fredericksburg, Virginia: Union wounded from the Wilderness fighting.

Armory Square Hospital, Washington, D.C., where Walt Whitman visited with patients.

"Condemned Yankees": the partially disabled soldiers of the 9th Veteran Reserve Corps at Washington in April, 1865, with the enlisted men in distinctive sky-blue uniforms.

Andersonville. This photograph was taken from just above the creek that washed through the prison camp; the top of the stockade wall is visible, out of focus, on the right.

Army of the Potomac engineers building a bridge over the North Anna River.

A house near Fort Stevens, on the fringe of Washington, that was struck by at least one artillery round during Jubal Early's raid.

Confederate defenses on the north side of Atlanta, showing abatis and the palings known among the infantry as "gut rippers."

Bombproofs inside Fort Sedgwick, on the Union lines at Petersburg.

Atlanta after its capture.

Alfred Waud's conceptual sketch of Phil Sheridan rallying fugitives to turn the tide at Cedar Creek, October 19, 1864.

Above: President Lincoln's chief cabinet officers, clockwise from top: Secretary of State William Seward, Secretary of the Navy Gideon Welles, Secretary of the Treasury (and later Chief Justice) Salmon Chase, and Secretary of War Edwin Stanton.

Left: Interior Secretary John P. Usher, who gratified railroad tycoons at the expense of his Indian wards.

Congressman Thaddeus Stevens of Pennsylvania, who organized the resistance to Andrew Johnson's Reconstruction policy and led the effort for impeachment.

Senator Ben Wade of Ohio, who vigorously opposed Lincoln's Reconstruction policy and threatened a revolt against his reelection.

PART II

THE BRAVEST PRESS'D TO
THE FRONT AND FELL

4

She with Thin Form
Presently Drest in Black

⋘ LESS THAN THREE months previously, Mr. Lincoln's administration had suffered temporary embarrassment at the hands of a young charlatan who arranged the publication of a fraudulent executive decree calling for four hundred thousand new conscripts and proclaiming the last Thursday of May as a day of fasting, humiliation, and prayer. The embarrassment had emanated from the impression of desperation implied by the appearance of that forgery during the then-apparent stalemate at Spotsylvania. Lincoln himself inadvertently created an even more convincing and legitimate atmosphere of despair when he actually did proclaim a day of fasting, humiliation, and prayer for the first Thursday of August, just eight days after the debacle at the Crater, especially since he had also just called for even more troops than had the bogus proclamation — half a million, this time, by draft if necessary. It had all begun innocently enough early in July, when there seemed no harm in complying with a congressional resolution asking for the special day: he never expected, when he signed the paper on July 7, that the next few weeks would bring a Confederate army into the suburbs of Washington, or see a battlefield defeat as conspicuous, complete, and unnecessary as Meade's army had endured on July 30.[1]

The draft call followed only a few days after Jubal Early bid farewell to the District of Columbia. Congress had revised the original draft law in the session that adjourned just before Early's appearance, allowing for the conscription of soldiers for terms shorter than three years if the president so chose, and on July 18 he indicated that the five hundred thousand men would be asked to serve for only one year. That was his fifth call for short-term troops since the beginning of the war, exclusive of the three-month men with whom he began the conflict, and most of those vacation volunteers had proven as expensive as they were inefficient. The provost marshal general, James Fry, thought of the one-year term as a reduction in the personal burden it posed for drafted men. Probably the president hoped the one-year commitment would alleviate the inevitable political backlash from yet another enormous draft barely eleven weeks after the final deadline on the last one. Surely, too, he hoped once again that it would raise enough men to win the war before they reached the end of their term, although soldiers again grieved that the green troops would hardly be broken in before the time came to send them home: the short enlistment represented another executive gamble that risked many lives and much money. The amelioration of the one-year term, meanwhile, was offset by the elimination of the commutation clause, which until this point had allowed any drafted man to buy his way out of that particular draft call for $300. Fry recommended dropping that means of escape because it stood so squarely in the way of raising men, and the congressional revisions removed it for nearly everyone except conscientious objectors. Those drafted under the July proclamation would have to either take arms themselves or find an eligible proxy.[2]

The commutation clause had cost a great deal of money already, either for men who paid it outright or for communities that voted to provide relief for their drafted citizens. Handing over $300 per man offered the easiest solution for avoiding service or meeting the local quota: no travel or other expense would be incurred in a quest for willing substitutes, who would often end up asking for more money than the simple fee. The drawback lay in the limited exemption it bestowed on the drafted citizen, whose name would go back into the tumbler for the next draft call. Since commutation brought no soldiers into the ranks, it only assured that the president would issue another call sooner, forcing town meetings and city councils (and sometimes individuals) to raise the same $300 all over again. The market for substitutes had pressed closely enough on the eligible population in May, before the most brutal epoch began, and the subsequent toll of death and mutilation had naturally reinforced the reluctance to serve. Had it not been for floods of desperate immigrants and boys growing just old or tall enough to pass muster, many more unfortunate, unwilling males would have had to wear the blue suit. As it was, many municipalities had already exhausted their first class of conscripts — that is, single men between twenty and forty-five and married men up to thirty-five, all of whom had either enlisted, hired substitutes, or been drafted themselves. That left only men over the age of thirty-five who had families, and in rural districts where the remaining men were too few or too heavily taxed to help their fellow residents out of the draft any longer, conscripts in their late thirties and early forties began saying goodbye to wives and children — including some who had contributed heavily to free their neighbors from earlier calls.[3]

Even if the shrinking population of eligible men and the soaring pace of the carnage had not heightened the demand for substitutes, the loss of the commutation option would have increased the prices they could ask, but in the summer of 1864 all three of those inflationary conditions coincided. Rumors of the impending demise of commutation and the inevitable approach of another draft levy leaked from Congress into the better social circles by the end of June, prompting those who could afford it to insure themselves by hiring a substitute in advance — before the rush, as it were. Francis Brooks, a well-connected gentleman farmer outside Boston, authorized his selectmen to spend $650, or more, if necessary, to hire a soldier who would fight in his name. Two weeks after Lincoln's proclamation, towns in cash-poor Vermont, where recruits had always come fairly cheaply, agreed to pay $500 per man, while in Connecticut voters offered $700 for anyone who would volunteer. A small coastal community in Maine raised record sums to meet this latest obligation with volunteers alone, but only three men had come forward by the end of August. One New Hampshire town that had paid an average of $319 for each of its recruits under the spring draft had to expend $836 apiece to meet its summer quota. As the September 5 deadline for the draft settled on deficient municipalities, the pressure created local and temporary inflation. George Templeton Strong, whose college classmate was killed leading a regiment in the Wilderness, periodically berated President Lincoln for hesitating to draft enough men, but late in August Strong readily peeled off $1,100 in greenbacks for the signature of "a big 'Dutch' boy of twenty or thereabouts," who went to war in place of that voluble Gramercy Park patriot. In Washington, where so many clerks and contractors fed at the government trough, a resident of Virginia Avenue recorded about the same time that substitute fees had jumped from the commutation-era price of $600 to $1,200 and $1,500.[4]

Boisterous support for the war, whether genuine or feigned, frequently coexisted with a firm determination not to serve, or to save one's conscriptable relatives from the government's deadly machinery, no matter how blatant the hypocrisy. Men who endured the rigors and peril of the front lines counseled their friends and siblings against entering the service, sometimes pleading with them to abandon the idea while simultaneously expounding bitterly on the other "stayathomes" who refused to enlist. A Michigan lad who entered West Point as a plebe that summer described the institution as "a perfect nest of Copperheads," which perhaps reflected his partisan reaction to Democratic opinion, but influential men may also have been using the Military Academy as a refuge for sons near the threshold of draft age who privately despised the war. One especially tight-fisted Ohio Quaker ignored his sect's apolitical principles enough to fully support the Lincoln administration, but he adhered to its pacifist doctrine sufficiently that he did not wish to fight, so he helped solicit substantial donations to use as bounties for those who would fight — or to hire substitutes for himself and any others of his community who might be selected.[5]

Suddenly everyone desperately wanted a substitute. Domestic sources were drying up: the reform schools had been cleaned out of inmates who were old enough to enlist but too young to be drafted — some of whom went as substitutes whether they wanted to enlist or not — and the more adventurous of that age group who were not incarcerated had already been recruited. The fear that there might not be "subs" enough to go around sent innovative principals or their brokers to experiment with distant markets. A Boston society dispatched agents to Germany to contract with eager emigrants for unspecified service at a price considerably lower than stateside bounty or substitute rates; the society paid their passage before delivering them to recruiting officers in Boston, which struck one conservative critic as eerily similar to the transatlantic slave trade. With tens of thousands of enlistments expiring, the army itself posed an inviting source of quota credits, and Jefferson Whitman, whose brother commanded a company in the 51st New York, asked if there might not be some weary veteran in that unit who would reenlist for another three years in the field so Jeff could continue to stay home. The commander of the 9th Vermont, which had just become eligible to reenlist after two years of service, suggested his own regiment as a means of satisfying his hometown quota. Southern refugees and Confederate deserters started responding to the munificent offers, and if they had signed no oaths to remain in the North for the duration, the provost marshals would take them as substitutes. A former lieutenant in an early six-month Ohio regiment perceived that he might be faced with real service in the shooting war, so he sent a hired man down to Knoxville to look for destitute freedmen who would come back to Cleveland and enlist as substitutes for himself and others, for each of whom he hoped to realize hundreds of dollars in markups. Such agents swarmed through the occupied South, hunting for unemployed black men who would respond to a fraction of the prevailing bounties. An employee of the Commissioner for the Organization of Colored Troops, in Nashville, wrote to a staff officer he knew with a plan to tap the contraband camp in Saint Louis, though apparently more for the profit they could glean from substitute fees than to augment the army.[6]

Maria Sargent, the wife of a New Hampshire soldier, had not seen her husband in nearly two years when she overheard several neighbors remark that they would make their way to Canada if drafted, and those neighbors included professed Republicans. Especially in regions close to the Canadian border, migration seemed a more appealing avenue in the era of costly and uncertain substitution than it had when $300 bought sure and swift exemption, and many started north while others thought seriously about it; others took to the gold fields of Montana and Idaho. Mrs. Sargent knew that her husband and his comrades resented the dwindling courage of those at home, and she shared that resentment, but she also seemed a bit sympathetic with the reluctance of the draft-shy. "I think men hate to go worse than ever," she said, "because so many have been killed this summer." A few weeks later, commenting on the phenomenal bounties that their town finally offered, she blurted out that no amount of money (and evidently no grandiloquent political principles) could persuade her to let her husband enlist, if only he were home again. Women, including soldiers' wives, sweethearts, and mothers, some of whom had soured on the endless brutality, often seemed more understanding of those who shunned the war. A pamphlet distributed by the ultra-Unionist Loyal League network urged women to encourage prospective suitors into uniform by rejecting "the coward who eludes the draft," but that idea seems not to have sold very well in a land where unmarried women now heavily outnumbered the eligible bachelors.[7]

From June, when the local districts started revising the militia enrollment lists, the topic of how many men were left at home started to interest the soldiers. Now and then a naïve private who had not been home for a couple of years imagined the cities and towns virtually empty of able-bodied denizens of military age, but in general the men living like troglodytes south of the Chattahoochee and the James knew from their families that plenty of potential conscripts still inhabited the North, and that most of them were desperately trying to convince someone else to join the army on their behalf, at almost any price. The men at the front felt betrayed and abandoned because so many refused to share their struggle, and as soldiers tend to do they often sneered at the cowardice they thought lay at the bottom of it. Major Roebling, the Fifth Corps staff officer, put a subtle twist on that viewpoint; as he explained it half seriously to his fiancée, the toils and trials of the private soldier were so onerous and dangerous that only a fool would undertake them, and all the fools had been killed already. The rest, he supposed, "think it is about played out to stand up and get shot."[8]

Others understood that political dissent, personal considerations, or fastidious sensibilities dissuaded many from enlisting, so they raged at "butternuts," "Copperheads," and "precious *gentlemen*" who still enjoyed the comforts of home, whom they wished could be forced to the cannon's mouth.[9] This sort of enmity could strain relationships between friends or relatives, like the Chandler brothers of Concord, New Hampshire: George, the major of the 9th New Hampshire, took umbrage when his brother William, the speaker of the New Hampshire House of Representatives, failed to come down to Petersburg to see him during a trip to Washington. In a letter to their mother, the major wondered that his brother had not found it appropriate to at least visit the regiment, since it inhabited a significant theater of "the *War* about which he and so many other New Hampshire politicians roar so loudly, and which they help along so earnestly by sending out now and then some fresh lot of Norwegians just imported at the highest expense." Writing directly to his brother, the major vented his spleen with bitter sarcasm, accusing him of base hypocrisy for publicly urging others to enlist in a token of patriotism that the honorable speaker did not find "susceptible of a personal application." Still recovering from his Spotsylvania wound in the division hospital, Major Chandler scolded his brother for talking about shedding blood for the flag as though "it all meant something." The colonel of the 22nd Massachusetts knew that patrician Southerners and their sons frequently carried muskets in the ranks of the Confederate army, while that class of Northern citizen rarely entered the Union army except as commissioned officers, preferring otherwise to stay home and make money. He belittled those whose support for the war consisted mainly of cheerfully paying high taxes and donating freely to soldiers' relief, and he implied an abiding contempt even for men like New York City's Squire Strong, the treasurer of the U.S. Sanitary Commission, who deemed their charitable efforts an adequate contribution. "When the government has called for men," wrote the colonel, "they have sent money." Six days before he was killed just outside Atlanta, one of Wisconsin's early volunteers made the same complaint in his last letter home.[10]

It therefore seemed frustratingly evident to the men with the army that their neighbors were going to meet their latest draft quotas the same way they had filled the others: they would offer so much cash that a volunteer or a substitute who committed himself to the single year of duty could put away more money than the earlier volunteers could save during their entire three years. That only added insult to injury for men who had not hung back, but had volunteered for bounties that inflation had later reduced to a pittance, and it particularly aggravated soldiers whose families had to pay massive property tax increases against the ballooning municipal debt created by escalating bounties.[11]

The predictable response to the president's July draft call severely bruised the morale of the troops, conveying the inescapable sense that everyone up North had turned their backs on them, including those who supplied the loudest vocal support. The previous year had seen widespread political opposition to the war, which the administration had successfully portrayed as the attempt of a disloyal faction to demoralize the troops, but that Copperhead phantasm had inspired more anger than discouragement in the army. The disparity between the abundant patriotic words and the slow, mercenary recruiting on the home front bespoke a universal malaise far more disheartening than the dissident antagonism of a presumed minority. Compared to the spring of 1863, or even the early autumn of that year, fewer men in the front lines that summer of 1864 doubted that the Confederacy could eventually be beaten, but a surprising number of them still did doubt it, despite seeing regular Confederate desertions and other signs of deteriorating resistance. Their persistent discouragement may have emanated from the more glaring evidence of withering civilian will in the North, and that was the one factor on which enemy hopes rested. A New York captain whose regiment had disembarked from transports fresh from Louisiana to join the futile hunt for Jubal Early expected the war to last years longer, primarily because the rebels fought with such earnest intent while the North could produce nothing but "gas and emptiness," and sent only "puny boys of fifteen and sixteen" in place of soldiers. More than a month later, a Sixth Corps private who was also tailing Early admitted that he saw no end in sight, hoping only that his luck would hold for one more year so he could leave the war behind. A lieutenant colonel on the North Carolina coast remembered having considered the Confederacy on the verge of collapse when he first entered the army, two years before, but that end seemed no closer in July of 1864 than it had in July of 1862. With Sherman's army at the Chattahoochee and Lee hemmed in at Richmond and Petersburg, a wounded man at the Chestnut Hill hospital still found the war news so bad that he fully expected to have to serve out the remaining two years of his term.[12]

Sherman's soldiers had seen more direct reason for hope, especially after John Bell Hood superseded Johnston, and their spirits reflected their fortunes in the field. The Army of the Potomac and the Army of the James harbored more lingering defeatism, partly because of the resilience and resourcefulness of Robert E. Lee, but also because the gains in Virginia had been accompanied with such maddening failures and fearsome mortality. One of Butler's brigade commanders sometimes wondered whether the war would ever end during his lifetime, and a Massachusetts sergeant in the same army perceived more evidence of weakening in the Union army and the Northern people than he could detect among the Confederates. David Hunter's chief of staff, in the Army of West Virginia, lapsed into such disgust with the "folly, faction, and feebleness" of the government that he concluded to leave the army. While his men perfected their trenches on the very outskirts of crucial Petersburg, an officer in the Iron Brigade who had already lost two brothers in the war held out no hope that it could be won while his government floundered in the hands of fanatics and fools. Well into October, a field officer in Meade's army entertained little hope that Petersburg or Richmond would be taken anytime soon.[13]

The average Union soldier may not have really lost heart, even in the historically unlucky Army of the Potomac, but most of them did feel they had already sacrificed about as much as anyone could expect of them. Thomas Cheney, an artilleryman with the 1st New Hampshire Battery, perhaps typified the veteran in the Petersburg trenches: he had taken part in every major engagement since Second Bull Run, but his devotion to the cause never flagged, and his faith in ultimate victory never failed. Cheney's enlistment would expire at the end of summer, however, and he was going home for good.[14]

It was probably not so much pessimism that pervaded the armies as an abiding cynicism. Most soldiers had seen enough to believe that those who were making money from the war hoped to drag it out as long as possible — and that this mercenary incentive infected generals and politicians who could manipulate either the prosecution of the war or the policies that might prolong it. A perennially discontented Polish captain in the 27th U.S. Colored Troops fumed over corruption in the medical departments, cursing the drivers and attendants for the wholesale theft of government goods and accusing the surgeons of negligence, profiteering, and pilferage. The department as a whole amounted to "a set of thieves and whoremasters," he insisted, "especially in the colored division," where avarice ruled and officers prospered according to the degree of their rascality. The peevish captain's indictment assumed a semblance of credibility when the War Department court-martialed Surgeon General William Hammond for conspiracy to defraud the government of half a million dollars through the purchase of shoddy blankets and drugs. Hammond's many supporters viewed the irregularities of his purchases as more technical than intentional, and Edwin Stanton's vindictive animus probably figured as prominently in the prosecution as any malfeasance, but Hammond's conviction and peremptory dismissal late in August corroborated at least the appearance of systemic corruption.[15]

Myron Underwood, an Iowa surgeon on duty along the lower Mississippi, might have disputed those slurs on the medical departments, but he concurred in the perception of pervasive corruption, at least in the relations between citizen speculators and contractors, whom he grew to loathe for their continual bilking of the army collectively and the soldiers individually. Enlisted men certainly coincided in the matter of civilians fleecing them, especially with the outrageous prices their sutlers charged them for minor comforts, but they found their own support personnel just as rapacious. Men detailed at the express offices regularly rifled the boxes of food and clothing sent to soldiers by their families, and a regimental commissary in Arkansas recognized that among the army's enlisted men his title was synonymous with "thief."[16] Indeed, quartermasters and commissaries frequently saw their careers marred or ended by allegations (and sometimes repeated allegations) of embezzlement, bribery, or simple larceny, and their superior officers often went down with them. A new general had hardly taken over the command of Natchez, Mississippi, where cotton posed a terrible temptation to morally lax officers, before his assistant adjutant general fell into a "thieving transaction" that ended in his transfer to a still-more-obscure outpost, though some had expected his outright dismissal.[17]

The odor of profiteering scented even legitimate enterprises, like the early version of carpetbagger cotton farming, in which Northern entrepreneurs leased abandoned or confiscated plantations. In North Carolina a Vermont field officer estimated the yield on one plantation at five hundred bales, which could bring half a million dollars at wartime prices, and most of that would represent the lessee's profit. The lure of such remunerative enterprises, and the air of collusion that clung to them, went right up the chain of command. General Grant, who had been made to blush earlier in the war by his own father's speculations within his official domain, dropped the commander at Vicksburg a note to hint that Grant's brother-in-law, who was engaged in a presumably legal cotton-planting enterprise on leased Mississippi land, deserved the same "favors" as were accorded to others engaged in that endeavor.[18]

An atmosphere of corruption drifted higher still, and reached beyond the effort to suppress secession. Secretary John P. Usher, of the Interior Department, enjoyed some valuable considerations from the Union Pacific Railroad because of the influence he exerted on its behalf, and for the information he funneled to its financiers. Usher's intrigues included swindling reservation land away from the Delawares and other tribes whose welfare he was pledged to oversee, in which he met with both cooperation and competition from James Lane, who was simultaneously a U.S. senator from Kansas and a brigadier general of volunteers. Lane must have had some ambition for the Interior Department himself, and he cultivated a correspondence with some aspiring officeholders who apparently intended to help him perpetuate the tradition of fraud against the various tribes in Kansas, so their lands could be settled by "enterprising white settlers" instead of languishing in the possession of the "indolent, improvident Red Man." Along the way, of course, the collaborating knaves would turn a pretty penny.[19]

Many of those who sacrificed so much for the preservation of the government could (or had to) turn a blind eye to the impression that it suffered from endemic graft, and a healthy proportion reflected that at least the chief representative of that government remained honest and devoted. That failed to satisfy everyone in the army, however, and few of those citizens who might have joined them in uniform would wish to risk their lives in the defense of institutions rife with dishonesty and opportunism, so corruption not only disheartened the troops directly but substantially impeded any augmentation of their numbers. So did the accelerating visibility of war-related tragedies on the home front, for by August of 1864 everyone — except perhaps a few who were isolated by their wealth, or the most recently arrived immigrants — knew people afflicted with the loss of sons, husbands, or fathers. Untold numbers of parents and friends had offered to take in a young war widow with a toddler or two; abundant stories circulated of neighbors who, with no suspicion that any disease or danger loomed, saw their last letter to their boy returned by his company commander, or received a final note from the soldier himself, written in a feeble hand and finished by someone else. Often a sick or wounded soldier would assure his kin of his steady and rapid recovery, only to have a thoughtful ward nurse describe his death, a day or two later. As disturbing as the numerical estimates of casualties and the long lists of names might be, it was the common sight of black crepe, widows' weeds, and funerals that drove home the hazards of impetuous patriotism. A Boston attorney who had lost his brother and three of his best friends within barely a year found it so terrible to contemplate that he felt grateful they had been gone so long before they died, lest their absence should "perpetually be calling out that they are dead."[20]

On the last Friday in July, Sarah Upton seated herself at her little house in Derry, New Hampshire, to give her husband the news from home. They were not a wealthy couple: George Upton had been working as a shoemaker and farming a few acres when he enlisted as a private early in the war — to defend the Constitution, he insisted, rather than to free any slaves. By conscientious effort he had risen through the ranks, finally, to first lieutenant, and with close economy they had managed to pay off all their debts, after which he continued scrimping on his living expenses to accumulate a secure cushion for his return to civilian life, in November. He had just written to her the day before, describing the preparations to explode Burnside's mine, but that letter had not yet left City Point. Sarah was answering his letter of July 10, in which he lamented the seventy-five thousand men Grant had squandered to resume the line of the James, only to allow Early an opening to strike at Washington. Sarah concentrated on the details of her housekeeping and gardening, which had always seemed to calm her husband after his diatribes against the generals and the government. She had transplanted cabbages in the cool of the previous evening, and she hoped for some rain that day so she could avoid carrying water to them, but the summer had been as dry in New England as it had been in Virginia. Because of the prolonged drought her beans were not doing very well, and she doubted they would climb to the tops of the poles. She had sold the hay in their pasture, and hoped to use the proceeds to buy some winter clothing for their three young children: as reluctant as she was to pay the outrageous prices, she feared they would only go higher if she waited. She closed the letter "hoping this will find you well," and probably dropped it at the post office that afternoon. By the time their last letters crossed in the mail, he was dead — shot through the head in the Crater. So intensely did she mourn that she expended a generous portion of their precious savings to bring his remains back to Derry for burial. All she had left of him, besides his grave, was the watch he had sent home months before, as a memento for posterity in case he did not return.[21]

Mrs. Upton's neighbors commiserated with her as she began her four decades of widowhood among them. Evidently they felt some of her loss, too, for her husband was well thought of there; when Derry's returning veterans established their post of the Grand Army of the Republic, they named it after Lieutenant Upton. The church bells of Saint Johnsbury, Vermont, tolled slowly as a long column of pedestrian mourners followed the flag-draped coffin of Colonel Addison Preston from there to Danville, eight miles away; Concord, Massachusetts, turned out en masse for the funeral of Colonel George Prescott, and the death of Colonel Charles Russell Lowell a few months later saddened many of the same people. Again and again, the fall of highly regarded citizens shocked whole towns, bringing a touch of sadness to every doorstep and reminding the most preoccupied households of the dangers awaiting those with the temerity to take up arms.[22]

The dread of losing family members especially tormented women, and they seldom hesitated to share the depths of their terror. A Michigan woman with three brothers in the army made a conscious effort not to "borrow trouble" over their safety, but she could not shake the nagging sense that something would happen to them as the 1864 campaigns opened, and as a result she absolutely refused to let her husband enlist; nine months after she first revealed her premonition, one of those brothers had been killed on the battlefield and the other had died after a long imprisonment. The news of every new battle revived a perpetual, lurking disquiet among the wives, mothers, and sisters of soldiers in that particular theater until the reassuring letters arrived, and village centers filled with milling crowds of "anxious faces" as people who had just learned of fresh fighting tarried in hopes of hearing about the casualties.[23]

Individual obituaries and lists of the killed and wounded filled whole pages in small dailies from the middle of May, when Union soldiers were falling at the rate of nearly ten thousand a week in Virginia, and although barely four thousand were lost at the Crater the reports of the savage struggle spread particular alarm. As the accounts of that melee filled the newspapers, a Vermont woman gasped with relief to learn that her husband had just been transferred away from the Army of the Potomac, but she begged him to resign and come home as soon as he could, for she could not stand the strain. On the other side of the Connecticut River, the wife of a Ninth Corps soldier paced her bedroom all night after learning of the Crater, wringing her hands and trying to hold back her tears; her husband's survival seemed unlikely in such a deathtrap, and in writing a letter while she knew not whether he was alive or dead she reflected that even if he had escaped he still had another year to serve, and she was certain she could never endure the constant worry. She rallied when a letter dated after the fight reached her, but two months later she had to bear the same anguish all over again when much of his brigade was overrun and captured, and ten days passed without word from him. A Connecticut woman admitted to her husband, whose regiment crossed swords repeatedly with Jubal Early that August, that she had spent the entire summer "in agony and suspence," and three days later her sister-in-law interpreted a lapse in letters from her own husband as evidence that evil had befallen him, too.[24]

Life remained equally uncertain at home, of course, with endemic tuberculosis and recurrent plagues like typhoid and diphtheria sweeping through neighborhoods, but that only drew a darker pall over the image of a soldier's existence, with its greater likelihood of violence, pestilence, and misery. In addition to the grinding emotional burden over the personal safety of a boy or man in the army, the chance that a struggling family might permanently lose its chief source of support posed a significant concern that was often accentuated by the inconvenience of that breadwinner's temporary absence. The rigors of taking over the absent volunteer's domestic and agricultural duties often contributed to health problems in the wives and mothers who were left behind, especially when combined with the stress of worry and the inability to afford medical care.[25] The accumulating hardships were usually difficult for neighbors to miss, even if the soldier's family strove to disguise acute poverty and the dire need for a man's strength and mechanical expertise. With the aid of her small son a woman might try to climb onto the roof of their prairie homestead in the midst of a tempest to reset their toppled stovepipe, and she might endure the agony of serial, untreated toothaches for months, but she could hardly fail to discuss the serious overextension of her credit with the local storekeeper, or with the landlord, and those conversations seldom earned confidentiality. Her travails might end, and her pecuniary situation might gradually improve, if the man of the house survived in condition to resume his occupation, but if he died, or came home with crippling illness or injury (an increasingly likely outcome, as 1864 progressed), a grateful nation would afford her only eight dollars a month to compensate for his loss; if she were the mother of the departed hero, rather than his widow, she ran a good chance of never drawing a penny.[26]

Little wonder, then, that many women stood squarely in the way of their husbands going into the army, or turned resentful and bitterly critical of those who did. The wives of men who entered the service as officers, or gained commissions after they enlisted, might belabor them with perennial pleas to resign, extracting promises that they would come home when they could find an interlude or an excuse that would allow them to do so honorably. Enlisted men's wives seldom urged them to desert, but they did frequently beg them not to reenlist, crafting pitiful appeals that only the heartless could have ignored — although some did ignore them. The wife of an Ohio surgeon who pestered her husband to come home hinted that she no longer missed him as much as she once had, attributing the waning of her loneliness to an unconscious impulse for self-protection: it might be fatal to continue feeling "so utterly forsaken," she explained, adding that their little boy was turning his filial affection to another young doctor because he fully expected that his long-absent father would never be back.[27] For some women, especially those who were newlyweds, without children, or who were victims of abusive marriages, the sense of having been cruelly abandoned seemed almost literal, and may have triggered a detachment that occasionally fractured the marital bond. Gossip sputtered from one campfire to another about wives who had taken to "sassing around" back home with other men, with particular stories sometimes filtering down to the husband himself, and the potential for infidelity may have posed a chronic concern to men who had so callously disregarded their wives' impassioned objections to their military ambitions.[28]

With the families of earlier volunteers so often suffering in such palpably wretched circumstances, prospective recruits with families of their own might understandably have demurred from offering themselves to the ideal of national unity. Their vacillation assumed an air of sagacity when, to many of those at home and even to some in the front lines, it seemed increasingly unlikely that the Unionist cause could overcome the stubborn resistance of a determined and resilient Confederacy.

Contrary to Horatio Wright's confident expectation, Jubal Early had not turned for home. Wright's abrupt departure from the lower Shenandoah Valley opened the way for Early to chastise the little Army of West Virginia again — which operated under George Crook now instead of the hated David Hunter, who remained at Harper's Ferry, periodically ordering the eviction of prominent citizens' families and the burning of their homes. One of Early's young division commanders, Stephen Ramseur, lost his chance to belabor William Averell's detachment at Stephenson's Depot, north of Winchester, when he underestimated its strength; in place of another smashing victory, Ramseur took a beating himself when his veterans crumbled before a surprise flank attack. With that single blemish on their winning record of the past five weeks, Early's Confederates fell back through Winchester and headed for the banks of Cedar Creek, nearly twenty miles beyond. There lay Massanutten Mountain — a long, narrow ridge that bisected the Shenandoah Valley lengthwise — and Early positioned his little army to block each of those narrow corridors. Union cavalry followed to within a few miles, only to be driven back to the vicinity of Kernstown, just up the valley from Winchester.[29]

Within a hundred hours of the defeat at Stephenson's Depot, Early took his revenge. On the morning of July 24 he started his whole force north on the Valley Turnpike, driving in Crook's advance pickets. Early moved along and beside the pike in separate parallel columns, with his cavalry leading, leaving the impression of a light force. His cavalry met Crook's at Kernstown, and Crook dealt out two of his four brigades of infantry to meet it. Twice he repulsed Early's main body of cavalry, supplemented finally by two divisions of infantry, and then Crook called back for one of his remaining brigades. Another Confederate division burst over a ridge on the extreme left of Crook's line, folding up Colonel Rutherford B. Hayes's brigade like a jackknife, but Hayes rallied his survivors behind a stone wall to shield what by then had become a retreat. The Union cavalry all but disintegrated at the surprise, much as Ramseur's Confederate infantry had scattered only four days before, and with nearly four hundred casualties in his brigade alone Hayes found himself covering the precipitous flight of Crook's little army. Through Winchester they went late in the afternoon, sprinting in the same panic that had gripped Nathaniel Banks's fugitives in 1862, Robert Milroy's in 1863, and Franz Sigel's just ten weeks back. Discouraged loyalist citizens in Winchester wondered if the Union army would ever show any fight, while Confederate sympathizers gazed with ill-disguised glee on the streams of Federals draining into town from the old forts to the south. Finally, civilians of both persuasions took to their houses as bullets started spattering through the streets.[30]

The retreat continued into the evening, with burning wagons lighting the way for the chase. Robert Rodes led the pursuit with his division of infantry, stopping finally at the scene of Ramseur's defeat at Stephenson's Depot, more than twenty miles from where his men had slept the night before. Early's cavalry kept up the pressure, and Crook only stopped at Bunker Hill, a dozen miles north of Winchester, well after nightfall. The next morning he dropped back to Martinsburg, West Virginia, in a soaking rain, skirmishing much of that day before retreating across the Potomac to Williamsport, Maryland, all the while shedding footsore stragglers and flushing hordes of refugees ahead of his haggard column. From there he marched down the Maryland side through Sharpsburg, finally reaching safety on the heights opposite Harper's Ferry, where he found General Hunter's headquarters in a dither with all their baggage packed and supplies sent away. David Strother, Hunter's chief of staff and a native Virginian of Unionist proclivity who had served in that same district during the earliest days of the war, remembered Robert Patterson's Union army abandoning the valley almost exactly three years before. This latest forcible expulsion seemed to seal his contempt for bumbling, ineffective leadership, and he noted that one of his staff colleagues had just quit the army; in a few days, so would Strother.[31]

Early followed Crook into Martinsburg, where he spent a couple of days tearing up the railroad on either side of that town, but then he loosed two little mounted brigades to ride into Pennsylvania and give the residents there a taste of the arson that Hunter had been inflicting on Confederate civilians since June. Brigadier General John McCausland's Virginia cavalry and Colonel Bradley Johnson's mixed brigade of Virginians and Marylanders crossed the Potomac at McCoy's Ford on July 29, spurring due north under cover of Ramseur and Rodes, who forded the river at Williamsport and pushed east toward Hagerstown to distract William Averell's cavalry. Skirmishers from Rodes and Ramseur pushed Averell and a gaggle of militia into Hagerstown, where they burned all their own equipment before scurrying north toward Pennsylvania ahead of a largely imaginary force of Confederates — for Rodes and Ramseur both fell back to the Virginia side that evening. McCausland and Johnson, meanwhile, rode for Mercersburg with nothing to slow them down except half a company of the 6th U.S. Cavalry under a lieutenant. Averell's cavalry and the militia stopped at Greencastle, Pennsylvania, and before dawn the next morning they heard artillery ten miles or more to the north, where

McCausland had reached the outskirts of Chambersburg. With only a few dozen men and a single fieldpiece for its defense, the town fell to the two thousand rebel horsemen by daylight, just as Union troops were spilling into the blown-up Confederate fort at Petersburg, a couple of hundred miles to the south.[32]

McCausland rode into the village square with about five hundred men and immediately rounded up the principal citizens to give them an ultimatum. In the spirit of General Hunter's war upon the homes of Southern civilians, General Early had decided that the citizens of Chambersburg must ransom the town for a hundred thousand dollars in gold or half a million in greenbacks, or McCausland would put it to the torch. No such amount of money could be found at short notice on a Saturday morning, they replied (and one defiant councilman said they would not pay five cents), so by midmorning the demolition parties had scattered through the community and started the burning on what was already the hottest day of the summer — and of his life, asserted Colonel Strother, who had spent nearly fifty years in the Potomac River valley. There was no time for more warning than would hurry people out of their homes, and with dozens of blazes simultaneously kindled across town the fire spread rapidly, depriving many of everything but the clothes they were wearing. The raiders left before noon, by which time flames had engulfed the entire town, consuming what some estimated as $1.5 million worth of mostly private property.[33]

Again the rumors circulated in Washington that Early had swept the Shenandoah Valley and invaded Pennsylvania with forty thousand men. Another estimate that there had been only five hundred raiders (likely based on the detachment that had accompanied McCausland into the center of Chambersburg) failed to counterbalance that wild exaggeration. General Halleck fully credited Early with forty thousand men, or more, and that credence inspired hysteria, while the competing talk of so much destruction by a mere five hundred men elicited scorn for military commanders and civilian administrators who were so easily overawed. The New York Times raved well into August about "The Invasion," and Early was expected to strike next near Frederick, Maryland, or at Wheeling, West Virginia, with the reinforcement of Longstreet's corps. Distraught War Department functionaries considered mobilizing soldiers who were passing through Washington on their way home, with only days to serve. Capital newspapers copied the frustrated invective of Pennsylvania journalists who characterized the Confederate raiders as "desperate, ferocious, and untamed" freebooters of "dark and malignant passions," and those quotes brought wry smiles to the faces of Southern sympathizers who had shuddered at three years of Union vandalism in the South, the latest round of which had been initiated by David Hunter himself.[34]

The destruction of Chambersburg led almost directly to the conclusion of David Hunter's connection with armies and battlefields: the secretary of war would continue to value Hunter's services in the manipulation of military tribunals, but his days in command of other soldiers had come to an end. The events of July 30, both in Pennsylvania and at Petersburg, had made both the administration and Ulysses Grant look bad, and that required some changes. At Petersburg the change was effected somewhat backhandedly, through a court of inquiry that laid all the blame for the Crater disaster on Burnside, Ledlie, and Ferrero, while effectively exonerating General Meade; Burnside asked for a leave of absence, and although Grant considered him for other commands he never called him back to duty. For the problem on the upper Potomac, where Early's rampage had elicited reproach for the lieutenant general's unimaginative strategy, Grant conferred with the president in a meeting at Fort Monroe on July 31. He had already decided to install a new commander in that sector with authority over all the troops operating against Early's troublesome little army, to avoid having the rebels fall on one independent army like Crook's while another — like Wright's — marched back toward Washington. It was only a matter of finding the right person. He had first named General Franklin, days after he escaped from Early's cavalry, but Halleck advised against him. Then Grant considered Meade for the job, perhaps not only because he was competent for it but also because it would have severed Meade's prickly relations with numerous subordinates. Meade conveyed his lack of enthusiasm for the position, and he supposed the president would prefer Halleck. The morning after his meeting with Lincoln, however, General Grant decided to send Meade's cavalry chief, Phil Sheridan.[35]

Sheridan was another of those who had tangled with the crabby Meade, aggravating the army commander with his insubordinate arrogance and insufferable self-promotion, so his departure helped eliminate much of the personality conflict that Meade's reassignment would have resolved. More to the point, though, Sheridan owned the dual traits of inexhaustible energy and insatiable ambition that drove him to perpetual activity and won him the admiration of Grant, who considered him one of the two best division commanders he had ever known. Grant might have thought less of Sheridan's cutthroat behavior toward competitors had Sheridan not been careful to cultivate close relationships with those who favored him and could advance his career, and had he not demonstrated the same ruthlessness toward his enemies — even a defenseless enemy of dubious antagonism.[36]

Mortified to have abandoned his pursuit just as Early resumed the offensive, Horatio Wright prodded his Sixth Corps and the Nineteenth Corps back to the valley by merciless forced marches that a Vermont corporal considered "a sin in the sight of God." When the head of the Sixth Corps marched into Harper's Ferry, said the corporal, half the corps still lay gasping along the roadside between there and Washington. General Hunter confidently took overall command of the troops as they came in, knowing nothing of Sheridan's impending arrival. Halleck assumed that Hunter would ask to be relieved if made to serve under a man half his age and his junior in rank: because he had cultivated a friendship with president-elect Lincoln, Hunter had held a major general's commission for a year while Sheridan remained a captain in the Quartermaster Department. Halleck judged Hunter well. Grant tried to salve the old man's pride, and Hunter acted the cordial host at dinner when Grant came along to introduce Sheridan, but he had probably already planned his escape on an excuse other than jealousy. The next day, responding to a four-day-old order in which the president countermanded Hunter's arbitrary eviction and arrest of Maryland citizens, Hunter asked to be relieved of his department. That eased matters considerably, and before the day was out Sheridan had been given command of a vast new entity called the Middle Military Division, encompassing Washington, Maryland, Hunter's old Department of West Virginia, and most of Pennsylvania.[37]

Sheridan wasted little time. Within forty-eight hours he had made all his assignments and issued marching orders for what he would soon christen the Army of the Shenandoah. From Harper's Ferry he struck south and west, on a course that would have cut Early off at Martinsburg, and Early — unaccustomed to facing much bold aggression under Hunter — packed up and started south, toward Winchester and beyond. Sheridan followed him up the valley to Cedar Creek, but then he detected the presence of Confederate reinforcements: to help Early make short work of the new Army of the Shenandoah, Lee had sent his nephew Fitzhugh Lee's division of cavalry and Joseph Kershaw's infantry division, from Longstreet's corps. Sheridan, feeling timid about the geography of his position, came striding back to Winchester again with Early, Kershaw, and the rebel cavalry right on his heels. In both directions Sheridan had to fight off irksome raids on his supply trains by a small battalion of Confederate cavalry under Lieutenant Colonel John Singleton Mosby.[38]

Before Hunter stepped out of the way, Grant had instructed him to strip the Shenandoah Valley of all provisions that might feed the Confederate army, from forage and grain to poultry and livestock; anything his own army could not use should be destroyed, Grant had insisted, al-

though he specifically cautioned against any willful damage to civilian
structures. Sheridan adopted those directions along with his new command, ignoring only the caveat about burning private property, at which
he winked, and as his troops started up the valley they found the old prohibition against foraging suddenly void. In fact, they were now often encouraged to steal anything they wanted to eat, both to reduce their dependence on vulnerable supply trains and to deprive the enemy of that much
provender. That enemy included the civilians living in the region, who
would lose their market crops as well as their own winter's sustenance.
Soldiers who had campaigned in the Louisiana swamps and in the tram-
pled districts of eastern Virginia found the valley a land of plenty, with
acres on acres of corn, luscious apples ripening overhead, flocks of deli-
cious fowl, and droves of pigs, sheep, and cattle. Whatever corn, grain, or
hay they could not consume or carry, they burned, whether it stood in the
field or lay in a barn.[39]

Sheridan, whose troops hanged a suspected spy after a drumhead
court-martial at Middletown on August 14, apparently also condoned
peremptory execution for prisoners of war, and Ulysses Grant sustained
him in that opinion, for on the afternoon of August 16 Grant instructed
Sheridan to hang the troublesome Mosby's men without trial whenever
he caught them. Sheridan anticipated him in that brutality, for he did not
receive that telegram until the morning of August 17, by which time he
had already hanged one of Mosby's captured horsemen and shot six more
to death. On August 19 he reported to Grant that he was "quietly dispos-
ing of numbers of" prisoners whom he called guerrillas, most of whom
were regularly enlisted members of Mosby's battalion, and three days
later he repeated that he had "disposed of quite a number of Mosby's
men." Nor did he stop there, for on September 11 he boasted that his
troops had "exterminated 3 officers and 27 men of Mosby's gang in the
last twelve days." That set the tone for Sheridan's valley campaign, for
which a lesser number of his own cavalrymen would meet a similar fate
when Mosby learned of those summary executions.[40]

His own encouraging reports notwithstanding, Sheridan had accomplished no spectacular feats by late August, although he had performed
the invisible service of keeping Early sufficiently amused in the lower valley to curb further depredations above the Potomac. Both of the major
Union armies had accomplished long, lunging offensives toward Atlanta
and Richmond that spring, but neither of those campaigns had involved
any significant battle that might have been singled out as a resounding
victory; no headlines had reported any dazzling Union triumph since
the unmitigated success at Missionary Ridge — nine long months and a
hundred thousand lives before. No strategic cities had fallen since then;

no Confederate army had fled the field in confusion. The determined Unionist who believed the optimistic newspaper reports and reinforced them by tracing a map with his finger might well suppose that the national forces were making slow but steady progress, but for the less ardent or hopeful it was all a deadly waltz, spiraling repeatedly around the same ballroom floor. One season the rebels might be crowded back into the lower tier of Gulf States, and the next they might be driving deep into Kentucky; at the beginning of summer the battlefront could lie at the gates of Richmond, and two months later it would shift to the suburbs of Washington. So long as the enemy held his vital centers and enough arable land to sustain an army, the fortunes of war remained fickle, and even if they failed to turn about completely, the rebellion seemed capable of eternal resistance. Once again the people grew weary of the war and doubtful of its success, as they had two winters previously.

In the first days of 1863 William Rosecrans had won the administration's praise for a drawn battle that had provided the best news the nation heard that season, and even greater adulation attended the conquest of Mobile Bay in that dismal August of 1864. General Grant had hoped for a campaign against Mobile as soon as he became general in chief, in March, but Nathaniel Banks had stymied those plans with an ill-managed expedition up the Red River. In May, Major General Edward R. S. Canby had come to New Orleans to take command of the new Military Division of West Mississippi, and he had brought with him Grant's designs on Mobile. In the War Department's new habit of combining several departments under intermediate regional administrations, Canby had assumed control over everything from the Rio Grande to the mouth of the Chattahoochee River at Apalachicola, Florida, and as far up the Mississippi River as the Iowa border. That sprawling bailiwick consumed Nathaniel Banks's former Department of the Gulf, reducing Banks to a subordinate of Canby, who gave him no field command. Canby had evidently shared Grant's wish to operate against Mobile, and then perhaps to move on to aid Sherman against Atlanta, as Grant had meant to do before Banks undertook his Red River frolic. Early in his tenure Canby had corresponded with Rear Admiral David Farragut on the subject of Mobile, but he had been forced to suspend his Gulf coast ambitions when Grant called on him to send the Nineteenth Corps to Virginia. Then Farragut proposed entering the mouth of Mobile Bay, thirty miles below the city itself: he had done some reconnaissance, including sending a party ashore to capture pickets, and he judged that it would only require about a thousand infantry to seize the smaller of the two forts guarding the entrance. That would secure their communications, and (Farragut implied) if Canby could spare more men later they could lay siege to the bigger bastion.[41]

Canby afforded Farragut a small brigade of infantry, with some heavy and light artillery and a battalion of engineers, totaling perhaps twenty-four hundred men, under the command of Major General Gordon Granger, whom an observer described as "a rough looking man with a very harsh voice." Most of those troops arrived off Petit Bois Island, twenty miles west of Mobile Bay, on August 3, and the next day Farragut issued his orders for the attack. The appearance of the armada warned the Confederate defenders that something more ambitious than routine blockade duty lay in the offing, and all day on August 4 rebel boats plied between Mobile and the coastal fortifications, bringing reinforcements and supplies.[42]

Mobile Bay lay broad and deep, a dozen miles wide at the mouth and half a dozen at the narrow end, thirty miles to the north, where sat the port of Mobile. A long, narrow peninsula stretched out from the mainland on the east, cutting the bay off from the Gulf of Mexico and ending at Mobile Point. A lighthouse occupied Mobile Point, and right behind it stood the pentagonal brick fortress guarding the main ship channel — Fort Morgan, with forty-six guns and six hundred men. Three miles of open water intervened between Mobile Point and Fort Gaines, on Dauphin Island, and that was the chute that Farragut had to run. He aligned his fourteen wooden ships in pairs, lashed together, with four ironclad monitors running in between those vulnerable vessels and Fort Morgan. The *Brooklyn* and the *Octorora* took the lead for the wooden ships, and Farragut followed on his flagship, *Hartford,* tied to the *Metacomet.* The *Tecumseh,* with two fifteen-inch smoothbore guns in its turret, led the monitors. The fleet started toward the inlet before 6:00 A.M., moving under a cloudy sky, and at 6:47 by Farragut's watch the *Tecumseh* threw the inaugural round. Fort Morgan withheld fire until just after 7:00, aiming first for the *Brooklyn,* which replied with its hundred-pounder bow chasers. Then everyone opened up.[43]

Obstructions and underwater mines — torpedoes, in the lexicon of the day — had been strung across the ship channel. Buoys marked those devices for friendly mariners who knew where to look, and the captain of the *Brooklyn* spotted some of those suspicious buoys. With that he backed his engines to clear them, blocking the entire column, and the impatient Farragut ordered the *Hartford* to veer around and take the lead, dragging the little *Metacomet* along. A moment later the *Tecumseh* detonated a mine, rolled on its side, and sank in seconds with all but a handful of its crew. At about that moment Farragut uttered (or was said to have uttered) his instruction to "damn" the torpedoes, ordering the *Metacomet* to send a boat for survivors before dashing through the presumed location of the mines toward the waiting Confederate fleet, if the term "fleet" could be applied to three wooden gunboats and one ironclad ram. Admiral Franklin Buchanan, aboard the ram *Tennessee*, met the enemy with only twenty-two guns and fewer than five hundred men on his four craft; Farragut's command carried nearly three thousand sailors and a couple of hundred guns, many of them in much heavier caliber than Buchanan's own. The fight did not last long: once inside the bay the Union ships cast apart from each other, several of them scattering after the three wooden gunboats; within half an hour one of them had been captured, while the other two ran for shoal water under the guns of Fort Morgan, where one of them soon settled by the stern.[44]

That left only the *Tennessee* to oppose thirteen gunboats and the three remaining monitors. Sixty-four-year-old Admiral Buchanan, who had been wounded in the leg while commanding the ironclad ram *Virginia* in its epic battle with the original *Monitor*, nearly two and a half years before, entered just as pugnaciously into the second-most-memorable naval duel in Southern waters. With the fate of his vessel a foregone conclusion, he steered for the biggest of Farragut's ships, while the rest of them swarmed around him and rammed the *Tennessee* from all angles. As each passed the ram it would unload a vicious broadside into the iron-plated casemate at a range of ten or twelve feet, and with such a flock of swirling targets the rebel boat could not concentrate enough firepower to sink any one of them. After an hour or so a collision smashed the ironclad's steering apparatus, leaving it crippled, and Buchanan, whose leg had been badly broken, authorized his executive officer to surrender.[45]

The presence of Farragut's vessels inside the bay ended Mobile's history as a port for blockade runners: the last one slipped in on August 4, darting past Farragut's gathering fleet. That left the Confederacy only the ports of Galveston and Brownsville, Texas, and Wilmington, North Carolina. Charleston remained open, but a dense cloud of warships usually darkened the approaches to its channels; with so few harbors open, the U.S. Navy could more effectively saturate each of them. That was the grounds on which the importance of this victory was sold, beginning with bold headlines announcing that for the first time in a great while there was some "Good News." The first reports came through a Confederate newspaper, three days after the battle, and editors gave it prime placement; even Gideon Welles had no better information at the Navy Department. Yankee soldiers in the trenches below Richmond heard about Mobile before any Northern sheets did, and they found comfort in how badly their foes took it. Richmond papers passing between fraternizing pickets continued to provide the North with details of the coup for a day or two longer, and by August 12 New Yorkers were being treated to inaccurate rumors that Mobile itself had fallen.[46]

Mobile would remain Confederate until the final days of the war, for Canby could not accumulate enough troops to hold the place even if Farragut could help him take it, but there still remained Fort Morgan and Fort Gaines, at either side of the main inlet, as well as Fort Powell, a smaller work guarding the other entrance to the bay at Grant's Pass. It was the ease with which the latter two fell that should perhaps have given Northerners more cheer than the occupation of Mobile Bay itself.

The Confederate troops at the inlet had been growing discontented for some time, as their department commander deduced by their tendency to desert, especially at Fort Morgan, and he attributed it to the length of time they had gone without a visit from the paymaster. The devaluation of the Confederate dollar casts some doubt on the importance of pay to those men, especially as they had little opportunity to spend any money, and the isolation and boredom of those forts may have had more to do with their restlessness. Except for some local militia, the garrisons consisted mainly of the 21st Alabama and the 1st Tennessee Heavy Artillery, and both of those regiments evinced a certain disquiet. Thomas Benton Alexander, one of the Tennessee privates at Fort Morgan, had asked for a transfer in the middle of May — presumably to some other fort in the Mobile defenses, and that request appears to have reflected his dissatisfaction with the location, rather than any resentment over his pay. Alexander had spent about half of his Confederate service as a prisoner or in a parole camp, having been captured at Fort Donelson early in 1862 and again at Port Hudson in 1863. He may have dreaded being trapped again as the approach of summer increased the likelihood of a Union attack on Mobile, and Fort Morgan would certainly leave its garrison trapped once the inlet had been breached. The same was true of the force at Fort Gaines, in its more vulnerable position and condition. The troops there were, besides, not much accustomed to fighting: the veterans of the 21st Alabama had only seen one battle, in the firestorm at Shiloh, more than two years before, and they were not exactly clamoring to see another.[47]

Two companies of the 21st held Fort Powell, under Lieutenant Colonel James Williams. While Farragut led his flotilla toward Mobile Point, five more Federal gunboats steamed toward Grant's Pass and assailed Fort Powell from the west, opening a steady fire with six heavy rifles. Colonel Williams fought his western battery for about an hour and a half, firing wildly and inflicting no damage whatever. Neither did his fort suffer much injury, but after Farragut's ships gained the bay behind him he grew frantic, signaling Brigadier General Richard Page at Fort Morgan that he would have to evacuate. Page ordered him to hold on as long as he could, but without firing another round Williams prepared to escape, slipping away under cover of darkness and blowing up his magazine. The next morning bell-bottomed Federals strode ashore there to raise the Stars and Stripes over the rubble.[48]

Colonel Charles D. Anderson of the 21st Alabama held Fort Gaines with 863 soldiers, militia, and Marines, with provisions enough to last for months. The garrison included forty-five other officers, mostly from Anderson's own regiment, and on August 6 all but two of those officers joined in presenting him with a resolution advising him to surrender, claiming that the enlisted men fully concurred in their belief that they could not resist effectively or with any benefit to their cause. General Granger's infantry and artillery had landed on the western end of Dauphin Island well before Farragut ran the forts, and they were already moving in on Fort Gaines. On his own initiative, Colonel Anderson raised a flag of truce at first light on August 7 and sent two officers out to the fleet to ask for terms.[49]

Back at Fort Morgan, General Page demanded by signal flag what the truce meant. No reply came from Gaines, even when Fort Morgan fired a signal gun. Telegraphing and signaling repeatedly for Anderson to hold his fort, Page waited until dark to take a boat across to Fort Gaines, where he learned, to his astonishment, that Colonel Anderson had gone aboard one of the Yankee ships to accept the surrender terms. Page was a first cousin to Robert E. Lee, and a former officer of the old navy himself, where he had been known as "Sir Ramrod." For him, the notion of surrendering without a fight ran completely against the grain; he could not believe that Anderson would initiate surrender proceedings from his subordinate position. Before starting back to Fort Morgan, Page instructed the senior major in the fort to relieve Anderson from command when he returned, and repudiate the surrender. At dawn the next day he tried signaling again with guns and flags, besides telegraphing, but at 9:30 that morning the U.S. flag fluttered up the flagpole over Fort Gaines.[50]

The 21st Alabama had been raised from the population of Mobile and the surrounding countryside. If entire rebel regiments declined to even stand the first fire in defense of their own home cities, Northern citizens might take heart, but the fragile morale of the Alabamians at Fort Powell and Fort Gaines merited only a sentence or two in newspaper reports, conveyed more as an amusing tale of official Confederate frustration over the surrender than as an example of flagging Southern will.[51]

Morale did not soar particularly at Fort Morgan, either. Canby had forwarded more infantry that he had collected from the coast of Texas, and Granger landed some of them on the peninsula to the east of Fort Morgan the day after Fort Gaines fell. Within twenty-four hours, a few of General Page's men began slipping away, and the only direction they could go was right into the arms of the Yankees. Page moved his command into the fort from their encampment outside, and for a fortnight the Federals crept ever closer, sniping at the rebels and wounding one now and then, while Union artillery played on them regularly during each day and sometimes through the night. The Union fleet remained fairly quiet, but the captured ram *Tennessee* limped down with a Union crew to toss a few token shells at the fort. The barrage intensified on August 22, with solid shot battering the gorge wall and one shell setting the interior barracks on fire. Page ordered the magazine flooded to avoid an explosion, and detailed men to spike the guns, dismount them, and destroy the carriages as effectively as he could. The next morning he, too, ran up a white flag, with smoke and flames billowing from the fort. Granger steamed ashore while a line of his troops formed across the peninsula, and out the sally port came six hundred tired, grimy, smoke-blackened Confederates, followed by the grizzled General Page — tall and straight in a straw hat and a bombazine coat, without sword or side arms. Again came the exchange of flags, the garrison laid down its mostly unserviceable rifles, and the prisoners shuffled aboard Union gunboats for the journey to prison.[52]

While the army and navy planned and implemented their joint operation against Mobile, Nathan Bedford Forrest remained active in the northern reaches of the same department. After the wreckage of Sturgis's column at Brice's Crossroads, Cadwallader Washburn had sent Andrew Jackson Smith after Forrest with eight brigades of infantry, two of cavalry, and nine batteries of artillery, amounting to fourteen thousand men. Smith, who had saved Nathaniel Banks's hash during the worst of the Red River campaign, started from the same railhead as Sturgis had used, making for the Mobile & Ohio at Tupelo by a different route, but part of Forrest's command caught up with him about fifteen miles from there and started following, occasionally striking at Smith's rear guard and once taking some of his wagon train, at least temporarily. That night, a mile or so short of Tupelo, Smith turned to fight, and prepared some breastworks for the purpose. The next morning, July 14, on the orders of his department commander, Forrest attacked with a force no more than half the size of Smith's: his men lunged forward with their old yell, sprinting in a mob rather than sweeping forward in column, and the barricaded Yankees cut them down like rows of grain. This time the blue ranks held, but the next morning Smith discovered that his bread ration had gone moldy, and on that account he decided to go back to Memphis ten days early, first tearing up a few miles of the railroad. Forrest had been wounded in the foot, and he dispatched a subordinate to pursue Smith's column for a couple of days, but this time there was no panic, and Smith escaped without further incident. Forrest, meanwhile, had lost a number of his best brigade and regimental commanders, besides about a quarter of his men, while inflicting only half as many casualties on his enemy.[53]

Five weeks later Forrest compensated for the disappointing results at Tupelo with a spectacular raid on Memphis itself. Early in August Smith directed most of his Tupelo army to Holly Springs and Oxford, in north-central Mississippi, where Forrest came to monitor his movements less aggressively than before. Finding so many of Washburn's troops in the field, Forrest must have availed himself of his Memphis information network to learn that district headquarters was defended only by a squadron of cavalry, a few scattered infantry detachments, and a couple of regiments of hundred-day men who were going home in two weeks. With four mounted regiments and one cavalry battalion, Forrest made a forced march of some eighty miles from the vicinity of Oxford, and before dawn on Sunday, August 21, he burst into Memphis, scattering the drowsy summer soldiers of the 137th Illinois, seizing scores of them as prisoners, and leaving fifty of them dead and wounded in their camp. Rebel horsemen rode straight into town through a thick fog, sending strong parties to surround General Washburn's residence on Union Street and the Gayoso House, where Major General Stephen Hurlbut had been visiting. Hurlbut was not in his room, however, and Washburn had been alerted by the local cavalry commander just in time to flee on foot, apparently in his nightclothes, without leaving a word of instruction. Forrest had to be satisfied with subjecting his nemesis to that indignity, for the shooting soon brought Union officers spilling into the streets, where they called out odd lots of enlisted men and started forming them in line. Stealing as many horses and mules as they could find, Forrest's impromptu brigade thundered out of Memphis on the road to Hernando, Mississippi, taking their prizes and prisoners with them and leaving the city in conniptions.[54]

Washburn gladly accepted inflated estimates of the number of Confederates who had followed Forrest into Memphis, and he blamed their escape on General Smith, seventy miles away.[55] The incident created more humiliation than anything else, and it disguised General Smith's success (and Washburn's) in continuing to detain Forrest in Mississippi while he could have been dissecting Sherman's umbilical to Chattanooga and Nashville. As the summer wore on, though, panic and humiliation were precisely the emotions that Confederates most wanted their enemies to feel.

Eight hundred miles to the east, Robert E. Lee's Army of Northern Virginia did its part in that vein by further foiling and discouraging the Union armies on either side of the James River. The heat and the long weeks without rain had made the summer unbearable enough without the uncomfortable confinement in the trenches, the random shell, and the periodic mortal combat, while the frustration of repeated defeats by an inferior foe tended to undermine the confidence that Meade's and Butler's men might have felt over a victory like Mobile Bay, or over Sherman's steadier, less costly progress in Georgia. August proved no kinder to those Tidewater armies than July had been, providing several more humbling lessons in courage and capacity from a Confederate army that was supposed to have been sorely reduced in strength and élan after three months of continual pounding.

It did not escape the notice of Grant's troops that the people back home paid little heed to the president's call for a day of fasting and prayer on August 4. The distressing events of July had perhaps distracted the Northern public from any recollection of that proclamation, and no encouraging prospects had yet emanated from Mobile, but one might have expected the dismal circumstances to have instilled a more somber spirit than seemed to prevail. Reading the *New York Herald,* a Connecticut captain detected that Gotham had observed the day with "fast driving fast sailing &c but very little fasting."[56]

Then, even as the captain commented on the accounts in the *Herald,* a Confederate agent smuggled a homemade time bomb aboard a heavily laden ammunition barge at the City Point dock, and an hour later it exploded with a resounding blast that the troops could hear in their trenches at Petersburg, ten miles away. An ominous cloud blossomed over the vicinity of Grant's headquarters, while shards of wood, pieces of bodies, and artillery projectiles showered the river and the various department headquarters scattered around the point. Colonel Orville Babcock of Grant's staff was wounded in the hand by a splinter of shell, a man in the provost marshal's office was hit in the leg, and in Grant's escort a mounted orderly was killed. A Regular Army sergeant with a decade of service was fatally injured by debris, and several others came out with lesser wounds. The toll was finally fixed at 43 killed and 126 wounded seriously enough to count, most of them black laborers, but so much was lost in ordnance, supplies, vessels, and buildings that no one ever counted the material damage. Ignorance diminished the demoralizing effect of the sabotage, though, because Union authorities mistook it for an accident.[57]

The other flops and fiascoes of that month could not be attributed to accident. A few days after the City Point explosion, Grant sent Winfield Hancock north of the James River at Deep Bottom with his Second Corps, with authority over the Tenth Corps, and with a division of cavalry, intending to surprise the enemy by an attack along the roads leading toward Richmond. Instead, the surprise fell to Hancock, who learned that the troops of his legendary corps had grown as timid and unreliable as many in the Ninth Corps were said to have been at the Crater.

Crediting intelligence that two of Lee's infantry divisions had gone to the valley, Grant supposed the Confederate lines there were held by barely eight thousand men, while Hancock would have at least twenty thousand. Only Kershaw's division had marched to Early's aid, however, and Hancock's troops flinched or fled at almost every challenge. It was the veterans of the Army of the Potomac who showed the greatest fear, too: those in the Tenth Corps, which had seen less action that summer, could not manage to hold the ground they took, but their retreat brought little of the disgrace felt in the Second Corps. Francis Barlow, who commanded the better part of two Second Corps divisions, found his troops wanting in pluck four times in succession: a regiment of New York heavy artillery declined to face a few rebel skirmishers, preferring to huddle behind their own skirmishers farther down the line. Then, when ordered to fill the gap abandoned by the heavy artillery, the famous Irish Brigade (the former commander of which lay in a drunken stupor back at City Point) sidled off behind a line of trees that protected them from any stray bullets. Barlow next turned his attention to a hill near a Mr. Fussell's millpond, sending the last two brigades of his own division to drive away the few Confederates who held the breastworks on that hill, but a little artillery fire on their flank so obviously unnerved both brigades that Barlow gave up on them; he turned to an oversized brigade from another division that had been among the best in the army, but that brigade also quailed before the spattering fire from the hilltop. The next day a division from the Tenth Corps carried a little fort near Fussell's Mill at considerable cost, but a countercharge soon swept it out of the work and back where it came from.[58]

The movement at Deep Bottom degenerated into a standoff, and a few days later Hancock withdrew to the Petersburg side with nothing to show for his labors beyond three thousand casualties. He returned, in part, because General Warren had encountered some surprisingly determined resistance south of Petersburg, where Grant had also sent him to take advantage of Lee's reported weakness. Still reasoning that those detachments to Early should have thinned Lee's lines somewhere, Grant hoped to seize one of Petersburg's last two rail connections to the rest of the Confederacy, or at least to persuade Lee to recall Early's reinforcements.[59]

Warren sidestepped to the Weldon Railroad, five miles south of the city, on August 18, leaving the trenches to the Ninth and Eighteenth Corps. He marched all four divisions of his Fifth Corps to the railroad at Six Mile Station, making his headquarters at nearby Globe Tavern before edging one division north, up the railroad toward Petersburg. Two lone Confederate brigades slammed into that northbound division before it had gone far, and forced it back toward Globe Tavern. Warren sent up a second division, and a brigade from a third, but those two rebel brigades fought them all to a standstill. The next day, in a steady rain, the same two brigades challenged Warren in front while a division of reinforcements emerged from a dense wood to strike him from behind: Warren's right flank crumbled, and two divisions of the Ninth Corps arrived just in time to save him from worse damage, but he still lost nearly three thousand men and a brigadier general. An orderly sergeant who had been transferred to the 155th Pennsylvania with the reenlisted men of his original unit found his new comrades "terrible cowards," with skulkers accounting for at least a third of the regiment; it was all he could do to keep his company in line during Warren's fight. One of Grant's staff officers who was on the scene called it "disheartening & disgusting" that so few Confederates could soundly pummel so many of their own men, who seemed "feebler" than the enemy.[60]

The Yankees spent August 20 building an extensive line of works along the railroad and perpendicular to it. On the twenty-first the still-outnumbered Confederates tried vainly to pry Warren out of those works, but their fiercest attacks shriveled under a steady roar of canister; after the last attempt Fifth Corps stretcher teams darted onto the field and fetched in a couple of hundred wounded rebels, who ranged from beardless boys who looked about fifteen to grey-haired men old enough to be grandfathers. In the end Warren kept his hold on the Weldon Railroad, at a cost of four thousand men in the Fifth Corps and five hundred in the Ninth, and the rebels had to establish a new wagon route that bypassed Warren's position. It caused them much inconvenience, but they continued to draw supplies from eastern North Carolina into the following spring.[61]

The last and worst evidence of deteriorating morale in the nation's principal army came a few days later and a few miles away, and once again the shame fell to Hancock's celebrated command. Almost immediately after he brought his men back from Deep Bottom, Hancock took his two best divisions — under Barlow and John Gibbon — to Warren's support; Barlow had reported himself sick, and Nelson Miles assumed command. David Gregg's division of cavalry accompanied them. The first of the infantry divisions reached the field on the afternoon of August 21, after Warren had repelled the last infantry assault, and the following morning the Second Corps started tearing up the railroad from just behind Warren toward the south. The line had not suffered much during the June foray, when the fatigue parties "merely threw the rails about," but Hancock's men piled all the ties into a pyre and set the rails on top of them, where they bent of their own weight when the ties were lighted. The wrecking continued all day on the twenty-third, after which Miles camped at the charred remains of Reams's Station, five miles below Warren's position at Globe Tavern. Gibbon showed up on the morning of August 24, falling behind a line of breastworks that the Sixth Corps had constructed late in June, during the first abortive attempt to seize the Weldon Railroad. Miles's division dismantled another two or three miles of track below Reams's that day, but late that night reports reached Hancock of a Confederate column as strong as ten thousand men that had left Petersburg headed for either Warren's position or his own. On Thursday morning, August 25, Hancock reconnoitered to the west with cavalry, but when that produced no sign of rebel infantry he still sent Gibbon out to wreak some more havoc with the Weldon line. Those troops had barely left camp when a division of Confederate infantry came rolling toward Reams's Station from the west.[62]

Hancock pulled Gibbon back behind those old entrenchments with Miles, who held the right of the line while Gibbon filed in on the left. Around noon A. P. Hill arrived with several brigades from two other divisions, and two hours later he launched an attack on Miles, who repulsed two successive charges. For a few hours Hancock thought he would be able to hold on until dark, when he hoped to slip away to the main army. Meade sent him a division from the Ninth Corps that was with Warren, as well as a brigade of Hancock's other division, from back at Petersburg, but it was all too late. As evening drew near Hill gathered his forces for one last grand effort, coming at Hancock from the front with infantry while Wade Hampton hovered on Hancock's left with what had been J. E. B. Stuart's cavalry. Rebels started spilling through a gap in front of Miles, who had arranged several New York regiments to cover that vulnerable spot only to see them break and run without firing a shot. Relatively few of the enemy had gotten inside his works, and Miles ordered a borrowed brigade from Gibbon to charge the intruders and hurl them back, but most of the brigade either fled to the rear or took cover. Hancock's line took the shape of a narrow horseshoe, so the rupture on Miles's side left Gibbon's men exposed to fire from the rear, and Gibbon ordered his division to jump to the other side of the parapet. From that position he tried to lead them in a charge against the mounting line of rebels, but most of them would have nothing to do with it. After falling back and reforming, Miles did finally manage to take the rebels in the flank and drive them out, but just then Hampton swept toward Gibbon with dismounted cavalry, forcing him to jump his troops back inside the breastworks. Miles's counterattack ran out of steam, or will, and fell back in confusion, and Gibbon's division fled the field as well. Only the intervention of Gregg's cavalry division stopped the exhilarated rebels from chasing the most famous corps in the Army of the Potomac all the way back to the Jerusalem Plank Road.[63]

The infantry of the Second Corps put up so poor a fight at Reams's Station that Hancock lost fewer than seven hundred in killed and wounded, while well over two thousand men — about one-third of his effective force on the field — threw down their arms and surrendered. He lost nine pieces of artillery, and his own adjutant general was captured, while another of his staff officers was killed. Reports of the shameful display by Hancock's corps spread through the army within hours, provoking more dismay and disgust. One of Grant's staff grumbled that he would rather have seen the two thousand prisoners killed than captured, because "that would look as if they fought," and an aide to Meade admitted that the sound of cannon did nothing any longer except to prepare him for reports of another wholesale surrender by their men. Only the previous day had that same officer commented on the Army of the Potomac's poor showing against Beauregard's little army in the impromptu new fieldworks before Petersburg on June 18: remembering the valiant capture of Confederate works at Kelly's Ford and Rappahannock Station the previous November, he supposed that the men who took those intimidating positions would have walked over Beauregard's makeshift line and shoved him into the Appomattox River. With implicit criticism of Grant's abattoir, though, he reflected that most of those men now filled graves between Petersburg and the Rapidan, or crowded the hospitals at the North.[64]

Probably without meaning to, Hancock corroborated that allusion to Grant's costly combativeness when he blamed the cause of troop failures at Deep Bottom and Reams's Station on the large numbers of new men in his regiments and on "their enormous losses during the campaign, especially in officers." He named several old New York regiments that were now composed almost entirely of recruits and substitutes, some of whom had come to the front in whole new companies under officers who could not even speak English. As much as it might have sounded like an excuse for his failures at Deep Bottom and his resounding defeat at Reams's Station, officers in Hancock's and other corps had begun to complain in growing numbers and greater volume about the caliber of replacements sent their way. A Connecticut captain who sometimes commanded his regiment observed that only fifty-six out of a hundred-man contingent sent from New Haven had even made it into camp; most of them looked healthy enough, but not one of them was an "American." The captain supposed he would be able to incorporate them eventually if they didn't all desert first, but clearly he expected they would. On the very day of Reams's Station an officer in the 9th New Hampshire described the "decimated & rapidly thinning ranks" of his regiment, which had lost half its men in the Crater, and he deplored the "aliens, vagabonds, outcasts & sneaking cowards" who were sent to take their places; his fellow officer in another company recalled that only thirty of the 9th's last hundred recruits had ever reported for duty. A private in the 11th New Hampshire, of the same brigade, felt personally insulted by the "foreigners" his state sent to replenish its veteran organizations.[65]

The problem was not unique to the Army of the Potomac, although the dreadful losses there made it more obvious; complaints about recruits were coming from everywhere that summer. While George Crook's army groped for Jubal Early, one substitute was found in the 23rd Ohio who had deserted earlier from the same regiment, after having initially deserted from the Confederate army in the Kanawha River valley. That man faced a firing squad within hours of his arrest, but Colonel Rutherford B. Hayes of the 23rd judged that their reinforcements included about as many professional bounty jumpers as willing recruits. A captain with the Twentieth Corps, before Atlanta, seemed content with his recruits earlier in the year, although he had no illusions about their pecuniary motives, but by mid-August he calculated that 60 percent of the men sent to Sherman's army deserted on the way. Similar rates of desertion encouraged provost marshals to send substitutes and volunteers alike to their regiments in closely guarded coffles — to the indignation of the reenlisted veterans and conscientious recruits among them.[66] Many, and sometimes most, of those who actually made it to the front either absconded soon thereafter or broke down under the strain of field service. Soaring bounties had lured so many men of frail health and so many underdeveloped boys (some of them as young as twelve) that whole contingents of recruits disappeared into the hospitals, never to return. Rarely, by August, did any of them show much real promise.[67]

Those dubious replacements would not have been so necessary, or perhaps so conspicuously unsatisfactory, without the staggering losses — particularly in Virginia, where unprecedented butchery had siphoned whole armies into the vortex from the Atlantic and Gulf coasts. For the prudent citizen, that campaign cooled the last embers of military ambition, and those who betrayed any whims in that direction risked having their friends in the army reprimand them for such lunacy. That only accelerated the cycle of draft levies, substitute enlistments, desertion, and more draft levies. Recruit-swollen regiments became so notorious for bad conduct under fire that the burden of battle fell all the more frequently to the veteran — as one reenlisted man noticed a few weeks before the first of his two wounds. From the shrinking number of staid and true veterans came outraged demands for "a vigorous, sweeping conscription," without exemptions of any kind, like the more comprehensive, continuous draft that kept the Confederate armies filled. Such a draft was never imposed on the Northern public, but the fear of it seriously dampened public enthusiasm for the contest. Marsena Patrick, Meade's provost marshal, understood from everyone he knew back home and everything he read that the North had fallen into "universal depression," and that any attempt at a real draft would be resisted, as it had been the summer before. An unlettered woman in southern New Hampshire, who feared conscription from both ends, corroborated that diagnosis: she dreaded that the lottery would take her sons, and that opposition to the draft would spark "sivil war all over the unitted states." She had heard that the "coper heads" were arming themselves for an uprising, and even that they had killed some Union men in her state.[68]

Confederate resilience and a draft-induced resurgence of interest in peace were not the only issues weighing against Lincoln's reelection. Corresponding with cunning if dubious representatives of the Confederate government, Horace Greeley had seriously compromised the administration with his quixotic effort at brokering peace negotiations. In his initial communications with those agents, Greeley withheld Lincoln's prerequisites of reunion and "the abandonment of slavery." Those two requirements only entered the dialogue when Greeley and Lincoln's private secretary crossed into Canada at Niagara Falls to meet the Confederate emissaries, who pounced on those last-minute demands as evidence of Northern perfidy. Rather than illustrating Lincoln's eagerness to make peace on the same grounds he had articulated since his congressional message of eight months before, Greeley's fruitless and disingenuous exchange made the president seem determined to prolong hostilities by insisting on impossible conditions. The opposition press made the most of that point, reminding the public that the president and his supporters had asserted, at the outset of hostilities, that reunion constituted their only aim in the war. In the face of imminent conscription — with an acute shortage of substitutes and no commutation — Lincoln's additional insistence on abolition seemed unreasonably stubborn to hundreds of thousands of voters liable to military service, most of whom still perceived no convincing evidence that the South could ever be beaten. In addition to steadfast opponents of the war and those of shaken confidence, that constituency now included those who embraced the cause of national unity only until their own active participation became effectively mandatory.[69]

The freelance diplomacy at Niagara nevertheless infuriated Confederate observers. Last-ditch advocates in Richmond and Charleston reproved the Southern participants for even suggesting an appeal for terms, and their intransigence might have fortified Northern arguments that the Confederacy was unconquerable, but some Southern critics hinted at their own preference for a settlement when they pondered what damage the episode might have done to the hope of installing a peace man in the White House. Accurately gauging the potential for Republican propaganda, they speculated that the conference could smear Northern proponents of peace with suspicions of being in league with the enemy.[70]

Greeley's blunder may have left his subscribers with the impression that Lincoln was too demanding of the enemy, but that did not stop him from criticizing Lincoln for precisely the opposite reason only a couple of weeks later. Taking umbrage at the president's failure to sign their joint bill for a more punitive reconstruction policy, Ben Wade and Henry Winter Davis composed a scathing rebuke that Greeley published in the *Tribune*. If Lincoln was too stringent in his peace discussions with Confederates, Greeley seemed willing to imply, he was also too lenient toward those same Confederates in his dealings with Congress. In what became known as the Wade-Davis Manifesto, the Radical pair claimed that Lincoln had defied and usurped the authority of Congress with his rejection of their bill, and that his proposal for establishing new Southern state governments with loyal minorities anticipated wielding their electoral votes for his own reelection. Every indictment and suspicion that conservative Democrats had borne against Lincoln over the previous three years was replicated, either in tone or content, by the two outraged Republicans, who clearly hoped to force the president to withdraw his name from the presidential contest. Failing that, Davis hoped that the peace men would reject George McClellan as the Democratic nominee, causing the War Democrats to bolt, in which case he hoped the Radicals could form an alliance with them as a means of "saving our principles & policy & the nation." The conservative Democratic press greeted the Wade-Davis attack with glee, relishing the damage it portended for Lincoln and his party. By the end of the month Greeley repented of having tried to unhorse Lincoln, and pledged himself to prevent a "Copperhead triumph," but at that point it seemed too late to undo the harm.[71]

Thurlow Weed, the political sage and champion of administration interests in New York, corroborated the bleak assessment of popular opinion. Early in August he had confided to President Lincoln that he considered his reelection "an impossibility," and that the same impression would soon be confirmed "through other channels." Henry Raymond, chairman of the Republican National Committee and editor of the Lincoln-friendly *New York Times*, had admitted to Weed that all was lost for Lincoln without some "prompt and bold" action, and to Lincoln's new secretary of the treasury Raymond had conceded that it would be "a work of very great labor to reelect" him; moments after he left Weed's presence, Raymond wrote the president directly to report that "the tide is setting strongly against us," and to suggest forming a committee to propose peace terms to Jefferson Davis, based on "the supremacy of the Constitution." "The people are wild for Peace," Weed had declared, adding that all the while the president seemed unwilling to make peace without the insurmountable demand for Southern acquiescence to abolition. Lincoln evidently concurred with Weed's pessimism, and between the battles at the Weldon Railroad and Reams's Station he admitted as much in a document that he asked his cabinet officers to endorse on the reverse, without allowing them to read it. Once they had signed, he sealed it tightly with glue and put it in his desk until the election. It pledged his cooperation with the new president-elect (whom he expected would be McClellan) in the effort to defeat the Confederacy before inauguration day. As Lincoln saw it, McClellan could only win the presidency by promising to end the war, which would leave them a mere four months to crush the rebellion together before McClellan had to begin making good on his promise.[72]

Disdain for Lincoln or despair for his chances came from every quarter. He grew more unpopular every day, thought George Templeton Strong, who saw the hardiest Republicans shaking their heads at the odds. Richard Henry Dana Jr., a conservative Whig of Lincoln's own school, doubted after meeting Lincoln in August that he was "up to the office" of president, and thought he should not have been nominated, at least until the final hour. "With him," Dana said, "there is but a step between the popular & the pitiable, and I am afraid the Nov. election may find him in the latter category." Noticing all the Republican newspapers that were harping on the issue of peace, to the apparent detriment of the administration, one Peace Democrat supposed they did so to steal the thunder of the Democratic nominee, who was to be chosen at the Chicago convention at the end of August.[73]

The draft, inflation, and the November election were the three main topics in many a civilian's letters at that juncture, and the three seemed inextricable from each other. Gold had climbed above 250 in July, while Early's army cavorted in Maryland, and it remained at 250 after his return to Virginia. Soldiers calculated their monthly pay in gold, and realized that it had fallen to barely a third of its original value; if a lieutenant exchanged greenbacks for gold, he found that he only earned about forty dollars a month, instead of a hundred. Every fluctuation in the price of gold ignited a panic that created its own crisis and closed one business after another. Uncertainty led to rampant speculation in gold, which contributed to its rise and fall on the slightest good or bad news, and that bred even more uncertainty. Credit tightened up in the financial centers, especially after the new government restrictions and taxes on the circulation of state banks discouraged investment in them, and prices everywhere soared higher still. Plenty of cash circulated at Council Bluffs, Iowa, if only because of westward migration, but costs had skyrocketed at that gateway to the Trans-Missouri. In far-off California farmers found seed costs high but grain prices low, and no one seemed to be spending anything if they could avoid it. The most basic commodities rose beyond the reach of the working class, and the poor blamed the greenback's increasing worthlessness on the government's massive war debt, raising a hue and cry for repudiation among the poor and their generally Democratic spokesmen. Jay Cooke, Secretary Chase's principal war bond salesman, had some difficulty trying to reassure his own father that the public credit remained sound, but within weeks Cooke had sold other Americans more than $70 million worth of the latest issue of government bonds, which paid 10 percent interest, redeemable in gold. Eventually army paymasters found that soldiers would accept small-denomination bonds in lieu of part of the cash that was owed to them, which saved the treasury from printing that much more currency.[74]

With the president's latest troop demand coming due in September, the draft increasingly rivaled the economy as a political issue, at least in households with eligible men. The more probable a draft seemed for the home district, the less likely would a correspondent be to express much enthusiasm, or hope, for Lincoln, or to find him very popular among the neighbors. For soldiers, though, the election certainly outweighed the draft as a matter of interest, but even the army's customary support for the administration was beginning to erode. Soldiers still praised the president or damned his critics, relentlessly comparing the most sincere of them to treacherous rebels, but in many cases the vigor and volume of those endorsements had withered since spring, and a growing number suddenly had little good — or something decidedly bad — to say about Mr. Lincoln.[75]

"Lincoln is losing ground in the Army daily," conceded an officer near Petersburg, who wanted peace only under honorable conditions and preferred to keep up the fight rather than accept disunion. That War Democrat feared only a peace platform at the Chicago convention, but that was precisely what some soldiers wanted, at least in the Army of the Potomac. "I have always thought our President is an old fogy and don't know his business," wrote a Maine lieutenant, barely two weeks before he was captured; with Lincoln at the helm, he considered the war "an outrageous waste of life and treasure," and declared that he would never vote for him. Watching the dead and wounded come in from a fight near Winchester, a New Hampshire soldier doubted that the South could be beaten if the war lasted a decade, and probably not then, so he hoped for a new president who would negotiate a settlement. A New York sergeant who despaired of Old Abe's reelection in mid-August acknowledged that McClellan's star rose steadily among the soldiers, and although he had not made up his own mind he nevertheless admitted that he and his discouraged comrades were prepared to support "any man that will put an end . . . to . . . this awful butchery." This man seems to have voted for Lincoln in 1860, but he suspected that to do so again would only assure endless and useless war.[76] A captain in the Regular Army, whose father was attending the Democratic convention as a delegate, adjured him to "go for McClellan *first, last,* and all the time," and a staff captain in the Ninth Corps admitted to a rapidly increasing disillusionment accompanied by growing sympathy for McClellan, although he retained some loyalty to Lincoln. A volunteer serving on detached duty with a battery of U.S. Regulars in the Ninth Corps found most of them betting on McClellan, especially if they had served under him. The commander of a short-term artillery company remarked on the opening day of the convention that the country would have been much better off "had Abraham Lincoln dropped into his grave two years ago," perhaps calculating that the complicating factor of emancipation would never have been introduced.[77]

In armies that had not paid so heavy a portion of the butcher's bill, the president could count on more loyalty. A Michigan man on duty at Decatur, Alabama, judged McClellan a firm enough Union man to cleave to, but he acknowledged that most of his comrades thought of Lincoln as "next to the Lord." A battery commander with Sherman assumed that if Lincoln were not reelected it would mean the soldiers would have to return home in disgrace, in which case he predicted that "Blood will flow like water at the North." John Chipman Gray Jr., a Bostonian of a conservative but nonpartisan bent, had recoiled in horror at the administration's arbitrary arrests in 1862, and he still viewed the Emancipation Proclamation as a radical and counterproductive doctrine. As August wore on, though, and as he watched the siege of Fort Morgan grind to a close, he hoped that McClellan would be nominated only because both Lincoln and McClellan were adamant that the Union had to be preserved. He deemed both the lanky Westerner and the stocky general honest, but considered them both unusually prone to surrounding themselves with poor advisors. He thought he would probably vote for Lincoln, since the "bulk of the republican party" seemed more devoted to reunion than the Democrats, but he wished there were a new man in the running who was not honor-bound to support immediate and universal emancipation. Colonel Hayes of the 23rd Ohio, who would stand as a presidential candidate himself only a dozen years hence, likewise hoped that McClellan would be the Democrats' nominee for the same reason as Gray — because he would still fight on to restore the Union; he also expected that Little Mac might win. Even outside Atlanta, though, a cavalryman accentuated his contempt for the Lincoln and Johnson ticket, and his esteem for McClellan, by swearing that he would vote for the general whether he was nominated or not — and that was before the disasters to Stoneman and McCook, which involved that trooper's own regiment. A Wisconsin soldier in the Army of the Tennessee backed Lincoln, but worried that Sherman's army would give McClellan "an overwhelming majority."[78]

Could the soldiers have voted, Lincoln's weakest support among them would have come from the prisoners in Confederate hands, masses of whom accused him of heartless indifference toward their plight, and at the end of August a diluted expression of their resentment surfaced in the memorial carried through the lines from Andersonville. For many who had languished so long and watched so many comrades die without any sign of sympathy from Washington, exasperation had reached such heights that they stood ready to forsake their flag and cast their lot with the Confederacy. The antagonism of those tens of thousands of interned unfortunates would cost Lincoln none of their votes at the polls, of course, but many of them had fathers and brothers who would be able to cast a ballot, as at least one prisoner's father and several other correspondents reminded Abraham Lincoln directly. The parents of a Vermont cavalryman who perished at Andersonville established a permanent rebuke to the chief executive on a cenotaph in their village cemetery, blaming their boy's death on the absolute neglect of President Lincoln.[79]

Mr. Raymond of the *Times* fully recognized the president's precarious electoral situation, both in the army and on the home front, where key states like Pennsylvania, Indiana, and Lincoln's own Illinois seemed ready to vote against him. Raymond did what he could to help, and like any experienced political partisan he first advised raising a great deal of money for the campaign, but most of his own contributions came in journalistic form. In one editorial he defended Lincoln's call for another draft, and in another he ridiculed the anger that the levy had reportedly aroused, but mainly he relied on the subtle misrepresentation of bad news. While whole brigades of Union soldiers refused to follow their officers to the attack, or gave themselves up at the first fire, Raymond's headlines focused on "Grant's tremendous tenacity." When an inferior Confederate force captured three thousand of Warren's men, the *Times* reported instead on the eight hundred rebels who fell into Union hands, belatedly admitting (on the back page) only that the enemy "claimed" to have captured the three thousand. After the whole story of Hancock's disaster had already come out, Raymond still insisted that the enemy had been repulsed at Reams's Station, and he strategically misplaced Edwin Stanton's hopeful estimate of total Confederate casualties for the past fortnight to make his readers think A. P. Hill had lost ten thousand men just in the contest with Hancock. Using the passive voice to keep his headlines encouraging, Raymond mentioned "several pieces of artillery captured," placing it in the column of headlines to imply that Hancock had taken the guns from the enemy, rather than the other way around. Remarking in his August 27 edition that only "reverses to our arms" could lead to Lincoln's defeat in November, Raymond marshaled style, vocabulary, and page composition to the task of disguising those reverses as they occurred.[80]

He might have saved himself the trouble, for in the end the Democrats restored Mr. Lincoln's popularity for him. The convention met on August 29, in the same Wigwam where Lincoln had been nominated four years and half a million soldiers' lives previously, and proceeded to tear their party in two just as the Democratic delegates of 1860 had done. That, cautioned former president Franklin Pierce, was precisely the danger Democrats must avoid, if they were to escape "absolute ruin." The November election would be a "tempest," Pierce warned, and unity was more important than which candidate the convention nominated. He particularly noted that "New York, Pennsylvania & Ohio must cordially concur."[81]

The convention split almost immediately into war and peace factions. Proponents of continuing the war, at least for the purpose of reunion, leaned heavily toward McClellan, but the peace men had gravitated behind no single candidate. Prospective nominees abounded, scheming with and against each other and denigrating McClellan all the while. Benjamin Harris, of Maryland, denounced McClellan as a tyrant because of his part in the arrest of the Maryland legislature in 1861, and said he would not vote for him if he won the convention's approval; one delegate called Harris a traitor to the party, at which Harris spun around and knocked the man out of his chair. Clement Vallandigham, the former congressman whom Lincoln had expelled from the country while he was a candidate for governor of Ohio, had come back to influence the direction of the convention, if nothing more, and with some assistance he managed to incorporate a plank in the platform declaring that the war was a failure and calling for an armistice pending negotiations. That provocative proposition had to abide alongside the more ambiguous, generally acceptable slogan of "Union under the Constitution," and a reproach to the administration for abandoning the captured soldier to indefinite confinement by suspending prisoner exchanges. With that hybrid philosophy articulated, the peace men acceded to McClellan's nomination, but they remained strong enough to insist on George Pendleton of Ohio, a firm advocate of peace, as his running mate.[82]

Some of McClellan's greatest admirers expected him to refuse the nomination over Vallandigham's call for an armistice, and the peace men may have anticipated the same result. Two weeks before the convention, a New Hampshire private who supposed that peace men dominated the Democratic Party believed McClellan would accept no call from them: "I have too much respect for him," he wrote. A Maine man in Sheridan's new army also doubted that McClellan would "be mixed with them." A battery commander who had spent most of his war in comfortable quarters near Washington opined to his brother that Mac was "done for in the Army" if he assented to the Chicago platform. While his champions and followers waited for his reply, McClellan privately promised that he would either take the nomination on his own terms or decline altogether. In his letter to the Democratic National Committee he espoused restoration of the Union as the only legitimate object of the war, but he claimed that both sides had already fought enough to satisfy their sectional honor, and he conceded the propriety of negotiations as soon as it became clear that "our present adversaries" were willing to accept restoration of the Union; if that failed, however, he would resume the contest to the bitter end. With that concession to the peace faction, he accepted the nomination.[83]

That letter appears to have doomed him among the soldiers. Cheers had been ringing through the North and throughout the army over the nomination of a firm Union man who would, unlike the incumbent, confine himself to saving the country and resist social revolution. From semiliterate privates to full generals had come gushing praise for the Democrats' candidate, especially before the details of the Chicago platform worked their way into the discussion. A Michigan private described regimental bands warming up their instruments for impromptu concerts to celebrate the nomination, and throngs of McClellan men making the woods echo with their shouts. The nomination moved an Indiana veteran with the Tenth Corps to reveal that he wanted all Republicans defeated, including his own hated governor, Oliver Morton. Joe Hooker bet that McClellan would glide to victory over Lincoln, thanks to Grant's brutal work, and another general's wife sent her husband tidings of the nomination with near-delirious relief. The father of a boy who was even then fighting Hood's army before Atlanta rejoiced at word of McClellan's selection, calling him "one of the best men in the nation" and welcoming his succession to the "failure" Lincoln.[84]

Then, by the time McClellan's acceptance letter reached its destination, the particulars of the party platform had emerged, and the mood changed abruptly. A New York Democrat confided to Samuel Barlow, the nominee's advisor, that "the enthusiasm with which the nomination of McClellan is received is dampened a little by the platform," and the 23rd Ohio's Colonel Hayes corroborated him, supposing that the general would have carried a flattering proportion of the soldier vote if only the party had backed him with a better platform. Men who had had enough of fighting stood behind him all the more, but firm Union men scowled at the peace plank. Colonel Charles Wainwright, a staunch War Democrat and a devoted admirer of McClellan, regretted the nomination on the grounds that Little Mac would never survive the "rascality" of Washington, concluding that "an honest, fair man has no more chance there than he has of making a fortune as a horse dealer." A New Hampshire captain in Butler's army explained that "McClellan is a very good man, but we *can't stand the Platform,*" and a fellow New Hampshireman in the Ninth Corps chided his sister for her "Copperhead Poison" when she complimented McClellan. "Peace Resolutions don't go down with Soldiers," he informed her. A Michigan soldier surmised that McClellan might win the soldiers over with some other running mate, but not with Pendleton. After reading the candidate's acceptance letter, a captain in one of Butler's black regiments offered to bet a hundred dollars that he could not win, and an officer with Sherman reported that "all gassing and enthusiasm for Mc" had evaporated with the reading of the Chicago platform. "Lincoln's stock here prior to this had been tremendously on the decline," he wrote, "but the inconsistencies of the party at Chicago has whirled everybody about again."[85]

This abrupt metamorphosis should have sparked immediate concern among McClellan's partisans, had they had time to assess it. Then, just as newspapers of all political stripes reproduced the text of the Chicago platform for their subscribers' consideration, came the news that Atlanta had fallen. Suddenly the end lay in sight again, and even some of the peace men — at home and in the ranks — began to question the wisdom of giving up the fight when pressing on to victory might be the shortest path to their goal.

5

Horseman and Horse They Knew

❧ THREE WEEKS AFTER sending Stoneman and McCook on the raid that nearly destroyed their respective commands, General Sherman made one more attempt to cut Atlanta's last rail lines with cavalry, and this time he sent his most flamboyant officer of that arm. Judson Kilpatrick had last been heard from during the failed raid on Richmond, the previous winter, which had resulted only in the death of Colonel Ulric Dahlgren, the loss of several hundred horses and men, and a nasty political contretemps over Colonel Dahlgren's evident plans to capture and kill the Confederate president and his cabinet. On August 18 Sherman gave him essentially the same mission as McCook had had in the mounted raid of late July, directing him to tear up the Atlanta & West Point tracks southwest of the city before moving on to the Macon & Western at Lovejoy's Station, where Stoneman and McCook were to have met. As in his previous escapades, Kilpatrick's accomplishment and glory in the undertaking were more evident in the telling than in the event. He whittled at the West Point rail line a little, then bounded over to the Macon road, below Jonesboro, where a combined force of infantry and cavalry drove him off, but he circled south to make another try at Lovejoy's. There he was almost treated to the fate of Stoneman and McCook, with the same infantry facing him in front while rebel cavalry assailed him from behind. He managed to fight his way through, but he could only get back to his own lines by making a complete circuit around Atlanta, by the east. For all his boasting of having disabled the railroads badly enough that service could not be restored within ten days, trains were running out of Atlanta the day after Kilpatrick turned for his own lines.[1]

After Wheeler dispersed both wings of the raid by Stoneman and

McCook, General Hood had sent him north with most of the cavalry, into Tennessee, to disrupt Sherman's supply line. Complaints of short rations started leaking into Atlanta from Sherman's lines during the third week of August, leading to the impression that Wheeler's raid had inflicted some damage. Sherman, meanwhile, planned to follow up the raids of McCook and Kilpatrick with his entire army, and when Union forces started disappearing from the works east and north of the city, Hood was left with too few horsemen for effective reconnaissance. The Yankees reappeared to the west a couple of days later, taking position from the Chattahoochee River, above the city, to the Atlanta & West Point, below it. Hood eventually deduced that they aimed to stretch their lines to Jonesboro, on the Macon & Western, which would have amounted to the chessboard equivalent of check: with all his rail lines either destroyed or in enemy hands, Hood would have no choice but to evacuate the city. Giving the preponderance of his army to General Hardee on the evening of August 30, Hood sent him to defend Jonesboro, twenty miles south of the city center.[2]

Sherman ordered the West Point line thoroughly destroyed, with the ties piled and burned beneath the rails, which his wrecking crews then twisted around trees to prevent them from being easily straightened and used again. A dozen miles of the track vanished in that way. In a hypocritical touch, Sherman filled in some of the railroad cuts with logs, dirt, and rocks, and he ordered the rubble surreptitiously mined with primed artillery shells, so they would explode if anyone tried to dig them out. When his own troops faced Confederate land mines a few months later, the general would regard them as uncivilized instruments of assassination, rather than legitimate weapons of war, and he would force rebel prisoners to dig them up at risk of their own lives.[3]

Once the railroad had been utterly eradicated, Sherman started swinging his three armies south and east in concentric arcs, with the southernmost of them headed for Jonesboro. O. O. Howard's Army of the Tennessee arrived first, crossing the Flint River and taking position on high ground east of it, with a marshy ravine in front. With his own corps and Stephen D. Lee's, Hardee lit into Howard in the afternoon of August 31, pounding at his line for hours without dislodging him. At considerable cost in casualties Patrick Cleburne, commanding Hardee's corps, gained a foothold on the left, as did Lee, on the right, but then Lee was driven back with two of his generals badly wounded. During the night, George Thomas's Army of the Cumberland began arriving on the field to join Howard, while Hood called Lee's demoralized and straggling corps back to Atlanta, leaving Hardee facing twice as many of the enemy with only half the force. Hardee pulled back nearer Jonesboro, built what breastworks he could in the few hours remaining, and awaited the inevitable. Four different corps attacked him, reaching so far around his right flank that he had to curl it back, stretching his front into a single rank, and by the afternoon his line was bent almost double. His left gave way, but rallied farther back, and the day ended with his two wings fighting virtually back-to-back. When Thomas's troops reached a road that cut him off from Atlanta altogether, Hardee fell back on Lovejoy's Station.[4]

Hardee's brave fight at Jonesboro saved what was left of Hood's army. Hood remained in the city with Alexander Stewart's corps and a few thousand Georgia militia under Major General Gustavus Smith — who had for one accidental day commanded what became the Army of Northern Virginia. Stephen Lee's corps spent the first of September marching back to Atlanta, and when it arrived Hood decided to abandon the place. That afternoon, as Hardee withdrew to Lovejoy's Station, Hood led the rest of the Army of Tennessee out of Atlanta on roads to the east, swinging south only after putting enough distance between his army and the enemy at Jonesboro. Union batteries languidly shelled the city, more for the sake of harassment, but the real noise came from Confederate saboteurs. All the extra ordnance, on more than eighty rail cars, went up in one enormous blast, simultaneously demolishing the arsenal, iron foundries, and the rolling mill where all those twisted rails might have been straightened. The explosion lighted the sky like the first glow of dawn for the few divisions of Yankees lingering in their camps on the Chattahoochee, while others heard it from a distance of twenty miles, and debris flew half a mile. The next afternoon Hood arrived at McDonough, a few miles east of Lovejoy's, where he reunited the remnants of his three corps. Hood sent the militia another dozen miles south, toward the prison camps, where they could guard against any cavalry threat in that direction.[5]

Federals who threw a few probing shells into Atlanta the next morning failed to raise any reply, and as the wavy blue lines of infantry started prowling thitherward out came the mayor and city council, looking for someone to whom they might surrender the city. They met the Eastern troops of the Twentieth Corps. The mayor identified himself as a nephew of John C. Calhoun, first among fire-eating Southern secessionists, but His Honor acknowledged that he had been a delegate for John Bell and Edward Everett in 1860 himself, and an opponent of secession. With the surrender, the troops fell into marching formation and filed into the city with their bands playing, and once inside they heard many of the citizens professing the same Union sentiments as their mayor, which may have explained how he came to be elected. Brigadier General Alpheus Williams rode at the head of his division as he led it into town that evening: he heard a window slide open, and then a woman's voice shouted, "Welcome!"[6]

The contending armies exchanged places as country dancers might execute a do-si-do, with the Federals moving north into the city from the western side while the Confederates marched out by the east and south, to hover on the perimeter as their enemies had. Sherman's Yankees had seen little in the way of civilization over the preceding four months (Georgia seemed half a century behind Ohio, thought a captain from Cleveland), and they toured the captured city with voracious curiosity whenever they could steal an hour from duty. Atlanta had obviously known prosperous times, they saw, but those days seemed long past: the dirt-encrusted tourists gaped at the devastation caused by the explosion of the ordnance train, and gawked at all the substantial houses pockmarked and perforated by shellfire — or knocked down altogether, or lying in cinders. Dugouts much like soldiers' bombproofs could be found in back yards where families had taken shelter against the shelling. A sprawling cemetery had been churned red with the dirt mounded over fresh graves. Three lines of intricate entrenchments surrounded the city, and the veterans among them recognized how many of them would have died had Sherman opted for a frontal assault.[7] Near the battlefields of Peachtree Creek and Atlanta they found crude tombs of fence rails and dirt, imperfectly covering heaps of Confederate dead whose flesh (as some could detect through the crevices) was already falling off the bones in the intense heat. A lieutenant came upon some of his men contemplating the skull of some Confederate Yorick. Atlanta residents who had fled during the siege started trickling back in, but they had no food and no means of buying any. Rather than use his barely adequate stream of rations to feed them, less than a week into the occupation Sherman ordered the inhabitants out of the city, loyal or not, and soon thereafter scores of wagons started leaving daily.[8]

Telegraph keys relayed confirmation of Atlanta's fall as far as Washington and Grant's headquarters late on the very night of its capture, and by morning it was all over the streets of New York. If the equivocation of the Democratic Party platform had not crippled McClellan's presidential ambitions, this news did, dispelling the image of a perpetual standoff that had blighted the military effort. The *Richmond Examiner* had predicted as much, three days before the city fell, assuring readers in the Confederate capital that Northern peace sentiments would evaporate with the capture of either Atlanta or Petersburg. As Lincoln's secretary of the navy noted, the idea of suing for peace rang an incongruous note in the wake of so significant a victory. There passed a brief interlude of doubt or disbelief, born of the false promises of earlier rumors, but those who worried most about waning enthusiasm for crushing the rebellion regarded Atlanta's demise as the end of the crisis, if only it proved true.[9]

Atlanta completely rejuvenated the drooping spirits of Union soldiers as soon as they heard it was theirs. "What glorious news we have from Sherman," wrote a staff lieutenant in the Ninth Corps, before Petersburg. "Everyone . . . feel[s] vastly more hopeful. . . . Things are so much better than a month ago." When a staff officer at New Orleans learned of Sherman's success he urged his wavering father to "stick hard to Lincoln," advising him that it was better to have "a poor pilot" than to replace him at a perilous stage in the voyage. A sergeant in Butler's army corroborated that "Sherman's victory is having a good effect on our rank & file." The news cheered men in hospitals behind the lines, who naively supposed that now it was just a matter of Grant strolling into Richmond before it was all over. Union officers in the Confederate prison at Charleston, South Carolina, rejoiced when they heard that Atlanta had been evacuated, and they learned of it only three days after their comrades marched into it. Even in Confederate hands they seemed to comprehend that the Northern war party's favor had been fading, and they understood how abruptly such a prize might reverse the tide of public opinion.[10]

The Union officers held at Charleston heard of Atlanta's demise about the same time the enlisted men at Andersonville did, despite Andersonville's relative proximity to the city. Hood positioned himself south of Atlanta to foil Sherman or any of his cavalry from making a dash at Andersonville — where, in evident ignorance of their physical condition, Hood supposed the prisoners could be released and armed to fight against him. Not until September 5 did orders go out to the Confederate commissary of prisoners, Brigadier General John Winder, to move his Macon and Andersonville inmates to Charleston and Savannah; by then the news of Hood's defeat was circulating inside the Andersonville stockade, courtesy of a handful of prisoners from the Jonesboro fight. The removal order came from the adjutant general in Richmond, who also enjoined Winder to hurry up the work on another stockade prison he had already begun at Millen, Georgia, on the other side of the state from Andersonville, about midway between Augusta and Savannah.[11]

Mortality alone had finally begun to alleviate the overcrowding at Andersonville. Since the peak population of 33,006, on August 9, the prisoners had been dying at the rate of more than a hundred per day, and on the morning of September 5 exactly 31,480 remained, of whom 2,325 lay in the prison hospital, outside the main stockade. Some shelter had at last been provided for at least some of those inside the stockade, in the form of five long, open sheds along the north wall of the prison, but those crude structures could not accommodate one man in twenty, even with two floors in each. A shortage of nails plagued the housing efforts: Union cavalry had burned the train carrying the last requisition of them. Lumber contractors had also been demanding prices 60 percent higher than the government's maximum permitted compensation, precluding the purchase of any more, and that dearth of materials prevented either the framing of new sheds or the siding of those that already stood. The post quartermaster had chosen to give as many men as possible as much cover as his supplies permitted, dedicating most of the boards and nails to roofing and flooring. Hammers were still ringing on the fifth shed even as the orders came to move everyone out.[12]

From his headquarters at Macon, Howell Cobb commanded the few regiments of Georgia Reserves, consisting mainly of teenaged boys too young for conscription and men who were just over the draft-age limit of forty-five. A couple of those regiments served as guards at Andersonville, and at Hood's order Cobb offered another one to help move the prisoners. The 5th Georgia Reserves came down by rail that night, and the ladies of Americus met them at Anderson Station with as lavish a banquet as the times permitted. Sergeants from the garrison held mandatory roll calls inside the stockade, misleading the prisoners with the rumor that they were going to be taken elsewhere for exchange, as a means of deterring them from trying to escape during the inevitable confusion of the transfer. The story of Hood's disaster had preceded that ruse by a full day, though, and the more skeptical Yankees saw through the deception, but wishful thinking lent the lie the aroma of truth. A sudden shortage of certain rations in the camp, and the distribution of some spoiled food — perhaps resulting from the extensive damage done to Southern railroads — only enhanced the willingness to believe.[13]

The prison had been divided into squads of ninety men apiece, with three squads constituting a detachment, and the guards instructed the first eighteen detachments to have their things ready to move by midnight. Excitement reigned all night, and many of those who had no orders to move found it difficult to sleep because of the constant chatter among those who did. The midnight warning notwithstanding, it was not until the morning of September 7 that anyone started out the gates. Those in the hospital, or those too sick or lame to walk, had to remain behind: only the healthy could pass through the gates, and that helped to perforate the pretense of exchange, since it would have been in Confederate interests to exchange the disabled first. That first day, nearly fifteen hundred ragged prisoners marched, shuffled, or limped the half mile to Anderson Station to board cattle cars for Macon, where civilian refugees crowded the depot. The prisoners were not allowed to disembark there during a long layover, after which the trains turned east toward Savannah. Not enough transportation could be rounded up to carry all those who marched out on September 7, even at sixty men to a car, and they came back inside that night intensely dejected, but the next day they all returned to the depot and started off. Three thousand more filed out of the prison that Thursday, and another thousand on the ninth, leaving one slope of Stockade Creek almost deserted. "Flankers" complicated the evacuation by slipping into lower-numbered detachments under the names of men who had died, and many who doubted the purported exchange sold their places to the more gullible. At least a few desperate men who had grown too weak or ill to cover the distance to the depot gambled on the exchange rumor and appealed for comrades to help them walk there and climb on the cars. By the tenth of September seventy-five hundred men had been shipped off to Savannah, filling a small new stockade in that city to its capacity, and over the next three days another ninety-five hundred were counted off at Andersonville for Augusta and Charleston. Somewhere along the way, depending on the candor of their guards, they all learned that the promise of exchange had been nothing but a hoax.[14]

That reduced Andersonville's population by more than half. The guards evicted all the healthy tenants from the five new sheds, installing the sickest men from the stockade in their places. Over the next few days Confederate surgeons examined them there for admission to the hospital, but the departure of so many of the most robust prisoners deprived many of their ailing comrades of their only conscientious caretakers. An Iowa sergeant whom a doctor entered on the hospital register could not take advantage of that consideration because his legs had drawn up with scurvy and he could no longer walk; none of his friends remained to carry him to the hospital, and neither would any of the strangers within earshot inquire around the prison for him to see if anyone from his regiment had been left behind.[15]

The rail line to Andersonville had borne far more than its share of traffic that year without much maintenance, for most of that region's available ties and rails had been funneled to the repair of damaged tracks elsewhere in the state, or in Alabama. The rolling stock needed attention, too, but parts were hard to come by. Accidents were not unusual on the Southwestern Railroad anymore: a month previously several people had been killed, and dozens of soldiers injured, in a mishap below Macon. The cars moved slowly, but the last train bound for Macon on September 13 went off the track about four miles into its journey, smashing several cars and killing a few guards and prisoners. The next morning, after sleeping on the railroad embankment under a close guard, several hundred men who had thought they were on their way home made the long march back to Andersonville; some of them could not make it on foot, and wagons or ambulances had to come out to cart them back. The deadly mishap ended the grand exodus that might have emptied the stockade altogether, and it was three days before any more trains could get through at all. Samuel Melvin, a young heavy-artilleryman from Massachusetts whose term of service had already expired, had rushed to join that last trainload in such haste that he left all his belongings behind; he returned to the stockade in an ambulance, almost completely destitute, and that night he came down with the first bout of an intestinal ailment that would kill him in ten days.[16]

Hood and Sherman agreed on an exchange of prisoners captured from each other on the battlefield — the only type of general exchange Edwin Stanton would still allow — and eighteen hundred of Sherman's men made their way from Andersonville back to Atlanta once the railroad had been repaired. Until the end of the month fewer than twenty-six hundred more left the stockade, but that brought the population down to a quarter of its August maximum, and closer to the number the prison could adequately contain. Had it not been for the disproportionate number of sick who had been left behind, mortality might have declined significantly, but by the end of September the prisoners were dying faster than ever. A Confederate surgeon who inspected the prison that summer had emphasized the crowding, advising a maximum density of fifteen thousand men, and he had recommended barracks, along with improvements in diet and sanitation. The barracks had started going up within days of that surgeon's report, and barely half the suggested fifteen thousand men occupied the prison, but with no salutary effect. On August 9, one prisoner died for every 343 in the prison, and on September 30, the death rate had risen to one prisoner in 107. On September 29 the number of Union soldiers buried in the prisoners' cemetery surpassed the number of living prisoners lying in the stockade and the hospital combined, and that circumstance was never reversed thereafter. Diarrhea, dysentery, and scurvy were claiming the preponderance of the victims by then, and the prison diet of unbolted cornmeal without vegetables had already been identified as the principal cause of those diseases. Most of the Yankees who were left behind already suffered from one or more of those complaints.[17]

General Winder had been at work for six weeks on the new stockade prison at Millen. Like Andersonville, it consisted of little more than a paling of upended pine logs in a huge quadrangle, more than half again the size of the Andersonville pen at fourteen hundred feet long and nearly as wide. Another stream ran through it for drinking water, washing, bathing, and sewage disposal. The interior was nominally divided into thirty-two rectangular lots that could each provide adequate campsites for a thousand men. Also like Andersonville, the prison bore an official name — Camp Lawton — and three weeks after Winder's order to remove the prisoners from western Georgia he reported that the Millen stockade was nearly finished. A week into October the ovens for the cookhouse had not yet been raised, for want of bricks, but just as the sun set on October 11 the first trainload of prisoners started spilling into the prison from Savannah, and hundreds more came in the next day, before either the hospitals or the cooking facilities had been completed. An Andersonville prisoner who reached Millen a month later admitted that it was still "a nice looking place," at least in comparison to his former abode.[18]

In Charleston, department commander Sam Jones soon found himself with far more prisoners than he could handle, and on September 12 he dispatched an officer to Florence, South Carolina, 130 miles north, to establish yet another stockade prison there. The first three thousand Andersonville alumni arrived at Florence only three days later, with nothing to confine them except a ring of guards. Right before those prisoners' eyes, gangs of slave laborers started digging trenches and cutting timber to form the palisade walls of their next open-air bastille.[19]

The Lincoln government suffered intense pressure from the friends and relatives of captured Union soldiers. The ever-helpful *New York Times* tried to redirect public outrage toward Confederate authorities, publishing a crude map of Andersonville and sworn statements of rebel cruelty, but it was the suspension of general exchanges that made prisoners vulnerable to any cruelty or disease. The exchange of equal numbers of prisoners in the wake of a battle, like that between Hood and Sherman after the capture of Atlanta, helped to alleviate the pressure on prisons as well as that exerted on the administration, but too few generals took advantage of battlefield exchanges. Grant, for instance, could hardly trade prisoners with Lee when he remained so personally adamant against exchanges — besides which, as he revealed in August, he viewed the breakdown of the exchange as a net Union gain because Northern forces could more easily bear the loss of manpower than the Southern armies could. Ben Butler had taken a hand in the negotiations, however, as a commissioner of exchange, and he proposed one scheme after another to release different classes of prisoners. While Andersonville emptied out he suggested to the Confederate commissioner that they periodically exchange all sick and wounded soldiers who, "in the judgment of the party holding them," would be unable to perform any duty for at least sixty days. The same day, he separately proposed exchanging all their respective merchant sailors. He had previously tried to effect an exchange of naval officers and seamen, as well as Marines. He seemed intent on rescinding the exchange prohibition by increments, and to some extent he succeeded, but then he complicated the problem by simultaneously announcing that he would arrest all white Southern males between the ages of seventeen and fifty as military prisoners because the Confederate Congress had officially conscripted all such citizens for the duration of the war.[20]

Besides haggling over the types of prisoners they would exchange, or the number, the commissioners often communicated about the treatment accorded prisoners. Rather than inquiring into the handling of their captured men, Union authorities more often chose to either exact retaliation on suspicion alone — like the reduction in rations issued to Confederate prisoners, on reports of short rations at Southern prisons — or to take other action, like suspending the exchange altogether, over the mistreatment of officers and enlisted men from the Colored Troops. Meanwhile, Confederate soldiers who were captured beyond the limits of the Confederacy, and cavalrymen in particular, often ended up in Northern penitentiaries, and sometimes in solitary confinement or in irons, for engaging in raids much like those carried out in the South by Benjamin Grierson and Judson Kilpatrick. Union generals also occasionally ordered the summary execution of suspected spies, some of whom were merely recruiting for their regiments in occupied territory, or were visiting their homes behind Union lines. All of that brought inquiries, accompanied by threats of retaliation, from the commissioner of exchange at Richmond. Beginning on August 16, the campaign in the Shenandoah Valley took a nasty turn when Phil Sheridan's cavalry hanged or shot seven prisoners from John Mosby's 43rd Virginia Cavalry Battalion, but no commissioners of exchange or commissary generals of prisoners ever seem to have inquired into those killings. It was left to the local commanders or their subordinates to resolve those issues, usually with reciprocal brutality.[21]

Believing himself heavily outnumbered, Sheridan retired to a secure position at Halltown, near Harper's Ferry, after his precipitate retreat from Cedar Creek. Eventually he started creeping back south, moving his infantry as far as Berryville, while Early held Winchester, ten miles away. At times the pickets dug their breastworks within sight of each other, and a Maine lieutenant merely expressed a common belief among Sheridan's men when he remarked to his wife that neither side seemed exactly raring to fight. In the middle of September, Kershaw's division and the artillery from Longstreet's corps started back for the Richmond defenses, and George Meade informed Sheridan of it as soon as he had the evidence. At first Sheridan replied, on September 18, that it was "impossible" for Kershaw to have returned, but that same day he learned that Early had marched on Martinsburg with two of his four infantry divisions. Sheridan decided to attack the two that were left at Winchester, under Ramseur and Breckinridge, and at two o'clock on the morning of September 19 three corps of Union infantry started toward Opequon Creek from the east, with one division of cavalry accompanying them and two more riding to their support from the north.[22]

Sheridan's infantry fell on Ramseur, who alone defended Winchester on the Berryville Pike. Breckinridge fought off the cavalry near Stephenson's Depot, where Ramseur had come to grief in July. Early arrived on the scene with the rest of the army after a night march, and he threw both Rodes's and Gordon's divisions in to bolster Ramseur just as the long blue lines were about to lap around his left flank. Late in the morning Rodes and Gordon pitched in with a furious counterattack that sent parts of the Sixth and Nineteenth Corps reeling half a mile backward, with stragglers racing toward the rear, where many of them remained hidden in the woods until the fighting ended. David Russell's Sixth Corps division caught the rebels in turn with an attack on their flank. Both Rodes and Russell fell mortally wounded, but their exchange brought the Union juggernaut to a momentary halt, and spontaneous cheers skirled over the Confederate ranks.[23]

Breckinridge pulled into line alongside Gordon, and the four divisions bent into a right angle northeast of Winchester, with nearly all Early's cavalry on the left under Fitz Lee, facing most of Sheridan's powerful mounted wing. After noon the din subsided, and Early appeared to have fought about twice his number in infantry to a draw, but late in the afternoon the Federals resumed the attack on all sides. Sheridan sent Crook's Army of West Virginia — known as the Eighth Corps, now — to swing around Early's left, and at the same time two cavalry divisions charged the Confederate left at full tilt, breaking through. The sound of gunfire behind their lines carried to Early's right wing, in front of the Sixth and Nineteenth Corps, causing the troops to start falling back without orders. After several hundred yards their officers rallied a portion of them in trenches that Joe Johnston had built to defend Winchester, more than three years before, and those few stopped the blue wave once more, but Union cavalry broke through the left flank again and Early had no choice but retreat: overpowering numbers and good luck had won the day. At sunset he turned his army south behind a rear guard, leaving three guns and thousands of dead and wounded on the field. A Maine officer who had fled through those same streets with Banks's beaten army in the spring of 1862 found the shame of that defeat "all wiped out" as he watched Early's valley army streaming south. Never again would Confederate columns march through Winchester, except as prisoners.[24]

Sheridan's men had been up since just after midnight, and had been engaged with the enemy for about ten hours when darkness descended, so they went immediately into camp after removing the wounded. In the morning, following some twilight browsing among the dead (a Vermont lieutenant took a watch worth fifty dollars from "a dead John's pocket"), the Army of the Shenandoah started after Jubal Early for the second time, leaving behind burial details to dispose of friend and foe. The town turned into one huge hospital, with the wounded crowded into hotels and churches. In a nonpartisan fashion that seemed peculiar to Winchester, which contained a leavening of Union loyalists, the citizens turned out to help without much concern for the politics of the wounded.[25]

Once again, Early took refuge on Fisher's Hill, between Little North Mountain and the northern extremity of Massanutten Mountain, known in that vicinity as Three Top Mountain. The North Fork of the Shenandoah River looped across half the valley's width there, leaving only a couple of miles for Early's badly reduced command to cover from behind earthworks, and from a vantage point on Three Top Confederate signalmen could see and report any flanking movements by their opponents. Sheridan overcame those disadvantages by concealing Crook's corps in the woods near Little North Mountain while he brought the Sixth and Nineteenth Corps out in the open for an apparent attack in front. On the afternoon of September 22 Crook led his two divisions to the slope of the mountain, still keeping to the woods, and bushwhacked around Early's extreme left. Late in the day, while the Sixth Corps and the Nineteenth pressed forward in front, the entire Eighth Corps swept out of the woods at the foot of the mountain, hitting the rebel cavalry that held Early's left and driving it backward. Once Crook had caved the Confederate line in far enough, a division of the Sixth Corps added its weight to help roll up that flank. For the second time in three days Early's line crumbled, but this time his men abandoned whole batteries of artillery, and hundreds of them threw aside their rifles, bounding away. Night came soon enough to minimize the disaster: Early lost fewer than three dozen killed and a couple of hundred wounded — attesting all the more to their demoralization — but a thousand men either sprinted into the forest or fell into enemy hands. Perhaps fifteen thousand Confederates of all arms made unseemly haste down the roads south. Yankees followed on their heels into the darkness, gathering in the slowest fugitives, deserted guns and wagons, and teams that had been cut from their traces. The pursuers described frantic Southern soldiers dispersing like chaff, or bounding away like so many sheep.[26]

While planning his attack at Fisher's Hill, Sheridan had sent two cavalry divisions around the eastern side of Massanutten, up the Luray Valley, in hopes that they could cross the mountain over a gap leading to New Market. There the horsemen might well have blocked Early's retreat and precipitated a fight to the finish, but that cavalry had turned back short of the gap when it reached a point where the Blue Ridge, Massanutten Mountain, and the South Fork of the Shenandoah choked the valley down to a narrow throat: there Early had posted a detachment of cavalry to prevent that very maneuver, and the precaution saved his army. During the night of the twenty-second, while Sheridan followed the retreating rebels in the opposite direction on the western side of the mountain, the Union cavalry rode back north to join him, and the next morning they stumbled across a little squadron of Mosby's men attacking Sheridan's ambulance train near Front Royal. The Federals swarmed down on the surprised rebels and drove them away, but a lieutenant of U.S. Regulars was killed in the action, and his comrades believed (perhaps with some reason) that he had been shot after surrendering. That initiated another round of summary executions for the half-dozen of Mosby's men who failed to get away. Most of the six were shot down where they stood, but at least one was left swinging from a walnut tree near the junction of the North and South Forks of the Shenandoah River. Civilian witnesses spotted a gaudily clad brigadier with long blond locks nearby whom they recognized as George Custer, and they mistakenly reported that he had personally ordered the men killed.[27]

Early reformed his troops in the daylight and continued on to Mount Jackson, more than twenty miles farther on, by September 24. From there he kept backpedaling, staving off repeated assaults by Sheridan's cavalry, until he reached Port Republic, at the southern end of Massanutten Mountain, sixty miles from Fisher's Hill. There Kershaw rejoined him, having turned back from Culpeper on orders from General Lee. Together they rushed up to Waynesboro, to chase away cavalry that had slipped behind them, before returning to the foot of Massanutten to bar Sheridan's main body from pushing farther south. Sheridan stopped at Harrisonburg, eight miles away, and for a long week the two armies faced each other down while Early waited for cavalry reinforcements that would allow him to turn about and follow Sheridan back down the valley yet again.[28]

The news from the Shenandoah Valley seemed too good to be true, especially after the capture of Atlanta, for past Union successes had usually been closely followed by significant setbacks, or humiliating fizzles. At Winchester, Sheridan had won the day with a cavalry charge reminiscent of medieval glory that mature observers had ceased to consider possible, and he had hounded his beaten foe for twenty miles, only to promptly scatter him again and chase him for another fifty miles; Union armies had never before followed up an advantage so tenaciously. Bold headlines greeted New Yorkers with "Victory!" proclaimed in capital letters, and "Victory again!" three days later. The Army of the Potomac fired a hundred-gun salute into Lee's lines after Winchester, and repeated it after Fisher's Hill. Winchester alone inspired fireworks displays across the North. Even the dropsical old commander emeritus of American armies Winfield Scott considered the week's work the masterpiece of the war so far.[29]

The euphoria of September seemed to wipe out the pervasive gloom of August, but the triumphs of Sherman and Sheridan told only part of the story, although they seemed to evoke the loudest applause from the soldiery. At home, the greater cause for celebration may have been the passage of the September 5 draft deadline without either violent uprising or the wholesale conscription of unwilling citizens. As always, money had gone a long way toward stirring an interest in military service, even amid the mayhem and dismay of midsummer, and its allure only soared with the invigorating headlines of summer's end. Bounties had reached their peaks, and to allay their quotas the poorest towns offered enormous cash bonuses for volunteers. Fathers more readily undertook the risk of letting their young boys enlist against a guarantee of nearly a thousand dollars than they might have for a few hundred. A patent medicine dealer in Waterbury, Vermont, deplored the youth of the volunteers who enlisted for the generous bounties in his town, and stripling Vermonters started flocking to the colors when their rural communities began offering thousand-dollar incentives. A New York sergeant in Sheridan's army implored his parents not to allow his younger brothers to join the army, however attractive the bounties might seem, but a few weeks later he discovered to his dismay that one brother, who had barely turned sixteen, had already enlisted in the sergeant's own company. Perhaps to accommodate this influx of puberulent boys, Edwin Stanton reduced the minimum height requirement for recruits by three inches, to a mere five feet even.[30]

Parental permission came more readily if easy victories made the army seem less dangerous, although mothers often interceded even then. The frock coats and shoulder scales of heavy artillery still conjured a vision of gentler duty, despite hundreds of rifle-toting heavies who had gone to manure Virginia soil, and so many New Hampshire residents showed interest in that branch that a new regiment materialized to accommodate them all. Albert Woolson, who would outlive every other soldier who served in the Civil War, enlisted in the brand-new 1st Minnesota Heavy Artillery that autumn, at the age of sixteen. And if a youth could find no opening in the heavy artillery, there was always the navy, which seemed relatively safe from combat in the absence of an effective Confederate fleet. Plenty of adults also sought refuge from the draft in the navy, if their communities showed no promise of paying for substitutes or raising attractive bounties.[31]

Old men sometimes took the bounty money for themselves. One sixty-three-year-old grandfather from New Hampshire joined a short-term artillery company for service in Portsmouth Harbor that August, and when his town voted a bounty of $600 on the eve of the draft he considered reenlisting for it. At least one elderly man did enlist in the 29th Michigan, a new unit raised to satisfy the quota, but the ladies of Flint who prepared a feast for that regiment judged far more of the recruits too young for the army than too old, with many no more than fifteen or sixteen. A New Jersey regiment seemed to have been filled entirely from the schoolroom, as both Union veterans and rebel soldiers noticed. "They all look like boys," commented a Connecticut officer, and Confederate pickets taunted them by asking when their vacation started.[32]

The September draft sparked dozens more of those new regiments, with most states attempting to raise at least one. The new organizations came with plenty of patronage for the state governors in the form of commissions, but many of those new officers lacked any training or experience. For that very reason a Wisconsin captain lamented the popular, traditional, and inefficient practice of raising virgin units, and he wondered why the dreadful losses in the spring crop of new regiments failed to discourage it. The 36th, 37th, and 38th Wisconsin had mustered in during April and May, and by the end of the war 370 of those men had been killed, or nearly eleven men per month, per regiment; the 2nd, 6th, and 7th Wisconsin had all entered the war in 1861, and had been through the worst of it in the Iron Brigade, but had barely lost six men apiece, per month. The Wisconsin captain clearly attributed the higher death rate among the new men to green officers. Still greater disparities prevailed between the old and new regiments in other states: the 17th Vermont, for example, lost nearly three times as many men per month as each of the state's five veteran regiments from 1861. The new regiments had come into the bloodiest year of the war with the greatest number of men, whereas many of the old regiments had been pared down to skeletons by 1864, but comparisons of wartime casualties to total enrollment told the same sad story. Twelve percent of the 17th Vermont's total enrollment perished under fire in eleven months of fighting, while the Vermont Brigade did not lose quite 11 percent from the first year of the war to the finish. An even more striking contrast distinguished the four new Massachusetts regiments that joined the Army of the Potomac in April of 1864, which lost 10.8 percent of their total enrollment in battle by April of 1865, compared to 8.9 percent combat deaths in the three Bay State regiments that served with the Army of the Potomac from 1861 until the end of the

war. Whether or not the Wisconsin captain's suspicions about inexperi-
enced officers accounted for it, new regiments were undeniably consign-
ing a disproportionate number of their men to burial details that summer.[33]

Those calculations occurred to few, if any, who hoped to delay their arrival at the front for the length of time a newborn unit might be expected
to remain under training. It was, after all, widely known by September
of 1864 that men who signed on as replacements in existing regiments
could find themselves sleeping in mud, drinking polluted river water, or
dodging shellfire in a matter of days or weeks.[34] Besides, a new organization offered the added comfort of going to war with one's acquaintances,
rather than being thrown into a battle-thinned unit among strangers. In
the camps where they gathered, the formation of new regiments resur-
rected the carnival atmosphere of the early war. Families and friends descended on Fort Snelling repeatedly during August and September to
visit with the recruits of the 11th Minnesota, enjoying romantic moonlit
nights around the campfires and sumptuous, raucous banquets. One of
those recruits relished that regiment's slow, peaceful journey down the
Mississippi River as "a perpetual treat," and it wasn't until late October
that he and his comrades reached their assigned guard posts along the
railroad, north of Nashville and out of harm's way.[35]

New regiments were all that saved New Hampshire from widespread
drafting. The New Hampshire legislature helped reduce the state's overall
quota by appropriating a $300-per-man state bounty, in addition to local
bounties, specifically to fill up a new regiment of cavalry. Hundreds of
Granite Staters also rushed to enlist in a new regiment of heavy artillery,
gambling that the imminent discharge of the hundred-day men would
empty out enough forts for them to occupy, and keep them out of the field.
Towns where someone was recruiting one of those big artillery companies
managed to collect their quota of volunteers a few days ahead of the draft
deadline, while the combination of massive bounties, battlefield victories, and new regiments afforded other communities the same intense
relief of retiring their obligations through volunteers. Elsewhere in the
state, many towns remained short of their magic number in spite of the
hefty bounties, and as September waned those residents whose names remained on the enrollment lists started buckling under the suspense. Sixteen eligible men from little New Boston left town as the draft date approached, presumably to cross into Canada, but local officials tricked
them into returning by spreading a rumor that enough nonresident volunteers had been secured; when the men came home they learned that it
was not quite true, and the provost marshal delivered a draft notice to at
least one of them.[36]

Unlike in the South, able-bodied men still abounded in the North, but most hung back, and in municipalities where support for the war had worn especially thin hardly a man had signed his name against the quota by the nominal deadline of September 5. That was the case in Conway, New Hampshire, where poorer citizens from the hardscrabble hill-farm districts had provided most of the town's soldiers for the first two years of the war, and out-of-state volunteers or recent immigrants had filled out the draft quotas during the third year. For the July 18 call, Conway owed the army thirty-two men for a year. A few shrewd Yankees had taken preventive action and hired a three-year substitute early, before they became scarce, and Conway voters ultimately allowed them $300 apiece toward that cost, since each substitute reduced the quota.[37]

The draft was a touchy subject in Conway: its debut, in 1863, had brought a rash of arson that destroyed the barns or homes of prominent officials, and no one wanted to see it imposed again. In a special town meeting held on September 19, voters acceded to almost three times the amount they had ever spent before to meet War Department demands, authorizing $800 apiece for each "citizen of this town who will fill our quota." With county and state bounties, and a prorated federal bounty of $100, that represented three years' wages for a Conway farm hand, in return for a single year of military service, but still no one leaped at the offer until William H. Allen took up the cause of convincing his fellow citizens to save their community from the anguish of direct conscription. Allen owned all or part of several businesses in the town, including a tannery and an interest in the big new hotel in the center of town, but his concern exceeded that of the average citizen. Not only did he stand to lose considerable property if political animosity revived the firebrand spirit, but Allen himself was eligible for the draft, and the dire shortage of potential substitutes left him in grave danger of having to go into the army. When the next draft call came, in December, he would take the preemptive course of hiring a substitute within twenty-four hours, but for the nonce his only hope lay in a patriotic appeal to his townsmen.[38]

The provost marshal for Conway's district had already held a draft lottery in Portsmouth; in order to have enough conscripts after all the inevitable exemptions, he had chosen the names of fifty enrolled residents. William Allen obtained the list, and on September 21 he appealed directly to those men, explaining that they could either realize an appealing windfall for a year's enlistment or risk an even chance that they would be drafted anyway, in which case they would be ineligible for the huge town bounty. They could all enlist in the state's new infantry regiment, he told them, for which one of his partner's sons was raising a company. The next day he met twenty-two of those men at the hotel, accompanying them and their nominal recruiter to Concord, where he treated them to dinner, bought them each a little gift, and made certain that they all enlisted in the 18th New Hampshire under the credit of Conway. Acting as agent for his town, he persuaded just enough additional recruits at the state draft rendezvous to forsake the towns they represented and sign on against Conway's quota, for the higher local bounty. Judging from the selectmen's report on the average cost of volunteers under that call, the town seems to have reimbursed Allen for his expenses, and perhaps for his time.[39]

The Conway residents who answered that call reflected an older, more established population than had the town's earlier volunteers. Their median age approached thirty years, and on average they, or their families, owned property valued at four times that of Conway residents who had enlisted under the last preconscription recruiting drive of 1862. None of those men had ever spent a day in the army when they enlisted, and some had allowed the town to pay commutation to excuse them from earlier calls; if the emergencies of 1861 and 1862 had not brought them into service, it seems unlikely that their enlistment in the encouraging month of September had its foundation in any sense of urgent patriotic duty. Just as smaller bounties had attracted less wealthy volunteers in the first eighteen months of the war, the highest bounties of the war tapped at least partially into a more affluent stratum of society after the poorer populations had been depleted. The shorter term and a more credible threat of compulsory service certainly helped — as, perhaps, did several weeks of optimistic reports from Georgia and Virginia.[40]

The combination of those four factors brought that sort of comfortable, middle-class citizen out of towns and villages all over the country. A Massachusetts woman acknowledged that her brother enlisted in the heavy artillery "for fear of being drafted," adding that by volunteering he took advantage of both a sizable bounty and the chance to enlist in a regiment that was already safely ensconced in a quiet sector. Dietrich Gerstein, a German immigrant who joined the new 29th Michigan that autumn, complained that after contributing to pay the commutation fees for drafted neighbors he had finally had to enlist himself, rather than be drafted. Gerstein was in the second enrollment class, too — over thirty-five and married, with several children, but most of the enrolled men of the first class in his community had either hired substitutes previously or enlisted for the bounty themselves, which he finally decided to do "so I could at least *make a little money.*" He also alluded to a shrewish wife whom he gladly escaped for a year, but while his family enjoyed a small state subsidy during his absence, his bounty remained unpaid long after he had been discharged.[41]

In a wavering hand, a hospitalized Pennsylvania cavalryman expressed his astonishment at a list of neighbors who had responded to profligate local inducements for volunteers that September, most of whom he thought would have been "the last ones to go." Similar surprises gratified many a soldier early that autumn, for among the newest recruits were men whom soldiers had been hoping to see fighting alongside them for the past two years, including large numbers who made it no secret that they had always voted Democrat and would continue to do so. A battery commander characterized a majority of his autumn replacements as Copperheads, and he supposed that they had only responded because the bounties had grown so large and the term of service had been shaved so short. An Ohio cavalryman at Camp Stoneman, outside Washington, noted the same phenomenon among the recruits there. The veterans would not be seeing most of those men in their own ranks, however, for the more mature and settled of the latest volunteers chose to associate themselves with fledgling infantry regiments or heavy-artillery companies.[42]

Country doctors and lawyers often earned less than a thousand dollars a year in 1864. It was therefore understandable, when a laborer or a modest tradesman who had sat out the war thus far suddenly committed himself to a year's duty for a thousand dollars in bounties and several hundred more in monthly pay and subsidies, that his neighbors believed he did it solely for the money. That suspicion grew all the stronger when those neighbors detected that a man's enlistment was attended with a conspicuous change in the volume or content of his politics.[43]

The bounties shrank as most municipalities completed their quotas, but wealthy men still sought substitutes to protect themselves for the future, and they might attract an enterprising young lad or an immigrant alien for $500 even without the pressure of an impending levy. Later that fall, as Union victories accumulated and the decline of the Confederacy seemed ever more obvious, military service began once again to appeal to the adventuresome, the undecided, and the impoverished as an acceptable alternative occupation — just as it had in the early days of the war, before it turned so deadly. The war machine had created a labor shortage that drove wages upward and made it easier for civilians to find work, but inflation had risen faster and higher, often leaving those with jobs unable to cover their living expenses. The promise of looming victory again persuaded those working poor to consider what seemed like the economic security of enlisting. One sailor who secured a berth as a signal quartermaster on a river gunboat congratulated himself that it brought him twenty-five dollars a month, plus keep, which he knew he could never have earned at home over the winter, and he supposed he would hire himself out as a substitute when his cruise ended. An aspiring young bard who tried peddling his self-published doggerel across Ohio failed miserably at it, and when his money ran out he finally started shopping around various recruiting stations. "I hate the army," he confessed, "but have to go blindly in it, I fear," and he, too, finally shipped as a landsman on a gunboat. As 1864 came to an end some one-year volunteers heard they could obtain discharges to join the Regular Army for enormous bounties, and they hastened to sign their names. The former major of a Rhode Island regiment, who had gone home just before Grant's brutal 1864 campaign began, found the offer inviting enough that he, too, joined the Regulars at the reduced rank of sergeant.[44]

Astronomical bounties enticed so many volunteers that provost marshals served relatively few men with the dreaded notices that they had been "legally drafted in the service of the United States." Adjustments for earlier credits and voluntary enlistments reduced the call for half a million men to fewer than fifty-five thousand, which made it a little easier to find substitutes for those who still demurred. Even in poor rural districts, substitute prices ran from $750 to $1,200 and more where voters agreed to subsidize the cost. To the glee of envious men in the army, who were already in a snit over the enormous bounties, barely half the men whose names were drawn could find anyone to take their places, and those who did hire proxies considered themselves especially fortunate regardless of the cost.[45]

So much money circulated among recruits from bounties and substitute payments that it inevitably attracted entrepreneurs intent on gleaning some of it for themselves. Selectmen, or their towns' appointed recruiting agents, sometimes tried to hold back some of the bounty money from volunteers who had already reported to their regiments, who could not return to complain about it. Soldiers on duty with the provost marshals' offices would themselves sometimes act as substitute brokers, signing men up from the pools of prospective recruits at the draft rendezvous against their hometown quotas, and often for larger bounties than they revealed to their unsuspecting dupes. Commissioned officers more often practiced that variety of larceny, but they disliked the competition of enlisted men and would punish them severely for intruding on their territory. Officers could also run into trouble for swindling ignorant or illiterate substitutes, however, like the captain and lieutenant whom Meade's provost marshal lodged on a prison ship.[46]

The officers of Colored Troops enjoyed particularly good pickings with so high a proportion of unlettered recruits, and numbers of them fell from grace for cheating their own men. Michael O'Brien, a teenaged lieutenant in the 23rd U.S. Colored Troops, had begun his own military career as a substitute, enlisting to evade prosecution for trying to shoot a policeman;

he bilked recruits in his company of some $2,000, went home without permission, and was entertaining himself at a local bordello when he was arrested in *flagrante delicto*. The army dismissed him for desertion a fortnight before his regiment was cut to pieces in the Crater, and the state tried to prosecute him for theft, but he posted bail and absconded.[47]

Others took more direct and violent measures for relieving recruits of the telltale bulges in their pockets, socks, or the lining of their clothing, and the substitutes themselves often produced the most vicious of the thugs. Guards at the conscript camps described the inmates as thieves, cutthroats, and pickpockets. One visitor had not stopped in the camp at Fairhaven, Connecticut, for two hours before his wallet disappeared. A member of the escort to a contingent of six hundred drafted men and substitutes on their way from Rutland, Vermont, to New Haven, Connecticut, thought them the meanest set of men he had ever seen, and the veterans who greeted them at the front found the assessment accurate. One September morning an officer at Bermuda Hundred reported that a fresh recruit who had been flashing $500 in cash the night before had been found murdered near his picket line.[48]

Their relative scarcity notwithstanding, substitutes continued to present disciplinary difficulties for provost marshals and other officers assigned to deliver them to their respective armies. The northeastern states seemed to provide the heaviest concentrations of unreliable substitutes, probably because the Atlantic port cities drew so many eligible aliens who lacked the community connections that bound others to their commitments. Deservedly or not, New Hampshire developed a reputation for sending the least trustworthy recruits of any state, perhaps because so large a proportion of the resident population vigorously opposed the war, or the administration, and declined to lend themselves to the cause even at the tempting bounties of September. Half of any town's substitutes might quickly desert, despite the heavy guards placed over them, and many of those who did finally report for duty could not even sign their names, or speak English. Renowned combat regiments like the 5th New Hampshire became better known for the droves of deserters who drained into Confederate lines from their ranks, taking their bounty money or substitute fees with them.[49]

Bounty jumpers and desperate or greedy recruits were not the only men who succumbed to the economic attraction of military service. Veterans who had secured a little rank or an acceptable job outside the line of fire often worried about leaving the army because they wondered how they would support themselves at home. Even those who had smelled a good deal of gunpowder delayed their discharges or reenlisted, even in the immediate presence of the enemy, because of the money they could earn. A Connecticut private in the Veteran Reserve Corps fattened his wallet speculating in substitutes through his job with the provost marshal, and he might have hired one for himself at any time, but he postponed doing so until he had looked into the employment situation at home. Leander Harris, of the 4th New Hampshire, typified that spirit among enlisted men: he reenlisted in 1864, despite his wife's pitiful pleading to come home, but his admissions that he coveted the cash stake and that he never again intended to work as a lowly shoemaker seemed more decisive than his repeated assertions of nationalistic devotion. Similar protestations of patriotic responsibility, as well as a professed disdain for the pay and benefits that he described as "sufficient," did not prevent another middle-aged New Hampshire soldier from inquiring persistently for his enlistment bounty and his wife's municipal subsistence stipend. An Ohio cavalryman who had taken sick insisted that he had originally entered the army from a sense of duty, but he eagerly applied for a disability discharge until he learned how much money he could make by reenlisting, whereupon he felt much better and signed on for another three years. A Kansas veteran underwent the opposite change of heart when his efforts to obtain a lucrative commission failed, after which he decided that civilian life beckoned far more vigorously than the army.[50]

Because of their higher pay, commissioned officers proved more vulnerable to the pecuniary considerations, although they, too, often cited their patriotic impulses or their aversion to slavery. Lieutenant Colonel Edward Wood of the 48th Indiana very much wanted to leave the army in the middle of the Atlanta campaign, but with legal activity "at a standstill" back home he wondered how he could make a living. When a sharpshooter killed a fellow officer from his home town, Wood's determination to resign intensified, but he still needed civilian employment. "I am only a little lost to know what to do," he explained to his wife, and he was still commanding his regiment four months after Atlanta had been captured. The infernal campaign along the James caused a New Hampshire captain to contemplate a return to the comforts of civil life, but he doubted the prospects of earning anything like the salary he drew in the army: "it would seem odd to do much hard work at present," he admitted to his mother, "after being three years in Uncle Sam's employ." He appealed to his brother for some occupation that would pay as well as his captain's bars did, but until something came up he thought he would not leave the service. Generals usually clung to their government stipends as long as they could, too: the following spring, when demobilization threatened to turn Major General Samuel Curtis back out into the world, he urged his wife to a strict economy to "prepare for the cessation of our present ample income."[51]

Instead of the rioting and revolts that some had feared from another draft, the president's call had visibly strengthened the national forces: personal avarice and military optimism were bringing recruits streaming down the rivers and railroads toward the armies by the end of September. Soldiers of all ranks who had betrayed deep despondency only three or four weeks before found their hope restored, both because of the victories Sherman and Sheridan had won and because the reinforcements that were pouring in had not yet begun to melt away with desertion and disability — as they soon would. Meeting the draft quotas calmed the potential for civil conflict at home, quieting the flagrant speech of those who bridled most at the threat of being conscripted. With less danger of a fire in the rear and better chances of success at the front, the month ended with most Union armies enjoying far better morale than they had at the beginning, including the perennially pessimistic Army of the Potomac. The soldiers' worst remaining concern lay in the coming election, and even that failed to trouble those who believed that George McClellan would carry the war through to the finish just as stubbornly as Abe Lincoln would.[52]

The firmest War Democrats, who welcomed Sheridan's victories as "a great gain to the country," recognized that the Shenandoah battles and the fall of Atlanta sorely diminished George McClellan's chances of winning the presidency. Nor were those military conquests the only successes accruing to the administration. The Radical attack on Mr. Lincoln had begun to disintegrate, removing the chances of a schism that could have cost the Republicans the White House — just as the split among Democrats had lost them the election of 1860. Postmaster General Montgomery Blair had seen it all coming, and had predicted the outcome: conservative Democrats had sympathized with the seceding states enough to let them go, Blair reasoned, while the Radicals hated slavery enough to accept secession themselves, so they both wanted someone besides Lincoln. It was precisely because Lincoln stood for the Union above all that the people at large would cleave to him, Blair concluded.[53]

Recognizing that their campaign to unhorse Lincoln might throw the election to the other party, the Radicals eventually gave it up. Horace Greeley had changed sides during the Chicago convention, but many supporters of the Wade-Davis Manifesto held out through most of September, hoping the early state elections would go against their party and dictate the replacement of their presidential candidate. Vermont came first that fall, on September 6, and it yielded a lopsided victory for so-called Union Party candidates for state and national office, but so many eyes were fixed on Maine that the Vermont governor's margin of more than two to one went virtually unnoticed outside the state. Maine attracted more notice, perhaps, because the race there seemed so much closer: a canvass of the state in early September estimated that the capture of Atlanta added only a thousand probable Republican votes to the doubtful expectations of August. A week later Maine nevertheless produced another resounding triumph for the administration's friends, although far less overwhelming than Vermont's, but it merited front-page treatment in major Republican dailies.[54]

The most heartening of September's gifts to the president may have been the one that coincided with the news of Fisher's Hill. Claiming that the presidential contest had come down to a question between outright disunion (or reunion with slavery intact) under the Democrats, and union without slavery under Lincoln, John Frémont announced on September 21 that he was withdrawing from the race. He refused to disavow his earlier assertions that Lincoln's administration was a failure, and in fact he repeated that it was, adding that he supported it with regret, but he considered the election of McClellan a worse calamity than continuing Lincoln in office. The same day that Frémont's letter reached the newspapers, the president wrote to his postmaster general and asked for his resignation, which he received within a few hours. The Blair family was as prominent in Missouri as it was in Maryland, and Montgomery Blair's younger brother Frank had run afoul of Frémont on a couple of occasions when General Frémont commanded the Department of Missouri in 1861. Montgomery Blair was also the most conservative of Unionists, scorning abolitionists like Frémont and his closest associates, and in his devotion to the administration Blair may have hinted to Frémont's friends that he would leave the cabinet if Frémont removed himself from the race. A friend of the postmaster general's later asked Frémont if his withdrawal had been conditioned on Blair's resignation, but Frémont denied it categorically. Lincoln himself probably took the initiative, recognizing that dismissing his most conservative cabinet officer would be seen as a courting gesture to the supporters whom Frémont had just cast loose. Within a few weeks the last Radical holdouts were falling in line, lambasting McClellan if not praising Lincoln, and with a united party and winning armies the November election no longer seemed quite so daunting.[55]

Still, as late as the second Thursday of October, the president jotted down his calculation of the outcome if the election had been held that day, concluding that he could win it only by the thinnest of margins. Discounting the four border states as lost, as well as New York, New Jersey, and Pennsylvania, plus his own home state of Illinois, he gave himself a three-vote electoral lead over McClellan; if any other state went over to the Democrats, the administration would be turned out, along with its policies of emancipation and unconditional surrender. The previous

March, Congress had authorized the sparsely settled territory of Nevada to form a convention and submit a constitution. It looked as though Nevada would vote safely Republican, and on October 31, eight days before the election, Lincoln padded his margin by proclaiming the admission of the undersized state, which dutifully delivered its three new electoral votes.[56]

When Grant learned how badly Sheridan had stunned Early, and that Kershaw's division had been ordered back again to reinforce the valley army, he supposed that Lee would be weak enough to warrant another offensive that might seize Petersburg, or even Richmond itself. Active operations along the line of the James River would, besides, dissuade Lee from sending any more troops to Early, and would allow Sheridan to devote more attention to the destruction of crops that would feed Confederate soldiers or their livestock.[57]

Leaving only one strong brigade to hold the trenches at Bermuda Hundred, Grant shifted the entire Tenth Corps and most of the Eighteenth to the north side of the James at Deep Bottom, a few miles closer to Richmond than Malvern Hill, on George McClellan's famous Peninsula. At the same time, Grant pulled the Fifth Corps and two divisions of the Ninth Corps out of their works to operate on the extreme left of his Petersburg lines, beyond the Weldon Railroad.

The men who shouldered their equipment for those marches weighed the ominous portents of a major movement against the relief of leaving their trenches. The drought of June and July had turned to frequent and sometimes heavy rain by August, including a veritable torrent that struck just after the middle of the month, causing a flash flood in the ravines of Bermuda Hundred where the Eighteenth Corps had camped; new entrenchments had trapped the runoff in ponds on the high ground, and when those inadvertent dams burst, the floodwaters washed entire campsites away — tents, knapsacks, rifles, and all — drowning and injuring a number of men.[58] The trenches filled with water that turned putrid, but troops still had to stand forty-eight-hour tours in them, and when the sun came back out it would bake the churned red clay into rock-hard clods that acted as supplementary shrapnel whenever an artillery round landed nearby. Rather than waste their ammunition on routine bombardment, rebel artillerists tended to choose inopportune moments like mealtimes to throw a well-directed shot, and sharpshooters waited at little portholes to drill someone through the head whenever he stepped on a high spot in the trench. When they retired to their camps for a day or so, there was still the chance of a stray shell fragment plunging through the tent and killing a man where he lay.[59]

By late September the nights had turned damp and chilly, too, adding to both the general discomfort and the odor of the earthworks where they spent most of their time. The Petersburg and Bermuda Hundred fronts had been transformed into a desert, with miles of fortifications in every direction; a veteran who remembered the ridicule McClellan had endured for constantly entrenching bet that Grant had done more digging that summer than had been done in the entire war. Pioneers denuded the landscape of trees to corduroy roads and build log revetments, bridges, the military railroad that ran from City Point to the Weldon Railroad, and tangles of sharpened abatis or chevaux-de-frise to ensnarl attacking columns — called "gut rippers" by some. Whatever small growth, waste wood, and stumps those projects had left went into campfires, for cooking and, on cool nights, for warmth. Nearly every house near the front that was not used for some general's headquarters had been burned or torn down, either to open a field of fire or to provide lumber for breastworks and bombproofs. The absence of trees made birds scarce, and the only other animals were the horses and mules that hauled the army's wagons and artillery. Every cow, hog, and chicken had disappeared, and as early as the beginning of August a Massachusetts corporal had thought it rare enough to spot an old hound slinking through the camps that he described it at length for his parents.[60]

The men north of the James, under Butler, took less enjoyment in their respite from the trenches than did the troops south of the river. Since spring the commanders of Butler's two corps — the pair who had counseled him to seize Petersburg by its lightly defended southern approach, back in May — had been replaced. Edward O. C. Ord, one of the more senior major generals in the army, led two divisions of the Eighteenth Corps across the river at Aiken's Landing, just upstream from Deep Bottom, and he waited until full darkness on September 28 to start them on the march. David Birney's Tenth Corps, fattened by a division of Colored Troops from Ord's corps, took the roads to Deep Bottom the same night. Birney was to follow the New Market Road toward Richmond, while Ord was expected to seize the extensive earthworks around Chaffin's Bluff, along the river, and prevent Lee from sending reinforcements from Petersburg.[61]

Birney ran into trouble first. New Market Heights towered above the road just beyond Deep Bottom, bristling with Confederate infantry, and Samuel Duncan's two-regiment brigade of Colored Troops tried to take it by storm, charging with muskets uncapped. Duncan estimated that he led seven hundred rifles into the fight, and in a twinkling he lost four hundred of them. Bullets ripped through his own hat and coat, nipping at his skin, and then a bullet smashed his ankle. One of his staff officers was killed, another lost a leg, and the other two had their horses shot from under them. The flag of the 4th U.S. Colored Infantry fluttered to the ground three times, and when one company commander reached the abatis just outside the works he could find only five men left with his company, out of twenty-five, and they declined his invitation to press on. Here and there men started fitting percussion caps on their rifles to return the enemy fire, and that robbed them of any remaining momentum: they continued to load and fire without advancing, giving the entrenched rebels the advantage over them. A larger brigade of black troops, with a regiment loaned from the third brigade, advanced over the same ground and fell victim to the same mistake of standing in the open to exchange fire with an enemy behind cover, but their officers eventually prodded them into motion again and they finally sent the Confederates hurrying off the heights and up the New Market Road. Birney's troops took up the chase past the empty works, in front of which an admiring New York sergeant found that "the slaughtered negroes lay piled in heaps." There they would lie for at least three more days, unburied by their white comrades.[62]

Pushing Confederate skirmishers ahead of him from Aiken's Landing, Ord reached the Chaffin's Bluff line a couple of hours after sunup and almost immediately pitched his leading division into the biggest bastion of that line, called Fort Harrison. His second division came up late, adding little vigor to the attack, but Hiram Burnham's brigade of New Hampshire, Connecticut, and New York regiments surged up nearly a mile of cleared slope to that imposing work. At first they marched in normal cadence, carrying their rifles at a right-shoulder shift as though on parade, uncapped, with bayonets fixed. Artillery punched gaping holes in their line, but then those bayonets dropped to the angle for a charge, the pace accelerated to a double-quick, and a cheer went up before the surviving Yankees climbed the parapet and dove in among the rebels. General Burnham fell mortally wounded inside the fort, and the colonel who succeeded him was wounded within minutes. The two Union divisions before Fort Harrison amounted to only eighteen regiments, but the Confederate garrison had been thinned out weeks previously, when Kershaw's division left to join Early, and after a brief struggle the occupants fled, leaving behind their guns and a few prisoners. Ord faced that division to the left, toward the river, to sweep the enemy out of the entire line of entrenchments, but he was wounded in the thigh himself, and without reinforcements his troops fell back into Fort Harrison, where they had turned all the ordnance around to bear on its previous owners.[63]

With his borrowed division of Ord's, General Birney commanded all the Colored Troops on the north side of the river. Those, and his two white divisions, gave him ten brigades, but many of those men had taken advantage of the night march to drift away from their regiments in fear of a fight. Following the retreating rebels up the New Market Road, Birney passed Ord's position at Fort Harrison early in the afternoon and ordered Robert Foster to take his division cross-country to charge Fort Gilmer, which lay just north of Harrison. When Foster lined up his fifteen regiments for the attack he found that shirkers had reduced the division to some fourteen hundred bayonets, but he strung all three brigades out abreast and sent them rolling forward across terrain serrated with marshy ravines full of underbrush and slash that disrupted his ranks and forced him to realign them under a raking fire of artillery. The division traversed a grove of thick woods where more of the men dropped out to take cover behind trees. As the remnants climbed out of the last ravine before Fort Gilmer, Foster dismounted and joined his men while they dressed ranks for the final charge. With a whoop they all broke into a run, trampling a cornfield as they went, until they reached the abatis, when Southern musketry joined the artillery, rippling across the division front and dropping most of those who had reached that far. Foster called a retreat, and Confederate reinforcements from the other side of the river helped him on his way. Late in the day William Birney, the elder brother of the Tenth Corps commander, made another stab at Gilmer from Foster's left, throwing three of his five black regiments at the fort piecemeal and getting them butchered for no good purpose. Thanks to a blunder somewhere along the chain of command, four companies of one regiment went in without supports and disappeared into the moat surrounding the fort. Not a man of them came back.[64]

General Lee moved his headquarters to Chaffin's Bluff as soon as the crossing had been detected on September 29. The next morning, while another Union force threatened his extreme right below Petersburg, he ordered an attempt to recover Fort Harrison. Brigadier General George Stannard, the Vermonter whose division had taken Harrison in the first place, still held it on September 30, although the previous day's battle had cost him one-fifth of his force in killed and wounded: casualties, and the skulking that seemed to infect every white division on that side of the river, left Stannard with little more than two thousand men. When he saw the rebel infantry gathering to assail him, just after noon, he also learned that all the artillery inside the fort had run out of ammunition. That left him only the musket to repel the assault, and when the dun lines of Confederate infantry reached close range the top of the fort blazed with a deafening volley that disintegrated into random but rapid firing. Stannard sent back for another battery, but none came. The first assault failed to gain his parapet, though, and the surviving rebels receded to find cover, leaving behind windrows of dead. Before long they came on again in even greater force, yipping their shrill yell. Stannard's men had begun running short of ammunition, and he had already asked for a fresh supply. In the midst of the second attack, just in the nick of time, a dauntless ordnance captain came bounding around the fort at the seat of a loaded wagon, pulling up at the old sally port of the fort, on the Confederate side and in full view of the oncoming rebels; he held his mules to a stop while soldiers came out to unload the boxes, and in the time it took to empty the wagon three of the mules were wounded. Stannard had an arm shattered, but his men held their ground and the second assault was the last. Fort Harrison would become part of a powerful new Federal line, and henceforth it would be called Fort Burnham.[65]

With Lee attending to his left flank, north of the river, Grant decided to test his right flank, below Petersburg, telling Meade that "the enemy must be weak enough at one or the other place to let us in." Warren, who held Meade's extreme left at Globe Tavern, on the Weldon Railroad, moved out of his works at midmorning. Once the tail of Warren's corps had filed onto the road, John Parke followed with two divisions of the Ninth Corps. Both corps suffered from the same preponderance of new men that had led to such unusual malingering on the north side of the James, with old regiments augmented by heavy concentrations of recruits and most brigades bolstered by entirely novice regiments. One Second Corps brigadier who would later join the expedition complained that half his men had never fired a gun, and many could not understand English; they came, he said, from "all nations but the Hottentots."[66]

Charles Griffin's division of the Fifth Corps led the way, striding westward past the railroad through a mile or more of thick woods into enemy territory. Just past a tiny, ramshackle chapel called Poplar Spring Church, Griffin flushed some rebel pickets who fired on him and retreated before his skirmishers, backing across the William Peebles farm to reveal a lightly defended line of entrenchments on the far side of a half-mile clearing. Without much fuss Griffin's men seized those works, taking a few prisoners and one of the two guns that stood in the embrasures, but then everyone seemed to sit down to wait for more orders. Parke set a regiment to work cutting a road to the west, as Meade had instructed him to do, but his main body hung beside Warren's new left flank.[67]

The Federals faced no more than cavalry here. The only Confederate infantry left at Petersburg consisted of A. P. Hill's corps and Bushrod Johnson's division, and most of those units began the campaign manning Petersburg's interior defenses. A couple of miles ahead of Warren and Parke lay the Boydton Plank Road, leading west and a little south of Petersburg, and a mile or so beyond that ran the South Side Railroad, paralleling the plank road; this was Petersburg's last direct rail connection to the rest of the Confederacy, and if Union forces could seize that corridor it should compel Lee to evacuate the city. A dozen brigades of Meade's infantry congregated around Mr. Peebles's farm, and two brigades of cavalry cooperated, comprising more than ninety regiments, with only five brigades of rebel horsemen opposing them, amounting to a score of mounted regiments, battalions, and emaciated "legions." General Meade and his staff reined up at Warren's headquarters in the middle of the afternoon, finding the troops burying their dead and waiting for something to happen.[68]

Around 4:00 P.M. Parke moved his divisions to the west of Warren's captured trenches and faced them north, toward the red-dirt fortifications that guarded the plank road. Stopping Orlando Willcox's division near Oscar Pegram's farm, Parke sent Robert Potter's two brigades ahead on the presumption that Warren would advance in concert, but Warren had lost touch with Parke's right flank. Simon Griffin's predominately New England brigade took the advance, with his three New Hampshire regiments — the 6th, 9th, and 11th — in the lead. During the wasted hours of the afternoon word had naturally drifted back to Petersburg of the powerful concentration of Yankees perched on the vulnerable right flank of the city, and reinforcements that had started on their way to join Lee north of the James had turned around to confront the new threat. As the sun neared the horizon the New Hampshire demibrigade had covered about a mile, pushing beyond Robert Jones's farm, and was advancing on the second line of earthworks, from which came a seemingly weak and defensive fire. Suddenly, though, the defenders turned aggressive. Two brigades of North and South Carolinians boiled out in a front overlapping the New Hampshiremen on both ends, and as they trotted forward the extremities of their line began to arc around the flanks of the three little regiments. Potter's second brigade, under John Curtin, had dropped behind on Griffin's left, as had the Fifth Corps on his right, so the Granite State soldiers abruptly found themselves penned in on both sides and in front as they backed toward the tall, columned portico of the Jones house.[69]

At least one other Confederate brigade dashed into the gap between Curtin and Griffin, separating them, and Curtin's first line of three regiments fell quickly within a similar encirclement. Survivors of the three New Hampshire regiments, which had hardly numbered six hundred to begin with, came bounding out of the closing gap between the Carolinians' pincers, starting a stampede in the regiments behind them. The 17th Vermont stepped up to stop the right arm of those pincers from closing around the trapped contingent, allowing a few more of their comrades to escape, but the Vermont regiment's commander and six of his officers were shot down in quick succession; scores of his men fell back within the fenced grounds of the Jones house, where they soon threw their hands into the air with three hundred of the New Hampshiremen. Curtin's three isolated regiments fared even worse, surrendering in droves. Griffin lost nearly five hundred prisoners from his brigade in a matter of minutes, and Curtin lost more than eight hundred. The reserve regiments of those two brigades offered little help, beyond fixing bayonets to try halting the fugitives. Hundreds of Potter's remaining troops, with recruits prominent among them, simply struck for the rear, and they never stopped running until they passed the Oscar Pegram farm, half a mile back. There Parke formed a new line on Willcox's division, parts of which also broke and ran. Night finally ended the fight, and under cover of the darkness Parke dropped back to join hands with Warren. Then it began to rain.[70]

A cold downpour continued all night and the next day, dampening chances of a fight, and the troops spent the day digging new works. A division of the Second Corps came out to aid Parke's battered corps, and on October 2 this reinforced wing pushed back out to the Pegram farm, where the men took up their axes and shovels again to establish a permanent string of fortifications. The three days' work had extended Grant's left two miles, and with the ground gained north of the James the Union cordon ran in an arc twenty-eight miles long. Neither Richmond nor Petersburg had fallen, however, and Potter's catastrophe had been "disgusting," according to a Regular Army officer. Potter's veteran division had been humiliated, with some of his regiments reduced again — just sixty days after the Crater — to company-sized remnants. Observers at home or in the army might focus on the failures, like one of Simon Griffin's demoralized New Hampshire captains, who concluded that for all the blood that had been spilled "we cannot take the Southside RR any more than we can take Petersburg." The echo of the Shenandoah victories still rang loud enough, though, to drown any discouraging words for the first failure of autumn, and close inspection put a brighter shine on the campaign, because Butler's men and Meade's held the ground they had gained. Fresh Yankee entrenchments reached within three miles of the South Side Railroad, and several miles onto the north side of the James. Lee's lines had been stretched several additional miles, while the army that defended them had been pared down a little more.[71]

However cheering news from the lower Shenandoah Valley might be, or however innocuous the deadly drudgery before Petersburg and Richmond, few could find anything redeeming about Union operations in southwestern Virginia just then, unless it was the scanty newspaper attention occasioned by the remoteness of that theater. The only event in that region that had caught the public's notice in months had actually happened in Tennessee, when the commander of the Confederate Department of Western Virginia and East Tennessee had been killed. John Hunt Morgan, whom residents of Indiana and Ohio had come to loathe because of his 1863 foray into their states, had ridden from his headquarters in Abingdon, Virginia, to Greeneville, Tennessee, to meet a raid by Michigan and Unionist Tennessee cavalry under Alvin Gillem. Thinking he had chased them away, Morgan retired on the intensely stormy night of September 3 to the brick mansion of a widow in Greeneville. The thunder and lightning must have disguised the gunfire of Gillem's cavalry as it chased Morgan's men out of town early in the morning, and the general himself rose too late: Federals had surrounded the house, and as he tried to slip out the back one of them dropped the general stone dead.[72]

Later in September, writing from his Kentucky headquarters, Brigadier General Stephen Burbridge enlisted General Gillem in a scheme to pinch the Confederates of southwestern Virginia between their respective commands. Burbridge, who took an undue share of the credit for wrecking Morgan's Bluegrass raid the previous June, proposed leading a mounted division into the region from Kentucky while Gillem pressed them up the Great Valley from east Tennessee. Initially Gillem agreed, and in company with two regiments of foot he paced his approach to match Burbridge's more arduous march over the grueling mountain roads. The combined forces would entail more than six thousand cavalry, mounted infantry, and infantry, while the Confederates could depend on fewer than two thousand, and those were scattered the length and breadth of the voluminous department.[73]

It was salt that gave the region its greatest importance. Salt was essential to the preservation of meat, and the Southern diet relied heavily on meat, so without salt the winter would bring starvation. The U.S. Navy's blockade had curtailed the importation of salt, and Union armies had seized most sources of the vital crystal by the autumn of 1864. That made Saltville, Virginia, all the more crucial to the Confederacy, several states of which had sent agents there to assure adequate and fair distribution of a commodity in such demand that it invited graft. The armies of Lee, Early, and Hood had nevertheless stripped troops from southwestern Virginia, which had been reduced to a number of small mounted brigades and independent companies, with some dubious militia for local defense. Burbridge's plan might well have brought salt production to an end there had William Sherman not called the expedition off at the last moment. Unfortunately for Burbridge, Sherman's message reached Gillem first, depriving Burbridge of the cooperation that would have virtually assured his success. Clambering over the mountains in blissful ignorance of the change, Burbridge sparred with a depleted brigade of the dead Morgan's cavalry until he came within six miles of the salt wells, on the evening of October 1.[74]

The next morning Burbridge started down the Holston River toward the saltworks. Henry Giltner's Kentucky and Virginia horsemen slowed his progress with harassing fire from either bank, but Burbridge pressed them to the last ridge before the town. Chestnut Ridge rose steep and tall northeast of Saltville, and there, on the left bank of the Holston, Giltner prepared to make his stand with the six hundred cavalry and mounted rifles in his brigade. The only other Confederates nearby consisted of about the same number of old men and boys of the Virginia Reserves, without training or uniforms, commanded by a colonel with a long white beard. Burbridge divided his three brigades into separate columns, sending one downriver past Giltner to approach the town from the northwest, deploying another to try crossing the river in Giltner's front, and sending the third across the river to surmount Chestnut Ridge and cut off Giltner's retreat. That third brigade included a regiment each of Ohio and Michigan cavalry and five or six hundred recruits of the 5th and 6th U.S. Colored Cavalry.[75]

Only at the last moment did three more small Confederate brigades come thundering up under Brigadier General John S. Williams, freed to face Burbridge when Gillem withdrew on Sherman's orders. Williams's tiny Kentucky brigade sped to the lower crossings of the Holston to hold back Burbridge's Kentucky Federals while his brigades of Confederate Regulars and Tennessee cavalry raced up to Chestnut Ridge and took position just over the crest, facing the Yankees on their side of the river. None of Burbridge's first brigade made it over the river downstream, northwest of town, but some did on Giltner's front, only to be driven back by a desperate countercharge. On Chestnut Ridge the white and black Union cavalry made a valiant attempt to carry the heights, where four mismatched cannon disputed their passage, but it was the two brigades of reinforcements from the Tennessee front that saved the day — or rather the night, for the fighting continued there until after sunset. Under cover of darkness Burbridge took as many of his wounded as could travel and started back over the tortuous roads and trails to Kentucky: first he justified his hasty retirement on a lack of ammunition, but later he insisted that Sherman's order to desist had just reached him. He left behind scores of wounded to be taken prisoner, including one of his brigadiers, and Williams's skirmishers flushed a few stragglers from the brush in the morning, but they refused to accept the surrender of many of the wounded black troopers, squads of whom they executed on the spot. Giltner tracked the fugitives for the next two days, picking up stragglers and those too badly wounded to go on, but with a head start and an energy born of apprehension the main body of Yankees escaped him. After a weeklong hegira on short rations and food stolen from the mountain folk, Burbridge reached the safety of his Lexington headquarters and transformed his utter failure into success by means of adroit literary gymnastics, but the ragtag rebels of the Alleghenies had won another round.[76]

Sherman had not wanted Burbridge to return to Kentucky, but rather to send every man he could spare to Nashville, immediately. John Bell Hood had come back to life again after a few indolent weeks outside the lost city of Atlanta, and Sherman feared for his army's long umbilical, with good reason. Bedford Forrest's cavalry had gone to work on the railroad from Memphis to Chattanooga, tearing up track and capturing railroad guards wholesale, and then he moved into middle Tennessee to cut the roads from Nashville. Joe Wheeler had been hacking away at Sherman's supply line as well, and Forrest hoped to cooperate with him, but Hood concluded that he would instead put his entire army across Sherman's communications. He ordered Wheeler to rejoin him at his new position just west of Atlanta, but Wheeler was on the far side of Alabama at the time, and from Richmond the adjutant general had taken half Wheeler's cavalry away to answer Burbridge's raid on Saltville. Leaving a lone brigade of cavalry to watch Sherman, and taking only one mounted division to ride with him, Hood started the Army of Tennessee back across the Chattahoochee River, headed north, on September 29.[77]

That same day, George Thomas left Atlanta for Chattanooga and Nashville, from which he would deal with Forrest's depredations, and with him went a single division of infantry from his Army of the Cumberland. He arrived at Chattanooga the next day, finding the place packed with furloughed officers and men who were trapped by Forrest's presence somewhere between them and Nashville. Then Sherman perceived that Hood was on the move against his lifeline, and he started most of his own army back up the railroad, leaving only one corps to garrison Atlanta.[78]

Hood moved faster. Alexander Stewart's infantry hit the railroad above Marietta on October 3, tearing up the tracks on their way up the line that day and the next, meanwhile capturing hundreds of Union soldiers guarding the different stations. On the evening of October 4 they came to Allatoona, just below the Etowah River. There the railroad bisected a mountain through a conspicuous manmade cut more than sixty feet deep, and there Brigadier General John Corse commanded about two thousand men to protect a massive intermediate supply depot where towering piles of rations stood amid lowing herds of beef cattle bound for Atlanta. The guard detachments at the other railroad depots had surrendered readily enough, so Stewart dispatched only Samuel French's division to seize

Allatoona, but Corse refused to capitulate, and when French attacked the next morning Corse mounted a pertinacious defense. While his troops mowed down repeated rebel assaults, his signalmen atop Allatoona Pass maintained constant communication with Sherman, who paced the crest of Kennesaw Mountain, a dozen miles south. Sherman ordered reinforcements up from Atlanta, but on foot they had no chance of reaching Allatoona in time. North of the Etowah, a train headed for Rome to pick up some of the garrison there, but it derailed on the way and those troops were farther away than those at Atlanta. Corse was entirely on his own, but with more than a third of his command down he retired to the strongest redoubt on the hillside and fought until his ammunition was nearly gone. A bullet glanced across his cheekbone, stunning him, but he retained command and continued defiant until, finally, French withdrew in fear of the column coming from Atlanta.[79]

Heralded in headlines, Corse's heroic stand at Allatoona went a long way toward compensating for the disconcerting intelligence of Hood's reappearance. The editors conveyed the story as though Hood had been badly whipped, and was leading his army in a desperate retreat, but could not cross the Tennessee River. Instead, as Hood had hoped, his march north had brought Sherman back over the same ground he had fought so hard to gain, and it threatened to rejuvenate the chorus of doubt that echoed across the North with each apparent loss of a presumed advantage. The movement worried everyone, including President Lincoln, Edwin Stanton, and General Grant, who disliked a new plan Sherman had begun to promote — of abandoning both Atlanta and his line of communications, and taking his entire army on a raid across Georgia to the coast.[80]

Such a campaign would seem to leave the region of the Tennessee River open for Hood to recover for the Confederacy, and even after the repulse at Allatoona he demonstrated that he could do a great deal of damage if left to himself. From Allatoona he darted westward, toward Alabama, but short of that state he turned north, crossing the Coosa River well downstream from Rome. He navigated the mountains above Rome and then veered east again, crossing the Oostanaula and intersecting with the railroad below Resaca, snapping up more prisoners and supplies. Stephen Lee tried to seize the larger garrison at Resaca, but his men showed a decided shyness about the earthworks there, and when the Union commander refused his demand for surrender Lee let it go at that. Drawing back to the same Snake Creek Gap where James McPherson had waited for Joe Johnston, Lee camped his troops that night where McPherson's men had lain in May, inside their old earthworks and amid the five-month-old graves of Union soldiers. Stewart had better luck a couple of miles above Resaca, taking a blockhouse and several hundred more prisoners, and his men destroyed the railroad nearly all the way to Dalton, where they had spent the previous winter.[81]

Sherman's leading corps found the Confederates holding Snake Creek Gap, but before the rest of his three armies could come up the rebels slipped away, on October 15, following the long valley that ran southwest beside Lookout Mountain all the way to Gadsden, Alabama, where they stopped to draw clothing and shoes from the depot. Sherman, recognizing that he would merely be playing into Hood's hands if he continued the chase, camped thirty miles away. There he waited for ten days so his men could fatten up on the abundant provisions in that country, for his own supplies came by wagon over roads that required him to cut government rations in half. Then, after he had convinced Grant that it was safe to leave Hood to General Thomas, Sherman stripped off another corps of infantry to remain behind with Thomas while he and all the rest of his troops returned to Atlanta.[82]

While Hood's tattered and weary veterans had been luring the three powerful Union armies back from Atlanta, another Confederate force had materialized as though from nowhere on the far side of the Mississippi to cast a little more doubt on the image of universal Union triumph. On the same day as Phil Sheridan's first impressive victory in the Shenandoah Valley, Major General Sterling Price entered the state of Missouri with three Confederate divisions of cavalry and mounted infantry numbering nearly twelve thousand men, almost all of them from Missouri and Arkansas. A full third of them carried no weapons, which left them a vulnerable impediment for a peripatetic army with limited supplies, but Price evidently hoped to find arms for them in Missouri, which he had served as both congressman and governor. Price also represented his state in his personal political contradictions, for he had never advocated secession until federal troops under a fanatical abolitionist essentially declared war on the state, undertaking a preemptive attack on its militia and driving the duly elected legislature into exile. At Wilson's Creek, less than four months into the war, the Missouri State Guard had fought under Price alongside Confederate troops, but some of them went into that battle carrying a United States flag, evidently defending states' rights under the Constitution just as colonials had begun the American Revolution by asserting their rights as Englishmen. Price had given up on the concept of regaining state sovereignty under U.S. control, just as the rebels of 1775 had turned their energies toward independence by 1776. By taking the unarmed troops along Price seemed to signal an intention to establish himself in the state and remain there for a while. By the second half of 1864 Missouri was alive with animosity for Union soldiers and their government, and Price hoped to attract recruits by the thousands.[83]

In New York, Squire George Strong remarked that Phil Sheridan had "knocked down" the price of gold and the prospects of George McClellan with his performance in the valley, but he acknowledged that "a reverse or two before November" could restore both. Sterling Price may have aspired to contribute such a reverse, for Southern confidence persisted in the region where he gathered his troops. A week into September, one Arkansas judge who had accepted secession reluctantly in 1861 saw much better odds for ultimate Confederate victory in early September, despite the steady devaluation of Richmond's paper money, and a Union general actually proposed abandoning the interior of that state, where the storehouses for their outposts served only to equip rebel forces. Once reports of the capture of Atlanta leaked into the region, Confederate hopefulness abated, but Price's invasion was also partly intended to afford a diversion for Hood, in Georgia. Lieutenant General Edmund Kirby Smith, commander of the Trans-Mississippi, later explained that he had found it impossible to transport reinforcements across the Union-held Mississippi River, and that he anticipated that Price would divert thousands of Yankees who had been, or were about to be, sent east to aid Sherman.[84]

The Army of Missouri, as Price styled his corps — further implying an aim to occupy the state — crossed the state line from Arkansas, about 125 miles south of Saint Louis. That city seemed to be his target, and from his headquarters there William Rosecrans tried to throw some troops in Price's way, meanwhile calling for reinforcements. In the city he imposed modified martial law, ordering all businesses to close every afternoon so the employees could drill with the militia, and his soldiers collared civilians on the street to make them attend the musters.[85]

Price traveled with the three divisions, under James Fagan, John Marmaduke, and Joseph Shelby, spread out in three columns. A week's march brought the Army of Missouri within reach of Ironton, and just north of there a thousand Union volunteers and militia took refuge in a little fort under William Sherman's brother-in-law, Thomas Ewing. Price concentrated Fagan's and Marmaduke's divisions against the little bastion, skirmishing with the garrison there all day September 27 and making one charge, which Ewing's men repulsed. That night the Yankees slipped away by the only route left open to them. Hearing of Union reinforcements at Saint Louis that greatly outnumbered him, Price maintained a northerly course toward that city, burning rail depots, destroying track and bridges, and capturing hundreds of Sharps breechloading rifles. On the first of October a brigade of Fagan's Arkansans ventured as far as Franklin, within twenty-five miles of Saint Louis proper, where a brigade of veteran Union infantry chased them away, but the rest of the army veered west, below the Missouri River, for the state capital at Jefferson

City. Price found the city stoutly defended by men behind solid earth-works, so he skirted that scene of his earlier glory to find another target, at Lexington, which he had captured three years before.[86]

Missouri guerrillas attached themselves to Price, who put them to use against railroads north of the Missouri, and their depredations raised a hue and cry in the loyal press. Even the less irregular troops with the main army took whatever they wanted all along their route, stripping farms of horses, livestock, and grain. In the plantation country of the Missouri River valley they also attracted hundreds of recruits, if not thousands — but more by conscription at gunpoint than by volunteering, according to one of their pursuers. Price started looking for armories where he might find weapons for the new men and for the unarmed division that had rid-den with him from Arkansas. A number of garrison towns on the river promised to supply them, and the first one he came to was Glasgow, on the far side of the river. At dawn of October 15 one of Fagan's brigades swam the river and attacked the town directly while Shelby opened on it with artillery from the right bank, but before they surrendered the de-fenders set fire to the town hall, where the rifles had been stored. The re-bels did gather in somewhat fewer than a thousand prisoners and their weapons, along with more than a thousand overcoats that would be wel-come in the cool autumn air. Leaving the captured Yankees behind on parole, Price proceeded upriver once again, blithely picking up recruits while Union infantry under Rosecrans raced to catch up with him.[87]

Ahead of Price lay a collection of volunteers and militia from Missouri, Kansas, and Colorado under the direction of Sam Curtis, who had fought Price at Pea Ridge in 1862. Curtis — the general whose family was living so comfortably on his army salary (and apparently from his cotton specu-lation, as well) — had come in from fighting Indians on the plains to meet Price. He made his initial headquarters at Kansas City and assured his wife, at Fort Leavenworth, that Price could not cross the river, but he doubted the outcome sufficiently that he warned her to send her valu-ables to safety with a woman who had decided to find a safer haven. A Leavenworth newspaperman on the border noted, the night after Glas-gow surrendered, that the "cold, clear light of the Hunter's Moon is shin-ing on the encampments of five thousand Kansas soldiers."[88]

The Trans-Mississippi, as the Confederate government so dismissively designated everything it claimed west of the Mississippi River, attracted little attention east of the Big Muddy. A Union soldier in northern Ar-kansas, whence Price's army had entered Missouri, remarked that their theater of operations was "out of the world," and unworthy of national no-tice. Unless they involved prominent cutthroats like William Quantrill or Bloody Bill Anderson, Easterners never heard of fierce little combats between motley brigades — like the one at Cabin Creek, Indian Territory, on the same day Price crossed the Missouri line, in which Texan, Cherokee, Creek, and Seminole Confederates trounced hundreds of Union soldiers and Indian Home Guards as they escorted a wagon train from Fort Scott to Fort Gibson. The grand march of the Army of Missouri aroused little more interest than those spats in the territory, warranting only a few column inches two or three times a week from the major dailies. New Yorkers first heard of Price's latest foray through a back-page piece two weeks into the invasion, after his bridge burners had already visited Franklin, but no one seemed very troubled about it, although he used the notorious bands of both Quantrill and Anderson for incidental sabotage.[89]

Price's raid, and to a lesser extent Hood's drive north, faded into the background with another bold-type announcement of "victory," at least on the front pages of Republican newspapers. Early elections in the bellwether states of Pennsylvania, Ohio, and Indiana had all gone to the Union Party, and administration papers crowed about it for days on end, quoting phenomenal landslides. They reported that Ohio had elected seventeen Republican congressmen and only two Democrats, with comfortable margins at home and overwhelming majorities among its soldiers, while Pennsylvania chose two Republicans for every Democrat. Soldiers and civilians reading such lopsided returns lapsed into either relief or dismay, for those three states alone accounted for more than a quarter of the country's electoral votes, and handy victories in worrisome states like Pennsylvania seemed to foretell the reelection of President Lincoln. A Republican daily in Iowa boasted that the McClellan candidacy was "up a spout." Then, for good measure, Phil Sheridan gave the country another thrilling battlefield performance from the Shenandoah Valley.[90]

Because his wagon train could support him no farther up the valley, Sheridan had taken the main body of his army only as far as Harrisonburg, and with the first of October he proposed to Grant that he could do the most damage by turning back down the valley. To deprive Lee's army of its agricultural bounty he would lay waste to the countryside all the way, destroying not only crops but even "the means of planting," and when he arrived at the Potomac he would leave Crook to hold the valley while the other two corps continued on to join Grant before Petersburg. That sounded right to Grant, and a few days later Sheridan's infantry started tramping back toward Winchester, filing past their own cavalry as it implemented Sheridan's drastic orders. As the 10th New York Heavy Artillery crested a hill on the Valley Pike, a lieutenant could see the smoke from five burning farms at once, and when their march carried them past another home the women who lived there stood weeping while Yankee horsemen drove off all their cattle and sheep. One woman tracked the army for ten miles looking in vain for a general who would order the return of her last cow, whom she called "Betty." Whatever the cavalrymen could not use to feed the army, they destroyed: a Vermont surgeon thought the devastation "beyond description," and caravans of refugees started north in company with the same vandals who had left them destitute. The victims included many families of divided or even loyal sentiments, some of whom had befriended certain of the Union soldiers when they first entered the Shenandoah Valley.[91]

Sheridan's orders implied that he should leave towns and villages unmolested, since they offered no agricultural benefit to the Confederacy, but when one of his engineers was killed in an isolated scrap with Virginia cavalrymen, the general used that as an excuse to exceed his orders. That engineer, Lieutenant John Meigs, happened to be the only son of Montgomery Meigs, the quartermaster general of the U.S. Army, and Sheridan accepted the rumor that Meigs had been murdered, so, to the disgust of some of his own officers and men, Sheridan ordered every house within a five-mile radius to be burned to the ground, including the village of Mount Crawford. Confederate cavalry shadowed his rear guard, finding to their frustration that other towns had been put to the torch as well. Outnumbered and outraged, they made a dash at George Custer's picket line one night, near Fisher's Hill, snaring three prisoners from the 1st New Hampshire Cavalry who were found hanging from tree limbs the next morning.[92]

With burly Tom Rosser leading them, the rebel horsemen badgered Sheridan's cavalry as vigorously as their worn-out stock and inferior equipment would allow. One of Rosser's two divisions lacked sabers, revolvers, or carbines, having to rely instead on rifles that forced them to dismount for reloading, and that made them vulnerable to mounted charges. While Early and the infantry bided their time at New Market, twenty-five miles away, Rosser strung his cavalry across the valley at Tom's Brook, south of Fisher's Hill. Alfred Torbert attacked him there with all three divisions of Sheridan's cavalry on October 9, and the tide turned early in the day against the Southern cavaliers: they fled up the valley as fast as their winded horses could carry them, leaving behind all their artillery, wagons, and ambulances. Torbert chased them until his own horses gave out, through Woodstock and beyond, sabering gunners and taking their guns when the horse artillery turned to curb the pursuit.[93]

"Desolation marks everything," reported a division quartermaster who traveled the valley a couple of weeks later. The swath that Sheridan incinerated made it clear that he did not then intend to return to the upper valley, and Early picked up the information that Sheridan meant to send two corps back to Grant. To prevent that he decided to attack again, despite his conspicuous disadvantage in numbers, and he reported that his infantry was "in good heart and condition" — perhaps with a vengeful edge after passing so many charred homes and burnt-over fields.[94]

Sheridan had fortified himself behind Cedar Creek, where it flowed into the Shenandoah. From his old position behind Fisher's Hill, Early found routes for two infantry columns to approach from the southeast and southwest while a small Southern cavalry division rode stealthily up Cedar Creek and came at the enemy camp from behind. His troops all moved into position in the dark of night, with John B. Gordon's corps marching single-file on a primitive track around the foot of Massanutten Mountain. Once in position, everyone lay waiting in the mist until 5:00 A.M. on October 19, when all three columns burst into the Union camps. They hit the Eighth Corps first, and most of that somnolent multitude opted for either immediate surrender or headlong retreat; the Nineteenth Corps showed as much surprise and little more grit, leaving behind only prisoners and spoils.[95]

Early had designated a cavalry detachment to race toward Belle Grove plantation, where he knew Sheridan to have made his headquarters, but Sheridan was not there: he had been called to Washington for a conference, and Horatio Wright was left in charge. Wright's Sixth Corps had more warning and showed a little more fight, forming a line under the Greek crosses of their battle flags and slowing the rebels for a couple of hours, but the weight of Early's two columns bent their line double, and over the course of the morning even Wright's divisions fell back a couple of miles.[96]

The Confederate onslaught netted a couple of dozen guns and well over a thousand prisoners whom guards hustled to the rear, on the first leg of a trek to prison camps some of them would not survive. The battle subsided to skirmishing while hungry rebels plundered the enemy camps, and then — as morning became afternoon — Phil Sheridan came tearing up the Valley Pike at a full gallop. Breakfasting nearly twenty miles away in Winchester, on his way back from Washington, he had heard reports of distant firing and leaped onto his favorite horse, spurring the animal without stint until he came within sight of the battle smoke, around noon. When he began passing stragglers he slowed to encourage them; they started turning around to follow him, and above Newtown he could see the Sixth Corps and the cavalry still contesting the field. Rallying the other two corps, he steadied the line through the early afternoon and then, about 4:00 P.M., he waved them into a counterattack. The rebels had been awake most of the night and fighting all day, while Sheridan's reconstituted army significantly outnumbered them, so when the Nineteenth Corps slammed into Early's left flank it caved in. General Ramseur went down, dying, and in a relative twinkling Early's entire army began flooding toward the rear behind a blazing screen of artillery. Union cavalry circled around to intercept the retreat, and when the sabers began slashing among them the erstwhile masters of the field broke and ran, leaving everything behind including their own artillery, as well as all they had captured. In half an hour the smashing battlefield triumph the Confederacy needed so badly had dissolved into an unmitigated rout. The fugitives sprinted unabashedly into the autumn darkness, with the shattered remnants of Stonewall Jackson's storied command among them. The presidential election lay less than three weeks away, and Sheridan had again demonstrated how badly the ostensibly invincible Confederate army could be beaten.[97]

6

From Charred Atlanta Marching

◈ TO AUGMENT THE electoral effect of Sherman's and Sheridan's accomplishments, President Lincoln's campaign enjoyed the propaganda benefits of a well-timed War Department report on treason. In an "investigation" that began with Lincoln's nomination for a second term and ended with his reelection, Edwin Stanton's favorite headsmen informed the secretary — who then informed the public — of an extensive seditious organization associated with the Democratic Party that was waiting to spring into revolt against the government.

The inspiration for this mummery appears to have originated in Saint Louis. Colonel John P. Sanderson, of the 13th U.S. Infantry, had come to that city late in the winter to serve as provost marshal for William Rosecrans in the Department of Missouri. Sanderson was not a soldier, but a politician. As a state senator in Pennsylvania he had cultivated a close friendship with Simon Cameron, and had personally visited President-elect Abraham Lincoln to urge Cameron for secretary of war. That mission had won him the chief clerkship in the War Department under Cameron, and later a direct field commission when Congress authorized nine new regiments for the Regular Army. His military career had consisted primarily of recruiting and staff duty thus far, and he had hardly donned his shoulder straps before he started reporting on the Knights of the Golden Circle, which Republican mythology touted as a fraternity for Northern advocates of secession who planned to overthrow the government.[1]

The brotherhood evidently did still exist, albeit only as the remnant of a scheme concocted by an antebellum charlatan who had promoted it as a fantasy filibustering expedition to Mexico, for the purpose of defrauding dues-paying members. With the help of Henry Carrington, the commander of the Military District of Indiana, Governor Oliver Morton had crafted a detailed image of the K.G.C. to serve as an effective political tool for smearing any who opposed government policy. Like Sanderson, Carrington had used political connections in the summer of 1861 to secure a direct appointment as colonel in the Regular Army. He compiled an imaginative report on an armed, ninety-two-thousand-man fifth column lurking in Indiana, and Morton prepared that novella for publication in pamphlet form by the nationwide network of Union Leagues — the main mission of which was to distribute Republican propaganda under the guise of nonpartisan "Union" literature. The K.G.C. pamphlets contributed substantially to the demonization of the Democratic Party and its candidates, helping to reverse the tide of opposition and to germinate lingering distrust of dissidence in general. The little booklets outlined the purported structure of the organization and the rituals of the order, thereby aiding anyone with a taste for political perjury to offer convincingly detailed testimony as further evidence.[2]

Sanderson took Carrington's example to the national level. Almost as soon as he arrived in Saint Louis he began compiling a dossier on what he characterized as a vast treasonable conspiracy under the auspices of the Order of American Knights, which he presented as the latest metamorphosis of the K.G.C. Most of his indictment consisted of testimony he claimed to have taken from incarcerated or paroled Confederate prisoners of war and political prisoners, whose names he refused to divulge, ostensibly to protect them from reprisals. He invented aliases for all of them except one, and included evidence given by a suspected impostor whom another provost marshal deemed "a great rascal," who seemed willing to incriminate anyone in return for his own freedom. Sanderson also appeared to give full credence to what he labeled "An Anonymous Letter from a Lady" who warned of a disloyal society called the "Knights of America" that reached all the way from New York into the West. Professed apostates of the order reported at least two hundred thousand members, with as many as a million followers, and they testified that the various councils were amassing weapons, ammunition, and "infernal machines" for their uprising. One week before the Republican convention, Sanderson presented General Rosecrans with a sheaf of hearsay, innuendo, and fairly obvious fabrication.[3]

Two days after Sanderson's first letter on the subject, Rosecrans wired the president immediately to say that he had information too secret to transmit by mail, and asked permission to send him the documents by the hand of a staff officer, probably thinking of Sanderson as the best emissary. Lincoln waited several days to respond, suggesting that Rosecrans ship the packet by express, but the general balked. He let the governors of Illinois, Indiana, Ohio, and Kentucky into the secret, and Illinois governor Richard Yates interceded with the president, urging him to allow either Rosecrans or Sanderson to come to Washington with the evidence. Suspecting that Rosecrans really had a favor to ask, Lincoln finally told one of his personal secretaries, John Hay, to prepare himself for a quick journey west, and invited Rosecrans to trust the young man with anything he would see fit to tell the president. Hay was nearly three days getting there, and Rosecrans met him at the Lindell House in Saint Louis the night of June 13, outlining the evidence in general and interspersing it with some by-the-way explanations of his ill-starred tenure commanding the Army of the Cumberland. Afterward, Sanderson led Hay across the hall to show him the thick wad of affidavits, examination transcripts, and letters that he had accumulated. Hay deduced that Sanderson very much wanted to see the president personally, the better to impress him with the importance of his discoveries. When Hay returned to Washington, four days later, his revelations evoked little concern from Lincoln. Annoyed that Rosecrans had not released the paperwork, he snorted at the idea of keeping secret from the chief magistrate what had already been revealed to four governors and their staffs, growing all the stronger in his suspicion of ulterior motives.[4]

According to Rosecrans, the uprising was supposed to begin on July 4, with the opening of the Democratic convention. As it happened, Jacob Thompson, a leading Confederate agent who worked out of a Toronto hotel, did hope for a general revolt on Independence Day from a group he called the Sons of Liberty. He also hoped for a number of other ambitious operations, however, like a plot to spring Confederate prisoners in Chicago and Indianapolis, or to set fire to major Northern cities, all of which either fizzled or had to be abandoned for lack of resources. In a report to Attorney General Judah P. Benjamin, Thompson said he met with men who identified themselves as leaders of the Sons of Liberty, but the most generous interpretation of those fraternal potentates would describe them as suffering from delusions of grandeur. Even Thompson understood them to represent far fewer people than Sanderson claimed, and — judging from the paucity of contemporary correspondence between actual members of the society, and from the dearth of credible confessional memoirs — those who met with Thompson were surely overestimating their membership as they presented it to him. For that matter, most of those who did belong to any of the various secret societies may not have taken the notion of armed revolt any more seriously than President Lincoln did. Considering the greenbacks and gold that Thompson doled out to real and pretended saboteurs and provocateurs, the presumed leaders of the conspiracy could well have misrepresented themselves altogether simply to filch a portion of his secret-service fortune: Thompson's report named at least one other stranger with an elaborate tale of an improbable, undocumented mission who had appeared in Toronto with the more obvious (and successful) aim of bilking Thompson out of some of his Confederate funds.[5]

To the extent that they existed at all, the secret societies would have provided little more than a private haven for the company of politically like-minded men, most of whom remained perfectly loyal but judged the war unconstitutional, a failure, or both. In that respect those fraternities mirrored the Union Leagues that flourished in almost every city and in many of the smaller towns, as a social rendezvous for men holding a common political viewpoint. When the expected rebellion of July 4 failed to take place, Thompson wrote Benjamin that his emissaries blamed it on the postponement of the Democratic convention. A "general Council" of the order scheduled a second plan for revolt later in July, but then canceled it and decided on a third for August 16 (or so the self-proclaimed insurgent moguls told Thompson), and the publicity around Horace Greeley's attempt at peacemaking supposedly caused the organization to abandon any orchestrated uprising at all, in favor of a political solution. The series of excuses that came Thompson's way carried the tone of a confidence game, for it would have been nearly impossible for a geographically widespread organization to hold executive meetings so frequently and convey the intelligence of such substantial changes of plan when it could not be trusted to either the mail or the telegraph.[6]

President Lincoln thought the Canadian Confederates were more intent on collaborating with Democratic leaders to field a peace candidate at the convention, or at least he wished the public to believe as much, in order to discredit any peace candidate or platform in advance. At no time did he give much weight to the report of pending revolt that Sanderson had submitted, or to any of the blizzard of similar material that followed. Neither did his immediate circle appear to find all the testimony terribly alarming, including Secretary Stanton, but that failed to deter Stanton from pursuing the matter with accelerating vigor and attention as the election approached. While the president tried to establish a political connection between enemy agents and Peace Democrats, his war minister charged the judge advocate general with finding an even more subversive association between the two.[7]

Stanton had chosen Joseph Holt as his judge advocate general in 1862. The two had much in common. Both men had been lifelong Democrats until the war began, and both had been cabinet officers under James Buchanan — Stanton as attorney general, and Holt as postmaster general.

In that administration they had purportedly been the strongest advocates of maintaining federal authority against the seceding states. When the fighting began, both men became unrelenting, and often unreasonable, in the administration of their duties. Prompted by Sanderson's stream of reports, Stanton sent Holt to Kentucky and Saint Louis to look for further evidence, and after a couple of weeks in Louisville Holt replied that yes, indeed, plenty of information had been collected to "dictate clearly" a conspiracy throughout Kentucky, Ohio, Indiana, and Illinois to rise up against the government. When Holt returned to Washington, early in August, he submitted his own report corroborating all Sanderson had claimed, and more. In an eerie foreshadowing of the McCarthy era, he charged that the traitors labored ceaselessly to infiltrate the government and ancillary services, like the telegraph office, both as a means of gleaning confidential information and generally injuring or betraying the government. Those who had been arrested and examined tended to deny all connection with any conspiracy, but Holt only viewed their denials as further evidence of their guilt, since "perjury is but one of the every-day phases of a traitor's life."[8]

Stanton's official inaction that summer belied any real terror over insurgent plots. The commander of the Northern Department, encompassing Ohio, Indiana, Illinois, and Michigan, asked for twenty-five thousand troops to defend those states against insurrection, but Ulysses Grant positively refused them — and the secretary of war made no objection to his refusal. In Indiana another general replaced Henry Carrington as commander of the military district, so Carrington could devote all his attention to the investigation and editorial condemnation of treasonable societies, but when that successor's provost marshal requested four thousand troops to "suppress incipient revolt," Stanton sent only $5,000 in secret-service funds. The governor and adjutant general of New York asked a former governor to intercede with Stanton for funds to buy ten thousand stand of arms to equip a home guard against insurgents and infiltrators from Canada. In reply Stanton denied the need for any home guard, or for any apprehension of trouble from that quarter, but all the while Colonel Sanderson's estimates of the number of plotting insurrectionists grew, and Carrington's reports of the supposed conspiracy made the rounds of Republican newspapers below the Great Lakes, throwing the old Northwest into a fluster.[9]

Not until August 31, 1864, when the Democratic convention nominated George McClellan for the presidency, did Stanton give Holt the latest packet of evidence from Sanderson. That installment included Sanderson's leading questions about an alleged New York society he called the "McClellan Minute Men" (about which his interrogations elicited nothing), as well as some benign-looking penciled notations that were supposed to have been minutes of O.A.K. meetings, in which members referred to each other as "Sir Knight." Inspired, perhaps, by Holt's reference to the publication of Carrington's "researches" in the Western press, Stanton instructed Holt to combine his own and Sanderson's accumulated bunkum into "a detailed report."[10]

With that, the investigation blossomed into its ultimate incarnation as a government-funded propaganda project dedicated to the defamation of Democratic candidates in general and George McClellan in particular.[11] According to Sanderson, and thus according to Holt, the supreme commander of those hundreds of thousands of Northern traitors was Clement Vallandigham. Vallandigham's alleged counterpart in the Confederate wing of the Sons of Liberty — or O.A.K., K.G.C., or Corps de Belgique — was supposed to be Sterling Price, whose passage through Missouri that autumn seemed consistent with the claim that Southern forces would coordinate their movements with those supposititious battalions of allies lying in wait behind Union lines. Holt must have approached Henry Carrington to help him compile the report, because, only four days after Stanton charged Holt with the project, Carrington informed a crony that he was preparing a comprehensive history of the secret societies to give the president "for the public," and indeed politically timely publication seemed to be the main purpose of Holt's report. Carrington also mentioned that he was about to begin a speaking tour of the state, obviously on his favorite subject of the conspiracy, since such a topic would inevitably aid Republican candidates without even naming them. While Carrington harangued crowds on the evil aspirations of myriad devils masquerading as Democrats, a military tribunal met in Indianapolis to decide the fate of several accused ringleaders of the plot in Indiana, all of whom were prominent Democrats. The government had found military courts particularly useful because they paid no heed to constitutional protections or the rules of evidence that prevailed in civil courts, so they leaned sharply toward conviction, and that was the prompt result in the Indianapolis trials.[12]

With Carrington's assistance, Holt punctually submitted his report on the secret societies on October 8, exactly one month before the election, and it was hastily prepared for widespread distribution in pamphlet form. According to that pamphlet, Vallandigham and one other conspirator had established the disloyal society in the fall of 1863, although Vallandigham had been expelled from the country months previously. The mysterious "McClellan Minute Guard" came in for particular notice: an anonymous witness had supposedly claimed that the chief officer of the Minute Guard admitted that the McClellan campaign preached insincere support for the war because that was what the voters wanted — and that seems to be exactly what the reputed leaders of the Sons of Liberty had told Jacob Thompson, to explain their equivocation. Holt's report listed the names of numerous leaders of the conspiracy, but many of those men were never arrested, or even interviewed, including the putative ringleader Vallandigham, who was responsible for the Democrats' peace plank. Big-city Union Leagues published similar pamphlets casting Vallandigham as the head of a subversive society, or otherwise associating Democrats with treason, and they often summarized the entire argument in the bold-print title on the front page, for the benefit of those who did not wish to bother reading any further. Charges of rank treason spawned pithy, pejorative slogans that trumped Democratic complaints about usurpation, abolition, or corruption.[13]

For all the accusations and named names, however, only in Indiana had any treason trial come to the public eye. That was the state where those seeking testimony had obtained $5,000 in secret-service funds, which was precisely the amount one self-professed conspirator had set as his price for giving Carrington and Governor Morton all the incriminating details. In that trial, most of the government's case came from a single detective who said he had infiltrated the order, and from a few reputed members who had been threatened with prosecution for the capital crime of treason, at least one of whom suffered a suspicious lapse of memory when asked repeatedly whether the government detective had coached him on his testimony. The election-eve charade filled Indianapolis newspapers day after day, terrifying and infuriating readers and voters who imagined they would have been the victims of the defendants' fiendish designs.[14]

The Indiana trials offered inspiration and a semblance of credibility to government officials who chose to bring charges of subversive activity against lesser figures, whose arrests might further stir the public paranoia, smear administration critics, and cow political opposition. Such may have been the motivation behind the mid-September arrest of a prominent draft opponent in Portsmouth, New Hampshire, for keeping a crate of rifles in his store. Although firearms constituted part of the merchant's wares, the provost marshal seized them all and arrested him on the assertion that the defendant planned to use his sixteen muskets to "resist the government."[15]

On November 4, Carrington assured Holt that the Sons of Liberty in New York intended to "create insurrection" if Lincoln were elected. "I am not mistaken in the infamous character of this order," that excitable desk general sternly advised Holt. "I make no assertion without proof." Still, no troops moved into the Northern states to address the threat Carrington deemed so imminent, and Holt seemed to ignore his dire warning altogether. With the election only four days away, the information could be put to no practical political use, so no more was heard of the pervasive, malignant conspiracy that Stanton's chief investigator had so recently judged a grave danger to the nation's survival. Only after the assassination of President Lincoln did the subject resurface in official circles, again implicating conservative Democrats by association with a supposedly resuscitated "Order of Knights of the Golden Circle."[16]

That some citizens from loyal states convened with Jacob Thompson is undeniable: Thompson and other rebel agents mentioned Judge Joshua Bullitt, of Kentucky, and one other officer in the Louisville temple of the Sons of Liberty. For all of that, even the army prosecutor in the Indiana treason trials admitted that the "more apparent treason" had been stricken from the oaths and rituals of the order because of the members' aversion to it, and his indictment of the organization described a fraternity of states'-rights Democrats whose political views differed from those of mainstream Democrats largely in their fear of and hostility toward a grasping central government. At a time when political activists of each faction were arming themselves against violence by the other, the Indianapolis prosecutor tried to present the possession of fewer than three hundred revolvers by members of the Indiana society as proof that the order intended a military takeover of the state, or at least to resist the draft. The testimony in Indianapolis instead suggests that most of the leaders fancied their order as a purely political association meant to imitate and counter the Union Leagues that served Republican interests, and those leaders counseled answering the draft with substitutes, rather than subversion. Meanwhile, however few or numerous the rank-and-file members may have been, most of them seemed to find nothing treasonable in their membership. Assuming that the more incriminating witnesses were even telling the truth (and perjury did taint the government's case in most military tribunals during the second half of the war), any plans for insurrection involved only a few megalomaniacal senior officers. The failure of anyone in the War Department to contemplate a military response to the peril of an armed revolt illustrates how little administration officials believed their own propaganda about the secret societies, and the timing of the trials just prior to the presidential election betrays the political motivation that underlay them.[17]

With little or no aid from Northern conspirators, a few Confederate operatives just over the Canadian border tried to implement their own desperate, harebrained schemes for cultivating Northern war weariness. Just as the leaders of the Sons of Liberty went on trial in Indianapolis, and as Phil Sheridan drove Early's rebels out of Winchester once and for all, a couple of dozen Confederates under Acting Master John Y. Beall seized the Lake Erie steamer *Philo Parsons,* from which they hoped to board the only gunboat the United States had on the lake — the side-wheel steamer *Michigan.* Their ludicrous scheme included using the gunboat to free the thousands of Confederate officers imprisoned on Johnson's Island, in Sandusky Bay, Ohio; after the prisoners had been mounted on stolen horses, they would ride diagonally across Ohio to Wheeling, and cross the Ohio River into what they still recognized as Virginia. This wild plan involved another escaped Confederate prisoner using the name Charles H. Cole, variously known as an officer of the 5th Tennessee Cavalry of Forrest's command and an officer in the C.S. Navy, who was supposed to abet the lake pirates by getting aboard the *Michigan* and disabling the officers with drugged wine poured into goblets around the wardroom. Someone tipped off the provost marshal in Detroit, who alerted Captain John Carter of the *Michigan,* and Carter steamed immediately to Sandusky to arrest Cole. In trying to explain his way free, Cole mentioned several citizens of Sandusky who were instantly arrested as suspected accomplices.[18]

Disappointed not to see the expected signal from the *Michigan,* the band on the *Philo Parsons* instead boarded another steamer, the *Island Queen,* laden with civilian passengers and a few dozen hundred-day soldiers on their way home. They paroled the soldiers, took them and the passengers aboard, sank the *Queen,* and landed everyone on an island in the Detroit River. Beall's crew balked at his proposal to take the *Michigan* without Cole's assistance, especially since the Union vessel was probably on the alert, so Beall abandoned the *Parsons.* He and his men dispersed on the Canadian side.[19]

A few weeks later more Confederates swooped out of Canada to give Northern citizens a taste of how quickly war could turn their peaceful lives upside down, as Phil Sheridan was demonstrating for the people of the Shenandoah Valley. Like Beall and Cole, those men inadvertently chose the same day as one of Sheridan's sweeping valley victories. The last yellow leaves of autumn still clung to the trees in the town of Saint Albans, Vermont, fifteen miles below the boundary with Canada East, when some strangers started drifting into town from the north, singly and in pairs, and took lodging at the American Hotel and the Tremont House. No one paid much attention to them, supposing they were speculators or substitute brokers who had been scouting over the line for potential recruits. Others arrived over the course of a day or two. The streets lay soggy from recent rains on the lowery afternoon of Wednesday, October 19, when a score or more of those men appeared in front of the American Hotel, wearing caped overcoats commonly associated with the cavalry. The bells had rung three o'clock, and then the half hour, at which each of the men drew a revolver or two from beneath those coats, and a young Kentuckian named Bennett Young started shouting orders. Young was merely a lieutenant, but the men addressed him as "Colonel," probably to suggest that they had come in greater numbers; some of his men herded startled pedestrians onto the village green across Main Street while a few others entered each of the three banks that sat directly opposite the green.[20]

Saint Albans had provided Mr. Lincoln with a good many soldiers. Still, a sizable number of vigorous young men worked as cashiers and clerks in the banks and in nearby stores when the rebels started waving their revolvers and barking gruffly at anyone who showed his — or her — head. In stark contrast to the demographics in Southern towns that season, only two of the residents walking or working on Main Street when the raid began had ever seen any military service in the war, and both of them had been nine-month soldiers who never faced an armed enemy.[21]

Inside the banks, the raiders held cashiers and customers at bay while they rifled the vaults. At the Saint Albans Bank, on the corner of Kingman Street and Main, a merchant who came in to make his afternoon deposit encountered a stranger who pointed a revolver at him and said that he accepted deposits. Another stranger entered the Franklin County Savings Bank, beside the American Hotel, at the other end of the same block, and engaged the cashier with an attempt to buy gold just before his comrades burst in brandishing their pistols, swearing they were going to burn the town after robbing the banks; they locked the cashier and one customer in the vault before leaving. A young store clerk saw the robberies and ran across Main Street to alert those inside the newly opened First National Bank, but some of the raiders caught him, dragged him over to the green, and relieved the institution of about $55,000 in legal tender and bonds; the take from all three banks totaled $150,000. Only when the gunmen emerged from the banks and started stealing horses did anyone seem to respond aggressively. A few men found weapons and fired at the raiders, wounding at least one of them, and his compatriots started firing back. From the street one of the rebels, whom a local woman remembered as a recent guest at the Tremont House, fatally shot a masonry contractor as he sought refuge in a Main Street shop. A passing pedestrian took a bullet in the hip when he ignored orders to join his fellow citizens on the village green. At last the bandits galloped out of town toward Sheldon, on a path that circled back into Canada. A couple of former officers in the 1st Vermont Cavalry, both of whom had come home after resigning their commissions, formed a posse to pursue them, chasing the party across the international boundary. The rebels scattered, and the posse caught up with a few of them, including Lieutenant Young, but had to turn them over to Canadian authorities, who jailed them while the two governments began a long dispute over the legitimacy of their status as belligerents and the jurisdiction of U.S. authorities.[22] Meanwhile, panic gripped towns all along the Canadian border. The War Department contributed enough weapons and cavalry tack to mount five hundred men, and the military rendezvous at Brattleboro shipped a few carloads of convalescent soldiers and guards from the Veteran Reserve Corps to comfort nervous bankers, businessmen, and harried politicians.[23]

Much like the raids north of the Potomac and the Ohio over the previous two years, the ineffective little intrigues hatched in Canada served primarily to anger the border population, and to corroborate the Radical Republican image of the Southern cause as one prosecuted by brigands and brutes. Combined with the serial misfortunes of Confederates on the battlefield, the raids tended to strengthen Northern resolve to crush the rebellion once and for all, rather than nurturing any war-weary conviction to let the Confederacy go its own way. An extensive campaign of guerrilla warfare might have reversed that effect, especially if it had been accompanied by a stubborn continuation of a stalemate in Virginia and Georgia, but Confederate resources could never have sustained such a campaign and Canadian neutrality would not have tolerated it.

The same could be said for Sterling Price's last pilgrimage through his adopted state of Missouri, which had reached its apogee by the time gunshots rang out on the streets of Saint Albans. Just as Lieutenant Young's men gathered on the porch of the American Hotel, Price's leading division ran into stubborn resistance at Lexington, Missouri, from the first of General Curtis's forces. Brigadier General James Blunt, who had been operating under something of a cloud for the past year, met Price with a couple of thousand Kansas and Wisconsin cavalry and some little mountain howitzers. Moderate Kansas politicians suspected that Curtis and Senator James Lane had called out the Kansas militia just to excite the Radical element for the coming election, and doubted that Price was still headed west, so the governor would not allow his militia to go any farther than the immediate vicinity of the Missouri border. Blaming that decision, Curtis informed Blunt that he could have no reinforcements, so Blunt skirmished with the Confederate advance until rifled guns forced him to withdraw. He backed toward Independence during the night, and Price kept coming. The next morning Blunt took position on high ground along the western bank of the Little Blue River, hoping to make a stand there until Rosecrans could overtake Price with his considerable little army of infantry and cavalry, but Curtis told Blunt to pull all the way back to Independence.[24]

Curtis meant to make his fight beyond the Big Blue River, with his back against the Kansas state line, for that was as far as the militia would go. He concentrated most of his troops before Kansas City and nearby Westport, on the roads from those towns to Independence. Blunt spread his own troops across several upstream fords on the Big Blue, in case Price decided to flank the main body. A terrified but determined militia-man from Paola, Kansas, wrote a hasty note to his wife the evening of the twenty-first, advising her to leave town with everything she could save. "The Rebels are on us," he told her, and the morning would bring the big battle. "I never expect to see My little family Again on the Earth but hope to meet you in heaven."[25]

Leaving Independence on the morning of October 22, Price sent a sin-gle brigade toward Kansas City to decoy Curtis while he and the rest of the Army of Missouri swerved southwest on the road to Fort Scott, which ran through the border settlement of Santa Fe. That brought them to the uppermost ford on the Big Blue, guarded by Kansas militia, and a Con-federate cavalry regiment from Missouri blundered into part of the 2nd Kansas State Militia between the Big Blue and Santa Fe. The militiamen, all of whom had remained comfortably at home barely ten days before, fended off the cavalry for a while with the help of a brass twenty-four-pounder, but Jo Shelby threw another brigade at them and scattered the lot of them, taking their brass fieldpiece into the bargain. Shelby turned north to confront the militia and Blunt's cavalry, driving them past the next crossing of the Big Blue, known as Byram's Ford. Blunt formed a line along Brush Creek, perpendicular to the river, and stopped Shelby there that night.[26]

The rest of the Confederate wagon train splashed across the Big Blue and headed down the road to Fort Scott, but the cavalry from Rosecrans's army had caught up with Price's main body and was pressing him from behind. On the clear, cold morning of Sunday, October 23, Price loosed Shelby once more against Curtis's mixture of militia and volunteers, which he started driving steadily northward. James Fagan's division followed Shelby in close support, and John Marmaduke turned to bar Byram's Ford to Rosecrans's cavalry, coming from the east now under Alfred Pleasonton. While Shelby splashed over Brush Creek and pushed Curtis across open prairie until they came within sight of Westport, Pleasonton slipped a mounted brigade upriver to flank Byram's Ford just as Shelby had flanked it the night before, and that brigade started toward Price's wagon train. Learning of it, Price instructed Shelby and Fagan to fall back to the Fort Scott road as soon as they could disengage, and until they could come to his aid Price threw his last little unattached brigade out as skirmishers, backing them up with his own escort company and the bluff of several thousand unarmed men standing in line of battle. That saved the train, but Marmaduke had to abandon the ford for lack of ammunition, allowing Pleasonton to squeeze Shelby and Fagan on the right flank while a few regiments of Kansas cavalry rode around their left. The prairie had turned "dark with Federals," Shelby said, and the Kansans came at a full gallop in a line twice as long as the dismounted brigade of Shelby's that met them, but with two rapid volleys at point-blank range the Confederates repelled first the Union horsemen directly in front of them, and then the others who were trying to swing around their left. The bold maneuver allowed Shelby and Fagan to escape, but with heavy losses, and only to fall in with Price for a night retreat. Hearing of the fight from his camp east of Independence, Rosecrans's infantry commander woke his men up around midnight and marched them all night toward the battlefield, but by sunrise the first of them had not yet reached the banks of the Big Blue River.[27]

Price's route for the next two days lay through Kansas. The dark, rainy evening of October 24 he camped on the Marais des Cygnes River, sixty miles from the Westport battlefield, and Curtis's column — minus the militia — ran upon him there at midnight. Creeping into position, the Yankees waited until the first glimmer of dawn to open with artillery. The rebels quickly fled, and Curtis started after them. Two brigades of Pleasonton's cavalry caught them at the slippery banks of Mine Creek a few miles later, and there the retreat turned to rout. Under brightening skies Lieutenant Colonel Frederick Benteen, who achieved notoriety at the Little Big Horn a dozen years later, charged Price's rear guard with a brigade of Missouri, Iowa, and Indiana cavalry. Benteen burst through their line and seized eight guns, while the Army of Missouri scattered to the winds. Hundreds of Price's men flung away their arms and ran, or threw up their hands and surrendered, along with General Marmaduke, two brigade commanders, and several colonels. Pleasonton's cavalry chased after the fugitives, hacking at them with sabers, until Jo Shelby's troopers turned around to face the torrent, breaking ranks to let their own stragglers through. Price again arrayed the unarmed division for the illusion of strength, and then Shelby unleashed his best brigade in a furious countercharge. That convinced Pleasonton that his horses were too exhausted, and he turned back to Fort Scott for forage. Price escaped again, after burning most of his wagons. James Blunt took up the pursuit where Pleasonton left off, attacking the rebels three days later at Newtonia, Missouri, and Shelby again covered the disintegrating army as it streamed farther south. With November, Price's survivors traversed northwest Arkansas, scattering finally into the Indian Territory and the

Red River country of Texas. Like the town of Winchester, Virginia, the state of Missouri would never feel the tread of another Confederate army.[28]

The final days before the presidential election saw Confederate fortunes at their lowest ebb yet. Price's bold gambit had failed to restore Missouri to the cause or to even gain enough recruits to compensate for his crippling losses, and the portion of his army that did return came back in terminal disarray. John Bell Hood and his Army of Tennessee languished in apparent impotency along the Tennessee River in northern Alabama, after having lost Atlanta at the crucial moment and been chased out of Georgia. The indefatigable General Forrest roamed West Tennessee with a few small brigades, seizing riverboats and some quartermaster stores, but even he failed to inspire his customary panic. Operations on the Atlantic coast had come to a standstill, each side having stripped the region for troops, and in Virginia Grant had made another leap to his left, trying again to close off Petersburg's last rail line, while simultaneously moving Butler against Richmond again from north of the James. For those at home who would be casting their ballots, every theater finally showed some promise.

Grant's late-October effort produced far more in the way of failure than his election-conscious official reports let on. Leaving only a skeleton guard in the trenches, he pulled most of the Second, Fifth, and Ninth Corps from the Petersburg line and spread them out three miles west of the last fieldworks built after the fighting around Poplar Spring Church. Well before dawn on October 27 they started forward under a cold, raw drizzle, mostly cross-country, with Hancock's Second Corps taking the left, Warren's Fifth Corps the center, and the Ninth Corps stretching between Warren and the last Union entrenchments. Hancock had orders to cross the Boydton Plank Road and keep going until he struck the Southside Railroad, but he ran into cavalry, and later he met infantry belonging to the same A. P. Hill who had handled him so roughly at Reams's Station, and who had sent much of the Ninth Corps packing at Poplar Spring Church, less than a month before. As the rain intensified, the outnumbered rebels managed to break between Hancock and Warren, catching several of Hancock's brigades from behind while they were under fire from the front. For a time it looked like a reprise of Reams's Station, but finally the rebels shrank back. A few hundred of them fell into Union hands, but one of Warren's staff admitted that they were captured "more by accident than by fighting." That concluded yet another attempt at the Southside Railroad, though, and the next day the three corps retired to their old lines, leaving the bodies of their dead comrades lying unburied. Those who watched Hancock's and Warren's men coming back into camp thought them especially demoralized.[29]

Butler had no better luck on the Union right. His men fought over the Fair Oaks battlefield of 1862, losing four hundred prisoners, gaining nothing, and leaving their own dead on the field when they withdrew. The dual movement, mimicking the late-September offensive, failed all around. Colonel Wainwright, the artilleryman, saw no accomplishment in it "save a few hundred more men laid under the sod." With the election eleven days away, Grant passed it off as a mere reconnaissance that had been intended to go out and return quickly: he called it "a decided success." That interpretation rang perfectly false to the men who had taken part in the expedition, one of whom remarked sarcastically about "Useless" Grant and the soldiers of either army, who "ran away from each other."[30]

Charles Mills, a division staff captain in the Ninth Corps, corroborated that poor opinion, at least from the perspective of his own army's effectiveness. He supposed that one good shove from Warren's Fifth Corps and the Ninth would have broken through the thin Confederate line, and he was probably right, but the Ninth Corps did no better than the others, and the entire operation had lacked vigor. It seemed obvious to Mills that "this army is not what it was in May by any means," and General Warren echoed that point when he explained that about a third of his corps had never loaded or fired a rifle before meeting the enemy on October 27. Mills estimated that atrocious casualties and the discharge of veterans who refused to reenlist had removed three-quarters of the men who had crossed the Rapidan less than six months previously, and clouds of recruits and new regiments had come nowhere near replacing them. He had complained weeks previously that the same attrition had caused a shortage of good line officers, as the more valorous fell in battle only to have less experienced subordinates who were more lucky — or more cautious — rise to the vacancy. Mills thought the army might overcome the deficiency by consolidating regiments, as the Confederate army did, but politics and privileges worked against such a solution. A major corroborated the poor quality of the recent Union levies, judging them "worthless as soldiers," and useful only to fill quotas. An older officer, who had marched through Baltimore with the 6th Massachusetts in 1861 and had been in the service ever since, revealed that even the veterans seemed more reluctant to face the enemy than they once had been. "I think they would not make a very good charge," he speculated that autumn, "as they have had enough of such work." The battle-hardened had now become understandably battle-weary.[31]

The Northern public heard none of that from army headquarters or the War Department. The administration's loyal newspapers dutifully reported Grant's transformation of the disappointing offensive into a useful reconnaissance in force, boasting that an attack on Hancock had been repulsed without mentioning that Hancock himself, as well as Warren, had been the ones repulsed in the end. In a subhead on the front page of the *New York Times,* edited by Republican National Committee chairman Henry Raymond, the "7 loaded teams" that Grant reported capturing became "seven wagon trains."[32]

Raymond's paper ran Grant's disingenuous account of his most recent offensive in the October 29 edition. He devoted more than half the front page of that same issue to his lead story on the War Department's latest show trial, in which a voting agent for the state of New York was accused of having forged soldiers' proxies. Joseph Holt appointed another of his military commissions to prosecute the case just prior to the election, and he appointed the Radical-friendly general Abner Doubleday to lead the court to a satisfactory conclusion. Curiously enough, the *Times* failed to name the defendant, instead identifying him only as a voting agent appointed by New York's Democratic governor, Horatio Seymour.[33]

Most states passed special legislation allowing their soldiers to vote in the field for the 1864 election, but those laws generally provided for officers of the individual units to act as registrars of the voting. In New York, Democratic fears that the War Department might concoct some kind of fraud with the soldier vote may have motivated the adoption of a proxy process, in which the soldier swore that he was a registered voter of his precinct, and authorized someone else in his home community to cast his vote "the same as if I was personally present at the general election." Voter agents went out from New York to swear soldiers and collect their proxies, and the arrest and court-martial of Seymour's agents replaced the suspicion of Republican fraud with the insinuation that the forged proxies were meant for use by Democrats. Marsena Patrick, the provost marshal of the Army of the Potomac, responded resentfully to an accusation that he had aided Democratic agents in the pursuit of their proxies, while giving Republican agents no assistance at all. It was Democratic agents in Washington, however, who had to navigate bureaucratic impediments to their work, and some regimental commanders at the front evidently refused to swear Democratic voters to the required affidavits, forcing them to go elsewhere if they were to have anyone cast their votes. Reciprocal predictions of malfeasance with New York's military vote persisted until the eve of the election, effectively tainting any lopsided outcome in advance. For that matter, suspicious party creatures retailed fears of opposition skullduggery throughout the election: Democratic papers, for instance, broadcast a warning that Republicans were "flooding the country" with bogus Democratic tickets that would be disqualified if cast as ballots.[34]

The partisan political use of military tribunals and perjured testimony to secure convictions against Democratic defendants provokes serious doubt whether government accusations of Democratic fraud had any foundation. The suggestion hardly tests the limits of credibility, but Edwin Stanton had once again brazenly bent the full power of the War Department to further the cause of Republican candidates, and New York Democrats exercised justifiable mistrust of the soldier vote if it was going to be administered entirely under the control of the federal government.

There was, for instance, the blatant hypocrisy in the treatment of officers who spoke for the different parties. Officers had been dismissed from the service often enough for publicly supporting Democratic candidates to discourage that sort of thing during the quadrennial of 1864, and the practice continued against those who so much as revealed their support for McClellan: even Republican soldiers acknowledged that any officer who backed the general ran that risk. For that reason, it took some nerve for officers to certify the affidavits of New York soldiers who wanted their votes to go to McClellan, and that may have been the cause of some commanders denying them the opportunity. Any who spoke for the president, meanwhile, had nothing to fear, and higher-ranking officers who supported the administration could anticipate governmental accommodation if they wished to take their politics to the people. Furloughs came easily to the more eloquent general officers who backed the president, and particularly to former Democrats who might lend some credence to Republican claims of nonpartisan support for their Union Party ticket. Cabinet officers did not shy from using their influence to secure political sabbaticals for popular soldiers who would stump for Republicans. General Carl Schurz campaigned widely for the president for weeks before the election, only reporting for duty after the voting ended. In New Hampshire, a lieutenant at home on recruiting duty had been summarily cashiered in 1863 for handing out Democratic ballots during the gubernatorial campaign, but Colonel Walter Harriman of the 11th New Hampshire came home in the fall of 1864 on a sanctioned campaign tour for President Lincoln.[35]

Besides the unofficial prohibition of Democratic rhetoric, there hovered some danger of physical abuse for those soldiers who favored McClellan, at least in those regiments where Lincoln men held an overwhelming majority, and that may have induced the silence that kept many officers wondering which way their men would decide. "A man dare not open his mouth for McClellan," observed an Iowan with Sherman. A trooper with the 4th U.S. Cavalry at Nashville feared the worst: "Lincolnism and Niggerism is on the ascendant," he told his parents, "and a poor fellow like me with McClellan on his mind stands a good show for being shot." He added that a man who interrupted a Republican celebration with cheers for McClellan had been killed, and he seemed to believe it.[36]

Such an intimidating atmosphere surely dissuaded many soldiers from voicing their preferences, and at least one artilleryman noticed that many Democrats in his battery feared to vote at all when the time came, characterizing them as the "weak kneed kind." Plenty of them still seemed to harbor sympathies for Little Mac, however, either from a sense of shared experience or from political affinity. "I am a McClellan man up to the handle," a drafted Vermont private informed his wife. "I have seen to[o] much trouble in this administration to vote for another like it." In isolated outposts where the men stood more evenly divided, actual discourse became possible. After a round of speeches and debates in their blockhouses along a Tennessee railroad, officers of the 4th Michigan Cavalry took a straw poll that revealed a dead heat, although Lincoln had led comfortably before the electioneering. Some regiments leaned heavily toward McClellan, and there no one shrank from speaking his mind. An Ohio cavalryman who had been ordered to Camp Stoneman, outside Washington, expressed surprise at the multitude of McClellan supporters there, but he ascribed it to the influx of recruits, whom he accused of enlisting for the prodigious bounties and to avoid being drafted into the infantry: he credited the Republican propaganda that McClellan would immediately end the war by recognizing the Southern Confederacy, and he supposed that the recruits hoped for that very outcome.[37]

That Buckeye horse soldier was not the only one who blamed the despised recruits for any concentrations of Democratic sentiment, but others thought it was instead the old soldiers who stuck by McClellan, as though from nostalgia, while freshly arrived "thousand-dollar patriots" went for Lincoln. Whether the Democrat was a veteran or a fresh volunteer, though, he attracted the scorn of the majority who would have Lincoln. The Democrats were "the ruffscuff of the lot," reported one man, and "cowards," said another, while a third insisted that they were all "traitors thieves and cut throats." It was generally assumed, and correctly so, that Confederates hoped McClellan would win. Prisoners who fell into Union hands through October either admitted or implied that they were "McClellan men," describing extensive destitution and depression in what epithet-coining Yankees began to call the "Cornfederacy," or the "Skedaderacy." The rebels saw Little Mac as their only prayer for a negotiated peace that Jefferson Davis's government could tolerate. A Virginia surgeon anxiously awaited the results of the election, which he thought would determine whether the war ground on under Lincoln or whether the South could entertain the "hope of better things from McClellan."[38]

It was not so much McClellan whom the enemy found so palatable as it was the Republicans' distorted image of McClellan, but that was also what turned many Union soldiers against him. Even Colonel Wainwright, a die-hard Democrat who appraised the defeatist slanders against McClellan as partisan effluvia, still considered not voting at all in protest of the Peace Democrat who shared the ticket with Little Mac. As Republicans painted it, Lincoln's reelection would extinguish the last hope of the reeling Confederacy and bring the rebellion to a rapid conclusion, which came true enough, but they also insisted that McClellan would submit to ignominious surrender at the threshold of victory, which was not so likely: the more credible argument held that McClellan would restore the Union with some form of slavery intact, thereby allowing the internal tension to persist and provoke future strife. Occasionally a simpleminded soldier found the difference too subtle to fathom — supposing that the war would end almost immediately if Lincoln were reelected, and that it would continue indefinitely if he were not — but most understood the concept of giving up a winning fight, even if many of them failed to appreciate the consequences of abandoning emancipation. The question among the troops was often whether they believed that McClellan would really accept peace without reunion: almost every soldier who supported him did not, but a majority of the army seemed convinced of it. They begged their friends and family to stick with Lincoln, and once in a while a young man would answer with astonishment or rebuke when his own father instead defended McClellan, or worse yet praised him.[39]

Of McClellan's friends who were serving with the armies, only those prone to partisan denial shared the candidate's expectation that he would at least take the soldier vote. Where stubborn nationalism, recent military successes, or Republican propaganda had persuaded a civilian, the man in uniform bore the more personal consideration of whether to squander the sacrifices already made by himself and his comrades, living and dead. Even after discounting for the suppression of Democratic sentiment in the army, the Lincoln spirit had clearly infected a majority of soldiers by midautumn.

When the army finally voted, the magnitude of the president's mandate from the troops nevertheless brought some surprises. Some of the older regiments managed sizable majorities for McClellan — 397 out of 424 in the 95th New York, claimed one Democratic soldier, and 112 to 6 in the 69th New York, while a Lincoln man in the 116th Pennsylvania lamented the majority his comrades gave McClellan — but Lincoln won most units, and frequently by margins of five, six, or seven to one. Early returns showed four New York regiments going unanimously for Lincoln. While McClellan carried the 25th Massachusetts, in the same brigade the 23rd Massachusetts went for Lincoln by nearly eight to one. The more decimated old regiments from New Hampshire registered as few as ten dozen votes apiece, but they ran five and six to one for Lincoln, and the 14th New Hampshire made it twelve to one, while the brand-new 18th New Hampshire cast more than three hundred ballots and yielded only three to one for the president.[40] The 20th Michigan voted 153 to 35 for Lincoln, while the 24th Michigan gave him 170 against only 50 for McClellan. In Sheridan's valley army, the 29th Maine chose Lincoln 174 to 40. A Missouri soldier saw only one Democratic ticket submitted in his company, while the ballot box of a nearby regiment contained none at all. Out in Arkansas, the 36th Iowa voted 233 to 4 for Lincoln. In Sherman's army, a staff officer doubted that McClellan's portion would exceed 10 percent, even among the New Jersey regiments that had originally served with the Army of the Potomac. A soldier in the 11th New Hampshire reported large numbers of "copper heads" in his regiment a couple of weeks before the election, basing his judgment on their denunciations of the administration, but on November 8 his company harbored only two votes for McClellan.[41]

Regiment by regiment, soldiers reported McClellan winning overwhelmingly or not at all: when the vote was close, Lincoln seldom lost. That curious trend hinted at the possibility of fraud in those regiments where Republicans held control, and sound Republican officers did draw the task of supervising the collection of votes in their commands. Major George Chandler, who had remained on light duty in the rear since a wound at Spotsylvania, finally returned to the headquarters of the 9th New Hampshire on the evening of November 7 to oversee the vote in his brigade, which included three New Hampshire regiments. Chandler's brother was William E. Chandler, a sly and slippery young Republican who had been Speaker of the House in the New Hampshire legislature, and he was also the son-in-law of his state's governor, who had appointed him an agent of the Granite State in Washington. The night before the election Major Chandler reported to his brother, for the benefit of the governor, that "I have got everything all straight for the 9th," in which he predicted "very few" votes for McClellan; he feared a slightly higher Democratic vote in the other two regiments because they had been lax about bringing in their many detailed men — thereby implying that those who had been favored with such safe and comfortable sinecures were reliable Republicans. The other regiments performed as desired, though, and while Lincoln enjoyed only a slim margin among New Hampshire's civilians, he won three-quarters of the soldier vote from that state. More than half a century later William Chandler took the credit for having finagled that result: by then retired from the U.S. Senate, he claimed responsibility for "securing the soldiers' vote in New Hampshire for President Lincoln in 1864."[42]

Senator Chandler's statement likely betrays more self-congratulatory invention than any secret manipulation of votes. Despite the wide disparity among individual regiments, the returns from different corps and from the armies as a whole proved too similar to arouse much suspicion of widespread dishonesty, although it would have been unusual had there been no fraud at all. The disproportionately lopsided tallies in many regiments more likely reflected the intimidation that Democrats complained of feeling wherever Republicans outnumbered them. McClellan backers risked official retribution, from summary dismissal of officers to extra duty or the denial of privileges for enlisted men, and they also frequently suffered the stern opprobrium of their comrades in arms. In such an atmosphere, it was understandable if public displays of support for the Democratic candidate fell off abruptly in any unit where McClellan men did not predominate, or at least approach equal numbers. Voting alone constituted public support, for ballots were cast in the open in 1864, for all to see.

McClellan averaged about 30 percent of the votes throughout the Army of the Potomac, where he had probably hoped for his greatest majority. Neither the U.S. War Department nor other prisoners could exercise any effective means of discouraging political expression in Southern prison camps, and government neglect had alienated many of the inmates, so captured Union soldiers revealed a bit more enthusiasm for McClellan. In a mock election inside the stockade at Florence, South Carolina, McClellan won the endorsement of a full third of the eighteen hundred who participated. Nine thousand prisoners took part in a similar contest at Millen, Georgia, and more than four thousand of them embraced McClellan. Lincoln's narrower margin among the Millen prisoners almost precisely matched the popular vote nationwide, of which he only won 55 percent. That translated into an electoral landslide of 223 to 21, but the country as a whole only supported Lincoln in the same proportion as the most wretched of Union prisoners, who had unavailingly presented public memorials begging their government to relent on the issue of exchange. McClellan won New Jersey, Delaware, and Kentucky, where he beat Lincoln by forty percentage points. A few other states came very close to falling in the McClellan camp, like New York, where Lincoln won by less than a percentage point, and the much-mistrusted soldier vote may have carried him over the top. In Connecticut — where the Republican governor habitually resorted to trickery to maintain a slim lead, and where a Republican ward heeler saw nothing wrong with candidly applying for cash to buy votes — Lincoln's majority amounted to a mere twenty-four hundred votes.[43] Nor was the president's 10 percent national lead in the popular vote all that comfortable, considering the bizarre quirks made possible by the electoral college: had fewer than forty-two thousand wavering War Democrats changed their votes in six close states — representing barely 1 percent of the total votes cast, and less than the total of McClellan's surplus majorities in the three states he did win — McClellan would have taken the presidency with an electoral victory of 120 to 114.[44]

Legislative permission to vote in the field did little good for many soldiers who had come of age in the army, because most of them had not been home to put their names on their communities' checklists since they enlisted. That probably explained the furloughs that were still granted to many soldiers in October and November, so they could go home to cast their first ballots. Convalescents from Sherman's scattered corps who could travel at all went home long enough to vote, and no longer.[45] Other troops had to spend the day of the election on the alert for trouble, either from the enemy in front of them or from the one they imagined in the rear. In the trenches below Petersburg, everyone rose at three o'clock in the morning in anticipation that Lee might schedule an election-day diversion, and a steamer loaded with Vermont and Connecticut soldiers tied up off New York City's Twenty-Fourth Street, ready to disembark at a moment's notice. To the surprise of all, the day passed quietly almost everywhere.[46] A college student in Ohio heard hardly a word on that riveting topic as the election neared, and in most towns it was not until the telegraph brought enough returns to suggest a healthy lead for Lincoln that anyone dared to celebrate; schoolboys in one New England town fired off a factory signal gun that night and burst it into fragments. Boston police turned out in force, expecting a riot, but the day turned out cloudy and wet; the only disturbance came from the bands and fireworks that greeted the arrival of the U.S.S. *Kearsarge,* with a boodle of Confederate naval officers taken from the C.S.S. *Alabama* and *Florida.*[47]

Lincoln's triumph failed to satisfy many of his more ardent supporters. One man who lived in central Connecticut — not far from either the Republican vote-buyer or the devious Republican governor — supposed that the narrowness of Lincoln's victory in New York reflected the fruit of Democratic "cheating." Ralph Waldo Emerson's daughter fumed that even 72 of Concord's 327 voters disgraced her beloved Massachusetts town by siding with McClellan, but the outcome seemed satisfactory enough for most Union soldiers, and their camps rang with cheers from

Tidewater Virginia to the Gulf of Mexico. The McClellan men among them bore their disappointment in silence, or grieved privately for their hero. "How the mighty are fallen," lamented an erstwhile colonel who had led a regiment under Little Mac, but one general of antebellum Democratic credentials parted with his former political associates — more over their reluctance to crush slavery than anything else. In a letter that conservatives might have used to document the war's misappropriated aims, he chastised McClellan supporters for not "keeping with the progress of the age . . . away up in the noon of the nineteenth century."[48]

As Lincoln's uniformed proponents had predicted, his reelection doused the last flickering hopes of all but the most obdurate rebels. Cavalier sons of genteel families in the border states had already begun to repent of embracing the Southern cause so impulsively, and families on the fringes of Union occupation were drifting in to take the oath in return for food. With the news of McClellan's defeat Confederate deserters hailed Union pickets more frequently, and even tough rebels who endured winter winds barefooted, in ragged clothing, could not hide their disappointment in the election when flags of truce brought them in contact with inquisitive Yankees. Quite a few Southerners tried to wait out the war in the city of Vera Cruz, on the Gulf coast of Mexico, where anti-imperialist guerrillas were closing in; confirmation of Lincoln's election reached there a full month after the event, whereupon the rebel refugees resigned themselves to defeat, shining up to the American consul for passage to New York.[49]

Similar dejection settled over the conservative camp in the North. A Michigan woman living northwest of Detroit observed "a good many long faces since Election," and she would have seen more widespread unhappiness in the border states. Tench Tilghman, the current patriarch of a gentrified Maryland family, had remained loyal while his sons went South, but he doubted the weakness of the Confederacy and so he deplored Lincoln's pertinacity, which he felt doomed the country to indefinite turmoil and financial ruin. One of Lincoln's own cousins, by marriage, seemed affectionate enough toward Old Abe personally, but admitted his deep regret at the president's reelection. Peace, he insisted, would be eminently preferable to Lincoln's endless war, even at the price of disunion. One week after the election an Ohio woman taunted a friend by admitting her entire family's continuing opposition to the war, to the point of proudly proclaiming that they were all "Copper heads."[50]

Notwithstanding the discouraging implications of a second term for Lincoln, there remained many Confederate soldiers (and some citizens) who literally preferred death to surrender, and who intended to resist as long as there remained a few comrades to whom they could cleave. A Vermont native working for the Quartermaster Department in Arkansas found the most unyielding defiance among transplanted Easterners, including presumably New Englanders, who had come South before the war, and a fellow Vermonter named William Spoor attested to that observation with his faithful service in a Confederate regiment from Missouri: although captured twice on the battlefield, Spoor refused to give up until the war was clearly over. Those who had endured Northern prisons often seemed particularly dogged. George Stedman had ridden with John Mosby in the Shenandoah Valley since escaping from a Union prison, after which he went marauding behind Union lines in Kentucky with five companions, all of whom had left him by the time of the presidential election. Stedman maintained a one-man war against the United States for several weeks, hoping that Lee would abandon Richmond so the army could disperse, and wear down Northern will through guerrilla warfare. He confided to an old friend that it was not for slavery that he fought: he wished to see every black person banished from the South, and only hoped for independence. At last he attached himself to a small brigade of recruits raised by one of Bedford Forrest's colonels, and was killed while leading those novices in an attack just before Christmas.[51]

Captain James Fitts, in Sheridan's army, understood the stubborn spirit that impelled enough of his enemies to keep the contest alive, and he anticipated no end to the struggle until the Confederacy and its armies lay prostrate. The fall of Richmond, Charleston, or any other Southern city would not bring peace, he admitted, as though acknowledging George Stedman's obstinacy. "On the 19th of September," he reminded his mother, "we beat them so thoroughly at Winchester that they fled in utter panic from the field; just one month from that day, that routed army came down on us at Cedar Creek, and drove us out of our camps." Less than sixteen weeks before Lee surrendered, Captain Fitts worried that the North was again growing overly optimistic.[52]

William Sherman concurred fully with Captain Fitts on the resilience of Southern arms, and as soon as the election had passed he initiated his plan to lay the Confederacy prostrate. From his headquarters at Tuscumbia, Alabama, John Bell Hood issued ominous orders for his troops to start crossing to the north side of the Tennessee River, but Sherman believed he had left enough men in Tennessee for George Thomas to handle any trouble Hood could make for him, and he turned his back on the foremost Confederate army of the West.[53]

Through the autumn Alpheus Williams had maintained his division headquarters at an empty Atlanta home. As he returned in the drizzle from casting his first ballot in four years, he discovered a single rose blooming fragrantly in the absent owner's yard, and he plucked it to flatten out inside the last letter he expected to send to his motherless daughters for some time. As everyone of General Williams's station in the army knew, the next campaign was about to begin, and it would take the army toward the Atlantic coast, away from all communication with the North, or with any other Union forces. Farther down the chain of command it was merely evident that "something huge is up," and that the last mail for some time would soon start up the railroad. Everyone sat down to reassure parents, or wives, and a good many officers used that opportunity to tender last-minute resignations, most of which quickly came back to their authors, denied.[54]

The night of November 10 the troops at Rome burned every building of any industrial capacity, from foundries and mills to individual tradesmen's shops, but it was not until November 12 that Sherman marched from Kingston with his rear guard, bound for Atlanta. At Cartersville that afternoon, Sherman sat on the porch of the town's hotel, writing his last dispatch to Chattanooga, and once the telegrapher had sent it Sherman ordered the line cut. The finality of the broken ends of the wire brought a moment of sober reflection to a staff major standing nearby, who thought the impending march as daring as anything since Hernando Cortes burned his ships and plunged into the interior of Mexico; it suddenly registered with him that they were now "away down South in Dixie," on their way to an unknown fate.[55]

Before Sherman's men took their first step, the Northern press laid out his entire plan for the enemy to read in detail. "Great Military March through Georgia," announced the *New York Times* headlines: "Atlanta as a Point of Advance upon the Atlantic." The November 10 issue of the *Times* revealed a slightly exaggerated estimate of the size of Sherman's mobile force, described his destruction at Rome before it even happened, and reported the precise path he intended to follow, touching at Macon as he rolled toward the coast; it was expected that he would reach Savannah in twenty-five days. The story ran in all the major dailies, and General Grant read that revelation of the high command's secrets the next day, at City Point. He warned the secretary of war that the enemy would probably have the information within another twenty-four hours, and start reacting accordingly. Stanton replied that the blunder was Sherman's own fault, for letting too many people in on his plans; that very day a letter had crossed Stanton's desk from a paymaster to another officer, outlining the campaign as he had heard it from Sherman's own lips. Sherman remained ignorant of the leaked information when he severed the telegraph line, and he continued to choreograph his movements in a fruitless effort to disguise his ultimate destination. At first the enemy supposed that he was retreating from Atlanta because of all the ordnance and equipment he had sent back to Chattanooga, but before he was halfway to Savannah he would find Southern newspapers repeating his itinerary from several Northern sheets. Had the Confederacy been able to marshal enough resources, the *Times* might have done his campaign enormous damage.[56]

Sherman took four infantry corps with him. Two of them marched as his left wing, under Henry Slocum, and at the outset of the campaign he christened them the Army of Georgia; two corps from the Army of the Tennessee, commanded by Oliver Otis Howard, formed his right wing. A single division of cavalry accompanied him, led by the boastful and impulsive Judson Kilpatrick, and the entire artillery train consisted of only sixteen batteries. At no time could Sherman have fielded as many as sixty-five thousand men all told, but he would have no supplies beyond those he carried from Atlanta, and he wanted no more troops than he could expect to feed from the provisions they foraged along the way. The Confederates in front of him could mobilize nothing to match either of his wings, and Hood was too far away to worry about, even if he had seemed inclined to interfere. Sherman suspected that political pressure from Georgia might well force Hood to turn back and defend the state, but Hood and his immediate superior, General Beauregard, hoped to force Sherman to return to Tennessee under a similar impetus.[57]

For two days the Yankees lingered at Atlanta, tearing up mile after mile of every railroad that came into the city from all directions, burning the ties, and bending the rails between trees or twisting them with the aid of a little tool invented by Sherman's chief engineer. Engineer troops from Michigan and Missouri burned the railroad depot and all its appurtenant sheds, repair shops, and storehouses, as well as the city's mills and machine shops. At Sherman's instructions, they left only homes and churches standing. "For military purposes the city of Atlanta has ceased to exist," reported the engineer in charge, and then on the fifteenth they started marching, continuing to tear up railroad tracks as they moved. The city was still blazing here and there, and smoking everywhere, when the last regiment filed out.[58]

Slocum moved east out of Atlanta, past the towering granite face of Stone Mountain to Social Circle and Madison, where he diverted John Geary's division to burn the railroad bridge over the Oconee River. From there he turned south toward the state capital at Milledgeville. A Massachusetts captain who was still limping from his fourth wound of the war followed near the tail of the left wing, grimacing at the burned or burning houses all along the road; none seemed to have been spared. In three years of war the captain had seen nothing like it, and it occurred to him how he might feel to see such destruction in his home state — which had felt the heel of a hostile army less than a century before. Pondering what his own reaction might be, he dreaded what might happen to any of his comrades who fell into rebel hands. One plantation they passed included enough slave cabins to resemble a town of its own, and the old man who owned all of it stood alongside the road in a light rain while soldiers burned his house. "He did not seem to see the joke," observed the captain.[59]

Howard's two corps marched parallel to Slocum from the south side of Atlanta, meeting no resistance beyond a little cavalry, which hampered their progress more by burning bridges than by armed confrontation. Three of Howard's staff officers and their orderlies were able to secure the town of McDonough on the afternoon of November 16 by charging into it with nothing but their revolvers and a single rifle. While Howard made camp at the home of a refined local widow, Kilpatrick swept down the railroad toward Macon with the cavalry. The mist and drizzle of November 20 turned to pouring rain that night, and continued throughout the next day, slowing the march and ruining shoes. Bitter cold descended with darkness on the twenty-first, and men who had shivered through the night found their canteens frozen at daylight. On the right wing, Kilpatrick lunged toward Macon, where William Hardee had gathered what troops were left in central Georgia. He could muster only a few little brigades of Georgia militia and Joe Wheeler's cavalry, but that was enough to repel Kilpatrick when he veered that way. Deducing that the move on Macon was merely a feint, Hardee ordered the militia toward Augusta on Monday, November 21, just before leaving for Savannah to take command there. By the frosty morning of November 22 it had become clear in Macon that Kilpatrick was riding ahead of a large portion of Sherman's army, and that the Georgia militia was going to run right into it, so orders went out for the militia to come back, but those instructions reached the moving column too late.[60]

The clash came at the tiny crossroads of Griswoldville, eight or ten miles east of Macon on the Georgia Central Railroad. The village had sprung up around a cotton gin and little factories where slave laborers and artisans produced soap, candles, and, more recently, brass-frame revolvers for the Confederate army on a variation of the Colt pattern. Michigan troopers from Kilpatrick's cavalry had burned the entire village the day before. Wheeler's cavalry — a few of them probably armed with Samuel Griswold's brass-frame revolvers — arrived too late to save the town, and the blackened timbers were still smoldering on Tuesday morning, when Wheeler attacked Kilpatrick's leading regiments near there. Wheeler was finally pushing them back in the middle of the afternoon when a fair-sized brigade of Union infantry came up, gliding along on the extreme right flank of Howard's wing. Those six regiments of Ohio, Indiana, Illinois, and Iowa infantry, led by a young brigadier named Charles Walcutt, took over the fight for their cavalry, but soon Wheeler's horsemen faded back as well, making way for the first Confederate infantry Sherman's main force had met. Three long lines of Southerners emerged from a dense wood less than half a mile away and, without further ceremony, started rolling across open fields toward Walcutt's brigade. The Yankees imagined themselves outnumbered by four to one or more, estimating the three enemy ranks at six or seven thousand strong, although they numbered fewer than half that many. Little realizing at first that they were only facing state militia, Walcutt's Westerners fabricated a hasty breastwork of fence rails while their own guns and Confederate artillery dueled, and when the militia came within range that breastwork erupted in a withering fire. The indifferently clad citizen-soldiers trudged into that musketry with surprising grit for troops with so little experience and training, approaching within a couple of hundred feet of those blazing muzzles before they began to flinch, and over the next two hours they made two more attempts, perfectly ignorant that Walcutt's brigade only represented the first of nearly thirty thousand Yankees. The sun set with the antagonists still blasting away at each other from a distance of five hundred feet, and in the darkness the militia finally retired on the authority of the tardy morning order. With Sherman's army blocking the Georgia Central, they had to retreat to the south by rail and foot nearly to the Florida border before taking trains east to Savannah, to wait for Sherman at the end of his march.[61]

Griswoldville marked the only real battle of the entire campaign. Multitudes of increasingly ragged Union soldiers bisected Georgia in a swath thirty miles wide, putting homes and businesses to the torch extensively and capriciously, if not consistently, and stripping the farms of all available provender to replenish or preserve their commissary supplies. They prodded cattle, sheep, and hogs into herds for future butchering, roasted turkeys, chickens, and ducks, fed their horses and mule teams on abundant corn cribs, carried off sweet potatoes by the wagonload, and feasted on what molasses they could consume, pouring the rest on the ground. A single meal might include eggs, chicken, potatoes with butter, and flapjacks; everything but green vegetables could be had for the taking. Nor did they confine their pilferage to food, often stealing anything of value or interest; an Illinois soldier with an intellectual bent stole a few volumes from each of the better libraries along the way. Sherman's men learned to search the plantation gardens for buried valuables, and to scour the woods around the towns, where farmers and grocers tried to hide their provisions from the locust-like swarms of soldiers. "We lived better on this trip than any time since this has been an army," reported an Indiana sergeant.[62]

While the combatants parted at Griswoldville, Slocum's vanguard reached the state capital at Milledgeville. The next day one of his rear brigades moved up to the front of the column, parading through the town with drums beating and flags unfurled and crossing the Oconee River before turning off to camp. The left wing passed the afternoon destroying railroads and anything else that might be useful for carrying on the war, while foraging parties ferreted out secret hoards of food in the woods; they ate well and slept soundly that night. General Howard camped only a dozen miles away, in the surprisingly polite hospitality of a local woman who visited companionably with the staff officers despite refusing to hide her hatred of those who laid waste to her homeland. The next evening, those who remembered to celebrate Thanksgiving did so (as one officer admitted) by drinking liberally of local whiskey and dining on fresh pork.[63]

Beyond Milledgeville frequent creeks and rivers corrugated the countryside, and rebel cavalry easily slowed the enemy's advance by burning one bridge after another, skirmishing occasionally with the leading Federals from the relative safety of the opposite bank. The success of Sherman's campaign, and for that matter the survival of his army, depended on how much territory his troops could cover each day, for once those sixty thousand voracious men came to rest they would quickly exhaust whatever the surrounding country could provide them for sustenance. The chief engineer therefore followed close behind the screen of cavalry with an ample corps of pioneers and a train of pontoons, to clear the roads of obstructions and extemporize bridges, which they accomplished with remarkable efficiency. The repeated delays still posed the only real threat of disaster that Sherman faced, and in pique or panic his soldiers began to burn down the houses nearest to the ruined bridges, ostensibly on the suspicion that the homeowners were responsible for the sabotage. At least two staff officers with the left wing implied that they doubted the citizens had anything to do with the burned bridges, one of them noting that not one of those "Southern braves" dared so much as fire a shot at the host of invaders who were burning their houses, barns, crops, and fences. The other officer, Sherman's own judge advocate general, objected to the destruction in his chief's presence, but Sherman authorized it anyway, arguing that it might dissuade Wheeler's cavalry from hindering the march even that much, lest nearby civilians suffer for it. With or without Sherman's approval, all too many civilians had already endured similar vandalism for no worse crime than residing in a seceded state, so the indiscriminate retribution failed to save any bridges for "Uncle Billy's" army.[64]

Sherman's assistant adjutant general, Henry Hitchcock, had only recently joined the army. He had not yet witnessed a battle, and perhaps retained more sensitivity about making war on civilians than men who had seen as much havoc as Sherman, but if he would argue for probable cause before destroying the home of even an ardent secessionist citizen he seemed supportive of Sherman's overall plan of widespread destruction. Hitchcock perceived the general as publicly gruff and privately tender, describing his exchange with an elderly woman in Sanderson, Georgia, who had badgered him somewhat: first Sherman chastised her politics with stern courtesy, but then he worried about her after leaving her home, sending back coffee and provisions for her household. This same man still ordered innocent country folk rendered homeless in an awkward and hopeless attempt to manipulate the behavior of enemy combatants, and he left almost everyone in the path of his army with neither livelihoods nor larders, yet Hitchcock considered that the appropriate strategy; largely because of it, he thought Sherman was "the right man to end this war." Until the summer of 1864, most digressions from civilized warfare had been punished with reprisals. David Hunter's depredations in the Shenandoah Valley, for instance, had prompted the burning of Chambersburg, but by November the Confederacy had been driven to its knees, leaving little chance that a rebel army could treat whole regions of the North to similar devastation. The absence of effective retaliation made it safer for Union generals to adopt a scorched-earth policy. Those who applauded Phil Sheridan's despoliation of the Shenandoah Valley did so with the near-certainty that Confederates could not respond in kind, and they sanctimoniously dismissed the few feeble attempts at reciprocation as the work of fiendish brutes.[65]

Sherman had hoped to free the thousands of Union prisoners who remained in Georgia, but Kilpatrick's feint at Macon had come after the last ambulatory patients had been removed from the prison hospital at Andersonville for transport to the new facility at Millen; the trains carrying them had slipped out, through Macon and Griswoldville, just ahead of Sherman's right wing. Only fifteen hundred of the sickest prisoners remained in the Andersonville hospital, with not a one in the stockade at the moment, and even if Kilpatrick had swooped down to rescue those inmates they would not have had the strength to march back with him. Ten thousand prisoners had spread out inside the larger stockade at Millen over the previous month, where sanitation had not yet deteriorated into the pestilential swamp that served as Andersonville's sewer, but the rations continued monotonous and the only shelter consisted of brush huts and mud burrows at a season when nights sometimes turned cruelly cold even in Georgia.[66]

While Slocum's wing dismantled fifty miles of the Georgia Railroad in the first days of the march, General Hardee began to conclude that the Yankees intended to strike for Augusta. That trajectory would bring them too close to Millen to refrain from liberating the place, so he ordered that stockade emptied out, too. Over several days baggage cars took the sickest of the prisoners to Savannah for exchange by flag of truce with the U.S. Navy, and some of them slept beneath the Stars and Stripes as early as November 20, sipping their first coffee in months. Then several trains came back to Millen to collect the rest of the ten thousand, taking them to Savannah under the illusion that they, too, would be exchanged, but in the city they changed cars and continued south on the Gulf Railroad, camping inside a perimeter of armed guards at Blackshear Station. Over the next month they moved west and north to Thomasville, Georgia, before undertaking a strenuous overland march and rail journey that brought them in a complete circuit back to Andersonville: most of them arrived there by Christmas, and there they remained — those who survived — until the war came to an end. When Sherman's troops finally reached Millen, on December 3, they found nothing there but the rude shelters the prisoners had fashioned to keep the rain off their backs, along with eight dead Yankees whom the last nervous rebels had neglected to bury.[67]

From Millen the four corps marched directly on Savannah. The terrain dissolved into marsh again as they descended the Savannah and Ogeechee Rivers, and the city's defenders had grown more ambitious about inconveniencing the oncoming horde of Yankees by dropping trees across the road. Occasional artillery bastions threatened resistance, but the blue host simply surged around those annoyances, forcing the occupants to retire. Hardee backed into Savannah with some ten thousand men, outnumbered about six to one; Beauregard estimated that Joe Wheeler had three thousand cavalry, some of which harried Union foraging parties when they ventured from the main body. Once it became obvious that Sherman aimed for Savannah rather than Augusta, Wheeler took most of his command over the Savannah River into South Carolina, to prevent Union troops on the coast from closing in on Savannah from that direction. Because the rebels still had the four-gun ironclad *Savannah* on its namesake river, Sherman dared not throw many of his own troops over on the South Carolina side to trap Hardee in the city, but by December 9 he had reached the infantry entrenchments outside the city and he soon cut off all communication between Savannah and the rest of Georgia. Once they stopped before those works his men had to depend on the food in their wagons, and commissaries quickly cut rations by three-quarters, so Union scouts made their way down the Ogeechee River in search of steamers from the blockading fleet. Before he tried an assault on the city's defenses, Sherman decided to open the Ogeechee for supply ships.[68]

Several miles upriver from where the Ogeechee emptied into Ossabaw Sound sat Fort McAllister, guarding against any incursions by the back door. Savannah lay about ten miles to the northeast of this key little bastion, over soft and soggy ground cut by several other rivers and creeks. The intervening terrain afforded its own defenses, although a few marsh batteries sat alongside some of the innumerable little inlets where smaller naval craft might intrude. Forts and obstructions on the Savannah River and the presence of the *Savannah* deterred Admiral John Dahlgren from deploying any of his blockading squadron against the city. A line of fortifications ran perpendicular to the Savannah River a couple of miles above town, and a ring of swamps and earthworks protected Savannah inside that. Even with the few thousand men Hardee could put in the works, he might have exacted an exorbitant price had he required Sherman to take the city by storm.

Fort McAllister posed a somewhat softer nut to crack: it mounted a few large guns and several smaller ones, but the garrison had been reduced to barely a couple of hundred infantry and artillery, half of whom were state troops who had seen no field service until this emergency. Judson Kilpatrick stopped there on his own way down the Ogeechee to communicate with the fleet, and he intended to take the fort with his own dismounted men, but Sherman preferred to use his infantry. He chose William Hazen's division, from the Fifteenth Corps, which outnumbered the Confederates in Fort McAllister by about twenty to one, and before noon of December 13 Hazen brought his three brigades within range of the little citadel. He aimed for the rear of the fort, where the guns that bore on his attack route all sat in barbette, atop the earthworks, with little or no protection, and he positioned sharpshooters to keep the gunners from their work. After several hours of arranging his troops he finally sent them all in at a rush, near dusk, across a minefield and over the usual infantry obstructions. Mines claimed a few of his men, but he fanned them out as far as the spongy approaches would allow, to give the fort's defenders a less inviting target, and that blue line surged right up the parapet, fighting the garrison hand to hand. Captain Stephen Grimes, of the 48th Illinois, engaged in a personal duel with Captain N. B. Clinch, who commanded a little battery of light artillery in the fort. For all their inexperience the Georgians contested every inch of their fort, only surrendering when cornered by superior numbers in their bombproofs, but the entire affair lasted only fifteen minutes.[69]

With the Ogeechee clear for the passage of transports, Sherman no longer had to worry that inertia would bring starvation. He could draw regular rations from the great supply depot on Hilton Head Island, below Charleston, but army rations offended the palate after the culinary diversity of the overland march, and rice offered the only alternative staple available in sufficient quantity. Threshing mills on the Savannah River and the Ogeechee resumed operation with Union labor, turning out enough rice to feed much of the army from the ubiquitous paddies above the city. More important than all, for men who had not heard from home in over a month, was the mail that arrived with the first ships up the Ogeechee River. After penetrating so deep into Dixie, Major Hitchcock, of Sherman's staff, felt peculiar to be able to read New York newspapers of recent vintage. It was like having risen from the dead, as he tried to explain it to his wife. "I have a real fellow feeling for Rip Van Winkle."[70]

As costly as it might be, Sherman concluded that he would have to take Savannah by direct assault, just as Hazen had stormed Fort McAllister. He ordered some heavy field guns up to batter the works, and crossed Ezra Carmen's three regiments of the Twentieth Corps to the South Carolina shore upstream from the city, where islands narrowed the channel and the ram might not interfere. From the banks of the Savannah River that detachment kept watch over the causeway that led from the river toward Charleston, providing Hardee his only avenue of retreat. Deserters had told Union officers of failing morale in the garrison at Savannah, where the militia refused to stand against an attack, but when Sherman sent in a demand for surrender Hardee refused. After ordering Slocum to prepare for an assault, Sherman hurried by river and sea to Port Royal, South Carolina, to urge the commander of that department to move his troops and close off the causeway. The position of Carmen's brigade near his escape route decided the issue for Hardee, and while his foes prepared to attack his works, he stretched a pontoon bridge between Savannah and Hutchinson's Island, and from there to little Pennyworth Island, and thence finally to the South Carolina shore. Beginning a couple of hours after dark on December 20, he spirited his little army over the river, escaping between the converging columns on the South Carolina side. All the while, General Sherman was trying to make his way back from Port Royal with Admiral Dahlgren. It was 3:00 A.M. before the pickets of John Geary's division noticed that their Confederate counterparts were scurrying off, and when Geary moved his own skirmishers ahead they found the rebel works empty. After a quick sweep of the vicinity he started toward the city on the Augusta road, and it was still dark when he met the mayor coming out to make the surrender. When the first of Geary's men started marching down the streets they found many of the houses sprouting

United States flags, revealing either the genuine loyalty or the insincere precaution of the inhabitants. Sherman was still with the admiral when they met a dispatch boat carrying the news that Savannah was his, minus Hardee's patchwork little army.[71]

By the shortest roads then available, some five hundred miles separated Sherman from the nearest Confederate army large enough to cause him any worry. When he arrived before Savannah, in fact, he was about as close to Lee's army as he was to Hood's, for the Army of Tennessee had returned to the heart of its namesake state in a vain attempt to draw Sherman back from Georgia.

After Hood lost Atlanta, the Confederate War Department created the Military Division of the West, consisting of nearly everything between the Chattahoochee and the Mississippi River, and assigned General Beauregard to command it. Only four months before, Beauregard had saved the city of Petersburg with a stellar performance in an unequal contest, but the new administrative position left him with no armies to lead: he only assumed a nebulous, general control over the armies within his mammoth bailiwick, and the impulsive Hood retained direct command of the Army of Tennessee — or what remained of it. Hood's position at Tuscumbia lay too far away from Sherman to overtake him when he started for Savannah, and Sherman's shipment of supplies back to Chattanooga had suggested until very late that he was returning there from Atlanta, as though Hood's movements had forced him to come back. Intelligence of Sherman's campaign to the coast, gleaned by scouts and confirmed by indiscreet Northern newspapers, did not reach Hood until the middle of November, by which time he had already undertaken an offensive into Tennessee designed to hasten Sherman's imagined retreat and compel the evacuation of Chattanooga, as well.[72]

Persistent rain delayed the start of Hood's northward invasion, raising the rivers and turning the roads to soup. While Sherman burned Atlanta and set off for Savannah, Hood sat at Florence, Alabama, with two of his infantry corps north of the river while the third lay at Tuscumbia, trapped below the river by high water. When Bedford Forrest returned from raiding in West Tennessee he assumed command of all Hood's cavalry and started crossing to the north bank of the Tennessee on November 16. The first of the infantry broke camp at Florence on November 20, heading for the Tennessee border in another driving rainstorm. The rest of the army followed the next day, as cold winds drove alternating flurries of snow and rain through threadbare clothing.[73]

Sherman's man in Tennessee, General Thomas, made his headquarters at Nashville, 125 miles north of Florence; with the permanent garrison and detached troops, he could have put about ten thousand men into line there. A brand-new Ohio regiment, just under a thousand strong, held the town of Columbia, fifty miles below Nashville. Most of the Fourth Corps and two divisions of the Twenty-Third, amounting to nearly twenty-five thousand, had gathered around Pulaski, thirty more miles south, with Major General John Schofield in general command. One division of three thousand cavalry and another loose brigade of a thousand or so patrolled south and west of Pulaski. The rest of Thomas's eighty thousand men were strung out along the railroads or held Chattanooga and other scattered posts between there and Fort Donelson, but with the cavalry and the forces at Nashville and Pulaski he could send about forty thousand men into the field — which gave him approximate parity with Hood's entire army, after its five weeks of rest and recruiting. Equal numbers had seldom brought Union victory in this war, so Thomas appealed to William Rosecrans for the return of Andrew Jackson Smith's two Sixteenth Corps divisions that had gone chasing after Sterling Price. Smith telegraphed from Saint Louis that his troops had arrived there, and would start boarding steamers November 22; he had more than twelve thousand very dependable infantry, but they were at least a week away from Nashville.[74]

As Hood crossed from Alabama into Tennessee he spread his three corps across three roads converging on Columbia, sweeping twenty miles west of Schofield's main body at Pulaski. Union cavalry detected the apparent advance of the whole Confederate army by the evening of November 22, and Schofield started to retreat toward Columbia the next morning, with the rain still falling and the roads sodden. The next day Forrest's cavalry pushed within a few miles of Columbia, putting him north of Schofield's army, but the leading Union infantry division cut across Forrest's path and delayed him long enough for Schofield to bring everyone safely into Columbia. The Duck River ran north of there, but Schofield wanted to hold Columbia if possible, so he fortified a line around the town and settled in to await reinforcements, while from Nashville General Thomas pestered everyone between there and Saint Louis for A. J. Smith's two divisions. Hood kept his infantry behind the screen of Forrest's cavalry, prompting concern that he was sliding east to interrupt the railroad to Chattanooga, which Schofield considered inevitable, but he thought he could stop Hood from going any farther north. There he sat until November 26, when he grew concerned that Hood planned to cross the Duck River upstream and get behind him again. Posting one reliable division in an abbreviated line before Columbia, Schofield started bringing everyone else north of the river that night. Darkness slowed the evacuation over his single pontoon bridge, and he had to finish the job on the night of the twenty-seventh, in another cold rain. The last man had just crossed on Monday morning, November 28, when Thomas apprised him that Smith's reinforcements would reach Nashville in two days. Once Smith arrived, said Thomas, they would have a strong enough field force to turn the tables and go after Hood.[75]

Schofield's intuition saved him. After wasting half a day, Hood — Schofield's West Point classmate — did cross upstream and try to put his army astride the path to Nashville, aiming to intersect with that road at Spring Hill, a dozen miles behind Columbia. He left Stephen Lee's corps at Columbia to decoy Schofield, and with the other two corps he started over the river at daylight on November 29. Ben Cheatham took the lead, with Patrick Cleburne's renowned division in front, but it was late afternoon before Cleburne reached the vicinity of Spring Hill. Forrest's cavalry was already there, sparring with the head of Schofield's column. A brigade from the Fourth Corps was just coming into town on the Nashville Pike, and trotted the last couple of furlongs to contest the crossroads. A second brigade soon followed, and then a third, joining forces in an arc east of town, but enough rebel infantry reached the field to overpower them had they hit the Union line square. Daylight did not last long three weeks before the winter solstice, and the sun had already sunk low in the west when Cleburne moved out to seize the pike. He ran afoul of the right extremity of that impromptu Union line, and wheeled to his right to engage it head-on. That confused the division behind him, led by William Bate. Darkness soon blackened the field, and Bate managed to lose his way. He fired once into the pike at the shadows of a moving column, and the column returned fire before shrinking back toward an alternate route, but Cheatham had not outrun the foremost elements of Schofield's army and so never blocked the road. Eventually Cheatham's entire corps bivouacked right on the field, with some of Bate's troops as close as two hundred yards from the pike. Alexander Stewart's corps came up right behind Bate before bedding down for another chilled night on the frozen ground, wet to the knees from fording a creek. Virtually the whole Army of Tennessee, from General Hood to the humblest private, fell asleep while Schofield's Yankees strode by, within easy musket range. When the sun rose on November 30, the turnpike stood perfectly empty.[76]

Next lay the town of Franklin, nearly fifteen miles farther on. A shaken Schofield arrived in that town with the sun on Wednesday morning, November 30, fully conscious of how close he had come to complete disaster. "I don't want to get into so tight a place again," he wired Thomas, who asked him in turn if he could hold out at Franklin for three more days, until Smith's troops had all come in. Schofield doubted it: he had enough infantry to handle Hood, if he remained on the defensive, but he feared Forrest, whom he credited with far more cavalry than remained with his own force. In that case, Thomas replied, Schofield should send his trains on to Nashville and follow with his entire command, collecting troops from the blockhouses along the railroad as he came. While his wagons crossed on improvised bridges, Schofield backed most of his army into the loop of the Harpeth River that encircles Franklin, anchoring his flanks on the river at either end and curving a line of works around the outskirts of town. He anticipated that Hood would appear on the Nashville Pike, known as the Columbia Pike by the residents of Franklin, and there, just beyond the brick home of Fountain B. Carter, he posted his men the thickest. In addition, he pushed a couple of brigades a quarter of a mile or more beyond the Carter house, where their flanks hung in the air as though they were meant to serve as a sacrifice.[77]

Hood showed up on cue that afternoon, right behind Schofield's rear guard. As at Columbia, he sent Forrest over the river again, upstream, to lash at Schofield's trains and try to intercept his retreat, while Cheatham's and Stewart's corps formed three ranks deep on either side of the Columbia — or Nashville — Pike. Between 3:30 and 4:00 P.M., by varying watches, those three lines surged forward. The two vulnerable brigades Schofield had advanced beyond the main line tried to stem that tide alone, failing quickly and understandably, and their injudicious position forced them to race back toward their main line, acting as an involuntary shield for the rebels until they sprang past the comrades behind them. The Confederates followed them at full tilt, momentarily safe from small arms and artillery fire, and when they hit Schofield's works on the heels of the sprinting Yankees they carried portions of the line. Most of the 183rd Ohio, a big one-year regiment that was barely a month old, and had only been with the army for two days, threw down their weapons and ran for dear life, leaving a void west of the pike that invited part of two Mississippi brigades over the works. Heavy concentrations from Cheatham's corps carried sections on either side of the pike, but a furious fire drove them back. Union officers and sergeants sat in the rifle pits, ripping open boxes of ammunition and percussion caps, loading rifles for the men on the line, or tearing cartridges for them to hasten the loading process, and the myriad volleys merged into a rolling thunder that forced Cheatham's veterans back, but then they rallied and came on again, and again, and again, into the dusk and then into the darkness.[78]

Within a thousand feet of the Carter house six Confederate generals fell dead or dying, including Cleburne, the best division commander in that army. Five more were wounded, and one made it over the Union works, only to be trapped with some of his men when the Yankees closed off the rupture. Hood, who had shown such lethargy the evening before, dashed his army relentlessly against Schofield's fortifications, losing more than six thousand men before the field fell silent. That represented a quarter of Hood's infantry, in addition to the dozen generals whose names were erased from his roster. Schofield's casualties ran something over two thousand. He quietly started his men over the Harpeth around midnight, leaving his dead and wounded behind.[79]

As Thomas had instructed him, Schofield picked up the detachments at railroad blockhouses along the way to Nashville, and those who were cut off found roundabout routes to other posts east or west of the capital. A. J. Smith's two divisions reached Nashville on the Cumberland River, by way of the Ohio and Mississippi, and a division came up the railroad from Chattanooga. By nightfall on the first of December Thomas could count on something like fifty thousand men within sight of the capitol building, with all his quartermaster details, convalescents, and Veteran Reserve Corps detachments in the trenches, while the erratic Hood appeared on the hills south of town the next evening, intent on besieging the place with about thirty thousand of all arms.[80]

Hood took high ground a couple of miles outside Nashville and started building his own extensive works, in the hope that Thomas would attack first and allow the Confederates to return the favor of Franklin. Thirty miles behind him, to the southeast, lay Murfreesboro, with a garrison of more than ten thousand men of the Twentieth Corps. Rather than turn his back on all the Yankees in that direction, Hood sent Bate's division toward Murfreesboro, to destroy the railroad from that place and guard against any attack from that direction; only afterward did Hood convey his idea of the number of Union soldiers who were said to hold Murfreesboro, and he seriously underestimated them. Bate dutifully turned in that direction and started down the tracks, seizing blockhouses and burning them as he dismantled the line. Then Hood sent Forrest, with the cavalry and two more infantry brigades, to join Bate and take command. On December 7 Forrest turned the raid into an assault, trying to take Murfreesboro from a fortified garrison stronger than his own command, with a serious advantage in artillery. Unnerved by the example of Franklin, perhaps, some of the rebel infantry balked and ran, and Forrest gave up the attempt. He remained before Murfreesboro, though, in company with Bate, while freezing rain and sleet started to turn the landscape into a solid sheet of ice.[81]

The rain and ice persisted for six days. Horses and mules could hardly move alone, and could gain no traction to pull wagons or caissons, so for most of a week the two armies sat staring at each other while Ulysses Grant badgered Thomas to attack immediately. Prompted by Edwin Stanton, who claimed that the president wanted an immediate movement against Hood, the general in chief urged Thomas as early as December 2 to attack before Hood fortified, and three days later he hinted again that it would be best to go after him sooner rather than later. Thomas wanted fresh horses and reinforcements for his outnumbered and worn-out cavalry, so he could contend with Forrest, but on December 6 Grant telegraphed him to "Attack at once, and wait no longer for a remount of your cavalry." Thomas read the order that night, and agreed to make the attack, although he considered it dangerous without a mounted force to cover his flanks. Grant involved the nominal chief of staff, Henry Halleck, telling him, "I want General Thomas reminded of the importance of immediate action." Halleck relayed Grant's dissatisfaction just after the ice storm commenced, and Thomas replied — first to Halleck, and then directly to Grant — that if they felt it necessary to relieve him he would "submit without a murmur." For a time that cooled Grant's impatience, for he knew that Thomas had given the Union its first noteworthy victory nearly three years before, and that he had almost single-handedly saved the Army of the Cumberland from destruction at Chickamauga, besides driving Braxton Bragg's army into complete rout at Missionary Ridge. "I am very unwilling to do injustice to an officer who has done as much good service as General Thomas," Grant told Halleck, and he suspended orders that he had just written for Thomas to hand his command over to Schofield. Two days later, though, in the middle of the ice storm, Grant started in again, telling Thomas to "delay no longer for weather or reinforcements."[82]

Lacking enough cavalry to penetrate Forrest's screen, Thomas had not been able to estimate his enemy's strength, and the ferocity of the assaults at Franklin implied a sizable force, so Thomas had some reason for caution. Considering that Hood had sent Forrest away with most of the cavalry, and that he did not call him back when the crisis finally came at Nashville, Thomas might well have made his attack before the ice storm. Hood's action defied logic, however, as it often did, and Thomas could not reasonably have predicted it. The weeklong storm would, besides, have hampered Thomas's ability to pursue Hood if he had defeated him before December 8. Grant's refusal to trust the judgment of so eminently trustworthy a subordinate reflected poorly on him as a commander, while the pressure from the War Department (and presumably the White House) demonstrated that political interference had not yet ceased to complicate and jeopardize the conduct of military operations.

Hood had recalled General Bate from Murfreesboro, and Bate described many of his men marching with bare, bleeding feet over frozen roads that had shredded their shoes. When they reached the army camps overlooking Nashville they found that their comrades had already consumed most of the firewood within convenient reach, and while the temperature did not drop low enough to produce frostbite it left the trenches chilly and miserable. Their opponents enjoyed better clothing, and after an idle week they began to wonder if there would be no more fighting at all: anticipating winter quarters, many of Thomas's troops demolished abandoned houses for lumber to build huts, so they passed the ice storm in far better comfort than the poorly clad rebels outside the city.[83]

Not until December 14 did the mercury begin to rise and the ice start to melt, and Thomas ordered his troops to prepare for a movement on the morrow. Under a dense fog on Thursday morning, December 15, he gathered most of his forces on his right while on his left the division from Chattanooga prepared to make a feint against Hood's extreme right. First Thomas opened a deafening barrage that echoed for forty miles even under that overcast. Then, once Hood had turned to face the feint, the rest of Thomas's army came crashing down on his left and center, with the greatest weight on his left. A. J. Smith's rugged veterans of the Sixteenth Corps, abetted by a flank guard of dismounted cavalry, swept the defenders out of one redoubt after another and turned the guns against their previous owners. Schofield, with the Twenty-Third Corps, swung out from behind Smith and reached even farther around to the Union right, overlapping the left of Hood's line and putting it to flight. Hood shifted Cheatham's corps to bolster the left, and as they crossed the Franklin Pike those reinforcements plowed through a flood of stragglers streaming back without weapons. By nightfall Hood had dropped back nearly two miles to a tighter perimeter across the Franklin road and the Granny White Pike, both of which ran south, where he felt so safe that he sent his artillery horses to the rear, leaving the guns in their fresh embrasures. The next day Thomas moved up everything he had and resumed the attack. On Hood's right Stephen Lee's artillery and infantry drove back the first assault of the Fourth Corps with stunning volleys of canister and musketry, but in the afternoon Smith's Sixteenth Corps and the Twenty-Third fell on his center and left, punching numerous holes in the rebel line and bursting through to nab guns by the dozen and prisoners by the hundred. Cheatham's and Stewart's corps dissolved and fled down the Franklin Pike, and Lee fell back to cover the inexorable retreat. The Sixteenth Corps alone scooped up twenty-seven guns and more than four thousand prisoners, including a major general and two brigadiers. Lee's rear guard held back one attack after another into the evening while the wreckage of Hood's army scurried south. At dusk Union cavalry caught up with some of Hood's, charging into the column and cutting out the rebel brigade commander, along with the colors of his division. The deep darkness of a cloudy night allowed the survivors of the Army of Tennessee to escape, but Thomas had lost barely half as many men as Hood despite having taken the offensive. The capture of more than five thousand men and fifty-four guns illustrated that the morale of that Confederate army had reached its nadir.[84]

Four days of rain slowed the pursuit, and then it began to snow. Hood destroyed any standing bridges at each river crossing, taking his pontoon bridges with him, while rising water flooded all the fords. Thomas's pontoon train, complete with its pioneers, was just then closing in on Savannah with Sherman, and Thomas had only hammered together a few makeshift pontoons during the wait at Nashville. His leading units usually built their own trestle bridges out of refuse lumber at the various rivers' edges. On December 17 Hood's rear guard, still under Lee, burned the bridge over the Harpeth River, at Franklin, and mounted a little defense there that gave their fleeing comrades a few hours' advantage. Several regiments of Thomas's cavalry swam the icy river and engaged two of Lee's brigades, incidentally wounding Lee in the foot and taking five battle flags with scores of prisoners; at Franklin the Yankees also found Hood's hospital, with more than fifteen hundred wounded from the fighting of November 30. The townsfolk at Franklin reported utter chaos and dejection in the rebel ranks. Deserters told of their comrades slogging along in independent squads, without officers and often with only a couple of rifles among them, for shooting the occasional cow. Hood admitted as much when he crossed the Duck River to Columbia, where he had hoped to winter over: as he put it two months afterward, "the condition of the army" necessitated crossing to the other side of the Tennessee as soon as he could get there. Forrest had rejoined him, and on December 21 Hood left him behind at Columbia with the cavalry and eight thinned-out brigades of infantry. Taking the rest, Hood pressed on to Pulaski and the Tennessee River, crossing at Muscle Shoals on Christmas Day. Forrest could only hold the Duck River for a day, but he staged one ambush after another all the way to Pulaski, and crossed the Tennessee himself on December 27. Thomas followed two days later, and there he gave up the chase. Hood did not stop until the remnants of his army reached Tupelo, Mississippi, and Thomas spread his army out along the line of the Tennessee, in northern Mississippi and Alabama, to go into winter quarters.[85]

It was poor country, but the conquerors set about stripping what nourishment it could offer. After only a few days there, a Minnesota private confessed with evident disgust that their army had become "nothing better than a legalized band of highwaymen." The Confederate army in that region had all but ceased to exist, and no one remained to exact either individual or collective retribution on Union soldiers for any imposition on the local population, so long as their officers looked the other way.[86]

Effective Confederate resistance had vanished across most of the South. While the shattered battalions of the Army of Tennessee staggered toward safety, George Stoneman thundered out of east Tennessee and into southwestern Virginia with two columns of mounted Federals who had things essentially their own way, literally running circles around their opponents. With inferior numbers, indifferent arms, and underfed, un-shod, exhausted horses, John Breckinridge's rebels could do little more than delay and harass Stoneman as he rolled steadily down the Great Valley along the Virginia & Tennessee Railroad. In Stoneman's path lay the crucial saltworks at Saltville, the Austinville lead mines near Wytheville, and the Confederacy's principal region for manufacturing niter, without which the domestic production of gunpowder would have ceased. Union cavalry from east Tennessee stormed over little hilltop citadels overlook-ing Saltville after dark on December 20, scattering a few hundred Vir-ginia Reserves and local militia. Just before dawn the next morning Ste-phen Burbridge followed the Tennesseans into town with his Kentucky troopers, including those of the 5th and 6th U.S. Colored Cavalry, many of whom had seen the place before, and thousands of men turned their hands to destruction — burning scores of salt sheds and distillery build-ings, plugging wells, and smashing machinery that the remaining Con-federate foundries would require months to replace. The smelting works at Austinville had already fared similarly, and when Stoneman turned lei-surely for home there was not a depot, a bridge, an engine, or a car on the Virginia & Tennessee line between Wytheville and the Tennessee bor-der that he had not destroyed. On Christmas Day a bureau chief in the War Department at Richmond confessed that the serial disasters at Nash-ville, Savannah, and in southwestern Virginia had "filled the land with gloom."[87]

Allatoona Pass, which John Corse successfully defended when John Bell Hood led his army against Sherman's supply line.

Republican political print insinuating that Democratic candidate George McClellan associated with peace men, Jefferson Davis, and the devil.

Union soldiers and civilians on the outskirts of Nashville watch the first day's fighting south of the city.

Sherman's march through South Carolina required his men to wade through miles of swamps like this.

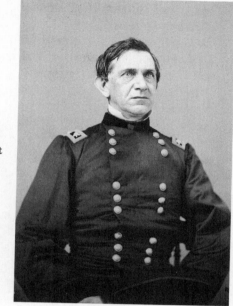

Edward R. S. Canby, who took Mobile and accepted the surrenders of the last Confederate armies.

The crowd in front of the U.S. Capitol for Lincoln's second inauguration.

Flag raising inside Fort Sumter, April 14, 1865.

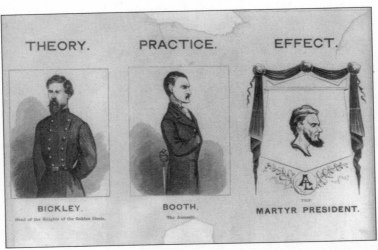

THEORY.   PRACTICE.   EFFECT.

BICKLEY.
Head of the Knights of the Golden Circle.

BOOTH.
The Assassin.

THE
MARTYR PRESIDENT.

A crude effort to link dissident Northern citizens to the purported Knights of the Golden Circle conspiracy and, by extension, to the assassination of Abraham Lincoln.

The Bennett farm near Durham, North Carolina, where Johnston surrendered.

The Andersonville Cemetery, soon after the war: more than 2 percent of the lives lost during the Civil War ended at Andersonville.

The *Sultana* stops at Helena, Arkansas, less than twenty-four hours before the steamboat exploded and burned, taking two-thirds of its passengers to their doom.

The second day of the Grand Review, May 24, 1865, looking up Pennsylvania Avenue from the Treasury Building, where the avenue turned up Fifteenth Street. The troops are Henry Slocum's Army of Georgia.

The military commission that condemned the Lincoln assassins. Judge Advocate General Joseph Holt sits at right; court president David Hunter, who waged more successful war against civilians than soldiers, is sixth from right.

THE VETERAN IN A NEW FIELD.—FROM A PAINTING BY HOMER.

A newspaper engraving of Winslow Homer's 1865 painting *The Veteran in a New Field*, depicting a Union soldier who had returned to the pursuits of peace.

Slavery restored: less than two years after the war, an indigent Florida freedman is sold into a period of servitude to pay his fine for some violation.

A former slave photographed in the summer of 1937, still awaiting effective freedom.

PART III

LIKE A TIRELESS
PHANTOM

7

With Burning Woods Our Skies Are Brass

⋘⋙ WHEN MOBILE BAY fell to Admiral Farragut, in August, that left the Confederacy only Wilmington, North Carolina, as a practical port east of the Mississippi for fitting out or receiving blockade runners, and within weeks that city on the Cape Fear River became the subject of scrutiny for another joint-service operation. On the first of September Quincy Gillmore and Assistant Navy Secretary Gustavus Fox consulted with General Grant about detaching a force to cooperate with the navy, but with the sieges of Atlanta and Petersburg Grant supposed that he already had enough on his mind. The news that Atlanta had been captured came immediately after this interview, but it failed to change his opinion, perhaps because he thought the naval commander who would lead the expedition unsatisfactory for the occasion. Grant vaguely pondered sending as many as ten thousand men to seal off the port, but the plan stalled there for months.[1]

Then, late in November, Ben Butler came up with a shortcut scheme for knocking down the forts below Wilmington, or in Charleston Harbor. Butler had become enamored of dubious projects of late, including the digging of a canal across the neck of Dutch Gap, on the James River, to allow navy gunboats upriver; Union naval officers feared that even if the canal did work, it might give the Confederate navy a better advantage than their own. Butler's plan for the coastal forts involved running a ship aground near them with hundreds of tons of gunpowder aboard, and exploding it. The chief engineer of the U.S. Army doubted that it would work at all, but naval officers seemed optimistic, and eager to try it.[2] Ultimately the planning focused on Fort Fisher, guarding New Inlet just north of Cape Fear, at the southern limit of Butler's geographical department. The day after Thanksgiving, Grant took George Meade and Gouverneur Warren to Butler's headquarters for dinner, where they must have discussed both Butler's project and a raid that might divert Confederate attention from Wilmington, or slow the transfer of troops there from Lee's army. Sixth Corps soldiers began trickling back from the Shenandoah Valley early in December, to the disgust of some who remembered Petersburg from July as "an ugly place." They moved right into the huts and trenches occupied by Warren's Fifth Corps, which bivouacked alongside the Jerusalem Plank Road, to make room. Before daybreak the next morning, December 7, Warren roused the three divisions of his corps, one from the Second Corps, four batteries of artillery, and a division of cavalry to start toward the North Carolina border and the Weldon Railroad. Each man carried four days' rations and sixty rounds, with another two days' provisions and forty rounds per man in wagons. The Weldon line provided the only direct rail corridor from Petersburg to the North Carolina coast: Warren's presence might divert any Confederate reinforcements from Wilmington, besides preventing them from using that railroad to get there. While Warren effaced the tracks on his way south, a smaller expedition ventured out from the Union base at New Bern, North Carolina, to sever the same line south of the Roanoke River.[3]

Warren's raid penetrated some forty miles, as far as the Meherrin River. Rain began on the first day of the march, but then buffeting north winds brought such biting cold that hospitals back on the Petersburg lines saw patients coming in with frozen hands and feet. On the second day out the raiders came up with the Weldon line at Jarratt's Station and started to work, burning a trestle over the Nottoway River and incinerating all the ties between that stream and the Meherrin. The third night the rain turned to sleet, or froze as it hit the ground, covering southern Virginia with the same thick sheet of ice that stalled military activity around Nashville that week. The troops suspected they were heading for the coast themselves, like Sherman, and in imitation of Sherman's scavengers they set fire to many of the houses they passed. There would be no march to the sea for them, however, for below the Meherrin stood three fortified batteries and enough Confederate infantry to discourage Warren from intruding farther with his rations half gone. With eighteen more miles of the Weldon line eliminated, he turned everyone back to Petersburg, where they had to build another little city of winter huts on fresh ground. The New Bern column met resistance, as well, and retired before doing much damage.[4]

The day Warren departed on his mission, Butler selected two divisions from the two newly organized corps in his army — one from the Twenty-Fourth Corps, which had been patched together from the defunct Tenth and Eighteenth, and one from the all-black Twenty-Fifth Corps. Butler marched these seven thousand men to the landing at Bermuda Hundred, putting them on deepwater transports the next day for Fort Monroe. There they sat, waiting aboard their steamships for nearly a week, perfectly ignorant of their destination while Admiral David Dixon Porter readied the massive fleet he had gathered. Porter had to fill all his ships' magazines at the Gosport Navy Yard, in Portsmouth, and the screw steamer *Louisiana*, which he had designated as the "powder ship," had to be stripped of its armament and loaded with thousands of kegs of gunpowder. The wind and rain that assailed Warren's troops churned the seas into a cauldron, slowing that work and wrinkling a few brows at the prospect of putting to sea in such a tempest. Porter finally left on December 13, and he planned to stop at Beaufort to load more ammunition, so Butler did not follow him out of Hampton Roads until the next day. Butler himself accompanied the flotilla, apparently against the wishes of General Grant, who had intended the commander of the Twenty-Fifth Corps, Godfrey Weitzel, to take charge of the enterprise. The sergeant major of the 3rd New York saw Butler tagging along, and cynically assumed that he had come to assure the failure of the campaign, but a staff officer at Twenty-Fifth Corps headquarters recognized that Butler came to assure "that there might be a proud flourish of trumpets at *his* success, in the papers."[5]

To delude spies ashore, Butler sailed the troop transports up Chesapeake Bay and the Potomac River, as though bound for Washington, before retracing his steps in the darkness and rounding Cape Henry for the open sea. Only when the ships hove to off New Inlet did the passengers realize that they were not going to Savannah, or Texas, but — because of fog and more trouble with the powder boat — another three days passed before Porter's armada reached the rendezvous from Beaufort. By then the troops had been trapped aboard their transports for more than ten days, racked with seasickness for much of the time. Those fortunate enough to secure a spot on deck or in a cabin enjoyed some impromptu entertainment from fiddlers, dancers, and an extemporaneous chorus, but many of them passed the voyage in the hold, with their days broken only by twice-daily rations of coffee, raw pork, and hardtack. It occurred to one well-educated soldier aboard the *Weybosset* that if Confederates were to house Union prisoners in such conditions, the press would howl of their brutality.[6]

The Cape Fear River flows twenty-five miles or more beyond Wilmington, leaving an increasingly narrow peninsula on the coastal side, and New Inlet had cut through that sandy barrier twenty miles below the city, where it tapered to half a mile. Ignoring that rupture, the river continued for a few more miles behind the island created by New Inlet. The extremity of that island still included Cape Fear and the treacherous Frying Pan Shoals, but Fort Fisher rose on the new tip of the peninsula known as Federal Point.[7]

Butler's first three days at the inlet passed with still winds and smooth seas, but no sooner had Porter arrived than the wind picked up enough to make it hazardous to land the troops, and for the next four days a gale whipped the cape. The troopships turned back to Beaufort to load coal and fresh water, and on December 23 Butler sent a messenger to Porter announcing that he would rejoin him on the morrow, but Porter replied that he would blow up the powder ship that night and start shelling Fort Fisher. Butler, of all people, understood that Porter wanted the glory of the victory for himself and the navy, but there was nothing he could do about it while his ships were still coaling. He started back the next day, and only came within sight of the battle as Porter's ships broke off their bombardment. The powder ship had spawned a spectacular if short-lived display of fireworks, but had apparently caused no damage to the defenses at all; inside the fort they thought a Union gunboat had exploded. During the barrage the garrison lost fewer than two dozen men out of 667, most of them slightly wounded, and that evening over four hundred reinforcements slipped in, three-quarters of whom consisted of sailors or teenaged Junior Reserves. That still left them outnumbered six to one by the Union army, aside from the naval firepower, and it seemed there might yet be a chance to carry the fort by infantry assault.[8]

That chance faded fast. Nine days of transports and gunboats lying off the cape had given the Carolinians plenty of time to respond, and now Robert Hoke's division of Lee's army stood nearby to lend a hand, with men enough to even the odds, at least among the land forces. Hoke had marched his men into Richmond on December 20 and 21, boarding them on the Danville train to avoid the break in the Weldon road, and by a roundabout route they had shuttled into Wilmington by December 23. The first brigade of that division, some sixteen hundred rifles, came trudging up to the sand hill known as Sugar Loaf, five miles above Fort Fisher on the river side, just at the close of the Christmas Eve bombardment. Christmas Day dawned cloudy but calm, with no breeze and only an occasional fold of the sea lapping at the dozens of hulls offshore. Porter started pounding the fort in the middle of the morning, inflicting little loss on the Carolinians huddled in their bombproofs. At noon, boat crews started lightering Butler's infantry ashore on the opposite side of the peninsula from Sugar Loaf. Five hundred men of Martin Curtis's brigade, New Yorkers all, leaped over the gunwales into icy water up to their waists, fanning out into a skirmish line before they set foot on the beach.

General Weitzel came ashore with them. While another thousand men landed under Brigadier General Adelbert Ames, Weitzel faced the first five hundred to the left, to patrol south toward Fisher. A sand-banked fieldpiece and a company of infantry lay directly in their path, but the gun had already burst and a white flag fluttered from the little embrasure before the Yankees came within musket range. Some of Porter's sailors on one of the closer gunboats saw the flag and jumped into a boat, pulling ashore so fast that they claimed the fort for themselves and started ferrying the prisoners out to their ship.[9]

General Weitzel interrogated some of the prisoners before the sailors led them away. He found that they belonged to the 42nd North Carolina, of Hoke's division, which Weitzel knew quite well from more than seven months of contact below Richmond. He was aware that Hoke had as many as six thousand men, and the prisoners said that some of the division had gone into Fort Fisher.[10]

With nothing more than his exaggerated skirmish line and a thin screen of flankers, Curtis strode past the battery, only stopping when he came within half a mile of Fort Fisher. There Weitzel and Cyrus Comstock, Grant's staff engineer, stopped to make a detailed examination of that massive battery, which they mistook for a square bastion: it actually consisted of a great L, with the short leg cutting almost completely across the peninsula from seaside to river's edge, and the long side stretching perpendicularly down the sea face of the point, nearly to the inlet. Weitzel could see that the sand parapets had hardly suffered at all under the naval barrage, and his experience told him that a land assault from the north could never succeed, with seventeen heavy guns arrayed against the beach. He turned back to his boat to deliver his disheartening news to Butler, but as the ships' firing abated Curtis ventured farther still, halting perhaps five hundred feet from the fort; his men trod among the remains of the post vegetable gardens, in the shadow of the unoccupied ramparts. One of his staff cut the telegraph line running up to Sugar Loaf and Wilmington, and a lieutenant who saw no enemy to challenge him crept to the very sally port to retrieve the garrison flag and the tip of its flagpole, which one of Porter's shells had snapped off. An enlisted man slipped right inside the fort. The navy's shells were still flying, and the Confederates had not yet emerged from their shelters, but Curtis seemed to think the place abandoned; he assured Comstock that he could take the fort with fifty men. He sent back to the landing place for two hundred, and General Ames ordered the rest of Curtis's brigade to join him, but Weitzel suspected that the whole garrison was still there, ready to come pouring out as soon as the shelling gave way to the infantry assault. His report prompted Butler to order a withdrawal, and that order overtook Curtis's reinforcements just in time, for just about then the garrison spilled into the palisade trenches and manned the guns to defend their work; even the Junior Reserves fell into line, although they required some special prodding to pry them from the bombproofs. Then came the darkness, as Curtis retired.[11]

Back near the landing, the troops under General Ames snared a couple of hundred young Carolina Reserves making their way to the fort. The boys, who averaged no more than seventeen years of age, threw down their rifles without a fight. They explained that they had been sent out of the fort because there was no room for them in the bombproofs, which implied (incorrectly) that the fort was fully manned, and they admitted the presence of at least two brigades from Hoke's division. Butler, who also remembered Hoke and his troops from operations along the James, concluded that he was outgunned and decided to call the entire operation off. Grant had ordered the troops to entrench on the peninsula if they could not seize the fort immediately, but Weitzel had apparently never seen those orders. Wind picked up out of the southeast that evening, and the sea started churning again in the middle of the debarkation, leaving nearly a thousand of Butler's men stranded onshore, with little food or water. One brigade lay ashore until December 27, through a drenching rain, coming in soaking wet: when the last man had climbed aboard, the whole flotilla of troopships steered for Fort Monroe.[12]

The fiasco disgusted General Grant when he learned of it the next evening, and his ire mounted when he heard from Colonel Comstock, who thought Butler could have landed his troops during the three days of pleasant weather after his arrival, and taken the undermanned fort without the help of the navy at all. Grant promptly issued instructions to renew the operation, asking Admiral Porter to hold his gunboats off New Inlet for a while yet, while he sent down more troops than before, "without the former Commander." Porter readily agreed, and by Wednesday morning, January 4, the troops who had just returned from Cape Fear were shuffling back aboard the transports, along with an additional brigade. While those men clattered up the gangplanks, Grant asked Stanton to remove Butler from the command of his department, lest he try to lead them through another failure. Butler almost certainly would have gone along again, for press criticism of his blundering in the first attempt had already provoked him to speak of making a second.[13]

"Very few tears will be shed," predicted a New York lieutenant when he learned of Butler's removal, and that sentiment seemed almost universal in the army. A Regular Army officer thought Butler should have been dismissed from the army altogether. "Thus endeth the military career of the hero of Wilmington & Dutch Gap Canal," chuckled an officer in the Twenty-Fifth Corps. Butler did not go quietly into the night, but he did go.[14]

The new commander was Alfred Terry, a brevet major general from Connecticut who, though a lawyer by profession, had shown much promise in high command. Weitzel did not accompany the second effort, choosing instead to stay behind and get married.[15]

Except for those who had gone ashore on Christmas Day, most of the troops who composed the second expedition had endured twenty-three days aboard those cramped steamers, only to disembark at their old camps, where their huts had been cannibalized for fuel by those left behind. Their knapsacks had gone elsewhere, so they lacked blankets or ponchos as another downpour turned to sloppy, wet snow. They had just begun to rebuild their winter quarters when, five days later, they were ordered back to the ships. The fleet steamed between the Virginia capes again on Friday, January 6, and anchored in the harbor at Beaufort on Sunday morning, after a tempestuous passage around Cape Hatteras. Bad weather kept them there several days, even without the jinx of Ben Butler's presence, and it was not until the evening of January 12 that the ships hauled up once again off Federal Point, just above where Curtis and Ames had landed on Christmas Day. A light wind from the northwest left the coast calm, and the transports lolled in such gentle swells that the soldiers dared open their ink bottles for those last letters home before another dangerous enterprise.[16]

Sergeant Major Edward King Wightman, of the 3rd New York in Martin Curtis's brigade, wrote two letters that day from his cramped cabin on the *Atlantic*. Wightman represented an uncommon soldier in the Union army: he held a graduate degree, and might have profited from influential connections, but he had made no attempt to secure a commission before entering the army, and he appears to have enlisted entirely from a sense of patriotic duty, without the economic or social pressure that had guided so many of his comrades into the ranks. His family enjoyed comfortable surroundings, and he left a satisfactory job to enter the army; he may have lusted for a little adventure, but the war had already become quite brutal when he donned the uniform of a private soldier. Having spent thirty-one of the past thirty-five days dining on the spare and revolting fare of a troopship, he lampooned the cruelly tempting courses of Christmas dinner described in a letter from home. The next Christmas might be all the jollier, he supposed, anticipating that the New Year would bring peace.[17]

The troops started going ashore right after the breakfast hour on Friday, the thirteenth, but no one seemed to regard the date as ominous. The surf was rolling heavier by then, wetting the men as they rowed ashore and dampening a lot of their paper-wrapped ammunition, but they met no opposition, and by the middle of the afternoon everyone had landed. By dark, one brigade had stretched the entire width of Federal Point, and had begun entrenching against any assault from Wilmington by Hoke's division. That isolated the defenders at Fort Fisher, who could only escape by sea if they failed to repel an assault. Up at Wilmington, Braxton Bragg, now commander of the Confederate Department of North Carolina, appeared to write the garrison off as lost.[18]

The next morning Admiral Porter moved five ironclad monitors within a thousand yards of the fort and opened on the long southern leg of Fort Fisher with them, gradually silencing one gun after another and tumbling much of the protective traverses between the embrasures. From the Cape Fear River, on the opposite side of the peninsula, the erstwhile blockade runner *Chickamauga,* now a Confederate cruiser, dropped occasional shells on Terry's soldiers as they improved their earthworks and reconnoitered the north wall of Fort Fisher. From a distance of five or six hundred yards Colonel Comstock saw that the steep, towering parapet of the fort was protected by a palisade of vertical logs running from the beach on the Atlantic side to a marsh near the riverbank. Naval gunnery had perforated the palisade extensively. Comstock argued against a siege for the difficulty of bringing in provisions — and because it would have to end in assault anyway — so Terry decided to make the attack the next day. Porter offered two thousand sailors and Marines for a separate storming party.[19]

Four hundred Marines armed with rifles and about sixteen hundred sailors with revolvers and cutlasses landed on the beach by noon of January 15, two miles above Fort Fisher. The army formed on their right, near the river. Adelbert Ames organized his three brigades in columns of fours, with Curtis in front, Galusha Pennypacker behind him, and Louis Bell's brigade in the rear: Ames and all three of his brigadiers had been in the war from the start, but none of them had yet reached the age of thirty. The division numbered about four thousand, and all were New Yorkers or Pennsylvanians except for the 4th New Hampshire and 13th Indiana, of Bell's brigade.[20]

The fire from the fleet dropped off around 3:00 P.M., and the two columns started forward, with the naval brigade in the lead and aiming for the northeast corner of the fort, where eight-inch rifles and smoothbores blasted them with canister. Sharpshooters picked off their officers, and when they reached closer range the Confederate infantry trotted into the exterior works to riddle them with musketry. The sailors' cutlasses did them no good at a distance, and few of them could come close enough even to use their revolvers effectively. In the end they fled in panic, back up the beach, but their sacrifice relieved the Union infantry of enough pressure that they poured through the gap-toothed palisade and gained a foothold on the northwest corner of the parapet, where the Wilmington road ran into the fort. The Junior Reserves and others in the garrison evidently balked at leaving their bombproofs to fight, which only increased the three-to-one odds presented by the naval column and Ames's division, but a struggle on the north wall continued at point-blank range after the sun went down. Finally Terry pulled Joseph Abbott's brigade out of the trenches facing Hoke, added the 27th U.S. Colored Troops, and threw those six regiments into the fort to fight in the moonlight. Abbott, whom Comstock thought reluctant to enter that cauldron, nevertheless punched through to the interior of the fort, where gunners farther down the sea face spun their pieces around to rake their own parade ground with grapeshot and canister. Abbott secured the last few embrasures in the north parapet before starting down the sea face, and once he had silenced the last gun, the remainder of the garrison either turned and ran or surrendered. The fort's commandant, Colonel William Lamb, and Major General William Whiting, the department commander whom Bragg had superseded, were both seriously wounded, and retired with most of the survivors to Battery Buchanan, a separate work at the extreme tip of Federal Point. Late that night the victors closed in and Whiting capitulated on behalf of everyone.[21]

The trophies consisted of over two thousand prisoners with as many small arms, more than fifteen dozen heavy guns and rifles, and control over the last major entrance for blockade runners east of Texas. The cost had been fifty thousand rounds of naval shells, four or five times that much in musket cartridges, and about a thousand casualties among soldiers and sailors — not counting scores who were killed and maimed the next morning, when some fool sauntered into one of the fort's magazines with a lighted candle. All three of the brigadiers in Ames's division had been shot in front of the parapet, or on it. Colonel Bell soon died, and nine regimental commanders in that division had been killed or wounded. Among the dead lay Sergeant Major Wightman, of the 3rd New York, who had been in the forefront of his regiment in the leading brigade. The next morning his comrades buried him in the sand outside the fort. Notification that the sergeant major had been killed may have reached Wightman's father in the same mail as his son's last missive, with its expectations of the joy he and his family would enjoy "if we all do see another Christmas," but the father was not home to receive either of those letters: the *New York Herald* had already published a report of his son's death, and he had taken passage south to bring the body home.[22]

Lieutenant Colonel Charles Francis Adams Jr. inquired of his father, the United States minister to Great Britain, how the people of England reacted to the capture of Fort Fisher. That blow had been struck "for the English market," he insisted, alluding to the serious dent it would make in the demand for British-built blockade runners and contraband goods; Colonel Adams assumed that the decline in economic interest would yield a commensurate withering in political sympathy with the Confederacy. His father replied that both private and public response had been extremely gratifying, especially following so soon after the fall of Savannah. A "very distinguished lady" who had never previously touched on the topic had congratulated Ambassador Adams on "the war coming to an end," and even the formerly pro-Confederate *Times* of London had dropped its sneering tone toward the government at Washington. "A quarrel might yet help the failing rebel cause," Minister Adams warned, but Parliament would dissolve by constitutional limitations in July, and with every member seeking reelection he doubted that any of them would support a military confrontation with the United States. The Confederacy would collapse before then, he presumed.[23]

In Washington, the only person who seemed unhappy about the fall of Fort Fisher was Ben Butler. The deposed general stopped at the capital at the behest of his Radical Republican friends on the Joint Committee on the Conduct of the War, who planned to rehabilitate their discredited hero and look into the reasons for his removal, all under the guise of an official investigation into military questions. Having abandoned Federal Point against the wishes of the general in chief, Butler intended to excuse himself by asserting that the fort could never be taken except by siege — which, after all, was why Grant had wanted the point held, even if an assault proved impractical. The swift seizure of the place by Terry and Porter demolished Butler's defense and implicitly impugned his judgment. Worst of all, from Butler's perspective, the victory severely undermined the joint committee's accommodating examination "into the causes of the failure of the late expedition against Wilmington," for the committee opened its testimony on January 17, 1865, at about the same hour the news of Fisher's capture reached Washington City. The committee did its best for their portly little hero, whom some had once eyed as a presidential candidate in place of Lincoln. Although their charge was confined to Butler's attempt at Fort Fisher, committee members asked him helpful questions about the alleged maladministration for which he had also been supplanted as department commander. In his conclusions, Chairman Ben Wade blamed others for the failure of Butler's powder boat, and implied that there had been a lack of naval cooperation with Butler's excursion. Finally, he highlighted written testimony from the dying General Whiting, who remarked that Terry's January success was only made possible by Braxton Bragg's inaction. The grist the committee provided for

Butler's defense came too late to be of any use, even if it had been more persuasive, and his discomfiture soured the midwinter triumph for him and his Radical champions.[24]

Some of the Confederacy's most famous travelers had embarked from, or landed at, Wilmington's docks. The city remained in Confederate hands for a while yet, but no longer would it provide Jefferson Davis's armies with ordnance and supplies from abroad. Only Galveston and Brownsville remained open, in Texas, and anything that slipped through the Union naval cordon there had no real hope of reaching Richmond, or even the ragged survivors of Hood's Nashville campaign. Charleston, surrounded by a cloud of U.S. warships, some of which patrolled inside the harbor, offered a poor haven: the Atlantic coast had effectively been won.[25]

Also won during that month of January was the matter of emancipation that had hung in doubt since President Lincoln's famous decree on the subject, two years before. Until then, the president had always insisted that the federal government could assert no authority over slavery in the states where it existed, maintaining that its continuation or abolition was an issue for each state to decide, and in his inaugural address he had promised not to interfere with it. He had issued his proclamation under the authority of the extraordinary war powers that he claimed as his right, but there had always been some doubt about whether he would carry through completely with the letter of that proclamation: if the Confederacy were conquered and the war ended, his assumed war powers would also end, and he might revert to his antebellum stance that the states had to decide the question individually. He had made it clear enough that he never intended to return anyone to slavery whom his order had set free, and all his subsequent discussions about peace negotiations had included a prerequisite for the abandonment of slavery. In June he had welcomed his party's endorsement of an antislavery amendment with his presidential nomination, and the November election had implied national concurrence with that sentiment, so in his annual message on December 6 Lincoln recommended that Congress reconsider the abolition bill that had died in the House during the previous session.[26]

Radicals who had feared the constitutional amendment was "dead" the previous summer thus found the supposedly resistant president their foremost ally in the cherished crusade. Three days into the session Representative James Ashley of Ohio announced that he intended to resurrect Senate Resolution 16, and he reserved January 6 for his introduction, opening early that morning with President Lincoln's own recorded comment that "if slavery is not wrong, nothing is wrong." The debate took up the entire first day, and six more full days over the course of the month.

Ashley remained the principal spokesman, and Robert Mallory of Kentucky led the opposition, basing his case on the social ramifications of emancipation but depending more on parliamentary delays and obstruction. The vote to reconsider S.R. 16 only came at the last minute, on January 31, with a tally of 112 to 57, and Mallory objected that it failed to win a two-thirds majority. Speaker Schuyler Colfax ruled that the motion to reconsider only needed a simple majority, while the final passage required two-thirds, and Mallory then asked for a postponement, since several Democrats were ill that day. Ashley refused to oblige, and John Dawson of Pennsylvania, an opponent of the amendment, called for the question to have it over with. As four o'clock approached, the clerk began calling the roll. Democrats John Ganson, of New York, and James English, of Pennsylvania, drew boisterous cheers from the Republican side of the aisle when they voted in favor, but the Speaker gaveled the members to order. Every Republican was present, but eight Democrats — any four of whom would have defeated the resolution — did not or could not show up to vote. The Speaker reminded the clerk to call his own name, and with his vote in favor the cheers soared again. When Colfax announced that the resolution had passed, 119 to 56, the House broke into pandemonium: congressmen, at least on the Republican side, leaped to their feet and applauded, as did the spectators in the brimming galleries. It was obvious there would be no more business that day, and the House adjourned at 4:20 P.M.[27]

"This year is going to close the war sure," wrote a jubilant New Hampshire lieutenant a few days after the capture of Fort Fisher, and that feat had evidently aroused equivalent suspicions among rebel officials in Richmond. "The prospect is growing darker & darker about us," remarked the chief of Confederate ordnance when he recorded the event. That evening he attended a dinner party at a family home on Richmond's Sixth Street, where he encountered his friend James P. Holcombe, formerly of the Confederate Congress and lately back from the secret Confederate mission in Canada West. Holcombe, who had represented a Unionist Virginia district himself, revealed that plenty of men in the Congress had given up hope of winning the war, and felt ready to rejoin the Union if they could make terms, and chief among those terms would have been the preservation of slavery in some form.[28]

Until the end of 1862, President Lincoln's only demand for peace had been submission to federal authority under the old Union, but since the first day of 1863 reunion and emancipation had become his tandem prerequisites for ending hostilities. Those had been the terms he conveyed through Horace Greeley the previous summer, which had been published in the newspapers, but Lincoln knew through private emissaries that Jefferson Davis had already rejected the former condition and that great political pressure forced him to refuse the latter. Of late, however, Southern leaders had heard rumors of a potential softening in Lincoln's demand for immediate and absolute abolition.[29]

On Thanksgiving Day of 1864 a quondam doctor, lawyer, and militia general from Illinois named James W. Singleton met with his lobbyist and townsman Orville Hickman Browning and told him that Lincoln had withdrawn his insistence on an end to slavery. Browning, who was an old friend of the president's, very much doubted Singleton's interpretation, and assured him that Lincoln would not budge on that issue, but Singleton insisted that he had it from the president himself, before the election. According to Singleton, who had numerous Southern connections and seems to have opposed the war, Lincoln told him that his demand for the "abandonment of slavery" in the Greeley correspondence had not accurately represented his real position. Two days later, the self-important Singleton added that the president had just sent him a note reasserting that point, and that Lincoln intended to say as much in his message to Congress, besides which he might send Singleton himself to Richmond as a peace commissioner. The president made no such clarification in his annual message, and no note from him to Singleton has ever surfaced, but on Christmas Eve Browning spoke personally with Lincoln, who showed him all the letters to and from Greeley. Lincoln confirmed Singleton's claim that "he had been misrepresented, and misunderstood[,] and that he had never entertained the purpose of making the abolition of slavery a condition precedent to the termination of the war, and the restoration of the Union." On December 27, Lincoln called Browning back to the White House on behalf of Singleton, whom he was going to allow through the lines to Richmond, purportedly to buy cotton.[30]

Indeed, Singleton did mean to buy cotton and bring it back through the lines at the customarily hefty profits (and revenue rates), but he also appears to have undertaken a more political errand, albeit nominally on his own hook, and ulterior political missions seem to have been in vogue that week. Even as the president discussed Mr. Singleton's trip to Richmond, he contemplated another unofficial envoy to that city who would also travel under the excuse of a personal quest, without authority of any kind to treat with the enemy, but without any prohibition against it. Old Preston Blair, patriarch of the political clan that had included Lincoln's loyal postmaster general, called on the president December 28 for a pass to Richmond. He said he was going to retrieve some property titles that had been taken from his home during Early's raid on Washington, but he and the president had previously discussed feeling out Blair's old friend

Jefferson Davis on the subject of appointing a peace commission. Lincoln gave Blair the pass, and when the old man reached Davis's office, on January 12, they discussed whether Lincoln would receive peace commissioners, and what conditions might stand in the way of a negotiated settlement. The Confederate president supplied him with a written message that he might show to Lincoln — thereby avoiding the impediment of an official letter that Lincoln would refuse to accept — in which he expressed his willingness to appoint a peace commissioner immediately to end hostilities between "the two countries." Blair took that back to Washington six days later, and Lincoln returned a note assuring that he would receive any agent who could bring peace to "our one common country." Lincoln must have supposed that his rejection of implied independence for the Confederacy would cause Davis to let the opportunity pass, but Davis may have surprised him. Blair returned to Richmond on January 21 to deliver the reply, and Davis read it over twice, apparently aloud. Blair pointed out the final words, noting that it was Lincoln's response to Davis's insistence on two separate countries. Davis acknowledged that he understood it that way. When Blair related this to Lincoln a week later, the president probably assumed that he would hear no more about it, but the next evening a flag of truce brought a letter for General Grant through the pickets of Orlando Willcox's division, below Petersburg, from three men calling themselves peace commissioners. They asked permission to cross the lines and go on to Washington for a conference with President Lincoln.[31]

Grant had ventured down to Federal Point to see General Terry, and had not yet returned when the message reached his headquarters. Major General Edward O. C. Ord, who had replaced Butler, received the note in Grant's absence as the senior general, and sought instructions from the secretary of war before allowing so unusual a visitation. Stanton, who may not have been privy to the correspondence between the presidents, replied late that same night that Ord should admit no such emissaries, but the next morning Stanton advised that the president was dispatching Major Thomas Eckert of the War Department telegraph office as a special messenger to speak to the Confederate trio before deciding whether they would enter Union lines. Eckert found the three already ensconced at City Point, for General Grant had returned on the morning of January 31 and allowed them to enter his lines; they had come in that evening near Fort Davis, on the Jerusalem Plank Road, alighting from a closed carriage at the rebel works and walking through the pickets of the 51st Pennsylvania. From there they had proceeded in an ambulance to Ninth Corps headquarters, where staff officers met them and accompanied them on the military railroad to City Point. At Lincoln's behest, William Seward started for Fort Monroe as his proxy with three "indispensable" terms, rather than just two: the restoration of national authority, no retreat from his position on slavery as expressed to Congress in December (or from the Thirteenth Amendment, passed only that day), and no armistice short of complete surrender and demobilization.[32]

The secretary of state arrived at Fort Monroe on the *River Queen* at 10:00 P.M. on February 1, but Major Eckert telegraphed at the same hour that the commissioners' reply was "not satisfactory," apparently because they declined to acknowledge Lincoln's reference to a common country. Lincoln was going to recall both Eckert and Seward in the morning, but early on February 2 Edwin Stanton came over from the War Department with a telegram from Grant, who interjected that the commissioners' letter to him had provided "all that the President's instructions contemplated" — besides which, Grant feared that it would produce "a bad influence" to refuse to even see them. In what may have been an attempt to discredit Seward, one of the Confederate commissioners later seemed to hint that Mrs. Grant had something to do with her husband's intervention, claiming that while the three Confederates waited at City Point she and some of Grant's staff expressed impatience to have the three envoys bypass Seward and meet Lincoln directly. Grant wrote that he thought the commissioners came with good intentions, and that it would be too bad if the president could not meet with them. At that Lincoln relented, and wired at 9:00 A.M. that he would come as quickly as he could and see them himself. Two hours later he left Washington in the company of a railroad official: the Baltimore & Ohio put a special engine and car at his service, on which he sped to Annapolis, boarded the packet *Thomas Collyer* at the Naval Academy dock, and headed downriver for Fort Monroe.[33]

Considering the men he appointed for the mission, one might have thought that Jefferson Davis also had good intentions. One of the three, Robert M. T. Hunter, was one of Virginia's foremost statesmen, and although he had favored leaving the Union in 1861 he represented a state that had resisted secession until the last moment. The other two had both opposed secession, and acceded to it only after their states went out of the Union. John Campbell had been a justice on the U.S. Supreme Court, and Alexander Stephens had served in the House of Representatives as a Whig ally of freshman congressman Abraham Lincoln. Stephens and Jefferson Davis had found more to disagree about as vice president and president of the Confederacy than as members of the U.S. Congress from opposing parties, and it seemed to say something about Davis's hopes for the conference that he overlooked his antagonism toward Stephens enough to benefit from Stephens's acquaintance with Lincoln. Davis's willingness to persist in discussions despite Lincoln's diplomatic insinuations of mandatory submission gave the impression that Davis might modify his insistence on independence somewhere along the way.

That impression was almost certainly mistaken. To the last ditch, Davis insisted on the sovereignty of his government as stubbornly as Lincoln asserted the authority of his own. Davis's own statements suggest his aversion to a negotiated settlement, and a hope that the peace mission would discredit Southern advocates of compromise.

Judging from their memoirs of the mission, the principal questions that Stephens and his associates had for Lincoln included whether some relic of slavery might not survive the conflict, and whether states returning to their allegiance would resume all their former rights of congressional representation. That they would ask the first question after Lincoln's repeated public statements implies that they had been informed of some equivocation on his demand for the "abandonment of slavery." Their anticipation clearly had no foundation, for Lincoln had signed the resolution launching the Thirteenth Amendment even while he pondered whether to see the commissioners, but they may have obtained such misinformation through the aspiring plenipotentiary James Singleton, who had left Richmond only two or three days before the Confederate commissioners started from that city. Senior officials in James Seddon's War Department knew that Singleton had spoken to someone high in the rebel government about a peace initiative, apparently suggesting that the best terms could be obtained if the negotiations were left to Grant and Lee. Meanwhile, the commissioners' readiness to talk in spite of Lincoln's stated conditions may have persuaded him that they were ready to yield on the subjects of reunion and slavery, but wanted to know whether a general amnesty might counter any popular demand for retribution — and on that matter he held full authority to answer, as well as a demonstrated inclination to act charitably. "General" Singleton's freelance diplomacy may also have been responsible for unjustified optimism on the president's part, for Lincoln reversed himself and decided to come to Fort Monroe barely twelve hours after Singleton dropped into his office to relate "who he saw, and what was said in Richmond" in relation to public affairs, all of which Mr. Browning thought the president would find "interesting to hear."[34]

Everyone across the country seemed to know from the start about the ostensibly secret missions of Blair and Singleton, which some understood to have been a joint venture, and few doubted Lincoln's hand in it, however solemnly he declared that each man had gone to conduct his own private business. The very inkling of unofficial preliminaries toward peace set the soldiers on both sides salivating for an end to their miseries. Plenty of men in both blue and grey concurred with the pacifist sentiments of one reluctant middle-aged recruit from Wisconsin who resented the martial ardor of politicians and citizens who had no idea of the hardships men suffered at the front. Line officers and enlisted men risked disciplinary action with a sudden surge in fraternization along the picket line. While the commissioners waited for permission to proceed, a Confederate soldier on the Ninth Corps front shouted that he and his compatriots were going home, having "sold out to the Yanks," and the word "peace" raced sibilantly up and down the long trench network when information spread that the three Southern statesmen had actually crossed into Union custody.[35]

Grant conveyed the commissioners to Fort Monroe on his dispatch boat the *Mary Martin*. Seward remained aboard his own steamer, and well after midnight on February 3 the *Collyer* anchored nearby. After daylight the *Mary Martin* and the *River Queen* sidled up to each other in the middle of Hampton Roads and their crews lashed the two vessels together. Lincoln joined his secretary of state in his stateroom on the *River Queen*, and that afternoon they welcomed the commissioners there.[36]

The only records of the meeting are some memoranda Campbell jotted down soon afterward, and recollections written by Stephens and Hunter a few years later, but in most respects those independent accounts agree with each other and with the tenor of Lincoln's public stance on the various issues. First came the inevitable exchange of amiable reminiscences between Lincoln and his diminutive former colleague Stephens, and then the president reiterated his foremost demand: that the Confederacy must cease hostilities, disband its armies, and submit to the restoration of federal authority. The commissioners tried to suggest a more gradual form of reunion, first involving a joint campaign against French imperialism in Mexico — a scheme eerily similar to Secretary Seward's 1861 suggestion of creating an international conflict to disarm the secession crisis. This was apparently Preston Blair's idea, passed on to the commissioners by President Davis. Lincoln firmly opposed any complicated postponement of that sort, or any preliminary armistice, and Campbell's inquiries about the rights Southern states might expect under reunification revealed that Campbell, at least, was willing to consider outright submission. When asked how that reunification would be accomplished, Lincoln replied that it was only necessary to disband the Confederate armies and allow the federal government to resume its functions. That statement seemed to offer immediate restoration of statehood, consonant with his persistent argument that the states had never left the Union, but had merely succumbed to insurrection. He acknowledged that Congress might refuse to admit elected representatives from the erstwhile Confederate states, as was its right, but his image of a reunion of the states still seemed not to include the reversion to territorial status favored by Radical Republicans.[37]

It was only on the matter of emancipation that Campbell's notes conflicted with Stephens's memory, and that subtle distinction may have amounted only to a slight misunderstanding or stylistic ambiguity. Stephens thought that Lincoln characterized his Emancipation Proclamation as a war measure that applied only to those who had actively attained freedom under its authority during the war; it would become void the moment peace returned, which would leave most slaves still in bondage. Campbell recorded Seward as having voiced that opinion, rather than Lincoln, and in reference to both the proclamation and the Thirteenth Amendment. In light of Lincoln's recent signature on the resolution approving that amendment for ratification, and his statements to Seward, to his private secretary, and to Congress, such a remark by him would have been disingenuous, but it did comport with James Singleton's claim, as confirmed by Lincoln's friend Browning. Hunter remembered no vacillation on emancipation, summarizing Lincoln's terms as mandatory reunion and abolition, but his was the last and the most jaundiced of the three men's accounts. Since the Thirteenth Amendment would not become operative nationally until it had been adopted by three-quarters of the states, Lincoln might well have felt safe contending that individual states would still determine the fate of slavery within their borders, as he had always maintained they should, but with twenty-three states already free (including Missouri and Maryland, by then), and numerous territories, it would not be long before the amendment became the law of the land. If Lincoln refrained from telling the commissioners that universal abolition would follow the Confederacy's dissolution, it may have been to avoid throwing an insurmountable obstruction in the path of peace — or to escape having it said again that he had done so.[38]

Lincoln did suggest that slave owners might be compensated for the loss of their investment. Judge Campbell remembered him acknowledging that the Northern states (some of which had still allowed slavery in the recent past) shared responsibility for the existence of slavery in the country, and Lincoln said he would happily pay a tax toward the elimination of slavery himself, although Seward grumbled a bit over the idea.[39]

After four hours, there seemed little else to discuss. The commissioners failed to introduce the question of whether the leaders of the rebellion would be prosecuted, but perhaps Lincoln's references to the generous application of his pardoning power satisfied that inevitable worry. Stephens asked Lincoln to reconsider his objections to declaring an amnesty, but the president said he doubted his mind would change. Before they parted, Stephens asked the personal favor of an exchange for his nephew, then a prisoner on Johnson's Island, which Lincoln readily granted. When the commissioners had climbed back aboard the *Mary Martin* the two steamers cast apart in the dusk, and the *River Queen* turned back for Annapolis, where it docked at an early hour on February 4. Lincoln and his secretary of state boarded the special train after breakfast, and arrived in Washington near half past nine.[40]

At noon that day the president gathered the rest of his cabinet, to brief everyone on the discussion aboard the *River Queen*. He had told them nothing about his plans before leaving for Hampton Roads, and perhaps a touch of pique over that impetuous junket had inclined them to disapprove of his presenting himself before his inferiors in the rebel government. The thrust of his briefing echoed the inconclusiveness that the newspapers were already announcing, but the next evening he called the cabinet back together to seek their opinion of a plan that obviously emanated from his conversation on the boat. He proposed offering a concession of several hundred million dollars to compensate slave owners, in return for giving up the fight by the first of April. The grant would equal only a fraction of what it would cost to prosecute the war for another year, he argued. It greatly resembled a proposal he had made to encourage the border states to abolish slavery, three years before: not one state had taken him up on it, although two had recently voted to end the institution without a penny in compensation. Gideon Welles perceived Lincoln's fervid wish to end the war, but he thought it would sound too eager to the Confederate leadership, and all of his ministers disapproved of the idea, so he filed it away for eternity.[41]

A few days later, Lincoln officially presented all the correspondence about the conference to Congress. Its publication served to silence those who might still say he refused to consider any overtures for peace, but that political cover was the only productive result of his efforts. At the same time, though, Jefferson Davis turned over copies of his correspondence to his own Congress, which proved useful in convincing his public that the North sought complete subjugation of the Confederacy, and the elevation of slaves to a level of equality with their masters. The Confederate Senate ordered five thousand copies printed.[42]

As attentively as Grant's soldiers had awaited the results of the conference, its failure surprised few and gratified many. Recuperating in one of the Naval Academy buildings that had been converted to a hospital, from which he might have seen Lincoln departing for or returning from Hampton Roads, the wounded Colonel Samuel Duncan, of the 4th U.S. Colored Infantry, cringed at the image of his president going to the rebels hat in hand, instead of dictating terms to them; the colonel hoped the meeting would come to nothing, so the outcome satisfied him. The Confederacy yet needed a little more humbling, a Vermont colonel concluded, and an Ohio captain in northern Alabama assured his friends that the only effective peace commissioners were "Grant, Thomas, Sheridan, Sherman, and Terry."[43] Enlisted men expressed similar sentiments, albeit often with less bravado or enthusiasm, but on the Petersburg front they noticed that the steady trickle of Confederate deserters coming into their lines had become a swollen stream.[44]

The Confederate armies suffered worse than their opponents from short rations and poor clothing, but they were not alone in hemorrhaging deserters. Twenty-nine men from the Second Corps alone underwent court-martial for desertion in the month of January. Most of the twenty-nine went free, but many a soldier wrote home that winter of parading out with his division to witness a hanging or firing-squad execution of some unfortunate whom the whim of military justice had selected as an appropriate example. The mandatory spectacles revolted the average veteran, who preferred going into battle to witnessing the execution of a helpless prisoner, but ghoulish curiosity could grip a man beset by boredom. The promised multiple hanging of some men from the 5th New Hampshire intrigued a Vermonter, who admitted his intention to "go and see them if I can." The once-renowned 5th New Hampshire developed an unenviable distinction because so many of its recruits disappeared each night. "How they do desert from that Regt," remarked the morbid Vermonter. A captain in another Vermont regiment ascribed it to the "roughs and rowdies" the Granite State was sending to fill its quota.[45]

Most Union armies were draining deserters, too, even in the Deep South, where there were no substantial Confederate armies in which a runaway Yankee might seek asylum. When the 2nd Massachusetts left Atlanta as the rear guard of Sherman's army, some recent recruits from that regiment remained surreptitiously behind; deserters and stragglers took their lives in their hands on the march through Georgia, but when that regiment reached the relative safety of Savannah the bounty jumpers started slipping away again. A Canadian recruit on the coast of North Carolina had worked his way into a hospital, but he tried to orchestrate a furlough that would allow him to go home, where he could remain with impunity. Toward that end he conspired with his wife, advising her to write him a fraudulent letter, addressed and mailed from the New York side of the Canadian border, that claimed she was dying and needed his signature on legal documents to place their children in a home.[46]

That man's ploy failed, but enough soldiers had taken French leave that Congress passed a law stripping deserters of their citizenship, or of their right to become citizens, in addition to any other penalties a court-martial might impose, as well as being "forever incapable of holding any office of trust or profit under the United States." Any citizen who moved from the district where he was enrolled, or left the United States altogether, in order to avoid the draft would suffer the same consequences. The president had issued another call for three hundred thousand men on December 19, and the approaching deadline for that levy had turned many a young man's mind to thoughts of travel, which served as the poor man's only form of draft insurance. John Giffen, a young Ohioan with a master's degree, moved to Harrietsville, Canada West, where he taught school instead of pursuing his medical ambitions, and his brother Jacob wandered west, across the Missouri, beyond finding by the post office or the provost marshal. Canada had appealed to many in the northern tier of states during the last draft, but New York City had its own charms, including both the anonymity of the teeming streets and a rising flood of immigrants that left pools of potential volunteers to diminish the city's obligations.[47]

New York also exercised an effective habit of claiming additional credits for volunteers, challenging the provost marshal's draft quotas, and otherwise questioning the equity of the demands placed on the city. In part, those challenges reflected sincere apprehension that a Republican administration in Washington might play foul with the largely Democratic metropolis, but that genuine fear seemed to coexist with a deliberate effort to delay or obstruct the selection of citizens for military service. One example of the latter tactic may have been the letter from a committee of the board of supervisors for New York County that came to Provost Marshal General James Fry's desk early in February. The signers included William Marcy Tweed — the "Boss" Tweed of later infamy — and they wanted to examine the documents Fry used to set New York's quota under the last call: the city's quota had been raised for the current draft, and Fry had provided documentation for that, but the committee wished to examine the previous figures to assure that the increase had been levied correctly. They also wanted to copy the enrollment figures for all the congressional districts in the loyal states, and the quotas of those districts for the previous draft and the current one, with the excesses or deficiencies of each. Fry could not see the point of reviewing records for quotas that had been abandoned, and he declined to do it on the grounds that digging up the information would force him to suspend his work on the draft. He passed the request on to Stanton, who agreed that the request seemed unreasonable and sent it to the president, who asked Fry to give the committee a few hours to copy the pertinent records. Fry repeated to Lincoln that it would only delay him from preparing the draft quotas for other districts that much longer, so Lincoln rescinded his request, but so many questions of that nature had arisen in New York and elsewhere that he appointed a board to look into the application of quotas and credits generally. Then he pressed Fry to start drafting for the December 19 call as soon after February 15 as he could.[48]

With the Confederate armies in disarray, and Federals victorious virtually everywhere they went, civilians across the North again had to dig into their pockets to keep from being forced into uniform. In his Canadian refuge, John Giffen thought it horrible that a neighbor back in Ohio had to pay $800 for a substitute, but prices had risen so high for the autumn draft that more established local men had begun signing on as substitutes instead of hiring their own. Such citizens would only consent to serve as long as the fees remained exorbitant. In one community in upstate New York the going rate ran to $1,000. Out on the prairie, where money was less plentiful, $300 or $400 might do the trick, but farmers whose homesteads would fall apart without them had to scrape up the money somehow. For this draft, central Kansas saw variations on the draft-insurance societies that had been so popular in the eastern states, before the advent of massive bounties made them too expensive.[49]

A nation that had so recently demonstrated its approval of the president's war again showed an unseemly disinclination to pay the personal cost of his policy. The last draft of the war demonstrated, even more clearly than the late-summer levy of 1864, how thoroughly the will to fight had atrophied across the political spectrum. Typical, perhaps, of the late-war Lincoln supporter was the foreman of a quartermaster's work gang in Arkansas, who told his family back in Vermont that he would not feel content staying home while the war lasted, but he had no intention of going into the army, either. In his letters he alternately damned rebels, praised Lincoln, and boasted his determination never to be drafted. "I will get out of it if I can," he told his parents, "and if not, I will get a substitute if it costs me one thousand dollars." As many as twenty eligible men resided in Sturgeon Bay, Wisconsin, but when the provost marshal assigned the town a quota of at least two men he goaded those twenty into an immediate, energetic campaign for volunteers. From everywhere came reports of collective horror at the threat of taking more men from communities that had already been drained of eligible males or money. "Pike has a great aversion to the draft," a Missourian said of his county, "and shell out the 'Greens' freely to prevent it coming on the people," but a woman in a poor Michigan district feared there would not be enough able men left to do the heavy farm work for all the women who remained. An Ohio man described his neighbors as "a buging there eyes" at a quota of seventeen soldiers from their town. A Wisconsin soldier who learned of the methods his neighbors would use to avoid service paid sardonic tribute to the "brave & true Patriots" at home, and a Massachusetts soldier proposed that the lyrics of "We Are Coming, Father Abraham, Three Hundred Thousand More" might be less apt than "who is the man that will go for me, $300 more."[50]

For over three years Alexander Christie had been reading his older brothers' letters about Vicksburg and the Atlanta campaign, most of which had conveyed more of glorious adventure than misery and mayhem, and by late January the Minnesota lad presented himself at Fort Snelling as a recruit. Except among such impressionable and often headstrong adolescents, misfortune and money provided the principal influences for making soldiers out of civilians, and those ingredients could motivate the youngest boys, too. Thomas Hogan, of Goshen, Vermont, had lost his mother before the war; his father enlisted in 1861, boarding the boy with relatives and sending money regularly for his keep. Then the father was captured in the early assaults on Petersburg, which stopped the regular flow of support, and at the end of January the son himself enlisted.[51]

The captain of a New York artillery battery upbraided his brother for his dread of the coming draft. The captain bore no grudge against those who raised fortunes to lure volunteers, or paid their own substitutes, so long as it brought capable soldiers into the service, but he strenuously objected to all the towns that appropriated money to meet their quotas. Raising bounty money from town coffers forced everyone who owned property to pay, he complained, including those men who had enlisted early in the war for comparatively small bounties, most of which they would not receive until they mustered out, or died. After serving through the worst of the war, those men would find their bounty money shrunken all the more by inflation, while their homes would be saddled with enormous debt for the exorbitant bounties paid to the latecomers. Others had been raising the same objections since the militia draft of 1862, which had inspired the first lavish bounties. The injustice they predicted frequently came to pass, but in most communities their logic failed to persuade a manifest majority of voters who shrank from the thought of mandatory service, or who wished to partake of such last-minute largesse.[52]

Those who had already been declared exempt from conscription looked on in smug contentment, except perhaps for those who would have to pay part of the tax burden. A young German citizen living in central Illinois enjoyed satisfactory wartime wages as a wagon maker, and while the $1,000 bounties offered to volunteers in that vicinity impressed him as extravagant, he sagely weighed the value of money to a dead man. He had no desire to sacrifice his life for abolition, he admitted, and if he had been required to serve he would instead have gone home to Germany. He suggested that he might return anyway when he lamented that the promise of America had been squandered on the war and the inflation it had created.[53]

Another German who had volunteered in the cause of Union, Brigadier General August Willich, tried to convince Senator John Sherman to submit a bill reorganizing the conscription law to avoid both the frightful expense and the multitude of undesirable recruits. He suggested dividing the entire population into classes by age, in increments of five years between twenty and forty-five (Willich himself was pushing fifty-five), eliminate the substitution clause, and gradually draft until each class had contributed proportionately, with a maximum bounty of $100. That should discourage mercenaries, he reasoned, which would avert the danger of a military coup posed by greedy soldiers who lacked ideological motivation. Willich's Prussian idea failed to win many converts, and his letter disappeared into the files of Senator Ben Wade.[54]

As always, local bounties reached their peaks as the oft-postponed draft dates ran down through the last possible delays, and this time the response to such munificence may have been enhanced by the increasing evidence of deterioration in the Confederate armies, just as the September victories had combined with the massive summer bounties to lure a new crop of recruits. About the middle of February came another flood of new soldiers, similar to that of September and October. The draft rendezvous all began to swell with recruits. In February alone, Illinois sent ten big new regiments to Nashville. Indiana mustered three new regiments that month, eight more in March, and another three in April. Ohio raised thirteen regiments in the same period, and New York fielded three. The last companies of the 1st Minnesota Heavy Artillery filled out in late February and started for Nashville, arriving in March.[55] The wife of a Pennsylvanian who enlisted in the second half of February told of so many neighbors who enlisted after his departure that he wondered if there would be anyone left to draft. Young Nettie Brown, from Wisconsin, shocked her relatives late in March with the news that her father had enlisted for $800. She doubted that he would have joined the army even for that much had he not feared that he would be drafted anyway; she had wanted him to hire a substitute, but he could not afford that, so he took the money himself. About the same time, a corporal who had survived three years in the 12th Michigan reenlisted in another regiment after barely two months at home, leaving his wife and children with a clear title to their farm. Then Nettie Brown heard from a friend whose brother had enlisted: the sister expected that he would "get good pay and not have to fight any either." Thomas Barnett had been enrolling eligible citizens for the draft in Fulton County, Indiana, since June of 1863, but eight weeks before the war came to an end he allowed two of his own sons to enlist for a generous bounty in the 151st Indiana, which was heavily laden with adventurous, well-paid lads when it mustered in on the third day of March.[56]

Most of those recruits would do little more than guard railroads and bridges against an enemy that had virtually disappeared, and many would not reach anything that might have been called hostile territory until after all organized hostilities had ceased. Those last recruits enjoyed a few weeks of travel through strange and sometimes fascinating scenery, all at government expense. They may have realized their good fortune in just missing the more apocalyptic struggles of the war, but without the opportunity to participate in stirring historical events they soon succumbed to monotony. John Augustine Johnson, a seventeen-year-old apprentice gunsmith from Providence, Rhode Island, heard of a generous bounty offer over the state line in Massachusetts and lied about his age to take advantage of it. He enlisted March 8, and three weeks later he started on his first sea voyage for the Gulf of Mexico and the siege of Mobile, Alabama. The ship docked at Key West on April 6, and from the deck young Johnson glimpsed a dream world of palm trees and coconuts. Two days later they stopped at lonely Dry Tortugas, to disembark prisoners bound for Fort Jefferson, before steaming across the Gulf and up the Mississippi River, where he watched his fellow recruits fire a few shots at an alligator that swam past. Not until April 11 did they reach New Orleans, just in time to learn that Mobile was already taken. Three long, indolent months later Private Johnson boarded the *H. S. Hagar* for Boston, where he arrived a few days before his eighteenth birthday and went ashore to resume civilian life.[57]

For those already serving with the armies, it was not over yet, and for some of Sherman's men the most grueling campaign was yet to come. That general next meant to sweep through South Carolina, which Grant had added to his gigantic Military Division of the Mississippi, and he communed with the department commander there, John Foster, to follow his progress with a parallel movement up the coast. Barely had the new year begun before Sherman ordered O. O. Howard to start ferrying Frank Blair's Seventeenth Corps from Savannah to Beaufort, on Port Royal Island, South Carolina, and on the morning of January 14 Blair crossed from the island to the mainland on a rickety, six-hundred-foot pontoon bridge, marching for Pocotaligo on the Charleston & Savannah Railroad. Lafayette McLaws, once a division commander under Longstreet, commanded the few thousand Carolina and Georgia troops who held

Pocotaligo, but after putting up a bold bluff from a position protected by swamps, he withdrew in the darkness, leaving the Yankees the supply base Sherman coveted for the start of his campaign.[58]

Henry Slocum, with the left wing of Sherman's army and most of the Fifteenth Corps of Howard's right wing, was supposed to cross the Savannah River by pontoon bridge and settle in alongside Howard before they started off together. Some five thousand men of Nathaniel Jackson's division tramped across on the bitterly cold day of January 17, deeply regretting having to leave Savannah behind as vicious winds drove through their clothing. That division had not finished crossing when a terrific storm kicked up and started to wash away the causeway they used to traverse the rice fields on the Carolina side. The rain raised the river so far out of its banks that the rest of Slocum's troops were trapped at a ferry landing above Savannah.[59]

Their discomfort may have put them in a bad humor, for as they set foot on South Carolina soil for the first time they seemed unanimous in deciding that the cradle of secession would suffer intensely for fomenting rebellion. Union sympathizers in Savannah had evidently voiced the hope that their fire-eating neighbors over the river would be punished for bringing on the conflict, and those who now regretted embracing the Confederate cause reportedly muttered similar sentiments. "There seems to be a prevailing opinion in the Army that the State of South Carolina should be destroyed," an Iowa captain revealed to a friend, and a New Jersey soldier pitied the people of that state as the day of retribution dawned. During the first night's soaking march inland, General Alpheus Williams hoped at least that he would be able to find dry lodging at the mansion of planter Langdon Cheves, but when he arrived there with his staff he found the home already a "smouldering ruins," and his entourage instead packed into a leaky slave cabin. All of South Carolina seemed inundated. The next morning Williams rode out to survey the road his troops were to take and found only water, stretching like a sea before him. The occasional spine of a dike broke the surface, like "the backs of sea monsters" in the biblical flood. His soldiers felled massive cypress and magnolias for timber to corduroy the narrow, slippery tops of those dikes for their wagons to use, and when General Slocum wanted to consult with Williams from the Georgia side he could only find the forward encampment in a rowboat. Not until early February, amid another severe cold snap, was Slocum able to bridge the river and undertake his role in Sherman's program.[60]

It required only a hint of the movement north to stimulate thoughts of home, for that was the direction the army was now headed, and Sherman's vagabonds began to talk of returning to "America," or "God's Country." They had become accustomed to moving where they pleased with little interference from Confederate forces, and they supposed that the only enemy before them consisted of a few thousand cavalry under Joe Wheeler and ten or twelve thousand second- and third-rate infantry, including garrison troops, Reserves, and militia, that Hardee had collected from along the coast.[61]

The ominous transfer of so many troops into South Carolina disabused Confederate authorities of any belief that the winter would give them respite from their woes, and they finally concluded to concentrate their forces against Sherman, rather than continue trying to distract him from his purpose. Unfortunately for them, there remained but few forces to concentrate. John Bell Hood had finally relinquished command of the army he had destroyed through obstinate, uninspired aggression, and General Beauregard shuttled what was left of that army from northern Mississippi to eastern Georgia. President Davis appointed Richard Taylor to nominal command of the Army of Tennessee, but Taylor was also commander of the Department of Alabama, Mississippi, and East Louisiana. He stayed there, with his headquarters at Montgomery, keeping only one broken-down division from Alexander Stewart's corps and three tiny brigades from Stephen Lee's; the rest he forwarded to Beauregard to confront Sherman. Depleted by desertion in addition to the losses in Tennessee, Cheatham and Stewart could put barely three thousand men apiece into the field — the dead Cleburne's fabled division had shrunk to a mere thousand — while Lee mustered about four thousand. Along with a fresh Alabama brigade that steamed up the Alabama River from the garrison at Mobile, those remnants gathered at Montgomery and made their way to Augusta through Columbus, Macon, and Milledgeville, climbing off the cars to march over the voids Sherman had left in Georgia's rail network. When the blue behemoth began to lumber northward again early in February, Beauregard began prodding the ghost of the Army of Tennessee on to Branchville, South Carolina, where the railroad to Charleston intersected with the line to Columbia and points north. Hardee, with something over ten thousand Confederate troops and about three thousand militia and Reserves, dug in behind the Salkehatchie River, across the Charleston & Savannah Railroad and right in front of Frank Blair's advanced corps at Pocotaligo.[62]

Sherman left Pocotaligo on the first of February, following the Coosawhatchie River upstream with John Logan's Fifteenth Corps while Blair and the Seventeenth Corps marched up the right bank of the Salkehatchie, flushing Wheeler's cavalry from one intersection or watercourse after another. The night of February 2 Sherman established his headquarters camp on Duck Creek, not far from where Slocum was still trying to cross his army from the Georgia side, and there the two generals conspired on Slocum's movements after the last of his wing had reached the South Carolina shore. That evening a staff major from General Foster caught up with Sherman after traversing the thirty barren miles that the army had covered in the first two days. The major took note that every building but one or two over that distance had been burned, from the barely smoking rubble near Pocotaligo to glowing embers farther on until, nearer the army's encampment, he saw houses with the flames licking out the broken windows. Over his route he reflected more than once that capture by any but regular Confederate troops might mean summary execution by Carolinians whose homeland the Yankees subjected to such indiscriminate destruction; by the time Sherman traversed the state, outraged Southerners were reportedly dispatching whole squads of captured foragers, including legitimate details commanded by commissioned officers. Sherman eventually threatened retaliation by the execution of Confederate prisoners, only to be told that such executions would be reciprocated in duplicate. Alpheus Williams, with more overt sensitivity to the rights of noncombatants, issued orders prohibiting enlisted men from leaving camp to forage indiscriminately, with daily company roll calls to detect any who wandered, but he admitted to his daughter that orders against rampant pillage were "not heeded at all."[63]

The Confederate general McLaws complained that Sherman's men emptied out even the homes of free Negroes, taking bedclothes for a night or two of comfort against the February cold and stealing the families' clothing in lieu of washing their own. Union soldiers and commissioned officers corroborated the accusation, which General Williams alluded to in his own orders. When the army lounged in camp after a rain, a Massachusetts lieutenant recorded the spectacle of all the stolen bed quilts drying over trees and bushes, "gay with all the colors of the rainbow."[64]

Blair's infantry forced a crossing of the Salkehatchie — more accurately a swamp than a river — in the face of entrenched defenders under McLaws. In a stiff skirmish at one bridge, the Yankees waded across up- and downstream in bone-chilling water as deep as the shoulder, with their cartridge boxes and rifles held over their heads. McLaws fell back on the railroad junction at Branchville, and Hardee warned Beauregard that he could not hold the railroad much longer. Sherman fanned his troops out so wide that no one could say for certain whether he aimed for Columbia, Augusta, or Charleston, but Beauregard guessed that Columbia was the target. Hardee turned back to Charleston to face Foster, who had begun landing troops on James Island. By February 7 Sherman's railroad crews were tearing up the tracks between Augusta and Branchville, cutting McLaws off from rail communication with the arriving corps of

Stewart, Cheatham, and Lee, which Beauregard started funneling toward Columbia; the first of those reinforcements had to foot it from Augusta, taking position behind the South Edisto River to provide token resistance against a foe that outnumbered them as much as four to one.[65]

Just above the forks of the Edisto River, behind substantial breastworks on the left bank of the south branch, lay the two brigades of Carter Stevenson's division, from the Army of Tennessee — all Georgians and Alabamians, except for one stray regiment of Virginians. When Frank Blair approached the river on the afternoon of February 9 with the eleven thousand men of his Seventeenth Corps, he estimated Stevenson's strength at about a thousand, and he easily outflanked the position by assembling a pontoon bridge a quarter of a mile downstream from the main road and pushing a division to the other side. From the riverbank those Yankees still had to wade a mile-wide swamp as deep as four feet, and after putting Stevenson's command to flight in the waning daylight they lay down to sleep through an "exceedingly cold" night on the bare ground, still dripping wet, without so much cover as their blankets.[66]

Hoping that the rest of the Army of Tennessee would reach them in time to offer more effective resistance, the Confederates retreated next behind the North Edisto, at and above Orangeburg. Georgia railroads, and perhaps Georgia railroad managers, were moving troops more slowly than ever before, and Cheatham's and Stewart's corps were only then arriving in Augusta. That allowed Blair and Logan to outflank Stevenson's division with relative ease again on February 12, near Orangeburg, by crossing another vast swamp; William Hazen's division of the Fifteenth Corps spent as long as seven hours immersed chest-deep, but when they emerged the Confederates took to their heels. With that, Beauregard sent every man who could be spared straight to Columbia, where he knew the next confrontation would come.[67]

Slocum's wing crossed farther upstream against little opposition, and with less travail, finding or building bridges or fording where the water ran only knee-deep. They suffered the same from the cold and the rain, though, and the accumulated misery may have aggravated the rank-and-file disposition to rob the inhabitants of everything they needed for mere survival, down to the last chicken and loaf. A first sergeant from Massachusetts who bore the name of a *Mayflower* passenger left no hint of shame as he described taking the last morsel of food from a relatively poor Lexington County family consisting only of a woman, her numerous children, and her mother. Besides their flock of chickens and a collection of honey-laden beehives, the women had only a barrel and a half of flour remaining, and some bacon, and the Bay State men took it all, besides smashing the beehives out of pure malice.[68]

By submitting completely to their fate, to the extreme of supplying the soldiers with string to tie the chickens' legs together for easier carrying, those women had at least saved the roof over their heads — assuming no other Yankees came later to burn their house down. Most others in the path of the invaders fared less fortunately: An Ohio soldier informed his parents proudly that "fire and smoke marked our way," and from the headquarters of the Twentieth Corps General Williams put it the same way, describing each corps revealing the line of its march with thousands of columns of smoke; when he caught a glimpse of the surrounding terrain from a hilltop, the awful grandeur of the sight momentarily distracted him from his pity for the helpless old men, women, and children who were thus left without bed, shelter, or crust of bread. An Indiana sergeant confirmed that Williams had not mistaken the meaning of those ubiquitous columns of smoke, boasting, "We burned nearly every house and barn . . . we came across," and after Sherman had passed out of South Carolina an Ohio soldier described the state as "utterly ruined." Abraham Lincoln had long maintained that Southern families of modest circumstances had been lured unwittingly into secession by slave-power aristocrats, but his soldiers seemed willing to punish every South Carolinian regardless of poverty, age, or gender, especially now that the Southern army had grown too weak to exact vengeance.[69]

The capital city of Columbia endured the brunt of that malicious spirit. In the arc that ran from Augusta through Columbia to Charleston, Beauregard estimated his command at twenty thousand "more or less demoralized" infantry and artillery, with most of them nearest Charleston: McLaws had turned for Charleston to aid Hardee, and Cheatham and Stewart were still on the way from Augusta. When Yankees approached Columbia during a storm of freezing rain, on February 16, the only force Beauregard could employ in the defense of the capital was Stephen Lee's corps, consisting primarily of Carter Stevenson's depleted division. Extensive swamps made the Congaree River impassible even to O. O. Howard's web-footed infantry downstream of the city, but the smaller Saluda River and the Broad River joined to form the Congaree above town, and these were more easily bridged. Once Logan's corps had crossed the Saluda, Beauregard tried to hold him at the Broad, but gave it up as hopeless during the night. On Friday morning, February 17, the head of Logan's corps tramped over a pontoon bridge three miles north of Columbia and met the mayor coming out in a carriage, with a white flag.[70]

Sherman and Howard rode across the pontoon bridge and through the streets. The ice storm had passed and the sky had turned clear, but Sherman later described "a perfect tempest of wind" blowing. It proved an ill wind, for that evening fires erupted here and there, spreading through the night until the conflagration threatened the entire city. After he had been accused of destroying Columbia through conscious order, passive connivance, or simple negligence, General Sherman blamed the conflagration on bales of cotton that retreating Confederates had dragged into the streets to burn, but Logan's division commander in the city claimed that the citizens had greeted the conquerors with buckets of liquor that had rendered their men unmanageable. Why the residents would have taken so foolish a course he did not attempt to explain, but at least part of George Stone's Iowa brigade did find alcohol somewhere while they stood guard over the city, and they grew so wild that they had to be relieved by other troops, who shot down dozens of the rioters, arrested hundreds, and tried in vain to quell the gale-driven inferno. By the morning of the eighteenth, about half of Columbia had been reduced to a charred ruin.[71]

Sherman alone, with the corroboration of one of his own staff officers, appears to have explained the fire by remembering the burning cotton. General Logan, who was in the city that night, made no mention of it. He passed on his division commander's report of citizens handing out whiskey by the cup and bucket, but he added — as though from personal observation — that liberated slaves also piloted soldiers into private homes where they could find liquor and wine. Logan admitted, too, that he saw drunken soldiers reeling around the streets with torches, as terrified civilians ran for their lives, but the exaggerated spirit of vindictiveness that Sherman's men had shown from the moment they crossed the Savannah River did not require inebriation, even if some of the troops did drink their fill. A staff officer in the Fourteenth Corps frankly conceded that Sherman's army "burned everything it came near in the State of South Carolina, not under orders, but in spite of orders," and there was no reason that the capital of the state would have enjoyed any greater mercy than the thousands of innocents who had been left homeless and starving over more than forty leagues of devastated country. The senior captain of the 4th Iowa, who commanded the regiment for much of the way through South Carolina and entered Columbia with Stone's miscreant brigade, had remarked early in the campaign on how many men in his command said that "South Carolina should be destroyed." Other Union soldiers who described the rampage, including one who may have been a participant, did not always represent the rioters as under the influence of anything but hatred. "As soon as we got possession of the town," one of Logan's corps confessed to his sister, "it was ransacked and burned to the ground," but he mentioned no drinking. Hearing the story from eyewitnesses, though, a Massachusetts captain did learn of widespread drunkenness among both officers and men. He relayed a tale of Western troops who "behaved like brutes," setting fire to houses as the women and children ran from them without a moment to save anything. It was other Westerners, though — from Michigan, Ohio, Illinois, Indiana, and Missouri — who tried to save the city. Some of those on guard wheeled out Columbia's fire engines to douse the flames, only to have the hoses cut by other soldiers who refused to see the place saved.[72]

When Sherman broke the railroad between Augusta and Charleston, Beauregard ordered Hardee to evacuate Charleston — the scene of Beauregard's first glory in the war — so they could consolidate their forces. Hardee hesitated to comply, but the capture of Columbia put the enemy between Beauregard and Hardee, so Beauregard instructed him again to abandon the city, which he did on the same night that Columbia burned. Hardee and McLaws took their troops north by railroads Sherman had missed, or had not yet struck, with the goal of meeting Beauregard at Greensboro, North Carolina. With the cavalry and Lee's little corps, Beauregard retreated up the railroad to Charlotte ahead of Sherman. Yankees continued to rifle private homes for liquor and valuables before applying the torch, and they began hanging captured rebel soldiers for daring to resist their advance. The expansive swath cut by the four Union corps kept Beauregard isolated from the pitiful remnants of Stewart's and Cheatham's corps: those thirty-two hundred men lingered forty miles west of Columbia, with Yankees lolling across their only practical corridor. Beauregard hoped they could slip behind Sherman after he had passed, making their way to Greensboro via the railroads in the eastern part of the state.[73]

On Saturday morning, February 18, Lieutenant Colonel Augustus G. Bennett, of the 21st U.S. Colored Troops, was the senior officer on Morris Island, just inside Charleston Harbor. When he heard rumors that the rebels were pulling out of their signature city he ordered a cutter toward Fort Sumter, but on the way it met a boatload of Confederate musicians who had been left behind. Bennett directed the commander of a special detail of "boat infantry" to row out to Fort Sumter and raise Old Glory over the battered ramparts. With a handful of men Bennett himself pulled for Mills's Wharf, in the city, landing there about 10:00 A.M. He scribbled a note for the mayor, demanding surrender, but by the sound of explosions and the reports of citizens he deduced that the last Confederates had not yet left town. Preferring not to risk the capture of his own party, he waited at the wharf until he saw a small craft scudding into the bay flying a white flag. Jumping into his own cutter with the oarsmen, Bennett overtook the sailboat and found that it bore the mayor's letter offering to turn his city over to either the commander of the Union fleet or the general commanding at Morris Island, and as the senior officer on that island Colonel Bennett accepted the surrender. His determination to be the man who received the capitulation provided a jarring twist to the event: not quite fifty months after the Charleston secession convention voted to preserve South Carolina's slave-based economy by taking the state out of the Union, the city fell into the hands of a man who commanded a regiment of freed South Carolina slaves.[74]

During the second half of January, while Sherman's corps commanders were struggling to cross the swollen Savannah River, John Schofield led his Twenty-Third Corps from deep in middle Tennessee to the Potomac River. The first regiments boarded transports at Clifton, Tennessee, on January 15 and steamed down the Tennessee River to the Ohio, and then upriver to Cincinnati, where they climbed into railroad cars for the journey east. Rather than leave Schofield's troops to guard against the unlikely resurgence of Hood's disheartened remnant, Grant wished to augment his forces on the North Carolina coast and work them inland, across what he supposed would be the path of Beauregard's retreat. Schofield and the last of his corps had reached Washington by the end of the month, just before Sherman began his South Carolina campaign in earnest, but so cold was the winter that the Potomac had frozen over, and another week passed before any seagoing transports could accommodate his troops from the Alexandria waterfront. Not until February 8 did the first of Schofield's Nashville veterans step onto the beach above Fort Fisher to join Alfred Terry's two corps. The infantry of Jacob Cox's division had landed by February 10, adding more than four thousand men to Terry's eight thousand, but Schofield accompanied that spearhead and took charge of everyone as the new commander of the Department of North Carolina. General Cox assumed nominal command of the Twenty-Third Corps from that moment, although none of the corps had arrived except his division.[75]

Braxton Bragg, who was absent from Wilmington at the time, later estimated his effective force below the city at about sixty-five hundred men, with two thousand of them positioned west of the Cape Fear River under Johnson Hagood and the rest in a fortified line at Sugar Loaf under Robert Hoke, blocking the troops on Federal Point. First, Schofield tried twice to sneak Cox past Sugar Loaf by a narrow sand spit that bordered Myrtle Sound, over which Cox was supposed to assemble a pontoon bridge. Heavy weather foiled the first attempt, and Cox thought they should have quit then. Schofield insisted on another try, but Hoke learned of it in time to mount an effective resistance. With several days wasted, Schofield gave up on that side of the river and crossed Cox to the right bank with his own and Adelbert Ames's divisions, plus another newly arrived brigade of the Twenty-Third Corps. Out with the fleet, a frustrated Admiral Porter grumbled to the assistant secretary of the navy that Wilmington would have been captured long before, had Grant only sent Terry more men and left Schofield in Washington.[76]

While Terry amused Hoke on the point, Cox started up the western side toward Fort Anderson, sitting astride the Wilmington road with big Orton Pond protecting its right flank. Navy gunboats were shelling the fort when Cox came within reach of it on February 18, but he and Schofield decided to make a flank march around Orton Pond rather than risk the casualties it would cost to bull through. Only when Cox arrived behind the fort, the next morning, did he find that the enemy had already evacuated it. Continuing on toward Wilmington, he ran up against Hagood again late in the day, behind a battery of artillery at the bridge over Town Creek. Yankees scouting the creek after dark found a little scow, and the next morning two of Cox's brigade commanders began slowly ferrying men across the creek, downstream from the artillery, while another brigade occupied Hagood's men at the bridge. By early afternoon the two brigades had crossed, and Cox decided to take a third one over himself. From the other bank they still had to slog through inundated rice fields, but late in the afternoon they came up on Hagood's left. Cox had sent one of the three brigades farther up the road to intercept the enemy's retreat, but it failed to come up in time. A few hundred South Carolina infantrymen stalled the advance of several times their number while Hagood withdrew the rest of his command toward Wilmington, less than ten miles away.[77]

By then General Terry was only about half as far from the city. Sensing the import of the bombardment across the river at Fort Anderson, Hoke had withdrawn from Sugar Loaf on the morning of February 19, and Terry followed him toward Wilmington with Charles Paine's black division and a single brigade of white troops. The next afternoon, while Cox was about to spring the trap on Hagood above Town Creek, Hoke took refuge in artillery-studded earthworks five miles outside Wilmington. There the two lines sat, plugging steadily away at each other until dark, and again all day on February 21. Cox glided down undefended roads, slowed only by burned bridges, and arrived on the bank of the Cape Fear River by noon that same day, chasing the last rebel pickets to an island in the river and then all the way to the other side. Smoke from massive stores of turpentine and other burning supplies billowed out of Wilmington during the evening, and at daybreak of Washington's Birthday, Cox sent a few Kentuckians across the river in a skiff to investigate. They found the city had been evacuated so hastily that the siege guns around the perimeter had not even been spiked. A few hours later the 3rd New Hampshire led Terry's column into the city from the other side, and by the time

Paine's nine regiments of U.S. Colored Troops tramped into the streets the city's erstwhile slaves had wound themselves into a delirium, shouting, "I'se broke my chain" as they greeted "the year of jubilo."[78]

Beauregard had advised Hardee to send his troops by rail to Florence, South Carolina, and then east through Wilmington before veering west again to Goldsboro, but Schofield's entrance into the town closed that avenue for him. Neither could Hardee turn west from Florence, reaching Goldsboro by way of Charlotte, for Sherman's horde sat astride that line. The only railroad still open to him was the route running straight north from Florence, but that one ended on the banks of the Pee Dee River at Cheraw, just below the North Carolina border. From there they would have to march between the converging Union armies. McLaws started with his division on February 24, the first day of a three-day downpour, with nearly as many men on top of the train as inside it; the crowd atop one car broke through the roof. Hardee collected every man and weapon at Cheraw that he could find, mobilizing even the sailors from the steamer *Pee Dee*, and for a week he occupied the town while civilian refugees crossed the river in flight from the Seventeenth Corps, on its way from the direction of Columbia and Camden at the forefront of Sherman's army. On the third day of March, Hardee finally put his little corps on the road to North Carolina, and Frank Blair's troops poured into Cheraw, throwing a pontoon bridge over the river in less than an hour. The next night, Sherman's vanguard slept just over the line in North Carolina.[79]

The eastward slide of Sherman's army finally opened the way for the three little corps of the Army of Tennessee to start for the railhead at Chester, South Carolina. From there the few slow and rickety cars of the Charlotte & South Carolina Railroad carried them on precarious tracks of mismatched gauges over the Catawba River into North Carolina. Schofield had moved twelve thousand men over a thousand miles in barely a fortnight, but the neglected Carolina rails required two weeks to transport barely half as many men less than one-quarter the distance, delivering them finally to a new point of concentration at Smithfield, midway between Raleigh and Goldsboro. As it happened, the next Union incursion would aim directly for Goldsboro.[80]

Now Sherman would be facing his old enemy of the previous spring. Robert E. Lee had assumed command over all Confederate armies early in February, although he also retained direct control of the Army of Northern Virginia, and Jefferson Davis used Lee's new authority to evade the unpleasant task of personally reinstating Joe Johnston to head the Confederacy's other main army. Not only did Davis and Johnston not get along personally (any better than Davis and Beauregard did), but restoring Johnston to command amounted to an acknowledgment that Davis had erred in replacing him with Hood the previous summer — and indeed it would be difficult to understand how Johnston could have performed worse than Hood, who had reduced the Army of Tennessee to a devitalized fragment in six months of fruitless aggression. After some prominent Southerners petitioned President Davis to reassign Johnston, he explained his lack of confidence in that general in a lengthy screed that he intended to present to Congress, but the next day General Lee urged Johnston for the position in a note to the new secretary of war, John Breckinridge. That did the trick: within seventy-two hours Johnston had orders to report to Lee for duty, and Lee promptly consigned to him the detritus of the army he had last commanded, along with all other Confederate troops below Virginia.[81]

Johnston proceeded immediately to Charlotte, where Beauregard gave him the tally: between Hardee and the Army of Tennessee they could count on a little more than seventeen thousand infantry and six thousand cavalry, curling before Sherman in a porous crescent more than a hundred miles long, from Newberry to Cheraw. Bragg led about six thousand more in retreat from Wilmington. Estimates of Sherman's strength ranged from forty thousand to forty-five thousand (in reality he had around fifty-seven thousand), and Johnston knew that their best hope was to bring all their own forces together and try to crush each of Sherman's two wings separately. Thus came his orders to converge on Smithfield, where Hardee could have the shortest march while Bragg and the Tennessee troops could move by train.[82]

Crossing into North Carolina, Sherman suggested that his wing commanders remind the troops that the population might respond to better restraint than had been shown to South Carolina, but he had no qualms about threatening through deliberate rumors to "deal harshly" with the town of Fayetteville if Hardee burned the bridge over the Cape Fear River as he retreated. Foragers, ranging ahead of the organized bodies to claim the best plunder, chased the last Confederates out of Fayetteville on March 11, and there all four weary Union corps lounged for the next three days. Couriers galloped for Wilmington to alert the garrison there, and Schofield's quartermaster started sending some vital supplies up the river on steamers — principally coffee, sugar, and some shoes. Better still, a navy gunboat came up and took back bags of mail from thousands of vagabonds who had not seen a chance to send a letter in five or six weeks.[83]

As one of Sherman's staff officers noted, all through the campaign so far none of the Confederate infantry had shown as much vigor as the Georgia militia had demonstrated at Griswoldville. Sherman expected that to change soon: predicting that Johnston had been able to bring Beauregard, Hardee, and Bragg together, and that he might feel strong enough to pounce on any isolated fragments, Sherman reverted to a defensive formation when he marched from Fayetteville. Instead of spreading the four corps out over a broad front, he put Slocum and Howard within a few miles of each other on different roads to Goldsboro. Howard took the right and Slocum the left, but each of them kept the preponderance of their infantry on the outside track, unencumbered by trains, while the wagons traveled on roads between those protective columns.[84]

Riding ahead on Slocum's route the evening of March 15, Judson Kilpatrick's cavalry ran into two brigades of entrenched Georgians and South Carolinians at the farm of John C. Smith, below Averasboro, on the road to Smithfield. The rebels were still there the next day. When the Union infantry came up, Alpheus Williams flung a brigade around to his left, and it came crashing down perpendicular to the Confederates' flank, sending them sprinting through a stand of open pine with all the haste Sherman's men had become accustomed to seeing. Behind them, screened by the trees, stood Lafayette McLaws with two more brigades of Georgians and South Carolinians and quite a bit of artillery, all ensconced behind breastworks built on the edge of a pine forest. That line gave the fugitives a place to rally, and the combined forces fought Williams to a standstill as a heavy rain began to fall. Williams waited for reinforcements from the Fourteenth Corps, but the skies were growing dark when those troops pulled into sight. In the morning, all the rebels were gone.[85]

The delaying action at Averasboro convinced the Yankees, up to and including Sherman, that Johnston had found it impossible to mount an offensive even after concentrating all his scattered troops. Feeling quite secure, Sherman allowed Howard to take a better road that swung a little wider of Slocum's route in their roughly parallel march to Goldsboro. Johnston detected that divergence, and saw it as the chance he had been waiting for. It was, he also knew, probably the only chance he would have to beat Sherman in detail, because Schofield was on his way from New Bern with several divisions and had reached Kinston, only fifty miles from his position at Smithfield. General Terry was also coming up the Wilmington & Weldon line with another column.[86]

All of the Tennessee troops had reached Smithfield except Ben Cheatham's original division, but they still numbered barely five thousand, including officers. With his two divisions from the Averasboro fight Hardee had more than six thousand of all ranks, and in front of Schofield, Bragg could call on nearly five thousand men from Robert Hoke's division, besides a little brigade of boys in the North Carolina Junior Reserves. The field returns for Wade Hampton's cavalry also showed five thousand men under Joe Wheeler and Matthew Calbraith Butler. Johnston called almost all of those troops, including most of those facing

Schofield, to congregate near the village of Bentonville, fifteen miles below Smithfield, to lie in ambush for Slocum's wing. His effective infantry
amounted to fewer than fifteen thousand bayonets — or muskets, since
many of them no longer carried bayonets — while Slocum's two corps
could have brought twenty-five thousand into line.[87]

As Slocum put his troops on the road the morning of March 19 he understood the cavalry hovering in front of him to be nothing more than the
routine harassment he had experienced since early February. He suspected nothing even after that cavalry retired behind entrenchments near
Bentonville, and he started stringing a few brigades of the Fourteenth
Corps out in line to brush away the annoyance. Johnston put the corps-
sized Army of Tennessee on his right, and when he rode before those few
thousand troops of his old command they cheered him lustily. Hardee's
men arrived through the morning, falling in on the left, but one of his
divisions started around behind the Tennessee troops toward the extreme
right, to overlap Slocum's left. That division's path lay through thick
blackjack on one narrow, bad road, and the afternoon was half over before
Johnston was content with his preparations. Then the advance began
against outnumbered and surprised Yankees who started to fall back
slowly, and then steadily, and finally in urgent haste. On Slocum's right,
his men made use of the Confederate entrenchments that had first
blocked the road, lying on the wrong side of them, but that gave them
enough protection to hold their ground. That strong point served as a
hinge on which the rest of Slocum's line swung back like a gate, for as
much as a mile. Reinforcements came up from the Twentieth Corps late
in the afternoon just in time to see the Westerners of William Carlin's
division sprinting unashamedly for the rear, throwing away their rifles
and knapsacks as they ran. Those fresh troops bolstered and extended
Slocum's line, bringing the attack to a halt as the day wore out, and the
Confederates dropped back to their entrenchments. During the night
Slocum brought up every man he had, dismounting foragers to go back
into the ranks and sending his trains toward Howard so he could deploy
the wagon guards.[88]

Satisfied now that the weight of numbers had turned too heavily
against him, Johnston waited all day March 20, hoping for an assault he
could punish, but none came, and on March 21 Howard reached the
field with the rest of Sherman's army. That afternoon one of Howard's
divisions struck close enough to threaten Johnston's escape route through
Bentonville: Hardee made a furious counterattack to repel it, losing his
own sixteen-year-old son in the front rank. Word came that Schofield
had reached Goldsboro, within a day's march of either the battlefield
or Smithfield, and once the last of the wounded had been carried off

Johnston turned back to the Smithfield depot. After their showing on the nineteenth Johnston reported his men in far better spirits than they had enjoyed in months, but his best opportunity for beating Sherman at all had vanished. The only remaining hope was to escape the closing cordon of Union corps and join forces with the Army of Northern Virginia. If Lee could break away from Grant, with incredible luck they still might deal with Sherman together and then turn back to face Grant.[89]

8

Forests of Bayonets

✎ ONCE THE PEACE conference at Hampton Roads dissolved, General Grant wasted no time resuming hostilities. Within hours after Confederate lines swallowed the three Richmond emissaries, and before President Lincoln had slept again in his White House bedroom, Union artillery along the Petersburg front served high-decibel notice of the parley's unsatisfactory conclusion. In addition to that symbolic barrage, Grant instructed Meade to strike a more productive blow at Lee's serpentine supply line on the following morning.[1]

The initial rupture in the Weldon Railroad the previous summer had forced rebel quartermasters and commissaries to extemporize a looping, thirty-mile wagon road through Dinwiddie Court House and up the Boydton Plank Road to deliver military supplies, forage, and food to Petersburg from Stony Creek Station. After Warren's December raid, those wagons had to reach another eighteen miles each way to bring provisions from the Meherrin River, but that roundabout caravan was still rolling in February, supplementing the supplies brought in on the Southside Railroad. Grant wanted to interrupt the wagon traffic by sending David Gregg's division of cavalry as far south as Belfield, a dozen miles from North Carolina, to seize or burn all he could, while a couple of infantry corps followed along as escort. Meade instead suggested intercepting the train around Dinwiddie, which would save the infantry a lot of marching and keep it close to Petersburg in case Lee took that opportunity to turn aggressive. Grant assented, and well before dawn on February 5 three brigades of cavalry trotted off on the Halifax Road through Reams's Station, turning later to Dinwiddie Court House. Warren's Fifth Corps followed after daylight. Andrew Humphreys had taken over for Hancock, whose

Gettysburg wound had reopened, and he led two divisions of the Second Corps down the Vaughan Road as far as Hatcher's Run, where he hung about five miles behind Warren and nearly three miles beyond their last stretch of occupied works.[2]

Confederate entrenchments had been extended that far after Grant's last, ill-fated offensive in that vicinity late in October, and when Humphreys forced his way across Hatcher's Run Lee started funneling heavy reinforcements down to strengthen those works. They came on the run, and late in the afternoon Henry Heth's division burst out of the defenses to investigate. The eerie, oscillating keen of the rebel yell vibrated over the leafless treetops, and Heth's brigades dashed at Humphreys through a gap in the Union line, as though to separate his command from the troops behind him and force him to fight in the open. Humphreys had but two brigades to fill that gap: the weight of the attack fell primarily on one of those brigades, belonging to Robert McAllister, but with only five regiments in line behind fresh breastworks McAllister managed to stop it. The rebels rallied, raised their yell once more, and started back, but McAllister repelled them again, and then a third time. Recognizing that the Yankees had begun entrenchments of their own, Lee brought Heth's troops back to their own lines. In the meantime, Union cavalry had found pitifully few wagons on the Boydton Plank Road at Dinwiddie Court House, taking some mail and a few dozen prisoners as well.[3]

In planning the operation with Grant, Meade had worried that the Northern public would perceive any major movement as just another failure if it did not achieve spectacular results. The particularly unspectacular trophies from Dinwiddie portended precisely that captious reaction, so Grant wired Meade to gather everyone for an attack on Lee's extreme right, in another attempt at the Southside Railroad. Meade countermarched both Warren and the cavalry back up the Vaughan Road to Hatcher's Run, and he stripped some reserve troops from the Sixth and Ninth Corps to fill in between Humphreys and the last of his main fieldworks, some three miles back at the Peebles farm, where the Ninth Corps had taken a thrashing on the last day of September.[4]

Diving temperatures robbed many a soldier of any sleep that night, and frostbite nipped at the toes and ears of some. February 6 dawned with the roads frozen solid. After noon Warren ventured ahead from the Vaughan Road toward the Boydton Plank Road with two divisions of his corps, looking for unprotected bodies of Confederate troops lying beyond Lee's fortifications, and he had not covered much ground before he found some. His leading brigade — consisting of the remainder of the old Iron Brigade, reinforced by three Pennsylvania regiments — rolled over a line of rebel picket pits and straight into three divisions of the enemy. Gregg's cavalry ran into trouble on Warren's left about the same time, and as the senior officer Warren shifted troops from his own and the Sixth Corps until he thought it safe to push ahead. His line disappeared into the woods below Hatcher's Run late in the afternoon, and brisk firing developed soon afterward as first one and then another of the Confederate divisions lunged at the Fifth Corps and at the cavalry, which gave way into the ranks of Samuel Crawford's division. Wounded started trailing back from the woods, singly or with assistance, and dusk was just settling over the scene when a mob of blue-clad men came pelting out of the forest "as fast as their legs would let them." Both of Warren's divisions had broken into shameless flight, streaming back to — and beyond — their temporary breastworks by the Vaughan Road. "I never see the 5th Corps do so badly before," confessed a lieutenant in Crawford's division, which seemed the fleetest-footed on the retreat. Some veteran regiments had been weakened once again by heavy infusions of recruits, many of whom had come into the army more or less reluctantly, under the tightening draft and rising bounties of the fall and winter: even the reconstituted Iron Brigade ran for dear life. By personal example Warren slowed the flood, rallying fugitives under fire and adroitly deploying enough reinforcements to finally stop the advancing Confederates.[5]

Bright moonlight brought another brutally cold night to Dinwiddie County, forcing men in swampy or open bivouacs without firewood to forgo sleep in favor of walking around to stave off freezing. Wet snow started falling late that night, turning to sleet and rain by daylight and freezing as it hit the ground. Those who did roll themselves into their blankets awoke encased in a thick film of ice. The rain quickly soaked into their clothing, and the first few steps in the slush served to wet their feet. Perhaps partly to keep them active, the generals set them to corduroying roads and building the rudiments of main-line earthworks. Warren sent Crawford's division back out to retrieve its reputation, and Crawford recovered the ground he had lost the day before, shoving right up against the rebel works in the chilling deluge, but after dark his shivering infantry crept back and built little fires to warm their hands over, between stints at the log-and-earth fortifications. In the end, three miles of those muddy new revetments represented the only advantage all their suffering had purchased. General Meade saw the adverse public reaction that he had anticipated, but seven weeks hence the control over that additional acreage would abet a more decisive movement.[6]

The failure of the peace commissioners appeared to have diverse effects on the Confederate soldier. For many, apparently, it rejuvenated the determination to resist an intractable foe, which may be what inspired the Confederates who scattered the big, recruit-laden Fifth Corps. The rebels defending Lee's right wing endured the same freezing weather and drenching precipitation as Meade's men during those three days, and in that entire time they had nothing to eat but hardtack. They had been suffering reduced rations for weeks, and from insufficient clothing all winter long, so they had done well to endure three days of numbing temperatures without shelter or meat, and they had stood their ground into the bargain. As Lee confided to his secretary of war, though, they could not even be rewarded with one good meal for what limited success they had managed, for the commissary department still could not find the first pound of beef or pork to feed them. Lee warned that even if the men's courage survived such neglect, their health could not sustain the physical rigors of the trenches without adequate nourishment. The secretary of war passed that letter on to Jefferson Davis, who endorsed it as scandalous evidence of negligence or incompetence. That sharp rebuke went to the commissary general, who brushed it off with a flurry of excuses.[7]

The courage of many could survive no longer, either. A few deserters always trickled into Union lines, and winter increased that traffic, especially as the war's fourth winter began. The shattering blow that Hood suffered seemed to balance the passage of deserters from one army to the other: absconding Union bounty jumpers had always vastly outnumbered rebel deserters, but in late December a Vermont captain in the Sixth Corps concluded that more of the enemy were coming in than they were losing in the other direction. As though to corroborate his observation, two days into the new year he reported that two "Johnnies" had entered their picket line the previous night, while a recruit in the 5th New Hampshire had bolted toward the Confederate works. A week later a New Yorker told of seven more from the 5th New Hampshire who made a run for the rebel lines on the same night that fifteen Confederates came the other way. By the middle of the month Meade's and Ord's pickets reported rebel deserters turning themselves in daily — or rather nightly — and sometimes several of them at once.[8]

The intense cold and abominable weather of early February opened the floodgates, and the failure of the Confederate meat ration had apparently added the last straw. A heavy-artillery captain on Bermuda Hundred counted seventeen Confederates who came through his own brigade line during the course of February 17, and a Sixth Corps soldier learned of thirty-two giving up two nights later. On February 20 a Pennsylvanian wrote that they were receiving deserters faster than ever before in the war, and a few days later a surgeon repeated a tale of an entire company of fifty-five Confederates surrendering together, complete with their officers.[9] That last story bore the scent of a rumor spawned as a jest, and a Maine officer surely overestimated when he claimed his brigade had been collecting a hundred deserters a night for two weeks running, but from the new works on Meade's left the Second Corps reported twenty-eight deserters over a twenty-four-hour period ending the afternoon of Washington's Birthday. On the last morning of February, a squad of seven rebels approached the Second Corps pickets during the night, along with a lieutenant, and just after noon that day four more privates and another officer joined them. General Meade counted seventy-five deserters along the length of his lines on March 4, including forty who brought their weapons with them for the advertised cash bounty of ten dollars. Lee's own adjutant calculated that their entire army was losing a hundred a night through March.[10]

Desertion had deprived the Army of Tennessee of at least as many men as Hood had lost to the Yankees in middle Tennessee, for all the carnage at Franklin and the wholesale roundup of prisoners at and after Nashville. Thousands of rebel soldiers had drifted away on the retreat through Tennessee, or during the furlough given to many of Hood's frazzled troops afterward, but Beauregard had still expected the three corps to total nearly eleven thousand men, counting artillery, when he ordered them east in early February. Stories of widespread desertion followed their migration across Georgia and the Carolinas, and when Beauregard turned those troops over to Johnston in March, there were fewer than seven thousand of them.[11]

So desperately did Confederate armies need men to carry rifles that General Lee proposed arming slaves, and rewarding them with freedom for themselves and their families in return for service; many of those slaves would only find their way to Union lines, he contended, where Northern substitute brokers would lure them into the Union army anyway. Between the degree of urgency and Lee's personal prestige, the concept of slave-soldiers came before the Congress in Richmond as a formal bill. For the sake of self-preservation, the would-be nation considered forsaking the very social and anthropological ideology on which it had been founded.[12]

As Confederate forces shrank, Union armies burgeoned: an Ohio soldier who had begun his service in the Shenandoah Valley only a few months before gaped in amazement at the size of Grant's army when his regiment moved to the trenches below Richmond. For all the hardships of the siege, that recruit also deemed it easier soldiering on the James River front than he had known in the valley, and the stories told by one of Sheridan's cavalrymen suggested that the difference lay with the army commanders, rather than in any variation of climate. Pliny Jewett, of the 1st Connecticut Cavalry, reported the same vicious cold, sleet, and freezing rain in the valley that Grant's armies endured at Petersburg, but

Sheridan seemed to keep them out in it more often. One raid toward Staunton took Jewett's regiment through such cold that he claimed, with a certain hyperbole, that two hundred men suffered some degree of frostbite, and when it came to a fight some of his comrades could not operate their carbines because the grease had frozen. He remarked with evident envy that at least their prisoners were able to keep warm by walking, but in their ill-supplied camps those rebels had enjoyed no such advantage. Like their comrades below Richmond and Petersburg, they lacked effective winter wardrobes: Jewett described the prisoners they took just before Christmas wearing "old pieces of carpet & other odds & ends picked up through the country."[13]

With February petering out, Sheridan mounted two divisions of his cavalry and headed up the valley one last time, planning to wreak further destruction on the Virginia Central and the James River Canal, seize Lynchburg with all its railroad shops and hospitals, and then ride on south into North Carolina, to join Sherman. Winfield Hancock, who had been recruiting a new First Army Corps in Washington, left that city very suddenly on the afternoon of February 26 for Winchester, where he assumed command of the Middle Military Division the next day in an order he did not wish made public. Sheridan struck off that same morning with ten thousand horsemen and a light train, consisting of only ordnance wagons, a few ambulances, and enough transportation for a fifteen-day supply of coffee, sugar, and salt. Each man carried rations in his haversack for five days, with thirty pounds of forage for his horse strapped to the saddle. That was supposed to last until they passed beyond the barren waste they had created in the Shenandoah; after that, Sheridan expected them to live off inhabitants whom they had not yet plundered.[14]

The first day they made thirty miles over roads already muddy from the spring thaw, recent rains, and a melting blanket of snow. In the afternoon they crossed Cedar Creek and Tom's Brook, the names of both streams evoking earlier victories over Jubal Early's Confederates, and that evening they camped at Woodstock, where Sheridan's cavalry had chased Tom Rosser's troopers through town twenty weeks before. Early's Valley Army, or what was left of it, lay sixty miles farther up the valley at Staunton, where a crowd of citizens had come to the Augusta County courthouse to hear stirring appeals for continued resistance from a Confederate naval commander and J. E. B. Stuart's brother. Most of the troops Early had originally brought into the valley, and those that had subsequently been sent to him, had gone back to the Army of Northern Virginia to fill the gaps in the siege trenches. His principal force consisted of Gabriel Wharton's weakened division of infantry, with no more than three thousand present for duty and perhaps as few as two thousand, while shortfalls in forage and numerous outposts left him with only a few dozen available cavalry. Some of those videttes came galloping up the valley on February 28 to let Early know that the Yankees were coming back, and his army hastily packed up to get out of town, but no one took their leave until noon on the incessantly rainy first of March. Early remained with his staff until late that afternoon, following the road east toward Waynesboro, at the foot of Rockfish Gap over the Blue Ridge. He made it known, as though by way of a medieval challenge, that he would fight Sheridan at Waynesboro.[15]

Sheridan rode into Staunton on March 2. Hearing instantly of Early's whereabouts, he hesitated to continue farther south with an enemy roosting in the mountains behind him. He turned George Custer's division east after Early, through mud that coated every horse and rider, and followed Custer up with his second division, but one turned out to be enough. With nearly five thousand men in three brigades, Custer found Early in front of Waynesboro with Wharton's infantry peering over a long line of breastworks. Behind him ran the swollen and turbulent South Fork of the Shenandoah River, spanned only by a footbridge and by the railroad bridge, sheathed over with boards. Alternating rain and sleet was falling when Custer's men fanned out a mile before town, and Early evidently hoped for a reckless frontal assault, but instead Custer dismounted one brigade and posted it between the riverbank and Early's dangling left flank — for he had not men enough to stretch his line to the water's edge. Under cover of fog and woods, those dismounted Union troopers edged within sprinting distance, with three regiments in the front rank carrying Spencer repeating carbines. In the middle of the afternoon Custer launched that brigade toward the rebels from his right, which served as the signal for his mounted brigades to charge in front. Almost before anyone could believe it was happening, Early's infantry began peeling away from the works on his left, unsettled by that flurry of carbine fire, and his other troops started to melt away as they saw their comrades abandoning the line. Yankee cavalry broke through and chased them down, bringing hundreds up short. With no Confederate cavalry or artillery on the other side of the river to cover the retreat it was every man for himself, and general officers whipped their own horses through the mob to take the forefront of the stampede. Only General Wharton stuck with his men, falling into enemy hands along with most of them, and those who did escape scampered up the mountainside or darted into houses to seek sanctuary in attics or cellars.[16]

The chilling downpour that soaked Early's vestigial army in its final defeat glided northeastward to drench Washington City, where crowds of visitors came to watch President Lincoln's second inauguration ceremony

— and perhaps to stay on afterward to petition the president or one of his ministers for some remunerative public office. General Halleck feared "mischief" might attend the inauguration, but beyond his fretful brow capital authorities seemed less apprehensive of trouble than they had four years before, when vigilant officers saw secessionist conspirators lurking behind every government building, plotting a coup.[17]

While rain soaked the White House grounds on March 3, the president held the last cabinet meeting of his first term, and the main order of business consisted of telling his department heads that he had decided to appoint Hugh McCulloch secretary of the treasury. Senator William Pitt Fessenden had taken over, quite reluctantly, after the resignation of Chase, but the Maine legislature had chosen to return him to the Senate, and with the Treasury Department somewhat stabilized Fessenden decided to accept the seat. McCulloch presented a problem for John Usher, the secretary of the interior, because both men were residents of Indiana, and it was not considered acceptable to give any one state duplicate representation in the cabinet. Usher had been worried about it since December, when McCulloch's name was first mentioned, and he had confided to Seward and Welles that he needed the money the position brought him. Considering the influence he exerted on behalf of certain powerful interests, he may have depended on the job bringing him more money than the salary, and indeed he would ultimately take a position with the Union Pacific Railroad, for which he had acted profitably as head of the Interior Department. The choice of McCulloch may have been Lincoln's way of allowing an unsavory subordinate an honorable escape, for when he introduced the new appointee's name he had already broached the subject with Usher, and he specifically mentioned that he did not want the resignation of any of his other department heads.[18]

Congress kept chattering away until the last moment of its constitutional limit, with barely a quorum holding together through the night of March 3. The Senate wrangled endlessly over amendments to the civil appropriations bill, finally passing it just before breakfast on Saturday, March 4, while a powerful gale blew through the city outside, uprooting trees and driving the rain with enough force to threaten windowpanes. The Senate reconvened at 10:00 A.M. after a three-hour adjournment, and Senator John Sherman reported disagreement with the House over the part of the bill that involved military arrests. The Senate concluded to send the bill back to the House with that disagreement noted, but without removing the problem appropriation, and then members entered a debate over the early admission of ladies for the swearing-in of the new vice president at noon. Ticket-holding guests filled the lobby, and a senator who had spent twenty minutes shouldering his way into the chamber complained of the crush, so the doors were opened. Women poured into the spectators' galleries overlooking the senators' desks, and the recorder noted that their "very audible conversation materially retarded the transaction of public business." While trying to discuss a bill prohibiting the enlistment of criminals, Senator Lyman Trumbull remarked that "it is impossible to hear anything." Late in the morning Vice President Hannibal Hamlin surrendered the chair and left the chamber, returning just before noon with Andrew Johnson, whom he escorted to a seat on the right hand of the presiding officer's chair. On the other side of the Capitol the House of Representatives considered the appropriations bill until the brink of noon, leaving that legislation undecided when Speaker Schuyler Colfax returned (perhaps from a nap), and gaveled the session to a close.[19]

Johnson, the uneducated, fiercely Unionist Democrat from east Tennessee, whom Republicans had included on their Union ticket as a gesture of bipartisan nationalism, made the unfortunate decision to offer an inaugural speech. Everyone who could hear him quickly deduced that he had fortified himself for the honor of his life with a bracer or two — or more. He launched into an embarrassingly didactic harangue on the sanctity of popular will and his pride in being a commoner. The assembled senators and the justices of the Supreme Court were "but creatures of the American people," he said. He reminded the various department heads of the same origins in their exalted positions, addressing them by name (and whispering to someone behind him for the name of the secretary of the navy). "Humble as I am," he continued, "plebeian as I may be deemed, permit me in the presence of this brilliant assemblage to enunciate the truth that courts and cabinets, the President and his advisers, derive their power and their greatness from the people." Hamlin prodded him from behind, and Johnson promised not to take much more time from "these intelligent and enlightened people," but added that he could not fail to remember those democratic fundamentals when he, "a plebeian," had come to discharge the duties of vice president of the United States. Rambling on, he confessed his ignorance of parliamentary procedure and appealed to the more experienced senators to guide him in the application of Senate rules. While cabinet officers muttered, Johnson yet again referred to himself as "a plebeian boy" before digressing into an awkward political rant involving the delicate (and henceforth capitalized) subject of Reconstruction: Tennessee, he asserted, had never left the Union. He conceded that "the operations of her government were for a time interrupted," but, he insisted, "she is still in the Union." That comment carried him from merely inappropriate deportment into an open political challenge of the Radical Republican agenda, and Hamlin interceded by thrusting the Bible toward him to administer the oath of office.

Johnson prolonged even the oath with superfluous interjections, and with the final phrase he took the book from Hamlin and kissed it ostentatiously.[20]

The boisterous discourse in the galleries at least drowned out much of Johnson's humiliating tirade, but in their choice seats the most prominent guests, including the president and some newspaper reporters, caught every word. After a few more unnecessary remarks, the new vice president took the chair while the clerk called the names of new senators and swore them in. Then the dignitaries proceeded to the east portico, where a platform had been raised similar to the one where Lincoln had stood on that same date in 1861. One of the president's secretaries guessed there were twice as many spectators as he had seen on the first inaugural, in spite of the rain and deep mud that discouraged women from stepping off the sidewalks. Every soldier who could beg leave from his post or his hospital had come to witness the event, and many of them milled about the steps at the bottom of the platform. The rain had receded to a drizzle, and then to a fine mist. Just as the presidential party ambled out onto the platform the clouds began to lighten, and the sun started burning through the thinning haze until that, too, faded away. It seemed so good an omen that people mumbled to each other about it, and jotted it down in their diaries. A similar rain ceased at precisely the same hour at General Grant's headquarters, at City Point.[21]

A band struck up "Hail to the Chief" as the president emerged from the Capitol. The sky had nearly cleared when the top-hatted congressmen, the cabinet ministers, and the Supreme Court justices in their voluminous robes all settled into their seats behind and beside the podium. Chief Justice Chase, who had always imagined himself standing some day on the other side of that Bible, rose to give the oath to the man who had twice squelched that hope for him. When he had completed his task, Chase rustled back into his chair, and the president took a folded paper from the pocket of his long coat.[22]

In his quadrennial as president, Abraham Lincoln had learned much, especially in the art of public address. His brief oration that day illustrated the skills he had honed, not least of all by its very brevity. In three paragraphs he summarized his view of the epic struggle that had transpired since his first, longer speech on those steps, describing the contest in mildly accusative tones as one between those who would accept war to preserve the Union and those who would "*make* war rather than let the nation survive." Without acknowledging the opponents who had foretold as much, he admitted that the conflict had escalated beyond anything he and most of its proponents had ever expected, but he justified the cost in terms more religious than rational. Plying the biblical rhetoric he found so politically persuasive, he devoted much of his third paragraph to a theory of divine intervention that he had been polishing for at least eleven months, with which he seemed to absolve all those who had "accepted" the war from any responsibility for the horrors that had followed. He theorized that God seemed to will the war should be so brutal, in order to punish North and South for allowing the evil of slavery to continue beyond "His appointed time." With the contorted logic of Old Testament doctrine, he proclaimed that if a supreme power prolonged the struggle "until every drop of blood drawn with the lash" had been "paid by another drawn with the sword," that would only illustrate how "true and righteous" were "the judgments of the Lord."23

The long sentence that formed the fourth and final paragraph revealed Lincoln at his polemic and personal zenith. While adjuring his fellow countrymen to firmness in seeing the contest through to victory, he bade them to seek that triumph "with malice toward none; with charity for all." In the time remaining to him he would demonstrate the sincerity of that sentiment, and pass it on to those generals who were likely to play the most prominent roles in the peacemaking. He had been the most stubborn and stern of opponents, but with the rebellion so clearly moribund he envisioned a generous and even gentle conquest, and with that implied promise he folded the paper on which he had written the little address and returned it to his pocket.24

Seated with the ladies of his party near the upper steps of the Capitol, Senator James Doolittle, of Wisconsin, caught only random words from the inaugural address, but he conveyed the sense of it with his general description of the president as "kind, approachable, and winning." Lincoln manifested great dignity, Doolittle explained — but not the "selfish, conceited, proud, imperial dignity" of Mr. Chase. Doolittle deemed Lincoln "a great man," adding that "his greatness as a ruler and a diplomatist has not dwarfed the kindness of his heart." While cannon roared in the distance to announce the conclusion of the ceremony, Doolittle watched Lincoln make his way to an open barouche with his son Tad for the ride back to the White House. The carriage spun through mud that had even veneered the paving stones on Pennsylvania Avenue, followed by streams of parade marshals, fire companies, and cavalry, all of which squeezed between teeming citizens waiting for a glimpse of the president. A soldier in the president's escort had recognized a multitude of officially forgiven rebel deserters rambling the streets of the capital in recent days, and he spied a few of them lifting their hats to the passing Lincolns and cheering "as loud as the bluecoats."25

That evening the greatest crowd any of Lincoln's staff had ever seen at the White House poured through the gates for the president's reception.

For nearly four hours Lincoln stood pumping one hand after another — averaging twenty-five hands to the minute, calculated the bored commissioner of public buildings, who tallied the line by hundreds, and timed each hundred: in the thickest of the throng the president afforded each guest less than two seconds, and never more than three. Mrs. Lincoln took great pleasure in the endless parade of admirers, declaring that she would rather stay all night than leave anyone outside, but the doors closed before midnight and many had to go away disappointed.[26]

Wet, violent weather coursed the entire southeastern quadrant of the continent that month, although on the fourth of March skies cleared nearly everywhere as though in honor of the inauguration. While the Lincoln family rested from the ceremony and prepared for the evening's reception, Brevet Major General James Wilson wrote from northwestern Alabama that the worst storm of the season had just ended, and that he would depart on a planned raid deep into that state as soon as the Tennessee River receded from its record flood level. Veritable monsoons reached all the way to the Gulf of Mexico for another fortnight, forcing the repeated postponement of Wilson's raid and several concurrent incursions into Mississippi and Alabama.[27]

General Grant wanted to send a division or two of cavalry raiding eastward into Mississippi from Vicksburg, and another from Memphis into North Mississippi, in conjunction with Wilson's descent into Alabama. All three cavalry columns were meant to take the heat off new operations against Mobile. The raid from Memphis did depart on schedule in the middle of a three-day torrent early in March, but no one else could move. Edward Canby, commander of the Military Division of West Mississippi, could see that no expedition was going to be able to traverse the saturated terrain between Vicksburg and Mobile, so he ordered all the Vicksburg-bound cavalry down to New Orleans. From there he ferried everyone by steamer to Mobile, but rain — and more rain — slowed the transportation, while gale-force winds and thick fog complicated the debarkation of troops at the forts guarding Mobile Bay. According to residents of the region, it was the worst weather in forty winters.[28]

Scanning maps of the Gulf States in his cozy headquarters cabin at City Point, General Grant seemed oblivious to the unprecedented storms down there, although he had certainly heard of them through other sources. He grew so irritated with the delays at Mobile that he dispatched his aide, Colonel Comstock — the engineer whom he had assigned as his personal envoy during the reduction of Fort Fisher. Comstock made Cairo by train in only three days, but the *Paulina Carroll* required a full week to negotiate the swollen Mississippi, only arriving in New Orleans on March

10. Comstock, unlike his chief, may have begun to appreciate General Canby's difficulties by the time he reported to him at Fort Gaines, on March 12. Instead of viewing Comstock as a headquarters snoop, Canby put him to work collecting information about local roads and enemy dispositions, in preparation for an advance that Canby planned to begin on March 17.[29]

The Alabama River and the Tombigbee meet just below the site of Fort Mims, where Creeks massacred scores of soldiers and settlers in 1813, and for more than thirty miles the two rivers intertwine in the pattern of a caduceus, swapping courses and names through a labyrinth of islands until they empty into Mobile Bay as six smaller rivers. Just there, on the western shore of the bay, sits the city of Mobile. During the course of the war three concentric tiers of fortifications had risen around the city, and surmounting them might have been a grim enterprise. Canby instead chose to ascend the bay on the eastern side, where two earthen bastions protected the back door to Mobile. Spanish Fort, below Bay Minette, bristled with more than two dozen siege guns and mortars, and Fort Blakely, above Bay Minette, included nine intimidating batteries in an arc two miles long. Either would have posed a serious obstacle if manned with determined garrisons. Canby's informants reckoned that Dick Taylor had as many as twenty thousand men for the defense of Mobile, and some credited wild estimates of forty thousand, with which he reputedly intended to defend the city "to the last." Canby's own force neared fifty thousand by the time the last troops had arrived from New Orleans, and he would enjoy the assistance of the U.S. Navy.[30]

The first of Gordon Granger's Thirteenth Corps, amounting to about nine thousand men by Canby's count, started from Mobile Point on March 17. Alerted by Canby, Admiral Henry Thatcher replied that morning from New Orleans that a fleet from his West Gulf Squadron stood ready to cooperate. Granger's route followed bad roads, there being no other kind in that vicinity, and those roads softened all the more when the skies opened up again, three days later. More than three hundred wagons and five batteries of artillery shambled along with Granger's column, none of which could move at more than a crawl, if at all, because the landscape east of the bay turned into a single sprawling swamp. On the morning of the twentieth a division of cavalry and five brigades of infantry started overland from Frederick Steele's command at Pensacola, Florida, while A. J. Smith's Sixteenth Corps crossed Mobile Bay by boat that same day to intersect with Granger at Fish Creek. Granger's roundabout march from the long point was supposed to frighten away any Confederates lying in ambush below Fish Creek, but if there were any there he never saw them, and his route left him twenty miles behind. In the latest crop of mud it took him three more days to cover that distance. His leading brigade stumbled into the rendezvous at Dannelly's Mills on Tuesday night, March 21, and the last of his column only reached that camp on Thursday.[31]

Steele, meanwhile, followed an indirect path up the Alabama & Florida Railroad, from which he was to turn back southwest along the tracks of the Mobile & Great Northern toward Fort Blakely. By March 23 his division lay stalled at Pine Barren Creek, about halfway to his first railroad intersection, where the bridge had been swept away and all the rivers had overflowed their banks. The Escambia River paralleled the first length of his route, and he used that as a source of supply from his depot at Pensacola, but he warned Canby that high water between him and Mobile Bay might foil their plans. Steele had more than a hundred miles yet to travel, and over most of it he would have no river access. Neither would he be able to live off the countryside, as poor and uncultivated as it was, and he reported having drawn the fire of rebel pickets. March had almost run out when Canby next heard from Steele, in the form of an urgent plea for provisions, and April had begun before the Pensacola column arrived within supporting distance.[32]

By then, James Wilson had burst out of extreme northwestern Alabama with twelve thousand cavalry to cut his way toward the heart of that state. Cannibalizing one division to equip the three he was taking with him, he armed all but a fraction of his command with seven-shot Spencer carbines, greatly simplifying the distribution of ammunition. Even the few hundred men who lacked Spencers carried breechloading weapons that fired brass cartridges, so each trooper surpassed any potential opponent in firepower and (more to the point, that sodden spring) entertained none of the Confederate soldier's fear that persistent rain would spoil his ammunition. Like Sherman in the Carolinas and Sheridan in the Shenandoah, Wilson pruned his train to a bare minimum, expecting to levy the countryside heavily for sustenance of man and beast. The northern tier of Alabama was already stripped clean, just as the valley of Virginia had been, so like Sheridan's troopers each man took enough light rations in his haversack for five days and tied twenty-four pounds of grain to his saddle for his horse, plus an extra set of horseshoes. Wilson prescribed that every man bring a hundred rounds of ammunition with him, and for Spencer carbines that would have meant two cylindrical cartridge boxes, each holding seven tubular magazines. Pack mules transported a supply of hardtack to carry the command through the blighted northern counties. Everything else — consisting primarily of the two essentials, a six-week supply of coffee and eighty extra rounds of ammunition per man — went into the wagons.[33]

Once across the Tennessee River, Wilson's three divisions moved east and south along parallel roads. For the first week they worried little about anyone contesting their advance, and the terrain acted as their worst enemy. Swamps had to be bridged, bottomless roads had to be corduroyed, and new roads had to be cut. Two branches of the Black Warrior River posed serious threats, each having cut deep, treacherous ravines in the surrounding plateau, and twelve thousand horsemen had to negotiate precarious trails descending to the water's edge while leaden skies threatened to lift the rivers beyond fording or the reach of Wilson's thirty-pontoon bridge train. No rain interfered, though, and but few horses were lost in the crossings. Just as dark fell on Tuesday night, March 28, Emory Upton led the first Union soldiers into Elyton, the county seat of Jefferson County. There his division encamped, spreading out on ground that local promoters would soon churn into the streets of Birmingham. Wilson followed the next evening with the other two divisions, while Upton's men collected forage and destroyed one of the iron foundries that would lure the Birmingham entrepreneurs.[34]

At Elyton, Wilson detached John Croxton's brigade from Edward McCook's division to ride southwest, to Tuscaloosa, with orders to burn bridges and factories and dismantle the railroad before veering back southeast to rejoin the main column on its march to Selma. Croxton ran into Forrest's cavalry on its way to confront the great raid, tangling with part of it and nearly winding up surrounded before he dodged first one way and then the other, convincing the rebels that he was on the run before circling back to seize Tuscaloosa. Wilson sent the rest of McCook's division to try to extract Croxton from his fix, but McCook returned without him: from Tuscaloosa Croxton led his command on a month-long hegira across the northern half of the state, backtracking repeatedly when faced with impossible streams or news of superior forces in his path. Not until May would Wilson lay eyes on him again, somewhere in Georgia.[35]

While McCook went looking for his lost lambs, Upton and Eli Long continued toward Selma with their divisions, pushing Forrest ahead of them through all of April Fools' Day. At Ebenezer Church, twenty-five miles north of Selma, Forrest came to a stand with about three thousand men: Wilson outnumbered him about two to one, but ten months previously Forrest had turned lopsided odds into unmitigated victory, while acting on the offensive. This time he decided to receive the attack, and Long struck him from the front while Upton sailed into him from the flank. An Indiana regiment of mounted infantry from Long's division drew sabers and charged head-on into the rebel line, breaking through and making for a second line of artillery that was playing on them. One captain and a handful of his troopers disappeared through that second line, too, but none of them ever came back. Hearing a train whistle that might mean more rebels, Upton also sent his men in on a saber charge. An Iowa cavalryman in Upton's division crossed blades with Forrest himself, striking him several times and demanding that he surrender, but Forrest shot him dead with his revolver. Upton's pressure from the flank sent the Confederates scurrying, leaving behind a few guns and a couple of hundred prisoners, some of whom seemed particularly well uniformed for so late in the war.[36]

Selma had become the largest supply depot west of the Savannah River, and by April of 1865 it was developing into a major industrial center for the Confederacy, with foundries for shot, shell, machinery, railroad car wheels, and a new rolling mill, besides a powder mill and a niter works. Long's division reined up outside the city on the afternoon of April 2, finding Forrest's men stretched thin to fill the five miles of complex, intimidating fieldworks that encircled the place. Forrest had mobilized all the Alabama militia he could find to join his troopers in the trenches, putting muskets in the hands of men as old as sixty. Upton prepared to join Long in an assault as the light faded, but Long detected that Forrest had worked a force around behind him, and rather than wait to be attacked he posted a rear guard, jumped the gun, and waved one brigade toward the center of Selma's defenses, on foot. Long went in with them, but fell with a head wound before reaching the trenches. With their repeating carbines his men made their numbers tell, and when they mounted the works the defenders could not bear the fusillade. As the rebels broke, Upton came at them from the side again, gathering in discouraged prisoners by the hundred. More than two thousand rebels, veterans and militia alike, surrendered as their comrades showed Yankee soldiers the heels of Forrest's celebrated command for the second time in two days.[37]

The day Wilson captured Selma was the same day General Steele finally joined Canby with his division, having had one serious exchange with rebels near the Florida line and another only the day before, on the Tensas River. His men camped amid blossoming peach trees, savoring the aroma and the scenery after two weeks' sojourn among acrid pine barrens, but Steele had not seen his first sunset over Fort Blakely before he began to quail before the Confederate chimera. He reported that the fort had just been reinforced, and called for someone to come up to his support before the garrison sallied out against him. From Pensacola Steele had brought three brigades of U.S. Colored Troops who presented well over five thousand muskets, along with two brigades of the Thirteenth Corps with better than five thousand more, and two brigades of cavalry that exceeded two thousand, giving him a total of over thirteen thousand men. Inside Blakely, the infantry and artillery combined amounted to fewer than three thousand. Canby, with the rest of the Thirteenth Corps, all of the Sixteenth Corps, an engineer brigade, and hundreds of siege artillerymen, had arrayed some thirty-two thousand troops in the vicinity of Spanish Fort, where the garrison fell short of two thousand men of all arms. Still, he sent another division to Steele, so he could completely invest Fort Blakely by land. There and at Spanish Fort, the only means of escape led across corduroyed plank roads over the marshes to an island where steamers plied back and forth to Mobile. In those two citadels and in Mobile itself, Dick Taylor had not been able to leave Major General Dabney Maury more than ten thousand Confederate soldiers.[38]

Canby learned all of this from deserters picked up by the navy. On the evening of April 3 Admiral Thatcher relayed information offered by three Confederates who had slipped away that afternoon from one of the island batteries between Mobile and the forts. They quite accurately averaged the two complements at Spanish Fort and Blakely at two thousand men apiece, and according to them both garrisons were equally short of ammunition and esprit. The officers might still attempt a stubborn resistance, but they assured the admiral that the enlisted men were nearly unanimous in wanting to give up and run. "Not one private in twenty would fight if they could get out of it," wrote the commander of the gunboat *Octorara*, who interrogated those rather willing prisoners.[39]

To Maury's surprise, Canby refrained from swooping down on Spanish Fort with irresistible force. Instead, he started digging regular approaches and locating his artillery to pound the place into submission. On April 4 he introduced the dejected rebels to the concept of siege with a two-hour barrage encompassing the dinner hour. The rebels took cover in their bombproofs, but one shot struck a magazine in the fort, lifting a few victims high enough into the air that Union officers saw them through their binoculars. Four miles away on the north side of Bay Minette, Steele reported during the bombardment that two steamers had delivered heavy reinforcements to Fort Blakely. Canby tried to calm him with the assurance that Steele would still have the superior force if every Confederate around Mobile concentrated against him. Only "sheer desperation" could move the troops in Blakely to come out and attack Steele's lines, remarked Canby's chief of staff.[40]

The next day Canby read about the capture of Selma, probably through Mobile newspapers; Wilson wrote Canby a letter on April 4, detailing his success, but the most daring and fleet-footed courier could not have delivered it overnight across two hundred miles of hostile territory. Colonel Comstock advised Canby to send a couple of divisions to secure Selma and help Wilson seize Montgomery, but Grant's earlier carping about his weather-induced delays may have dissuaded Canby from depriving himself of the irresistible strength he needed to sweep Mobile clean. With what Comstock saw as excessive caution, Canby kept inching his trenches nearer and positioning more heavy artillery to bear on Spanish Fort. Confederate crews had seeded the mouths of the rivers with hundreds of torpedoes, and light-draft Union vessels dredged them from the water as fast as they detected them, although half a dozen craft found them the hard way. The last runoff from the March monsoons had flowed out to sea, and dropping water levels in the rivers behind the forts prevented Admiral Thatcher from running any gunboats in to harass them from the rear.[41]

Not until April 8 did Canby feel ready to launch an infantry assault, but once he began, he made short work of it. At 5:30 P.M. he opened fifty-three guns on Spanish Fort and moved part of Smith's Sixteenth Corps against it. An Iowa regiment crept close to a bend in the rebels' entrenchments and swept a length of them with enfilading fire. The occupants instantly bolted from that line, and the Iowans took their places. Daylight faded out, but a bright moon cast enough light to continue the fight. Canby wanted to overrun the fort, but Smith hesitated, especially after the garrison pushed back a little. Smith asked to wait until morning, assuring he could take the fort before noon, but his troops had caved in the left flank of the fort and were threatening to close off the only avenue of retreat. Randall Gibson, the post commander, recalled his orders not to hold Spanish Fort if it meant the capture of the garrison, and he quietly started his Louisiana, Alabama, and Texas troops across the causeway General Maury had given them. Darkness protected them from the canister and musketry of the Yankees in the fort, and most of them reached the safety of the adjacent island. Smith suspiciously eased his pickets forward around midnight, and when their movement drew no fire the Union line began to ripple with cheers. About three hundred of Gibson's men fell behind, or remained behind intentionally, and surrendered.[42]

Drinks and salutes coursed the fleet while Canby shifted troops and guns in front of Fort Blakely. He spread seven divisions, representing forty thousand men, over a four-mile front, with four of those divisions forming for the attack and three waiting in reserve. His arrangements took most of the day, but they need not have. Blakely stood on better ground than Spanish Fort, with a good angle of fire and obstructions as intricate as rows of sharpened stakes to snare or impale assailants, telegraph wire strung between stumps at ankle height, and fields of buried torpedoes, but it was the spirit of the garrison that mattered, and that had perished. The attack began at half past five with the long lines surging forward at a run. The row of flags in the front rank descended into ravines, rolled over ridges, and finally climbed up and over the parapet of the fort. Relatively few men fell, mainly at the eruption of a land mine here and there. Roaring cheers applauded the appearance of blue uniforms and the U.S. flag inside the embrasures, and soon it was all over. About twenty minutes elapsed between the moment the Yankees first lurched into motion and the sound of the last shot. The thick, dark semicircle of Canby's assault reached the riverbank on either side of the fort, and almost no one inside escaped.[43]

The capture of Fort Blakely cut Maury's command in half. Batteries on the river islands kept Canby at bay for another day, and he brought up more guns to contend with them, meanwhile appealing to Admiral Thatcher for boats to land an amphibious force behind them, but before that could be arranged the gunners inside those works abandoned them. The next day Maury evacuated Mobile, too, leaving with about five thousand men to join General Taylor. Canby's first troops marched into the city at noon on April 12.[44]

Canby had finally received Wilson's April 4 dispatch, asking him to take over the occupation of Selma and — by then — Montgomery. With his own goal secure, Canby put Smith's corps on the road to Selma the same morning he occupied Mobile, and he ordered enough steamers to carry Steele's division up the Alabama River.[45]

Minus the wandering Croxton, Wilson's cavalry rode into Montgomery — the first capital of the Confederacy, and the city where Jefferson Davis had been inaugurated as president — that same April 12, exactly four years after Confederate batteries opened fire on Fort Sumter. Smoke spiraled over Montgomery from warehouses holding ninety thousand bales of cotton, burned by the retreating rebels to keep it out of Yankee hands. After another orgy of destruction, Wilson divided his column as he left Montgomery on Good Friday, April 14, sending Upton due east through Tuskegee toward Columbus while Colonel Oscar LaGrange led a brigade northwestward, to Opelika and West Point, Georgia. Each was to seek his own way across the Chattahoochee River, but each would also meet serious opposition.[46]

LaGrange ran into parts of Forrest's old command that first day, skirmishing with them over a distance of nearly forty miles and picking up scores of prisoners in the process. On the fifteenth his five regiments made another twenty-five miles, camping at Auburn. Not long after midnight he roused two Indiana regiments and started them toward West Point, where they found the bridges over the Chattahoochee guarded on their side by an imposing fort with massive ditches and parapets, sitting on a hill overlooking the river. More than three hours later the rest of the brigade cantered up, and dismounted cavalrymen clambered up the hill toward the fort. Rebel cavalry appeared across the river, but one of the Indiana regiments galloped down to seize the bridges and stave off those reinforcements while the rest of LaGrange's brigade swarmed over and into the work, which they later came to know as Fort Tyler. It was named after Brigadier General Robert Tyler, who had lost a leg at Missionary Ridge but who commanded the 265 men holding his namesake fort. Tyler lay among the dead inside when the Yankees entered, earning his only enduring distinction as the last Confederate general killed in the war. In a spectacular action after dark that same night, Upton's column overcame a fair-sized garrison at Columbus, driving in their first line and finally dispersing the entire force and capturing about half of it. He characterized the affair at Columbus as "the closing conflict of the war," and for him it was.[47]

Stopping to write a letter on the inundated roads from Mobile Point to Fort Blakely, early in Canby's campaign, a homesick Indiana soldier inquired about affairs back on the farm, and in particular he wanted to know how the sugaring was going. Tapping maple trees was the ritual that March brought to mind in boys from the upper latitudes, where long winters made them appreciate spring as they did no other season. The sugaring tradition had necessarily withered on the treeless prairies beyond the Wabash, where so many of the Western armies had been raised, but it exerted an almost visceral attraction for most of the Union soldiers in Virginia. They wanted to know what day the first good run came, and when their families boiled, and how many pounds of syrup and sugar they made. At no other time did they yearn more to go home, and the inevitable approach of another deadly campaign only intensified that seasonal allure. Soldiers desperate for furloughs more often hinted toward the end of winter that one of those falsified letters claiming fatal illness in the family might tweak the sympathy of their company commanders, and officers who mainly wanted to return to the bosom of their families usually found it judicious to submit their resignations by April, lest a later attempt provoke the suspicion that they wished to evade the impending dangers of field service. Enlisted men who could neither resort to the privilege of resignation nor cajole a furlough from their superiors often took matters into their own hands, and it was in March that the president usually issued his periodic amnesty for deserters, if they would only return to duty.[48]

Although that winter's weather had been the worst of the war, spring came early and in full flower. The rain abated somewhat after the middle of March, and a warm sun made the dry days seem more like May. It was, thought a New Yorker who was greeting his fourth spring under Virginia skies, unusually mild even for that climate. Good news from just about everywhere complimented and enhanced the vernal exhilaration. Before Mobile, and before the news of Bentonville, most citizens north of the Potomac supposed that the Confederacy could hold out for a while longer. From Gramercy Park, George Templeton Strong allowed that the rebellion had "at the very least, another year's fight in it," but he added that it might succumb to "inward disease" within a month, noting in particular that the narrow vote to raise slave armies amounted to "a confession of utter exhaustion." The price of gold was dropping steadily with each report that Sherman had reached another strategic milestone; the greenback that had been worth barely forty cents the previous summer climbed toward sixty cents by the middle of March, and that alone improved the public's reception of the war.[49]

The jubilation of the season and of the epoch brought numerous parties of celebrities and their ladies gallivanting down to see the Army of the Potomac. General Meade and his staff entertained one group on March 8, and three days later General Grant brought another entourage to see a review of the Second Corps. If there was one ritual of spring in that army it was the Saint Patrick's Day celebration that the Irish Brigade of the Second Corps always orchestrated, and for what many suspected would be the last such event of the war even Secretary Stanton came down, bringing his wife. The Regular Army major who commanded the 3rd U.S. Infantry drew his men and another regiment of the provost guard up for inspection by the secretary just after lunch on March 16, and the major paid particular attention to the female members of the party as they climbed into an ambulance to leave, when their legs necessarily peeked out from beneath their skirts. "One leg was beautiful as far as it went," he observed, "which was a little above the garter."[50]

The next day General Ord and the Twenty-Fourth Corps provided the Washington entourage with a grand review, overseen by General Grant. After that the Irish Brigade held its Saint Patrick's Day festival, with horseracing galore and the usual assortment of accidents, though nothing quite fatal to horse, rider, or spectator. The day passed with a conspicuous absence of excessive inebriation, perhaps in response to the mere presence of the exalted visitors, who may not have even attended the races. The Stantons left the next morning, to the disappointment of General Meade, who apparently wanted to bend the secretary's ear a little. Meade's own wife and those of some of his staff came down to visit the army next, and Meade slipped quietly away from his headquarters for a few days while he escorted his wife around the lines and on at least one James River cruise.[51]

Then came the most prominent visitor of all. Gideon Welles thought that Washington might have grown too warm for President Lincoln toward the end of March, for even the admiring secretary of the navy had been hounding his chief over executive interference in the trial of a pair of contractors who had been skinning the government in the manufacture of naval goods. Benjamin and Franklin Smith, of Boston, had sold the navy anchors and other equipment made with substandard iron at excessive prices, and prosecutors had their letter to an iron manufacturer in which they specifically asked for the weakest and cheapest product that could pass inspection. The Smith brothers, however, enjoyed a close bond with numerous Radical Republicans. They appealed to those connections, including Senator Charles Sumner and at least one member of the Joint Committee on the Conduct of the War, to have their trials transferred from a military tribunal to the civil system; after they were convicted, they asked those same acquaintances to lobby for what amounted to presidential clemency. Under the threat of losing the support of three congressional districts, Lincoln applied the same mercy to the cheating contractors that he did to so many condemned soldiers, and nullified their convictions. Secretary Welles then started to annoy him about other cases in which contractors had confessed their malfeasance and made restitution, asking whether those prosecutions should be pursued now that the Smith brothers, who had never repented or repaid the government, had been pardoned. The president's response to this and a host of other perplexing entreaties was to accept General Grant's invitation to take a little vacation at City Point, and he left the White House after the midday meal on Thursday, March 23.[52]

Welles also suspected that, in addition to avoiding difficult questions, the president wanted to apprise Grant of his wishes for easy terms if Lee, or any other Confederate commander, could be brought to ask for them: Lincoln had evidently remarked to cabinet members that he feared the generals might not be as avid as he was to end the fighting, and Welles supposed he did not want harsh demands to stand in the way of any possible surrender. With the early spring, the last few days of March might be the last time Grant could be found at his City Point headquarters. The president took Mary and Tad with him, to have a little family reunion, for forty days previously he had commissioned his twenty-one-year-old son Robert a captain and sent him to serve on General Grant's staff. A tremendous windstorm kicked up that afternoon, ripping the canvas roofs off many a soldier's shanty in the army camps, knocking down entire rows of trees, blinding men with whirlwinds of sand, and injuring them with limbs blown from trees. For safety's sake, the president's boat anchored in the Potomac overnight, and docked at City Point a couple of hours after dark on March 24.[53]

Much of the Army of the Potomac was supposed to fall in for a review by the president on the following day, but Robert E. Lee had other plans. Ever aggressive, Lee had used his remaining telegraphic connection with

Johnston's headquarters in North Carolina to develop a joint strategy against the Yankees on the James and the converging armies of Sherman. First he had to dissuade Grant from his habit of extending either end of his lines, as he had at Hatcher's Run, and convince him instead to either abandon or at least shorten those lines so Lee could hold Petersburg and Richmond with a fraction of his army. Then, when Sherman drew near, he might be able to detach heavy reinforcements for Johnston: if those troops could move without being detected, and if the remnant left in the trenches could hold Grant's entire attention, it might be possible to fight Sherman with something approaching equal numbers. If Sherman were quickly defeated, Johnston could return to Petersburg and relieve Lee. Johnston and Lee both knew that this was their only chance, and the first step in that long-shot gamble was to strike a blow that would convince Grant to reel in his extended lines, or evacuate them.[54]

That blow would be aimed at Fort Stedman, near the extreme right of the Army of the Potomac. The fort stood atop Hare's Hill, a mile south of the Appomattox River and nearly a mile north of the infamous Crater, overlooking the spot where so much of the 1st Maine Heavy Artillery had been butchered, nine months before. About two hundred yards separated the main trench lines of either army there, and the pickets might have thrown stones at each other. Lee chose John B. Gordon to lead the attack, and Gordon took advantage of the Union ploy of buying deserters' weapons to assure that he could overwhelm the fort before any warning could be sounded. So many Confederates had crept out to turn themselves in and collect ten dollars apiece for their rifles that none of the Ninth Corps pickets below Hare's Hill thought it unusual to hear a few rebels ask to come in with arms in their hands more than an hour before dawn in the piercing chill of March 25. In that way the entire picket line fell without a sound, and Gordon's infantry swept up over the hill, wheeling to the right — south — to overwhelm the battalion of heavy-artillerymen in Fort Stedman, capturing a couple of hundred of them along with a few hundred infantrymen in the trenches. The Union brigadier who commanded the vicinity of Fort Stedman darted into the fort in the darkness and began barking orders at men scrambling over the parapet, supposing they were his own returning pickets. Those men obeyed him, thinking him a rebel, but with the first hint of dawn he detected a grey uniform and demanded that soldier's regiment — at which the reciprocal mistakes became apparent, and the general followed his men into Petersburg as a prisoner. More of Gordon's Confederates turned to the left, trying to roll that short fragment of the Union line into the Appomattox River, and by daybreak a broad gap had been opened in the Union trenches. Rebel artillerists then turned captured cannon on the adjacent forts.[55]

All the noise failed to wake some slumbering veterans on the front line. John Parke, the commander of the Ninth Corps since Ambrose Burnside's departure, learned of the rupture around 5:15 A.M. — as much as an hour after the first faux deserters surprised their opponents. In response, he ordered John Hartranft's division of six big, relatively green Pennsylvania regiments up to confront the intruders. He also telegraphed repeatedly to alert army headquarters, only to read, after six o'clock, that General Meade was not even there: he was still aboard the steamer at City Point, with his wife. That left Parke unwittingly in command of the army, so it was that much longer before anyone began ordering troops from elsewhere in the line to help seal off the breach. Meade's chief of staff offered the provisional brigade from headquarters, and once Parke knew he held the command he called for assistance from Warren's corps, along with a division from Wright's Sixth Corps.[56]

In the end, reinforcements proved unnecessary: the Ninth Corps alone managed to drive the rebels out. Gordon's thrust sank deep behind Parke's trenches, but Gordon lacked enough men (or his men lacked enough temerity) to widen their foothold. Union forces on either side refused their flanks to meet the attack, and their artillery stopped it cold. Hartranft assembled his Pennsylvania regiments, all of which had joined the army the previous autumn, and three hours after the first pickets had been overcome he sent those Pennsylvanians forward. As soon as his first regiment charged head-on toward the contested works the rebel line showed signs of caving in, and when the rest of his division rushed in from the flanks a freshet of ragged grey uniforms began pouring out of Stedman. Volleys of canister made that a dangerous gauntlet, and hundreds of those who dared not run it surrendered, but when the battle lines receded scores of bodies littered the fort and its field of fire. Gordon fell back to his own trenches with about three thousand fewer men than he had led out. As some in the Army of the Potomac contentedly observed, the attack amounted to the Crater disaster in reverse, and they took nearly as much satisfaction in noting the shabby wardrobes of most of the prisoners, and how ravenously they devoured hardtack.[57]

The attack interrupted the telegraph line to City Point, and by the time General Meade heard about the fighting on Parke's front it was nearly over. Knowing that Lee must have weakened his line somewhere to throw so many men at Parke, Meade ordered Andrew Humphreys to press the lines in his front, on the left of the army, to see if they seemed soft. Parke reported having taken prisoners from Bushrod Johnson's Confederate division, which had previously faced Humphreys, so Humphreys started prodding the pickets in front of him. By afternoon a small but persistent battle had begun on the Union left, where Humphreys and Wright tried to pierce the thinned-out rebel defenses. An assortment of assaults and counterattacks dragged the lines one way and another into the evening, when a cold rain moved in. Some of the tired-out troops who had strengthened Gordon's morning offensive trotted back in time to protect their main works, but Lee lost his picket line there, and Union infantry pressed uncomfortably close.[58]

General Meade sent his wife home at the first inkling of trouble, and made it back to his usual headquarters before noon. While the fight was in progress on the left, and while Confederates were burying their dead at Fort Stedman under a flag of truce, Meade attended to his celebrated guests, including Mr. and Mrs. Lincoln as well as General Grant and his wife. The grand review could not be had, so the luminaries had to satisfy themselves with an inspection of Samuel Crawford's division of the Fifth Corps, but the rumble of battle so nearby piqued the adventurous spirits of the civilians, who asked to be taken within sight of it. Meade obliged them with a visit to Fort Wadsworth, on the ground where Warren fought his battle of the Weldon Railroad, seven months previously, where they could stand on the parapet and watch the struggle through a glass. The following day was Sunday, the soldier's only real day of rest in camp, but much of Ord's Army of the James spent it waiting for the first families of the country and the army to ride over to the left bank of the James for an abbreviated version of their grand review.[59]

Phil Sheridan arrived at City Point, fresh from his last raid, on Monday evening, March 27. General Sherman showed up from North Carolina. The docks at City Point teemed with quartermaster, commissary, and ordnance details unloading transport after transport of ammunition and supplies. Whole boatloads of horses arrived to replace Sheridan's exhausted mounts. Ord was bringing most of his troops from Bermuda Hundred down to the Petersburg front. It was beginning to look like business, and the president lingered amid the hubbub to chat with his senior military men before they sprang at the enemy again.[60]

Sherman had not been ashore long when he and General Grant joined the president on the *River Queen* — meeting in the aft cabin, which was probably where the Confederate peace commissioners had talked with Lincoln and Seward. The cabin saw another peace convention that afternoon of March 27, as Lincoln explained his preference for offering liberal terms if Lee or Johnston should consider surrender. He wanted nothing more than for the rebel forces to lay down their arms and return to their homes, adding that he would then be willing to allow the civil authorities of the states to resume control under federal authority. He still seemed ready to abide by his oft-repeated promise of a speedy restoration of the antebellum Union, insisting only on the eradication of slavery. Retribution played no visible part in his plan, in contrast to the Radical Republican agenda, and he hinted that he might be happiest if the more prominent political leaders of the rebellion escaped into exile. He reiterated those wishes in another interview aboard the *River Queen* on the morning of March 28, after which the generals took their leave of him. Before dawn the next morning, the Second Corps, the Fifth Corps, and all three divisions of cavalry started moving to the west, as inconspicuously as fifty thousand men could move.[61]

From his first collision with Lee the previous spring, Grant had relied on the same tactic of flanking impregnable positions, usually by going around his opponent's right. The campaign that began before daybreak on March 29, 1865, reflected that habit, essentially duplicating the February expedition to Hatcher's Run. Sheridan took the cavalry to Dinwiddie Court House; Warren followed after him, while Humphreys sidled to his left to occupy the works across Hatcher's Run. The Twenty-Fourth Corps, from Ord's army, filled the void Humphreys had left. Warren led his corps down the familiar Vaughan Road, past the battlefields of early February, until he reached the Quaker Road — named after the Gravelly Run Meeting of the Society of Friends, which had their meetinghouse in that neighborhood. The Quaker Road, alternately and contradictorily known as the Military Road, ran straight north into the Boydton Plank Road just below Burgess's Mill and the scene of the October fighting. Lee's field entrenchments petered out two or three miles beyond Burgess's Mill, after bending a couple of miles to the west along the White Oak Road. When Warren turned northward up the Quaker Road early in the afternoon, with Charles Griffin's division feeling the way, he was aiming straight for the Confederate right flank, threatening both the Weldon Railroad detour on the Boydton Plank Road and, a couple of miles beyond that, the tracks of the Southside Railroad. Knowing that Sheridan had proceeded even farther west than Warren, to Dinwiddie Court House or beyond, Lee responded by gathering most of his available cavalry in that sector and sending much of George Pickett's infantry division to join it there.[62]

The Ohio-born Confederate general Bushrod Johnson commanded the division covering those last earthworks along the White Oak Road, and he threw a couple of brigades down the Quaker Road to meet Warren. South of the plank road Johnson's lead brigade ran into another pair of those big, high-numbered autumn regiments — one from Pennsylvania and one from New York — under Joshua Chamberlain, and they sparred a little in the middle of the afternoon. Chamberlain pushed his opponents into and through a line of woods, but Johnson brought up another brigade and recovered the lost ground, whereupon Griffin hurried more of his own troops into the fight and swung the tide back the other way. By dark Johnson had stalled the Federal drive and left a picket line, drawing most of his troops back to his works.[63]

Dusk of March 29 delivered a driving rain that turned the roads back into a deep slurry, and it kept up with mounting intensity all through the following day. Thus far in the program, Grant had hoped to either force Lee out of his works or to at least distract him long enough for Sheridan to obliterate his two railroad connections to Lynchburg and Danville. Those two lines crossed at Burkeville Junction, where Sheridan was supposed to focus his destruction before either returning to Grant or reining south to join Sherman at Goldsboro. With five corps of infantry and one of cavalry positioned on an unbroken line from the mouth of the Appomattox River to Dinwiddie Court House, Grant felt the impulse to transform the operation into a more devastating blow, and he bade Sheridan to give up the railroad errand in favor of an attempt to circle behind Lee's right flank.[64]

Lee had already decided to bolster his right with part of George Pickett's division, and later he concluded to send all of it. Those troops rushed down from the Richmond front through the night, and by morning Pickett had concentrated three brigades of his division at Five Forks, four miles out the White Oak Road from the plank road and Hatcher's Run. Johnson sent two of his brigades slogging out to join Pickett in the deluge of March 30, and with Fitzhugh Lee's cavalry that should have given him nearly nine thousand men. That evening two more divisions of cavalry came out to join them, bringing perhaps three thousand more horsemen, including those Tom Rosser had salvaged from the valley. Their camp at Five Forks put them protectively between Sheridan, at Dinwiddie Court House, and the Southside Railroad, but their left flank hung in midair, several miles from the nearest support. That nearest support was Johnson, back at the other end of the White Oak Road, who had only his two remaining brigades and one of Pickett's that had lagged behind. With those three brigades, Johnson still had to face nine brigades in the Fifth Corps.[65]

General Lee rode out to Burgess's Mill on the morning of March 31 to supervise a counterattack personally. From farther up the Boydton Plank Road he commandeered a brigade from A. P. Hill's corps to add a little strength to the punch, and late in the morning Johnson started arranging sixteen regiments from Alabama, Virginia, and South Carolina for an attack, just as the rain drizzled to a stop. Warren had posted Romeyn Ayres's division above the plank road and near the White Oak Road, and Johnson's drive caught Ayres sidelong, propelling him through Crawford's division, after which both Ayres and Crawford came reeling back on

Griffin. That expended the momentum of the four rebel brigades, and Warren sifted his less disorganized troops for enough firepower to make another advance. Meade, who witnessed the collapse of those two divisions, sent a division of the Second Corps in to help plug the gap, and Griffin bulled ahead to reclaim the contested territory.[66]

General Sheridan's luck had been worse still. Brigades from two of his divisions had ventured out toward Five Forks that morning and met Confederate horse and foot under Fitz Lee and Pickett, who handled the dismounted troopers rather roughly and then did the same to the reinforcements Sheridan sent to their aid. That afternoon they drove the Yankees steadily back toward Dinwiddie Court House, and when Warren heard the firing receding behind his left he deduced that Sheridan was in trouble and sent a brigade of infantry marching off to his aid.[67]

Grant had been directing much of the action himself, and not without creating some confusion for Meade and his corps commanders. Grant communicated directly with Sheridan, who did not get on well with Meade, and late on the night of March 31 Grant decided to give Sheridan command over Warren and his corps, in addition to the cavalry. He had considered giving Sheridan the Fifth Corps for a vigorous attack on the Confederate right the day before, if Pickett's position had proven vulnerable, but Sheridan didn't like Warren, either: he wanted the Sixth Corps, with which he had had such good luck in the valley. The Sixth Corps was too far away, and Grant — ever solicitous of Sheridan, and down on Warren himself — offered to have the Fifth Corps change places with the Second in a muddy left-and-right sashay. Lee's four-brigade counterattack had quashed that option, though, and at 9:45 P.M. Meade suggested sending Warren to help Sheridan smash Pickett and Fitz Lee. Grant agreed, but added that he wanted Sheridan to have charge of the whole. Warren was junior to Sheridan by several months anyway, and Grant's insistence on it only betrayed his disdain for the eternally cautious Warren, whose interactions with his superiors tended to be more fraternal and argumentative than subordinate.[68]

The one-day alliance between Sheridan and Warren started off wrong, perhaps partly because Grant optimistically assured Sheridan that Warren would be with him by midnight. The orders only reached Warren, through Meade, a few minutes before eleven that night, and Warren issued his own instructions at that hour. His men slept so close to the enemy that they had to be wakened individually, by a touch on the shoulder, and his columns had to march about five miles over abominably muddy roads on a pitch-dark night, with at least some resistance from the enemy. With two days of rain Gravelly Run had swollen far too deep for fording, and pioneers had to bridge the stream; Warren ordered an abandoned house dismantled to provide the materials. It was full daylight on April 1 before the Fifth Corps came within reach of Sheridan's cavalry, and when Warren reported to Sheridan he found his new commander in a rather surly mood. Neither had slept much — Warren had not slept at all — but Sheridan had taken an unaccustomed beating the day previously. He also may have borne a lingering grudge against Warren for a collision between his cavalry and Warren's infantry at Spotsylvania, where Meade's own tensions with Sheridan began. Grant, as usual, had taken Sheridan's side back then, and now he seemed to be growing acutely impatient over serial misunderstandings about Warren's location and that of the enemy; around the time Warren finally presented himself to Sheridan, a staff officer showed up from Grant with verbal instructions for Sheridan to relieve Warren from command if he thought the infantry would do better under another officer. Sheridan must not have thought so at the time, and there was a battle in the offing.[69]

The evening before, when Pickett captured a few men from the brigade Warren had sent to Sheridan's aid, he realized that Union infantry was coming to catch him out in the open, and he retired to an entrenched line along the White Oak Road, on either side of Five Forks. Finding him dug in there on the first of April, Sheridan lined up two divisions of cavalry on his left, with more than five thousand repeating carbines, but he loaded his right with Warren's three divisions, over fifteen thousand strong, with which he hoped to bend Pickett's left back and cut him off from the rest of Lee's army.[70]

The morning of April 1 passed in relative quiet, and toward noon Pickett rode with Fitz Lee a couple of miles to the rear, where they remained with General Rosser for several hours, evidently without informing anyone where they would be. Dismounted Union cavalry started pressing Pickett's front in the afternoon while Warren deployed his infantry, but Sheridan had overestimated the length of Pickett's line, and Warren overshot the target. When the dense blue lines rolled forward late that afternoon, most of the Fifth Corps strode right past Pickett's left flank and into the woods. Those on the left extremity of either line saw their foes: the brigade on the rebel left had swung back to protect the flank, and threw a raking volley into Ayres's division, on Warren's left. Ayres wheeled to the left to face this, but the three brigades under Samuel Crawford — the least liked and easily the least competent of Warren's three division commanders — just kept on tramping deeper into the woods until Warren himself rode out and set them on the right path. Griffin, who had deployed behind Crawford, swung in beside Ayres and overlapped the Confederate flank, which started to crumble. Crawford's infantry turned completely about and came at the rest of Pickett's line from behind, and that was the end of any further resistance. With Pickett still absent, rebel regiments burst apart like milkweed pods, scattering into the woods to the rear or surging down the road past their cavalry, which could do nothing to stop them. At last Fitz Lee and Pickett heard the firing, and Lee ordered his squadrons into a charge, to slow the pursuit, but the Yankees gathered in more than five thousand of the same rebels who had whipped them so soundly only the day before. A Massachusetts soldier saw one impressive contingent of towering North Carolina prisoners, some of them as tall as six foot six.[71]

Only after the battle had been safely won did Sheridan decide to wield the peremptory authority Grant had given him. For a litany of inaccurate, insufficient, and apparently insincere reasons that he only listed later, Sheridan ordered Warren to surrender command of his corps to General Griffin and report to Grant's headquarters. Most of his own and Warren's subordinates, as well as a roving artist for an illustrated weekly, suspected that Sheridan simply meant to eliminate the only other man who might have taken credit for a victory that Sheridan wanted for himself and his cavalry. Sheridan would go on to become general in chief of the U.S. Army, with four stars on his shoulder. Warren — who had saved Meade's flank at Gettysburg, knocked A. P. Hill into a cocked hat at Bristoe Station, and transformed his last battle with the Fifth Corps into its most decisive triumph — would go back to his Regular Army rank, and would not even don the silver leaves of a lieutenant colonel until three years before he died.[72]

With Pickett's sizable command in abject retreat to the north and west, unable to return to their main body, Grant ordered all the artillery along his Petersburg lines to open fire on Lee's works, and he directed the infantry across that front to look for an inviting spot to assault. Late that night the guns in Fort Wadsworth initiated a barrage that deafened bystanders and lighted the sky across a ten-mile quadrant. After midnight, dark ranks of riflemen started creeping toward the black, ominous trenches, stopping just short of the rebel picket lines to wait for the horizon to lighten, but between the din and the dread few could avail themselves of sleep. A fortnight previously, a Vermont soldier in the Sixth Corps had warned his wife that "if we charge the works in front of us their will not be enough of us left to tell the tale," and the rout of Pickett's command did little to change that opinion. The notion of a frontal assault made some very courageous soldiers "heartsick at the prospect."[73]

A frontal assault was, however, exactly what Grant intended, and it began at first light. From the Appomattox River to Hatcher's Run, Union artillery belched a final fanfare and the serried lines swept forward, swallowing rebel pickets and provoking lethal protest from flaming embrasures. The muzzles of rebel rifles flickered over the brow of the looming works, blending quickly into a solid blaze, but valiant Yankee officers prodded their men or pushed through them to lead from the front in the terrifying twilight. Defending against the massed infantry assault they had hoped for since June, the ill-clad and chronically hungry Confederates took a heavy toll on the society of shoulder straps — especially among field officers, noted General Parke. Parke's best division commander, Robert Potter, went down with a bullet through the bladder while leading his men from one traverse to another at Fort Mahone, near the Jerusalem Plank Road. It was in front of Fort Welch, five miles farther down the line and five miles from the last entrenchments on the White Oak Road, that Horatio Wright's Sixth Corps pierced the defenses most effectively. It began with a lone, mettlesome Yankee leaping over the parapet here and there, followed by little squads and then a billow of blue. Any reserves Lee might have thrown into the breach had marched to Five Forks, whence none of them would return, and once the tide of U.S. flags reached their works the outnumbered defenders lost their last advantage. Singly and then by units, rebel soldiers abandoned their trenches where Wright broke through, swinging back to the right and left to contain the flood. Lieutenant General A. P. Hill galloped down the Boydton Plank Road to see what damage had been done in that sector, and rode right into the outermost fringe of the breakthrough, where a stray Union soldier shot him out of the saddle. His death left his subordinate commanders mounting a disjointed defense as daylight revealed shoals of men in blue pouring through the gap. Most of the Sixth Corps wheeled to the left down the plank road and started driving that part of Lee's army toward Burgess's Mill, away from their friends in Petersburg.[74]

Caught between Hatcher's Run, the Appomattox River, and overwhelming numbers of Yankees, the survivors of that fragment of Hill's corps scattered, swam, or surrendered. Ord worked his own troops through to the right of the Sixth Corps and spun them to the east, in the direction of Petersburg, where a few hundred determined rebels in two little forts stopped him cold through much of the afternoon. Sacrificing themselves to inevitable death or capture, they bought Lee enough time to bring some reinforcements down from Longstreet, before Richmond, and the sun set on that fateful Sunday with the victors still just outside Petersburg, but New York artillerymen camped in the yard of the house where Lee had last slept.[75]

Lee spent the night of April 2 funneling the residue of his army out of Petersburg. Except for the disorganized survivors now west of Five Forks, the only safe escape lay between the big rivers — north of the Appomattox and south of the James. Into that corridor, from Petersburg, came John B.

Gordon with his corps and James Longstreet, with his own corps and Hill's. From Richmond, Jefferson Davis and his government fled for Danville by train while a promiscuous column of miscellaneous troops marched in the same direction under one-legged Richard Ewell, whose own wife had gone over to the Yankees with her daughter a month previously, giving the cause up as lost. All were to rendezvous at Amelia Court House, forty miles down the Richmond & Danville line.[76]

The Ninth Corps lay closest to Petersburg, and early on Monday morning, April 3, the 1st Michigan Sharpshooters filed out in front of Orlando Willcox's division as skirmishers, shivering through the darkness in anticipation of another dawn charge. The glow of fires and one rumbling explosion gave away Lee's intent, but no one knew how much longer he would linger. At 3:10 A.M. the Wolverines eased forward, tentatively at first, but they broke into a trot when no picket fire challenged them. In nervous relief and exhilaration they lifted a little cheer that the heavy lines of infantry behind them could easily interpret. Soon enough they were sprinting over the rebels' muddy, empty parapets and racing each other into the city. The 1st and 2nd Michigan beat everyone, loping across the Jerusalem Plank Road and into the town just as the clocks would have struck four. In faint light half an hour later, Michigan flags decorated the cupolas of the courthouse and customs house, and jubilant Western soldiers started the town's bells ringing. The bridges over the Appomattox had been burned, so the only thing to do was ferret out Confederate stragglers and secure the city. Crowds of erstwhile slaves, cheering madly, met columns of the Ninth Corps as they started marching into the city.[77]

The Sixth Corps came into town from the west, and the rest of the Ninth Corps from the east and south. Once order had been restored, most of those troops turned around and went back to their camps to collect their belongings before joining the chase for Lee. One of Wright's brigades was just leaving Petersburg in the middle of the morning when the soldiers saw a cavalry troop escorting two dignitaries, and more cheers erupted when curious gawkers recognized President Lincoln in the company of Admiral Porter. Around noon Potter's division, led now by his senior brigadier, Simon Griffin, started out of town behind Griffin's brigade band — formerly the Nashua Cornet Band, from New Hampshire. The horns were tooting the "Faust Quickstep" to lighten their comrades' steps when the bandsmen learned, through whispers flying from the rear ranks, that the president was bringing up the rear of the division.[78]

A more apocalyptic scene greeted the first victors into Richmond. At a late hour Sunday night the last train had crawled out of the depot bound for Danville, carrying President Davis and the principal administrators of the Confederate bureaucracy. Throughout the night, long lines of Confederate soldiers slipped away from the fortifications below the capital, passing through the city in the darkness while looters of both genders pillaged government stores. The columns filed down to the Mayo Bridge, within sight of the island that once teemed with thousands of Union prisoners, and there they crossed the James River on their way out of the foremost symbol of Confederate resistance. By dawn fires roared at the river's edge, where the tobacco warehouses had been ignited, and began spreading uphill toward the capitol, consuming hundreds of homes, businesses, and government warehouses. It was primarily women who remained behind, many of them now homeless and half-crazed at the thought of the Yankee horde that would soon descend upon them.[79]

That Yankee horde, far less numerous than the one before Petersburg, also rose early for the anticipated assault. The roar of exploding ammunition and the detonation of the James River gunboat fleet startled some, who feared they were listening to the first artillery fire from rebels who intended to fight to the death, but as the sky began to lighten pickets near Fort Harrison eased forward, finding nothing but dank, deserted earthworks. As at Petersburg, it became a race from there, with different officers striving to be the first into the enemy's principal city; one infantry regiment ran nearly the entire seven miles to the outskirts of town, wearing knapsacks. They found a cordon of white cavalry waiting at the city limits, barring anyone from going farther for the moment. From their hilltop they could see Richmond burning, along with the Mayo Bridge, and occasional shells exploded in the fire; the last gunboat blew up while they watched. General Weitzel rode ahead with a squadron of the 4th Massachusetts Cavalry to accept the surrender from the mayor, and only then did the 5th Massachusetts Cavalry — black troopers — ride into Richmond at the head of a division of U.S. Colored Troops, with drums beating and flags flying; some of the soldiers bellowed "The Battle Cry of Freedom." Throngs of black Richmonders pressed the line of march from either side, going wild to see men of their own color taking their city back into the Union and lifting the shackles from their lives. A few white faces scowled from upper windows.[80]

The next day Lincoln came to Richmond, too. Amid an adoring swarm of people whom his words had freed, he came to the mansion where Jefferson Davis had spent nearly four years of his life. He walked the rooms his opponent had paced, and sat in the chair where Davis had worked. Before leaving, he consented to see one of Davis's associates. John Campbell, once a justice of the U.S. Supreme Court and now a former assistant secretary of war for the Confederacy, had met Lincoln at Hampton Roads in February; he wished to renew peace negotiations, but Lincoln simply repeated that in order to have peace and enjoy their old rights the people of

the Confederacy need only lay down their arms, recognize federal authority, and give up any hope of retaining slavery. He suggested again that his
power to pardon any criminal would prevent the vindictive prosecution of
repentant rebels, and he also offered a particularly inviting proposition: if
the "gentlemen who have acted as" the Virginia legislature would convene
and rescind the act of secession, the war might end abruptly for that state.
On April 6, just before he returned to Washington, Lincoln instructed
General Weitzel to allow the Virginia solons to meet for that purpose if
they chose, and he told Weitzel to show Campbell that order. The rebellion had lasted four years, and in as many days it had crumbled so completely that Lincoln seemed overwhelmed with joy and generosity, all of
which he might marshal to craft a smooth and prompt restoration of the
old Union.[81]

The news raced up the East Coast on the wires, and bounded from telegraph offices by word of mouth. At noon on Monday a Bostonian sauntering down Winter Street greeted an acquaintance who apprised him of the
captures, and as he turned up Washington Street he noticed that every
pedestrian was reading a newspaper; knots of people blocked the sidewalk in front of the *Herald, Journal,* and *Transcript* offices on Washington, and he encountered a curious mob on State Street; later there was a
"jubilee meeting" at Faneuil Hall. Textile mills closed along New Hampshire's rivers, and volunteer artillerymen manned antiquated cannon in
town commons. More orchestrated demonstrations celebrated the events
in New York the next day, when a resident described Broadway as "a river
of flags," and in Washington City that night all the government buildings
and private homes combined to present a grand, candlelit illumination.
"*All Washington* was in the streets," recorded the commissioner of public
buildings, who had stretched a huge, gaslit transparency across the western portico of the Library of Congress reading, "This is the Lord's doing; it
is marvelous in our eyes."[82]

The soldiers in the Army of the Potomac and the Army of the James
might have contended that the credit belonged to more terrestrial agents,
but for them — and even for much of the Army of Northern Virginia —
the end was not yet. Grant estimated that his opponent began the campaign with about seventy thousand men. With the repatriation of thousands of exchanged prisoners, Lee might have been able to put that many
in line after the fighting of March 25, but he lost about thirteen thousand
more from March 29 through April 2. Thousands more dropped out of
the ranks during the evacuation of Petersburg and Richmond (mostly
Virginians and North Carolinians whose homes lay within easier range),
and the Yankees only picked up a fraction of them; most just melted away
in the confusion and distraction of the evacuation. After crossing to the

south side of the Appomattox once again, the vanguard of the Petersburg pilgrims staggered into Amelia Court House on April 4, weary and hungry, but provisions that Lee had expected to have waiting there had never been delivered. He nevertheless waited a full day for Ewell's Richmond column, including a division commanded by his own son, George Washington Custis Lee; Ewell had been detained at the Appomattox by the lack of a pontoon bridge that Lee had ordered up as a contingency, well in advance of the retreat, but once again someone had blundered. Some forty-five thousand Confederate troops probably gathered at Amelia, which was as many as Lee had led back from Gettysburg, but these were a mixed and dubious group with much less stamina and experience than the survivors of the Pennsylvania campaign. Custis Lee's division, for instance, consisted of one small brigade of infantry augmented with converted heavy-artillerymen and local militia, and there was a naval brigade composed of sailors and Marines unaccustomed either to marching or to the close-order drill necessary for fighting in the field. To chase them down, Grant led about eighty thousand men west from Petersburg.[83]

From Amelia Court House, Lee meant to march down the railroad to Burkeville Junction, where carloads of food had been sidetracked, and from there he would press on to his big supply depot at Danville, but the daylong layover allowed Grant to catch up. With the old enemy so clearly reeling, morale in the Army of the Potomac soared at last, and the blue columns strode with an eager gait unmatched since Gettysburg. Sheridan's cavalry sped west below the Appomattox, taking position at Jetersville, just in front of Amelia Court House, on April 4. By the time Lee felt ready to move, on the afternoon of April 5, four divisions of dismounted cavalry and at least three divisions of Union infantry stood ready to dispute his passage, with the Second Corps coming up fast to stiffen the barrier. That forced the fugitives into a long, roundabout night march over narrow back roads.[84]

The next day the Second Corps and the Sixth dogged the tail of Lee's column, which stretched unduly from widespread straggling. Sheridan again raced for the head of it, but in the afternoon he struck the middle of the attenuated rebel cavalcade, again falling upon the hapless Pickett and Bushrod Johnson. That stopped everyone behind them: Ewell's Richmond troops found their path blocked as they crested a hill beyond Sailor's Creek, and when John Gordon came up behind Ewell he guided his corps around a parallel road that crossed the same creek downstream. The Sixth Corps spread out to attack Ewell, while the Second Corps chased Gordon on his detour and caught him where the creek created a bottleneck. The Sixth Corps gave Ewell a drubbing with their artillery before surging up the hill for a savage close-quarters fight in which the Confederate sailors and heavy artillery held to the last moment alongside the veteran infantry, but when the longer blue line bent around Ewell's the bullets started coming from every direction. Sheridan's cavalry had dispersed both Pickett's division and Johnson's, and was bearing down on Ewell's doomed command from behind, so white rags and handkerchiefs flourished here and there until the firing ground to a halt. Seven thousand men surrendered, with a wagonload of generals. On the other road Gordon lost most of his trains when the Second Corps charged him, but he managed to fight his way out with his diminished corps and rejoin Longstreet, who had outdistanced Pickett before the fight began, and knew nothing of it.[85]

Their long detour brought them out to the Southside Railroad, on the way to Lynchburg, a few miles west of Burkeville Junction. Still hoping to join forces with Johnston, Lee wanted to backtrack to Burkeville and turn onto the Danville line, but Ord already held the junction with a couple of divisions. Lee had no choice but to turn west again, until he could find another route leading south. That night he crossed back to the north side of the Appomattox on the long, towering railroad trestle known as High Bridge, passing through Farmville on April 7; the former colonel of a Virginia regiment, who had returned home to Farmville, accurately estimated Lee's army at somewhere between thirty and forty thousand men, at least a third of them without weapons, and most of them greatly dispirited. Saboteurs who were supposed to burn the bridge botched the job, and Humphreys still trailed right behind his prey with the Second Corps, attacking at every opportunity. In the afternoon, Lee established a defensive line north of Farmville, at Cumberland Church. From those breastworks Longstreet held off an evening assault while Gordon and the refuse of Pickett's and Johnson's divisions gained some distance on the Lynchburg Stage Road, toward Appomattox Court House and Appomattox Station, where they next hoped to outdistance their tormentors and make for Danville. During the night Longstreet's divisions pulled out, too, for their third consecutive night march.[86]

Humphreys, and later Wright, took up the pursuit on the stage road while Sheridan, Ord, and the Fifth Corps hurried west below the river. Late in the afternoon Union cavalry rode into Appomattox Station, where they found railroad cars full of the food that the famished rebels desperately needed. Beyond the station they also spotted the encampment of Lee's entire artillery reserve, which had given both armies a wide berth on a northern route, bound for Lynchburg. In the gloaming the gunners ran to their pieces and set their muzzles in a dense arc to greet Sheridan's sabreurs, and with serial volleys of canister they held him off long enough for the column to start moving again toward the mountains. Just then the head of Lee's main column was trudging into the shire town of Clover Hill, three miles away. There they stopped, dropping out to forage in local gardens or just to collapse in sleep. Longstreet still brought up the rear a few miles back, near a home called Rose Bower, where he, Lee, and Gordon decided that they would try to break through the cavalry in the morning and continue on their ever-wider circuit to Danville. Between the campfires on Clover Hill and those at Rose Bower slept the majority of Lee's soldiers, most of whom had lost or thrown away their rifles, and who clung to the army from little more than habit.[87]

Before dawn of April 9 Gordon strung out a line of battle just outside Appomattox Court House and put it in motion toward the railroad station. At first he flushed the Yankee cavalry ahead of him, but halfway to the station heavy ranks of men on foot appeared before him and started firing at rifle range, bringing him to a halt and then pushing him backward. This was the Twenty-Fourth Corps of Ord's army, with some of the black troops of the Twenty-Fifth Corps, and the Fifth Corps was coming up on Ord's right. Heavily outnumbered, Gordon's own infantry put up a fierce reply for their numbers, creating scores of new widowers and pensioners for the care of the federal government, but soon Gordon was backing over the ridge into the village again, and he could see Union cavalry circling behind his left flank. Through the village his infantry marched, firing and retiring, down the abrupt valley carved by the creek-sized headwaters of the Appomattox and up the other side where, at the crest, Gordon bade them halt and dig in. At the rear, a couple of miles back, Longstreet had advanced to a church called New Hope, but there he found no hope at all: his veterans also raised their last fieldworks as a tide of blue uniforms spread out in front of them. When Lee heard of the Union infantry in front of Gordon he knew he was trapped, and couriers went out with improvised white flags to ask General Grant for an interview.[88]

9

No More to Know the Drum

⟨⟩ STAFF OFFICERS FOUND a comfortable parlor in the courthouse village where the two generals could hold their conference, and General Grant did not forget Mr. Lincoln's wish to treat the conquered foe gently. For those who had come the last mile with Lee, there would be no prison: each would go directly home, and with transportation from the U.S. government, if that would help. Those who claimed horses could take them home to start the first crop, for it was planting time, and none of them was to be molested by federal authority so long as he obeyed the law and abided by his parole.[1]

About 4:30 that afternoon a Union officer spurred through the camps of the Sixth and Second Corps at full tilt, waving his hat and shouting that Lee had surrendered. His path was followed by little volcanic eruptions of caps, canteens, blankets, haversacks, and knapsacks as giddy Yankees exploded with glee. Other messengers sped eastward, back through Farmville and Burkeville Junction, carrying news of the surrender.[2] New York City had the story late that night, and newsboys strode the sidewalks by midnight, hawking extras. A doctor and his wife in Portland, Maine, rose from bed when a scream on the street roused them: the watchmen started blowing their whistles, and church bells rang the whole city into the streets to hear that the most illustrious Confederate army was no more. Pistols substituted for firecrackers, presumably with blank loads, and windows across the city glowed with candles until dawn. By morning everyone in Washington, Philadelphia, New York, and New England knew about it, and the bells tolled again everywhere, longer and louder than ever. Salutes boomed through the capital from Lafayette Square, breaking window glass again in the residences of perfectly loyal folks who nevertheless wished for an end to the raucous celebrations of Union victories. Governors ordered hundred-gun announcements of their own, and town selectmen scrambled for powder to match the state tributes. Prudence succumbed to patriotism, and now and then another amateur artilleryman blew his cannon, or himself, to pieces.[3] Work ceased entirely, and stores closed; flags unfurled in brilliant splendor from every building, bands blared, bonfires roared in the streets, and torchlight processions blazed through the evening. The sun had not set on April 10 before the news reached deep into Tennessee and west of the Mississippi. After so many false reports and reversals of fortune, it was almost more than some could believe: a skeptical Michigan editor had seen so many of his pessimistic predictions realized that on the very morning of the surrender he reproved Grant for "manifest" failure in allowing Lee to escape Petersburg, which he assured his readers would prolong the war indefinitely.[4]

Most of Lee's cavalry escaped before he capitulated, but those that remained passed through the village in a formal surrender ceremony the day after Lee signed Grant's articles, piling their carbines, rifles, and sabers like cordwood alongside the road. The artillery came through the next day, and on April 12 the infantry passed between two ranks of Joseph Bartlett's Fifth Corps division to stack their flags and the few thousand rifles they had not thrown into the woods that side of Farmville. With that they marched away as paroled prisoners under their own officers, down whatever road offered their shortest route home. Here and there remained a bitter, defiant subaltern or field officer, but most of the defeated rebels seemed content to have done with it, and not a few demonstrated actual satisfaction. When the prisoners from Sailor's Creek heard of the surrender some of them cheered along with their captors, although they were not included in the Appomattox parole and had ten weeks of prison life ahead of them.[5]

Lee's surrender only appeared to end it. For two months past he had exercised command over all Confederate armies, but Grant would not allow him to negotiate a general capitulation, and several other armies survived, at least in name. Johnston led the only one left in the field, though, and he desperately wished to avoid further bloodshed. The elimination of the Army of Northern Virginia extinguished the last spark of hope, and Union generals would portray it that way with great effect in their communications with the remaining rebel commanders. Chaplains and hospital attendants would still have to write a few sad letters for victims of random ailments or late complications from wounds, but for families across the North the news from Appomattox gave near-certain assurance that their young men would come home safe, and soon.[6]

Grant's generous terms went a long way toward easing the bitterness of the vanquished, and a New York lieutenant on provost duty in Petersburg described great relief among the citizens once they learned how kindly their conquerors would treat them. This was the spirit Lincoln wanted to cultivate, to convince as many as possible to take the oath of allegiance and restore national relations with all practical haste. He said as much in his last speech, delivered to an admiring throng from a White House window the night of April 11, in which he argued for the acceptance of Louisiana's new state government, spawned under the terms of his 10 percent plan. There might have been only twelve thousand loyal Louisiana voters willing to take the oath and proceed, he admitted, but they had adopted the Thirteenth Amendment and ended slavery forever: should that bold gesture be rejected? This was his first volley in what he knew would be his next great struggle — the battle against Radical Republicans who wished the former Confederate states reduced to conquered provinces that could be remolded in the Radical image. Intertwined with that was his suggestion that the Confederate Virginia legislature convene once more to rescind the act of secession; he was beginning to admit that this idea might have been a mistake, since his administration had always recognized the improvised, postsecession Virginia government under Francis Peirpoint. He had only wished to have those prominent Virginia Confederates renounce rebellion for the public influence it might offer, but as they made no immediate move to take advantage of the opportunity, he instructed Weitzel to withdraw the offer. Still, the episode had illustrated his zeal to restore the machinery of the old Union as rapidly as possible — perhaps before the beginning of December, for more than one of his associates remarked on Lincoln's satisfaction that Congress was not in session.[7]

Chief Justice Chase had been pestering the president with his Radical vision for restoring the rebel states, and in the final cabinet meeting on April 14 Lincoln's secretary of war proposed his own model plan for Virginia: Stanton suggested dual administrators, one of whom would restore federal authority while the other organized a state government, apparently by appointment rather than by election. Secretary Welles objected to the lack of self-direction, and reminded the president of the recognized Virginia state government of Governor Peirpoint, which Lincoln acknowledged, but before the meeting adjourned he asked everyone to consider Stanton's scheme carefully. They also discussed a new, "legal" government for North Carolina.[8]

Stanton had also come up with a scheme for commemorating the Union victories with a ceremony amid the rubble of Fort Sumter on the fourth anniversary of its evacuation by Major Anderson's garrison. Anderson, promoted to brevet major general, would attend the ceremony himself and run the same flag up a new flagpole that he had ordered taken down on that long-ago day in 1861. Anderson had been allowed to salute his flag before leaving the fort, although the observance had to be cut short when a premature explosion killed the war's first victim, but this time the salute would echo not only from Fort Sumter but from all the Confederate forts and batteries that had fired upon it. The president had approved of it, and Stanton invited a host of dignitaries, including Henry Ward Beecher. Originally it was to be a small affair but it grew into a fair collection of celebrities and their families. Stanton hoped to go himself, but he was foiled by the president's long sojourn at City Point, because someone had to stay behind to keep the government running: the attorney general had also left town, Stanton's assistant secretary of war was reporting to the department from down on the James, and William Seward had gone to his bed with a broken arm and jaw after a carriage accident. Stanton delayed the departure of the entourage from New York by a day, hoping yet to join in the festivities, but the president only returned to Washington on the same afternoon that the steamer *Arago* touched at Fort Monroe with Beecher and the delegation, on its way to South Carolina.[9]

Many hundreds of guests sought passes to attend the ceremony, and the steamer *Oceanus* brought down a mob of communicants from Reverend Beecher's church. The *Arago* landed at Hilton Head early in the week, and perhaps to celebrate the firing on Fort Sumter the post commander got up a ball for them on the evening of April 12, but a dearth of both food and female dancing partners made it a dull affair. The next night the steamers took everyone to Charleston, and as they lay off the bar a tender brought word of Lee's surrender. The next morning, Good Friday, the visitors came ashore or took lighters out to the ruined fort. The city itself had lost most of its antebellum charm: a devastating fire had leveled a portion of it in 1861, and the rubble remained undisturbed, along with the damage from Union shellfire. People had started returning after the occupation, filling empty houses and reopening closed businesses. Pentagonal Fort Sumter had been reduced to rubble on four sides, leaving only the face toward Charleston to represent the illusion of invulnerability it had reflected four years before. Major John Gray, of Quincy Gillmore's staff, could not restrain his admiration for the Confederates who had still held the place in its vulnerable condition; he interpreted the pulverized fort as a reproof to the "feeble and half-hearted defence" by Robert Anderson, whom he had never held in very high esteem. The entire morning passed in delivering passengers to the wharf at Sumter, where they climbed an extemporized wooden stairway over the remains of the parapet and descended to the constricted amphitheater that had once been the Sumter parade. There stood a new flagpole, heavily braced to support its height, with a rough lumber rostrum for the speakers and notables.[10]

Secretary Stanton had specified that the flag was to be raised at precisely noon, but guests were still coming over the parapet at that hour. Spectators covered the ramparts at Sumter and Fort Moultrie, the waterfront at Charleston, and batteries on Morris and James Islands. As many as three thousand people crowded the little manmade island in the middle of the harbor, including several hundred women, Admiral Dahlgren and two hundred other naval officers, governors, ex-governors, and lieutenant governors. Senator Henry Wilson of Massachusetts attended, as well as Boston abolitionist William Lloyd Garrison (whom Stanton had personally invited), and the black soldiers of the 54th Massachusetts Volunteers, which had seen its baptism of fire just over the water on Morris Island, twenty-one months previously. A chorus demanded the attention of the multitude with a song called "Victory At Last," after which the chaplain who had accompanied the garrison to Sumter in 1860 read a flurry of prayers and psalms. Then came General Anderson with his heavy garrison flag; he delivered a few brief and reluctant words before the thick canvas banner glided up the staff. When it reached the peak, the first of a hundred guns opened atop the crumbling bricks, signaling the commencement of the sham battle. When the last echo subsided, Reverend Beecher embarked on a long-winded oration that positively bored Major Gray.[11]

"As long as it was not filled with buffoonery," the major advised his mother, "I suppose we have reason to be grateful." The ceremony closed with a rendition of "Old Hundred," which had been sung at Gettysburg two Novembers before, and with yet another prayer from the former Sumter chaplain. That night, in Charleston, one of Gillmore's subordinates threw a much more satisfactory ball in the same mansion where the fall of Sumter had been celebrated with similar festivities, but the flood of Northern visitors tested the diminished accommodations of South Carolina's once-most-hospitable city, and Major Gray had to share a bed with Senator Wilson. After exorcising the Confederate spirit from as many repugnant anniversaries as they could, many of the visitors spent Saturday on pilgrimages to infamous wartime sites, but the limited amenities of a city that had endured so many months of siege drove most of them homeward by Easter Sunday.[12]

Before they embarked from Charleston that Sunday, the celebrants knew that Abraham Lincoln was dead. He had concluded his final cabinet meeting while the guns roared around Sumter, or perhaps while Reverend Beecher was droning on, during the course of which the president had revealed to his ministers, and to General Grant, his recurring war dream, with which he had often awakened on the eve of stirring military news. In the dream he occupied an indistinct craft floating on a water body that was drifting speedily toward "an indefinite shore," and he had had that dream again the preceding night. He ascribed it to anticipated good news from Sherman, but Gideon Welles gave the dream a more somber significance within twenty-four hours.[13]

That evening, with everything going so well, Lincoln chose to relax. Ford's Theater, on Tenth Street, was presenting a comedy called *Our American Cousin,* starring Laura Keene and Harry Hawk, and the president decided to see it. As company for himself and Mary, he invited Clara Harris, the daughter of Senator Ira Harris, of New York, who came with her stepbrother and future husband, Major Henry Rathbone, of the 12th U.S. Infantry. They arrived after the play had begun, and their entrance interrupted the performance with a burst of spontaneous applause from the audience. They climbed the stairs on the right of the theater and filed into the box that hung above stage left. The president evidently followed the fatal courtesy of waving the others into the box ahead of him: Clara and Major Rathbone sat to the right of the box, with Mary between them and her husband, who sat in what would thereafter always be called a Lincoln rocker, almost in front of the door. Flags decorated the front of the box, and hung beside it.[14]

John Wilkes Booth, a young actor of thespian pedigree, Maryland birth, and Confederate sentiments, came into the theater late in the play. Like many Marylanders of his political leanings, he bore a particular hatred for Lincoln, considering him an uncivilized tyrant. That hatred may have germinated as early as the federal occupation of Baltimore, at the beginning of the war, or more likely with the military arrest of the Maryland legislature, in September of 1861, on the most dubious evidence of a secessionist plot. Excessive and unconstitutional reactions to imagined dangers had particularly marred the opening months of Lincoln's presidency, and the vicarious continuation of those excesses by ministers like Seward and Stanton had aggravated the offense in the eyes of the dissident, turning many of them against the government altogether. Booth may have needed no aggravation to transform his disaffection to outright disloyalty, but he had apparently needed some impetus to reconfigure a months-old kidnapping scheme into wholesale assassination. Over the winter he had involved a handful of hangers-on in a plan to seize Lincoln and deliver him into the Confederacy, but that evening — with Confederate armies surrendering and the new nation in collapse — he had murder on his mind. Like the rest of Washington, he expected Lincoln to attend Ford's Theater on April 14, and he had prepared his way by boring a peephole in the door to the likely presidential box. The seating arrangement that he saw through that hole failed to discourage him, so he swung the door open, pointed a .44 caliber derringer at the back of Lincoln's head, and pulled the trigger. As Lincoln slumped forward, Booth turned a knife on Major Rathbone, probably expecting to find General Grant, who had been announced as the Lincolns' guest.[15]

Charles Sanford, a young civilian in the audience, heard the shot and glanced around, but he thought it was some exuberant drunk. Since no excitement followed, he looked back to the stage, where Harry Hawk stood alone, gazing up at the president's box, to see a stranger throw back the flags. With that Sanford saw him, too, still holding a knife in his hand and (or so Sanford thought) a revolver in the other; Hawk spotted only the knife. From the balcony the man shouted something that Sanford couldn't hear, but Hawk made it out as the state motto of Virginia: "Sic semper tyrannis." Then the figure leaped to the stage, seizing one of the flags as though to rip it down in his descent. He landed with a little slip of his foot, but up came the dagger again, and another shout: "The South shall be free," whereupon Hawk recognized the man as his colleague Booth, who ran toward him as though to avenge some unforgivable professional discourtesy. Hawk fled offstage, and Booth sprinted through the back door into the alley, where he mounted a horse held by a companion, with whom he sped away. Five hours later, Booth and his accomplice were thirty miles away in southern Maryland, looking for someone to treat the leg Booth had broken when his horse stumbled in the darkness and landed on him.[16]

Booth had converted some of his henchmen in the kidnapping plot to the mission of assassination, including one who was supposed to shoot Andrew Johnson, but lost his nerve. The only other conspirator bold enough to carry out his part of the program was Lewis Powell, a tall, strapping Floridian who had escaped from a Northern prison camp but had later taken the oath of allegiance under the alias of Lewis Paine. Pretending to deliver medicine to the injured William Seward, Powell burst into the Seward home on Fifteenth Street, beat the secretary's son over the head with a revolver, and struck viciously at the invalid with a knife, gashing his face before Seward's other son and a Veteran Reserve Corps attendant drove him from the home.[17]

Wakened by messengers, Gideon Welles and Edwin Stanton rushed to the Seward home, where Stanton started asking questions of the occupants in a tone so loud that one of the doctors asked him to lower his voice. He and Welles then mounted a carriage and directed the driver to Tenth Street, where they had to push their way through a dense throng. They quickly learned that Lincoln had been carried across the street to a boarding house, where he was not expected to live more than a few hours. Stanton settled in at the house as temporary head of the government, and as de facto chief of the murder investigation, ordering witnesses interrogated or held in custody until they could be interviewed. He tried to direct the pursuit of the assassin, or assassins, and for three hours after the attacks he was not yet certain whether the same man had struck twice, a few minutes and a few blocks apart, or whether there had been a conspiracy. James Speed, the attorney general, arrived later to join him in taking evidence.[18]

Stanton wrote what would later have been called a press release about the assassination, sending it to General John Dix in New York for telegraphic distribution, and toward the end of it he inserted an account of the previous afternoon's cabinet meeting that seemed slightly out of place among the details of the crimes. "The President was very cheerful and hopeful," he remembered; "spoke very kindly of General Lee and others in the Confederacy, and the establishment of government in Virginia." That description comported with the navy secretary's rendition of the meeting, and with Lincoln's mood of the foregoing fortnight, but the inclusion of that passage with the report of his murder seemed almost to invite reflection on the ingratitude of those conquered countrymen whom Lincoln had treated so benevolently, who were already suspected of having taken a part in the assassination. Stanton, for one, would strive to prove that Confederate officials had been involved, and his 1:30 A.M. dispatch of April 15 may constitute evidence that he had made the decision to do so before the president had breathed his last. He was one of those who bridled at Lincoln's gentle hand with vanquished enemies, and if the architects and artisans of secession could somehow be implicated in the assassination, they and their ideological kindred would face such a firestorm of political discredit and public disfavor that for the foreseeable future all political power would swing to the party that cloaked itself in Lincoln's mantle. A nurse at the former naval academy in Annapolis underscored the latent political power of such a connection when she asked a colleague how they would ever be able to "forget the loss, or forgive the outrage."[19]

The public needed little prodding to link the lost cause to the lamentable crime. "Did we need this one new adder sting from the serpent slavery?" wrote a New Hampshire woman the day Lincoln died, automatically and perhaps naturally associating the murder with the enemy below the Potomac. Sanitary Commission treasurer George Templeton Strong learned of it at nine o'clock that morning and immediately entered the tragedy in his diary, adding that the "South has nearly filled up the measure of her iniquities at last!" The assumption of Confederate involvement surfaced everywhere over the next few days in the venomous letters sent home by soldiers who had, until then, begun to show a certain tolerance or even admiration for the beaten rebel army. There flourished vows to take no more prisoners among those who still resisted, and threats of a "war of extermination" that would spare no Southerner, soldier or civilian. A colonel swore that if any of his men ever brought in a live prisoner, he would shoot both of them. A brigadier general recanted his support for moderation and conciliation, regretting that he "ever treated a Rebel magnanimously."[20] "Wo[e] to the rebel that falls into our hands," wrote a soldier on the march from Mobile to Montgomery, beyond the reach of the telegraph, and when his column carried the news to those already in Montgomery they, too, stood ready to avenge Lincoln's murder, although they no longer had an enemy on whom to take their vengeance. Transporting a boatload of paroled Confederates homeward on the Tennessee River, the crew of a navy steamer suddenly started snarling viciously at their passengers, who had no idea why. "We dont ask for any more surrender," remarked one of Sherman's men. "If this army moves on the enemy from here, it will leave a mark that will never be effaced."[21] An Indiana Quaker who habitually made no mention of the war in his diary recorded his own sadness at the assassination, and his concern that the soldiers could not be restrained from "indiscriminate Slaughter," while a Michigan woman who had lost one son in the war seemed willing to see it done. Reminding her other soldier-son that she had adjured him to forsake retribution over his brother's death, with the murder of Lincoln she advised him to "take that check off."[22]

Similar universal fury licensed widespread intimidation of dissident citizens and opposition newspapers in the North, with a fair amount of violence. Police had to come to the rescue of the *Age,* a Democratic paper near Philadelphia, when a mob surrounded it on the night of Lincoln's death. The same night rowdies in Westminster, Maryland, destroyed the office of the *Westminster Democrat* and warned the editor to get out of town: he did not, and another throng of thugs returned to his home a few nights later to drag him from it; other newspapers reported that the Westminster editor tried to defend himself, firing into the crowd and wounding one of his tormentors, whose accomplices overwhelmed their victim and killed him. The *Evening Bulletin* recklessly headlined its account of an antiwar speech by Philadelphian Edward Ingersoll as "The Ingersoll and Booth Doctrine," and when Ingersoll came into town on the Germantown Railroad a crowd of hecklers surrounded him, demanding an apology. Ingersoll told them to go to hell, at which one of them attacked him with a cane; Ingersoll responded with his own walking stick, but when the crowd grew more threatening he drew a pistol, the sight of which scattered his assailants. Ingersoll was the one arrested, however, and when his unarmed, sixty-year-old brother came to the police station to attend to him the mob jumped him and beat him savagely until the police, fearing he would be killed, interfered. It was, as a repatriated prisoner of war admitted, worth a man's life to say something critical of Lincoln in Philadelphia, and the same intolerant spirit prevailed everywhere. Three days after the assassination, when some infraction moved police to take a man into custody outside a government office in Washington, a gathering crowd assumed that he was one of the conspirators and started stoning him, while calling for his head.[23]

Just as abolitionists had brazenly advocated secession from the slave states, even while it was considered treasonable to support Southern secession, abolitionists alone seemed daring enough to find fault with Lincoln in the wake of his death. Just before leaving Charleston with the fresh news of the assassination, Henry Ward Beecher revealed his unhappiness with the president's lenient policy toward the conquered South, and he insinuated his satisfaction with the exchange of Lincoln for Andrew Johnson, admitting to an army officer his belief that "Johnson's little finger was stronger than Lincoln's loins." That inflammatory remark raised little more than eyebrows, but Beecher seemed to convey a common sentiment in Radical circles. Adopting Lincoln's own theme of divine orchestration, one abolitionist in the Treasury Department explained his conviction that Booth had acted as an instrument of God, who recognized that the president was about to embrace a policy that might have thwarted the sacred object of emancipation; Lincoln's death simply made room for someone else who was "already molded to his purpose," reasoned that Radical bureaucrat. A quartermaster of similar political slant did not share the pervasive sense of irreparable loss, although he had liked Lincoln well enough, because he suspected (as did many others, in Congress and out) that Johnson's rabid nationalism had marked him as one of "the radical school," and he thought the new president "perfectly sound on the anti-slavery question." Like many who had never gushed over Lincoln, George Templeton Strong took the news hard, as though it were "a fearful personal calamity," but he also understood that the assassination, "occurring just at this time, may be overruled to our great good."[24]

As many former rebels and Northern citizens phrased it, the man who killed Lincoln had robbed the South of its best friend. Among those who put it that way were William Sherman and Joseph Johnston, who were then negotiating for the surrender of the forces under Johnston's command, which Sherman's much larger army had pushed steadily back from Smithfield to Raleigh, Durham, and Hillsboro, forty miles from the latest refuge of the peripatetic rebel government.[25]

At the very moment Lincoln sat with his cabinet, interpreting his last dream as a portent of good news from Sherman, Johnston's appeal for peace was in the hands of a courier on the way to Sherman's headquarters. Sherman opened it at midnight, less than two hours after the president had been shot. At first Johnston, who had just returned from a meeting with his fugitive president at Greensboro, asked only for an armistice to allow negotiations between the civil authorities. Lincoln had specifically and repeatedly rejected any cease-fire without immediate surrender and submission to federal authority, but Sherman halted his troops and agreed to a noon meeting with Johnston near Durham on April 17. At that meeting, where no one yet knew of the assassination, their discussion ranged far beyond the realm Lincoln had authorized, to the extent of immediately restoring the political rights and privileges of all citizens, preserving the existing state governments, and requiring a general amnesty against prosecution, or other penalties, for taking part in the rebellion. Those three topics all fell within the authority Lincoln had claimed for himself, but the next day the generals met again at the same place, joined this time by the Confederacy's new secretary of war, John Breckinridge, and they agreed to hold their respective armies stationary until they could obtain the approval of their governments. Sherman and Johnston each took the view that their convention essentially ended the war, and both feared only that desertions from Confederate ranks would fill the countryside with destitute bands of desperadoes for whom robbery would provide the only source of sustenance.[26]

General Grant immediately realized that such broad terms would be disapproved, having had more conversation and correspondence with the president on that subject than Sherman had. He forwarded the document to Washington with inevitable apprehension of the results, for Sherman was one of Grant's closest friends, but he may not have anticipated so harsh a response as Edwin Stanton's. That Sherman had exceeded his authority could not be denied, and even his brother, Senator Sherman, wrote Stanton to express his dismay, although he pointed out that the general had only been too liberal in his terms to Johnston, as both Lincoln and Grant had been to Lee. The secretary of war responded as though General Sherman had committed treason himself: he produced another of his press releases to General Dix, declaring that President Johnson, every cabinet member, and even General Grant had disapproved of the terms, and he charged that Sherman's armistice had probably allowed Jefferson Davis to escape the country "with his plunder," consisting of the gold from the Confederate treasury.[27]

Davis and the remnants of his government had, in fact, slipped out of Greensboro on Saturday night, April 15, before the truce began, while George Stoneman's cavalry burned bridges and tore up railroad tracks between there and Salisbury. The little caravan evaded Stoneman, arriving at Charlotte on April 19, and for a few days an impromptu Confederate capital flourished there. After much hindrance from paroled men and deserters from his own army, Breckinridge reached Charlotte and delivered a copy of the Johnston-Sherman convention to his president. Davis asked his cabinet for their opinions, and all present advised him to accept the terms. The cause was lost, they chorused, and although he still seemed reluctant to give up the fight he consented. On April 24 he approved those parts of the agreement that required whatever survived of his authority, but the next day they heard through their remaining telegraph line that Sherman's generous terms had been rejected, and with it the promise of amnesty — which might not have been necessary even for government officials, had Abraham Lincoln still lived to wield the executive pen. The next morning they learned from the same source that Johnston intended to surrender his army at noon that day, April 26, on the same terms Lee had accepted, and early that afternoon the Confederate government dissolved, every man for himself. Clerks, assistant department heads, and scores of Confederate officials in and out of uniform scattered toward their homes. President Davis and his small party moved south, with most of his cabinet officers and a cavalry escort, into South Carolina, where even the firmest female rebels had given up all hope. The president would sup that night with some of his poorer constituents in his flight to parts unknown.[28]

The next evening Horatio Wright led the Sixth Corps into Danville without a shot fired, despite the presence of hundreds of Confederate soldiers. The conquerors found the city populated mostly by black people, with a conspicuous portion of the white minority dressed in mourning. John Mosby, the "grey ghost" of northern Virginia, had disbanded his battalion of raiders after a final week of defiance, and most of them had ridden into Winchester to ask for their paroles. Even a band of recalcitrants hiding in Shenandoah Valley caverns emerged to find their way home. By the last of April, Virginia and North Carolina were free of any organized Confederate troops.[29]

Even with so much Confederate territory overrun by Union armies, thousands of Yankees still languished in rebel prisons. Nathan Bedford Forrest had already sent about two thousand of them to prison camps in the summer of 1864, and in the fourth week of September he had embarked on a raid into northern Alabama and middle Tennessee. There he snared well over a thousand more captives from isolated garrisons like one at Athens, Alabama, where he took hundreds of men from Michigan, Ohio, Tennessee, and from the 110th U.S. Colored Troops, which had been raised along the Alabama portion of the Tennessee River. All the black prisoners went to Mobile, where Confederate authorities put them to work on the city's defenses and advertised them by name in the local newspapers, probably so former owners could identify them. Unlike the prisoners Forrest had run down after Brice's Crossroads, the Athens contingent never saw the inside of Andersonville, which had been emptied of all but the sick early in September, in fear of Sherman. Instead, their escort delivered the Athens captives to Cahaba, nine miles below Selma on a tall bluff over the Alabama River. Cahaba provided a much smaller version of Andersonville, with fewer than two hundred guards and only a couple of thousand other inmates after Forrest's latest contribution arrived. Except for the size, though, Cahaba resembled the typical Confederate stockade prison, with a twelve-foot plank fence surrounding an incomplete cotton shed, a few other makeshift shelters, and a small prison yard with water and latrine facilities, all packed into less than an acre of ground that the river could reach during prolonged periods of heavy rain. In the last winter of the war a great deal of heavy rain fell on Alabama.[30]

Still, the administrators at Cahaba facilitated correspondence with families in the North, and the prisoners reported decent treatment in spite of the cramped conditions. Edwin Ford assured his parents in Hillsdale, Michigan, that steady activity in the way of collecting wood and rations, cooking, and washing fended off the monotony that might breed melancholy, and they had plenty to eat. It was nothing like he had heard about the dire conditions in rebel pens, for they drew meal, beef, rice, and sometimes flour, and on the evening of December 8 his mess was cooking a relatively sumptuous beef and rice soup. He and seventeen other soldiers of his family's acquaintance had come to Cahaba: only one had died, while two others had been sent away, sick, to be exchanged. The remaining fifteen enjoyed good health, he wrote, and seven weeks later they were all still well. All that remained to round out the diet was vegetables, but at least a portion of the Cahaba population had lain in prison long enough that an inspector discovered some evidence of scurvy by the middle of October.[31]

The drenching rains that inundated Alabama through late February and early March of 1865 raised the Alabama River to record heights, threatening the prison, which sat just below the mouth of the Cahaba River. A Confederate nurse steaming up the river to Montgomery on the once-opulent *Southern Republic* saw whole towns under water, including Cahaba, where she noted townspeople getting about in boats. The stockade also had a couple of feet of water in it, but from the shrieks of the prisoners she supposed they were cavorting in it; the prisoners themselves did not remember the flood that fondly, after days of roosting in the rafters for a dry place to sleep. The two governments had finally decided to resume prisoner exchanges by that time, though, and transports started taking the prisoners away as the waters receded. Perhaps prompted by the flood at Cahaba, Union officers in Vicksburg and Confederate exchange officials took the unusual step of establishing a neutral camp on the Big Black River, east of Vicksburg, where the paroled prisoners could await exchange in a more salubrious climate. They even gave the place an independent name: "Camp Townsend, Aubrey Territory," where they began with a proposal to exchange three thousand men, representing the estimate of prisoners in Cahaba. About a thousand left the bluff in the first load, steaming down the Alabama River to the Tombigbee and upstream from there to Demopolis, on the Alabama & Mississippi Railroad. The remainder of the prisoners followed by the end of March, before James Wilson's cavalry could swing down to liberate them. The trains from Demopolis delivered their Cahaba passengers to Jackson, but Sherman had destroyed the railroad between Jackson and the Big Black in 1863: as unaccustomed as they were to marching, the prisoners had to hoof it about forty miles from there. The Union army loaned the rebel agents ambulances to bring back the frail and the sick.[32]

Because no Confederate prisoners had yet arrived at Vicksburg, most of the men from Cahaba lay at the camp on the Big Black day after day, staring at their own flag billowing at the far end of the pontoon bridge and fattening up on better rations than they had known for months; one six-foot Michigan man reported proudly that he weighed 170 pounds. Toward the end of March a new procession of "walking skeletons" limped in from Andersonville, and at least one of the borrowed ambulances came in overloaded with four of them, all of whom were dead, or nearly so, when attendants unloaded them at the river's edge. These were the worst of the sick from the Georgia prison, who may have been sent first so they could benefit from the earliest medical care, but the trek had nearly done them in. Later arrivals from Andersonville proved increasingly hardy, and the Union commander at Vicksburg, Major General Napoleon Dana, described most of the denizens of the exchange camp as "in excellent health, the Cahaba prisoners particularly." The sick were all Andersonville survivors, Dana believed, and his adjutant thought them "more dead than alive," but a few of the Cahaba men were dying, as well.[33]

With their infant nation crumbling around them, Confederate officials agreed on the day after Lee's surrender to release all Union prisoners anywhere they were held, without waiting for an actual exchange. Under that agreement General Dana's adjutant general, Captain Frederic Speed, asked the rebel exchange agent at Camp Townsend on April 13 if he could send enough prisoners to make up a boatload by noon of the next day.

Presumably there was then a steamboat at Vicksburg on which he could ship a thousand or so men north, but it took much longer than Speed supposed to prepare rolls of the prisoners' names and regiments for use in recording their exchange, so more than a week passed before any of them started north.[34]

The transportation of prisoners fell within the responsibility of the quartermaster at Vicksburg, where corruption had evidently been running rampant since the city fell into Union hands — and the Quartermaster Department won its share of accusations for fraud and graft. Formal inquiries into civil and military venality at Vicksburg had been scuttled by changes of command nearly a year before, and officers awaiting transportation there in the spring of 1866 firmly believed that Vicksburg's quartermaster was still favoring certain steamboats with government passengers in return for a cash tribute. Similar suspicions hovered around the lucrative task of carrying the paroled prisoners upriver that spring of 1865, with quartermasters and staff officers pointing fingers at each other in either righteous indignation or jealous competition. Dana's department quartermaster, Colonel Reuben Hatch, only enhanced the odor of malfeasance by his presence. Hatch had been investigated earlier in the war by none other than Ulysses Grant himself, who thought Hatch guilty of "great frauds," but Hatch's brother was secretary of state for Illinois — besides being a neighbor, good friend, and political benefactor to Abraham Lincoln, who had appointed Colonel Hatch in the first place. Lincoln interested himself in the colonel's fraud case (as he did later in the prosecution of the Smith brothers of Boston), appointing a commission of his own old friends who ultimately blessed all of Hatch's dubious expenditures.[35]

Captain Speed had stepped into the exchange process in place of Dana's commissary of musters, Captain George Williams, who had gone looking for rebel prisoners whom he could trade for the men at Camp Townsend. Speed had not been long on the job when he approached General Dana with an allegation against Hatch's "master of transportation" at Vicksburg, Captain William Kerns, whom he suspected of taking a bribe for funneling as many prisoners as he could to a particular steamship line.[36]

This Speed was an ambitious character, eternally on the lookout for the next opportunity. In 1861 he had recruited part of a company for a Maine regiment, just missing a commission, and since then he had spent most of the war pestering his father for political help in getting promotions or a Regular Army appointment, and on more than one occasion he had insinuated that he was willing to pay a bribe to secure those ends. When he took over the transfer of prisoners from Camp Townsend to Vicksburg, he was mulling the prospects of going into the ice business with his father, who would ship Maine ice to Mississippi, where Frederic would warehouse and sell it.[37]

The first load of prisoners boarded the steamer *Henry Ames,* which pulled away from Vicksburg on the evening of April 22 with thirteen hundred prisoners. The *Olive Branch* arrived in the wake of the *Henry Ames,* taking seven hundred more. It was then that Captain Speed complained of the quartermaster holding prisoners for a later boat when Speed wanted them to go on the *Olive Branch.* The next boat behind the *Olive Branch* was the *Sultana.*[38]

The *Sultana,* a side-wheel riverboat 260 feet long and more than 40 feet wide, had been carrying freight and passengers up and down western waterways since it was launched in Cincinnati, early in 1863. It was the *Sultana,* speeding down the swollen Mississippi from Cairo, Illinois, that had brought the news of President Lincoln's assassination to the river cities, including Vicksburg and New Orleans, where the boat arrived draped in mourning on April 19, four days out from Cairo.[39]

The *Sultana* left New Orleans before noon on Friday, April 21, struggling against the highest water and strongest current Louisiana had seen in years. It took more than two days to reach Vicksburg, where Colonel Hatch had previously promised the *Sultana*'s captain a boatload of prisoners at government rates. Captain Speed, who had until then acted as though he needed every possible transport to convey a multitude of prisoners, suddenly reversed himself and claimed that only about three hundred were ready: they might as well wait for the next boat, he contended, which could be filled out with all the prisoners he processed in the interim. The next morning, however, Colonel Hatch called very early at Captain Speed's quarters, and they apparently talked for some time before Hatch converted the hesitant captain, who went promptly to General Dana and said he could put all the passengers on the *Sultana* after all. He told Dana he had spoken with Captain Williams, who had just returned, and said they had decided to take the names of the men as they went aboard, rather than preparing complete lists beforehand, but after Speed left, Williams came to General Dana to complain that Speed seemed to be dawdling unjustifiably, probably so he could withhold prisoners for a later boat in expectation of "a pecuniary consideration." Dana doubted it, and told Williams of Speed's similar charge against Captain Kerns, so Williams said he would look into it. The next time he saw Dana, Williams recanted completely, assuring the general that he had entirely misjudged Speed, who had delivered nearly two thousand potential passengers in short order.[40]

Three trainloads of those men came in from the Big Black through the rest of the day, and after two of those trains had emptied their passengers onto the *Sultana* Captain Kerns began complaining to Colonel Hatch and to the commander of the post at Vicksburg that there were already too many men aboard it. He pointed out other boats that could transport the surplus, but the captain of one of those boats was already suspected, accurately, of offering a bribe to have some of the business thrown his way, so both Williams and Speed invoked principle and refused to give him any passengers. Not until the morning of April 25, half a day after the *Sultana* had left Vicksburg, did Speed reveal to an astonished General Dana that about nineteen hundred men had been packed onto the boat, disingenuously reassuring the general that the boat could handle the load, and that the passengers were not overcrowded.[41]

There was, in fact, little room to move on the *Sultana*. By official admission, 1,886 paroled prisoners covered the decks, besides the civilian passengers and the crew. For all those people, many of whom were suffering from dysentery or diarrhea, the *Sultana* afforded only six double toilets that emptied directly into the river. Survivors of Andersonville and Cahaba had become accustomed to crowding and hardship, however, and the scent of home filled their nostrils. Samuel Boysell, of Ohio, had spent nearly a year in Andersonville and a variety of South Carolina prisons since Forrest took him at Brice's Crossroads, and he could hardly wait to see the wife and children whose faces he had begun to forget. David Millspaugh, of Tecumseh, Michigan — a Cahaba prisoner captured by Forrest at Athens — was about to realize his dream of "one country one Government and that free," which he had inscribed on the diary he took to war in 1862. "Our union at any cost," he had written then, but that cost was not yet entirely paid. The *Sultana* touched at Helena, Arkansas, on the morning of April 26, where a local photographer captured the image of the teeming passengers tilting the boat to port, evidently as they swarmed to see what he was doing, or to get into the picture. That evening the boat stopped at Memphis, but started back upriver later that night.[42]

An hour or two after midnight on April 27, a few miles above Memphis, one of the boilers exploded. The pilothouse and some of the cabins dropped through to the boiler deck, killing and pinning those below. Fire spread quickly through the mortally wounded craft, forcing terrified passengers on the windward end of the boat to take to the water; when the current spun the burning craft about, those at the other end had to jump, too. The rest of the cabins fell through, and the paddlewheel housings keeled over on top of survivors struggling to stay afloat. The explosion and fire killed hundreds, or burned them beyond recovery, and many more drowned. Even those who could swim ran the risk of being pulled under by panicking comrades. Spring runoff had filled the river with cold water and pushed it over its banks, and chilled swimmers floundered vainly toward the distant safety of shore. Most of those who survived clung to flotsam and drifted downstream until they ran aground, or encountered rescue boats steaming up from Memphis, but hours passed before the alarm reached that city. W. B. Snow, freshly elected to the U.S. Senate from Arkansas under Lincoln's loyal minority government and bound for a capital where he would not be allowed to take his seat, decided not to leap toward the Tennessee shore: "a sea of heads" bobbed in the water there, so he jumped off the Arkansas side and swam to a half-submerged log, where he perched until picked up by a boat. The cold water alone killed some of those who clung to fallen trees and planks. First reports estimated that the *Sultana* was carrying 2,200 passengers overall, and that only 786 had been found alive, but many of those perished from their injuries. Overall, about two-thirds of those who took passage on the *Sultana* did not survive. That proportion held true for the enlisted men, and for the male passengers. Twelve members of a Louisiana family named Spikes were on their way north with the family fortune in gold coin, but the gold went down and eight of the twelve family members died; their family Bible was found in a pile of debris, listing the 1837 marriage of the parents, who were both lost. Eighty percent or more of the crew died in the wreck, however, and of nearly two dozen women aboard no more than two survived. Rank may have had its privileges, for two-thirds of the commissioned army officers on the boat made it to Memphis alive.[43]

Unaware of the disaster upriver, Captain Speed and Captain Williams emptied the camp in "Aubrey Territory" of Union prisoners and sent them home on other transports. Speed had begun delivering Confederate prisoners to their agents on the Big Black River when he informed his sister of a business arrangement that promised a chance "for my getting a hand in the money making war, in which so many are engaged down here." He referred to it too vaguely for the arrangement to involve the ice enterprise he had contemplated with their father, which he might have named overtly, but he implied that he had accumulated enough money for an investment. Before he entered upon his exchange duties, though, he had evidently been depending on his father to stake him in any business venture they undertook. Once he learned of the explosion of the *Sultana*, he fell silent about his business prospects.[44]

A battery of investigations naturally followed, and evidence accumulated of an assortment of bribe offers, but no proof surfaced that any money had actually changed hands. Some blame accrued to the captain of the *Sultana* for allowing his boat to travel after patching one of his boilers at Vicksburg, but he died in the wreck, and overloading was still deemed to be a significant factor in the explosion despite the mended boiler. Captain Speed found himself censured in an early report for putting so many men on the boat: in reply he insisted that he had supported Captain Kerns's effort to have part of the men board another boat, only to be overruled by Williams, but that statement clashed with his personal assurance to General Dana that the boat was not crowded.[45] Speed finally endured the only court-martial associated with the *Sultana,* in which the court found him guilty of negligence and ordered him dismissed from the service. Everyone up the line approved the findings and sentence except Judge Advocate General Joseph Holt, who had approved numerous convictions for treason and murder on much less convincing grounds, but he overturned the court's verdict on logic that was contradicted in the testimony, at least in part. That freed the captain from any consequences, and he resigned immediately.[46]

Forty Union prisoners still remained at Andersonville the day the *Sultana* went down. Two dozen of them languished in the prison hospital, but the others had the stockade to themselves. Knud Hanson, a Norwegian immigrant who had been drafted into the 1st Wisconsin Cavalry seventeen months before, died on April 28 of chronic diarrhea, filling the last marked grave in the vast prison cemetery. Two days later, five cobblers who had volunteered to work in a Confederate quartermaster's shoe shop came back to the prison because the shop had ceased operation. James Wilson's cavalry had passed fifty miles north of the prison on the way to Macon, and had remained in Macon since, observing General Sherman's truce. With Johnston's surrender Wilson grew restless again, and on May 2 he sent Lieutenant Henry Noyes, of his staff, down the Southwestern Railroad with dispatches. The train took on wood and water at Anderson Station, and Noyes stretched his legs while he waited. He noticed a group of Federals standing nearby in ragged attire, listening to a Confederate captain who was trying to convince them to sign their parole forms, so he could send them home. They hesitated, perhaps thinking it a trick, and the aggravated captain warned them that they might still die at Andersonville if they persisted. The train whistle blew to recall the passengers, so Noyes climbed aboard, and the rebel captain — Henry Wirz — finally succeeded in sending those fifteen prisoners to Florida for exchange. The next day he shipped off another half-dozen, but after that Wirz was entirely on his own: the post commander left for his home in Florida, and that night the remains of the garrison decamped after raiding the post storehouses and corral, leaving no food or transportation for the handful of prisoners. Two of those prisoners died on May 4. They were the last of Andersonville's victims, at least among the prisoners; some of their own comrades, probably, dropped those bodies into the trench beside the freshly mounded grave of Knud Hanson, with a few perfunctory shovelfuls of red clay sprinkled over them and no attention to recording their identity.[47]

Wirz, who lived nearby with his family, was the only Confederate of any rank who stayed on at the prison to the bitter end, and for him the end would be very bitter. On his return to Macon, Lieutenant Noyes mentioned his observations at Andersonville, and Wilson sent him back to the deserted post with a guard detail. Wirz was the Confederate most familiar to Andersonville prisoners, because the stockade had been his particular domain; the survivors had seldom seen or heard of the post commanders, quartermasters, or commissaries. It was the Swiss captain with the sinister, sibilant name who represented all the misery they had suffered, although he was not responsible for the breakdown of the exchange system, the crowding, the shortages of food, or the lack of shelter. It was he whom the prisoners hated, and he was the one Union authorities could find. On the morning of May 7 Lieutenant Noyes and his detail arrived at Wirz's home and arrested him while his wife and daughters wailed. Noyes took him to Macon — where, six days later, Wilson's cavalry brought Jefferson Davis in to join him.[48]

Paroled prisoners had been coming back into Union lines for weeks at Wilmington, North Carolina, and sometimes in very rough condition. At Danville and Salisbury, where most of the prisoners had enjoyed dry housing and enough food through the summer of 1864, the diet deteriorated through the winter, and before the exchanges began a day's ration might consist of bread alone. Officers had fared better, sometimes receiving boxes of clothing, shoes, and comfort items from home, with the lack of coffee constituting the worst deprivation, but a few men in every exchange came across the lines too frail to survive the journey to the parole camp at Annapolis, or with just enough strength to reach friendly soil before the light flickered out. The advertised return of prisoners, giving their names, regiments, hospitals, and homes, prompted thousands of inquiries from the families of those who had not yet come back, or who never would.[49] When Vermont newspapers announced the return home of Corporal Alson Blake, after fourteen months as a prisoner, letters flooded into the Milton post office asking if he could supply any information about this or that missing soldier, last heard from at Andersonville. Almost all the men sought in those letters were dead, and some had never made it to prison. A Montpelier woman claimed that the last word from her husband had come from Andersonville, but he had been killed outright at Spotsylvania.[50] Caleb Dodge's family pestered his comrades for more than a year after his capture at Olustee, Florida, trying first to find him and later to confirm reports that he had died at Andersonville in the summer of 1864, only to learn finally that it was true.[51]

With handwritten records scattered across the country, it often took years to learn the fate of those who had died even in friendly custody, like Elisha Douglass, who had succumbed to wounds in a Union hospital in Fredericksburg twelve days into the 1864 campaign; nine months later, New Hampshire's adjutant general could give his widow no information about him, although he had written to the commander of Douglass's regiment and numerous state agents.[52] Sometimes the story of a soldier's end could never be firmly established, and at least one family suffered that uncertainty twice. Gilman Aldrich fell into enemy hands at Williamsburg, early in 1862, and was never seen again, but years later his father heard that Gilman had fallen from the parole boat and drowned in the James River while on his way back to Union lines. Gilman's young brother Asa enlisted in the spring of 1864, against his mother's wishes, and months after Asa's death his family had to reconcile conflicting reports that he had died of disease and that he had been killed in battle.[53]

Once Union forces controlled all of Virginia, survivors of the killed flocked to the battlefields, searching for the graves of their husbands, fathers, sons, and brothers. Soldiers or chaplains often wrote detailed descriptions of gravesites for the convenience of their comrades' kin. All too often the landscape had been drastically altered as the armies leveled forests and lacerated the earth with fortifications, and the resting places of men killed in the final battles were often the easiest to find. The enemy had frequently held the ground in the wake of the earlier battles, burying the Union dead as unknown strangers, and many families already knew they would never be able to find the final resting place of their lost ones. Only after his clerks had spent ten days leafing through captured Confederate records did one Union general manage to locate the grave of a Connecticut man's son, in the cemetery of a Richmond prison.[54]

For many mourners it was enough just to see the grave and decorate it somehow, but often a father or widow simply had to bring the remains home. Ammi Williams, a farmer from Fremont, Ohio, had lost two sons in the war: dysentery killed Joseph in 1862, and Gilbert died when an epidemic decimated his regiment in 1864. Gilbert already lay in the family plot when the war ended, after which the father had Joseph disinterred and brought home to lie beside his brother. Doubting (as many did) the identity of the body in the coffin, he made the mistake of opening the lid to assure himself that he was burying his own son. "I thought there would be some feature that I could recognize," he explained to one of his surviving sons, "but there was nothing except the shape of the forehead and the hair which was distinguishable. The rest was a mass of matter." That last grisly glimpse of his son unnerved him completely. "Almighty God," he gasped, "must we come to this?"[55]

Thanks to the efforts of her husband's friends to mark his grave in the Wilderness, Frances Bixby was able to disinter the body and rebury it near their home in Royalton, Vermont, after the fighting ended. "What a satisfaction it must be to you," a cousin wrote Frances, "that you can visit that grave with that little one." The cousin herself had lost a "dear one" in the war, and lamented that she had been forced to leave him buried on the banks of the Mississippi.[56]

It would have been the disruption in communications and transportation, rather than continued hostilities, that prevented Mrs. Bixby's cousin from transporting a body from the Mississippi, for the war had essentially ended on the eastern half of the continent. "We have nothing left to *Fight*," reported a happy Indiana officer in northern Alabama in early May, and in Kentucky Confederate soldiers were coming in by the score and the hundred to ask for paroles. Tennessee was so secure that a lone sailor from a U.S. gunboat could saunter safely over the Shiloh battlefield, where human bones lay scattered and weathered boards identified graves only by the number of men they contained.[57]

April had not ended when Lieutenant General Richard Taylor, the son of President Zachary Taylor and the commander of all Confederate troops left east of the Mississippi, met with General Canby. Their first interview might have ended things had it not been for the delayed and confusing news of the convention between Sherman and Johnston, and then by the rejection of that convention. On May 4, after those interruptions, the pair convened again at Citronelle, Alabama, thirty miles north of Mobile. From Canby the terms were as generous as Sherman had given, with no formal surrender ceremony before victorious troops: the men would turn their weapons in to their own ordnance officers and be paroled in their own camps over the next few days; then they would go home by units, under their officers, with transportation at the expense of the United States on whatever conveyances remained functioning. Returning to his headquarters at Meridian, Taylor urged his men to abide scrupulously by Canby's terms. "His liberality and fairness make it the duty of each and all of us to faithfully execute our part of the contract," read his last general order. Even the defiant Nathan Bedford Forrest submitted, bidding his horse soldiers farewell at Gainesville, Alabama, on May 9. That same day, Union troops returning to Mobile from McIntosh Bluffs, on the Tombigbee, had their last skirmish with a party of rebels who may not have heard about the surrender. "Gurilas," a Vermont boy called them, and by federal decree they would be considered outlaws. A couple of men died on each side, and each took away their wounded.[58]

That left only the Trans-Mississippi Department with an active Confederate army. Edmund Kirby Smith commanded there, with nominal authority over five states and territories, but his domain spilled into two large Union bailiwicks. His Union counterpart at Saint Louis, John Pope, held sway over the Military Division of the Missouri, which included Missouri, Arkansas, and the Indian Territory, where Smith exercised the least control. No organized Confederate force existed in Missouri, where the greatest danger came from bushwhackers who had turned brigand; Missourians feared another invasion from Sterling Price, but Price's rebels were surrendering all over Arkansas. Stand Watie still commanded a nominal Confederate division of Choctaw, Chickasaw, and Cherokee regiments in the Indian Territory, but they remained idle while their tribal councils pondered peace treaties. Most of Kirby Smith's army occupied distant locations in Louisiana and Texas, which fell within E. R. S. Canby's Union Department of the Gulf. Pope, probably still seeking to rehabilitate the tarnished record he had carried out of the Virginia theater, wrote to Smith as soon as he heard of Lee's surrender and Sherman's armistice to ask him to capitulate, too, gratuitously intimating that the whole weight of the unemployed Union armies would fall on him if he declined. Had Smith consented, Pope would have had the honor of receiving the last Confederate surrender of the war. Instead Smith stalled, perhaps calculating that he could strike a better deal with Canby, but at the same time he was negotiating with Mexican officials in Maximilian's imperial government to seek refuge and employment there for himself and his soldiers if the Confederacy should collapse. On May 9 Smith returned a theatrically indignant refusal to Pope, knowing that it would not reach Saint Louis for some days.[59]

During the winter General Grant had sent Lew Wallace, a major general of known political instincts, to the mouth of the Rio Grande to see if he could not subvert any imperial Mexican alliance. Toward that end Wallace arranged an interview with the two senior Confederate officers in south Texas — Brigadier General James Slaughter and Colonel John Ford — both of whom Wallace described as reluctant Confederates who hoped for an honorable avenue to peace and renewed citizenship. Meeting them late in March, Wallace presented them with tentative terms reflecting the benevolence President Lincoln had been exuding, and they seemed receptive to it, but they suspected that Kirby Smith would stand in the way. In fact it was the commander of the District of Texas, John Walker, who rejected the terms before they ever reached Smith, and the department commander never partook of that discussion. Wallace's mission therefore failed, but because of it an unofficial truce prevailed along the lower Rio Grande through April and into May, and that was just as well for Slaughter and Ford, who could not have collected a thousand fighting men between the Gulf of Mexico and Laredo, two hundred miles away.[60]

Slaughter's territory included most of Texas below San Antonio. He kept his headquarters at Brownsville, thirty miles upriver from the gulf by land, and much farther by the winding river. Union troops had occupied the town the year before, finding it squalid. Matamoras lay on the Mexican side, and Confederates at Brownsville probably enjoyed the same frequent view their Yankee predecessors remembered, of señoritas sauntering down to the river's edge and nonchalantly stripping down in broad daylight for a bath, au naturel. Colonel Ford also lodged in Brownsville, but he kept an outpost of about two hundred cavalry near Palmetto Ranch, half the distance to the mouth of the river. The road to Palmetto Ranch followed roughly parallel to the river, past a place called White's Ranch, ending at Boca Chica, where the Rio Grande opened into the gulf. To the north, between Boca Chica and the long sand bank known as Padre Island, sat the smaller island of Brazos Santiago, where a Union brigade had wintered over.[61]

Colonel Theodore Barrett, of the 62nd U.S. Colored Troops, had commanded at Brazos Santiago since early April, with something fewer than two thousand men of his own and another black regiment, a battalion of dismounted cavalry recently recruited among loyal Texans, and the 34th Indiana, which had gone to war in 1861 wearing a muted Zouave uniform. Colonel Barrett had never led troops in combat, and had never seen any action himself, although that was no fault of his; he had commanded a company of Minnesota troops on guard duty in Missouri for a year before taking command of a regiment of freed Missouri slaves in 1863. The war was obviously about to end, given all the news coming into Brazos Santiago on supply ships, and the thirty-year-old Barrett may have dreaded missing his last chance to seize some glory. Nothing else seems to explain his sudden decision to make a stab at Brownsville, which his predecessor had recently been discouraged from trying, but on the stormy evening of May 11, 1865, Barrett risked ferrying more than three hundred men of his own regiment, along with the little Texas battalion, across to Boca Chica, whence he put them on the road up the river. Barrett's lieutenant colonel, David Branson, led a four-hour night march to White's Ranch, which an Iowa lieutenant had described the previous summer as consisting of "a little house the size of a hen coop" lying amid "patches of cactus and chapperal on a barren sandy plain." Branson expected to catch the forward Confederate picket post there, but his trap sprang on thin air.[62]

After hiding in the brush until daylight, the three hundred Missouri freedmen and Unionist Texans pressed on to Palmetto Ranch, but by then suspicious rebel cavalrymen had trotted out to see what was up. Encountering many times their number in Yankee infantry, they fell back shooting, alerting the rest of the outpost at Palmetto Ranch. At noon Union skirmishers came up over the hill where the ranch sat, driving the still-outnumbered rebel cavalry away. There Branson rested his troops until the middle of the afternoon, when the Texas colonel in charge of the outpost returned with all his collected pickets, and by nightfall those Confederates had pushed the intruders all the way back to White's Ranch. Branson sent back to Brazos Santiago for help, and Barrett ferried another two hundred of the 34th Indiana across in the darkness, accompanying them personally and marching through the night.[63]

With the added weight of the Indiana detachment, the tide of battle turned again. Barrett reached Branson's combined force at White's Ranch around dawn of May 13: allowing the men who had been marching all night half an hour to cook some coffee, he ordered Branson to proceed with most of his three hundred. Branson reached the hill at Palmetto early in the morning, but the Confederates made no special effort to defend it that time, and the Federals all stacked arms there to eat breakfast while the 34th Indiana caught up. An hour or two later Barrett resumed the march, throwing two of the weary Indiana companies ahead as skirmishers and later adding the two companies of Texas recruits to their line. They skirmished forward a couple of miles over the course of several hours with the detachment of Barrett's regiment supporting them, but then Colonel Ford came up with some more men from Brownsville, giving him a total force that he calculated at no more than three hundred, including a few volunteers to operate a battery of guns. That stiffened the resistance enough that by the middle of the afternoon Barrett decided to fall back to a hill a mile from Palmetto Ranch, where the Indiana regiment waited, and everyone sat down to eat another meal.[64]

While they ate, rebel cavalry rode straight for them from Brownsville, and a smaller force started circling around their right, as though to gain a loop in the river behind them and cut off their retreat. Ford's artillery started to play on them, and Barrett ordered a retreat, hastening both regiments to a quickstep, and then to a double-quick, to reach the bend of the river before the enemy did. The skirmishers tried to hold off the main attack, and both regiments of infantry made it to Palmetto Ranch and around the river bend safely, but the flanking column cut off the skirmishers and captured dozens of them. Barrett replaced them with two companies of black troops, adding more until half the regiment was covering the retreat. Once the main flanking threat had been averted, the Yankees slackened their pace to a steady route-step, and Ford pressed his more numerous prey as long as daylight lasted, all the way to Boca Chica. General Slaughter finally joined him near there with ten dozen more cavalry, but they satisfied themselves with driving the enemy to their boats. Colonel Barrett, who had seemed ambitious to report winning the last battle of the war against Confederate troops, had to be content with boasting that his regiment had fired the last volley, albeit while in retreat.[65]

Leaving John Schofield behind while Johnston's troops disbanded at Greensboro, General Sherman pointed his army north. By May 9 his men were marching through Petersburg, and two days later they passed through Richmond on the way to Washington. The Army of the Potomac was headed the same way, and once the two armies crossed paths the march turned into a race. With no reason for haste save rivalry, they covered as much as twenty-six miles a day under a sun hot enough to prostrate men by the dozens, when even the idle soldiers around Washington vied with each other for some shade. Rumors of men dying to appease the pride of corps commanders embittered veterans who had expected a leisurely jaunt toward a hero's welcome.[66]

It was mainly the officers, and particularly field or staff officers on horseback, who found enough leisure during that marathon march to tour some of the more storied sites they passed along the roads the Army of the Potomac had followed. They reached the field of Spotsylvania during the anniversary of that two-week confrontation, and a Michigan surgeon rode out to the Mule Shoe, where he marveled at trees that had been cut down by musketry. He revealed some of the competitive spirit that had always marked the Eastern and Western soldiers' impressions of each other when he noted that he "saw more signs of *running* than fighting," especially on the Chancellorsville battlefield, where the moldy remnants of two-year-old knapsacks, blankets, and other impedimenta lay scattered all over the forest floor. The doctor spotted graves everywhere.[67] An Ohio lieutenant who visited Spotsylvania on the same day as the Michigan surgeon also reported finding hundreds of skeletons lying on the ground, never having been buried at all.[68]

The head of Sherman's army started pouring into Alexandria on May 19, while much of the Army of the Potomac had already camped a few miles to the west, around Bailey's Crossroads. Conflicting rumors predicted that they were all about to be mustered out and sent home, or that the men or regiments with a year or more to serve might be sent to Texas, or even into Mexico, to deal with Maximilian; a few considered reenlisting for a year, just to take advantage of that opportunity to see the West. Amid the excitement and uncertainty of their arrival, they learned that the War Department planned a final grand review of Meade's army, Sherman's, and the troops that had served in the Shenandoah Valley; as early as May 20 engineers were planning the route and inspecting bridges to be sure they could bear the weight.[69]

When the newspapers announced the Grand Review, everyone seemed to want to go. For the sake of the soldiers, Mr. Raymond of the *New York Times* thought it desirable to have as many spectators as possible, and he urged all the railroads within reach of Washington to issue cheaper excursion tickets. Generals differed on the wisdom of summoning their families to witness so historic an event. Robert McAllister, a brigade commander in the Second Corps, telegraphed for his wife and daughter to come at once, advising them that they needed only a pillow for each of them, as he could provide the rest of their bedding. Alpheus Williams, of the Twentieth Corps, advised his daughters not to come at all: it was, he wrote, "nothing but a march through Washington" by multitudes of men in blue, "all looking alike, for hours and hours, till everybody will be tired to death of seeing soldiers." At first, when he was just starting from North Carolina, Sherman had hoped his wife would bring his family to see the army enter Washington because he thought the sight would be "a prize in the memory" to their children, but the secretary of war's insulting reaction to Sherman's broad surrender terms pursued the general during his march through Virginia: along the way he learned that Henry Halleck had proposed instructing other generals under Sherman's command not to obey his orders, and Edwin Stanton had released Halleck's telegram to the public press. Long before he reached the Potomac, Sherman wrote his wife not to meet him in Washington, after all.[70]

The review was to start on Tuesday, May 23, with the Virginia armies, and continue the next day with Sherman's, but rain or showers prevailed during the four preceding days, and it appeared that mud would spoil the splendor of the show. The city did fill up, as the commander of Fifth Corps artillery learned to his dismay at two o'clock on a dreadfully humid Sunday morning, when the desk clerk at Willard's Hotel roused him to say that he had been assigned the wrong room, asking him to surrender it to five young ladies who had just arrived. "Many a poor visitor took his rest in a chair for want of a bed," reported a Wisconsin colonel, who noted that plenty of soldiers touring the town curled up in a doorway to sleep out of the rain. General Halleck, who had moved to Richmond for his new assignment, offered the use of his Washington house to Grant's wife, who was stuck in a steamy hotel herself, with her children.[71]

As though on cue, the sky cleared off completely early Tuesday morning, and a light breeze dried most of the mud. Meade's infantry rose long before dawn and marched up the Columbia Pike to the Long Bridge, crossing the Potomac there and following Maryland Avenue toward the Capitol. The Ninth Corps was already camped on that side, and had formed in ranks on East Capitol Street by six o'clock, with three hours to wait. A couple of hours later, hundreds of Washington's schoolchildren climbed the stairs to staging on the north side of the Capitol, immaculate in bright white, and armed with bouquets to throw at the soldiers as they passed. Though still draped and beribboned in mourning for Lincoln, the building had been decorated with flags and slogans welcoming the heroes home. One conspicuous banner had been stretched across the north end of the Capitol, announcing that the one debt the nation could never repay was the one it owed to its soldiers. Waiting to turn his artillery brigade into the line of march, Colonel Charles Wainwright wondered whether the congressmen for whom the banner presumably spoke would make no effort to even try repaying that debt, since they had already determined the feat to be impossible.[72]

A canvas-topped reviewing stand draped in red, white, and blue had been built in front of the White House, where the route would jog up Fifteenth Street and down G Street before the nation's chief men; in response to the nation's first presidential assassination, a phalanx from the Veteran Reserve Corps stood before the stand with fixed bayonets. As nine o'clock approached, the president and his cabinet filed in. Edwin Stanton perched on President Johnson's right, and General Grant settled in on his left while his two young sons flitted about in light-colored suits and caps. Gideon Welles and Admiral Dahlgren took seats on the other side of Grant.[73]

At 9:00 A.M. sharp, General Meade and his staff started down Pennsylvania Avenue from the Capitol to begin the parade. The cavalry followed, without Phil Sheridan, who had already left Washington for his new assignment in Texas. Increasing intervals separated regiments, brigades, and divisions, with as much as three minutes between corps, but the horsemen who led the procession rode unevenly, sometimes cantering ahead to close up, and that caused the ranks behind them to bunch and stretch like an accordion. Making his usual spectacle, George Custer in particular allowed his horse to prance proudly and bolt forward occasionally, reining him in with what may have been feigned difficulty. Behind the cavalry came the engineers, the provost guard, and the Ninth Corps with the first of the infantry, twenty men abreast. Ahead of the wounded Robert Potter's division, still under Simon Griffin, marched the combined bands of the 56th Massachusetts and the 9th New Hampshire, blaring a musical program they had planned without much joint rehearsal. They strode between the overflowing sidewalks of Pennsylvania Avenue playing the "Faust Quickstep" and the "Ypsilanti Quickstep," and when they reached the president's reviewing stand they planned to launch into the "Door Latch Quickstep." They marched so briskly in the mounting morning heat to catch up with the cavalry — at nearly a double-quick, between selections — that the final notes of the "Ypsilanti" had just faded away when they came upon the bunting-shaded bleachers. The bandmasters somehow confused their signals, inviting a dissonant clash instead of the intricate "Door Latch," and to smother their blunder the disappointed musicians lapsed back into the more familiar "Faust," missing their cherished chance to distinguish themselves.[74]

The bigwigs ignored the fumbled melody, if they noticed it at all. Some brigades had collected dozens of drummers and fifers to precede them — Walt Whitman was able to recognize "Lannigan's Ball" in the cacophony — and the din they made alongside the cheering crowds may have dulled the dignitaries' eardrums. Once past the stand, the Ninth Corps veered left, winding its way back to camp by a roundabout route. Behind it came the Nineteenth Corps, from the valley, or at least one division of it, marching with the Ninth Corps infantry and trotting after it, once beyond sight of the reviewing stand. The Fifth Corps swung onto the avenue right behind the Ninth Corps artillery brigade. They found the buildings decorated with wreaths and the avenue crossed with more banners; spectators hung from windows and balconies, and shouted from the streets to men they recognized. Bouquets of flowers soared toward the commanders and their staffs in a blizzard that diminished to squalls and flurries as the endless procession outlasted the expectations of bystanders who had not fathomed how far seventy thousand men might sprawl. Those standing on the steps of the fortress-like Treasury Building, just before the White House, could see more than a mile of Pennsylvania Avenue filled with troops from the time General Meade reached them with the head of the column until well past the middle of the afternoon. Most of the soldiers glanced toward the Treasury, where a sign identified the flag John Wilkes Booth had grasped, or snagged, when he leaped to the stage of Ford's Theater.[75]

The Fifth Corps rolled past the reviewing stand and bent back onto Pennsylvania, toward the narrower streets of old Georgetown, crossing back into Virginia on the aqueduct to make room for the Second Corps, which concluded that day's parade. These men and the horses that served them had been marching, shuffling, and waiting in the streets east of the Capitol for as much as eight hours. For all the renown of the Second Corps, its ranks included thousands who had seen only the last six months of the war, or as little as six weeks. Most of those who had bought the corps its good name had stopped a bullet somewhere between Antietam and the Bloody Angle, but a few tanned veterans who had repulsed Longstreet at Cemetery Ridge still marched amid the thousands of bounty men and substitutes, some of whom had run at Reams's Station. The recruits in Robert McAllister's brigade had stood firm with the veterans at Hatcher's Run, less than four months before, and those five regiments trod at the tail of the column, followed by their artillery brigade.

After the batteries had passed, the crowd swelled into the street behind them. Some inevitably stood watching until the last caisson rolled out of sight, knowing that it was the world's last glimpse of the Army of the Potomac.[76]

The armies of the West had gathered in the streets converging on the Capitol by sunrise on Wednesday. The morning dawned unseasonably cool, but soon warmed enough to raise dust from what had been puddles and congealed mud the morning before. The president, cabinet, and generals took the same seats they had held throughout the previous day. Additional banners had arisen during the night to welcome these men specifically, and again the windows and balconies bulged with waving throngs, while others stood on the rooftops. Inevitable comparisons made their way into that day's diaries, like the predominance of forage caps and kepis in Tuesday's review, and the preference for slouch hats among Sherman's Westerners; only the transplanted Twentieth Corps stuck to the caps they had worn at Chancellorsville and Gettysburg. In the Western regiments men seemed generally taller and more rugged, probably because they had spent the winter marching instead of hibernating, but some attributed it to the "American type" that prevailed west of the Appalachians. Given their reputation for informality bordering on anarchy, Sherman's nomads marched in surprisingly good order, albeit with more faded uniforms and ragged cuffs. The color guards in particular drew admiring cheers because of their tattered, often shredded flags, although time and the elements had wrought worse damage to them than shot and shell. Colonel Wainwright deduced that Sherman's men marched so well because relatively light casualties had left him with a solid majority of experienced, well-trained troops: judging perhaps by the infrequency of fresh uniforms, Wainwright estimated 80 percent of the whole as veterans. Grant's brutal campaigns, meanwhile, had forced the Army of the Potomac to swell up with recruits, at least half of whom had not carried their weapons for a year yet.[77]

Once he had saluted the president from the head of the column, General Sherman doubled back with his staff to take his place in the reviewing stand and receive the salutes of his two army commanders. President Johnson, Grant, and the department heads rose to greet him with extended hands and warm smiles when he climbed up among them. Sherman shook every hand until he came to Stanton, before whom his face turned stern and rigid; one onlooker thought he bowed slightly in acknowledgment of Stanton's presence, but he left the war secretary's hand dangling conspicuously in the air. Observers in a subordinate stand across the street caught the slight through their opera glasses, gasped, and began buzzing the news to those who had missed it. Sherman took his place at the end of the front row, as far from Stanton as he could sit.[78]

In the heat of late morning and early afternoon the men who had subdued Georgia and the Carolinas moved through a thin haze of dust that lent an ethereal atmosphere to their last march, as though the gauzy dimension of unimaginable experience veiled them from their audience. They elicited louder cheers than their comrades had heard the day before; like the rest of the nation, the people shouldering together along the parade route had read and heard nothing but glorious news from Sherman's exploits over the past eight months, while the Army of the Potomac had been maneuvering ingloriously and with barely perceptible progress against Robert E. Lee. In the time it had taken Grant to capture one withered rebel army, Sherman had conquered three entire states with fewer men, and the feats of his army seemed somehow more heroic. The Westerners marched in near-perfect order, but with an ease that had not been obvious among Tuesday's columns. They bowed and nodded gratefully to those lining the sides of the avenue. If the infantry and artillery provoked the most noise, though, it was the pack train following the different divisions in Henry Slocum's Army of Georgia that won the broadest smiles. In the course of the review Sherman was moving his camps over the river to the more spacious ground outside the city, so the mules ambled beneath their customary burden of provisions, pots, and pans — on top of which there usually rode a chicken liberated from some Carolina family, or a raccoon, rooster, possum, or squirrel, kept as a pet, with cows, goats, or dogs trailing behind. A cavalcade of genuine bummers brought up the rear, perched on their own mules or ponies and accompanied by the erstwhile slaves who had followed them across as many as four states.[79]

Each army required more than six hours to pass the president's gaze, although many of the batteries had been left out, and neither the noncommissioned staff nor the detailed men had been required to march. A Fifth Corps hospital steward who enjoyed the option of remaining in camp did so, finding enough satisfaction in the vast panorama of camps he could see from the heights of the former Lee mansion, at Arlington. A commissary sergeant with the Twentieth Corps made no effort to watch the review, even while seeking refreshment in a Pennsylvania Avenue saloon; he was sick of reviews, he insisted, and never wanted to see another one again. Yet for all the long day's march and the inevitable hours of waiting, most would not have missed this culminating celebration of peace and victory. One Pennsylvanian judged it the most magnificent sight he had ever witnessed. A Maine corporal who regretted only that

Lincoln had not lived to sit in the reviewing stand surmised that this grand gathering of the Republic's two great armies would live forever in the memory of those who took part in it. "Talk about big Things," scribbled one of those late-war volunteers in the Army of the Potomac, on the evening of May 23; "this takes The Cap sheaf off of all big times." For four years a soldier had not amounted to much in the eyes of his countrymen, in spite of all the patriotic rhetoric and the brandishing of flags: the mobs of enlisted men seemed indistinguishable from one another, and officers came by the gross. During those two jubilant days in May it had finally become a matter of intense congratulation to be wearing the blue suit with the brass buttons, however frayed or devoid of stripes and braid, and most of those who felt that pride would never let it go, even if they had striven mightily to avoid the call to arms.[80]

With the final clatter of their heels and wagon wheels on the paving stones of Pennsylvania Avenue, the reconstructed remnants of the fabled armies faded into memory, disappearing from the front pages of the newspapers and eventually from the suburbs of Washington City. The craftsman in his shop who had fretted over finding a substitute, the mother who had worried that her teenaged son might succumb to the martial spirit, and the veteran pegging his tent on a gentle slope near Alexandria or Silver Spring all began to absorb the incomprehensible — that the war that had dominated their lives for four years was over and done with, as quick as that. There would be no more mythic battles, or killing marches, or pestilential encampments. A few days after the Grand Review, headlines proclaimed the surrender of Kirby Smith, who had sent a subordinate to New Orleans to bring Canby's terms to him, and Smith signed them onboard a gunboat in Galveston Harbor on June 2, before departing for exile in Mexico rather than submit to the possibility of prosecution at home. Troops from Brazos Santiago had already occupied Brownsville the day before, and United States warships entered Galveston Harbor, at last, on June 5. On June 23 Brigadier General Stand Watie signed a new treaty with the federal government at Doaksville, in the Choctaw Nation, assenting to peaceful deportment until the grand council could ratify the agreement in September. After that, the only organized Confederates on the entire continent consisted of no more than a few hundred border horsemen riding with Jo Shelby, who was making his way to Mexico with Sterling Price and a collection of prominent fellow Missourians. A few other generals and politicians followed them, crossing the border in late June, just ahead of the Yankees.[81]

Back in Washington, the War Department had already ordered all white soldiers mustered out who had four months or less left to serve, and that spelled freedom for those hundreds of thousands who had enlisted in the spring and summer of 1862. The same order applied to the one-year recruits from the summer of 1864, some of whom had served only eight months. Regiments and batteries familiar to every adult in their home states began winking out of existence within days of the Grand Review: batteries turned in their guns, caissons, and horses, and officers pored over the records of their companies and regiments to complete their final muster rolls and get their men paid.[82]

All the paperwork took a few days, or weeks. While they waited, unoccupied soldiers sought passes to visit Washington, where they gawked at the buildings or bought an unaccustomed drink, and with more drinks came the search for women, which often proved fruitful in a city crawling with prostitutes. A favorite diversion, at least for those with shoulder straps or connections, was the trial of those accused in the conspiracy to murder Lincoln. The proceedings were held in the old penitentiary, under the reliable animus of Major General David Hunter, the vandal of the Shenandoah Valley. Officers who had questioned the legality of the military tribunal had been excused from participating in the court, which would have been held behind locked doors if one of those officers had not gone to the president about it, and the unwashed defendants were displayed on a raised platform in their rumpled, malodorous clothing, where the public and the fourth estate could observe their manifest villainy at leisure. The wife of a colonel awaiting discharge dropped in at the Washington Arsenal to see the wretches in captivity, reporting to her son that "they are the ugliest looking set I ever saw."[83]

The glee at going home did not entirely quell complaints that the War Department was discharging the troops at Washington to save the cost of paying them until they reached home. The loss of a few days' pay mattered more to officers, who earned several times as much as any of the enlisted men, and surgeons seemed especially concerned about drawing army pay as long as they could, calculating that they could never realize that much in private practice.[84] Any married man, or any who did not live on a family farm, had cause to worry about how to earn a living once he was liberated from military service. Already the closing of the war had slackened industries that supplied the armies, and soon the North would be mobbed with veterans looking for work. Henry Brown, a lieutenant in the 1st U.S. Colored Troops, hoped to remain with his regiment for a while yet, since black soldiers were being retained as a means of providing them with support; "I do not wish to be suddenly thrown out of employment with the two or three hundred thousand others that will also be relieved," he told his mother. Brevet Major General Adin Underwood, who had been an attorney before the war, had to contend with his wife, who opposed his return to the bar because he had made so little money. Neither did she want him turning to manufacturing, fearing that he would not find that satisfying, but, with one leg lamed and shortened by a bullet, he could choose no more active profession.[85] James Brisbin, who had risen from private to brevet major general in the volunteer service, used his friendship with Ben Wade's son to lobby for the vacant position of assistant secretary of war; Senator Wade did not facilitate that appointment, however, and Brisbin had to make do with a captain's commission in the Regular Army.[86]

More common than those men of greater means was the tenant farmer who had tried to build a stake from his bounty money and army pay, only to realize at war's end that his wife had had to spend most of the cash to satisfy wartime inflation. The price of land in New England had risen so high that a young man coming home from the army could not hope to buy his own farm, even with parental assistance; the best a veteran could do was strike a bargain with his father to take on the home place in return for old-age security. Out in Minnesota, the price of sheep was dropping so fast that farmers had to rush them to market to break even, while grain, oxen, and horses cost more than ever.[87]

In such an economic climate the army seemed more attractive than it might have otherwise, and indeed many a man had originally enlisted in the hope of bettering his pecuniary situation, or surviving an acute financial crisis. For most, though, that illusion had dissolved, and they itched to go home regardless of the economic conditions. Deep in Dixie and on the plains many who had anticipated an early release from their commitments at the close of the conflict learned to their dismay that much would still be required of them. Up on the North Platte River, in what was still Dakota Territory, Kansas cavalrymen guarding the Overland Stage Road wondered when they might be sent home, but they had yet to endure another summer of peril and an occasional skirmish with the Cheyenne or Sioux. Once he heard of all his old comrades coming home, a young disabled veteran who had taken advantage of the pay and benefits of the Veteran Reserve Corps thoroughly resented being held to his term of service, and a Maine corporal for whom the Grand Review had marked a welcome ending reported ubiquitous grumbling at the discovery that the men in his regiment were expected to serve out the second half of their enlistment.[88] After only a few months of reefing topsails in howling gales and broiling under a tropical sun, a young sailor from Vermont yearned to exchange the Florida Keys for the Champlain Valley, but he would wait a while longer. A veteran from farther down that same valley had just accepted a commission in a black regiment, and as peace came he faced the prospect of nearly three more years in uniform.[89]

Exhilaration at their better fortune sometimes overwhelmed the homeward-bound troops camping along the Potomac, and the air would occasionally ring with spontaneous whooping and cheering at nothing in particular. An amiable insubordination gradually supplanted the discipline that had come so grudgingly when first they went to war, but after the major landmarks of demobilization they grew pensive, realizing already that the most memorable experience of their lives had come and gone. In the absence of danger their interlude as soldiers seemed once again romantic beyond all imagination, as it had in the camps where they first gathered. An unexpected sadness attended the pending dissolution of regiments, which would abruptly sunder friendships forged under intense tribulation, and men raised on dirt roads beyond the sound of a train whistle expected their parting to be permanent. The early evenings of late spring filled them with these bittersweet reflections, and most of the encampments around the capital acknowledged the sentiment with their own rustic illuminations whenever they received their monthly candle ration. The Grand Review, the turning in of equipment, or the last mustering for pay often sparked such a display, and as darkness settled each pair of soldiers would drive a bayonet into the ground at the head of their tent, insert a candle in the socket, and light it. Each tent would glow like a lantern, and as regiment after regiment followed suit the effect would spread, until the landscape glimmered for miles around. "Oh," wrote a sentimental bugler to his sister, "I wish you could see it." Elaborating on the concept, whole divisions stuck candles in the muzzles of their rifles and held nighttime dress parades. Converted to peaceful utility as cumbersome candlesticks and held at shoulder arms, the muskets described a flickering battleground ballet, with regiments and brigades wheeling into line, parading en masse, and dividing into fragments again in a forest of flame. Nostalgic country boys who would never see such sights again thought the spectacle grand and dreamy, and knew it was something they could remember forever.[90]

Epilogue

❦ Some of the veterans came home to celebrations and parades, applauded by clamoring crowds and escorted by firemen and militia eager to greet anyone else in uniform, but in most communities the enthusiasm for extravagant homecoming festivities had waned over four years. The governor and a few political aspirants might praise a returning regiment at the statehouse, and treat the officers to a meal at a local hotel, but the enlisted men usually retired to a deserted draft rendezvous to wait for less palatable fare and their final pay.[1] For most, the war ended with a journey by train and stagecoach, often followed by a visit to a livery stable or a long walk to a familiar house, where life resumed with a round of visiting, courting, and farm chores, as though it had never been interrupted. The day after reaching home, or the day after that, men with limbs still stiff from old wounds took up scythes to help their fathers and brothers get the hay in.[2]

Frequently the return proved less joyous. A German immigrant who had enlisted for a year in the autumn of 1864 regretted having to come home at all, especially after he discovered that his local bounty had never been paid, and that his wife was "more of a battle-axe than ever." A Michigan farmer whose march through Georgia and the Carolinas had led him to cherish the peace and solitude of his woodland homestead knew that his easily discontented wife hated the isolation, and he had already resigned himself to selling out for her sake. A more vagabond veteran, meanwhile, wanted to profit from the appreciated value of his Minnesota farm and start over on cheaper land even farther west, and when his wife resisted being uprooted from another new community he intimated that he would move on without her. Hints of infidelities confessed or discovered occasionally marred the correspondence of soldiers who were about to come home, and it was not always the lonely wife who aroused suspicion. A middle-aged lieutenant from Maine with a wife and several children had to face their neighbor's teenaged daughter, who named him as the father of the child she had borne about nine months after his last furlough.[3]

In her Minnesota community Nellie Brown rejoiced to see the streets filled with men again, and to watch neglected farms blossom back to life, but she detected an ominous uneasiness among the veterans, as though they had grown too accustomed to excitement and adventure to care for tilling the soil. Minnesota swarmed with recent immigrants, she added, and as many of them may have come from Mrs. Brown's New England as from the Old World, looking for cheaper, more level, more arable land where municipal bounty appropriations had not driven property taxes sky high. Hearing corrupted explanations of the Homestead Act, sometimes in combination with dubious real estate promotions, soldiers discharged in the spring of 1865 believed they could buy farm-sized tracts of land in the West for as little as twenty dollars in surveying expenses, so long as they made some improvements, and there would be no taxes for the first five years. Army officers with entrepreneurial instincts often followed the immigrants, hoping to find some lucrative market among them.[4]

From the upper Mississippi Mrs. Brown saw only the edge of that flood, for although her town and others along the river were filled with strangers, most migrants kept moving into the western portions of her state and Iowa, and into Dakota Territory. Little houses were popping up, and horse-drawn mowing machines were turning the wild grass into hay all across prairies that no one but Sioux hunting parties had traveled a few years before. Some of those Sioux had returned, causing a few of the settlers to regret having come, but soldiers freed from duty east of the Mississippi marched west to protect the newcomers and the roads they traveled. Veterans who had reenlisted too late to go home with their comrades, or who had secured army commissions in a quest for career opportunities, settled into distant, obscure little posts on the plains of Kansas or Nebraska, along the upper Missouri, or in Albert Bierstadt landscapes among the Rockies.[5] Railroad executives and investors ventured west to examine the progress and the potential dividends of the Union Pacific. In the last days of that first summer after the war, the Butterfield Stage Line opened a new route through the tallgrass prairie of central Kansas to Denver, along the Smoky Hill River. Farmers in Abilene, Salina, and Ellsworth put up hundreds of tons of hay in anticipation of daily coach traffic, and streams of wagons carried supplies and goods to New Mexico or the forts in the mountains.[6]

With no war news to thrill the public in bold headlines, it was west-ward expansion, the laying of the transatlantic cable, and the amenities at the various watering places in the East that earned headlines that sum-mer, with an occasional report on political activity in the conquered states and the progress of the new Freedmen's Bureau. Republican editors and politicians tried to keep the war fever alive with excerpts of Henry Wirz's trial or accounts of the "disloyal" attitudes held by pardoned Confeder-ates, and they denounced opposition to the Republican agenda — in-cluding early arguments for universal male suffrage — as evidence of the "Copperhead" spirit they had scorned as treason only months before. The Democratic press continued its own wartime tone, as well, characterizing Republicans as "Union Leaguers" who were clinging to public sinecures and serving the interests of the rich. The interests of those rich men, as many a Democratic sheet explained, included the tax-free proceeds of government bonds they had bought to fund the war, which the farmer and workingman would have to redeem with taxes on everything they bought or owned; the only way to resolve that inequity would be to repu-diate the federal debt, and repudiation would compete with citizenship and suffrage for the freed slave as the next principal topic for political mastication.[7]

An Illinois soldier finishing up his enlistment in the capital of Alabama that spring had seen so many thousands of displaced freedmen that he could predict the first major problem the country would face — namely, "what to do with the nigger." That topic nevertheless drew little attention for seven months after Lee's surrender, either from an unsympathetic ad-ministration or from a public too relieved by the return of peace to con-sider the people whose condition had been the cause of the war.[8]

Andrew Johnson seemed to be following the forgiving example of Abraham Lincoln when, as early as May 29, 1865, he issued an amnesty proclamation to most Southern rebels. He also appeared to act as Lincoln would have wished when, between May 29 and July 13, he named provi-sional governors for all seven Confederate states that did not already have loyal governors whom Lincoln had either appointed or recognized. As he installed those governors, Johnson called on them to hold constitutional conventions aimed at restoring their states' "constitutional relations to the Federal Government," with delegates to be elected by those who had taken the amnesty oath. That snatched the reformation of loyal govern-ments from the hands of Congress, which was evidently Johnson's inten-tion — as it had at least seemed to be Lincoln's, in the final week of his life. The president tried that summer to persuade Southern leaders to support token suffrage rights for the most educated black citizens, merely to un-dermine Radical opposition and facilitate acceptance of the new state governments. The Thirty-Ninth Congress would not meet until December, and those members who wished to impose the Republican agenda on returning states feared that Reconstruction might be effected in time to challenge their veto-proof majority at the first session, so Radicals started organizing their counteroffensive before Johnson announced his second provisional governor.[9]

Virginia needed no proclamation, already having the Peirpoint government in place at Alexandria when the war ended. Throughout the war that vestigial legislature had been filled mainly by loyal men from the counties of what became West Virginia, but by administration recognition it remained the governing body of the eastern half of the state after its partition, and in a special session in the old capitol at Richmond that June those minority legislators scheduled an October election for vacancies in the General Assembly of the Old Dominion, and for Congress. In those elections candidates who had supported secession or served in the Confederate army won many of the seats, and sometimes by overwhelming margins. The new legislature therefore bore a decidedly conservative flavor, however willing its members might be to bow to federal authority, and in their first session they addressed the social issue of transient, unemployed freedmen with more emphasis on control than on liberty. Their solution was to outlaw vagrancy, specifying a jail sentence for anyone without evident employment, or who refused to work for "the usual and common wages given to other laborers." That not only rid the roads of suspicious itinerants and provided planters with a more motivated labor pool, but it stripped the prospective plantation hand of any leverage in negotiating for higher pay. Wanderers, and anyone who held out for better wages, would simply be bound over to the sheriff. No sooner had the bill become law than Virginia farmers, who had been complaining about the lack of willing workers, reported a sudden wave of freedmen signing annual labor contracts.[10]

Similarly repressive measures soon appeared across the South, including enticement laws that made it a crime for anyone to lure workers away with an offer of higher wages, or for a laborer to leave one employer for a more generous one. Patrician Southerners who had shuddered at the prospect of racial equality, and had lobbied in May for gradual emancipation as the best they could hope for, suddenly realized a means of avoiding practical emancipation altogether.[11]

Within weeks of Johnson's first proclamation, North Carolinians who claimed to have remained loyal during the war complained that President Johnson was rapidly pardoning all the state's rebel leaders who were not covered by his amnesty, and warned that they were likely to dominate the constitutional convention in that state. Across the former Confederacy,

Johnson's pardons and apparent sympathies seemed to restore a spirit of defiance and bitterness to a population that had been almost entirely subdued by crushing military defeat the previous spring. According to those who described themselves as loyal, only rigorous application of the confiscation laws could stop such antebellum aristocrats from restoring the ancien régime.[12]

He who had been a slave might now be free, at least in name, but he was not necessarily safe if he chose to exercise the independence that freedom implies. John Richard Dennett, a young correspondent for *The Nation*, began a nine-month-long private inspection tour of the South less than three months after Lee's surrender, and early in his ambitious sojourn he learned that random violence maintained the subservience of the nominally liberated bondsmen in North Carolina. The officer who served as the Freedmen's Bureau superintendent at Greensboro reported that six black victims had been shot over the summer, with three fatalities and one man crippled. At least one assault was reported every day, he added, "always without sufficient cause," and he predicted that if the troops were ever withdrawn from the South "a reign of violence and oppression" would descend on the region. His counterparts in other states agreed, and congressional investigators found widespread reports, spanning the breadth of the onetime slave states, of brutal whippings and other cruelties inflicted as punishment for perceived insubordination or negligence, with frequent accounts of murder. Nor did the danger come entirely from former rebels: the commander of federal troops in Tennessee detected the most violent antagonism toward freedmen in the Unionist population of the eastern part of the state, where few slaves had been held.[13]

Dennett, a Massachusetts man, found it a common belief in Virginia by August of 1865 that the South would soon be fully represented in Congress, and that either Congress would then restore slavery "in some way" or the Supreme Court would declare uncompensated emancipation unconstitutional. Residents and observers in the South corroborated as much, testifying to the manifest aim of using the vagrancy laws and other infringements to reduce the freed slave to a condition worse than slavery, in which his labor could still be exploited without the expense of supporting him; they said it was also commonly believed that conservative congressmen from both sections would combine to repudiate the national debt. Judging from the political stances of favored candidates, and of those who finally did win, those were not unreasonable expectations. Recognition of the eleven former Confederate states would have seriously threatened the ultimate ratification of the Thirteenth Amendment, and had President Johnson's personal brand of Reconstruction not galvanized the Radicals to aggressive action, a much more conservative Congress might have convened that December.[14]

As President Lincoln had warned the peace commissioners at Hampton Roads, though, Congress had the ultimate right to determine whether a particular member had been legitimately elected. When Congress finally met, the Radicals caucused with other Republicans to simply ignore the Southern representatives, refusing to hear their objections on the grounds that they were not members, and Thaddeus Stevens of Pennsylvania almost immediately proposed a joint committee of Congress to oversee Reconstruction. From his unfortunate inaugural address, Andrew Johnson had maintained (as Abraham Lincoln always had) that no state had ever left the Union, because he insisted that secession was illegal. Two weeks into the new session, however, Stevens outlined his theory that the Southern states should be treated as territories, or conquered provinces, without rights of representation until readmitted by Congress. Evidently Stevens applied the same logic to Tennessee, although he had not made that objection the year before, when President Lincoln chose a running mate from that state.[15]

Executive pardons and opposition to equal political rights moved Northern citizens of a Radical bent to adopt the late Copperhead opinion that the war had been a complete failure, and even moderate Republicans regretted the pardons that were meant to restore the political rights of some of the most rabid secessionists, whose confidence instantly revived. A Unionist judge in Alabama warned President Johnson personally that the ex-rebels there had boasted they would kill all the Union men once the troops left. Stevens would use the reaction to Johnson's lenient Reconstruction policies to mobilize a congressional supermajority that would neutralize and reverse those policies, exacting harsh political demands from the conquered states while attempting to elevate the freed slave to a position of immediate political equality. That abrupt reversal would breed its own backlash in due time.[16]

The Stevens engine pushed through an extension of authority for the Freedmen's Bureau in February of 1866, losing it to a presidential veto. Bureau officers oversaw the construction, operation, and protection of schools for black children, collected accounts of violence against freedmen, and either monitored court cases prosecuted against them or tried the cases in Freedmen's Bureau courts, as they had done in minor cases before the civil courts resumed operation. Inspectors often reported that judicial proceedings against freedmen seemed fair, but suspected that the defendants' confessions were often extorted, and they believed that the courts avoided overt partiality primarily to avoid intervention by the bureau or the federal troops posted in each district.[17]

In March, responding to early testimony before the Joint Committee on Reconstruction, Congress passed a civil rights bill designed to counter repressive legislation in the Southern states. Johnson vetoed that, too, but he had alienated enough moderates by then that Radicals secured the votes to override it on the first anniversary of Lee's surrender. Until then Congress had almost never overridden a presidential veto, but under Johnson the spectacle would become routine.[18]

The tensions between president and Congress were matched and aggravated by mounting hostilities between the races in the South. Individual violence escalated that spring, exploding into a full-scale race riot in Memphis. Thaddeus Stevens called for a congressional inquiry, and the next month the House and Senate agreed on a final version of the Fourteenth Amendment, awarding equality of citizenship to all, reducing the representation of states that withheld the right to vote from any group of citizens, disqualifying anyone from office who had violated an oath to the United States by aiding the rebellion, and prohibiting repudiation of the federal war debt. The resolution did not require the president's signature, but it would not have mattered: the next month a new Freedmen's Bureau bill landed on Johnson's desk, which he reflexively vetoed, but Congress immediately passed it again over his veto without further discussion. When Unionist Louisiana delegates convened in an unauthorized convention to form a constitution compatible with the amendment, another riot erupted that left dozens of delegates and black citizens dead.[19]

Northern annoyance with Southern recalcitrance and the intransigent president rivaled that of the Radicals, and the biennial elections of 1866 augmented the overwhelming Republican majorities in the House and Senate. Early in 1867, with reports of violence against Union men and freedmen still rampant, Congress re-passed the first Reconstruction Act before the sun had set on Johnson's veto. That formally reduced the former Confederate states to occupied territories under military commanders — excepting only Tennessee, which had been readmitted. Three weeks later a second Reconstruction Act also overcame a veto, requiring the generals in command of Southern districts to organize elections for state convention delegates, in which they were to prohibit ex-Confederate soldiers and officials from voting or running in those elections. Over the course of the next year Congress passed two more supplements to the Reconstruction Act, each designed to assure that it was the minority of white and black Republicans in each of the Southern states who created the new state constitutions.[20]

How effectively Lincoln would have handled Reconstruction remains one of the more interesting of the unanswerable questions from that era, but it seems improbable that anyone of his political instincts would have pursued so antagonistic and self-defeating a course as Johnson, whose relentless pugnacity augmented the Radicals' ranks and fortified their arguments until both became insurmountable. Inevitably those Radicals would also have opposed Lincoln's preference for prompt and relatively painless Reconstruction as stubbornly as they flouted and frustrated Johnson's, but Lincoln's prestige and diplomacy would probably have ameliorated both the Radicals' obstinacy and the pace of their reforms, which in turn might have had a mollifying effect on Republican moderates and Southern whites.[21] Lincoln's promised lenience would probably have had the same effect of reviving Southern defiance as Johnson's did, but with early examples of violent repression Lincoln might have been more inclined to support the Radical agenda. A more moderate and gradual application of that agenda under Lincoln's guidance could conceivably have avoided so widespread a campaign of terror as finally arose to combat it, and Lincoln would likely have responded more effectively to such intimidation. Had he lived he would almost surely have chosen to leave office in 1869 — and, even if someone of equal talents had succeeded him, White House and congressional attention to racial equality would eventually have withered, just as the Radical spirit finally flickered out under the seductive distractions of the Gilded Age.

The prohibitions and requirements of the Reconstruction Acts bred the Republican state legislatures and governors the Radicals desired in the South, and by the summer of 1868 most of the Confederate states had been readmitted in time for the presidential election. The installation of those minority governments was soon followed by predictable violence from Southern Democrats, who had been deprived of any political voice after holding complete power for decades. Ultimately that violence succeeded in cowing enough black and white Republicans in Georgia and Louisiana to prevent many of them from voting, and the Democrats won those two states while the rest went to Ulysses Grant, as congressional Republicans had intended. The partial success of terrorist tactics in 1868 encouraged their proliferation over the next few years, and as more legislatures fell back into Democratic hands those bodies began exercising unsavory strategies learned from Republicans during and after the war — expelling opposition members and initiating impeachment proceedings against Republican governors on flimsy pretexts that failed to disguise the ulterior partisan motivation.[22]

The Grant administration reacted inconsistently to the Democratic takeovers and to the violence that made them possible. In North Carolina, for instance, the president declined to intercede when it might have been justified to uphold the popular will or federal law, but in Louisiana he finally deployed troops against what was perceived as the legitimate government in order to restore a faction friendly to his administration. Congress passed a series of increasingly intrusive enforcement acts to combat voter intimidation, allowing the federal supervision of elections, complete with fixed bayonets and the suspension of habeas corpus, but Northerners who had resented enduring those impositions themselves during the war frowned on their application in peacetime, even in the land of the former enemy. As popular support for such measures crumbled, enforcement of those various laws diminished and their deterrent effect evaporated; in the final year of Grant's presidency, the Supreme Court struck down some of the provisions as unconstitutional. In supportive response to those rulings, the moderately Republican *New York Times* interpreted it to mean that "the United States has neither the power nor the obligation to do police duty in the States." Southern states sent more Democrats to Congress every year — even returning Andrew Johnson to the U.S. Senate in 1875 — and their control of state and local government mushroomed as Republicans of both colors migrated, abstained from voting, or voted Democrat.[23]

The approaching centennial of American independence probably helped to inspire an orchestrated spirit of reconciliation between North and South. The new Memorial Day tradition served as an early vehicle for cultivating that atmosphere, with veterans from either army decorating the graves of their wartime opponents and performing exaggerated rituals of mutual respect. Even Nathan Bedford Forrest took part in a Memorial Day observance in Memphis. George Cary Eggleston published his memoirs of Confederate service in the autumn of 1874, explicitly hoping to help ease the animosity between North and South, and he bent his recollections toward that end. Elihu Washburne, the U.S. minister to France, would have just read about the Memorial Day services of 1874 when he described his experience at Appomattox for a Southern acquaintance. Washburne, a close friend of Grant's, had been a congressman when he witnessed the surrender ceremony; looking back on the event after nearly a decade, he focused on the camaraderie between Union and Confederate soldiers there, remembering a prevailing air of brotherhood among the recent enemies, who seemed to recognize that "after all the bloody struggle of the past, they were still all Americans." The celebration of early Revolutionary anniversaries offered wonderful opportunities for New England organizers to further the conciliatory cause by inviting legendary ex-Confederates to praise their common nationalism before Northern audiences.[24]

That strained effort at reconciliation became apparent just as Democrats made remarkable electoral gains across the country, finally winning a majority in Congress and seizing control of numerous legislatures; the fraternal trend necessarily ignored and excluded the South's former slaves. By the summer of 1876 only South Carolina, Florida, and Mississippi remained under Republican control within the former Confederacy, and serious racial violence persisted in those states as Democrats strove to regain dominance. An affray between black and white militia in South Carolina turned into a pitched battle in July, with several black men killed in the fracas or murdered afterward. The *New York Times* remarked sardonically on the slaughter as one way to reduce the black vote, adding an election-season warning that massacres of that sort could be expected regularly if Democrat Samuel Tilden were chosen president in November. South Carolina saw more widespread violence in September, but Republicans in that state could elicit no effective protection from Washington. The presidential vote there, in Florida, and in Louisiana threw the election into question. The negotiations that followed gave Republican Rutherford B. Hayes the presidency, but he had already indicated his hostility to the use of federal troops in the states. Hayes moved into the White House, and Democrats occupied the gubernatorial offices of every state in the not-so-old Confederacy.[25]

President Hayes lived up to his promise to keep the U.S. Army out of the South, regardless of racial violence, although he did not hesitate to use troops to quell labor disturbances in the North, where industrialization brought social and economic conflict reminiscent of the battle over slavery. That immunity to intervention gave the Southern legislatures carte blanche to reinstate the black codes they had enacted as a substitute for slavery, and black prisoners in striped uniforms became the new commodity that slaves had once been. Generations of black men, and women as well, lived in fear of arrest for minor or invented offenses, for which they would be sentenced to a period of confinement and to fines and court costs they could not hope to pay. An unlettered defendant might serve a few additional months at hard labor to work off the monetary penalty, during which he effectively became the property of the state, through the agency of the sheriff, who could use or lease convicts for agricultural or industrial labor at bargain rates. The system survived well into the twentieth century, and the shadow of the chain gang exacted subservience and an acceptance of inferior economic conditions from a black population for which lynching posed the only more terrifying fate.[26]

Long after Appomattox, racial issues fueled sectional conflict at least as rancorous as the antebellum battle over slavery. That prolonged struggle tried public patience with the enhanced centralized power conservatives had always dreaded, and eroded the national will for the decades-long federal occupation that 1861 opponents of military intervention had warned would be necessary to reestablish any fraternity with the seceded states. Almost a century had to pass, with several international wars to gradually restore a sense of shared nationality, before those sectional animosities began to dissipate. Effective substitutes for slavery and social intimidation persisted for almost all of that century, and many more years of battle had to be waged before any semblance of racial equality began to emerge. Between 1865 and 1877 the nation's leaders squandered the enormous sacrifices of Mr. Lincoln's war, precisely as the early critics of a military solution had anticipated they would.

Samuel Turner, an aging Vermont farmer who had longed to see the end of slavery, rejoiced in 1865 to think that his dream had been realized. Wartime taxes and inflated prices posed a worrisome burden, and the human cost of the war pained him deeply, but while the soldiers were coming home he explained to his children that emancipation seemed to compensate, "at least in part," for all the death and destruction. In the immediate wake of the 1876 presidential election Turner assumed that Tilden had won, and he feared that the Democratic victory would consign the freedmen to "a state little better than slavery." That was precisely what happened, despite Tilden's negotiated defeat. Mr. Turner did not outlive the honeymoon of the Hayes presidency, so he did not recognize the realization of his worst apprehension, and he was unable to retract his 1865 conclusion that the long, terrible war had nearly been worth the cost.[27]

NOTES

BIBLIOGRAPHY

SOURCES AND
ACKNOWLEDGMENTS

INDEX

Notes

AAS: American Antiquarian Society
ACHNHP: Appomattox Court House National Historic Park
AJP: Graf, Haskins, and Bergeron, eds., *The Papers of Andrew Johnson*
ALPL: Abraham Lincoln Presidential Library
ANHS: Andersonville National Historic Site
BGSU: Bowling Green State University
BL: University of Michigan, Bentley Library
BPL: Boston Public Library
CCHS: Chautauqua County Historical Society
CG: U.S. Congress, *Congressional Globe*
ChiHS: Chicago Historical Society
CHS: Connecticut Historical Society
CinHS: Cincinnati Historical Society
CL: University of Michigan, Clements Library
CPL: Conway Public Library
CWL: Basler, *The Collected Works of Abraham Lincoln*
DC: Dartmouth College
DRBL: D. R. Barker Library
FM: Fairbanks Museum and Planetarium
FSNMP: Fredericksburg and Spotsylvania National Military Park
HL: Huntington Library
HLHS: Hudson Library and Historical Society
IHS: Indiana Historical Society
ISL: Indiana State Library
IU: Indiana University
KSHS: Kansas State Historical Society
KU: University of Kansas
LC: Library of Congress
MC: William Marvel, Private Collection
MEHS: Maine Historical Society
MHS: Massachusetts Historical Society
MNHS: Minnesota Historical Society
MOC: Museum of the Confederacy
MOHS: Missouri Historical Society

MSSM: Massachusetts Soldiers, Sailors, and Marines in the Civil War
NA: National Archives
NCDAH: North Carolina Department of Archives and History
ND: University of Notre Dame
NHHS: New Hampshire Historical Society
NHS: Northfield Historical Society
NHSL: New Hampshire State Library
NSHS: Nebraska State Historical Society
NYHS: North Yarmouth Historical Society
OHS: Ohio Historical Society
OR: War of the Rebellion: A Compilation of the Official Records of the Union and Confederate
    Armies (all citations from Series 1 unless otherwise noted)
OR Atlas: Atlas to Accompany the Official Records of the Union and Confederate Armies
ORN: Official Records of the Union and Confederate Navies in the War of the Rebellion
    (all citations from Series 1 unless otherwise noted)
ORS: Supplement to the Official Records of the Union and Confederate Armies (all citations
    from Part 1 unless otherwise noted)
PEM: Peabody Essex Museum
RBHPL: Rutherford B. Hayes Presidential Library
RCCW: Report of the Committee on the Conduct of the War of the Attack on Petersburg, on
    the 30th Day of July, 1864
RG: Record Group
RIHS: Rhode Island Historical Society
RJCCW: Report of the Joint Committee on the Conduct of the War (37th Congress)
RJCCW2: Report of the Joint Committee on the Conduct of the War at the Second Session
    Thirty-Eighth Congress
RJCR: Report of the Joint Committee on Reconstruction at the First Session Thirty-Ninth
    Congress
RU: Rutgers University
SHC: University of North Carolina, Southern Historical Collection
SHSI-DM: State Historical Society of Iowa, Des Moines
SHSI-IC: State Historical Society of Iowa, Iowa City
SM: Sheldon Museum
UG: University of Georgia
UIA: University of Iowa
UME: University of Maine
UNH: University of New Hampshire
UR: University of Rochester
USAMHI: U.S. Army Military History Institute
USC: University of South Carolina
USG: Simon, The Papers of Ulysses S. Grant
UVA: University of Virginia
UVM: University of Vermont
VHS: Virginia Historical Society
VTHS: Vermont Historical Society
WHMC: University of Missouri, Western Historical Manuscript Collection
WHS: Wisconsin Historical Society
WRHS: Western Reserve Historical Society

PREFACE

1. Cutrer, *Goree Letters*, 123.
2. Nevins and Thomas, *Strong Diary*, 3:431, 435.
3. Davis, *Butler Letters*, 69–70, 76; Butler, *Private and Official Correspondence*, 4:418; Meade, *Life and Letters*, 2:190; *CWL*, 7:281.
4. *Democratic Standard*, May 4, 1861; *New Hampshire Patriot*, August 14, 1861.

NOTES TO PAGES 3–9

1. Inscription Rude in Virginia's Woods

1. Edgar Powers Diary, March 9–April 11, 1864, Bethel Historical Society; Francis Brooks Diary, April 10, 12, and 20, 1864, MHS; *Daily Chronicle*, April 16, 1864; Austin Morgan to George Morgan, April 17, 1864, DC; David Rugg Diary, April 26 and 27, 1864, VTHS.

2. *Dakotian*, March 29, April 5, and May 3, 1864; Joseph Swift to "My Dearest Eliza," May 15 and 16, 1864, Yale; *OR*, 34(2):766–67, 34(3):579–80, and 34(4):331, 497.

3. Chesson, *Dyer Journal*, 74; *OR*, 25(1):351–52, 34(3):579–80, and 34(4):331, 497; *Dakotian*, May 3, 1864.

4. *Dakotian*, August 18, 1863; *OR*, Series 3, 4:72–75, 1264–69.

5. Bemis to "Dear Steph," April 3, 1864, MOHS; Seventh Census of Jefferson County, Ky., Reel 205, p. 182 (M-432) RG 29, NA; Tax Assessment for Missouri, 1864, Reel 4, p. 110 (M-776), RG 58, NA.

6. Jacob Giffen to "Dear Father," June 20, 1864, and John Giffen to same, February 20, 1865, OHS.

7. Catherine Fisk to "Dear Cousin," May 16, 1864, Schwab Letters, CinHS.

8. *OR*, Series 3, 4:59, 181, 927–28; E. A. Miller to "My dear Clason," May 15, 1864, CinHS. Of the 85,861 men examined under that levy, 41,094 were exempted and 41,349 either hired substitutes or paid the $300 commutation fee, leaving only 3,418 who donned a uniform (*OR*, Series 3, 4:928).

9. Edgar Powers Diary, March 30, 1864, Bethel Historical Society; *Report of the Adjutant General of the State of Maine*, 553–54; Elisha Cowan to "Dear Brother," May 24, 1864, "Letters," MNHS.

10. Chauncey Hill to "My Dear Wife," March 2, 1864, and Sarah Hill to "Dear Chauncey," March 9, 1864, MNHS; Ninth Census of Winona County, Minn., Reel 719, p. 16 (M-593), RG 29, NA.

11. Davidson, *Hartley Letters*, 87; affidavits of B. F. and J. B. Mathews, pension certificate 362,390, RG 15, NA; Muster-in roll of Company A, 37th Wisconsin, RG 94, NA; Edward Van Deusen to "Dear friends," July 10, 1864, Sterns Family Papers, UIA. A photo of the slightly built Edward Van Deusen is in the Sterns Family Papers.

12. McCrae and Bradford, *No Place for Little Boys*, 58, 89; Cora Benton to Charles Benton, January 31, 1864, ND; George Monks to "Dear Mother," "May" [June] 8, 1864, and Zerah Monks to "My dear Hattie," November 13, 1864, WRHS; Isaac Roberts to Benjamin Wade, June 25, 1864, LC; *OR*, Series 3, 3:326 and 4:131, 473.

13. Nevins and Thomas, *Strong Diary*, 3:434; William Ford to James Knowlton, April 30, 1864, NHHS.

14. John Wilmot to "My Dear Wife," April 22, 1864, VTHS; Elijah Cavins to "Dear Ann," May 8, 1864, IHS; William Clayton to "My Dearest Mother," May 27, 1864, MNHS; A. W. Luther to "My Dear Father," April 27, 1864, ISL; Dyer, *Compendium*, 1155–56, 1227–28, 1267, 1654, 1687; Samuel Wilkinson Diary, April 12–16, 1864, UNH.

15. Peck, *Revised Roster*, 382, 396; Sylvester Bishop to "Dear Mother," May 3, 1864, ISL; Benjamin Ashenfelter to "Father Churchman," April 23, 1864, USAMHI; James Brown to "Dear Sister," April 28, 1864, MEHS; *OR*, 33:925.

16. Martin Clark to Wealthy Field, April 22, 1864, VTHS; Edwin Horton to "Dear Ellen," April 26, 1864, VTHS; Maria Sargent to "Dear Ransom," July, 1864, DC; George Watts to "My dear Father," May 3, 1864, MHS; George Jones to "Dear Friends at Home," April 29, 1864, UVM; Thomas Willis to "Dear Mother," May 1, 1864, CL; Marshall Phillips to "Dear Wife," April 21, 1864, MEHS; Alfred Keith to "My dear Sister," May 1, 1864, VTHS; Oscar Robinson to "Dear Mother," May 3, 1864, DC.

17. Racine, *Mattocks Journal*, 110, 112–13, 125–26; Charles Mattocks to George C. Kimball, April 7, 14, 21, 1864, AAS; George Jones to "Dear Friends at Home," March 3, 1864, UVM.

18. *OR*, 33:717–18; Daniel Spofford to "Dear Mother," March 30, 1864, MHS; Washington Roebling to "Dear Em," April 10, 1864, RU.

19. Union armies were usually named after rivers, and Confederate armies after states.

20. Simpson and Berlin, *Sherman Correspondence*, 611; Frank Collins to "Dear Father," April 8, 1864, SHSI-IC.

21. Sumner, *Comstock Diary*, 263; *OR*, 37(1):368–70, 401.

22. *OR*, 33:1048; George Bates to "Dear Parents," May 11, 1864, CL; George Wheeler to "Dear Mother," April 28, 1864, NSHS; Eugene Houghton to "Dear Cousin Hattie," May 10, 1864, CL; Charles Hadsall Diary, April 8, 10, 25, 1864, NSHS.

23. *USG*, 10:335; John Peirce to "Dear Wife," April 28 and May 1, 1864, PEM; Dyer, *Compendium*, 1242; *OR*, 36(2):384.

24. *OR*, Series 3, 4:181, 1266, and 5:636–37.

25. On the nine-month regiments see Marvel, *Lincoln's Darkest Year*, especially 323–26.

26. *OR*, Series 3, 4:237–39.

27. Edwin Vancise Journal, May 4, 15, 1864, LC; Christopher Keller to "Dear Parents," May 22, 1864, CL; W. N. Fast to Amanda Fast, May 7, 1864, BGSU; Davis, *Butler Letters*, 78, 81, 87–88.

28. Larimer, *Ritner Letters*, 271.

29. Catherine Fisk to "Dear Cousin," May 16, 1864, Schwab Letters, CinHS; Maggie Wade to "My Dear Aunt," May 13, 1864, LC; E. A. Miller to "My dear Clason," May 15, 1864, and Sallie Miller to "My dear Brother," July 21, 1864, CinHS; George Monks to "Dear Mother," "May" [June] 8, 1864, WRHS; W. N. Fast to Amanda Fast, May 7, 1864, BGSU.

30. Alonzo Cushman to "Dear Sister," April 28, 1864, Civil War Collection, AAS; Thomas Brown to "Dear Wif," April 20, 1864, VTHS; John Wilmot to "My Dear Wife," April 22, 1864, VTHS; Daniel Webster Brown to "Dear Brother F," May 1, 1864, MEHS; Engert, *Lamson Letters*, 95.

31. Duncan, *Neil Letters*, 23, 25; *OR*, 37(1):363–64; Mahon, *Chase and Lee Diaries*, 140–42.

32. *OR*, 37(1):10, 41.

33. Longacre, *Wightman Letters*, 171–73; Basile, *Stearns Diary*, 46.

34. Charles Richardson Diary, May 2, 1864, LC; Charles Reed Diary, May 2, 1864, LC; *OR*, 36(2):331–34.

35. Charles Reed Diary, May 3, 1864, LC; Forbes, *Diary*, 5; Meade, *Life and Letters*, 2:193; Orville Bixby to "My Dear Frances," May 1, 1864, VTHS, and to same, May 3, 1864, UVM.

36. Peck, *Revised Roster*, 31–66; William Stow to "Dear Mother," April 14, 1864, UVM.

37. On Meade's plan for the Wilderness battle, and for the battle generally, see Rhea, *Battle of the Wilderness*.

38. *OR*, 33:1036, 1045, 1297, and 36(2):940.

39. Meade, *Life and Letters*, 2:189.

40. *OR*, 36(1):639; Charles Reed Diary, May 4, 1864; LC; Henry Keiser Diary, May 4, 1864, USAMHI; Floyd, *Dear Friends at Home*, 25; *OR*, 36(1):305–6.

41. Agassiz, *Lyman Letters*, 87; John Wilcox Diary, May 4, 1864, NHHS; *OR*, 36(1):917, 990, and 36(2):380.

42. *OR*, 36(1):1081, and 36(2):953; Meade, *Life and Letters*, 2:193. Gordon Rhea argues the strategic benefits of posting Burnside at the upstream fords (*Battle of the Wilderness*, 56).

43. *OR*, 36(2):374–75, 378, 390; Blight, *Brewster Letters*, 292; Nevins, *Wainwright Journals*, 348–49; Levi Standly to "Dear Sister," May 9, 1864, Critchett Family Papers, NHHS.

44. Sumner, *Comstock Diary*, 264; *OR*, 36(2):371.

45. *OR*, 36(2):406, 407, 415–16, 418; Agassiz, *Lyman Letters*, 88–89.

46. *OR*, 36(1):539–40.

47. Ibid., 127, 696–98; Charles Richardson Diary, May 5, 1864, LC; Henry Hayward to "Mrs. Bixby," May 16, 1864, UVM; Lorenzo Miles Diary, May 5, 1864, VTHS; M. J. Sargent to "Mrs. Bixby," June 6, 1864, VTHS; Feidner, *Leach Letters*, 206; Samuel Pingree to "Cousin Hunton," June 10, 1864, VTHS; Olive Cheney to Jane Watts and Olive Corliss, May 22, 1864, VTHS.

48. *OR*, 36(1):190; Blight, *Brewster Letters*, 292.

49. *OR*, 36(1):190; Sumner, *Comstock Diary*, 264; Nevins, *Wainwright Journals*, 352–53; Robertson, *McAllister Letters*, 416; Agassiz, *Lyman Letters*, 94–97; Coco, *Mills Letters*, 78–79; Lorenzo Miles Diary, May 6, 1864, VTHS; Andrew Linscott to "Dear Parents," May 19, 1864, MHS.

50. Weld, *War Diary*, 287–88; Sparks, *Patrick Diary*, 368. A Massachusetts lieutenant contended that the new regiments ran just as vigorously as the veterans (Blight, *Brewster Letters*, 294), but Wilbur Fisk, a reenlisted veteran of the 2nd Vermont, admitted that he ran from Longstreet's flank attack that day, and remained in the rear until near the end of the fighting. Fisk may instead have disappeared from the fight of May 5, remaining absent through the evening of May 6: his transcribed diary asserts that the regiment went into action on May 6 under his own company commander, Captain Bixby, but Bixby had been killed the previous afternoon — which Fisk would surely have known, had he been with his company in or after the bloody fight of May 5 (Rosenblatt and Rosenblatt, *Fisk Letters*, 216; Fisk Diary, May 5 and 6, 1864, LC).

51. Charles Cummings to "My Dear Wife," May 15, 1864, VTHS; Josiah Jones Diary, May 6, 1864, NHHS; Levi Standly to "Dear Sister," May 9, 1864, Critchett Family Papers, NHHS; Willard Templeton to "Dear Brother James," May 10, 1864, NHSL.

52. Menge and Shimrak, *Chisholm Notebook*, 13; Chesson, *Dyer Journal*, 150; Sparks, *Patrick Diary*, 369.

53. Sparks, *Patrick Diary*, 369; John Bailey Journal, May 6, 1864, NHHS; *OR*, 36(1):190.

54. Agassiz, *Lyman Letters*, 90, 94; John Bailey Journal, May 6, 1864, NHHS; Chesson, *Dyer Journal*, 150–51; Joseph Leighty to "Dear Father and Mother," May 11, 1864, KU; George Howard to "My Dear," May 10, 1864, VTHS.

55. John Judd Diary, May 8, 1864, KSHS; Charles McCreery to William Fenton, May 20, 1864, BL; Jaquette, *Hancock Letters*, 88.

56. Samuel Fiske to "Dear Lizzie," May 11, 1864, and Asa Fiske to "My precious Lizzie," May 21, 1864, Stephenson Collection, LC; Francis Barlow to "My dear mother," May 18, 1864, MHS; *OR*, 36(1):133, and 36(2):652–53; Jaquette, *Hancock Letters*, 86.

57. Susan Forbes Diary, May 8, 1864, AAS.

58. *OR*, 36(1):190–91; Edward Taylor to "Dear Mother," May 16, 1864, BL; Blight, *Brewster Letters*, 294; Luther Furst Diary, May 9, 1864, USAMHI; Coco, *Mills Letters*, 81–82; Theodore Lyman to "my dearest," May 21, 1864, MHS; Weld, *War Diary*, 290.

59. Nevins, *Wainwright Journals*, 362–64; Howe, *Holmes Letters*, 112–13; Lorenzo Miles Diary, May 10, 1864, VTHS; Agassiz, *Lyman Letters*, 109–10. Gordon Rhea's two books on the fighting in this vicinity — *The Battles for Spotsylvania Court House* and *To the North Anna River* — are the best modern studies.

60. Greenleaf, *Letters to Eliza*, 90; William Hogan to "Dear Son" May 13, 1864, VTHS; Willis Porter to "Dear Etta," May 13, 1864, MEHS; Josiah Jones, John Wilcox, and Sewell D. Tilton Diaries, May 12, 1864, NHHS; Ransom Sargent to "Dear Maria," May 19, 1864, DC; Willard J. Templeton to "Dear Brother," May 16, 1864, NHSL; Conrad Noll Diary, May 12, 1864, BL; Charles Todd Diary, May 12, 1864, RBHPL; Britton and Reed, *Hartwell Letters*, 227; Edwin Hall to "Dear Parents," May 17, 1864, VTHS; Howard Hanson Diary, May 12 and 13, 1864, UNH; Howe, *Holmes Letters*, 115–17; Blight, *Brewster Letters*, 298–99; Henry Keiser Diary, May 12, 1864, USAMHI.

61. *OR,* 36(2):34–35, 112–17, 172–73; Andrew Byrne Diary, May 5–20, 1864, CHS; George Julian to "My dear Parents & Sister," May 11, 1864, UNH; Mushkat, *Voris Letters,* 166–69; Basile, *Stearns Diary,* 46–48; Longacre, *Wightman Letters,* 175–81; Leander Harris to Emily Harris, May 11 and 17, 1864, UNH; Louis Bell to "Dear George," August 12, 1864, NHHS; Washington Vosburgh to "My own dearest Ella," May 18, 1864, BL; William Willoughby to "My Dear Wife," May [13], 15, and 22, 1864, AAS; Charles Paine to "Dear Father," May 17, 1864, MHS; Edwin Bearse to "Dear Sister," May 17, 1864, MHS; Trimble, *Jones Letters,* 79–81; John Gallison to "Dear Mother," May 11 and 19, 1864, and Gallison Diary, May 16, 1864, MHS. For competing assessments of this theater, see Robertson, *Back Door to Richmond,* and Schiller, *The Bermuda Hundred Campaign.* Petersburg authority A. Wilson Greene saved me from several errors in this paragraph alone, not least of all the popular but inaccurate characterization of Butler as "sealed up" in Bermuda Hundred.

62. Halleck to Francis Lieber, May 21, 1864, HL.

63. *OR,* 36(1):789–92; William Hills Diary, May 11 and 12, 1864, LC; Clement Hoffman to "Dear Mother," May 17 and 20, 1864, USAMHI; Aaron Tompkins to "Dear Mother," May 24, 1864, LC.

64. *OR,* 37(1):10–12, 41–42; Williams, *Hayes Diary and Letters,* 2:456–58; Albert A. Wright Diary, May 8–14, 1864, USAMHI; *Daily Virginian,* May 10 and 13, 1864.

65. *OR,* 37(1):89, 407, 713, 715–16; Eby, *Strother Diaries,* 225. One travels southward "up" the Shenandoah Valley.

66. Duncan, *Neil Letters,* 28–32; Eby, *Strother Diaries,* 226–27; James Cady to "Dear Friends," May 22, 1864, Providence Public Library; *OR,* 37(1):76–77, 80–87, 90–91; Mahon, *Chase and Lee Diaries,* 146.

67. William Bradbury to "My dearest wife," May 6, 1864, LC; Joshua Breyfogle Diary, May 6, 1864, DC; Francis Crowninshield Journal, May 6, 1864, PEM; Quaife, *Williams Letters,* 306; W. C. Patton Diary, May 5, 1864, ISL.

68. Quaife, *Williams Letters,* 306; George Cobham Diary, May 6, 1864, CCHS; *OR,* 38(1):62–63. Estimates of Confederate numbers remain nebulous.

69. *OR,* 38(1):63–64, 139–40; George Hodges to "Dear Wife," May 20, 1864, WRHS; J. B. Dawley to "Dear Brother," June 1, 1864, Yale.

70. *OR,* 38(1):64, 140, 38(3):614, and 38(4):106, 112; Henry Duffield to "My own darling Fannie," May 11, 1864, CL.

71. *OR,* 38(1):64, 38(3):615; George Cobham Diary, May 14–15, 1864, CCHS; William Fordyce Diary, May 15, 1864, ISL; Franklin Warner to "Dear uncle and Aunt," August 21, 1864, Bennett-Stites-Fay Family Papers, OHS; Francis Crowninshield Journal, May 15–16, 1864, PEM; James Miller to "Dear Brother," May 17, 1864, CL; Marcellus Darling to "Dear Friends," May 21, 1864, UIA.

72. James White to "Dear Sis," May 20, 1864, CHS; Charles Senior to "Dear Father," May 17, 1864, UVA; Albert Slack to "Dear Father and Mother," May 18, 1864, OHS. The most extensive study of the Atlanta campaign, encompassing most of 1864, is Castel, *Decision in the West;* McMurry, *Atlanta 1864,* is more concise.

73. Thomas Fox to "Dear brother," May 12, 1864, WHS; Charles Boyle to "Dear Home," May 21, 1864, CHS; John Perley to "Dear Jenny," May 28, 1864, CL; *OR,* 35(1):400–401.

74. *OR,* 34(1):1–8, 670, 923–30.

75. *OR,* 36(1):133, 149, 36(2): 652–53, 695–97; J. M. Woodbury to "Dear Brother," May 18, 1864, MEHS; Ethan Allen Hitchcock to "Dear Henry," May 16, 1864, LC.

76. Edmund Townsend to Samuel Townsend, May 16, 1864, CL; A. Welsh to "Friend William," May 19, 1864, Bonner Family Papers, CCHS; Albert Huntington to "Dear Mother," May 15, 1864, UR; David Leigh to Herman Drumgold, May 31, 1864, DC.

77. Roe, *Melvin Memorial,* 98–99; Hilon Parker to "Folks at Home," May 28, 1864, CL; Charles Abbey Diary, May 19 and 20, 1864, AAS; Josiah Corban to "Dear Wife and Children," May 19, 1864, CHS; Michael Kelly Diary, May 19, 1864, CHS.

78. Martin Clark to "Dear Friend Wealthy," May 11, 1864, VTHS; Charles Hadsall Diary, May 16, 1864, NSHS; *OR*, 36(1):140, 143.

79. George French to "Dear Friends at Home," May 14, 1864, VTHS; Charles Cummings to "My Dear Wife," May 15, 1864, VTHS; Aldace Walker to unidentified recipient, May 15, 1864, VTHS; Feidner, *Leach Letters*, 207; Jerome Cutler to "My dear Emily," May 19, 1864, Bennington Museum; Samuel Pingree to "Cousin Hunton," June 10, 1864, VTHS.

80. Sparks, *Patrick Diary*, 374; Chandler Watts Diary, May 14, 1864, Cheney-Watts Collection, VTHS; John Bailey Journal, May 15, 1864, NHHS; Edward Roberts Diary, May 20, 1864, CHS; George Howe to "Dear Lorette," June 12, 1864, SM.

81. Charles Gould to "Dear Parents," May 15, 1864, UVM; Josiah Jones Diary, May 14, 1864, NHHS.

82. *OR*, 36(1):192, 600, 1073; McCrae and Bradford, *No Place for Little Boys*, 85–86; Roe, *Melvin Memorial*, 99; George Prescott to "My dearest Sallie," May 20, 1864, MHS; Nevins, *Wainwright Journals*, 378–79; Howe, *Holmes Letters*, 127; Washington Roebling to "Darling," May 21, 1864, RU; George Howe to "Dear Lorette," June 12, 1864, SM.

83. Meade, *Life and Letters*, 2:195; Sumner, *Comstock Diary*, 267; Washington Roebling to "My Darling," May 15, 1864, RU.

84. Albert Huntington to "Dear Mother," May 15, 1864, UR; Britton and Reed, *Hartwell Letters*, 228, 230; Oscar Robinson to "My Darling Sister," May 20, 1864, DC; Charles Cummings to "My Dear Wife," May 20, 1864, VTHS.

85. "Web" to "Dear Brother," April 14, 1864, and J. Warren Flint to "Dear Friend Frank," May 31, 1864, Daniel Webster Brown Correspondence, MEHS; John Macomber to "My Own Dear Wife," May 19, 1864, MNHS; Peck, *Revised Roster*, 421.

86. Francis E. Gray to Caroline Wentworth, May 25, 1864, LC; Edward Wade to "Dear Nell," [May 15, 1864], CL; Blair, *Geary Letters*, 177; Charles Henry Wilson to "My Dear Wife, May 7, 9, 11, 13, and 15, 1864, NSHS; Bradford Sparrow to "Parents & Brothers," May 13, 1864, UVM; Willard Thayer to "my dear wife & children," May 19 and 20, 1864, VTHS; Robert Moyle to "Dear father and Mother," May 20, and "dear Mother," June 17, 1864, UIA; Marcellus Darling to "Dear Mother," June 7, 1864, UIA; Greenleaf, *Letters to Eliza*, 97.

87. Blight, *Brewster Letters*, 307; Howe, *Holmes Letters*, 121–22, 125; Daniel Larned to "My Dear Sister," May 13 and 17, 1864, LC; Washington Roebling to "My Darling," May 15, 1864, RU.

88. Coco, *Mills Letters*, 83; Francis Barlow to "My dear mother," May 18, 1864, and to "My dear Edward," May 20, 1864, MHS.

89. *OR*, 36(1):119–49, and 38(1):85.

90. Gavin, *Pettit Letters*, 62; Coco, *Mills Letters*, 82, 151; *OR*, 36(1):147–48; George Hawkes Diary, May 12 and June 17, 1864, USAMHI; Weld, *War Diary*, 296–97, 311–12. Leasure never again led the regiment in battle, and he never received the brevet that most acting brigadiers were accorded.

91. George Chandler to "Dear Mother," May 17, 1864, E. C. Babb to Chandler, June 21, 1864, Charles Copp to Chandler, July 3, 1864, and William Brown to Chandler, August 7, 1864, all in George H. Chandler Papers, NHHS.

92. *OR*, 36(2):652–53; William Owner Diary, May 12, 1864, LC; Thomas Richards to Thaddeus Stevens, June 3, 1864, LC; Horatio Taft Diary, May 12, 1864, LC.

93. Wilbur Dubois to John Wesley Longyear, May 23 and June 21, 1864, BL; Blight, *Brewster Letters*, 307.

94. Fisk Diary, May 5, 6, 22–31, 1864, LC; Rosenblatt and Rosenblatt, *Fisk Letters*, 222–25.

95. George Howe to "Dear Lorette," June 12, 1864, SM; John Sheahan to "My Dear Father," June 7, 1864, MEHS; James Rickard to "D. Brother," July 14, 1864, AAS; William Harris Journal, July 13, 1864, VHS.

96. William Brown to George Chandler, July 6, 1864, NHHS; John Marshall Brown to "My dear Nellie," May 25, 1864, MEHS; William Barker to "Luther," June 4, 1864, Lunt Family Papers, MEHS. The unappreciated colonel of the 32nd Maine, Mark Wentworth, was awarded a Medal of Honor in 1863, along with several hundred other members of the 27th Maine, for agreeing to remain in Washington a few days beyond the regiment's term during Lee's invasion of Pennsylvania, but those frivolously issued medals were all called back later by the War Department; Wentworth redeemed himself from the standpoint of courage, if not competence, by leading his regiment into battle at Petersburg, where he suffered a wound that led to his resignation. Perhaps because of his medal, he later drew a brevet promotion to brigadier general.

97. Holden, Ross, and Slomba, *Cross Writings*, 136–37; *OR*, 36(1):435–36; Charles Dana to Edwin Stanton, June 12, 1864, LC; Edward Bragg to "My Dear Wife," September 16, 1864, WHS.

98. Henry Young to "Dear Delia," September 12, 1864, WHS.

99. Longacre, *Wightman Letters*, 175–79, 200, 207; Edward Hall to "My dear wife and son," June 7, 1864, NHHS; Henry Snow to "My Dear Mother," May 28, 1864, CHS; *Daily Chronicle*, June 22, 1864; Ayling, *Register*, 158, 162; William Badger to Louis Bell, June 21, 1864, UNH.

100. Frank Collins to "Dear Father," June 25, 1864, SHSI-IC. On the influence of community see, for instance, McPherson, *For Cause and Comrades*, 80.

101. *OR*, 38(2):340, 344, 375; Henry Langdon to "My dear Sister," July 30, 1864, CinHS; William Brown to George Chandler, July 18, 1864, NHHS.

102. Weld, *War Diary*, 296–97, 311–12; Henry Snow to "Dear friend," May 23, 1864, CHS; George Huckins to Louis Bell, August 25, 1864, UNH; *OR*, 39(1):172, 176, 181, 197, 198, 215–16.

2. The Mouldering Coat and Cuddled-up Skeleton

1. David Bates Diary, May 13–20, 1864, LC; Nevins and Thomas, *Strong Diary*, 3:446.

2. Edward Hall to Susan Hall, June 7, 20, and July 18, 1864, NHHS; Rufus Kinsley to "Dear Father," May 29, 1864, VTHS; Tench Tilghman to Hamilton Fish, May 28, 1864, LC.

3. Martha Conpropst and Hannah Rohrer to Zerah Monks, April 24, 1864, WRHS; Emily Thompson to "Dear Brother & Sister," June 3, "1863" [1864], Aldrich-Thompson Papers, NHHS; Butler, *Butler Correspondence*, 4:418.

4. Almira C. Barker to "My dear Charles," August 14, 1864, Lunt Family Papers, MEHS.

5. *New Hampshire Patriot*, April 24, 1861, and July 8, 1863; Franklin Pierce to Thomas Seymour, June 22, 1861, LC; Hawthorne, "Chiefly about War Matters."

6. Sophia Hawthorne to Annie Fields, April 29, 1864, and to James Fields, May 5, 1864, BPL; Sophia Hawthorne to Pierce, May 6, 1864, NHHS. See Wallner, *Franklin Pierce*, on the friendship between Pierce and Hawthorne.

7. Pierce to Mary Aiken, May 19, 1864, quoted in Skinner Catalogue, 22.

8. *New Hampshire Gazette*, October 10, 1863; Parker Pillsbury to "My Dear Friends," July 17, 1864, BPL; "your loving Huldah" to Elizabeth Saunders, May 18, 1864, CHS; Lizzie Corning Diary, especially April 30, May 2, and May 14–21, 1864, NHHS.

9. Carolyn White Diary, August 25, 1864, AAS.

10. *OR*, 34(2):756.

11. T. J. Barnett to Barlow, March 20, 1864, HL; *OR*, Series 3, 4:386–87.

12. Nevins and Thomas, *Strong Diary*, 3:449; Barlow to George McClellan, May 18, 1864, HL; *OR*, Series 3, 4:388–89.

13. *OR*, Series 3, 4:389–95, 636; Nevins and Thomas, *Strong Diary*, 3:449; Barlow to Montgomery Blair, May 28, 1864, HL.

14. *CWL*, 7:393, 493, and 8:187.

15. Alexander McClure to Stevens, March 9, 1864, LC; Nevins and Thomas, *Strong Diary*, 3:453.

16. *RJCCW*, 1:3–66; *OR*, 12(2, supplement):821–1135; Sears, *McClellan Papers*, 554, 567–69, 573; T. J. Barnett to Samuel Barlow, September 5, 1864, HL.

17. *CWL*, 7:50–56; *CG*, 38th Cong., 1st sess., part 3:2095–2108.

18. Amos Tuck to William Chandler, January 6 and May 5, 1864, NHHS; Niven, *Chase Papers*, 4:329–32; Chase to Albert G. Riddle, March 11, 1864, WRHS.

19. H. C. Ingersoll to "Dear Brother," June 9, 1864, MEHS; Henry Brown to unidentified addressee, June 14, 1864, CHS; Burlingame and Ettlinger, *Hay Diary*, 199; Horatio Taft Diary, June 8, 1864, LC.

20. Burlingame, *Nicolay Letters*, 145; Samuel Curtis to "Dear Sam," May 26, 1864, Yale; John Pugh to "Dear Sister," June 11, 1864, Earlham; Horatio Taft Diary, June 8, 1864, LC.

21. *CWL*, 7:49–50; Barlow to T. J. Barnett, June 6 and 14, 1864, HL.

22. *OR*, 38(3):615–16; James Goodnow to "My Dear Wife," May 29, 1864, LC; Robert Moyle to "Dear father and Mother," May 20, 1864, UIA.

23. James Miller to "Dear Brother," May 17, 1864, CL; Edward Edes to "My dear Mother," May 20, 1864, MHS; Benjamin Bordner to "Brother George," May 22, 1864, BL; Marcellus Darling to "Dear Friends in Catteraugus," June 1, 1864, UIA; Quaife, *Williams Letters*, 310, 316; Chauncey Mead to "Dear Kate," May 21, 1864, WRHS; John Lane to "Dear Ellen," May 22, 1864, Crist Manuscripts, IU.

24. *OR*, 38(3):947–48, and 38(4):303–4, 306.

25. Quaife, *Williams Letters*, 311–15; George Hodges to "Dear Wife," May 20, 1864, WRHS; William Bradbury to "My dear wife," May 30, 1864, LC; James Goodnow to "My Dear Wife," May 29, 1864, LC; Silas Strickland to "My dear Wife," May 29, 1864, NSHS; William Fordyce Diary, May 25–30, 1864, ISL; George Cobham Diary, May 25-June 1, 1864, CCHS; Stephen Green to "My Dear Wife," May 31, 1864, CCHS; James White to "Dear Father," June 9, 1864, CHS.

26. *OR*, 38(1):60–61, and 38(3):616–17; Quaife, *Williams Letters*, 317, 320–21; William Bradbury to "My dear wife," June 12, 1864, LC; Robert Moyle to "dear Mother," June 17, 1864, UIA; Edward Edes to "Dear Mother," June 5, 1864, to "Dear Father," June 12 and 20, 1864, and Surgeon E. B. Collins to Commander of Company B, 33rd Mass., July 4, 1864, MHS; John Lane to "Dear Ellen," June 25, 1864, Crist Manuscripts, IU; R. H. Foord Diary, June 9–19, 1864, BGSU; Francis Crowninshield to "Dear Mother," June 15, 1864, PEM; Thomas Coffman to "Dear Gal," June 17, 1864, SHSI-IC; Albion Gross to "Dear Wife," June 17, 1864, MNHS; George Cobham Diary, June 19, 1864, CCHS.

27. *OR*, 39(1):64–65, 39((2):42, 44, and 52(2):651–52; Edward Guerrant Diary, May 31–June 2, 1864, SHC; "O" to Clement Vallandigham, June 9, 1864, and "JPP" to Vallandigham, June 12, 1864, Stanton Papers, LC.

28. Edward Guerrant Diary, June 7–12, 1864, SHC; Henry Giltner Report, July 5, 1864, Morgan Papers, SHC; *OR*, 39(1):33–34, 37–38, 44–45, 46–48, 56–58, 63, 69, and 39(2):87–88; David Bates Diary, June 9, 1864, LC; *CWL*, 7:390.

29. Simpson and Berlin, *Sherman Correspondence*, 647; *OR*, 32(1):693–701.

30. *OR*, 39(2):59, 73–74, 628, and 38(4):750.

31. Record of Events, 9th Minnesota Infantry, Reel 91, Compiled Records Showing Service of Military Units (M-594), RG 94, NA; *OR*, 34(2):322, and 34(3):655.

32. *OR*, 38(4):750, 39(1):85, 221–22, 39(2):619, 628.

33. *OR*, 32(1):698, 39(1):86, 90, 152, 172, 176, 178, 179, 181, 197, 198, 215–16, 219.

34. *OR*, 39(1):222, and 39(2):74.

35. Chauncey Hill to "My Dear Wife," June 9, 1864, MNHS; *OR*, 39(2):74, 90–91, 188.

36. *OR*, 39(1):129, 153, 163, 165, 172.

37. Ibid., 129, 153–54, 165, 222–23; Peter Perry Diary, June 10, 1864, MC; Simon Duck Diary, June 10, 1864, USAMHI; Nehemiah Solon Diary, June 10, 1864, CHS.

38. *OR*, 39(1):129, 154–55, 174, 175–76, 213, 223–24; Simon Duck Diary, June 10–11, 1864, USAMHI; Peter Perry Diary, June 10, 1864, MC; Chauncey Hill to "My Own Dear Wife," June 17, 1864, MNHS.

39. *OR*, 39(1):106, 133, 140, 226–27, 230–31; Nehemiah Solon Diary, June 16, 1864, CHS; Chauncey Hill to "My Own Dear Wife," June 17, 1864, MNHS.

40. Albert Ritter to "Cousin Helen & Lib," September 5, 1864, UR; *OR*, 39(1):147–220, and 39(2):121, 123.

41. *OR*, 39(2):659, 665. Edwin Bearss makes this point in *Forrest at Brice's Cross Roads*.

42. Simpson and Berlin, *Sherman Correspondence*, 647, 657, 659; Chauncey Mead to unidentified addressee, June 24, 1864, WRHS; Rufus Mead to "Dear Folks at Home," July 13, 1864, LC; *OR*, 38(3):620, 994–1008, and 38(4):801.

43. R. H. Foord Diary, June 9–19, 1864, BGSU; Blair, *Geary Letters*, 182; *Southern Recorder*, July 12, 1864, quoted in *ORS*, Series 1, 7:89–90; James White to "Dear Father," June 9, "1863" [1864], CHS; *OR*, 38(1):67–68; 196, and 38(3):120; David Bates Diary, June 15, 1864, LC.

44. *OR*, 38(1):67–68, 879, 38(3):617, and 38(4):519; Quaife, *Williams Letters*, 320–21; Thomas Coffman to "Dear Gal," June 17, 1864, SHSI-IC; George Cobham Diary, June 19, 1864, CCHS.

45. *OR*, 38(1):68–69, 38(2):513, 38(3):762, and 38(4):582; Henry Guyer to "Dear Brother," June 24, 1864, Yale; Blair, *Geary Letters*, 183.

46. *OR*, 38(1):151, 38(2):514, 570, and 38(4):588, 607; John Boardman to "Father," July 4, 1864, BL; R. H. Foord Diary, June 24–27, 1864, BGSU; George Hudson to unidentified addressee, June "27" [29?], 1864, LC; Dexter Cotton to "My dear wife," June 29, 1864, LC; L. W. Costellow to "My Dear Brother," September 18, 1864, MEHS; James Goodnow to "My dear Wife," July 2, 1864, LC; Harvey Cutter to "Dear Mother," June 29, 1864, WRHS.

47. Charles Smith to "Dear Father," June 26, 1864, WHS; Henry Comey to "Dear Father," May 27, 1864, AAS; *OR*, 38(4):607.

48. Simpson and Berlin, *Sherman Correspondence*, 657; R. H. Foord Diary, July 3 and 4, 1864, BGSU; William Lowes to "Dear Bro & Sister," July 8, 1864, OHS; James Goodnow to "My dear Wife," July 5, 1864, LC; Joseph Kohout to "Dear Father and Mother and Sister," July 4, 1864, UIA; Marcellus Darling to "Dear Friends and companions in Leon," July 9, 1864, UIA.

49. *OR*, 36(1):193, and 36(3):145, 167–68, 198–99; Washington Roebling to Emily Warren, May 24 [1864], RU; Jedediah Hotchkiss Journal, May 24–25, 1864, LC; Rufus Dawes to "My dear Wife," May 23, 1864, WHS; Nevins, *Wainwright Journals*, 387; George Hawkes Diary, May 24, 1864, USAMHI; Coco, *Mills Letters*, 89–90; Julius Whitney Diary, May 24, 1864, USAMHI; Weld, *War Diary*, 296–97; Agassiz, *Lyman Letters*, 127; Tower, *Taylor Letters*, 164.

50. *OR*, 36(3):169, 206; Nevins, *Wainwright Journals*, 388.

51. *OR*, 36(3):206; Charles Reed Diary, May 24, 1864, LC; Blight, *Brewster Letters*, 303–4.

52. Agassiz, *Lyman Letters*, 128–31; Nevins, *Wainwright Journals*, 390; A. S. Boyce to "Dear Mary," May 31, 1864, BL; Elmer Wallace to "My Dear Parents," May 30, 1864, BL; George Fowle to "Dear Eliza," June 15, 1864, MHS; James Perry Diary, May 22, 1864, WHS; Webster Eaton to Gilbert Reynolds, June 1, 1864, UR.

53. Charles Cummings to "My Dear Wife," July 23, 1864, VTHS; Daniel Larned to "My Dear Sister," June 15, 1864, LC; William Harris Diary, June 14, 1864, VHS; *Boston Evening Transcript*, June 30, 1864.

54. *OR*, 36(1):998; Agassiz, *Lyman Letters*, 136; David Bates Diary, June 5, 1864, LC.

55. Charles Cummings to "My Dear Wife," May 30, 1864, VTHS; Agassiz, *Lyman Letters*, 137–41; Washington Roebling to "Dear Em," [May 31, 1864], RU; William White to Jacob Wead, June 9, 1864, VTHS.

56. Nevins, *Wainwright Journals*, 402, 404; *OR*, 36(1):194; Agassiz, *Lyman Letters*, 143–45; Brown, *Tilden Letters*, 59; James Howes to "My Dear Wife," June 6, 1864, NHHS; Ransom Sargent to "Dear Maria," June 4, 1864, DC.

57. Brown, *Tilden Letters*, 59; James Brown to "My Dear Friends," June 8 [1864], MEHS; Lorenzo Miles Diary, June 6 and 7, 1864, VTHS; Aldace Walker to "Dear Father," June 7, 1864, VTHS; Hosea Towne to "Dear Friends," June 9, 1864, NHHS; Joseph Cross to "Dear Emma," June 5, 1864, AAS; Carleton Felch Diary, June 4, 1864, FM; Harrison George to "Dear Sister," June 10, 1864, VTHS; Ray, *Diary of a Dead Man*, 196, 198.

58. Charles Coit to "Dear All," June 9, 1864, Yale; Andrew Byrne Diary, June 1–9, 1864, CHS; James Brown to "Dear Brother," June 6, 1864, MEHS; Lorenzo Miles Diary, June 10, 1864, VTHS; Blight, *Brewster Letters*, 314–15; Feidner, *Leach Letters*, 211–13; William Barker to "Luther," June 4, 1864, Lunt Papers, MEHS; Michael Kelly Diary, June 1–3, 1864, CHS; Josiah Corban to "Dear Wife and precious Children," June 7, 1864, CHS; Charles Gould to "Sister Ellen," June 8, 1864, UVM; Avery Cain to "Dear Mother," June 1, 1864, VTHS; Wells Fox to Robert Crouse, June 8, 1864, BL; Zerah Monks to "Dear Hattie," June 11, 1864, WRHS; Washington Roebling to "Dearest Emmie," June 7 [1864], RU; Joseph Clough to Abiah Clough, June 10, 1864, DC; Oscar Robinson to "Dear Mother," June 6, 1864, DC.

59. Tabor Parcher to "Dear Wife," June 7, 1864, UVM; Nevins, *Wainwright Journals*, 412, 419–20; Charles Bates to "Dear Parents," June 20, 1864, VHS; Washington Roebling to "My dear old woman," May 29, 1864, RU; Martin Smith to Sarah Nisbet Smith, May 29, 1864, CL.

60. Longacre, *Wightman Letters*, 191–92, 194; Mushkat, *Voris Letters*, 183; James Hale to "Brother Geo.," June 19, 1864, CL; Loving, *Whitman Letters*, 123.

61. George Upton to "My Dear Sarah," July 10, 1864, NHHS; Beale, *Welles Diary*, 2:78; Rosenblatt and Rosenblatt, *Fisk Letters*, 228; William B. Franklin to William F. Smith, June 29, 1864, VTHS; Zerah Monks to "Dear Hattie," June 19, 1864, WRHS; William Boston to "Dear Aunt," September 8, 1864, BL; James K. Hale to "Brother Geo.," June 19, 1864, CL; Luigi di Cesnola to Hiram Hitchcock, May 28, 1864, and to "My dear Friend," June 30, 1864, DC; William Harris Journal, June 13, 1864, VHS; Howe, *Holmes Letters*, 150.

62. James Irwin to "Dear Mother," June 9, 1864, BL; Edward Hall to "Dear Susan," June 20, 1864, NHHS; Rufus Dawes to "My dear Wife," June 15, 1864, WHS.

63. *OR*, 36(1):22–23, and 36(3):745–46; [Franklin Candee] to Horace Fenn, June 21, 1864, CHS; George Fowle to "Dear Eliza," June 21, 1864, MHS; Dowdey and Manarin, *Lee Papers*, 777–78.

64. *OR*, 36(1):186–87, 784–85, 868, 1095–96, 37(1):94–97, 598; David Cushman Diary, June 5–10, 1864, AAS; Nathan Webb Journal, June 16–18, 1864, CL; Floyd, *Dear Friends at Home*, 44.

65. *OR*, 37(1):99–102, 160; Cutrer, *Goree Letters*, 124; Charles Babbitt to "Dear Father," July 4, 1864, RBHPL; Henry Converse to Hiram Converse, July 12, 1864, AAS; Eby, *Strother Diaries*, 266–75; Duncan, *Neil Letters*, 38–39.

66. Andrew Linscott to "Dear Parents," June 19, 1864, MHS; Samuel Gilpin Diary, June 14, 1864, LC; Charles Putnam to unidentified recipient, June 18, 1864, VTHS; James Perry Diary, June 17, 1864, WHS; Albert Rogall Diary, June 17, 1864, OHS; *OR*, 40(1):303, and 40(2):57–58; Meade, *Life and Letters*, 2:204; Charles Greenleaf to "Dear Father & Mother," June 20, 1864, CHS.

67. *OR*, 40(1):705, 721, 724; Hilon Parker to "Dear Sister," June 19, 1864, CL;

Longacre, *Wightman Letters*, 192. This little action, known as the battle of Baylor's Farm, is immortalized in André Castaigne's painting *Charge of the 22nd Negro Regiment, Petersburg*, in the West Point Museum.

68. *OR*, 40(1):705, 721–22; David Kendall to "Dear Ones at Home," June 21, 1864, BL; Andrew Byrne Diary, June 15, 1864, CHS; Charles Coit to "Dear Sis & all," June 16, 1864, Yale; John Bassett Diary, June 15, 1864, MHS; Longacre, *Wightman Letters*, 192–93; Nicholas Bowen and Maurice Lamprey diaries, June 15, 1864, both in Smith Papers, VTHS; Louis Bell to "Dear George," August 12, 1864, NHHS.

69. Charles Merrill to "Dear Annie," June 16, 1864, Yale; Charles Paine to "Dear Father," June 17, 1864, MHS; Hilon Parker to "Dear Sister," June 19, 1864, CL; Carlos Lyman to "Dear Ones at Home," June 19, 1864, WRHS; George Bates to "Dear Parents," June 19, 1864, CL. For this and other Petersburg actions, see Greene, *Civil War Petersburg*, and Hess, *In the Trenches at Petersburg*.

70. *OR*, 40(1):317, 705, 40(2):675–78. Winfield Hancock complained as early as June 26 that official sources seemed to hold him, rather than Smith, responsible for the lethargy on the evening of June 15 (*OR*, 40[1]:313–14), and General Grant reported critically on Smith's June 15 performance in his end-of-war report (*OR*, 40[1]:25). In 1897 a former Signal Corps sergeant produced signalmen's diaries that indicated Smith had halted in obedience to an order transmitted from Ben Butler, at Bermuda Hundred — but, as exculpatory as that evidence seemed, Smith could not recall receiving such an order. No original was ever found, and Smith never mentioned it in his report to Butler, who later blamed Smith for the failure. See Thomas Baird's affidavit, the diaries of Archibald Thompson and Maurice Lamprey, and Smith's "Story of the Suppressed Dispatch," in Smith's papers, VTHS. The surviving dispatches from Butler in *OR*, 40(2):83, instruct Smith to continue the attack.

71. *OR*, 40(1):306–7, 40(2):53, 74, 78–79, 659, 660, 665; Sullivan Green Diary, June 16, 1864, WHS; Thomas Burnham to "Dear Friends," June 19, 1864, VTHS; James Perry Diary, June 16, 1864, WHS; Sparks, *Patrick Diary*, 382–84.

72. *OR*, 40(1):306, and 40(2):98–99, 106–7; George Stearns to "Dear Mother," June 18, 1864, NHHS; Longacre, *Wightman Letters*, 193–94; George Benton Codman to "Dear Sister," June 28, 1864, DC; Nicholas Bowen Diary, June 16, 1864, Smith Papers, VTHS. On his way to Petersburg Hancock could find no inhabitants who knew of a Harrison's Creek in the vicinity (*OR*, 40[1]:303–4), but today the stream is known by that name.

73. *OR*, 40(1):306–7, 522, 532–33; Agassiz, *Lyman Letters*, 166–67; Charles Cummings to "My Dear Wife," June 18, 1864, VTHS; Ransom Sargent to "My darling Wife," June 18, 1864, DC; Willard Templeton to "Dear Friends at Home," June 18, 1864, NHSL; Henry White Diary, June 17, 1864, AAS; Sewell Tilton Diary, June 17, 1864, NHHS; George Hawkes Diary, June 17, 1864, USAMHI; Weld, *War Diary*, 311–12.

74. *OR*, 40(2):664–67; Dowdey and Manarin, *Lee Papers*, 790.

75. Coco, *Mills Letters*, 115; William Harris Diary, June 18, 1864, VHS; Andrew Linscott to "Dear Parents," June 19, 1864, MHS; Weld, *War Diary*, 313; *OR*, 40(1):572–73, and 40(2):668; Lyman Jackman Diary, June 18, 1864, NHHS; John Irwin to "Mother dear Mother," June 18, 1864, BL.

76. Frederic Howes to "My Dear Wife," June 18, 1864, MNHS.

77. Aldace Walker to "Dear Father," June 18, 1864, VTHS; Hunter, "Ferguson Diaries," 211; *OR*, 40(1):572–73, and 40(2):167, 179; Nevins, *Wainwright Journals*, 424–25; Meade, *Life and Letters*, 2:207; Lyman Jackman Diary, June 18, 1864, NHHS.

78. Robertson, *McAllister Letters*, 443–44; *OR*, 36(1):140, 156, 169, and 40(1):222; Messent and Courtney, *Twichell Letters*, 306.

79. E. S. Wardwell to Mary Howes, June 28, 1864, MNHS.

80. Agassiz, *Lyman Letters*, 168; George Codman to "Dear Sister," June 28, 1864, DC; Britton and Reed, *Hartwell Letters*, 240.

81. For more on skulking officers see, for instance, Longacre, *Wightman Letters*, 193, and Edward Hall to "My dear wife and son," June 7, 1864, NHHS. Casualty figures are taken from Dyer, *Compendium*. An infantry regiment was allowed three officers for each of its ten 100-man companies, or 3 percent; a heavy-artillery regiment had five company officers for each of eighteen companies with as many as 156 men apiece, or 3.21 percent (*OR* Series 3, 1:155–56).

82. Horatio Taft Diary, May 12, 1864, LC; Blight, *Brewster Letters*, 313; Rufus Dawes to "My dear Wife," June 19, 1864, WHS; Elmer Wallace to "My Dear Parents," June 24, 1864, BL.

83. Albert Luther to "My Dear Father," June 21, 1864, ISL; George Monks to "Dear Sister Maggie," June 24, 1864, WRHS; James Rickard to "Dear Sister," July 5, 1864, AAS; George Barnard to "Dear Father," June 23, 1864, MHS; Francis Barlow to "My very dear mother and brother," June 23, 1864, MHS; Zerah Monks to "Dear Hattie," June 19, 1864, WRHS; Washington Roebling to "My dear Emily," August 26, 1864, RU.

84. *OR*, 40(1):620–21, and 40(2):232, 233; Samuel Gilpin Diary, June 22, 1864, LC. A. Wilson Greene, the preeminent student of the Petersburg campaign, notes in *Civil War Petersburg* (p. 4) that the official name of the railroad to Weldon was the Petersburg Railroad; Confederate maps identify it as the Petersburg & Weldon Railroad, but in conformity with the shorthand of most official reports and secondary histories it is referred to here as the Weldon Railroad.

85. *OR*, 40(1):501–3, and 40(2):281–82; Lorenzo Miles Diary, June 21–23, 1864, VTHS; Ransom Towle Diary, June 21–23, 1864, VTHS; Lyman Jackman Diary, June 22, 1864, NHHS; Aldace Walker to "Dear Father," June 26, 1864, VTHS; Carlos Lyman to "Dear Ones at Home," June 24, 1864, WRHS; Isaac Watts Diary, June 23 and 24, 1864, UVM; Darius Safford to "Dear Sister," August 2, 1864, VTHS; Peter Abbott to "Friends at Home," June 25, 1864, VTHS; Destler, "Ross Diary," 231; Nevins, *Wainwright Journals*, 427; William West Diary, June 21–24, 1864, MHS.

86. *OR*, 40(1):232, 237–38, 620–24; Samuel Gilpin Diary, June 22–July 1, 1864, LC; George Stevens to "Darling Hattie," July 1, 1864, CL; Flavius Bellamy to "Dear Parents," July 3, 1864, ISL.

87. See Greene, *Civil War Petersburg*, for the civilian experience in the besieged city as well as for military operations.

88. *OR*, 36(2):18–19, 133, 149, 164, 180, and 40(1):238; Longacre, *Wightman Letters*, 198; Elmer Wallace to "My Dear Parents," June 24, 1864, BL; George Upton to "My Dear Sarah," July 10, 1864, NHHS; Collier and Collier, *Chase Letters*, 354–55. Meade's and Butler's armies suffered 75,573 casualties between May 4 and June 30.

3. From Their Graves in the Trenches

1. Nevins and Thomas, *Strong Diary*, 3:458, 459, 460, 466; Niven, *Chase Papers*, 1:461, 470–71; *New York Times*, June 21–23, 1864. The price of gold, though usually quoted without a dollar sign, refers to the number of paper dollars required to buy one hundred dollars in gold coin.

2. *OR*, Series 3, 4:448–49; George Marden to unidentified correspondent, July 16, 1864, DC; "Mary" to "My Dear Sister," April 25, 1864, Savage Papers, UVM; Maria Sargent to Ransom Sargent, July 5, and August 19, 1864, DC; Sarah Low to "Dear Aunt," July 10, 1864, NHHS; Wainwright, *Fisher Diary*, 479.

3. *Evening News*, May 25, 1864; B. F. Knowles to Moses Southard, November 20, 1864, MEHS; E. Cooke to "My Dear Jay," July 12, 1864, RBHPL.

4. James Burrows to "Dear Brother," June 17, 1864, CCHS; Harlan Chapman to "Dear Mother," June 1, 1864, WRHS; Emily Harris to "My Dear Husband," February 23, 1864, UNH; *Portland Daily Press*, June 24, 1864; E. A. Miller to "My dear Child," April 16, 1864, CinHS; Horatio Wordsworth to "My Dear Mother," July 3, 1864, UR;

Gilbert Gulbrandson to "Brother Hans," November 15, 1864, USAMHI; Dennis Townsend to "Dear Parents Brothers & Sisters," January 10, 1865, VTHS.

5. Charles Merrill to "Dear Father," February 19, 1865, Yale.

6. Blair, *Geary Letters*, 178–79; Ellen Horton to Edwin Horton, May 6, 1864, VTHS; John Arnold to "Dear wife and family," May 19, June 5, July 7, and August 28, 1864, LC; James Uhler to "Provost marshal," October 11, 1864, Cumberland County Historical Society; Rachel Woods to "Beloved Father & Mother," January 17, 1865, Beard Papers, VTHS; Emily Harris to "My dear husband," April 3, 1865, UNH.

7. Orra Bailey to his wife, March 25, 1863, CHS, and to "My Dear Wife," June 6, July 31, August 7, and August 31, 1864, LC.

8. Eugene Hadley to "My Dear Wife" and to "Capt. Cunningham," both October 2, 1864, Jewett Papers, LC.

9. John McCoy to "Dear Martha," June 25, 1864, DC; John Peirce to "My Dear Wife," June 2 and 23, 1864, PEM; Kohl, *Welsh Letters*, 87, 88; Frederick Hooker to Mary and Nancy Hooker, April 14, April 22, May 9, June 10, July 3, and July 26, 1864, CHS.

10. J. B. Dawley to "Dear Brother," January 15, "1864" [1865], Yale; Joseph Lester to "Dear Father and Sister," June 5, 1864, LC; William Willoughby to "My Dear Wife," May 13 and 22, June 17 and 18, and September 22, 1864, AAS; Benjamin Wright to "My Dear Abbie," June 19, 1864, WHS; William Henry to "My own darling wife," July 25, 1864, VTHS; Blair, *Geary Letters*, 179. Earlier in the war, the military governor of Arkansas accused Major General Samuel Curtis of neglecting his duties to speculate extensively in cotton (John S. Phelps to Edwin Stanton, October 20, 1862, LC).

11. Charles Tillison to Dudley Tillison, May 31 and November 22, 1863, VTHS; Rufus Mead to "Dear Folks at Home," May 9 and August 29, 1863, LC; William Bradbury to his wife, June 27, July 5, and October 10, 1863, June 12, 1864, and June 4 and July 15, 1865, and to "Dear Frederic," June 28, 1864, LC.

12. Chauncey Hill to Sarah Hill, June 17, 1864, MNHS.

13. *OR*, 24(3):460, 470, and Series 2, 6:78–79, 279–80, 601.

14. *OR*, Series 2, 6: 471–73, 594–600.

15. John Hatch to E. A. Hitchcock, May 12, 1864, CL; *OR*, Series 2, 7:606–7.

16. *OR*, Series 2, 8:991–94. Roger Pickenpaugh's *Captives in Gray* provides the only study of Union military prisons overall.

17. *OR*, Series 2, 7:424–25, 467, 488–89, 8:997–98, and Series 3, 4:188; Allen Dauchey to Mary Saunders, November 28, 1864, CHS; Samuel Burnham to "My Dear Mother," July 1, 1864, NHHS.

18. *OR*, Series 2, 7:205, 208–9, 401–2, 441–42, 458, 467.

19. Bradford Sparrow Diary, July 12, 1864, UVM; John Gallison Diary, May 30, 1864, MHS; William McKell Journal, May 26, 1864, RBHPL; William Keys Diary, July 1, August 8, 1864, RU; Henry Adams Diary, July 1, 1864, CHS; George Crosby Diary, August 19, 1864, VTHS; Henry Stone Diary, July 1, 1864, USAMHI; Samuel Grosvenor Diary, July 1, 1864, CHS; John Converse Diary, July 1, 1864, KSHS; Consolidated Morning Reports, July 1–August 9, 1864, RG 249, NA; *OR*, Series 2, 7:441–44. For a complete history of this prison, see Marvel, *Andersonville: The Last Depot*.

20. George Crosby Diary, May 22 and June 19, 1864, VTHS; John Whitten Diary, June 15, 16, and July 2, 1864, SHSI-DM; Bradford Sparrow Diary, July 13–22, 1864, UVM; David Kennedy Diary, July 13, 1864, MNHS; Asa Root Diary, May 25, June 9, 18, and 20, 1864, DRBL; Edmund Pope Diary, July 30, 1864, NHS; John Pride Diary, July 10 and 18, 1864, MNHS; Basile, *Stearns Diary*, 68.

21. Robert Kellogg Diary, May 14, June 29 and 30, 1864, CHS; Helmreich, "Lee Diary," 17–20; Samuel Gibson Diary, May 27, June 18 and 30, 1864, LC; James Vance Diary, June 25, 29, 30, and July 1, 1864, OHS; John Whitten Diary, June 30, 1864, SHSI-DM; Samuel Grosvenor Diary, June 29, 1864, CHS; Henry Adams Diary, June 29 and 30, 1864, CHS; John Converse Diary, June 29 and 30, 1864, KSHS; Alfred Burdick Diary, June 30,

1864, WHS; George Crosby Diary, June 29 and 30, 1864, VTHS; Forbes, *Diary*, 25–26; Henry Tisdale Diary, June 28 and 30, 1864, BPL; William Tritt Diary, June 29–July 1, 1864, USAMHI; John Gallison Diary, June 29 and 30, 1864, MHS; Asa Root Diary, June 29–July 1, 1864, DRBL; Oliver Gates Diary, June 30, 1864, CHS.

22. Forbes, *Diary*, 29; Alfred Burdick Diary, June 30, 1864, WHS; Oliver Gates Diary, July 11, 1864, CHS; John Whitten Diary, July 11, 1864, SHSI-DM; John Gallison Diary, July 11, 1864, MHS; Helmreich, "Lee Diary," 21; Edmund Pope Diary, July 11, 1864, NHS; Peter Perry Diary, July 11, 1864, MC; George Crosby Diary, July 11, 1864, VTHS; Asa Root Diary, July 11, 1864, DRBL; James Buckley Diary, July 11, 1864, ALPL.

23. *OR*, Series 2, 7:113–14, 150–51, 183–84; Samuel Gibson Diary, May 4, 5, and 10, 1864, LC; David Kennedy Diary, July 12, 1864, MNHS; Dennison, *Diary*, 58; Alfred Burdick Diary, May 30 and June 5, 1864, WHS; J. A. Mendenhall Diary, August 31, 1864, IHS; George Crosby Diary, May 24, 1864, VTHS.

24. Edmund Pope Diary, August 20, 1864, NHS; David Kennedy Diary, June 12, 15, and August 9, 1864, MNHS; Samuel Foust Diary, July 13, 1864, USAMHI; Helmreich, "Lee Diary," 22; J. A. Mendenhall Diary, August 28 and September 3, 1864, IHS; James Vance Diary, August 9, 1864, OHS; Charles Chapin Diary, August 1 and 7, 1864, VTHS; William Keys Diary, July 21 and August 24, 1864, RU; Forbes, *Diary*, 34, 36.

25. David Kennedy Diary, June 22 and July 27, 1864, MNHS; Bradford Sparrow Diary, July 27, 1864, UVM; William Keys Diary, June 22 and July 27, 1864, RU; Basile, *Stearns Diary*, 67, 72; Albert Shatzell Diary, July 27, 1864, NSHS; Ira Forbes Diary, July 27 and August 6, 1864, Yale; James Buckley Diary, August 6, 1864, ALPL; Samuel Grosvenor Diary, July 13, 1864, CHS; Otis Knight Diary, July 13, 1864, USAMHI; Forbes, *Diary*, 34; Oliver Gates Diary, June 22, 1864, CHS; John Pride Diary, August 6, 1864, MNHS; Alvah Skilton Diary, July 29, 1864, RBHPL; Oliver McNary Diary, June 11, 1864, KU.

26. *OR*, Series 2, 6:855, 856, 884–85, 7:163–65, 385, 452–54, 1241, 1246, 1252–56, and 8:66–67, 115–16, 508–10, 692–93; George Buffum to "Dear Wife and Family," [undated, but late summer, 1864], WHS.

27. William Coe to "My dear Neine," March 19, 1864, LC; Samuel Foust Diary, July 13, 1864, USAMHI.

28. James Vance Diary, July 10, 1864, OHS; David Kennedy Diary, July 8, 1864, MNHS; John Gallison Diary, August 7, 1864, MHS; Kendrick R. Howard Diary, August 3, 1864, VTHS; Charles Hunt to John Longyear, July 12, 1864, BL; William Tritt Diary, July 8, 1864, USAMHI; William Keys Diary, August 29, 31, and September 4, 1864, RU.

29. Alvah Skilton Diary, August 30, 1864, RBHPL; Abner Small Diary, December 5, 1864, MEHS; J. G. Wood et al. to James Doolittle, December 16, 1864, WHS.

30. William Keys Diary, July 16, RU; William T. Peabody Diary, July 16, 1864, USAMHI; Forbes, *Diary*, 32; George Crosby Diary, July 18, 1864, VTHS; Peter Perry Diary, July 18 and 19, 1864, MC; Ira Forbes Diary, July 20, 1864, Yale; *OR*, Series 2, 7:615–23.

31. Peter Perry Diary, June 19, 1864, MC; Nehemiah Solon Diary, June 19, 1864, CHS; David Kennedy Diary, June 20, MNHS; Consolidated Morning Reports, June 15–19, 1864, RG 249, NA; Sarah Hill to "My Dear Husband," June 19, 1864, and Chauncey Hill to Sarah, June 17, 1864, MNHS.

32. Robert Kellogg Diary, May 3, 1864, CHS; Ira Sampson Diary, April 30, 1864, SHC; Destler, "Ross Diary," 233–34; Samuel Foust Diary, July 19, 24, and 25, 1864, USAMHI; Ransom Chadwick Diary, July 26, 1864, MNHS; Ira Forbes Diary, July 25, 1864, Yale; Albert Shatzell Diary, July 19 and August 2, 1864, NSHS; Lawson Carley Diary, July 31 and August 5, 1864, SHSI-IC.

33. Samuel Foust Diary, July 8, 10, 15, and 22, 1864, USAMHI; Roe, *Melvin Memorial*, 132–33; Miron Tower Diary excerpt, August 17, 1864, Hill Family Papers, MNHS; Atwater, *Report*, 26.

34. Warren, *Rogers Letters*, 89; John Wilcox Diary, May 12–16, 1864, NHHS; Edward Waite to "Dear Father," June 10, 1864, MEHS.

35. Jaquette, *Hancock Letters*, 88–89; Wilcox Diary, May 17, 1864, NHHS; George Chandler to "My Dear Mother," May 17, 1864, NHHS.

36. William Woodward to "Friend Em," May 23, 1864, USAMHI; Luther Furst Diary, May 15, 1864, USAMHI; Julius Hayden to "Dear Mother," May 14, 1864, AAS.

37. *MSSM*, 4:291, 5:326; Edward Bartlett to "Dear Martha," May 14, 1864, MHS; Nevins and Thomas, *Strong Diary*, 3:450.

38. William Henry to "My blessed darling wife," June 25, 1864, VTHS; Joseph Clough to Abiah Clough, November 8, 1863, DC; Andrew Robeson to "My dear Mother," August 28, 1864, MHS; Charles Cummings to "My Dear Wife," June 28, 1864, VTHS; Charles Bolton Diary, MHS, July 27–August 20, 1864.

39. Rebecca Usher to "Dear Ellen," March 31, 1865, MEHS; John Peirce to "My Dear Wife," August 13, 1864, PEM; W. H. Gay to Elizabeth Shenton, November 24, 1864, VHS; S. P. Bonner to George H. Nye, October 2, 1864, MEHS; Henry Whitney to "Dear Mrs. P.," January 30, 1865, MHS. The letters enclosed in comfort bags may help account for the occasional manuscript collection of correspondence between one woman and numerous soldiers who seem to have been strangers to her.

40. Albert Stearns to "Dear Parents," May 31, 1864, NHHS; Jaquette, *Hancock Letters*, 95–96, 98–99.

41. Thomas Cheney to "Dear Brother," June 11, 1864, UNH; William Henry to Mary Jane Henry, June 4 and 18, 1864, VTHS. The tracing of Colonel Henry's hand is in his papers.

42. Isaiah Robbins Diary, June 3–7, 1864, NHHS; *OR*, Series 3, 4:791; Pease and Randall, *Browning Diary*, 1:676; William Owner Diary, May 12 and 13, 1864, LC; Edward Waite to "Dear Father," June 11, 1864, MEHS.

43. Miller, *Whitman Writings*, 1:224; Sarah Low to "Dear Mother," June 22, 1864, NHHS; James Moore to "My Dr" [Juliet Fellows], May 27, 1864, UR; *OR*, Series 3, 5:239–40; John Warner to "Dear Parents," May 22, 1864, UNH.

44. Miller, *Whitman Writings*, 1:223; George Morgan to Austin Morgan, June 7, 1864, DC; Albert Stearns to "Dear Parents," May 31, 1864, NHHS; Charles Coit to "Dear All," July 6, 1864, Yale. See, for instance, court-martial findings against James Avery, 9th New Hampshire, October 25, 1862, for shooting himself in the hand at Antietam, John E. Mason Memorandum Book, NHHS.

45. George Morgan to Austin Morgan, June 7, 1864, DC; Miller, *Whitman Writings*, 1:227, 228, 230, 231; Charles Chace to "Dear Mother," June 14, 1864, UVM; *MSSM*, 5:648; Sarah Low to "Dear Mother," June 22, 1864, NHHS.

46. Sarah Low to "Dear Aunt," June 7, 1864, NHHS; Barnes, *Medical and Surgical History*, 11:127, 331, 333, 368–69.

47. Wilbur Dubois to John Longyear, June 21, 1864, BL; Lucius Gilmore to "My Dear Brother," June 27, 1864, NHHS; Leander Harris to "Dear Emmy," September 7, 1864, UNH; George Morgan to Austin Morgan, July 11, 1864, DC.

48. *OR*, 37(1):174, 766, 768, 769, and 37(2):6, 11; Mahon, *Chase and Lee Diaries*, 151–52.

49. *OR*, 37(1):174–77, 347, 686; Beale, *Welles Diary*, 2:69–70; David Bates Diary, July 7, 1864, LC; James Moore to "My Kind Friend," July 8, 1864, Fellows Papers, UR; Arthur Nesmith to "Sister Nan," July 17, 1864, DC; Laas, *Lee Letters*, 402; Horatio Taft Diary, July 11, 1864, LC; Pease and Randall, *Browning Diary*, 1:675.

50. *OR*, 37(2):77–79, 98, 130; *New York Times*, July 6, 1864; William McVey Diary, July 7, 1864, OHS; Washington Roebling to Emily Warren, July 7, 1864, RU; Quaife, *Williams Letters*, 335.

51. *OR*, 37(1):193–97, 199–200, 347–48, 350–51; William McVey Diary, July 8 and 9,

1864, OHS; William Henry to "My Darling Wife," July 12, 1864, VTHS; D. B. Harmon to E. N. Thomas, July 22, 1864, AAS; Atwater, *Report*, 18, 44–50.

52. David Bates Diary, July 10, 1864, LC; Bailey and Cottom, *Dunn and Randolph Letters*, 70–71; Lyman Holford Diary, July 10–11, 1864, LC; Horatio Taft Diary, July 10, 1864, LC; Beale, *Welles Diary*, 2:71–72; Eliza Swift to Joseph Swift, July 15, 1864, Yale.

53. Beale, *Welles Diary*, 72, 73, 74, 78; Pease and Randall, *Browning Diary*, 1:676; Stanton to Lincoln, July 9, 1864, in Randall Papers, LC.

54. *OR*, 37(1):767–68, and Series 2, 7:153–54; Younger, *Kean Diary*, 164.

55. *OR*, 37(1):348–49; George Suckley to William Smith, July 12, 1864, VTHS; Pease and Randall, *Browning Diary*, 1: 675–76. General Franklin quickly escaped.

56. Horatio Taft Diary, July 10, 1864, LC; Sarah Low to "Dear Mother," July 11, 1864, NHHS; David Bates Diary, July 11, 1864, LC; Richard Auchmuty to Samuel Wylie Crawford, July 25, 1864, CL; *OR*, 37(1):348; Lyman Holford Diary, July 11, 1864, LC; Beale, *Welles Diary*, 2:72; John Peirce to "My Dear Wife," July 15, 1864, PEM.

57. *OR*, 37(1):348; Horatio Taft Diary, July 10 and 11, 1864, LC; Lorenzo Miles Diary, July 11, 1864, VTHS; Chandler Watts Diary, July 12, 1864, Cheney-Watts Collection, VTHS; Edward Roberts Diary, July 12, 1864, CHS; William H. West Diary, July 12, 1864, MHS; William Adams Diary, July 12, 1864, and Adams to "Dear Father," July 12, 1864, MEHS.

58. George Stevens to "Darling Hattie," July 12, 1864, CL; Lyman Holford Diary, July 12, 1864, LC; Beale, *Welles Diary*, 2:74–76; Benjamin French to "My Dear Sister," July 17, 1864, NHHS; Henry Keiser Diary, July 12, 1864, USAMHI; Lorenzo Miles Diary, July 12, 1864, VTHS; Lyman Williams to "Dear Sister," July 17, 1864, VTHS; David Bates Diary, July 13, 1864, LC; Benjamin Hulburd to Juliana Hulburd, July 12, 1864, VTHS.

59. *OR*, 37(1):265, 37(2):259, 40(2):559, and 40(3):122–23; Franklin Fitts to "Dear Sister," July 13, 1864, UNH; Sylvester Bishop to "Dear Mother," July 29, 1864, ISL.

60. Lyman Williams to "Dear Sister," July 17, 1864, VTHS; *OR*, 37(1):268–69, 37(2):285, 368, 596–97; George Bates to "Dear Parents," July 15 and 24, 1864, CL; Edward Belville to "Dear mother," July 26, 1864, Rutherford Papers, UVM; Lorenzo Miles Diary, July 13–15, 1864, VTHS; Benjamin Hulburd to "Wife and friends," July 23, 1864, VTHS.

61. Benjamin French to "My Dear Sister," July 17, 1864, NHHS; Beale, *Bates Diary*, 385; Beale, *Welles Diary*, 2:77; Pease and Randall, *Browning Diary*, 1:676.

62. Charles Merrill to "Dear Annie," July 15, 1864, Yale; Wiggins, *Gorgas Journals*, 122; Younger, *Kean Diary*, 164.

63. Jones, *Diary*, 229.

64. *OR*, 38(1):70–71, and 38(5):104; Charles Cady to "Dear Brother," July 11, 1864; UIA; James Miller to "Dear Brother," July 15, 1864, CL; James Proudfit to "Dearest Emelie," June 27, 1864, KU; William Lowes to "Dear Bro & Sister," September 14, 1864, OHS; Sylvester, "Cox Letters," 200. For the effect of mail on morale see, for instance, B. F. Fellows to Sarah Marston, July 8, 1864, DC; Horatio Fish to W. H. Potter, March 26, 1864, CHS.

65. *OR*, 38(3):618–19, and 38(5):878, 881, 888; Rufus Mead to "Dear Folk at Home," July 19, 1864, LC.

66. *OR*, 38(1):71–72, 38(3):630–31, 697–99, 871, and 38(5):196–201, 892–97; Andrew Harris to "Dear Parents," July 22, 1864, KU; George Hudson to "Dear Mother," July 24, 1864, LC; Blair, *Geary Letters*, 188–89; Quaife, *Williams Letters*, 335.

67. *OR*, 38(1):72–75, 38(2):761–62, 38(3):564, 631, 38(5):929; A. E. Kinney to "Mrs. Boughton," July 26, 1864, CL; Marshall Miller to "Ever Dear Wife," July 22, 1864, LC; L. W. Costellow to "My Dear Brother," September 18, 1864, MEHS; Albion Gross to "My Dearest Companion," July 25, 1864, MNHS; Charles Smith to "Dear Father," July 26, 1864, WHS; Thomas Christie to "Dear Sandy," July 25, 1864, MNHS; John Boardman to

"Father," July 25, 1864, BL; Alvah Skilton Diary, July 22, 1864, RBHPL; Chauncey Mead to "Dear Kate," July 25, 1864, WRHS.

68. *OR*, 39(1):77–78, 39(2):914–18, 953–57, 963–65, 38(3):688–89; Lawson Carley Diary, July 30–August 7, 1864, SHSI-IC; J. A. Mendenhall Diary, August 6–9, 1864, IHS; William Keys Diary, August 3 and 4, 1864, RU.

69. *OR*, 38(1):77–78, and 38(5):917–19, 925, 946; Charles Smith to "Dear Father," July 31, 1864, WHS; Charles Senior to "Dear Father," July 31, 1864, UVA.

70. Marshall Miller to "Ever Dear Wife," July 22 (July 23 addendum), 1864, LC; Henry Guyer to "Dear Brother," August 6, 1864, Yale; Joseph Kohout to "Dear Father," August 23, 1864, UIA; George Beadle to "Dear Miss," August 25, 1864, WRHS; Isaiah Harris to "Dear Parents," August 23, 1864, KU; Blair, *Geary Letters*, 196.

71. Marshall Miller to "Ever Dear Wife," August 14, "1865" [1864], LC; James Congleton Diary, August 20, 1864, LC; Clason Miller to "My Dear Mother," August 28, 1864, CinHS; James Giauque to "Brother Alf," August 10, 1864, UIA.

72. Blair, *Geary Letters*, 197; Rufus Mead to "Dear Folks at Home," August 20, 1864, LC; Nevins and Thomas, *Strong Diary*, 3:467.

73. *CWL*, 6:314–16, 7:435, 440–42, 451, 459–60; *New York Times*, July 23, 1864; Meade, *Life and Letters*, 2:215–16. It seems possible that the increasingly reduced circumstances of the embattled Southern population would have persuaded a majority to accept reunion prior to complete military collapse — perhaps as early as November of 1864 — had it not been for the added demand of abolition. Fear of worsening the resistance had originally motivated many Northern citizens and Union soldiers to oppose emancipation policy.

74. *RCCW*, 126–28; Henry Heisler to "Dear Sister," July 20, 26, and 29, 1864, LC; Ransom Sargent to "My Darling Wife," July 27, 1864, DC; Greenleaf, *Letters to Eliza*, 117; James Rickard to "Dear Sister Lizzie," July 24, 1864, and to "Dear Brother," July 28, 1864, AAS; William Barker to "Luther," July 15, 1864, Lunt Papers, MEHS; Charles Cummings to "My Dear Wife," July 23, 1864, VTHS; John Sheahan to "My Dear Father," July 6 and 27, 1864, MEHS; *Portland Daily Press*, July 29, 1864.

75. Sumner, *Comstock Diary*, 279; Nevins, *Wainwright Journals*, 439; Sparks, *Patrick Diary*, 403–4; Meade, *Life and Letters*, 2:217. Grant's optimism ("So fair an opportunity will probably never occur again. . . .") was expressed after the fact, but seemed almost universal.

76. James Coe to Robert Crouse, July 24, 1864, BL; William Tilton Diary, August 1, 1864, MHS; *RCCW*, 17, 42, 98, 125. For the most recent and thorough account of the Crater episode see Hess, *Into the Crater*.

77. Andrew Robeson to "My dear Mother," July 31, 1864, MHS; Leander Harris to "My Darling," August 3, 1864, UNH; Longacre, *Wightman Letters*, 203; James Wade to "Dear Mother," August 1, 1864, LC; Wesley Darling to "Dear Father," August 1, 1864, WRHS; William Willoughby Diary, July 30, 1864, AAS; *OR*, 40(3):568; Sparks, *Patrick Diary*, 404–5.

78. *RCCW*, 16–17.

79. John Bassett Diary, July 30, 1864, MHS; Henry Muchmore Diary, July 28 and 29, 1864, DC; George Wheeler Diary, July 29, 1864, NSHS; Howard Hanson Diary, July 30, 1864, UNH; Henry White Diary, July 29, 1864, AAS; Conrad Noll Diary, July 30, 1864, BL; William Childs to "Dear Friend Spalding," July 27 and August 1, 1864, BL; Lyman Jackman Diary, July 29 and 30, 1864, NHHS; Caleb Beal to "Dear Uncle," August 5, 1864, MHS; Rufus Dawes to "My Dear Wife," July 30, 1864, WHS; Henry Young to "Dear Delia," August 4, 1864, WHS; James Perry Diary, July 30, 1864, WHS; Weld, *War Diary*, 353; Austin Kendall to "Dear Friends at Home," August 7, 1864, BL. The reported time of the explosion varies by more than an hour among eyewitnesses.

80. William Hamilton to "My dear Mother," July 31, 1864, LC; Henry Heisler to "Dear Sister," July 31, 1864, LC; George Codman to "Dear Sister," July 31, 1864, DC; *OR*,

40(3):820; Weld, *War Diary*, 352–53; *RCCW*, 206–22; William Harris Diary, July 30, 1864, VHS; Henry White Diary, July 30, 1864, AAS; George Harrington to William Pitt Fessenden, August 1, 1864, Abraham Lincoln Papers, Yale.

81. Charles Cummings to "My Dear Wife," July 31, 1864, VTHS; Claudius Grant to "My Dear Carrie," August 1, 1864, BL; Caleb Beal to "Dear Uncle," August 5, 1864, MHS; Josiah Jones Diary, July 30, 1864, NHHS; Charles Maxim to "My Dear Mother," July 31, 1864, CL; William Childs to "Dear Friend Spalding," July 27 and August 1, 1864, BL; Fred Ployer to "Friend Israel," August 3, 1864, USAMHI; *OR*, 40(3):657–60; Coco, *Mills Letters*, 139; Henry Young to "Dear Delia," August 4, 1864, WHS; Avery Cain to "Dear Mother," August 4, 1864, VTHS; William Tilton Diary, July 30, 1864, MHS; Henry White Diary, July 30, 1864, AAS; James Rickard to "Dear Sister," July 31, 1864, AAS; Louis Bell to "Dear George," August 12, 1864, NHHS.

82. William Tilton Diary, July 31, 1864, MHS; Henry Heisler to "Dear Sister," July 31, 1864, LC; Albert Rogall Diary, July 30, 1864, OHS; William Harris Diary, July 30, 1864, VHS; Henry Metzger to "Dear Sister," USAMHI; *OR*, 40(1):246–48. After deducting those who were captured, officers composed 10.9 percent of the casualties in the white divisions, but only 6.1 percent in Ferrero's.

83. Longacre, *Wightman Letters*, 204; William Brown to George Chandler, August 7, 1864, NHHS; *OR*, 40(3):662; Claudius Grant to "My Dear Carrie," August 1, 1864, BL; Charles Coit to "Dear All," August 3, 1864, Yale; George Fowle to "Dear Eliza," July 31, 1864, MHS; William Harris Diary, July 30, 1864, VHS; Loving, *Whitman Letters*, 128; Zerah Monks to "My Dear Sister," August 2, 1864, WRHS; Weld, *War Diary*, 354.

84. George Codman to "Dear Sister," July 31, 1864, DC; William Harris Diary, July 30, 1864, VHS; Ransom Sargent to "My own sweet Wife," August 1 and 9, 1864, DC; John Bailey Journal, July 30, 1864, NHHS; Lewis Simonds Diary, August 1, 1864, DC. In 1989 that spot of gore still clung to Burnside's withdrawal order (Burnside to Julius White, July 30, 1864, Box 18, Burnside Papers, RG 94, NA), and it is probably there yet.

85. William Harris Diary, July 30, 1864, VHS; *OR*, 40(3):691, 821; Charles Merrill to "Dear Father," August 2, 1864, Yale; Ransom Sargent Diary, August 1, 1864, DC; Howard Hanson Diary, August 1, 1864, UNH; John Irwin to "Dear Sister," August 3, 1864, BL; Caleb Beal to "Dear Uncle," August 5, 1864, MHS; William Boston to "Dear Aunt," August 1, 1864, BL; Josiah Jones Diary, August 1, 1864, NHHS. Captain Jones does not specify whether it was a Union or Confederate soldier who proposed going home.

86. Coco, *Mills Letters*, 140–45; John Bassett Diary, July 30, 1864, MHS; Austin Kendall to "Dear Friends at Home," August 7, 1864, BL; Alfred Milnes to "Dear Father," August 3, 1864, BL; Lyman Barton to Mary Melissa Barton, August 12, 1864, VTHS.

87. George Julian to "My Dear Parents," August 10, 1864, UNH; Henry Snow to "My Dear Mother," August 3, 1864, CHS; Oscar Robinson to "Dear Sister," August 5, 1864, DC; Theodore Lyman to "My Own Dearest," July 31, 1864, MHS; *USG*, 11:363.

88. Luther Lawrence to "My Dear Frank," August 9, 1864, NYHS; Oscar Robinson to "Dear Sister," August 3, 1864, DC.

4. She with Thin Form Presently Drest in Black

1. *OR*, Series 3, 4:386–87, 475–76, 515–16; David Bates Diary, August 4, 1864, LC.

2. *OR*, Series 3, 4:421, 5:784; J. B. Dawley to "Dear Brother," September 21, 1864, Yale.

3. Hiram Ketcham Diary, November 13, 1864, and May 10, 1865, BGSU; Kamphoefner and Helbich, *Germans in the Civil War*, 284.

4. Francis Brooks Diary, June 29, 1864, MHS; Mary Jane Henry to William Henry, August 3 and 5, 1864, VTHS; Frederick Bill to H. C. Holmes, August 2, 1864, CHS; James Milliken to "Dear Charles," August 17 and 28, 1864, MEHS; "Copy of Returns to Provost

Marshall [*sic*]," Old Town Records, CPL; Nevins and Thomas, *Strong Diary*, 3:449, 450, 472, 479; William Owner Diary, August 24, 1864, LC.

5. Horatio Wordsworth to "Dear Juliet," September 19, 1864, UR; Joseph Pollard to "Dear Cyrus," September 2, 1864, CL; Kamphoefner and Helbich, *Germans in the Civil War*, 112; E. A. Kelley to Joseph Colton, July 31, 1864, VTHS; George French to "Friends at Home," August 18, 1864, and to "Father," August 25, 1864 and January 22, 1865, VTHS; Harrison Weeks to "Dear Father," July 6, 1864, IU; Clarkson Butterworth Diary, August 18–24, September 16, and October 21, 1864, Earlham.

6. William Owner Diary, September 7, 1864, LC; Loving, *Whitman Letters*, 129; Valentine Barney to "My dear Wife M —," July 31, 1864, VTHS; Ohio Provost Marshal's Papers, 238, OHS; Virgil Taylor to Andrew Foster, July 25 (two letters) and August 2, 1864, Bunt Papers, WRHS; John White to Lucien Eaton, August 8, 1864, MOHS. See Ray, *Diary of a Dead Man*, 249–50, for the affidavit of a reform school inmate who was involuntarily sold to a minister as a substitute for a mere five dollars monthly.

7. Maria Sargent to Ransom Sargent, undated (between July 19 and 24) and September 8, 1864, DC; Mary Foreman to Francis Stewart, August 17, 1864, and January 5, 1865, BGSU; Horatio Wordsworth to "Dear Juliet," September 19, 1864, UR; John Jones to "Dear Brother," September 20, 1864, LC; Nellie Johnson to George Aplin, August 14, 1864, CL; Almyra Barker to "My dear Charles," August 14, 1864, Lunt Papers, MEHS; Elvira Aplin to George Aplin, September 26 and October 22, 1864, CL; Emily Thompson to "Dear Brother & Sister," June 3, "1863" [1864], NHHS; Rachel Aldrich to Asa Aldrich, April 29, 1864, Brownson Papers, NHHS; Myron Underwood to "My Dear Wife," October 5, 1863, UIA; Horatio Wordsworth to "My Dear Mother," July 3, 1864, Fellows Papers, UR; *A Few Words on Behalf of the Loyal Women*, 23. For a particularly rancorous political correspondence between a soldier and his antiwar wife, see the two Leander Harris collections, at DC and UNH.

8. Thomas Barnett Diary, June 18, 1864, Earlham; Claude Goings to Mary Goings, June 2, 1864, DC; Ann Cotton to "My dear Husband," June 2, 1864, LC; Silas Hall to Edwin Hall, August 17, 1864, VTHS; James Fitts to "Dear Mother," August 7, 1864, UNH; Gilbert Gulbrandson to "Parents and Siblings," July 16, 1864, USAMHI; Washington Roebling to "Dearest Emily," June 23, 1864, RU.

9. Ann Cotton to "My dear Husband," June 2, 1864, LC; Mary Foreman to Francis Stewart, August 17, 1864, BGSU; Joseph Hawley to Charles Dudley Warner, August 8, 1864, CHS; George French to "Father," January 22, 1865, VTHS; William Henry to "My darling wife," July 30, 1864, VTHS.

10. George Chandler to "My dear Mother," September 17, 1864, and to "My dear William," September 22, 1864, NHHS; William Tilton Diary, July 4, 1864, MHS; Clement Boughton to "Mother," July 15, 1864, CL.

11. Jonathan Allen to "Dear Father," August 9, 1864, VTHS; A. B. Jewett to William Henry, August 14, 1864, VTHS; Edwin Horton to "Dear Ellen" August 19, 1864, VTHS; Silas Hall to Edwin Hall, August 17, 1864, VTHS.

12. James Fitts to "Dear Mother," July 24, 1864, UNH; William Cheney to "Dear Parents," August 28, 1864, VTHS; Valentine Barney to "My dear Maria," July 3, 1864, VTHS; Edwin Horton to "Dearest Ellen," July 7 and August 1, 1864, VTHS.

13. Louis Bell to his wife (no salutation), August 4, 1864, UNH; Samuel Putnam to "Dear Brother Ote," July 2, 1864, AAS; Eby, *Strother Diaries*, 279–80, 287; Sullivan Green to "Dear Father & Mother," June 30, 1864, and to "Dear Mother," July 10, 1864, BL; George Chandler to "My dear Mother," October 10, 1864, NHHS.

14. Cheney to "Dear Brother," June 23, 1864, and "Dear Sister," September 18, 1864, UNH.

15. Albert Rogall Diary, June 14–17, 1864, OHS; undated specification of charges against Hammond, Reel 8, Stanton Papers, LC; Nevins and Thomas, *Strong Diary*, 3:476.

16. Myron Underwood to "Dear Sophia," June 22, 1864, UIA; Leander Harris to "My

Dear Emmy," June 29, 1864, UNH; Joseph Cross to "My Dear Wife," March 16, 1865, CHS; Amos Currier to "Dear Bro. Stoddard," December 21, 1864, SHSI-IC.

17. John Bowles to Mrs. James Lane, January 15, 1865, KU; R. W. Thompson to Conrad Baker, March 6, 1864, IU; Richard Thompson to Abraham Lincoln, July 29, 1864, ISL; B. G. Farrar to "Dear Brother," August 19, 1864, Sweringen Papers, MOHS.

18. Valentine Barney to "My dear Wife M[aria]," July 31, 1864, VTHS; Grant to Cadwallader Washburn, December 18, 1864, CL.

19. H. E. Lowman to Thomas Carney, August 18, 1864, and F. Johnson to Carney, December 10, 1864, KU; Thomas Murphy to James Lane, October 25, 1864, and Wood Davis to Lane, November 28, 1864, KU. For some details on Usher's skullduggery, see Bain, *Empire Express.*

20. "Annette" to Frances Bixby, undated (summer 1864), VTHS; John Norris to "My Dear Boy," May 24, 1865, Tuttle Manuscripts, IU; Elbridge Searles to Alfred Searles, July 3, 1864, Stanton/Searles Papers, BGSU; Byron McClain to William McClain, July 26, 1864, William McClain to Byron McClain, and George Fluent to William McClain, both August 26, 1864, UIA; Rachel Stevens to "My darling Ann," June 27, 1864, SM; Rose Smelledge to Cynthia French, June 10, 1864, CPL; Emily Thompson to Hannah Aldrich, September 29, 1864, Aldrich-Thompson Family Papers, NHHS; Francis Loud to Julia Comey, July 22, 1864, Brownson Papers, NHHS; William Wilder to Austen Wilder, March 11, 1865, and unsigned note to Austen Wilder, March 13, 1865, HLHS; Gray, *War Letters,* 203–4.

21. Sarah Upton to George Upton, July 29, 1864, George to Sarah, January "18" [25], February 17, and December 13, 1863, July 10 and 28, 1864, George Osgood to Sarah Upton, July 30, 1864, and J. S. Dore to Sarah Upton, December 30, 1864, NHHS; Eighth U.S. Census of Rockingham County, N.H. (M-653, Reel 678), p. 21, and Ninth U.S. Census of Rockingham County, N.H. (M-593, Reel 847), p. 8, RG 29, NA.

22. Sue Gould to "Dear Little Nell," June 5, 1864, UVM; Ellen Emerson to "My dear Alice," September 1, 1864, and to "My dear Haven," October 25, 1864, AAS; Lucy Webb Hayes to Rutherford B. Hayes, June 15 and September 4, 1864, RBHPL.

23. Lucinda Collins to Persis Blanchard, May 8, 1864, and Nelly Fogg to Persis Blanchard, May 9, 1865, MEHS; Lucy Webb Hayes to Rutherford B. Hayes, September 4, 1864, RBHPL; Olive Cheney to Jane Watts, May 22, 1864, VTHS; E. M. Lee to "Dear Lennie," June 21, 1864, Holmes Letters, MHS; "Mother" to Loring Winslow, February 21, 1865, WHS; Buckingham, *All's for the Best,* 295.

24. *Portland Daily Press,* June 24, 25, 29, and 30, 1864; Mary Jane Henry to William Henry, August 3 and 9, 1864, VTHS; Maria Sargent to Ransom Sargent, August 3, 7, and October 9, 1864, DC; Martha Blanchard to "Dear Caleb," August 21, 1864, and Hannah Blanchard to "Dear Sister," August 24, 1864, CHS.

25. Laura Plimpton to Mary Richards and "Lizzie" to same, both October 2, 1864, MNHS; Susan Hooker to "My dear Husband," August 21, 1864, UR; Amanda Chittenden to "My dear husband," June 17, 1863, ISL; Mary Foreman to Francis Stewart, August 17 and December 21, 1864, BGSU.

26. Emma Mitchell to "My Dear Husband," November 20, 1864, April 6 and 9, 1865, MNHS; Thomas Hyatt to "Dear wife," August 6 and 19, 1864, WRHS; William Combs to "Dear Wife," March 21, 1865, ND; Henry Robinson to Eliza Robinson, May 5 and June 8, 1864, and Eliza A. Robinson pension certificate, ISL; assorted affidavits of Lydia A. Wilder, Mother's Pension Application No. 296842, RG15, NA.

27. Amanda Chittenden to "My dear husband," June 17, 1863, ISL; Netta Taylor to Thomas T. Taylor, August 18, September 4, 14, and 28, and November 6, 1864, OHS; Ann Cotton to Dexter Cotton, May 1, 15, and 29, 1864, LC; Emily Harris to "Darling Husband," December 6, 1863, UNH; John Yowell to Caleb Core, January 18, 1864, OHS; Lucinda Sisk to Thomas Poe, April 12, [1864], IHS.

28. *Daily Chronicle,* February 11 and 20, 1865; Tabor Parcher to "Dearest of all dear

wives," April 9, 1864, UVM; Ransom Sargent to "My darling Wife," July 14, 1864, DC; Edwin Horton to Ellen Horton, January 14 and January 29, 1865, VTHS.

29. *OR,* 37(1):326–27, 353–54, 37(2):386, 402–3, 410, 43(1):1022; Eby, *Strother Diaries,* 280–81; Mahon, *Chase and Lee Diaries,* 157.

30. *OR,* 37(1):286, 309–12, 43(1):1022–23; Williams, *Hayes Diary and Letters,* 2:485–86; Mahon, *Chase and Lee Diaries,* 158–59; Duncan, *Neil Letters,* 54–55.

31. *OR,* 37(1):286, 328, 43(1):1023; Williams, *Hayes Diary and Letters,* 2:485; Duncan, *Neil Letters,* 55; John Hamer to "Dear Sister," August 5, 1864, USAMHI; Eby, *Strother Diaries,* 282–83.

32. *OR,* 37(1):330–33, 354–55, 37(2):506–9, 43(1):1023; William Collier to "Miss Mary" [Chapin], August 31, 1864, AAS.

33. *OR,* 37(1):333–37, 354–55; Eby, *Strother Diaries,* 284; A. A. Rutherford to Elizabeth Tuttle, August 8, 1864, IU.

34. *New York Times,* August 8, 1864; Samuel Gilpin Diary, July 30, 1864, LC; William Owner Diary, August 1, 1864, LC; *OR,* 37(2):582–83. As early as July of 1861, Union soldiers on the way to Bull Run completely destroyed the unoffending village of Germantown, Virginia.

35. *RCCW,* 137–232; *USG,* 11:274, 286, 309, 356; Meade, *Life and Letters,* 2:212–13, 216–17; *OR,* 37(2):558.

36. *OR,* 34(4):527. For a highly critical view of Sheridan, see Wittenberg, *Little Phil.*

37. Peter Abbott to "Friends at Home," July 30, 1864, VTHS; *OR,* 37(2):511–12, 564, 43(1):573, 719, 723; Eby, *Strother Diaries,* 286; *CWL,* 7:477.

38. *OR,* 43(1):739–40, 783, 811, 822, 995, 1000–1001; Duncan, *Neil Letters,* 58–59; George Bates to "Dear Parents," August 18, 1864, CL; Mahon, *Chase and Lee Diaries,* 162–65; Richard Anderson Report, Lee Papers, VHS.

39. *OR,* 43(1):697–98, 822; James Fitts to "Dear Father," August 19, 1864, UNH; George Bates to "Dear Parents," August 1 and 18, 1864, CL; Isaac Pierce to "Dear Sister Julia," August 19, 1864, OHS; Wesley Darling to "Dear Father," August 20, 1864, WRHS.

40. *OR,* 43(1): 811, 822, 841, 880, 43(2):69, 920; Houston, *Smith Correspondence,* 219; Kallgren and Crouthamel, *Dear Friend Anna,* 95.

41. *OR,* 34(3):490, 34(4):185; William Eastman to "Dear Sister Carrie," June 22, 1864, MHS; *ORN,* 21:340–41, 357, 379, 386.

42. *ORN,* 21:390, 404, 416; Gray, *War Letters,* 380; *OR,* 39(2):222.

43. *OR Atlas,* 147:1; *OR,* 39(1):404, 419–20; *ORN,* 21:417, 445, 465.

44. *ORN,* 21:417, 445, 576–77, 588–90; Thomas Alexander Diary, August 5, 1864, ND.

45. *ORN,* 21:418–19, 577.

46. Thomas Alexander Diary, August 4, 1864, ND; *New York Times,* August 9, 11, and 12, 1864; Beale, *Welles Diary,* 2:101; Luther Lawrence to "My Dear Frank," August 9, 1864, NYHS.

47. Dabney Maury to Braxton Bragg, July 29, 1864, CL; Thomas Alexander Diary, May 7, 9, and 14, 1864, ND.

48. *OR,* 39(1):427–28, 436; *ORN,* 21:502–3.

49. *OR,* 39(1):403, 417, 426–28, 436–37; *ORN,* 21:414, 801.

50. *OR,* 39(1):436–37; Gray, *War Letters,* 382.

51. See, for instance, *New York Times,* August 12, 1864. Incidentally, volunteers from the 21st Alabama had supplied the last crew of the Confederate submarine *Hunley.*

52. Thomas Alexander Diary, August 9–23, 1864, ND; *OR,* 39(1):418–19, 438–41; Gray, *War Letters,* 380–84.

53. *OR,* 39(1):250–56, 321–24.

54. Ibid., 371, 386–87, 400, 472, 475–84.

55. Ibid., 468–71.

56. Charles Coit to "Dear All," August 9, 1864, Yale.

57. Sullivan Green Diary, August 9, 1864, WHS; Floyd, *Owen Letters,* 49; Avery Cain to "Dear Father," August 9, 1864, VTHS; Sparks, *Patrick Diary,* 412; *OR,* 42(1):17, 954–55.

58. *USG,* 11:402, 404; *OR,* 42(1):216–19, 248–49, 850, and 43(1):43; Sparks, *Patrick Diary,* 414–15; Henry Fowler to "Dear Parents," August 28, 1864, PEM; Leander Harris to "Dear Emmy," August 19, 1864, UNH; Washington Vosburgh to "My own dear Ella," August 22, 1864, BL; Edwin Bearse to "Dear Mother," August 16, 1864, MHS; Mushkat, *Voris Letters,* 211–12; George Towle Diary, August 16, 1864, NHHS.

59. *OR,* 42(1):121, 42(2):244; Henry Fowler to "Dear Parents," August 28, 1864, PEM; *USG,* 11:411–12.

60. *OR,* 42(1):428–29, 851, 857–58, 42(2):244; Nevins, *Wainwright Journals,* 452; Andrew Linscott to "Dear Mary," August 24, 1864, MHS; Greenleaf, *Letters to Eliza,* 129–30; Reid-Green, *Matrau Letters,* 94–95; Elmer Wallace to "My Dear Parents," August 20, 1864, BL; A. Welsh to "Friend William," August 22, 1864, Bonner Papers, CCHS; Zerah Monks to "My Dear Sister," August 25, 1864, WRHS; William Boston Diary, August 19, 1864, BL; John Irwin to "Dear Mother," August 22, 1864, BL; Zerah Monks to "My dear Hattie," August 27, 1864, WRHS; Sumner, *Comstock Diary,* 286.

61. *OR,* 42(1):429–32, 851, 42(2):451; Nevins, *Wainwright Journals,* 453–55; Andrew Linscott to "Dear Mary," August 24, 1864, MHS; Zerah Monks to "My Dear Sister," August 25, 1864, WRHS; Scott, *Willcox Letters,* 571; William Boston Diary, August 21, 1864, BL; John Irwin to "Dear Mother," August 22, 1864, BL; Greenleaf, *Letters to Eliza,* 131; Tower, *Taylor Letters,* 186; Dowdey and Manarin, *Lee Papers,* 922.

62. *OR,* 42(1):222–23, 42(2):363, 368–69, 449, 452, 481–82; Chesson, *Dyer Journal,* 192.

63. *OR,* 42(1):223–29, 252–53, 293–94; Child, *Letters,* 257; Chesson, *Dyer Journal,* 193; Agassiz, *Lyman Letters,* 224–25; Scott, *Willcox Letters,* 571–72; Robertson, *McAllister Letters,* 488; Nevins, *Wainwright Journals,* 457.

64. *OR,* 42(1):131, 228; Washington Roebling to "My dear Emily," August 26, 1864, RU; Sumner, *Comstock Diary,* 287; Agassiz, *Lyman Letters,* 224–25.

65. *OR,* 42(1):218, 227; Charles Coit to "Dear All," August 10, 1864, Yale; Oscar Robinson to "Dear Friends," August 25, 1864, DC; Charles Copp to George Chandler, July 3, 1864, NHHS; Joseph Cross to "Dear Wife & Children," August 28, 1864, AAS.

66. Williams, *Hayes Diary and Letters,* 2:490, 492; Henry Comey to "My Dear Sister," July 16 and 17, 1864, and to "Dear Father," August 13, 1864, AAS; John McIntosh to "Dear Mother," August 9, 1864, WRHS.

67. James Fitts to "Dear Mother," July 24, 1864, UNH; William Henry to Mary Jane Henry, August 3, 1864, VTHS; Quintus Foster to Robert Crouse, undated (but summer 1864), BL; Silas Allen to "Cousin Julett," August 18, 1864, Fellows Papers, UR.

68. Samuel Howe to William Kinerson, August 16, 1864, UVM; Andrew Parsons to "Dearest Friend," June 6, 1864, CL; William Henry to "My own darling wife," July 25, 1864, VTHS; Samuel Bartlett to "Dear sister Hannah," July 2, 1864, CHS; James Fitts to "Dear Mother," July 24, 1864, UNH; Sparks, *Patrick Diary,* 415; Mary Triplett to Mehetabel Loveren, August 21, 1864, DC. The more universal Confederate draft certainly met resistance, mainly in the form of evasion, but it failed to excite such widespread animosity as the Northern version — probably because the Confederate armies were more obviously defending their homeland than invading "foreign" territory.

69. Burlingame and Ettlinger, *Hay Diary,* 224–29; *New York Herald,* July 21 and 22, 1864; *New York World,* July 22, 1864; Beale, *Welles Diary,* 2:83.

70. *Richmond Sentinel,* July 26 and 27, 1864; *Richmond Examiner,* July 26, 1864; *Charleston Mercury,* August 1, 1864. Larry Nelson interprets this episode in *Bullets, Ballots, and Rhetoric,* 64–73.

71. *New York Tribune,* August 5, 1864; Winter Davis to Wade, undated (but August 2

or 3, 1864), LC; *New York World,* August 6, 1864; *Prairie du Chien Courier,* August 25, 1864; Greeley to "My Friend," August 30, 1864, Palmer Collection, WRHS.

72. *CWL,* 7:514–15; Henry Raymond to William Fessenden, August 11, 1864, Goodyear Collection, Yale; Raymond to Lincoln, August 22, 1864, Lincoln Papers, LC; Burlingame and Ettlinger, *Hay Diary,* 247–48.

73. Nevins and Thomas, *Strong Diary,* 3:478; Dana to "Dear Father," August 6, 1864, MHS; William Owner Diary, August 26, 1864, LC.

74. Nevins and Thomas, *Strong Diary,* 3:466; George Marden to unidentified addressee, July 16, 1864, DC; Charles Hogan to James Sweringen, October 6, 1864, MOHS; James Gallatin to James Doolittle, May 10, 1864, WHS; N. B. Cobb to "Brother Walter," December 29, 1864, UVM; A. Washburne to Edward Washburne, September 19, 1864, CL; Aaron Core to Caleb Core, September 18, 1864, OHS; E. Cooke to "My Dear Jay," July 12, 1864, RBHPL; *Portland Daily Press,* June 28, 1864; W. P. Gould to William Fessenden, September 16, 1864, CL.

75. Mary Ritter to "Dear Lib," July 29, 1864, and "Sarah" to "Dear Girls," September 3, 1864, Chandler Papers, UR; George Anthony to "Kind Brother," June 17, 1864, CL; George French to "Dear Father," August 28, 1864, VTHS; John Luther to "My dear Father," August 8, 1864, ISL; William Rudolph to "Dear Cousin Helen," August 30, 1864, IU.

76. John Berry to Samuel Barlow, August 12, 1864, HL; John Sheahan to "My Dear Father," July 14, 1864, MEHS; Christopher Hoyt to "Dear brother and sister," August 25, 1864, NHHS; Britten and Reed, *Hartwell Letters,* 265, 270.

77. Avery Cain to "Dear Father," August 9, 1864, VTHS; Coco, *Mills Letters,* 158; Warren, *Rogers Letters,* 104; Sylvanus Cobb to "Robert B.," August 29, 1864, CL.

78. Alonzo Van Vlack to "Dear Father & Mother," August 11, 1864, BL; William Clayton to "Dear Brot. Charles," August 22, 1864, MNHS; Gray, *War Letters,* 376; Williams, *Hayes Diary and Letters,* 2:499–500; Charles Bates to "Dear Parents," June 20, 1864, VHS; Charles Smith to "Dear Father," September 14, 1864, WHS.

79. Charles M. Colvin Notebook, April 30, 1864, ChiHS; William T. Peabody Diary, July 16, 1864, USAMHI; John Whitten Diary, June 20, July 17, and September 3, 1864, SHSI-DM; Henry Stone Diary, July 16 and August 8, 1864, ANHS; William Keys Diary, July 16, September 1–4, 1864, RU; George Crosby Diary, July 23, 1864, VTHS; Anonymous Diary, August 15, 19, and 31, 1864, ANHS; Roe, *Melvin Memorial,* 123; *New York Times,* August 30, 1864; *OR,* Series 2, 7:767–68, 816, 821; Joseph P. Brainerd epitaph, Greenwood Cemetery, Saint Albans, Vt.

80. Raymond to William Fessenden, August 11, 1864, Goodyear Collection, Yale, and to Lincoln, August 22, 1864, Lincoln Papers, LC; *New York Times,* August 24–28, 1864; *Washington Star,* August 27, 1864.

81. Pierce to John Taylor, August 15, 1864, NHHS.

82. George F. Hoffer to Alexander Long, June 17, 1864, CinHS; *New York Times,* August 31 and September 1, 1864; Burlingame, *Brooks Dispatches,* 132–36. John Waugh provides a close, highly readable account of election-year politics in 1864, including the Democratic convention, in *Reelecting Lincoln.*

83. Warren, *Rogers Letters,* 104; Kallgren and Crouthamel, *Dear Friend Anna,* 100; George Anthony to "Dear Brother," September 4, 1864, CL; McClellan to William Aspinwall, "11PM" [otherwise undated], CL; Sears, *McClellan Papers,* 590–92.

84. Elmer Wallace to "Dear Mother," September 2, 1864, BL; James Coe to Robert Crouse, September 5, 1864, BL; John Majors to "Carrie," September 3, 1864, ISL; Hooker to B. N. Stevens, September 1, 1864, CL; "Lou" to James Denver, September 4, 1864, KU; Henry Winterstein to "Dear Clinton," September 1, 1864, OHS.

85. William Cassidy to Barlow, September 5, 1864, HL; Williams, *Hayes Diary and Letters,* 2:504; M. H. Hart to "Friends Alph & Sarah," September 15, 1864, CCHS; Nevins, *Wainwright Journals,* 461; George Stearns to "Dear Mother," September 18, 1864, NHHS; George Codman to "Little Sissey," September 11, 1864, DC; William Boston to

"Dear Aunt," September 23, 1864, BL; James Rickard to "Dear Brother," September 12, 1864, AAS; "John" [Aughe?] to "Forrest," September 14, 1864, William Hunter Papers, OHS.

5. Horseman and Horse They Knew

1. *OR*, 38(1):79–80, 38(3):691–92, and 38(5):624, 628; Blair, *Geary Letters*, 197.

2. *OR*, 38(3):691, 38(5):990, 997, 1000–1001; Mumford Dixon Diary, August 30, 1864, Duke, quoted in *ORS*, 7:73–74.

3. *OR*, 38(1):80–81; Howe, *Hitchcock Letters*, 161. Hitchcock tried to justify Sherman's inconsistency on a technicality that did not convincingly excuse him for having ordered this mining operation.

4. Mumford Dixon Diary, August 31–September 1, 1864, Duke, quoted in *ORS*, 7:73–74; *OR*, 38(3):694–95, 696; Wynne and Taylor, *Williams Diary*, 110–11.

5. *OR*, 38(3):694–95; Joshua Breyfogle Diary, September 1, 1864, DC; Rufus Mead Diary, September 2, 1864, and Mead to "Dear Folks at Home," September 4, 1864, LC; Henry Comey to "My Dear Father," September 3, 1864, AAS; Dexter Cotton to "My dear wife," September 4, 1864, LC.

6. Joshua Breyfogle Diary, September 2, 1864, DC; Henry Comey to "My Dear Father," September 3, 1864, AAS; Quaife, *Williams Letters*, 341; Wimer Bedford Diary, September 2, 1864, LC.

7. Daniel Hopper to "Dear Brother & Sister," September 16, 1864, WRHS; Judson Austin to "My Dear Wife," September 4, 1864, BL; George Hodges to "Dear Marana," September 9, 1864, WRHS; Blair, *Geary Letters*, 199–200; James Stillwell to "My Dear 'loved one,'" September 3, 1864, OHS; Henry Archer Langdon to "My dear Sister," September 19, 1864, CinHS.

8. Charles Smith to "Dear Father," September 29, 1864, WHS; Nathaniel Parmeter Diary, September 6, 1864, OHS; Mathias Schwab to "Dear Mother," September 10, 1864, CinHS; *OR*, Series 2, 7:791; George DeHart to "Dear Sister," September 16, 1864, SHSI-IC.

9. Beale, *Welles Diary*, 2:135–36; Nevins, *Wainwright Journals*, 460–61; Nevins and Thomas, *Strong Diary*, 3:480–88; *Richmond Examiner*, August 1, 1864.

10. Coco, *Mills Letters*, 163; Frederic Speed to "Dear Anna," September 8, 1864, CL; Benjamin Hill to "Friend Alfred," September 10, 1864, Filley Papers, CHS; Trimble, *Jones Letters*, 109–10; Racine, *Mattocks Journal*, 196.

11. *OR*, 38(3):633, Series 2, 7:773; Henry Adams Diary, September 5, 1864, CHS; Albert Shatzell Diary, September 5, 1864, NSHS.

12. Consolidated Morning Reports, Entry 111, RG 249, NA; *OR*, 38(2):908, Series 2, 7:624, 8:603; Richard Winder to F. W. Dillard, undated and August 12, 1864, Winder Letterbook, RG 153, NA; John Converse Diary, August 8, 22, and September 4, 1864, KSHS; George Crosby Diary, August 19, 1864, VTHS; Samuel Foust Diary, September 2–6, 1864, USAMHI.

13. *OR*, 38(3):1025; Cobb to John Winder, September 6, 1864, UG; *Sumter Republican*, September 10, 1864; J. A. Mendenhall Diary, September 2, 6, and 7, 1864, IHS; Samuel Foust Diary, September 2–6, 1864, USAMHI; Destler, "Ross Diary," 239; Helmreich, "Lee Diary," 24; John Whitten Diary, September 6 and 7, 1864, SHSI-DM.

14. William Keys Diary, September 6–9, 1864, RU; Henry Adams Diary, September 6–8, 1864, CHS; John Whitten Diary, September 6, 8, and 9, 1864, SHSI-DM; Lawson Carley Diary, September 7–9, 1864, SHSI-IC; Hunter, "Ferguson Diary," 221; Consolidated Morning Reports, Entry 111, RG 249, NA; Robert Kellogg Diary, September 6–10, 1864, CHS; Forbes, *Diary*, 44–45; Henry Adams Diary, September 10 and 11, 1864, CHS; Samuel Gibson Diary, September 10 and 11, 1864, LC; "Diary of a Prisoner," 6; John Converse Diary, September 8–15, 1864, KSHS; Alfred Burdick Diary, September 7–12, 1864,

WHS; Futch, "J. M. Burdick Journal," 291; David Kennedy Diary, September 12–14, 1864, MNHS.

15. Forbes, *Diary*, 44–45; John Whitten Diary, September 11–13, 1864, SHSI-DM; William Keys Diary, September 9, 1864, RU.

16. William Keys Diary, September 9, 1864, RU; *Sumter Republican*, August 6, 1864; Roe, *Melvin Memorial*, 132–33; Smith, "Lyth Diary," 23–24; James Vance Diary, September 13 and 14, 1864, OHS.

17. *OR*, 38(5):808, 822, and Series 2, 7:557–66; Consolidated Morning Reports, Entry 111, RG 249, NA.

18. *OR*, Series 2, 7:514, 593, 678, 881–82, 955–56, 993; Lawson Carley Diary, October 11 and 12, 1864, SHSI-IC; John Whitten Diary, November 12, 1864, SHSI-DM.

19. *OR*, Series 2, 7:817; Forbes, *Diary*, 46.

20. *New York Times*, September 5, 1864; *OR*, Series 2, 7:606–7, 790, 793–94, 1070–73; John Whitten Diary, October 12, November 14–18, 1864, SHSI-DM.

21. *OR*, 43(1):822; Series 2, 7:792–93.

22. *OR*, 43(1):45–47, 43(2):102, 107; J. A. Blodgett to "Dear Brother," September 6, 1864, UNH; William Jackman to "Dear Nancy," September 10, 1864, RBHPL; George Bates to "Dear Parents," September 7, 1864, CL; Richard Anderson Report, Lee Papers, VHS; William Davis Diary, September 19, 1864, MEHS; Benjamin Hulburd to "Well Juliana," September 23, 1864, VTHS.

23. *OR*, 43(1):46–47, 150, 554–55; Henry Keiser Diary, September 19, 1864, USAMHI; Jordan, *Gould Journals*, 400–401; Britton and Reed, *Hartwell Letters*, 286–87; Williams, *Hayes Diary and Letters*, 2:508–9; George Burrows to "Dear Mother," September 25, 1864, AAS; Thomas Porter Report, October 4, 1864, Yale; Jonathan Allen to unidentified addressee, September 22, 1864, VTHS; Chapin Warner to "Dear Father & Mother," September 21, 1864, MHS.

24. *OR*, 43(1):46–47, 150, 361–62, 554–55, and 43(2):118–19, 159; Williams, *Hayes Diary and Letters*, 2:509–10; Jonathan Allen to unidentified addressee, September 22, 1864, VTHS; Britton and Reed, *Hartwell Letters*, 287; James Fitts to "Dear Mother," September 21, 1864, UNH; William Hills Diary, September 21, 1864, LC; John Arnold to "Dear Wife and Family," September 23, 1864, LC; Jordan, *Gould Journals*, 402.

25. George French to unidentified addressee, September 22, 1864, VTHS; William Davis Diary, September 20, 1864, MEHS; Jonathan Allen to unidentified addressee, September 22, 1864, VTHS; Williams, *Hayes Diary and Letters*, 2:495; Mahon, *Chase and Lee Diaries*, 167–69; George Bates to "Dear Parents," September 24, 1864, CL.

26. Jonathan Allen to unidentified addressee, September 22, 1864, VTHS; *OR*, 43(1):48–49, 361–62, 556, and 43(2):162; Britton and Reed, *Hartwell Letters*, 290; James Fitts to "Dear Mother," September 23, 1864, UNH; Williams, *Hayes Diary and Letters*, 2:513.

27. *OR*, 43(1):441, 43(2):909–10, 920. Details of these executions appeared in Virginia newspapers decades later: see, for instance, *Richmond Times*, March 14, 1897.

28. *OR*, 43(1):49–50, 556, 558–59, 43(2):877, and 51(2):1041; Richard Anderson Report, Lee Papers, VHS; James Fitts to "Dear Father," September 26, 1864, UNH; Duncan, *Neil Letters*, 67.

29. *New York Times*, September 21 and 24, 1864; *OR*, 43(2):118, 152; Nevins and Thomas, *Strong Diary*, 3:491, 493; Davis, *Butler Letters*, 121.

30. Davis, *Butler Letters*, 123; Eli Johnson to William Henry, July 29, 1864, and Mary Jane Henry to same, August 18, 1864, VTHS; Bender, *Grass before the Scythe*, 122–23, 125; *OR*, Series 3, 4:966.

31. Joseph Cross to "Dear Wife & Son," July 26, 1864, AAS; Florilla Hayden to "My Dear Husband," August 28, 1864, AAS; John McCoy to "Dear Wife," undated, DC; *Keene Sentinel*, September 15, 1864; *New York Times*, August 3, 1956; Lawrence Joyce to "My Dear Wife and Children," October 30, 1864, MEHS; Adelaide Fowler to "My dear

Brother," September 11, 1864, PEM; "Mother" to Thomas Willis, August 14, 1864, CL; Allie Monson to "Dear Friend Nettie," December 20, 1864, Oblinger Papers, NSHS. Although Albert Woolson later remembered that he was born in 1847, early census records instead suggest that he was born in 1848; he died August 2, 1956.

32. Albert Putnam to Eleazer Putnam, September 2, 1864, DC; Sarah Aplin to "Brother George," October 9, 1864, CL; Henry Marshall to "My Dear Hattie," September 26, 1864, CL.

33. Henry Young to "Dear Father," September 19, 1864, WHS; Peck, *Roster*, 29, 105, 141, 176, 213, 597; Higginson, *Massachusetts in the Army and Navy*, 1:216–17, 230–33, 302–9. Other statistics are from tallies of killed or mortally wounded in Dyer's *Compendium*.

34. Joseph Tarbell to "Dear Father & Mother," October 6, 1864, VTHS; Edwin Flagg to "Dear Sister," November 26, 1864, WHS; Warren Goodale to "Dear Children," October 12, 25, and 28, 1864, MHS.

35. Margaret Howe to J. B. Howe, October 16, 1864, MNHS; Chester Evans to "Dear Wife," September 24, 1864, MNHS; John Shumway to "My Dear Wife," October 25 and December 8, 1864, MNHS.

36. John Thompson to "Dear Father," August 4, 1864, NHHS; Richard Kent Diary, August 29, 31, and September 3–5, 1864, NHHS; Emily Thompson to Hannah Aldrich, September 29, 1864, NHHS; *Daily Chronicle*, October 5, 1864.

37. "Bounties Paid to Volunteers," CPL; Ayling, *Register*, 820.

38. *Daily Chronicle*, November 14, 17, 18, and 27, 1863; "Certified Votes of Town Meetings" and "Bounties Paid to Volunteers," CPL. Allen's substitute, a German immigrant going by the name of Charles Miller, also deserted (Ayling, *Register*, 186).

39. *Daily Chronicle*, October 4 and 10, 1864; "Returns to Provost Marshall [*sic*] of Acct of Money Paid for Soldiers, 1863 & 1864," CPL.

40. Marvel, "A Poor Man's Fight," 37–38; *Report of the Treasurer and Selectmen*, 11–14.

41. "Lizzie" to Mary Richards, October 2, 1864, MNHS; Kamphoefner and Helbich, *Germans in the Civil War*, 284, 287, 289.

42. Bradford Darling to "Dear Father," October 3, 1864, WRHS; George Anthony to "Kind Brother," October 24, 1864, CL; Thomas Covert to "My Dear Wife," October 13, 1864, WRHS; Thomas Townsend to "Dear Friend," October 8, 1864, Richmond Papers, WHS; Chester Plimpton to Mary Richards, September 14, 1864, MNHS; Bender, *Grass before the Scythe*, 122–23.

43. Gideon Allen to Annie Cox, December 5, 1864, WHS; Maria Sargent to Ransom Sargent, September 8, 1864, DC; Jonathan Joseph to James Boals, August 4, 1864, ISL.

44. Edward Penney to "Dear Friends," December 5, 1864, Jewett Papers, LC; "Sam" to "Dear Bro.," January 2, 1865, Driver Papers, CL; Norman Carr to "Dear Father," November 20, 1864, and to "Dear Brother," January 7, 1865, UR; John Dickie Journal, December 23, 1864–February 2, 1865, CL; William Phillips to "Dear Father and Mother," January 31, 1865, WHS; Thomas Tobey to "My dear Father," February 27 and March 1, 1865, Yale.

45. Draft Notices of George Leonard, WHMC, and George Cramer, CL; *OR*, Series 3, 5:637; B. F. Knowles to Moses Southard, November 20, 1864, MEHS; Ama Hibbard to "My Dear Uncle and Aunt," September 4, 1864, Beard Papers, VTHS; Gilbert Gulbrandson to unidentified addressee, November 30, 1864, USAMHI; Thomas Honnel to "My Friend," October 17, 1864, OHS; Richard Elder to "Dear Sister," November 3, 1864, OHS; Isaac Down to Hannah Burkett, October 31, 1864, RBHPL.

46. Leander Harris to "My Dear Emmy," December 31, 1864, UNH; Norman Carr to "Dear Parents," February 16, 1865, UR; Orra Bailey to "My Dear Wife," September 19, 25, October 10, and November 27, 1864, LC; Edwin Turner to "My Dear Addie," February 1, 1864, in Turner and Turner, *Letters*, unpaginated; Sparks, *Patrick Diary*, 422.

47. Ayling, *Register*, 541, 1022; *Daily Chronicle*, August 27, 1864; C. W. Rand to L. C.

Turner, August 15, 30, and September 9, 1864, Case 3707, Turner and Baker Case Files (M-797), Roll 105, RG 94, NA.

48. Moses Parker to "Dear Friends," September 11, 1864, and to "Friend Eliza," September 16 [1864], Parker Family Papers, UVM; E. A. Kelley to Joseph Colton, July 18, 1864, VTHS; James Rickard to "Dear Sister Lizzie," September 11, 1864, AAS.

49. Substitute lists, Alexandria Recruiting Records, NHHS; "Bounties Paid to Volunteers," CPL; *Daily Chronicle*, August 28, 1864; Henry Comey to "Dear Father," August 13, 1864, AAS; Warren Goodale to "Dear Children," October 12, 1864, MHS; Charles Copp to George Chandler, July 3, 1864, NHHS; Sewell Tilton Diary, October 20–23, 1864, NHHS; *OR*, 42(3):780, 1036, 1065.

50. Orra Bailey to "My Dear Wife," October 3 and December 11 and 25, 1864, LC; Leander Harris to Emily Harris, January 6, February 7, and September 2, 1864, UNH; Joseph Cross to "Dear Wife & Children," September 23, October 23, and November 30, 1862, and January 18, 1865, and to "Dear Wife & Son," July 26, 1864, AAS; Thomas Covert to "My Dear Wife," July 8–11 and 17, 1864, WRHS; Samuel McCrea to Samuel Hanway, August 2, 1864, KSHS.

51. John Owen to "My Dear Mother," July 4, 1864, MHS; Rufus Kinsley to "Dear Brother," December 11, 1864, VTHS; Towne, *Wood Letters*, 191–92, 197, 198–99; George Stearns to "Dear Mother," July 25 and August 22, 1864, and to "Dear Brother," July 26, 1864, NHHS; Samuel Curtis to "My dear wife," May 3, 1865, Yale.

52. Nevins and Thomas, *Strong Diary*, 3:484; Coco, *Mills Letters*, 147, 163, 168, 176–77; Thomas Honnel to "My Friend," September 25, 1864, OHS; William Boston to "Dear Aunt," September 18 and November 8, 1864, BL; Davis, *Butler Letters*, 123; Nevins, *Wainwright Journals*, 465–66; Mushkat, *Voris Letters*, 223–24.

53. Hammond, *Diary of a Union Lady*, 304; Blair to Berton Able, August 22, 1864, LC.

54. Alphonso Taft to Benjamin Wade, September 8, 1864, LC; H. C. Ingersoll to "Dear Brother," September 8, 1864, MEHS; James Milliken to "Dear Charles," September 14, 1864, MEHS; *New York Times*, September 13 and 14, 1864; *Oxford Democrat*, September 16, 1864.

55. *New York Times*, September 23, 1864; *CWL*, 8:18–19; Laas, *Lee Letters*, 83, 433; John McKay to Montgomery Blair, December 14, 1864, LC; Palmer, *Sumner Letters*, 2:252–53; John Frazier to John Cresswell, October 5, 1864, LC.

56. *CWL*, 8:46, 83–84.

57. *OR*, 42(1):20, 43(2):157, 163, 183.

58. John Irwin to "Dear Mother," August 20, 1864, BL; Ransom Sargent to "My Own Dear Wife," August 17, 1864, DC; Andrew Linscott to "Dear Parents," August 16, 1864, MHS; John E. Bassett Diary, August 15, 1864, MHS; Edwin Bearse to "Dear Mother," August 16, 1864, MHS; Charles Coit to "Dear All," August 18, 1864, Yale; Buckingham, *All's for the Best*, 299–300.

59. Andrew Robeson to "My dear Alice," September 11, 1864, MHS; Benjamin Hill to "Friend Alfred," September 10, 1864, and to "Brother Filley," September 16, 1864, Filley Family Papers, CHS.

60. Charles Merrill to "Dear Father," September 25 and October 10, 1864, Yale; William Boston to "Dear Aunt," September 8 and 10, 1864, BL; Oscar Robinson to "Dear Mother," September 19, 1864, DC; Elmer Wallace to "My Dear Parents," September 13, 1864, BL; Henry Heisler to "Dear Sister," September 2, 1864, LC; Andrew R. Linscott to "Dear Parents," August 7, 1864, MHS.

61. *OR*, 42(1):760, 793; Henry Marshall to "Dear Folks at Home," October 2, 1864, CL; Longacre, *Wightman Letters*, 209; George Anthony to "Dear Brother," October 1, 1864, CL. Richard Sommers's history of this offensive, *Richmond Redeemed*, may be the most thorough and thoughtful study of any Civil War campaign.

62. Samuel Duncan to "Miss Julia," October 22, 1864, NHHS; James Wickes to "My

NOTES TO PAGES 188-195

dear Father," October 2, 4, and 18, 1864, BPL; Henry Marshall to "Dear Folks at Home," October 2, 1864, CL; Longacre, *Wightman Letters*, 209.

63. *OR*, 42(1):135, 793–94, 797; Andrew Byrne Diary, September 29, 1864, CHS; Charles Coit to "Dear All," September 30, 1864, Yale; George Julian to "My dear Parents & Sister," October 5, 1864, UNH; Henry Snow to "My Dear Mother," October 3, 1864, CHS.

64. *OR*, 42(1):760–61, 769, 772; Longacre, *Wightman Letters*, 209–11; Henry Marshall to "Dear Folks at Home," October 2, 1864, CL; Henry Brown to "Dear Friends at Home," October 5, 1864, CHS; Joseph O. Cross to "My Dear wife," October 4, 1864, CHS.

65. *OR*, 42(1):800–801; Charles Coit to "Dear All," September 1, 1864, Yale; Andrew Byrne Diary, September 30, 1864, CHS; Henry Marshall to "Dear Folks at Home," October 2, 1864, and to "My Dear Hattie," October 5, 1864, CL; Sumner, *Comstock Diary*, 291; Henry Brown Diary, September 30, 1864, and to "Dear Friends at Home," October 5, 1864, CHS; Valentine Barney to "My dear Maria," October 17, 1864, VTHS; George Anthony to "Dear Brother," October 14, 1864, CL; Buckingham, *All's for the Best*, 305.

66. *OR*, 42(2):1118; Zerah Monks to "My Dear Sister," October 3, 1864, WRHS; William Boston Diary, September 30, 1864, BL; Lyman Jackman Diary, September 30, 1864, NHHS; Coco, *Mills Letters*, 180; Robertson, *McAllister Letters*, 511–12.

67. Zerah Monks to "My Dear Sister," October 3, 1864, WRHS; Nevins, *Wainwright Journals*, 467; Agassiz, *Lyman Letters*, 235; OR, 42(2):1120; Coco, *Mills Letters*, 180–81; *OR*, 42(2):1137.

68. *OR*, 42(1):138–43, 42(2):1310; Coco, *Mills Letters*, 181; Agassiz, *Lyman Letters*, 235–36; Nevins, *Wainwright Journals*, 467–68.

69. Coco, *Mills Letters*, 181; Nevins, *Wainwright Journals*, 468; Josiah Jones Diary, September 30, 1864, NHHS; Ransom Sargent to "My own dear Wife," September 30 and October 2, 1864, DC; *OR*, 42(1):578–79, 582, 587.

70. Caleb Beal to "Dear Parents," October 5, 1864, MHS; *OR*, 42(1):546, 553, 579; Lyman Jackman Diary, September 30, 1864, NHHS; Oscar Robinson to "My Dear Mother," October 3, 1864, and to "Dear Sister," October 15, 1864, DC; Simon Griffin to Mrs. Charles Cummings, October 2, 1864, VTHS; Charles Manson to "Dear Mother," October 3, 1864, UVM; Jared Potter Diary, September 30–October 1, 1864, USAMHI; John Bailey Journal, September 30, 1864, NHHS; William Lamont to "Dear Sister," October 2, 1864, and to "Friend Daniel," October 6, 1864, WHS; Coco, *Mills Letters*, 181; Charles Reed to "Dear Mother," October 1, 1864, LC.

71. William Boston Diary, October 1, 1864, BL; Josiah Jones Diary, October 1 and 2, 1864, NHHS; *OR*, 42(1):546–47; Robertson, *McAllister Letters*, 511–12; Sumner, *Comstock Diary*, 291; Joseph Cross to "Dear Wife," October 3, 1864, AAS.

72. *OR*, 39(1):488–92; Edward Guerrant Diary, September 3 and 4, 1864, SHC.

73. *OR*, 39(1):555, 558, 39(2):360–61, 398, 408–9; Edward Guerrant Diary, September 29, 1864, SHC.

74. *OR*, 39(1):552–58. On the importance of salt and Saltville, see Lonn, *Salt as a Factor in the Confederacy*.

75. Edward Guerrant Diary, October 2, 1864, SHC; *OR*, 39(1):552–56.

76. *OR*, 39(1):560–62, 566; Edward Guerrant Diary, October 2–4, 1864, SHC; Moore, *Rebellion Record*, 11:454–55; *Daily Virginian*, October 7, 1864, *Richmond Dispatch*, October 12, 1864; *Richmond Whig*, October 7, 1864. Based on an analysis of surgeons' reports, service records, and carded casualty lists of the 5th and 6th Colored Cavalry in the National Archives, I concluded two decades ago that the Saltville "massacre" had been greatly exaggerated by newspapers like the *Virginian*, the *Whig*, and the *Dispatch*, which claimed that as many as 157 black soldiers had been killed (See Marvel, *Southwest Virginia in the Civil War*, 144–48). From those records I could positively identify no more than a dozen men who might have been murdered after the fight, but further research into muster rolls, descriptive lists, and pension records by Bryce Suderow and David Brown has since turned up an additional thirty-four names that may represent men who re-

mained missing after the battle. As in the records I reviewed, duplication and error may still account for many of those thirty-four, but at least eight of them almost certainly disappeared at Saltville in October, and were probably murdered — and more may have been. The legend of the incident did involve much exaggeration, but the execution of twenty or more prisoners better fits the common connotation of a massacre.

77. *OR*, 39(1):801, 39(2):513, 844, 849, 861, 863, 866, 870, 877–79.

78. *OR*, 39(1):585, 594, 39(2):532, and 39(3):69, 70, 73; Angle, *Connolly Letters*, 267–68.

79. *OR*, 39(1):761–66, 813–18, 39(3):55, 69, 70, 73, 92–93; Charles Senior to "Dear Father," October 22, 1864, UVA.

80. *New York Times*, October 7 and 8, 1864; Nevins and Thomas, *Strong Diary*, 3:496–97; *OR*, 39(3):3, 174, 202, 222.

81. *OR*, 39(1):806–7, 810, 812; Wynne and Taylor, *Williams Diary*, 115–17.

82. *OR*, 39(1):582–83, 807, and 39(3):304, 324, 394; Wynne and Taylor, *Williams Letters*, 117–18; Andrew Harris to "Dear Parents," October 26, 1864, KU. See Anne Bailey's thoughtful composite study of the Nashville and Savannah campaigns, *The Chessboard of War*.

83. *OR*, 3:68, 41(1):623; Henry Crawford to "Dear Friends," August 5, 1864, WHMC; "Mrs. Stillman" to "My Dear Brother," undated, WHMC.

84. Nevins and Thomas, *Strong Diary*, 3:494; John Brown Diary, September 6 and 7, 1864, USAMHI; Napoleon Buford to E. R. S. Canby, July 8, 1864, and Kirby Smith to Jefferson Davis, March 11, 1865, Stanton Papers, LC.

85. *OR*, 41(1):307–8; Helen Adams to "Dear Mother Adams," October 5, 1864, UNH.

86. *OR*, 41(1):322, 446–47, 628–31, 644–45.

87. *Weekly Herald*, October 6, 1864; *OR*, 41(1):632; Henry Fike to "Dear Cimbaline and Ellie," October 13 and 17, 1864, KU; Andrew Parsons to "Dearest Friend," October 18, 1864, CL; *OR*, 41(1):645–46, 632–33, 681–82.

88. *OR*, 41(1):472–74; Samuel Curtis to "My dear wife," October 13, 1864, Yale; *Daily Times*, October 16, 1864.

89. Milton Chambers to "Dear brother," July 7, 1864, KU; P. W. Service to Samuel Hanway, September 23, 1864, James Hanway Collection, KSHS; *Kansas Daily Tribune*, October 1, 1864; OR, 41(1):783–91; *New York Times*, October 2, 3, and 8, 1864.

90. *New York Times*, October 12–15, 1864; Thomas Barnett Diary, October 11, 1864, Earlham; John Rice to Sarah Rice, October 13, 1864, RBHPL; Williams, *Hayes Diary and Letters*, 2:526; Dexter Cotton to "My dear wife," October 31, 1864, LC; James Rickard to "Dear Brother," October 16, 1864, AAS; Horatio Taft Diary, October 11, 1864, LC; *Daily Gate City*, October 12, 1864.

91. *OR*, 43(2):249–50, 266; Hilon Parker to "Folks at Home," October 2, 1864, CL; Jordan, *Gould Journals*, 413; Joseph Rutherford to "My dear Wife," October 2, 1864, UVM; James Hale to "Brother Geo.," October 4, 1864, CL; Duncan, *Neil Letters*, 68; William Phillips to "Dear Cousin," January 25, 1865, WHS.

92. *OR*, 43(1):30, 612; James Hale to "Brother Geo.," October 4, 1864, CL; Williams, *Hayes Diary and Letters*, 2:522; Ayling, *Register*, 849, 871, 875, 885.

93. *OR*, 43(1):447–48, 559–60, 612–13, 43(2):329; John Thompson to "Dear Father," October 14, 1864, NHHS.

94. Horatio King Journal, November 2, 1864, Dickinson College; *OR*, 43(1):559–60.

95. Jedediah Hotchkiss Journal, October 18 and 19, 1864, LC; William Newton to "My Dear Wife," October 23, 1864, OHS; Williams, *Hayes Diary and Letters*, 2:527; T. L. Eastman and William Davis Diaries, October 19, 1864, MEHS; Jordan, *Gould Journals*, 419; William Rigby to "Dear Brother," October 22, 1864, UIA; George Dodge to George D. Lamb, November 10, 1864, VTHS; Kallgren and Crouthamel, *Dear Friend Anna*, 104–5; William Hills Diary, October 19, 1864, LC. For Cedar Creek see Wert, *From Winchester to Cedar Creek*.

96. Jedediah Hotchkiss Journal, October 19, 1864, LC; Charles Gould to "Brother Marcus," undated [October 20, 1864], UVM; Isaac Watts to "Dear Friends," October 20, 1864, UVM; Darius Safford to "Dear Sister," October 23, 1864, VTHS; George French to "My Dear Mother," October 20, 1864, VTHS; Henry Keiser Diary, October 19, 1864; USAMHI; Joshua Whiteman to "Dear Wife," October 20, 1864, OHS; William McVey Diary, October 19, 1864, OHS; William Adams to "Sister Dora," October 25, 1864, MEHS; Thomas Porter Report, October 23, 1864, Yale.

97. William Davis Diary, October 19–27, 1864, MEHS; William Hills Diary, October 19, 1864, LC; John Rhoades to "My Dear Wife," October 20, 1864, RBHPL; Lyman Williams to "Dear Sister," October 23 [1864], VTHS; William Rigby to "Dear Father," October 20, 1864, UIA; Wesley Darling to "Dear Father," October 28, 1864, WRHS; William Wells to "Dear Parents," October 21, 1864, and to "Dear Anna," October 27, 1864, UVM; Charles Munroe Diary, October 19, 1864, AAS; Britton and Reed, *Hartwell Letters*, 299–331; William Henry to Mary Jane Henry, October 19 and 20, 1864, VTHS.

6. From Charred Atlanta Marching

1. *CWL*, 4:166, and 7:198; *OR*, Series 2, 2:223–24, and Series 3, 1:206, and 4:577.

2. George W. Bickley to William Seward, August 14, 1863, Case 1649, Reel 48, Case Files of Investigation (M-797), RG 94, NA; *OR*, Series 2, 5:363–67; "Outline of Disloyal Organizations OAK and OSL in Indiana and Adjoining States," Morton Collection, ISL; Wayne Morris to "My Beloved Companion," May 27, 1863, BL; Jonathan Joseph to "Dear Sister," April 10, 1864, and to James Boals, August 4, 1864, ISL. See Frank Klement, *Dark Lanterns,* on Republican exploitation of conspiracy hysteria. Jennifer Weber's *Copperheads* and Frank van der Linden's *The Dark Intrigue* attempt to revive the belief in extensive, serious collusion between disloyal Northerners and Confederates.

3. H. W. Reid to Rosecrans, March 8, 1864, Sanderson to Rosecrans, May 31 and June 12, 1864, with attachments, OHS. Much of this is published in *OR*, Series 2, 7:228–366.

4. *CWL*, 7:379, 386–88; Burlingame and Ettlinger, *Hay Diary,* 200–208.

5. *OR*, 43(2):930–36. Oddly enough, a handwritten copy of Thompson's eighteen-page report resides in the Hamilton Fish Papers, LC; Fish was chairman of the New York Union League's "defense committee."

6. More than one Confederate operative in Canada saw through the grandiose fantasies of pretended insurgent organizers (*ORN*, Series 2, 3:1235, 1238).

7. See Lincoln's effort to convince the editor of the *New York Herald* of Confederate involvement in the formulation of the Democrats' platform, *CWL*, 7:461. Confederate agents did, of course, hope to encourage the nomination of a peace candidate: see Nelson, *Bullets, Ballots, and Rhetoric,* 80–83, 92–96.

8. *OR*, Series 3, 4:488, 577–79; Holt to Stanton, July 29, 1864, Stanton Papers, LC.

9. *OR*, 42(2):193–94, Series 2, 7:802, and Series 3, 4:578, 702–3, 711–12, 714, 716–17, 1286–87; Stanton to Edwin Morgan, September 4, 1864, LC; Anna Newton to "Dear Brother and Sister," August 23, 1864, USAMHI.

10. Stanton to Holt, August 31, 1864, LC; Sanderson to Rosecrans, August 20, 1864, with attachments, OHS; *OR*, Series 2, 7:626–60, and Series 3, 7:578.

11. The investigation also offered opportunities for vengeance against personal enemies and business rivals: one New York speculator approached the provost marshal of Saint Louis for potential informers who could form a case against his competitor in the pork trade (Charles Partridge to Lucien Eaton, December 9, 1864, MOHS).

12. *OR*, Series 2, 8:7, and Series 3, 4:578–79; Carrington to Richard W. Thompson, September 4, 1864, ISL.

13. *Report of the Judge Advocate General; OR*, 43(2):931, and Series 2, 7:930–53. For other pamphlets spawned by the investigation and Holt's report see, for instance, *Copper-*

head Conspiracy in the North-West; George H. Pendleton: The Copperhead Candidate; and *The Chicago Copperhead Convention.* Amos Kendall's anti-Lincoln *Letters,* which appeared in a large pamphlet about the same time as Holt's *Report,* illustrates the cumbersome complexity of a typical Democratic campaign document, and suggests the greater cost involved in producing it for popular consumption, which made the opposition argument much less accessible than those of the Union League network.

14. *OR,* Series 2, 7:270, and Series 3, 4:716; Pitman, *Trials for Treason,* 19-37, 47-49, 136-37,114; Davis, *Butler Letters,* 128.

15. *Daily Chronicle,* September 10, 1864; *New Hampshire Patriot,* September 14, 1864.

16. *OR,* Series 2, 7:1089, and 8:523-25. The principal Indiana defendant escaped from halfhearted confinement soon after the election, while several codefendants remained imprisoned under sentence of death until 1866, when the Supreme Court ruled the entire proceeding against them unconstitutional.

17. *OR,* 43(2):931, and Series 2, 8:523-25; *ORN,* Series 2, 3:1235; Pitman, *Trials for Treason,* 49, 104, 106, 119, 176, 177.

18. *Detroit Free Press,* September 21 and 22, 1864; *ORN,* 3:220-21, 716; *OR,* 39(2):427, and Series 2, 7:850-51, 864-65, 901-6. Postwar accounts of the incident usually describe Cole being arrested while dining with Union officers aboard the *Michigan,* but Captain Carter reported that the *Michigan* steamed to Sandusky especially to arrest Cole; most of his presumed accomplices were soon released, and none appear to have been convicted.

19. *Detroit Free Press,* September 21 and 22, 1864; *ORN,* 3:220-21, 716.

20. *Burlington Free Press,* October 20, 1864; *Saint Albans Messenger,* October 20, 1864; *Eastern Townships Gazette,* October 21, 1864; *Advertiser,* October 27, 1864; OR, 43(2):421, 914-15, and Series 4, 3:491.

21. The two nine-month veterans were Charles A. Marvin, of Franklin, Vt., and Edward Nettleton, of Newport, N.H.: see Peck, *Roster,* 501, and Ayling, *Register,* 781.

22. *Burlington Free Press,* October 20 and 21, 1864; *Portland Daily Press,* October 20, 1864; Ann Pierce to Marshall Pierce, October 19, 1864, and Ann Smith to "My Dearest," October 20, 1864, both in Saint Albans Historical Museum; *Advertiser,* December 15, 1864; *Eastern Townships Gazette,* October 21, November 4, and December 16, 1864, February 24, 1865; *OR,* 43(2):422, 443-44, 914-16.

23. Augustus Paddock to "Dear Mother," October 19, 1864, and to "My dear Mary," March 31, 1865, UVM; Henry Vaughn to "Brother Vol," November 26 [1864], VTHS; Aaron Thurber Diary, October 26, 1864, AAS; N. B. Cobb to "Brother Walter," October 21, 1864, UVM; *OR,* 43(2):444, 452; *Eastern Townships Gazette,* October 28, 1864; *Portland Daily Press,* November 22, 1864.

24. *OR,* 41(1):465, 572-74, 659; Charles Robinson to Sara Robinson, October 16, 1864, KSHS; Henry Fike to "Dear Cimbaline," October 22 and 27, 1864, KU.

25. *OR,* 41(1):479, 575; Thomas Hedges to Emma Hedges, October 21, 1864, Duncan Papers, KSHS.

26. *OR,* 41(1):575, 634-35, 658, 675-76; Samuel Reader Diary, October 22, 1864, KSHS.

27. *OR,* 41(1):485-86, 575-76, 635-36, 658-59, 676; Henry Fike to "Dear Cimbaline," October 27, 1864, KU.

28. *OR,* 41(2):332-33, 336, 337-38, 636-39, 660-61; Samuel Curtis to "My dear wife," October 30, 1864, Yale; John Brown Diary, November 22 and 30, 1864, USAMHI.

29. *OR,* 42(1):230-32, 434, 437-39, 548-49, 853; Robertson, *McAllister Letters,* 527-29; Winfield Hancock to Francis Barlow, November 3, 1864, MHS; Samuel Cauller to "My Dear and Loving wife," October 29, 1864, USAMHI; Albert Stearns to "Dear Sister," October 31, 1864, NHHS; Coco, *Mills Letters,* 207-8; William Boston to "Dear Aunt," October 28, 1864, BL; Washington Roebling to "My dear Girl," October 29, 1864, RU.

30. Valentine Barney to "My dear Maria," October 29, 1864, VTHS; Edward Bacon to "Dear Father," October 28, 1864, and to "Dear Kate," October 31, 1864, AAS; *OR*, 42(1):23; Coco, *Mills Letters*, 219; Washington Roebling to "My Dear Girl," October 29, 1864, and to "My dearest love," same date, RU.

31. Coco, *Mills Letters*, 177, 219; *OR*, 42(2):434; George Chandler to "My dear Mother," October 10, 1864, NHHS; Josiah Jones Diary, October 8, 1864, NHHS.

32. *New York Times*, October 29, 1864; *OR*, 42(2):22–23.

33. *New York Times*, October 29, 1864; *Burlington Free Press*, November 5 and 7, 1864.

34. George Anthony to "Kind Brother," October 16, 1864, CL; Voter authorization of William Bennit, CL; George Stevens to "My Darling Hattie," November 6, 1864, CL; Sparks, *Patrick Diary*, 435–37; Nevins, *Wainwright Journals*, 476; *Burlington Free Press*, November 7, 1864; *Prairie du Chien Courier*, November 3, 1864.

35. Sparks, *Patrick Diary*, 455; Rufus Mead to "Dear Folks at Home," November 3, 1864, LC; Henry Waterman to "Dear Eliza," October 30, 1864, Townsend Papers, VTHS; William P. Fessenden to Benjamin Butler, August 22, 1864, Shepley Papers, MEHS; Carl Schurz to Theodore Petrasch, October 12, 1864, WHS; Richard Kent Diary, October 19, 1864, NHHS.

36. Charles Senior to "Dear Father," October 22, 1864, UVA; Charles Bates to "Dear Parents," November 15, 1864, VHS.

37. Collier and Collier, *Chase Letters*, 376; Edwin Horton to "Dear Ellen," November 6, 1864, VTHS; Franklin Bailey to "Dear Father," October 8, 1864, BL; Perkins Bartholomew to "Dear Mother," October 15, 1864, CHS; Thomas Covert to "My Dear Wife," October 13, 1864, WRHS.

38. George Anthony to "Kind Brother," October 16, 1864, CL; Nevins, *Wainwright Journals*, 476; Isaac Watts to "Dear Sister," November 10, 1864, UVM; Thomas Covert to "My Dear Wife," November 10, 1864, WRHS; Caleb Blanchard to "Dear Mattie," October 20, 1864, CHS; James Hale to "Brother Geo.," August 21, 1864, CL; Zerah Monks to "My dear Hattie," October 9, 1864, WRHS; William Stewart to "My Dear General," November 10, 1864, CL.

39. Nevins, *Wainwright Journals*, 476–77; Charles Manson to "Dear Mother," October 22, 1864, UVM; George Hanson to "Dear Mother," September 16, 1864, KSHS; Zerah Monks to "Dear Sister Margaret," October 23, 1864, WRHS; Gilbert Gulbrandson to "Parents and Siblings," November 1, 1864, USAMHI; Joseph Kohout to "Dear Father and Mother and Sister," October 28, 1864, UIA; Marcellus Darling to "Kind Mother," November 4, 1864, UIA; George French to "Father," September 11, 1864, VTHS.

40. William Hamilton to "Dear Mother," November 7, 1864, LC; Menge and Shimrak, *Chisholm Notebook*, 144; *New York Times*, November 11, 1864; Charles Maxim to "Dear Mother," November 11, 1864, CL; *Keene Sentinel*, November 11, 1864; Houston, *Smith Correspondence*, 255.

41. John Irwin to "Dear Sister," November 10, 1864, BL; Elmer Wallace to "Dear Parents," November 9, 1864, BL; Kallgren and Crouthamel, *Dear Friend Anna*, 107; Henry Crawford to "Dear Friends," November 19, 1864, WHMC; Elder, *Vermillion Letters*, 295; Henry Hitchcock to "My darling Wife," October 31, 1864, LC; Joseph Cross to "Dear Emma," October 23, 1864, and to "My Dear Boy Henry," November 13, 1864, AAS.

42. George Anthony to "Kind Brother," October 16, 1864, CL; George Chandler to "My dear William," November 7, 1864, George Chandler Papers, NHHS; Josiah Jones Diary, November 8, 1864, NHHS; William Chandler to J. H. Benton, February 24, 1916, William Chandler Papers, NHHS. On the New Hampshire popular and soldier vote, see Renda, *Running on the Record*, 129–30.

43. Winfield Scott to Samuel W. Crawford, November 9, 1864, CL; Meade, *Life and Letters*, 2:239; Basile, *Stearns Diary*, 93; Watson, *Hitchcock Diary*, 268; R. D. Lane to George S. Gilman, October 28, November 4 and 5, 1864, CHS. For Connecticut governor

William Buckingham's election-related shenanigans involving special furloughs and government transportation for identifiably Republican soldiers, see Marvel, *Great Task Remaining*, 20–21, 261.

44. An electoral victory for McClellan would have required the reversal of 41,892 votes, distributed as follows: Connecticut, 1,203; New Hampshire, 1,782; New York, 3,375; Pennsylvania, 10,038; Indiana, 10,095; Illinois, 15,399.

45. George Anthony to "Kind Brother," October 16, 1864, CL; Henry Marshall to "Dear Folks at Home," October 10, 1864, CL; Willis Porter to "Dear Friend Etta," September 5, 1864, and Porter Diary, November 7–12, 1864, MEHS; *OR*, 39(3):732–33.

46. John Arnold to "Dearest and Beloved Family," November 26, 1864, LC; Ransom Sargent to "My dear Wife," November 9, 1864, DC; Valentine Barney to "My dear Maria," November 7 and 10, 1864, VTHS.

47. Charles Wilson to "Dear Father," November 6, 1864, RBHPL; Henry Herrick Diary, November 8, 1864, Fairbanks Museum; Maria Sargent to "My dear Ransom," November 13, 1864, DC; "Mollie" to Charles Parker, November 8, 1864, UVM; Almira Miller Diary, November 8, 1864, USAMHI; *Boston Evening Transcript*, November 8 and 10, 1864.

48. James Pratt to Rufus L. Baker, November 16, 1864, CL; Ellen Emerson to "My dear Haven," November 18, 1864, AAS; Palladino, *Westervelt Diary*, 186; John Work to "Dear Uncle," November 17, 1864, WRHS; Wesley Darling to "Dear Father," November 18, 1864, WRHS; Rufus Kinsley to "Dear Father," November 27, 1864, VTHS; Darius Safford to "Dear Sister," November 13, 1864, VTHS; Franklin Sawyer to Samuel Sexton, November 13, 1864, OHS; Blair, *Geary Letters*, 217.

49. Edward White and Frank P. Blair to Montgomery Blair, October 10, 1864, LC; Charles Blanchard to "Dear Cousin Persis," November 24, 1864, MEHS; Marquis de Lafayette Lane to "Dear Lissie," November 6–21 and December 11 and 25, 1864, MEHS.

50. Nellie Johnson to "My Dear George," November 20, 1864, Aplin Papers, CL; Tilghman to Hamilton Fish, December 18, 1864, LC; R. Y. Bush to John F. Hall, December 3, 1864, quoted in Sandburg, *Lincoln Collector*, 109; Rachel Hunt to "Dear friend Almeda," November 15, 1864, Bennett-Stites-Fay Papers, OHS.

51. Albert Harris to "Dear Father," November 6, 1864, VTHS; "Historic Roll" of Co. E, 2nd Missouri, and oath of allegiance dated April 29, 1865, William B. Spoor file, Compiled Service Records of Confederate Soldiers Who Served in Organizations from the State of Missouri (M-322), Reel 111, RG 109, NA; George Stedman to William Harris, November 9, 1864, and E. H. Stedman to Harris, January 2, 1865, MOHS.

52. Fitts to "Dear Mother," December 21, 1864, UNH.

53. *OR*, 39(3):740, 904–5.

54. Quaife, *Williams Letters*, 351; James Proudfit to "Dear Wife," November 9, 1864, KU; Henry Hitchcock to "My darling Wife," October 31 and November 11, 1864, LC; Angle, *Connolly Letters*, 294.

55. *OR*, 39(3):740; Angle, *Connolly Letters*, 295–97.

56. *New York Times*, November 10, 1864; *OR*, 39(3):740; Howe, *Hitchcock Letters*, 100–101.

57. *OR*, 39(1):802–3, 39(3):742, 743, 746–47, and 44:15–16, 19–25.

58. James A. Congleton Diary, November 13–16, 1864, LC; Nathaniel Parmeter Diary, November 14, 1864, OHS; *OR*, 44:56; Henry Comey to "My Dear Sister," December 17, 1864, AAS.

59. *OR*, 44:157; Francis Crowninshield Diary, November 16–20, 1864, PEM.

60. *OR*, 44:66, 362–63, 405–7, 414, 886; Anderson, *Geer Diary*, 177; Wimer Bedford Diary, November 16, 1864, LC; Joshua Breyfogle to "Dear Wife & children," [December] 17, 1864, DC; Francis Crowninshield Diary, November 20–21, 1864, PEM.

61. Edwards, *Civil War Guns*, 354–55; *OR*, 44:105–9, 363, 386, 414.

62. John Lane to Barbara Ellen Crist, December 25, 1864, IU; Francis Crowninshield Diary, November 27, 1864, PEM; Henry Comey to "My Dear Sister," December 17, 1864,

AAS; James Congleton Diary, November 14–23, 1864, LC; Anderson, *Geer Diary*, 177, 179; Bohrnstedt, *Cram Letters*, 151; Nathaniel Parmeter Diary, November 19 and 23, 1864, OHS.

63. James Congleton Diary, November 22 and 23, 1864, LC; *OR*, 44:48; Francis Crowninshield Diary, November 23 and 24, 1864, PEM; Nathaniel Parmeter Diary, November 23, 1864, OHS; Wimer Bedford Diary, November 24, 1864, LC.

64. *OR*, 44:48, 50, 51; Francis Crowninshield Diary, November 25, 1864, PEM; James Congleton Diary, November 26, 1864, LC; Angle, *Connolly Letters*, 321–22; Howe, *Hitchcock Letters*, 92–93.

65. Howe, *Hitchcock Letters*, 96–97. Joseph Glatthaar delves into the behavior and attitudes of Sherman's men during the campaigns to Savannah and through the Carolinas in *The March to the Sea and Beyond*.

66. *OR*, Series 2, 7:1145; John Whitten Diary, November 16, 1864, SHSI-DM.

67. *OR*, Series 2, 7:1145, 1148; Lawson Carley Diary, November 19 and 20, 1864, SHSI-IC; John Whitten Diary, November 20–25, December 6 and 23, 1864, SHSI-DM; Amos Ames Diary, November 21–23, December 10, 19, and 25, 1864, SHSI-DM; Peter Perry Diary, November 24, December 25–26, 1864, MC; George Shearer Diary, December 19 and 25, 1864, SHSI-IC; *OR*, 44:959; Marcellus Darling to "Dear Friends," December 16, 1864, UIA; Francis Crowninshield Diary, December 3, 1864, PEM.

68. James Congleton Diary, December 8–10, 1864, LC; *OR*, 44:9, 410–11, 959, 965; Francis Crowninshield Diary, December 9 and 14, 1864, PEM; *ORN*, 16:129, 478.

69. *OR*, 44:110–11, 122, 698; James Congleton Diary, December 13, 1864, LC.

70. Henry Comey to "My Dear Sister," December 17, 1864, AAS; Francis Crowninshield Diary, December 9 and 19, 1864, PEM; *OR*, 44:10; James Congleton Diary, December 17, 1864, LC; Henry Hitchcock to "My darling Mary," December 16, 1864, LC.

71. *OR*, 44:11–12, 158, 208–9, 279–80, 972; Francis Crowninshield Diary, December 19, 1864, PEM; Walton, *Weller Letters*, 134; Wimer Bedford Diary, December 17, 1864, LC; Oeffinger, *McLaws Letters*, 245.

72. *OR*, 45(1):1206, 1213; Howe, *Hitchcock Letters*, 100–101.

73. *OR*, 45(1):357, 687, 752, 763, 966, 970, 972, 1208–11; Mumford Dixon Diary, November 21, 1864, Duke, quoted in *ORS*, 7:684.

74. *OR*, 45(1):52, 54, 56, 572, 575, 969, 1104.

75. Ibid., 341, 357–58, 994–95, 1005–6, 1017, 1020, 1029, 1055, 1057, 1058, 1087, 1105–7. For a cohesive account of this campaign, see Sword, *Embrace an Angry Wind*.

76. *OR*, 45(1):239–40, 255, 268, 742, 753; Silas Strickland to "My dear Wife," December 1, 1864, NSHS. Interpretations explaining this lost opportunity include directional disorientation and the crippled Hood's fatigue, laudanum use, or loose command style: see Horn, "The Spring Hill Legend," and McMurry, *John Bell Hood*, 172–74.

77. *OR*, 45(1):342, 1168–71; Wayne Morris to "My Dear Companion," November 30, 1864, BL.

78. *OR* 45(1):343–44, 358, 379–80, 653–54, 1171; Wayne Morris to "Dear Libby," December 2, 1864, BL; George Hodges to "Dear Wife," December 2, 1864, WRHS; Silas Strickland to "My dear wife," December 1, 1864, NSHS.

79. *OR* 45(1):343–44, 1171; *New York Herald*, December 2 and 3, 1864.

80. *OR*, 45(1):358, 502–3, 1168, 1171; Carlos Lyman to "Dear Brother," November 30, 1864, WRHS; Marshall Miller to "Ever Dear Wife," December 5, 1864, LC; Ralph Dorrance to "Dear Father & Mother," December 2, 1864, MNHS.

81. *OR*, 45(1):613, 744–47, 755–56.

82. *OR*, 45(1):359, 45(2):16–17, 55, 70, 96–97, 114–16, 143.

83. *OR*, 45(1):747; Myron Underwood to "My Dear Wife," December 28, 1864, UIA; Henry Fike to "Dear Cimbaline," December 12, 1864, KU.

84. *OR*, 45(1):38–40, 345–46, 360, 436, 578, 655, 767; George Hodges to "Dear Wife,"

January 15, 1865, WRHS; Andrew Parsons to "Dear Aunt," December 16, 1864, CL; Amasa Richards to "Dear Mary," December 21, 1864, MNHS; Carlos Lyman to "Dear Ones at Home," December 15, 1864, and to "My Dear Father and Mother," December 17, 1864, WRHS; Ralph Dorrance to "Dear Parents," December 23, 1864, MNHS; Henry Fike to "Dear Cimbaline," December 19, 1864, KU.

85. *OR*, 45(1):41–44, 360–61, 655, 690, 726, 758–59, 45(2):228–29; Henry Fike to "Dear Cimbaline," December 21, 1864, KU; Thomas Wood to William Whipple, December 30, 1864, CL; Jonathan Harrington to "Brother L," December 27, 1864, RBHPL.

86. Thomas Martin to "Dear Parents," January 12, 1865, IU; Moses Greenleaf to "My dear folks at Home," January 5, 1865, and to "My dear People," January 16, 1865, MNHS.

87. *OR*, 45(1):807–14, 824–27; *Daily Virginian,* December 17, 28, 30, and 31, 1864, and January 5 and 6, 1865; "Diary of Major R. C. M. Page," 64–65; Younger, *Kean Diary,* 181.

7. With Burning Woods Our Skies Are Brass

1. Beale, *Welles Diary,* 2:133, 146; *USG*, 12:141–42, 154; *RJCCW2*, 2:3–4, 51.

2. *ORN*, 11:66; *RJCCW2*, 2:51; Sumner, *Comstock Diary,* 296. Comstock's remark that "the navy are full of it" probably reflected the nineteenth-century connotation of voluble enthusiasm, rather than the pejorative modern meaning of conspicuous misapprehension.

3. Sumner, *Comstock Diary,* 297; *OR*, 42(1):443, 42(3):803–6; Chandler Watts to "My Dear Wife," October 16, 1864, Cheney-Watts Collection, VTHS; Peter Abbott to "Friends at Home," December 14, 1864, VTHS; Elmer Wallace to "My Dear Parents," December 14, 1864, BL. Warren's raid and the Wilmington expedition seem not to have been previously recognized as two parts of a concerted plan.

4. Elmer Wallace to "My Dear Parents," December 14, 1864 and January 1, 1865, BL; Stokes Jones to "Dear friend Lillie," December 18, 1864, USAMHI; *OR*, 42(1):443–46, 449, and 42(3):1271; Freeman, *Lee's Dispatches,* 306–7. The Weldon Railroad superintendent reported to Lee that only six miles of track were actually destroyed.

5. *OR*, 42(1):966–67; *ORN*, 11:150, 191; Sumner, *Comstock Diary,* 297; *RJCCW2*, 2:52, 73; Longacre, *Wightman Letters,* 219–20; James Wickes to "My dear Father," January 16, 1865, BPL.

6. Longacre, *Wightman Letters,* 220–21; *OR*, 42(1):966–67, 980–81; *RJCCW2*, 2:83.

7. The history of Fort Fisher and the defense of Wilmington are described in engaging detail in Fonvielle's *Wilmington Campaign,* which includes many wonderful maps of the area. A. Wilson Greene, a fount of knowledge about Civil War sites renowned and obscure, points out that during the war Federal Point was known locally as Confederate Point.

8. Sumner, *Comstock Letters,* 297–99; McPherson and McPherson, *Lamson Letters,* 216; *OR*, 42(1):967, 993–94; *RJCCW2*, 2:106–7. Six days afterward, the commander at Wilmington dated the reinforcement on December 24; two months later, while mortally wounded and a prisoner, he mistook it for December 23.

9. *OR*, 42(1):982–83, 986–87, 42(3):1282–83, 1285, 1303, 1306–9; Longacre, *Wightman Letters,* 222–24; *ORN*, 11:281–82.

10. *RJCCW2*, 2:75.

11. *OR*, 42(1):968–69, 981, 982–83, 986, 994–95; Sumner, *Comstock Diary,* 299; *RJCCW2*, 2:72–73, 75–77, 84–85; Longacre, *Wightman Letters,* 224–25; *ORN*, 11:250–51.

12. Sumner, *Comstock Diary,* 299; *OR*, 42(1):968–69, 981, 984; *ORN*, 11:251; *RJCCW2*, 2:73, 75, 79; Longacre, *Wightman Letters,* 225–26.

13. *USG*, 12:177–78, 183–85, 197–98, 215, 223; James Wickes to "My dear Father," January 5, 1865, BPL.

14. Hilon Parker to "Dear Sister," January 14, 1865, CL; Avery Cain to "Dear Mother,"

January 6, 1865, VTHS; James Wickes to "My dear Lottie," January 11, 1865, BPL. See also "G. C. T." to "Dear Charlie," February 12, 1865, Shepley Papers, MEHS, on Butler's efforts to find scapegoats for his various failures.

15. *OR,* 46(2):11, 25; James Wickes to "My dear Father," January 16, 1864, BPL.

16. Longacre, *Wightman Letters,* 227–28; Sumner, *Comstock Diary,* 301.

17. Longacre, *Wightman Letters,* 227–28.

18. Ibid., 226–27; Sumner, *Comstock Diary,* 301; *OR,* 46(1):396, 440–42.

19. *ORN,* 11:432–33; Sumner, *Comstock Letters,* 301–2; *OR,* 46(1):397, 407.

20. *ORN,* 11:439; George Towle Diary, January 15, 1865, NHHS; *OR,* 46(1):403, 415–16. Pennypacker, purportedly the youngest general in the war, was supposedly only sixteen when he enlisted in 1861, and only twenty during the attack on Fort Fisher, but census records suggest that Pennypacker was older than he claimed.

21. *ORN,* 11:439; George Towle Diary, January 15, 1865, NHHS; *OR,* 46(1):398–400, 403, 415–16, 425; McPherson and McPherson, *Lamson Letters,* 223–25; Sumner, *Comstock Diary,* 302–5; Henry Gill to "Dear Brother John," January 16, 1865, Yale.

22. *OR,* 46, 399, 403–5, 425–31; *ORN,* 11:441–44; Longacre, *Wightman Letters,* 228–31.

23. Ford, *Adams Letters,* 2:247–48, 253–56; Beale, *Welles Diary,* 2:226–27.

24. Beale, *Welles Diary,* 2:226–27; *RJCCW2,* 2:vii–viii, 3–51.

25. *ORN,* 16: 29–32, 37, 42, 112–14, 246, and 22:190, 193, 216–17.

26. *CWL,* 7:380; *OR,* Series 3, 4:979–80.

27. Henry Winter Davis to Benjamin Wade, undated (but filed between June 19 and 22, 1864), LC; *CG,* 2 sess., 38 Cong., part 1:53–54, 138–56, 168–83, 189–202, 214–25, 257–67, 478–88, 523–31; Burlingame, *Nicolay Letters,* 173.

28. John Sturtevant to "Dear Friends at Home," January 21, 1865, DC; Wiggins, *Gorgas Journals,* 149; *OR,* Series 4, 3:636–40.

29. *CWL,* 5:553; 7:435, 461.

30. Pease and Randall, *Browning Diary,* 1:15, 694–95, 699.

31. *CWL,* 8:275–76; *OR,* 46(2):297; James Seddon to Francis P. Blair Sr., December 31, 1864, LC.

32. *CWL,* 8:276–80; Scott, *Willcox Letters,* 604; Sauers, *Bolton Journal,* 243; Charles Manson to "Dear Mother," February 1, 1865, UVM; Herbert Titus to George Chandler, January 31, 1865, NHHS; Nevins, *Wainwright Journals,* 496.

33. *CWL,* 8:280–82; *New York Times,* February 3–5, 1865; Hunter, "Peace Commission," 172; *CWL,* 8:282. Grant scholar Brooks Simpson also doubts Hunter's story of Mrs. Grant's involvement.

34. David Bates Diary, February 1, 1865, LC; Burlingame, *Nicolay Letters,* 172; *CWL,* 8:200–1; Younger, *Kean Diary,* 191; Pease and Randall, *Browning Diary,* 2:4–5.

35. William Rudolph to "Dear Cousin," January 22, 1865, IU; Chandler Watts to "My Dear Jane," January 22, 1865, Cheney-Watts Collection, VTHS; Hiram Ketcham Diary, January 31, 1864, BGSU; George Buffum to "Dear Wife," December 22, 1864, WHS; Thomas Covert to "My Dear Wife," January 21, 1865, WRHS; Bradford Darling to "Dear Father," January 22, 1865, WRHS; Peter Abbott to "Friends at Home," January 29, 1865, VTHS; Wilbur Hinman to "Dear Friends," February 1, 1865, WRHS; Addison Parlin to Merinda Houghton, February 3, 1865, MEHS; Herbert Titus to George Chandler, January 31, 1865, NHHS.

36. *New York Times,* February 3, 4, and 5, 1865.

37. "Papers of Hon. John A. Campbell," 45–47; Hunter, "Peace Commission," 173.

38. Stephens, *A Constitutional View,* 2:610–12; "Papers of Hon. John A. Campbell," 48–49; Hunter, "Peace Commission," 173–74; Burlingame, *Nicolay Letters,* 173; *CWL,* 8:279, 284. In *Lincoln,* 559–60, David Donald similarly speculated that Lincoln misled the three so they would carry back the idea that slavery could be saved by a prompt capitulation.

39. "Papers of Hon. John A. Campbell," 51; Hunter, "Peace Commission," 174.

40. "Papers of Hon. John A. Campbell," 49, 51–52; Stephens, *A Constitutional View,* 2:618–19; *CWL,* 8: 259, 287–88; *New York Times,* February 5, 1865.

41. Beale, *Welles Diary,* 2:235–36, 237; *CWL,* 8:260–61.

42. *CWL,* 8:274–85; Burlingame, *Nicolay Letters,* 174; Henry Ward Beecher to Lincoln, February 4, 1865, AAS; Nevins and Thomas, *Strong Diary,* 3:552; "Proceedings of the Second Confederate Congress," 300, 307.

43. Samuel Duncan to "My Dear Julia," January 30, 1865, NHHS; Valentine Barney to "My dear Maria," February 5, 1865, VTHS; Wilbur Hinman to "Dear Friends," February 15, 1865, WRHS; Darius Safford to "My Dear Sister," February 8, 1865, VTHS.

44. George Howard to "My Dear," February 26, 1865, VTHS; Christopher Keller to "Dear Parents," February 11, 1865, CL; William Boston to "Dear Aunt," January 24, 1865, BL; William Rudolph to "Dear Cousin," January 22, 1865, IU.

45. *OR,* 42(3):1036, 1065, 46(2):273, 354; Carleton Felch Diary, December 23, 1864, Fairbanks Museum; George Howard to "My Dear Daughter," January 1, 1865, VTHS; John Bailey Journal, January 6 and February 9, 1865, NHHS; Oscar Robinson to "Dear Mother," January 7, 1865, DC; George Bates to "Dear Parents," January 8, 1865, CL; Joseph Cross to "Dear Wife & Children," January 8, 1865, AAS; Sparks, *Patrick Diary,* 456–57; Chandler Watts to "Dear Jane," December 28, 1864, Cheney-Watts Collection, VTHS; Darius Safford to "Dear Sister," January 2, 1865, VTHS.

46. Francis Crowninshield Diary, November 16, 1864, and Crowninshield to "Dear Ned," January 12, 1865, PEM; John McCoy to "Dear Martha," January 26, 1865, DC.

47. *OR,* Series 3, 4:1225; John Giffen to "Dear Father," February 20 and April 18, 1865, and Jacob Giffen to "Dear Father," June 20, 1864, and March 20, 1865, OHS; Nellie Johnson to George Aplin, August 14, 1864, CL; Valentine Barney to "My dear Maria," August 4, 1864, VTHS; Kamphoefner and Helbich, *Germans in the Civil War,* 68, 69.

48. *OR,* Series 3, 4:1128–34; *CWL,* 8:262.

49. John Giffen to "Dear Father," February 20, 1865, OHS; Jane Fellows to "Dear Cousin," December 11, 1864, UR; Lester Fales to Richard Taft, January 21, 1865, RIHS; Robert Muir to "Dear Brother," March 1, 1865, Salina Public Library.

50. Albert Harris to "Dear Father," May 29, August 7, and October 23, 1864, to "Dear Father & Mother and All," January 29, 1865, and to "Dear Brother," February 19, 1865, VTHS; Gideon Allen to "Darling little girl," December 27, 1864, WHS; William Boston to "Dear Aunt," January 24, 1865, BL; D. L. Caldwell to Henry Carroll, March 13, 1865, USAMHI; Nellie Johnson to George Aplin, January 18, 1865, CL; Henry Winterstein to Clinton Winterstein, February 11, 1865, OHS; Loring Winslow to "Dear Parents," January 26, 1865, WHS; Lyman Holyoke to Samuel Henderson, January 15, 1865, MHS.

51. Alexander Christie to Sarah J. Christie, January 24, 1865, MNHS; William Hogan to "Dear Son," May 30, 1864, VTHS; Peck, *Roster,* 275.

52. George Anthony to "Dear Brother," March 3, 1865, CL.

53. Kamphoefner and Helbich, *Germans in the Civil War,* 329.

54. Willich to John Sherman, February 10, 1865, Wade Papers, LC.

55. Sewell Tilton to "My Dear Sister," February 10, 1865, NHHS; Fred Phillips to "Dear Sister," March 3, 1865, CL; Dyer, *Compendium,* 1102–3, 1157–58, 1294, 1471, 1554–55.

56. James Lockwood to "Dear Wife," March 8, 1865, MNHS; Jacob Gauchnauer to "Dear Wife and Mother and Benny," March 17, 1865, USAMHI; Nettie Brown to Hubert and Laura Tupper Brown, March 24, 1865, VTHS; Abram Parmenter Diary, March 20–22, 1865, LC; Thomas Barnett Diary, February 16 and 28, March 23–24, 1865, Earlham.

57. John A. Johnson Diary, March 8–July 17, 1865, LC; *MSSM,* 5:515.

58. *OR,* 47(1):191–92, 1068, 47(2):35; William Henry to "Dear Eunice," January 16, 1865, WHS.

59. *OR*, 47(1):17, 419–20; Francis Crowninshield to "Dearest Mother," January 31, 1865, PEM; Blair, *Geary Letters*, 228.

60. Blair, *Geary Letters*, 230; Henry Guyer to "Dear Brother," January 17, 1865, Yale; Randolph Sry to Ith Beall, January 29, 1865, KU; George DeHart to "Dear Sister," January 27, 1865, SHSI-IC; Quaife, *Williams Letters*, 367–69; Angle, *Connolly Letters*, 380; Samuel Storrow Diary, February 1, 1865, MHS; *OR*, 47(1):420.

61. Sylvester, "Cox Letters," 224; George Russ to "Dear Sister," March 30, 1865, Shumway Papers, MNHS; Howe, *Hitchcock Letters*, 214.

62. *OR*, 47(2):1043, 1049, 1058–60, 1083, 1163, 49(1):940; Wynne and Taylor, *Williams Diary*, 124.

63. *OR*, 47(1):19, 47(2):184–85, 546, 596–97; James Congleton Diary, February 2 and 27, 1865, LC; Gray, *War Letters*, 454–56; Howe, *Hitchcock Letters*, 236–47; Quaife, *Williams Letters*, 374.

64. Oeffinger, *McLaws Letters*, 250; *OR*, 47(2):184; Thomas Larue to "Dear Parents," February 1, 1865, USAMHI; Samuel Storrow Diary, February 26, 1865, MHS.

65. Howe, *Hitchcock Letters*, 253; *OR*, 47(1):19, 194, 375–77, 1046–47; James Congleton Diary, February 9 and 10, 1865, LC; Wynne and Taylor, *Williams Diary*, 124.

66. *OR*, 47(1):42–43, 377–78, 1047, 47(2):1143–44.

67. *OR*, 47(1):1047, 47(2):1176; L. W. Costellow to "My Dear Brother," July 10, 1865, MEHS; Wynne and Taylor, *Williams Diary*, 124.

68. Thomas Howland to "Dear sister," March 30, 1865, MHS.

69. Ibid.; Albert Slack to "Dear Father and Mother," March 19, 1865, OHS; Quaife, *Williams Letters*, 373–74; John Lane to Barbara Ellen Crist, March 28, 1865, IU; Joseph Hoffhines to "Dear wife," March 14, 1865, OHS.

70. *OR*, 47(1):21, 227, 1048; Oeffinger, *McLaws Letters*, 251; James Congleton Diary, February 16, 1865, LC.

71. *OR*, 47(1):21, 47, 227–28, 243, 252, 310, 47(2):457–58; Henry Hitchcock to "My own darling," March 12, 1865, LC.

72. *OR*, 47(1):47, 227–28, 238; Howe, *Hitchcock Letters*, 268, 270; Angle, *Connolly Letters*, 384; Randolph Sry to Ith Beall, January 29, 1864, KU; William Garrett to "Dear Sister," March 29, 1865, USAMHI; Francis Crowninshield to "Dearest Mother," March 12, 1865, PEM. In *Sherman and the Burning of Columbia*, Marion Brunson Lucas blames Confederates for leaving burning cotton in the streets, but it was hours after Union soldiers took control of the town that houses started burning, and only when drunken soldiers began looting them. Perhaps to save his wife worry, Lafayette McLaws informed her that Sherman's men were invariably courteous and well-behaved toward civilians, and that he always advised the women of a family to remain at home, while their men hid in the woods (Oeffinger, *McLaws Letters*, 251).

73. *OR*, 47(1):1048–49, 1079; Oeffinger, *McLaws Letters*, 250–51; Affidavits of B. F. DeBow and John J. Cantine, Hughes Papers, OHS; Patrick and Willey, *Miller Diary*, 309–12; Wynne and Taylor, *Williams Diary*, 124–25.

74. *OR*, 47(1):1018–20; 47(2):508.

75. *OR*, 47(1):909, 958, 965, 47(2):355–56; Sumner, *Comstock Diary*, 309.

76. *OR*, 47(1):924, 928–29, 960–61, 1077; Sumner, *Comstock Diary*, 309–10; Thompson and Wainwright, *Fox Correspondence*, 2:200–201.

77. *OR*, 47(1):924, 929–30, 961–63, 47(2):483, 509; *ORN*, 12:32–34.

78. *OR*, 47(1):921, 925, 930, 963–64, 47(2):521–23; Sumner, *Comstock Diary*, 311; Samuel Duncan to "My Dear Bro.," February 25, 1865, DC, and Duncan to "My Dear friend," March 15, 1865, NHHS.

79. *OR*, 47(1):380–81, 47(2):1231, 1242; Oeffinger, *McLaws Letters*, 254–59; A. A. McBryde to "Dear Ma," February 28, 1865, Henry Hitchcock Papers, LC; William Henry to "Dear Eunice," April 9, 1865, WHS; James Congleton Diary, March 4, 1865, LC.

80. *OR*, 47(1):1049, 1053, 1082, 47(2):1266; Wynne and Taylor, *Williams Diary*, 126–27.

81. *OR*, 47(1):1044, 47(2):1247, 1304–11.

82. *OR*, 47(1):1053, 47(2):43, 1257, 1271.

83. *OR*, 47(1):23, 204, 47(2):703–4, 852; James Congleton Diary, March 11–13, 1865, LC; Quaife, *Williams Letters*, 373–75; Henry Hitchcock to "My own darling," March 12, 1865, LC; Angle, *Connolly Letters*, 383–84.

84. Henry Hitchcock to "My own darling," March 12, 1865, LC; *OR*, 47(1):23, 204–5, 422.

85. *OR*, 47(1):422, 585–86, 862, 1084–86; Judson Austin to "Dear Wife," March 27, 1865, BL; James Congleton Diary, March 16, 1865, LC; Oeffinger, *McLaws Letters*, 266–67.

86. *OR*, 47(1):25–26, 1054, 1055–56, 1079; Francis Crowninshield to "Dearest Mother," March 25, 1865, PEM; Oeffinger, *McLaws Letters*, 268–69.

87. *OR*, 47(1):43, 66, 75, 1058.

88. *OR*, 47(1):423–24, 1056–57, 1088; Oeffinger, *McLaws Letters*, 268–71; Angle, *Connolly Letters*, 385–86; Henry Hitchcock to "My darling Mary," March 21, 1865, LC; Francis Crowninshield to "Dearest Mother," March 25, 1865, PEM; James Congleton Diary, March 19, 1865, LC; Charles Senior to "Dear Father," March 29, 1865, UVA. Several studies of Bentonville exist: Bradley's *Last Stand in the Carolinas*, Hughes's *Bentonville*, and Moore's more technical *Historical Guide to the Battle of Bentonville*.

89. *OR*, 47(1):424, 1055–57; Henry Hitchcock to "My darling Mary," March 23, 1865, LC; Nathaniel Parmeter Diary, March 20, 1865, OHS.

8. Forests of Bayonets

1. Meade, *Life and Letters*, 2:260–61; *OR*, 46(2):367.

2. *OR*, 46(1):149, 253, 365–66, 46(2):367–71, 389; Charles Reed to "Dear Mother," February 18, 1865, LC.

3. *OR*, 46(2):389, 391–92, 397–99, 401, 1206; John Heitman Diary, February 5, 1865, Duke; Robertson, *McAllister Letters*, 581–83.

4. *OR*, 46(2):368, 390–92; Charles Reed to "Dear Mother," February 18, 1865, LC.

5. George Fowle to "Dear Eliza," February 9, 1865, MHS; Henry Metzger to "Dear Father," February 17, 1865, USAMHI; Britton and Reed, *Hartwell Letters*, 331; *OR*, 46(1):254–55; Charles Reed to "Dear Mother," February 18, 1865, LC; William Phillips to "Dear Parents," February 8, 1865, WHS; George Fowle to "Dear Eliza," February 9, 1865, MHS; George Buffum to "Dear Wife and fammoly," February 8, 1865, WHS. See Greene, *Breaking the Backbone of the Rebellion*, 143–49, on Hatcher's Run.

6. *OR*, 46(1):256; John Heitman Diary, February 7, 1865, Duke; Floyd, *Owen Letters*, 75; George Fowle to "Dear Eliza," February 9, 1865, MHS; Britton and Reed, *Hartwell Letters*, 332; William Phillips to "Dear Parents," February 8, 1865, WHS; Edwin Flagg to "Dear Sister," February 14, 1865, WHS; William McVey Diary, February 7, 1865, OHS; Charles Reed to "Dear Mother," February 18, 1865, LC; Loring Winslow to "Dear Parents," February 18, 1865, WHS; Meade, *Life and Letters*, 2:261–62.

7. Wiggins, *Gorgas Journals*, 151; Jones, *Diary*, 493–94; *OR*, 46(1):381–82; Younger, *Kean Diary*, 200.

8. Henry Marshall to "Hattie," December 2, 1864, and to "Dear Folks at Home," December 21, 1864, CL; Warren Goodale to "Dear Children," December 23, 1864, MHS; Darius Safford to "Dear Sister," December 17, 1864, and to "My Dear Sister," January 2, 1865, VTHS; James Hale to "Brother Geo.," CL; Peter Abbott to "Friends at Home," January 15, 1865, VTHS; James Wickes to "My dear Father," January 15, 1865, BPL.

9. George Bates to "Dear Parents," February 4, 1865, CL; Hilon Parker to "Dear Father," February 17, 1865, CL; Edwin Horton to "Dearest Ellen," February 20, 1865, VTHS;

Henry Metzger to "Dear Sister," February 20, 1865, USAMHI; Joseph Rutherford to "My dear Wife," February 25, 1865, UVM.

10. William Adams to "Sister Dora," February 26, 1865, MEHS; Timothy O'Sullivan to "Dear Mother & Sister," March 14, 1865, CHS; *OR*, 46(2):635, 730; Meade, *Life and Letters*, 2:266; Taylor, *Four Years with General Lee*, 187.

11. *OR*, 47(1):1053, 47(2):1084, 49(1):906; Wiggins, *Gorgas Journals*, 153.

12. *OR*, Series 4, 3:1012–13, 1161–62; Younger, *Kean Diary*, 192; Jones, *Diary*, 496–97.

13. James Wilson to "Dear Sister," February 2, 1865, WRHS; Jewett to "Dear Lizzie," December 27, 1864, and to "Dear Uncle," December 28, 1864, VHS.

14. Meade, *Life and Letters*, 2:264; *OR*, 46(1):475; 46(2):592, 712, 724.

15. *OR*, 46(1):475–76, 515.

16. *OR*, 46(1):476, 485–86, 502–3, 516–17; John Thompson to "Dear father," March 9, 1865, NHHS; William Weeks to "Dear Father," March 21, 1865, IU.

17. David Bates Diary, March 4, 1865, LC; Burlingame, *Nicolay Letters*, 175; Beale, *Welles Diary*, 2:250–51.

18. Beale, *Welles Diary*, 2:194–95, 251. On Usher see Bain, *Empire Express*, 108, 131–32, 168, 186.

19. *CG*, 2nd sess., 38th Cong., part 2, 1338–1424; *Washington Star*, March 4, 1865.

20. Beale, *Welles Diary*, 2:251–52; Pease and Randall, *Browning Diary*, 2:9; *CG*, 2nd sess., 38th Cong., part 2, 1394–95; *New York Times*, March 5, 1865; Burlingame, *Brooks Dispatches*, 166.

21. *New York Times*, March 5, 1865; Burlingame, *Nicolay Letters*, 175; Beale, *Welles Diary*, 2:252; James Moore to "My Kind Friend," March 7, 1865, Fellows Papers, UR; David Bates and Jeremiah Lockwood Diaries, March 4, 1865, LC; Sparks, *Patrick Diary*, 476.

22. *New York Times*, March 5, 1865.

23. *CWL*, 8:332–33. See Lincoln's attempts to frame nearly the same argument in April of 1864, and earlier: *CWL*, 5:403–4, 7:281–82.

24. *CWL*, 8:333; *New York Times*, March 5, 1865.

25. Doolittle to his brother, undated (first page missing), but March, 1865, WHS; Brun, "Fleming Letters," 37–38.

26. Burlingame, *Nicolay Letters*, 175; French, *Journals*, 466; Beale, *Welles Diary*, 2:252.

27. *OR*, 49(1):825, 49(2):66.

28. *OR*, 49(1):76–80, 708–9, 812, 819, 824, 902, 909.

29. *OR*, 48(1):1164; Sumner, *Comstock Diary*, 311–12.

30. *OR*, 49(1):92, 712, 859–60, 865, 49(2):49, 66; *ORN*, 22:59–60.

31. Sumner, *Comstock Diary*, 312; *OR*, 49(1):141, 49(2):7–8, 13, 58, 59, 69.

32. *OR*, 49(2):70, 89; Sumner, *Comstock Diary*, 313–14.

33. *OR*, 46(3):67, 49(1):355–56, 49(2):72–73.

34. *OR*, 49(1):419, 49(2):125, 137.

35. *OR*, 49(1):419–24, 49(2):137, 173, 174.

36. *OR*, 49 (1):359, 388, 437, 473; E. N. Gilpin Journal, April 1, 1865, LC.

37. *OR*, 49(1):438, 473, 49(2):238–39; E. N. Gilpin Journal, April 3, 1865, LC. Jones, *Yankee Blitzkrieg*, scrutinizes Wilson's raid into Alabama and Georgia.

38. Edward Davis to "Sallie," April 16, 1865, UIA; Sumner, *Comstock Diary*, 313–14; Francis McGregor to Susan Brown, March 15–April 6, 1865, OHS; *OR*, 49((1):92, 49(2):195; Maury's Report, Lee Papers, VHS.

39. *ORN*, 22:79–80.

40. Maury's Report, Lee Papers, VHS; Sumner, *Comstock Diary*, 314; *OR*, 49(2):226–32.

41. Sumner, *Comstock Diary*, 314; *OR*, 49(1):95–96; *ORN*, 22:128–29; Dabney Maury's Report, Lee Papers, VHS; Milton Chambers to "Dear brother," April 3, 1865, KU.

42. *OR*, 49(1):96, 316–17, 49(2):283–88; Andrew Parsons to "Dear wife," April 10, 1865, CL; Sumner, *Comstock Diary*, 314; Henry Fike to "Dear Cimbaline," April 10, 1865, KU.

43. *ORN*, 22:86–87; Ferdinand Winslow to "Dearest Wife," April 10, 1865, UIA; *OR*, 49(1):97–99; Thomas Marshall Diary, April 9, 1865, OHS; Lorin Dame to "My dear Belle," April 10, 1865, MHS; Edward Davis to "Sallie," April 16, 1865, UIA; John Nelson Diary, April 9 and 10, 1865, MNHS; Dabney Maury's Report, Lee Papers, VHS.

44. *OR*, 49(1):98–99, 49(2):324, 327–28, 334; Dabney Maury's Report, Lee Papers, VHS.

45. *OR*, 49(2):323, 325–26, 335; Sumner, *Comstock Diary*, 315.

46. *OR*, 49(1):362–63.

47. *OR*, 49(1):428–29, 474–75; E. N. Gilpin Journal, April 15 and 16, 1865, LC.

48. Charles Harper to "Dear All," March 23, 1865, IHS; John Norris to Ira Norris, April 7, 1865, Tuttle Manuscripts, IU; Joseph O. Cross to "My Dear wife," March 10, 1865, CHS; John McCoy to "Dear Martha," January 26 and March 18, 1865, DC; *OR*, 46(2):926–27.

49. Nevins, *Wainwright Journals*, 501; Beale, *Welles Diary*, 2:201; Nevins and Thomas, *Strong Diary*, 3:503–5.

50. Meade, *Life and Letters*, 2:266–67; Agassiz, *Lyman Letters*, 314–16, 321–22; John Wilkins to "My dear Child," March 17, 1865, CL.

51. Hiram Ketcham Diary, March 17, 1864, BGSU; Agassiz, *Lyman Letters*, 321–22; *OR*, 46(3):28; Meade, *Life and Letters*, 2:267–68.

52. Beale, *Welles Diary*, 2:260–64, 266–67; *CWL*, 7:522–23, 8:364, 367.

53. Beale, *Welles Diary*, 2:264, 269; *CWL*, 8:223–24, 372–73; James Perry Diary, March 23, 1865, WHS; Oscar Robinson to "Dear Mother," March 25, 1865, DC; Carleton Felch Diary, March 23, 1865, Fairbanks Museum.

54. *OR*, 47(2):1453–54, 47(3):682. The prevailing impression — that Lee intended this offensive as a means of escaping Petersburg with his entire army — seems mistaken. Not only does Lee's subsequent letter to Jefferson Davis make no reference to escape (Freeman, *Lee's Dispatches*, 341–46), but his failure to inform Davis of the assault beforehand suggests that he did not mean to leave his government behind, unprotected.

55. *OR*, 46(1):70, 317, 331–32, 346, 391; J. F. Lovering Diary, March 25, 1865, IU. See Greene, *Breaking the Backbone of the Rebellion*, 156–60, 183, for Fort Stedman.

56. Nevins, *Wainwright Journals*, 503; *OR*, 46(1):318, 345, 46(3):146–48; Agassiz, *Lyman Letters*, 322, Meade, *Life and Letters*, 2:268.

57. *OR*, 46(1):322–24, 346–48, 46(3):148–50; Bushrod Johnson Diary, March 25, 1865, RG 109, NA; William Boston to "Dear Aunt," March 25, 1865, BL; Warren Goodale to "Dear Children," March 25, 1865, MHS; Agassiz, *Lyman Letters*, 323; Oscar Robinson to "Dear Mother," March 25, 1865, DC; Joseph Rutherford to "The Newport Express," March 27, 1865, UVM; Ransom Sargent to "My ever dear Maria," March 26, 1865, DC.

58. *OR*, 46(3):121–29, 143–44, 148; *CWL*, 8:373; George Bates to "Dear Parents," March 27, 1865, CL; Zerah Monks to "Dear Hattie," March 26, 1865, WRHS; Henry Rinker to "My Dear Mary," March 26, 1865, USAMHI; Brown, *Tilden Letters*, 65; Britton and Reed, *Hartwell Letters*, 344; Edward Roberts Diary, March 25, 1865, CHS; Sylvester Norton to Fanny Norton, March 28, 1865, MNHS; Warren Phillips to "Dear Father and Mother," March 26, 1865, WHS; J. Warren Keifer to "My Dear Wife," March 25, 1865, LC.

59. *OR*, 46(3):132; Agassiz, *Lyman Letters*, 322–23; Meade, *Life and Letters*, 2:268; Coco, *Mills Letters*, 250; Frank Morse to "My dear Nellie," March 27, 1865, MHS; Henry Keiser Diary, March 25, 1865, USAMHI; George Bates to "Dear Parents," March 31, 1865, CL; Daniel Nelson Diary, March 26, 1865, VHS; James Rickard to "Dear Father," March 28, 1865, AAS.

60. Aaron Tompkins to "Dear Sister," March 27, 1865, LC; J. R. Hamilton to "Dear Swinton," March 28, 1865, VHS.

NOTES TO PAGES 313-318

61. Like the Hampton Roads conference, the March meetings aboard the *River Queen* are recorded only in memoirs. Admiral Porter, who was more famous for self-promotion than for strict veracity, left a detailed account with General Sherman, who seemed to endorse the gist of it although he disputed the date: he thought Porter described the conference of March 27, while he only remembered Porter being present on the morning of March 28. Both their accounts appeared in Sherman's *Memoirs* (2:324-31), first published in 1875, while Grant was able to correct any errors or exaggerations, had he been so inclined. Grant failed to do so, or to mention the meetings in his own memoirs. William Crook, the presidential bodyguard on the *River Queen*, dated the principal conference March 27, and included only the president, Grant, and Sherman (Gerry, *Through Five Administrations*, 43). A newspaper reporter hovering around City Point mentioned the meeting in a letter of March 28 as having occurred "last night," but he thought Sheridan was part of it (J. R. Hamilton to "Dear Swinton," March 28, 1865, VHS). Grant did summon Sheridan the afternoon of March 27, specifically to meet with him and Sherman: *OR*, 46(3):215.

62. *OR*, 46(1):1286, and 46(3):224, 799-800, 1360, 1363. For this and all operations around Petersburg through April 3, see Greene, *Breaking the Backbone of the Rebellion*.

63. Bushrod Johnson Diary, March "28" [29], 1865, RG 109, NA; *OR*, 46(1):800-801, 1286-87, 1364-65; Agassiz, *Lyman Letters*, 330.

64. Hiram Ketcham Diary, March 29 and 30, 1865, BGSU; Alexander Rose Diary, March 29, 1865, USAMHI; Henry Brown Diary, March 30, 1865, USAMHI; J. F. Lovering Diary, March 30, 1865, IU; *OR*, 46(3):234, 266.

65. *OR* 46(1):388-90, 1299, and 46(3):1363-65; William Alexander Diary, March 29, 1865, SHC; Bushrod Johnson Diary, March 29 and 30, 1865, RG 109, NA; Holcomb Harvey Diary, March 29 and 30, 1865, Duke.

66. Holcomb Harvey Diary, March 31, 1864, Duke; Bushrod Johnson Diary, March 31, 1865, RG 109, NA; J. F. Lovering Diary, March 31, 1865, IU; *OR*, 46(1):814-15, 1287-88; Agassiz, *Lyman Letters*, 331-32.

67. *OR*, 46(1):817, 1110; *ORS*, Part 1, 7:780-81; Francis Sherman Diary, March 31, 1865, UVA.

68. *OR*, 46(3):325, 340-42, 380-81.

69. *OR*, 46(1):820-23, Alexander Rose Diary, March 31, 1865, USAMHI; *ORS*, 8:741-42, 9:901; Agassiz, *Lyman Letters*, 105-6. The best analysis of the infamous episode between Sheridan and Warren is Sears, *Controversies and Commanders*, 255-87.

70. Francis Sherman Diary, March 31 and April 1, 1865, UVA; *OR*, 46(1):62, 869, 1101-4.

71. *ORS* 8:471-72; Francis Sherman Diary, April 1, 1865, UVA; *OR*, 46(1):869-70, 1105; George Griggs Diary, April 1, 1865, MOC; Nevins, *Wainwright Journals*, 512-14; William Livermore Diary, April 1, 1865, VHS; Hiram Harding Diary, April 1, 1865, MOC; Pearce, *Chambers Diary*, 258-59; Benjamin Sims Journal, April 1, 1865, NCDAH; Andrew Linscott to "Dear Parents," April 12, 1865, MHS. Twenty years later Rosser alleged that Pickett and Lee had joined him for a feast of freshly caught shad (*Philadelphia Weekly Times*, April 5, 1885); Pickett was dead by then, but Lee seems not to have denied the story.

72. Nevins, *Wainwright Journals*, 514; *ORS*, Part 1, 9:1561, 1601-2. Under Grant's protection, Sheridan avoided a court of inquiry until 1881. With the help of General in Chief William T. Sherman and Grant's onetime staff officer Secretary of War Robert Lincoln, Warren did not see the court's vindication published during his lifetime.

73. Edward Roberts Diary, April 1 and 2, 1865, CHS; Judson Andrews Diary, April 1, 1865, FSNMP; Edwin Horton to "Dearest Ellen," March 17, 1865, VTHS; J. F. Lovering Diary, April 2, 1865, IU; George A. Bowen Diary, April 1, 1865, FSNMP; Henry Whitney to "Dear All," April 4, 1865, MHS.

74. *OR*, 46(1):902-4, 1017, 46(3):515, 521; Barnes, *Medical and Surgical History*,

9:264; Ransom Sargent to "My own darling Maria," April 2, 1865, DC; Carleton Felch Diary, April 2, 1865, Fairbanks Museum; John Brincklé Diary, April 2, 1865, LC; Lothrop Lewis Diary, April 2, 1865, LC; Caleb Beal to "Dear Parents," April 3, 1865, MHS; Britton and Reed, *Hartwell Letters*, 347; John Macomber Diary, April 1 and 2, 1865, MNHS; Robert Larimer Diary, April 2, 1865, UVA; Hiram Ketcham Diary, April 2, 1865, BGSU; Agassiz, *Lyman Letters*, 341.

75. Britton and Reed, *Hartwell Letters*, 347; Hiram Ketcham Diary, April 2, 1865, BGSU; Reports of Henry Heth, Cadmus Wilcox, and William McComb, Lee Papers, VHS; E. K. Russell to "Dear Mother," April 17, 1865, FSNMP; Daniel Himes Diary, April 2, 1865, USAMHI; Alexander Rose Diary, April 2, 1865, USAMHI.

76. Thomas Gantt to "My dear Blair," March 15, 1865, IU.

77. *OR*, 46(1):1019, 1047; William Boston to "Dear Aunt," April 9, 1865, BL; John Irwin to "Dear Mother," April 6, 1865, BL; James Boughton to Edwin March, April 4, 1865, BL; Luke and Charles Ostrye to "Dear Father," April 6, 1865, USAMHI.

78. Edward Roberts Diary, April 3, 1865, CHS; John Bailey Journal, April 3, 1865, NHHS.

79. Younger, *Kean Diary*, 205; Kena Chapman Diary, April 3, 1865, SHC; John Richardson Porter Diary, April 2 and 3, 1865, Duke; Frances Hunt Diary, April 3 and 4, 1865, F. H. Bullard to "Dear Friend Mary," April 13, 1865, Samuel Root to "My dear Wife," April 14, 1865, and Jacob Graham to "Dear Cousins," April 8, 1865, all in USAMHI; Valentine Barney to "My dear Maria," April 3, 1865, VTHS.

80. Henry Marshall to "Dear Folks at Home," April 3, 1865, CL; Edward Bartlett to "Dear Martha," April 3, 1865, MHS; Warren Goodale to "Dear Children," April 6 and 15, 1865, MHS; James Rickard to "Dear Brother," April 2 and 3, 1865, AAS; John Burrill to "Dear Ell," April 4, 1865, USAMHI; Herman Lewis to "Dear Sister," April 4, 1865, USAMHI; Jones, *Diary*, 528–30; Loren Kingsbury to Rachel and Viola Kingsbury, April 3 and 5, 1865, VTHS. In *Richmond Burning*, Nelson Lankford minutely examines the fall of Confederate Richmond.

81. Jones, *Diary*, 531–32; Henry Marshall to "Dear Folks at Home," April 5, 1865, CL; *New York Herald*, April 9, 1865; *RJCR*, Part 2:273; *CWL*, 8:386–87, 389; *OR*, 46(3):575.

82. John Thayer to Lorin Dame, April 5, 1865, MHS; *American Traveler*, April 8, 1865; "Anne" to Arthur Nesmith, April 7, 1865, DC; Nevins and Thomas, *Strong Diary*, 3:576; Alonzo Richards Diary, April 5, 1865, WHS; French, *Journals*, 468–69.

83. Charles Dana to Edwin Stanton, April 12, 1865 (1:30 P.M.), LC; *OR*, 46(1):1288, 1291, 46(3):529, and Series 2, 8:352–54; John Warr Diary, April 4 and 5, 1865, ACHNHP; Hiram Harding Diary, April 4, 1864, MOC; Creed Davis, James Phillips, and John Vincent Diaries, all April 4, 1865, all in VHS; John Coleman Diary, April 4, 1865, USAMHI. See Marvel, *Lee's Last Retreat*, 201–6, for a discussion of Lee's strength.

84. Isaac Ressler Diary, April 5, 1865, USAMHI; Robert Bell to "My Dear Wife," April 5, 1865, ACHNHP; Leonard Goodwin to Horace Fenn, April 4, 1865, CHS; George Bowen Diary, April 5, 1865, FSNMP; Alexander Rose Diary, April 5, 1865, USAMHI; Stephen Chase Diary, April 5, 1865, USAMHI.

85. Stephen Chase and Alexander Rose Diaries, April 6, 1865, both USAMHI; George Bowen Diary, April 6, 1865, FSNMP; Francis Sherman Diary, April 6, 1865, UVA; James Albright Diary, April 6, 1865, SHC; Holcomb Harvey Diary, April 6, 1865, Duke; Bushrod Johnson Diary, April 6, 1865, RG 109, NA; Judson Andrews Diary, April 6, 1865, FSNMP; John Brincklé Diary, April 6, 1865, LC; Warren Keifer to "My Dear Wife," April 7, 1865, LC.

86. Willis Porter to Etta Porter, April 6 and 10, 1865, MEHS; Robert Larimer Diary, April 6, 1865, UVA; Charles Field to Hattie Burleigh, April 16, 1865, USAMHI; Robertson, *McAllister Letters*, 606; Alexander Rose Diary, April 7, 1865, USAMHI; Darius Safford to "Dear Father & Mother," April 9, 1865, VTHS; Bushrod Johnson Diary, April 7, 1865, RG 109, NA.

87. Eri Woodbury Diary, April 8, 1865, and Woodbury to "Dear Father," April 25, 1865, DC; John Clark to "My Kind Friend," April 16, 1865, CL; John Council Diary, April 8, 1865, NCDAH; Anonymous Diary, April 8, 1865, UVA; Dowdey and Manarin, *Lee Papers*, 937.

88. Thomas Covert to "My Dear Wife," April 12, 1865, WRHS; Hiram Ketcham Diary, April 9, 1865, BGSU; Gordon's Report, Lee Papers, VHS; Chapin Warner to "Dear Mother & Father," April 15, 1865, MHS; Daniel Nelson Diary, April 13, 1865, VHS; Osmun Latrobe Diary, April 9, 1865, VHS; William Wells to "Dearest Anna," April 11, 1865, UVM.

9. No More to Know the Drum

1. George Anthony to "Dear Brother," April 9, 1865, CL; *OR*, 46(3):665–66.

2. Thomas Wilson to his wife, April (no day), 1865, LC; Henry Keiser Diary, April 9, 1865, USAMHI; Jared Potter Diary, April 10, 1865, USAMHI; John Bailey Journal, April 10, 1865, NHHS.

3. Hammond, *Diary of a Union Lady*, 351–52; E. U. Bacon to "Dear Bess," April 12, 1865, Usher Collection, MEHS; Jeremiah Lockwood Diary, April 10, 1865, LC; Brun, "Fleming Letters," 38; Burlingame, *Brooks Dispatches*, 181–82; Nevins and Thomas, *Strong Diary*, 3:578–79; Wainwright, *Fisher Diary*, 491; Elizabeth Livermore Diary, April 10, 1865, NHHS; Carolyn White Diary, April 10, 1865, AAS; Almira Miller Diary, April 10, 1865, USAMHI; Richard Kent Diary, April 10–14, 1865, NHHS; *Oxford Democrat*, April 14, 1865.

4. Henry Herrick Diary, April 10, 1865, Fairbanks Museum; Susan Forbes Diary, April 10, 1865, AAS; Chester Evans to "My Dear Little Wiffie," April 10, 1865, MNHS; Samuel Curtis to "My dear Son," April 10, 1865, Yale; Thomas Gantt to "My dear Blair," April 10, 1865, Blair Manuscripts, IU; *Boston Herald*, April 11, 1865; *Detroit Free Press*, April 7, 9, and 10, 1865.

5. William Hinson Diary, April 10, 1865, Charleston Library Society; Britton and Reed, *Hartwell Letters*, 349; Elihu Washburne Diary, April 10–12, 1865, Yale; John Bailey Journal, April 10, 1865, NHHS; Oscar Robinson to "Dear Mother," April 14, 1865, DC.

6. Perkins Smith to J. F. Phillips, April 3, 1865, and S. Brimhall to Phillips, May 15, 1865, WHS; Sylvester Norton to "My most beloved Fanny," April 22, 1865, MNHS; G. B. Gillett to C. B. Royall, April 29, 1865, Shaw Letters, CL.

7. *OR*, 46(3):716–17; Hilon Parker to "Dear Father," April 9, 1865, CL; *Boston Herald*, April 12, 1865; Burlingame, *Brooks Dispatches*, 183–84; *CWL*, 8:399–405; Beale, *Welles Diary*, 2:279–81. "Governor" Peirpoint changed the spelling of his name in 1881.

8. *CWL*, 8:399–401; Beale, *Welles Diary*, 2:281. Peirpoint's minority government had been elected from and by residents of western Virginia in 1861, but the Lincoln administration continued to recognize it as the government of the Old Dominion after the formation of West Virginia and the election of a government for that state.

9. *OR*, 47(3):18, 28, 59, 74, 109, 139–40; *CWL*, 8:375–76.

10. *New York Times*, April 18, 1865; Gray, *War Letters*, 192, 391, 469; Wallace Sanborn to "My dear Pastor," March 24, 1865, AAS.

11. *OR*, 47(3):161; *New York Times*, April 18, 1865; Franklin, *Ayers Diary*, 93.

12. Gray, *War Letters*, 469–70; *New York Times*, April 18, 1865.

13. Gray, *War Letters*, 472; Beale, *Welles Diary*, 2:282–83.

14. *Washington Star*, April 14, 1865. Of all the books about Lincoln's assassination, the most engaging and thoroughly researched is probably Kauffman, *American Brutus*.

15. *Washington Star*, April 17, 1865; *New York Times*, April 15, 16, and 26, 1865; *OR*, 46(3):780.

16. Charles Sanford to "Dear Goodrich," April 15, 1865, CL; *New York Times*, April 26, 1865. Newspapers reported by April 24 that Booth broke his leg when his horse fell, but an ambiguous passage in his diary abetted the tale that he broke it leaping to the stage, which became current within two days of his capture (see, for instance, *Bos-*

ton Herald, April 24 and 28, 1865). Kauffman, *American Brutus,* 273–75, debunks that myth.

17. *Washington Star,* April 15, 1865; *New York Times,* April 15, 1865; Beale, *Welles Diary,* 2:283–85.

18. Beale, *Welles Diary,* 2:283–88; *OR,* 46(3):780; *New York Times,* April 15 and 26, 1865; French, *Journals,* 469–70.

19. *OR,* 46(3):780; Louise Titcomb to Rebecca Usher, April 20, 1865, MEHS.

20. Elizabeth Livermore Diary, April 15, 1865, NHHS; Nevins and Thomas, *Strong Diary,* 3:582; J. F. Lovering Diary, April 16, 1865, IU; Oscar Robinson to "Dear Mother," April 24, 1865, DC; Washington Vosburgh to "My own dear Ella," April 25, 1865, BL; Warren Goodale to "Dear Children," April 15, 1865, MHS; J. Warren Keifer to his wife, April 15, 1865, LC.

21. Christopher Keller to "My Dear Carrie," May 5, 1865, CL; Albert Ritter to "Dear Cousin Helen," May 9, 1865, Chandler Papers, UR; Norman Carr to "Dear Father," April 18, 1865, UR; Thomas Honnel to "Dear Brother Eli," April 18, 1865, OHS.

22. Francis Thomas Diary, April 15, 1865, Earlham; Elvira Aplin to "Dear son George," April 18, 1865, CL.

23. Wainwright, *Fisher Diary,* 492–93, 495–96; *New York Times,* April 26, 1865; Dennis Aley to "Dear Brother," April 24, 1865, Yale; Thomas Trefry to "My dear Mother," April 18, 1865, Cole Papers, PEM.

24. Gray, *War Letters,* 472; G. Buckingham to "Dear Sister," April 21, 1865, Curtis Papers, Yale; Andrew Young to "My Dear Susan," April 20, 1865, DC; Nevins and Thomas, *Strong Diary,* 3:582–83.

25. Christopher Keller to "My Dear Carrie," May 5, 1865, CL; Oscar Robinson to "Dear Mother," April 24, 1865, DC; Hilon Parker to "Folks at Home," April 22, 1865, CL; Wainwright, *Fisher Diary,* 492–93; *OR,* 47(3):245, 287.

26. *OR,* 47(3):206–7, 237, 304, 788, 791, 802; James Stillwell to "My dear wife," April 18, 1865, OHS. See Bradley, *This Astounding Close,* on Johnston's surrender.

27. *OR,* 47(3):277–78, 285–86; John Sherman to Stanton, April 27, 1865, LC.

28. Younger, *Kean Diary,* 206–7; Wiggins, *Gorgas Journals,* 160–62; OR, 47(3):821–28, 830–31, 832–34, 834–35; Ellen Ravenel to "My dear Aunt Rosa," April 23, 1865, USC (original in South Carolina Historical Society). William C. Davis's *An Honorable Defeat* vividly describes the flight of the Confederate government.

29. *OR,* 46(1):1315, 46(3):910, 1396; Joshua Whiteman to "Dear Wife," April 28, 1865, OHS; John Amadon to "Dear Wife," April 30, 1865, VTHS; William Russell to George Chapman, April 13, 1865, CL; Thomas Shriver to "My dear Mother," April 16, 1865, ND.

30. *OR,* 39(1):227, 471, 506, 513, 520–21, 533–34, 542–45, 39(2):454–56, 859, 870, Series 2, 7:998–1002, and 8:803; Harwell, *Cumming Journal,* 259.

31. Edwin Ford to "Dear Parents," December 8, 1864, and to "Dear Sister," January 24, 1865, BL; *OR,* Series 2, 7:999.

32. Harwell, *Cumming Journal,* 259; William Fast to "Editor of the [Toledo] Blade," December 6, 1885, BGSU; Alonzo Van Vlack to "Dear Father & Mother," March 20, 1865, BL; *OR,* Series 2, 8:284–85, 404–5, 437. Four decades later, deep in the era of sectional reconciliation, one of the Confederate exchange commissioners claimed that he insisted on calling the neutral area Camp Fisk, in honor of a Union counterpart who suggested its creation (Henderson, "Lincoln's Assassination and Camp Fisk"). Some soldiers' letters use that name, but contemporary official correspondence does not.

33. Alonzo Van Vlack to "Dear Father & Mother," April 5, 1865, BL; Amos Ames and John Whitten Diaries, March 18–27, 1865, both SHSI-DM; Thomas Horan to unidentified recipient, March 27, 1865, IHS; D. A. Johnston to Abby Stafford, April 9, 1865, Duke; *OR,* Series 2, 8:492–93; Frederic Speed to "Dear Father," April 4, 1865, CL; unidentified correspondent to Peter Joslyn, April 9, 1865, AAS.

34. *OR,* Series 2, 8:488–89.

35. Joseph Geiger to Abraham Lincoln, May 28, 1864, Wade Papers, LC; W. F. Dubois to "Dear Uncle," March 20, "1865" [1866], Longyear Papers, BL; *CWL*, 4:461, 5:116, 177.

36. *OR*, Series 2, 8:211.

37. Frederic Speed to his mother, April 2, 1862, and February 2, 1863, to his father, May 15 and November 3, 1862, May 26, 1863, and April 4, 1865, CL.

38. *OR*, 48(1):211.

39. *Cincinnati Daily Commercial*, February 4, 1863; *Daily Bulletin*, April 16 and 17, 1865; *Daily Picayune*, April 19, 1865.

40. *Daily Picayune*, April 21, 1865; Sarah Wadley Diary, April 26, 1865, SHC; *OR*, 48(1):211, 219; Transcript of Frederic Speed Court-Martial, 193, RG 153, NA, cited in Potter, *The Sultana Tragedy*, 55; *OR*, 48(1):211.

41. *OR*, 48(1):211, 214–15, 219. There are several books on the *Sultana*, the best of which are Potter's *The Sultana Tragedy* and Salecker's *Disaster on the Mississippi*.

42. *OR*, 48(1):217; Alonzo Van Vlack to "Dear Father & Mother," April 28, 1865, BL; Sultana Engineering Plans, OHS; Samuel Boysell to "Dear Wife," April 7, 1865, OHS; David Millspaugh Diary, title page, BL; *Daily Bulletin*, April 28, 1865.

43. Alonzo Van Vlack to "Dear Father & Mother," April 28, 1865, BL; *Daily Bulletin*, April 28, 1865; *Chicago Tribune*, April 29 and 30, 1865; *Detroit Free Press*, April 29, 30, and May 2, 1865. Potter, *The Sultana Tragedy*, 131, 196–260, lists 2,317 soldiers who were on the *Sultana*, besides a crew of 85 and "approximately 100 civilian passengers," which suggests a death toll of more than 1,547; he counts only one female survivor, whose husband and baby drowned, but the Memphis *Daily Bulletin* and the *Chicago Tribune* reported another woman clutching a dead child who was rescued "opposite Beal street."

44. *OR*, Series 2, 8:537; Frederic Speed to "My Dear Lotty," April 28, 1865, CL.

45. *OR*, 48(1):212–13; Frederic Speed to "Colonel," May 28, 1865, CL. One theory of Confederate sabotage surfaced years later (Michael, "Explosion of the Sultana," 257).

46. *OR*, 48(1):217–20, and Series 2, 8:964–65; *American Traveler*, June 3, 1865; *Memphis Daily Avalanche*, February 1, 1866. Holt's unilateral decision "exonerated" Speed, but Potter (*The Sultana Tragedy*, 180) considered Speed culpable for underestimating the number of prisoners on the boat. Suspicions of graft appear to have centered mainly on Colonel Hatch, but his strangely persuasive interview with Speed on April 24 could well have included an offer to share a portion of the abundant bribe money, which would explain Speed's curious reference to prospects of war-related profits a few days later.

47. Consolidated Morning Reports, April 28–May 5, 1865, RG 249, NA; Atwater, *Report*, 69; Descriptive Roll of Company F, 1st Wisconsin Cavalry, Knud Hanson military service record, RG 94, NA; *OR*, 49(2):580, and Series 2, 8:532; *Trial of Henry Wirz*, 19, 315, 384.

48. *Trial of Henry Wirz*, 19–20; *OR*, 49(2):721–22, 743. Wirz would hang six months later, after a perjury-filled trial before a biased court-martial, but Judge Advocate General Holt found no fault with this verdict (*OR*, Series 2, 8:794).

49. Joseph Leavitt Diary, February 22–March 1, 1865, BPL; John Faller to "Dear Father," March 14, 1865, USAMHI; Alvah Skilton Diary, March 20–24, 1865, RBHPL; Walter Graham to "Dear Parents," July 31 and November 15, 1864, VTHS; William Howard to "Dear Friends at Home," August 4 and September 14, 1864, VTHS; Robert Cowden Diary, February 5, 1865, CCHS; Benjamin Calef to John Calef, November 13, 1864, DC; Abner Small Diary, February 17 and 18, 1865, MEHS; Nelly Fogg to Persis Blanchard, May 9, 1865, MEHS.

50. Neil Dodge, S. Morse, L. F. Southard, Mary Mahoney, and Mrs. Henry Sanborn to Alson Blake, May 29, 1865, VTHS. The collection contains scores of such letters.

51. Paul Whipple to "Friend Sophia," April 24, 1864 (in Caleb Dodge Correspondence), A. J. Bennett to William Dodge, February 25, 1865, and William Dodge to Samuel Kennison, May, 1865, NHHS.

52. Natt Head to Elvira Douglass, February 28, 1865, NHHS.

53. D. F. Young to Julia Comey, August 8, 1862, Francis Loud to Julia Comey, July 22, 1864, James Hollins to E. O. Kenney, November 6, 1864, and W. A. Start to "Sir," November 16, 1864, Brownson Papers, NHHS; Ayling, *Register*, 30; *MSSM*, 5:30.

54. John Mulford to Mark Glines, June 16, 1865, and C. P. Blackman to Glines, June 24, 1865, Yale; J. S. Dore to Sarah Upton, December 30, 1864, NHHS; Joseph Hawley to Charles Dudley Warner, October 12, 1865, CHS; G. W. Ball to "Mr. Moulton," January 29, 1865, NHHS.

55. Ammi Williams to Henry Williams, December 3, 1862, July 28, 1864, and April 29, 1865, RBHPL.

56. John Roberts to "Mrs. Bixby," May 21, 1864, Mark Sargent to "Mrs. Bixby," June 6, 1864, Henry Osgood to "Mrs. Bixby," October 14, 1864, and "EWC" to "Dear Cousin Frances," June 22 [presumably 1865], VTHS; Henry Hayward to "Mrs. Bixby," May 20, 1864, UVM. The UVM collection includes a lock of dark brown hair fastened to a letter addressed to Frances Bixby.

57. Job Brockman to "Dear Flora," May 2, 1865, IHS; Joseph Davidson to Sarah Davis, May 3, 1865, David Scott Letters, IHS; Norman Carr to "Dear Mother," May 5, 1865, UR.

58. *OR*, 49(2):558–59, 1263–64, 1283–84, 1289–90; Joseph Tarbell to "Dear Father & Mother," May 15, 1865, VTHS.

59. *OR*, 48(1):186–90, 1359, 1380, 48(2):1292–93; William Crawford to "Dear Son," March 13, 1865, WHMC; Mary Dodge to "Dear friend," March 26, 1865, Ball Papers, Aldrich Public Library; Albert Harris to "Dear Mother," April 16, 1865, VTHS.

60. *USG*, 13:282–90; *OR*, 48(1):1275–76, 1280, 1456, 48(2):17–18, 516–17.

61. *OR*, 48(2):516–17; Edward Davis to "Dear Mother," July 11, 1864, UIA.

62. *OR*, 48(1):265–68, 1219, 48(2):18; Tilley, *McIntyre Diary*, 380.

63. *OR*, 48(1):266, 268; Transcript of Robert Morrison Court-Martial, RG 153, NA, 19, 146, 182, 230 (page numbers from the version published in *ORS*, 10:1–276).

64. *OR*, 48(1):266, 268; Transcript of Robert Morrison Court-Martial, RG 153, NA, 19–20, 79–80, 147–52, 154–56, 182–83.

65. *OR*, 48(1):266–67, 268–69; Transcript of Robert Morrison Court-Martial, RG 153, NA, 80–81, 157–60, 183–87.

66. Simpson and Berlin, *Sherman Letters*, 883, 896; John Lester Diary, April 29, May 9 and 17, 1865, ISL; Henry Guyer to "Dear Brother," June 8, 1865, Yale; Jordan, *Gould Journals*, 466; Charles Reed to "Dear Mother," May 22 [1865], LC.

67. George Trowbridge to "Dear Wife," May 11, 15, and 16, 1865, CL.

68. Nathaniel Parmeter Diary, May 15, 1865, OHS.

69. Rosenblatt and Rosenblatt, *Fisk Letters*, 327; Quaife, *Williams Letters*, 388; Kallgren and Crouthamel, *Dear Friend Anna*, 127; John Thompson to "Dear father," May 3, 1865, NHHS; *OR*, 46(3):1169–71, 1181.

70. *New York Times*, May 21 and 22, 1865; Robertson, *McAllister Letters*, 618–19; Quaife, *Williams Letters*, 388; Simpson and Berlin, *Sherman Letters*, 883, 892, 897.

71. Jordan, *Gould Journals*, 466–67; Nevins, *Wainwright Journals*, 525; Francis Crowninshield to "Dearest Mother," May 23, 1865, PEM; Edward Bragg to "My Dear Wife," May 26, 1865, WHS; *OR*, 46(3):1169.

72. Jordan, *Gould Journals*, 468; Nevins, *Wainwright Journals*, 526–27; Albion Gross to "My Dear Companion," May 23, 1865, MNHS; John Bailey Journal, May 22 and 23, 1865, NHHS; Kallgren and Crouthamel, *Dear Friend Anna*, 127–28; Willis Porter to "My dear Wife," May 25, 1865, MEHS.

73. Lucy Hayes to "My dear Mother," May 26, 1865, RBHPL.

74. John Bailey Journal, May 23, 1865, NHHS; Horatio Taft Diary, May 23, 1865, LC; Jordan, *Gould Journals*, 468; Nevins, *Wainwright Journals*, 528.

75. John Peirce to "My Dear Wife," May 24, 1865, PEM; Miller, *Whitman Writings*, 1:261; John Bailey Journal, May 23, 1865, NHHS; William Boston Diary, May 23, 1865, BL; Jordan, *Gould Journals*, 467; Nevins, *Wainwright Journals*, 528; Horatio Taft Diary,

May 23, 1865, LC; William Porter to "My dear Wife," May 25, 1865, MEHS; Jeremiah Lockwood Diary, May 23, 1865, LC.

76. J. F. Lovering Diary, May 23, 1865, IU; *New York Times*, May 24, 1865; *OR*, 46(3):1195–96.

77. John Cushman Diary, May 24, 1865, NSHS; Joseph Hoffhines to Nancy Hoffhines, undated fragment, OHS; Nathaniel Parmeter Diary, May 24, 1865, OHS; John McIntosh to "Dear Sister," May 26, 1865, WRHS; Charles Smith to "Dear Father," May 26, 1865, WHS; Horatio Taft Diary, May 24, 1865, LC; Nevins, *Wainwright Journals*, 529–30.

78. *New York Times*, May 25, 1865; Horatio Taft Diary, May 24, 1865, LC; Henry Hitchcock to "My darling," May 26, 1865, LC; Jordan, *Gould Journals*, 468; *Chicago Tribune*, May 25, 1865; John Jamison and Lyman Trumbull to Edwin Stanton, both May 25, 1865, LC.

79. *New York Times*, May 25, 1865; Nevins, *Wainwright Journals*, 529–30; James Stillwell to "My dear wife and Children," May 24, 1865, OHS; Horatio Taft Diary, May 24, 1865, LC; Nathaniel Parmeter Diary, May 24, 1865, OHS.

80. Lyman Holyoke to Samuel Henderson, May 23, 1865, MHS; Rufus Mead Diary, May 24, 1865, LC; Samuel Cauller to "Dear Wife," May 30, 1865, USAMHI; Kallgren and Crouthamel, *Dear Friend Anna*, 128–29; Menge and Shimrak, *Chisholm Notebook*, 91.

81. *OR*, 48(2):600–602, 1067–68, 1100–1101; *ORN*, 22:216–17; Mosby Parsons to "My Dear Father & Mother," June 5, 1865, and L. A. Pindall to unidentified recipient, February 3, 1869, Parsons Papers, MOHS; Trusten Polk Diary, May 26–July 9, 1865, SHC.

82. *OR*, 46(3):1164–65, 1182–83.

83. George Trowbridge to "My Dear Wife," May 27, 1865, CL; Daniel Nelson Journal, June 23, 1865, VHS; Sumner, *Comstock Diary*, 317–18; Horatio Taft Diary, May 22, 1865, LC; Abiah Clough to "Dear Little Son," June 4, 1865, DC.

84. George Trowbridge to "Dear Wife," June 5, 1865, CL; Child, *Letters*, 357, 359.

85. William Nichols to David Thayer, April 8, 1865, MHS; Henry Brown to "Dear Mother," April 22, 1865, CHS; Jane Underwood to "My dear Adin," June 25, 1865, MHS.

86. James Brisbin to Benjamin Wade, May 23, 1865, LC.

87. Shannon, *Andrus Letters*, 136; Leander Harris to Emily Harris, July 26, 1865, UNH; Roswell Holbrook to "Dear Cosin Malinda," July 30, 1865, VTHS; Lorenzo Miles Diary, August 29, 1865, VTHS; Charles Marples to "Dear Wife," April 12, 1865, and Peter Isley to Jane Marples, April 28, 1865, MNHS.

88. William Haynes to "Dearest One," May 15, 1865, and to "My Dear," June 18, 1865, KSHS; *OR*, 48(1):164–65; Thomas Trefry to "Dear Mother," July 1, 1865, Cole Papers, PEM; Kallgren and Crouthamel, *Dear Friend Anna*, 129.

89. Alfred Parkhurst to "Friend Geo.," April 18, 1865, Wheaton Papers, UVM; William Proctor to "Father," March 14, 1865, Fairbanks Museum.

90. Charles Reed to "Dear Sister," May 23 and 25, 1865, LC; John Irwin to "Dear Mother," May 11, 1865, BL; William Livermore Diary, May 26, 1865, VHS; F. Schneider to Edwin March, June 21, 1865, BL.

Epilogue

1. J. F. Lovering Diary, June 8, 1865, IU; John Bailey Journal, June 13 and 14, 1865, NHHS; Daniel Himes Diary, June 14, 1865, USAMHI.

2. John Lester Diary, July 22 and 23, 1865, ISL; David Himes Diary, June 16, 1865, USAMHI; John Wilcox Diary, June 16–20, 1865, NHHS; Lorenzo Miles Diary, July 23, 1865, VTHS; Roswell Holbrook to "Dear Cosin Malinda," July 30, 1865, VTHS; John Bailey Journal, June 15 and 16, 1865, NHHS; Melzar Beard to "Dear Cousin," April 29, 1866, VTHS; Josiah Brown to "Dear Brother," August 27, 1865, UME. Winslow Homer's 1865 painting *The Veteran in a New Field*, depicting a young man who has tossed his blue

army jacket on the ground to begin cutting grain, was surely inspired by the literal sight of soldiers discharged from an army that had disbanded between the beginning of the haying season and the eve of the harvest.

3. Kamphoefner and Helbich, *Germans in the Civil War,* 287, 289; Judson Austin to "Dear Wife," April 24, 1865, BL; Sarah Gross to "My Dear Husband," May 17, 1865, and Albion Gross to "Dear family," May 31, 1865, MNHS; James Milliken to "Dear Charles," August 17, 1865, MEHS.

4. Nellie Brown to "My Dear Sister," August 1, 1865, MNHS; George Bates memorandum, included in letter to "Dear Parents," May 6, 1865, CL; C. H. Champney to Enoch Adams, February 14, 1866, UNH; Wimer Bedford Diary, May 9–July 9, 1865, LC.

5. *Prairie du Chien Courier,* August 24 and 31, 1865; Chester Plimpton to Mary Richards, April 16, 1865, MNHS; *Union and Dakotian,* August 26, 1865; Nellie McKeen to John Nelson, April 30, 1865, MNHS; Charles Howe to "Dear Sister," August 23, 1865, and February 13, 1867, NHHS; Thomas Tobey to "My darling Carrie," November 14, 1865, Yale.

6. William Palmer to "My dear Charley," September 22, 1865, Yale; Robert Muir to "Dear Brother," September 10, 1865, Salina Public Library.

7. *New York Times,* August 1, September 1 and 2, 1865; *Union and Dakotian,* August 19, 26, and September 2, 1865; *Prairie du Chien Courier,* August 17, 24, and 31, 1865.

8. Christopher Keller to "Dear Carrie," May 21, 1865, CL.

9. *OR,* Series 2, 8:578–80, and Series 3, 5:37–39; *AJP,* 8:599–600; Charles Sumner to Benjamin Wade, June 9 and 12, 1865, LC; Palmer, *Sumner Letters,* 307–8.

10. *Acts of the General Assembly, 1865,* 6; *Daily Virginian,* October 19 and December 30, 1865; *Acts of the General Assembly, 1865–66,* 91–93; Dennett, *The South As It Is,* 70–72, 76; Circular, November 4, 1865, General Orders, Special Orders, and Letters Sent, Entry 3800, RG 105, NA.

11. *RJCR,* 2:126, 3:41, 143, 163; J. D. Aiken to "Dear Wyatt," May 20, 1865, USC. See also Cohen, "Negro Involuntary Servitude," especially 35–36.

12. *New York Times,* August 1, 1865; *North Missouri Courier,* May 24 and June 6, 1865; *RJCR,* 3:116.

13. Dennett, *The South As It Is,* 110–11; *RJCR,* 1:112, 2:208, 209, 211, 222–29, 3:145–48, 4:46–48, 86.

14. Dennett, *The South As It Is,* 76, 91–92; *RJCR,* 2:62, 126, 208, 3:109, 143, 4:75; *Daily Virginian,* October 19, 1865.

15. Williams, *Hayes Diary and Letters,* 3:7; *CG,* 39th Cong., 1st sess., 3–6, 6–7, 72–75; *New York Tribune,* December 2, 5, and 6, 1865.

16. C. W. Milliken to George Kimball, October 8, 1865, AAS; *New York Times,* August 1, 1865; *AJP,* 8:582–83.

17. Beale, *Welles Diary,* 2:434–35, 554. For the activities of the Freedmen's Bureau see, for example, Louis N. Stevenson to C. W. McMahon, January 5 and 9, 1865, Letters Sent, Entry 4082, RG 105, N.A.; R. S. Lacey to Orlando Brown, March 9 and 22, 1866, Press Copies of Letters Sent, Entry 4072, RG 105, NA; R. S. Lacey reports of March 20 and April 30, 1866, Descriptive Lists of Reports of Outrages, March to June, 1866, Records Relating to Murders and Outrages, M-1048, RG 105, NA; Louis N. Stevenson to Orlando Brown, January 31 and February 28, 1867, Narrative Reports of Criminal Cases, Entry 3806, RG 105, NA.

18. Beale, *Welles Diary,* 2:479.

19. *Memphis Daily Avalanche,* May 2–4, 1866; *CG,* 39th Cong., 1st sess., 2544, 2572; *New Orleans Times,* July 31 and August 1, 1866; *New Orleans Daily Picayune,* August 1, 1866.

20. Beale, *Welles Diary,* 2:554, 615–16; *USG,* 17:38. The text of each Reconstruction Act is quoted in Trefousse, *Reconstruction,* 103–14, 128–29.

21. Hans Trefousse, for instance, noted that Johnson's counterproductive veto of the

Freedmen's Bureau bill spurred Thaddeus Stevens to reverse his support for the readmission of Tennessee (*Stevens*, 183–84), while it seems unlikely that Lincoln would have made that blunder.

22. *New York Times*, September 4, 1868, August 1 and 2, 1870, March 4 and 11, 1871; *Raleigh Standard*, August 10, 1870, quoted in Gillette, *Retreat from Reconstruction*, 92; Victor Barringer to Albion Tourgée, undated, Tourgée to Emma Tourgée, June 9, 1869, and Tourgée to Barringer, February 7, 1871, CCHS. On the political effectiveness of violence during Reconstruction see Rable, *But There Was No Peace* (72–79, for the 1868 election in particular); Gillette (xii, 363) is especially critical of Grant; while Brooks Simpson (*Let Us Have Peace*, 263) concluded that it was Grant's "tragedy" that he "reluctantly accepted the perpetuation of racial injustice as the price of sectional reconciliation."

23. *New York Times*, August 1, 2, 6, and 8, 1870; *New York Herald*, December 12, 1872.

24. *New York Tribune*, April 29, 1874, and May 31, 1875; *New York Times*, May 31, 1875; *Boston Daily Advertiser*, June 2, 1875; Eggleston, *A Rebel's Recollections*, 19, 22–23; Washburne to John L. Winston, June 17, 1874, UVA.

25. *New York Times*, July 14 and September 22, 1876; *New York Herald*, September 27, 1876, and May 1, 1877. For general works on Reconstruction see Franklin, *Reconstruction: After the Civil War*, Trefousse, *Reconstruction*, or Foner's *Reconstruction*. Many modern and more detailed state studies are available.

26. Blackmon, *Slavery By Another Name*, is the most recent book on the topic of convict leasing; Mancini, in *One Dies, Get Another*, notes that the same servitude was imposed on white convicts, and Richard Morris observed that all the repressive laws were imposed on poor whites as well as blacks in "The Measure of Bondage," 224–25.

27. Samuel Turner to "My Dear Children," June 4, 1865, and to "Dear Harrison," November 12, 1876, Turner and Turner, *Turner Letters*, unpaginated.

Bibliography

Manuscripts

Aldrich Public Library, Barre, Vt.
  Ball Family Papers
American Antiquarian Society, Worcester, Mass.
  Charles Edgar Abbey Papers
  Edward W. Bacon Papers
  Civil War Collection
    Henry Ward Beecher Letter
    George P. Burrows Letters
    Henry Converse Letters
    Alonzo S. Cushman Letters
    David F. Cushman Diary
    Samuel H. Putnam Letter
    Wallace W. Sanborn Letter
    Letters to Hon. Eron N. Thomas
  William B. Collier Letter (Miscellaneous Correspondence)
  Comey Family Papers
  Joseph Cross Letters
  Ellen Tucker Emerson Letters
  Susan E. P. Brown Forbes Diary
  Sidney Hayden Papers
  Joslyn-Burditt Family Papers
  Letters to George C. Kimball
  Charles M. Munroe Diaries
  James Helme Rickard Letters
  Aaron Scott Thurber Diary
  Carolyn Barrett White Diary
  Henry White Diary

William A. Willoughby Papers
Andersonville National Historical Site, Andersonville, Ga.
    Anonymous Diary
    Henry H. Stone Diary
Appomattox Court House National Historic Park, Appomattox, Va.
    Robert Bell Letters
    John Wilson Warr Diary
D. R. Barker Library, Fredonia, N.Y.
    Asa W. Root Diary
Bennington Museum, Bennington, Vt.
    Letters of Jerome Cutler
Bethel Historical Society, Bethel, Maine
    Edgar Harvey Powers Diary
Boston Public Library
    Sophia and Una Hawthorne Letters
    Joseph Ward Leavitt Diary
    Parker Pillsbury Letter
    Henry Tisdale Diaries
    James Henry Wickes Letters
Bowling Green State University, Bowling Green, Ohio
    Fast Family Letters
    R. H. Foord Diary
    Hiram Ketcham Diary
    Rachel Stanton/Searles Family Papers
    Francis R. Stewart Papers
Charleston Library Society, Charleston, S.C.
    William G. Hinson Diary
Chautauqua County Historical Society, Westfield, N.Y.
    Bonner Family Papers
    James Burrows Letters
    George A. Cobham Jr. Diary
    Robert Isaac Cowden Diary
    Stephen R. Green Letters
    M. H. Hart Letter
    Albion W. Tourgée Papers
Chicago Historical Society
    Charles M. Colvin Notebook
Cincinnati Historical Society, Cincinnati, Ohio
    Henry Archer Langdon Letters
    Alexander Long Papers
    Miller Family Collection
    Mathias Schwab Letters
Connecticut Historical Society, Hartford
    Henry H. Adams Diary
    Orra B. Bailey Letters
    Perkins Bartholomew Letters

    John S. and Samuel Bartlett Papers
    Frederick Bill Letter
    Caleb and Horatio Blanchard Papers
    Charles A. Boyle Letters
    Henry H. Brown Papers
    Andrew Byrne Diary
    Josiah B. Corban Letters
    Joseph O. Cross Letters
    Horace Fenn Letters
    Filley Family Papers
    Horatio N. Fish Papers
    Oliver Gates Diary
    Julius S. and George S. Gilman Papers
    Charles H. Greenleaf Papers
    Samuel E. Grosvenor Diary
    Joseph Roswell Hawley Papers
    Frederick Hooker Letters
    Robert Hale Kellogg Papers
    Michael Kelly Diary
    Timothy O'Sullivan Letters
    Edward S. Roberts Diary
    Mary Elizabeth Saunders Letters
    Henry Snow Letters
    Nehemiah Solon Diary
    James White Papers
Conway Public Library, Conway, N.H.
    Letters of Cynthia French (John N. Willey File)
    Old Town Records
Cumberland County Historical Society, Carlisle, Pa.
    James Uhler Letters
Dartmouth College, Hanover, N.H.
    Joshua D. Breyfogle Papers
    Benjamin Shreve Calef Correspondence
    Luigi di Cesnola Letters
    Joseph Messer Clough Letters
    George Benton Codman Letters
    Samuel Duncan Letters (in Duncan Family Papers)
    Claude Goings Papers
    Leander Harris Letters
    David Leigh Letters
    Mehetabel Loveren Letters
    George Marden Letters
    Oliver H. Marston Papers
    John McCoy Letters
    George Morgan Letters
    Henry S. Muchmore Diary

Arthur Sidney Nesmith Letters
Albert M. Putnam Letters
Oscar D. Robinson Papers
Ransom F. Sargent Papers
Lewis Simonds Diary
John W. Sturtevant Papers
Eri D. Woodbury Papers
Andrew Hale Young Correspondence
Dickinson College, Carlisle, Pa.
Horatio Collins King Journal
Duke University, Durham, N.C.
Mumford H. Dixon Diary
Holcomb P. Harvey Diary (in William Clifton Harvey Papers)
John Franklin Heitman Diary
John Richardson Porter Diary
Abby E. Stafford Papers
Earlham College, Richmond, Ind.
Thomas W. Barnett Diary
Clarkson Butterworth Diary
Achilles Pugh Papers
Francis W. Thomas Papers
Fairbanks Museum and Planetarium, Saint Johnsbury, Vt.
Carleton Felch Diaries
W. Henry Herrick Diaries
William Henry Proctor Papers
Fredericksburg and Spotsylvania National Military Park, Fredericksburg, Va.
Judson B. Andrews Diary
George A. Bowen Diary
E. K. Russell Letters
Rutherford B. Hayes Presidential Library, Fremont, Ohio
Charles Babbitt Letters
Hannah Burkett Letter
Cooke Family Papers
Harrington Collection
Rutherford B. Hayes Papers
William Jackman Letters
William J. McKell Journal
John R. Rhoades Letters
John B. and Sarah E. Rice Letters
Alvah Stone Skilton Diary
Charles D. Todd Diary (in Frederick Swift Collection)
Ammi Williams Letters
James W. Wilson Family Correspondence
Hudson Library and Historical Society, Hudson, Ohio
William W. Wilder Letters
Huntington Library, San Marino, Calif.

Samuel L. M. Barlow Papers
James T. Eldridge Civil War Collection
Francis Lieber Collection
Indiana Historical Society, Indianapolis
    Job Brockman Papers
    Elijah H. C. Cavins Papers
    Charles A. Harper Papers
    Thomas W. Horan Papers
    J. A. Mendenhall Diary
    Thomas B. Poe Papers
    David S. Scott Letters
Indiana State Library, Indianapolis
    Flavius Bellamy Papers
    Sylvester C. Bishop Letters
    Chittenden Papers
    William F. Fordyce Diary
    Jonathan Joseph Letters
    John F. Lester Papers
    James H. Luther Collection
    John S. Majors Letters
    Oliver P. Morton Collection
    W. C. Patton Diaries
    Henry A. Robinson Letters
    Richard W. Thompson Collection
Indiana University, Bloomington
    Blair Manuscripts
    Barbara Ellen Crist Manuscripts
    J. F. Lovering Diary
    T. H. Martin Manuscripts
    William H. Rudolph Manuscripts
    R. W. Thompson Manuscripts
    Elizabeth A. Tuttle Manuscripts
    William C. and Harrison S. Weeks Manuscripts
Kansas State Historical Society
    John Melvin Converse Diaries
    Margie Duncan Papers
    George Washington Hanson Papers
    James Hanway Collection
    William Casper Haynes Papers
    Judd Family Diaries
    Samuel J. Reader Diary
    Charles and Sara T. D. Robinson Papers
Library of Congress, Washington, D.C.
    John Carvel Arnold Papers
    Orra B. Bailey Letters
    David Homer Bates Papers

Wimer Bedford Diary
Blair Family Papers
William H. Bradbury Papers
John Rumsey Brincklé Papers
William P. Coe Correspondence
James A. Congleton Diary
J. Dexter Cotton Papers
John Allen James Cresswell Papers
Hamilton Fish Papers
Wilbur Fisk Diary
Samuel Fiske Letters (in John Aldrich Stephenson Collection)
Samuel J. Gibson Diary
E. N. Gilpin Papers
    E. N. Gilpin Journal
    Samuel J. B. V. Gilpin Diary
James Harrison Goodnow Papers
William Hamilton Papers
Henry Clay Heisler Papers
William G. Hills Diary
Henry Hitchcock Papers
Lyman Holford Diary
Jedediah Hotchkiss Journal
George A. Hudson Letters
George O. Jewett Papers
John Augustine Johnson Diary
John Griffith Jones Papers
J. Warren Keifer Papers
Daniel Reed Larned Papers
Joseph Lester Papers
Lothrop Lincoln Lewis Papers
Jeremiah T. Lockwood Diary
Rufus Mead Papers
Marshall Mortimer Miller Papers
William Owner Diary
Abram Verrick Parmenter Papers
Franklin Pierce Papers
James G. Randall Papers
Charles Wellington Reed Papers
Charles H. Richardson Diary
Edwin M. Stanton Papers
Thaddeus Stevens Papers
Horatio N. Taft Diary
Aaron C. Tompkins Papers
Edwin A. Vancise Journal
Benjamin Wade Papers
Edwin O. Wentworth Papers

Thomas Wilson Letter
Abraham Lincoln Presidential Library, Springfield, Ill.
    James Buckley Diary
Maine Historical Society, Portland
    William Bryant Adams Collection
    Blanchard Family Collection
    Daniel Webster Brown Correspondence
    James Brown Papers
    John Marshall Brown Papers
    L. W. Costellow Correspondence
    William Y. Davis Diary (in Roger B. Ray Collection)
    T. L. Eastman Diary (in Roger B. Ray Collection)
    H. C. Ingersoll Collection
    Lawrence Joyce Papers
    Marquis de Lafayette Lane Papers
    Lunt Family Papers
    James A. Milliken Collection
    George H. Nye Collection
    Letters of Addison G. Parlin
    Marshall Phillips Correspondence
    Willis M. Porter Collection
    John Parris Sheahan Collection
    George Foster Shepley Papers
    Abner Small Collection
    Letters to Moses Southard (in Carl Knowles Moses Letters)
    Rebecca Usher Collection
    Edward F. Waite Correspondence
    J. M. Woodbury Collection
William Marvel, Private Collection, South Conway, N.H.
    Peter B. Perry Diary
Massachusetts Historical Society, Boston
    Francis Channing Barlow Papers
    George W. Barnard Correspondence
    Edward J. Bartlett Papers
    John E. Bassett Diary
    Caleb Hadley Beal Papers
    Edwin W. Bearse Letters
    Charles Bolton Papers
    Francis Brooks Papers
    Lorin Low Dame Correspondence
    Dana Family Papers
    William H. Eastman Correspondence
    Edward L. Edes Letters
    George Edward Fowle Correspondence
    John B. Gallison Papers
    Warren Goodale Letters

Henderson Family Papers
James Edward Holmes Letters
Thomas S. Howland Letters
Andrew R. Linscott Papers
Theodore Lyman Letters and Diary
Frank C. Morse Papers
John Owen Jr. Letters
Charles J. Paine Letters
George L. Prescott Papers
Andrew Robeson Letters
Daniel H. Spofford Letters
Samuel Storrow Papers
David Thayer Papers II
William S. Tilton Diary
Adin Ballou Underwood Letters
J. Chapin Warner Letters
George Watts Letter
William H. West Diaries
Henry M. Whitney Correspondence
Minnesota Historical Society, Saint Paul
Nellie Brown Letters
Ransom Chadwick Diary
Christie Family Papers
William Z. Clayton Papers
"Letters Written by Elias and Elisha Cowan to Their Mother and Brother"
Ralph L. Dorrance Letters
Letters of Chester E. Evans
Greenleaf Family Papers
Albion Otis Gross Letters
Chauncey J. Hill Family Papers
Jonas Holland Howe and Family Papers
Frederic Carr Howes Letters
David Kennedy Diary
James Lockwood and Family Papers
John H. Macomber Papers
Charles Marples and Family Correspondence
John H. Mitchell and Family Papers
John Nelson Papers
Sylvester H. Norton and Family Correspondence
John W. Pride Diary (in Arthur D. Caswell Papers)
Mary E. Richards and Family Papers
John P. Shumway Papers
Missouri Historical Society, Saint Louis
Bemis Family Papers
Lucien Eaton Papers
William Torrey Harris Papers

Mosby Monroe Parsons Papers
Sweringen Family Papers
Museum of the Confederacy, Richmond, Va.
    George K. Griggs Diary
    Hiram W. Harding Diary
National Archives, Washington, D.C.
  Record Group 15, Records of the Veterans Administration
    Individual Pension Files
  Record Group 29, Records of the Bureau of the Census
    Seventh Census of the United States (M-432)
    Eighth Census of the United States (M-653)
    Ninth Census of the United States (M-593)
  Record Group 58, Records of the Internal Revenue Service
    Tax Assessment Lists, 1862–1918 (M-776)
  Record Group 94, Records of the Adjutant General's Office
    Ambrose Burnside Papers, Entry 159
    Case Files of Investigations by Levi C. Turner and Lafayette C. Baker, 1861–1866
        (M-797)
    Compiled Records Showing Service of Military Units in Volunteer Union Orga-
        nizations (M-594)
    Individual Military Service Records
    Record and Pension Office: Carded Medical Records, 5th U.S. Colored Cavalry
  Record Group 105, Records of the Bureau of Refugees, Freedmen, and Abandoned
        Lands
    General Orders, Special Orders, and Letters Sent, Entry 3800
    Letters Received, May 31, 1866 to January 9, 1867; Letters Sent, January 14,
        1867 to August 12, 1868, Entry 4082
    Narrative Reports of Criminal Cases Involving Freedmen, March, 1866, to Feb-
        ruary, 1867, Entry 3806
    Press Copies of Letters Sent, Entry 4072
    Records Relating to Murders and Outrages Against Freedmen, M-1048
        Descriptive Lists of Reports of Outrages, March to June, 1866
  Record Group 109, War Department Collection of Confederate Records
    Compiled Service Records of Confederate Soldiers Who Served in Organizations
        from the State of Missouri (M-322)
    Bushrod Rust Johnson Papers
  Record Group 153, Records of the Office of the Judge Advocate General
    Transcript of Robert G. Morrison Court-Martial
    Transcript of Frederic Speed Court-Martial
    R. B. Winder Letterbook
  Record Group 249, Records of the Commissary General of Prisoners
    Consolidated Morning Reports of Prisoners at Andersonville, Entry 111
Nebraska State Historical Society, Lincoln
    John Lewis Cushman Diaries
    Charles Hadsall Diary
    Uriah Oblinger Papers

Albert H. Shatzell Diary
Silas Allen Strickland Papers
George R. Wheeler Papers
Charles Henry Wilson Papers
New Hampshire Historical Society, Concord
Aldrich-Thompson Family Papers
Alexandria Recruiting Records
John Batchelder Bailey Journal
Louis Bell Papers
Orrin Brownson Papers
Samuel Burnham Letters (in the Stearns-Burnham Family Papers)
George H. Chandler Papers
William E. Chandler Papers
Lizzie Corning Diary
Critchett Family Papers
Caleb F. Dodge Correspondence
Elisha Douglass Letters
Duncan-Jones Papers
Benjamin B. and Henry F. French Correspondence
Joseph Gilmore Papers
Edward F. Hall Letters
Charles Emerson Howe Papers
James S. Howes Letters
Christopher Hoyt Papers
Lyman Jackman Diary
Josiah N. Jones Diary
Richard Peabody Kent Diary
James S. Knowlton Papers
Elizabeth Livermore Diary
Sarah Low Papers
John E. Mason Memorandum Book
Moulton Family Papers
Franklin Pierce Papers
Isaiah Robbins Jr. Diaries
Albert B. Stearns Papers
George Stearns Papers
John Leverett Thompson Letters (in Thompson Family Papers)
Sewell D. Tilton Papers
George F. Towle Diary
Hosea Towne Letters
George Upton Letters
John E. Wilcox Diary
New Hampshire State Library, Concord
Willard J. Templeton Letters
North Carolina Department of Archives and History, Raleigh
John Willis Council Diary

    Benjamin H. Sims Journal
Northfield Historical Society, Northfield, Vt.
    Edmund Pope Diary
North Yarmouth Historical Society, North Yarmouth, Maine
    Luther Lawrence Letter
Ohio Historical Society, Columbus
    Bennett-Stites-Fay Family Papers
    Samuel W. Boysell Letter
    Core-Porter Papers
    Richard Newell Elder Papers
    Joseph and John Giffen Papers
    Joseph Hoffhines Letters
    Thomas C. Honnel Papers
    James Hughes Papers
    William F. Hunter Papers
    William W. Lowes Papers
    Thomas Brainard Marshall Diary
    Francis Norman Ross McGregor Papers
    William McVey Papers
    William S. Newton Papers
    Ohio Provost Marshal's Papers
    Nathaniel L. Parmeter Diary
    Isaac Pierce Papers
    Albert Rogall Papers
    John P. Sanderson Papers
    Samuel Sexton Papers
    Albert L. Slack Letters
    James R. Stillwell Papers
    Sultana Engineering Plans
    Thomas T. Taylor Diary and Letters
    James Vance Diary
    Joshua H. Whiteman Diary and Letters
    Clinton B. Winterstein Papers
Peabody Essex Museum, Salem, Mass.
    John Cole Papers
    Francis Crowninshield Papers
    Letters of Adelaide, Sally, and Henry Fowler: Fowler Family Manuscripts
    John Peirce Letters
Providence Public Library, Providence, R.I.
    James Cady Letters
Rhode Island Historical Society, Providence
    Lester P. Fales Papers
Rutgers University, Brunswick, N.J.
    William Farrand Keys Diary
    Roebling Family Papers
Saint Albans Historical Society, Saint Albans, Vt.

Ann Pierce Papers
Smith Family Papers
Salina Public Library, Salina, Kan.
Robert Muir Letters
Sheldon Museum, Middlebury, Vt.
Howe-Wolcott Collection
William B. Stevens Letters (Rokeby Museum/Robinson Family Collection)
State Historical Society of Iowa, Des Moines
Amos W. Ames Diary
John Whitten Diary
State Historical Society of Iowa, Iowa City
Lawson H. Carley Diary
Thomas Coffman Papers
Frank Collins Letters
Amos Noyes Currier Letters
George DeHart Letters
George Marion Shearer Diary
University of Georgia, Athens
Cobb-Erwin-Lamar Papers
University of Iowa, Iowa City
Papers of Charles C. Cady
Papers of Marcellus W. Darling
Edward E. Davis Papers
Papers of the Giauque Family
Joseph Kohout Papers
Byron McClain Letters
Robert Moyle Correspondence
Papers of William and Titus Rigby
Papers of the Sterns Family
Myron Underwood Papers
Ferdinand Sophus Winslow Papers
University of Kansas, Lawrence
Ith S. Beall Collection
Thomas Carney Papers
Amory K. Chambers Collection
James William Denver Papers
Henry C. Fike Papers
Isaiah Morris Harris Correspondence
James Henry Lane Papers
Joseph Henry Leighty Collection
Oliver R. McNary Diary
James Kerr Proudfit Letters
University of Maine, Orono
Brown Family Letters
University of Michigan, Ann Arbor
Bentley Library

Judson L. Austin Letters
Franklin H. Bailey Letters
Boardman Family Papers
Benjamin F. Bordner Letters
William Boston Papers
A. S. Boyce Letters
Robert Crouse Papers
Edwin Ford Letters
Claudius Buchanan Grant Papers
Sullivan Dexter Green Papers
Irwin Family Papers
Letters of Austin Kendall
John Wesley Longyear Papers
Edwin J. March Letters
McCreery-Fenton Family Papers
David Millspaugh Diary
Alfred Milnes Papers
Wayne E. Morris Papers
Conrad Noll Papers
Spalding Family Papers
Edward Henry Taylor Correspondence
Van Vlack Family Papers
Washington Vosburgh Letters
Elmer D. Wallace Letters
Clements Library
George Tobey Anthony Letters
Aplin Family Papers
George Henry Bates Letters
William Bennit Voter Authorization
Clement Abner Boughton Papers
Braxton Bragg Letters
John A. Clark Letter
Sylvanus Cobb Letter
George Cramer Draft Notice
Samuel Wylie Crawford Letters
John A. Dickie Journal
George Driver Papers
Henry Martyn Duffield Letters
William Pitt Fessenden Letters
Ulysses S. Grant Letters
James K. Hale Letters
Winfield Scott Hancock Papers
Ethan Allen Hitchcock Letters
Joseph Hooker Letters
Eugene C. Houghton Letter
Christopher Keller Letters

Henry Grimes Marshall Letters
Charles Maxim Letters
George B. McClellan Letters
James T. and Robert E. Miller Letters
Hilon Adelbert Parker Papers
Andrew S. Parsons Papers
John L. Perley Papers
Fred H. Phillips Letter
Pollard Family Papers
James T. Pratt Letter
William L. Russell Letter
Charles A. Sanford Letter
William Henry Shaw Letters
Martin L. Smith Letter
Frederic Speed Letters
George T. Stevens Letters
William F. Stewart Letter
Edmund Townsend Papers
George M. Trowbridge Letters
Edward H. Wade Letters
Washburne Family Papers
Nathan B. Webb Journal
John Darrah Wilkins Letters
Thomas W. Willis Letters
Thomas J. Wood Letter
University of Missouri, Western Historical Manuscripts Collection, Columbia
Henry C. and W. H. Crawford Letters
George Leonard Draft Notice
Stillman Letters
University of New Hampshire, Durham
Adams Family Papers
Louis Bell Papers
J. A. Blodgett Letter
Thomas Carleton Cheney Papers
James Franklin Fitts Papers
Howard M. Hanson Papers
Leander Harris Letters
George Naylor Julian Papers
John W. Warner Letters
Samuel Wilkinson Diary
University of North Carolina, Southern Historical Collection, Chapel Hill
James W. Albright Diary
William D. Alexander Diary
Kena King Chapman Diary
Edward O. Guerrant Diary
John Hunt Morgan Papers

Trusten Polk Papers
Ira B. Sampson Diary
Sarah Wadley Diary
University of Notre Dame, Notre Dame, Ind.
Thomas Benton Alexander Diary
Benton-Beach Correspondence
William Combs Letters
Shriver Family Letters
University of Rochester, Rochester, N.Y.
Norman Carr Papers
Lyman Chandler Family Papers
Fellows Family Papers
Huntington-Hooker Papers
Gilbert H. Reynolds Papers
Albert Ritter Letters (in Lyman Chandler Family Papers)
Letters of William W. Wordsworth
University of South Carolina, South Caroliniana Library, Columbia
David Wyatt Aiken Collection
Ellen Maria Ravenel Collection
University of Vermont, Burlington
Orville Bixby Letters
Charles E. Chace Letters
Cobb Family Papers
Charles Gilbert Gould Letters
George N. Jones Papers
Kinerson Family Papers
Charles Manson Letters
Augustus Paddock Papers
Tabor Parcher Letters
Charles E. Parker Papers
Parker Family Papers
Joseph C. Rutherford Papers
Savage Family Papers
Bradford P. Sparrow Papers
William Stow Letters
Isaac N. Watts Papers
William Wells Papers
Wheaton Family Papers
University of Virginia, Charlottesville
Anonymous C.S. Officer Diary (in James B. Blackford Collection)
Robert Larimer Diary
Charles B. Senior Letters
Francis T. Sherman Diary
Elihu B. Washburne Letter
U.S. Army Military History Institute, Carlisle, Pa.
Benjamin F. Ashenfelter Papers

John Brown Diary
F. H. Bullard Letter
Hattie Burleigh Papers
John H. Burrill Letters
Henry Carroll Papers
Samuel Y. Cauller Letters
Stephen P. Chase Diary
John Kennedy Coleman Diary
Simon Peter Duck Diary
John and Leo Faller Letters
Samuel L. Foust Diary
Luther C. Furst Diary
William Garrett Letters
Jacob Gauchnauer Letter
Jacob L. Graham Letter
Gilbert Gulbrandson Letters
John Hamer Letters
George P. Hawkes Diary
Daniel Himes Diary
Clement Hoffman Papers
Frances Calderon de la Barca Hunt Diary
A. Stokes Jones Papers
Henry Keiser Diary
Otis Knight Diary
Thomas P. Larue Letters
Herman J. Lewis Letter
Henry C. Metzger Papers
Almira K. Miller Diary
Edmund Newton Papers
Luke and Charles Ostrye Letters
William T. Peabody Diary
Fred K. Ployer Papers
Jared J. Potter Diary
Isaac H. Ressler Diary
Henry Rinker Letters
Samuel H. Root Letter
Alexander Grant Rose Diaries
Henry H. Stone Diary (transcript)
William Tritt Diary
Julius Whitney Diary
William H. Woodward Papers
Albert A. Wright Diary
Vermont Historical Society, Barre
Peter M. Abbott Papers
Allen Family Papers
John Q. Amadon Papers

Valentine G. Barney Papers
Barton Family Letters
Beard Family Papers
Bixby Family Papers
Alson H. Blake Letters
Hubert and Laura Tupper Brown Letters
Thomas H. Brown Letters
Thomas Jefferson Burnham Letters (in Clark Family Papers)
Avery B. Cain Letters
Charles B. Chapin Diary
Cheney-Watts Collection
Clark Family Papers
Colton Family Papers
George R. Crosby Diaries (in Civil War Papers)
Charles Cummings Papers
Letters to Wealthy Field
George Oscar French Papers
Harrison B. George Letters
Walter Graham Papers
Edwin C. Hall Papers
Albert Harris Papers
William Wirt Henry Papers
William Hogan Letters
Roswell Holbrook Letters
Edwin Horton Papers
George J. Howard Letters
Kendrick R. Howard Diary
William Elmore Howard Letters
Benjamin F. Hulburd Papers
Alfred Horton Keith Papers
Loren Kingsbury Letters
Rufus Kinsley Letters (in Civil War Papers)
Letters of Lewis H. Lamb
Lorenzo Miles Diary
Pingree-Hunton-Stickney Family Papers (in Lyndon State College Collection)
Charles B. Putnam Papers
David F. Rugg Diary
Darius Safford Letters (in Sherman-Safford Papers)
William F. Smith Papers
Joseph Tarbell Letters
Willard Thayer Letters
Dudley Tillison Letters
Ransom W. Towle Diary
William Townsend Family Papers
Henry J. Vaughn Letters
Aldace Walker Letters

William White Letters
Lyman Williams Papers
John Wilmot Papers
Virginia Historical Society, Richmond
Edward Bates Papers
Creed Thomas Davis Diary
J. R. Hamilton Letter
William Hamilton Harris Journal
Jewett Family Papers
Osmun Latrobe Papers
R. E. Lee Headquarters Papers
William T. Livermore Diary
Daniel Thurber Nelson Papers
James Eldred Phillips Diary
Elizabeth Shenton Letters
John Bell Vincent Diary
Western Reserve Historical Society, Cleveland, Ohio
George W. Beadle Papers
Alexander Bunt Family Papers
Harlan P. Chapman Letters
Thomas A. Covert Papers
Harvey Cutter Letters
Darling Family Papers
Wilbur F. Hinman Papers
George W. Hodges Letters
Daniel D. Hopper Papers
Hyatt Family Papers
Carlos Parsons Lyman Papers
John A. McIntosh Letters
Chauncey W. Mead Papers
Zerah Coston Monks Papers
William R. Palmer Collection
Albert Gallatin Riddle Papers
James Wilson Letters
John Smith Work Letter
Wisconsin Historical Society, Madison
Gideon Winan Allen Letters
Edward S. Bragg Papers
George W. Buffum Papers
Alfred D. Burdick Diary
Rufus Dawes Papers
James Rood Doolittle Papers
Edwin H. Flagg Papers
Thomas Fox Papers
Sullivan D. Green Diaries
William I. Henry Papers

William Lamont Papers
James M. Perry Diaries
William L. Phillips Papers
Alonzo V. Richards Papers
Edgar Richmond Papers
Carl Schurz Papers
Charles M. Smith Papers
Loring B. F. Winslow Papers
Benjamin T. Wright Correspondence
Henry F. Young Papers
Yale University, New Haven, Conn.
    Civil War Manuscripts Collection
        Dennis Aley Letters
        J. B. Dawley Correspondence
        Gill Family Letters
        Henry C. Glines Letters
        Thomas W. Porter Reports
    Charles Morgan Coit Papers
    Samuel Ryan Curtis Papers
    Ira Emory Forbes Diary
    A. Conger Goodyear Collection
    Civil War Letters to Anna and Jacob Guyer
    Abraham Lincoln Papers
    Charles G. Merrill Papers
    William Jackson Palmer Letters
    Joseph Swift Collection (in Nancy Tattnall Fuller Research)
    Thomas Fry Tobey Papers
    Elihu Washburne Diary

Published Works

Acts of the General Assembly of the State of Virginia Passed at the Extra Session (June, 1865). Richmond: Republican Book and Job Office, 1865.

Acts of the General Assembly of the State of Virginia Passed in 1865–66. Richmond: Allegre and Goode, 1866.

A Few Words on Behalf of the Loyal Women of the United States, by One of Themselves. [New York]: Loyal Publication Society, [1864].

Agassiz, George R., ed. *Meade's Headquarters, 1863–1865: Letters of Colonel Theodore Lyman from the Wilderness to Appomattox.* Boston, Mass.: Atlantic Monthly Press, 1922.

Anderson, Mary Ann, ed. *The Civil War Diary of Allen Morgan Geer, Twentieth Regiment, Illinois Volunteers.* Denver, Co.: Robert C. Appelman, 1977.

Angle, Paul M., ed. *Three Years in the Army of the Cumberland: The Letters and Diary of Major James A. Connolly.* Bloomington: Indiana University Press, 1959.

Atlas to Accompany the Official Records of the Union and Confederate Armies. Washington, D.C.: Government Printing Office, 1891–1895.

[Atwater, Dorence.] *The Atwater Report: List of Prisoners Who Died in 1864–65 at Andersonville Prison.* Andersonville, Ga.: National Society of Andersonville, 1981.

Ayling, Augustus D., comp. *Revised Register of the Soldiers and Sailors of New Hampshire in the War of the Rebellion, 1861–1866.* Concord, N.H.: Ira C. Evans, 1895.

Bailey, Anne J. *The Chessboard of War: Sherman and Hood in the Autumn Campaigns of 1864.* Lincoln: University of Nebraska Press, 2000.

Bailey, Judith A., and Robert I. Cottom, eds. *After Chancellorsville: The Civil War Letters of Private Walter G. Dunn and Emma Randolph.* Baltimore: Maryland Historical Society, 1998.

Bain, David Haward. *Empire Express: Building the First Transcontinental Railroad.* New York: Viking, 1999.

Barnes, Joseph K. *The Medical and Surgical History of the War of the Rebellion (1861–65).* 15 vols. 1870. Reprint, Wilmington, N.C.: Broadfoot Publishing, 1990.

Basile, Leon, ed. *The Civil War Diary of Amos E. Stearns, a Prisoner at Andersonville.* Rutherford, N.J.: Fairleigh Dickinson University Press, 1981.

Basler, Roy P., ed. *The Collected Works of Abraham Lincoln.* 8 vols. New Brunswick, N.J.: Rutgers University Press, 1953.

Beale, Howard K., ed. *The Diary of Edward Bates.* Washington, D.C.: Government Printing Office, 1933.

——, ed. *The Diary of Gideon Welles, Secretary of the Navy Under Lincoln and Johnson.* 3 vols. New York: W. W. Norton and Company, 1960.

Bearss, Edwin C. *Forrest at Brice's Cross Roads and in North Mississippi in 1864.* Dayton, Ohio: Morningside Press, 1979.

Bender, Robert Patrick, ed. *Like Grass before the Scythe: The Life and Death of Sgt. William Remmel, 121st New York Infantry.* Tuscaloosa: University of Alabama Press, 2007.

Blackmon, Douglas A. *Slavery By Another Name: The Re-enslavement of Black Americans from the Civil War to World War II.* New York: Doubleday, 2008.

Blair, William Alan, ed. *A Politician Goes to War: The Civil War Letters of John White Geary.* University Park: Pennsylvania State University Press, 1995.

Blight, David W., ed. *When This Cruel War Is Over: The Civil War Letters of Charles Harvey Brewster.* Amherst: University of Massachusetts Press, 1992.

Bohrnstedt, Jennifer Cain, ed. *Soldiering with Sherman: Civil War Letters of George F. Cram.* DeKalb: Northern Illinois University Press, 2000.

Bradley, Mark L. *Last Stand in the Carolinas: The Battle of Bentonville.* Campbell, Calif.: Savas Publishing, 1996.

——. *This Astounding Close: The Road to Bennett Place.* Chapel Hill: University of North Carolina Press, 2000.

Britton, Ann Hartwell, and Thomas J. Reed, eds. *To My Beloved Wife and Boy at Home: The Letters and Diaries of Orderly Sergeant John F. L. Hartwell.* Madison, N.J.: Fairleigh Dickinson University Press, 1997.

Brown, Farwell T., comp. *Tilden Family Letters.* Ames, Iowa: privately printed, 1989.

Brun, Christian. "A Palace Guard View of Lincoln (The Civil War Letters of John H. Fleming)." *Soundings* 3, no. 1 (May, 1971), 18–39.

Buckingham, Peter H., ed. *All's for the Best: The Civil War Reminiscences and Letters of Daniel W. Sawtelle, Eighth Maine Volunteer Infantry.* Knoxville: University of Tennessee Press, 2001.

Burlingame, Michael, ed. *Lincoln Observed: Civil War Dispatches of Noah Brooks.* Baltimore: Johns Hopkins University Press, 1998.

——, ed. *With Lincoln in the White House: Letters, Memoranda, and Other Writings of John G. Nicolay, 1860–65.* Carbondale: Southern Illinois University Press, 2000.

Burlingame, Michael, and John R. Turner Ettlinger, eds. *Inside Lincoln's White House: The Complete Civil War Diary of John Hay.* Carbondale: Southern Illinois University Press, 1997.

Butler, Benjamin F. *Private and Official Correspondence of Gen. Benjamin F. Butler, during the Period of the Civil War.* 5 vols. [Norwood, Mass.: Plimpton Press, privately printed], 1917.

Castel, Albert. *Decision in the West: The Atlanta Campaign of 1864.* Lawrence: University Press of Kansas, 1992.

Chesson, Michael B., ed. *J. Franklin Dyer: The Journal of a Civil War Surgeon.* Lincoln: University of Nebraska Press, 2003.

The Chicago Copperhead Convention: Treasonable and Revolutionary Utterances of the Men Who Composed It. Washington: Union Congressional Committee, 1864.

Child, William. *Letters from a Civil War Surgeon.* Solon, Maine: Polar Bear & Co., 1995.

Coco, Gregory A., ed. *Through Blood and Fire: The Civil War Letters of Major Charles J. Mills, 1862–1865.* Gettysburg, Pa.: privately published, 1982.

Cohen, William. "Negro Involuntary Servitude in the South, 1865–1940: A Preliminary Analysis." *Journal of Southern History* 42, no. 1 (February, 1976), 31–60.

Collier, John S., and Bonnie B. Collier, eds. *Yours for the Union: The Civil War Letters of John W. Chase, First Massachusetts Light Artillery.* New York: Fordham University Press, 2004.

Copperhead Conspiracy in the North-West. An Exposé of the Treasonable Order of the "Sons of Liberty." Vallandigham, Supreme Commander. New York: Union Congressional Committee, 1864.

Cutrer, Thomas W., ed. *Longstreet's Aide: The Civil War Letters of Major Thomas J. Goree.* Charlottesville: University of Virginia Press, 1995.

Davidson, Garber A., ed. *The Civil War Letters of the Late 1st Lieut. James J. Hartley, 122nd Ohio Infantry Regiment.* Jefferson, N.C.: McFarland & Co., [1998].

Davis, Barbara Butler, ed. *Affectionately Yours: The Civil War Home-Front Letters of the Ovid Butler Family.* Indianapolis: Indiana Historical Society, 2004.

Davis, William C. *An Honorable Defeat: The Last Days of the Confederate Government.* New York: Harcourt, 2001.

Dennett, John Richard. *The South As It Is, 1865–1866.* 1866. Reprint, with an introduction by Henry M. Christman. Baton Rouge: Louisiana University Press, 1986.

Dennison, James H. *Dennison's Andersonville Diary.* Kankakee, Ill.: Kankakee County Historical Society, 1957.

Destler, C. M., ed. "A Vermonter at Andersonville: Diary of Charles Ross, 1864." *Vermont History* 25, no. 3 (July, 1957), 229–45.

"Diary of a Prisoner." *Historical Magazine* 9, no. 1 (January, 1871), 1–6.

"Diary of Major R. C. M. Page, Chief of Confederate States Artillery, Department of Southwest Virginia and East Tennessee, from October, 1864, to May, 1865." *Southern Historical Society Papers* 16 (1888), 58–68.

Donald, David Herbert. *Lincoln.* New York: Simon & Schuster, 1995.

Dowdey, Clifford, and Louis H. Manarin, eds. *The Wartime Papers of R. E. Lee.* New York: Virginia Civil War Commission, 1961.

Duncan, Richard R., ed. *Alexander Neil and the Last Shenandoah Valley Campaign: Letters of an Army Surgeon to His Family, 1864.* Shippensburg, Pa.: White Mane, 1996.

Dyer, Frederick H. *A Compendium of the War of the Rebellion.* 1908. Reprint, with an introduction by Lee A. Wallace Jr. Dayton, Ohio: Morningside Press, 1978.

Eby, Cecil B., Jr., ed. *A Virginia Yankee in the Civil War: The Diaries of David Hunter Strother.* Chapel Hill: University of North Carolina Press, 1961.

Edwards, William B. *Civil War Guns.* Harrisburg, Pa.: Stackpole, 1962.

Eggleston, George Cary. *A Rebel's Recollections.* 1874. Reprint, with an introduction by Gaines M. Foster. Baton Rouge: Louisiana State University Press, 1996.

Elder, Donald C., III, ed. *Love Amid the Turmoil: The Civil War Letters of William and Mary Vermillion.* Iowa City: University of Iowa Press, 2003.

Engert, Roderick M., ed. *Maine in the Wilderness: The Civil War Letters of Pvt. William Lamson, 20th Maine Infantry.* Orange, Va.: Publisher's Press, 1993.

Feidner, Edward J., ed. *"Dear Wife": The Civil War Letters of Charles K. Leach.* Burlington: Center for Research on Vermont, 2002.

Floyd, Dale E., ed. *Dear Friends at Home: The Letters and Diary of Thomas James Owen, Fiftieth Volunteer Engineer Regiment, during the Civil War.* Washington, D.C.: Government Printing Office, 1985.

Foner, Eric. *Reconstruction: America's Unfinished Revolution, 1863–1877.* New York: Harper & Row, 1988.

Fonvielle, Chris E., Jr. *The Wilmington Campaign: Last Rays of Departing Hope.* Campbell, Calif.: Savas Publishing, 1997.

Forbes, Eugene. *Diary of a Soldier and Prisoner of War in Rebel Prisons.* Trenton, N.J.: Murphy & Bechtel, 1865.

Ford, William Chauncey, ed. *A Cycle of Adams Letters.* 2 vols. London: Constable, 1921.

Franklin, John Hope, ed. *The Diary of James T. Ayers, Civil War Recruiter.* 1947. Reprint, with an introduction by John David Smith. Baton Rouge: Louisiana State University Press, 1999.

———. *Reconstruction: After the Civil War.* Chicago: University of Chicago Press, 1961.

Freeman, Douglas Southall, ed. *Lee's Dispatches: Unpublished Letters of General Robert E. Lee, C.S.A., to Jefferson Davis and the War Department of the Confederate States of America, 1862-65.* 1957. Reprint, with a foreword by Grady McWhiney. Baton Rouge: Louisiana State University Press, 1994.

French, Benjamin Brown. *Witness to the Young Republic: A Yankee's Journals, 1828-1870.* Hanover, N.H.: University Press of New England, 1989.

Futch, Ovid L. "The Andersonville Journal of J. M. Burdick." *Georgia Historical Quarterly* 45, no. 3 (September, 1961), 287-94.

Gavin, William Gilfillan, ed. *Infantryman Pettit: The Civil War Letters of Corporal Frederick Pettit.* New York: Avon Books, 1991.

George H. Pendleton, The Copperhead Candidate for Vice-President. Washington, D.C.: Union Congressional Committee, 1864.

Gerry, Margarita Spalding, ed. *Through Five Administrations: Reminiscences of Colonel William H. Crook, Body-Guard to President Lincoln.* New York: Harper & Brothers, 1910.

Gillette, William. *Retreat from Reconstruction, 1869-1879.* Baton Rouge: Louisiana State University Press, 1979.

Glatthaar, Joseph T. *The March to the Sea and Beyond: Sherman's Troops in the Savannah and Carolinas Campaigns.* New York: New York University Press, 1985.

Graf, LeRoy P., Ralph W. Haskins, and Paul H. Bergeron, eds. *The Papers of Andrew Johnson.* 16 vols. Knoxville: University of Tennessee Press, 1967-2000.

Gray, John Chipman, and John Codman Ropes. *War Letters, 1862-1865, of John Chipman Gray and John Codman Ropes.* Cambridge: Massachusetts Historical Society, 1927.

Greene, A. Wilson. *Breaking the Backbone of the Rebellion: The Final Battles of the Petersburg Campaign.* Mason City, Iowa: Savas Publishing, 2000.

———. *Civil War Petersburg: Confederate City in the Crucible of War.* Charlottesville: University of Virginia Press, 2006.

Greenleaf, Margery, ed. *Letters to Eliza from a Union Soldier.* Chicago: Follett Publishing Company, 1970.

Hammond, Harold Earl, ed. *Diary of a Union Lady, 1861-1865.* 1962. Reprint, with an introduction by Jean V. Berlin. Lincoln: University of Nebraska Press, 2000.

Harwell, Richard Barksdale, ed. *Kate: The Journal of a Confederate Nurse, by Kate Cumming.* 1959. Reprint. Baton Rouge: Louisiana State University Press, 1998.

Hawthorne, Nathaniel. "Chiefly about War Matters." *Atlantic Monthly* 10, no. 57 (July, 1862), 43-61.

Helmreich, Paul C., ed. "The Diary of Charles G. Lee in the Andersonville and Florence Prison Camps, 1864." *Connecticut Historical Society Bulletin* 41, no. 1 (January, 1976), 12-28.

Henderson, Howard A. M. "Lincoln's Assassination and Camp Fisk." *Confederate Veteran* 15, no. 4 (April, 1907), 170-71.

Hess, Earl J. *In the Trenches at Petersburg: Field Fortifications and Confederate Defeat.* Chapel Hill: University of North Carolina Press, 2009.

———. *Into the Crater: The Mine Attack at Petersburg.* Columbia: University of South Carolina Press, 2010.

Higginson, Thomas Wentworth. *Massachusetts in the Army and Navy During the War of 1861–65.* 2 vols. Boston: Wright & Potter, 1896.

Holden, Walter, William E. Ross, and Elizabeth Slomba, eds. *Stand Firm and Fire Low: The Civil War Writings of Colonel Charles E. Cross.* Hanover, N.H.: University Press of New England, 2003.

Horn, Stanley F. "The Spring Hill Legend." *Civil War Times Illustrated* 8, no. 1 (April, 1969), 20–32.

Houston, Alan Fraser, ed. *Keep Up Good Courage, a Yankee Family and the Civil War: The Correspondence of Cpl. Lewis Q. Smith, of Sandwich, New Hampshire, Fourteenth Regiment New Hampshire Volunteers, 1862–1865.* Portsmouth, N.H.: Peter E. Randall, 2006.

Howe, Mark De Wolfe, ed. *Marching with Sherman: Passages from the Letters and Campaign Diaries of Henry Hitchcock, Major and Assistant Adjutant General of Volunteers.* 1927. Reprint. Lincoln: University of Nebraska Press, 1995.

———, ed. *Touched with Fire: Civil War Letters and Diary of Oliver Wendell Holmes, Jr. 1861–1864.* 1947. Reprint. New York: Da Capo Press, 1969.

Hughes, Nathaniel Cheairs, Jr. *Bentonville: The Final Battle of Sherman and Johnston.* Chapel Hill: University of North Carolina Press, 1996.

Hunter, R. M. T. "The Peace Commission of 1865." *Southern Historical Society Papers* 3, no. 4 (April, 1877), 168–76.

Hunter, William A., ed. "The Civil War Diaries of Leonard C. Ferguson." *Pennsylvania History* 14, no. 3 (July, 1947), 196–224, no. 4 (October, 1947), 289–313.

Jaquette, Henrietta Stratton, ed. *South after Gettysburg: Letters of Cornelia Hancock from the Army of the Potomac, 1863–1865.* Philadelphia: University of Pennsylvania Press, 1937.

Jones, James Pickett. *Yankee Blitzkrieg: Wilson's Raid through Alabama and Georgia.* Athens: University of Georgia Press, 1976.

Jones, John B. *A Rebel War Clerk's Diary.* 2 vols. 1866. Reprint (2 vols. in 1), edited and annotated by Earl Schenck Miers. New York: Sagamore Press, 1958.

Jordan, William B., Jr., ed. *The Civil War Journals of John Mead Gould, 1861–1866.* Baltimore: Butternut and Blue, 1997.

Kallgren, Beverly Hayes, and James L. Crouthamel, eds. *Dear Friend Anna: The Civil War Letters of a Common Soldier from Maine.* Orono: University of Maine Press, 1992.

Kamphoefner, Walter D., and Wolfgang Helbich, eds. *Germans in the Civil War: The Letters They Wrote Home.* Translated by Susan Carter Vogel. Chapel Hill: University of North Carolina Press, 2006.

Kauffman, Michael W. *American Brutus: John Wilkes Booth and the Lincoln Conspiracies.* New York: Random House, 2004.

Kendall, Amos. *Letters Exposing the Mismanagement of Public Affairs by Abraham Lincoln and the Political Combinations to Secure His Re-election.* Washington, D.C.: Constitutional Union, 1864.

Klement, Frank L. *Dark Lanterns: Secret Political Societies, Conspiracies, and Treason Trials in the Civil War.* Baton Rouge: Louisiana State University Press, 1984.

Kohl, Lawrence Frederick, ed. *Irish Green and Union Blue: The Civil War Letters of Peter Welsh*. New York: Fordham University Press, 1986.

Laas, Virginia Jean, ed. *Wartime Washington: The Civil War Letters of Elizabeth Blair Lee*. Urbana: University of Illinois Press, 1991.

Lankford, Nelson. *Richmond Burning: The Last Days of the Confederate Capital*. New York: Viking, 2002.

Larimer, Charles F., ed. *Love and Valor: The Intimate Civil War Letters between Captain Jacob and Emeline Ritner*. Western Springs, Ill.: Sigourney Press, 2000.

Longacre, Edward G., ed. *From Antietam to Fort Fisher: The Civil War Letters of Edward King Wightman, 1862–1865*. Rutherford, N.J.: Fairleigh Dickinson University Press, 1985.

Lonn, Ella. *Salt as a Factor in the Confederacy*. New York: Neale Publishing, 1933.

Loving, Jerome M., ed. *Civil War Letters of George Washington Whitman*. Durham, N.C.: Duke University Press, 1975.

Lucas, Marion Brunson. *Sherman and the Burning of Columbia*. College Station: Texas A&M University Press, 1976.

Mahon, Michael G., ed. *Winchester Divided: The Civil War Diaries of Julia Chase and Laura Lee*. Mechanicsburg, Pa.: Stackpole Books, 2002.

Mancini, Matthew J. *One Dies, Get Another: Convict Leasing in the American South, 1866–1928*. Columbia: University of South Carolina Press, 1996.

Marvel, William. *Andersonville: The Last Depot*. Chapel Hill: University of North Carolina Press, 1994.

——. *The Great Task Remaining: The Third Year of Lincoln's War*. Boston: Houghton Mifflin Harcourt, 2010.

——. *Lee's Last Retreat: The Flight to Appomattox*. Chapel Hill: University of North Carolina Press, 2002.

——. *Lincoln's Darkest Year: The War in 1862*. Boston: Houghton Mifflin, 2008.

——. "A Poor Man's Fight: Civil War Enlistment Patterns in Conway, New Hampshire." *Historical New Hampshire* 43, no. 1 (Spring, 1988), 21–40.

——. *Southwest Virginia in the Civil War: The Battles for Saltville*. Lynchburg, Va.: H. E. Howard, 1992.

Massachusetts Soldiers, Sailors, and Marines in the Civil War. 8 vols. Norwood, Mass.: Massachusetts Adjutant General, 1932.

McCrae, Melissa, and Maureen Bradford, eds. *No Place for Little Boys: Civil War Letters of a Union Soldier*. Brewer, Maine: Goddess Publications, 1997.

McMurry, Richard M. *Atlanta 1864: Last Chance for the Confederacy*. Lincoln: University of Nebraska Press, 2000.

——. *John Bell Hood and the War for Southern Independence*. Lexington: University Press of Kentucky, 1982.

McPherson, James M. *For Cause and Comrades: Why Men Fought in the Civil War*. New York: Oxford University Press, 1997.

McPherson, James M., and Patricia R. McPherson, eds. *Lamson of the Gettysburg: The Civil War Letters of Lieutenant Roswell H. Lamson, U.S. Navy*. New York: Oxford University Press, 1997.

Meade, George. *The Life and Letters of George Gordon Meade, Major-General United States Army*. 2 vols. New York: Charles Scribner's Sons, 1913.

Menge, W. Springer, and J. August Shimrak, eds. *The Civil War Notebook of Daniel Chisholm: A Chronicle of Daily Life in the Union Army, 1864–1865.* New York: Ballantine Books, 1989.

Messent, Peter, and Steve Courtney, eds. *The Civil War Letters of Joseph Hopkins Twichell: A Chaplain's Story.* Athens: University of Georgia Press, 2006.

Michael, William H. C. "Explosion of the Sultana." In *Civil War Sketches and Incidents: Papers Read by Companions of the Commandery of the State of Nebraska, Military Order of the Loyal Legion of the United States.* Omaha: Nebraska Commandery, 1902, 253–57.

Miller, Edwin Haviland, ed. *The Collected Writings of Walt Whitman.* 6 vols. New York: New York University Press, 1961–1969.

Moore, Frank, ed. *The Rebellion Record, a Diary of Events with Documents, Narratives, Illustrative Incidents, Poetry, etc.* 12 vols. 1861–69. Reprint. New York: Arno Press, 1977.

Moore, Mark A. *Moore's Historical Guide to the Battle of Bentonville.* Campbell, Calif.: Savas Publishing, 1997.

Morris, Richard B. "The Measure of Bondage in the Slave States." *Mississippi Valley Historical Review* 41, no. 2 (September, 1954), 219–40.

Mushkat, Jerome, ed. *A Citizen-Soldier's Civil War: The Letters of Brevet Major General Alvin C. Voris.* DeKalb: Northern Illinois University Press, 2002.

Nelson, Larry E. *Bullets, Ballots, and Rhetoric: Confederate Policy for the United States Presidential Contest of 1864.* Tuscaloosa: University of Alabama Press, 1980.

Nevins, Allan, ed. *A Diary of Battle: The Personal Journals of Colonel Charles S. Wainwright, 1861–1865.* New York: Harcourt, Brace & World [1962].

———. *The War for the Union.* 4 vols. New York: Charles Scribner's Sons, 1959–71.

Nevins, Allan, and Milton Halsey Thomas, eds. *The Diary of George Templeton Strong.* 4 vols. New York: Macmillan Company, 1952.

Niven, John, ed. *The Salmon P. Chase Papers.* 5 vols. Kent, Ohio: Kent State University Press, 1993–1998.

Oeffinger, John C., ed. *A Soldier's General: The Civil War Letters of Major General Lafayette McLaws.* Chapel Hill: University of North Carolina Press, 2002.

Official Records of the Union and Confederate Navies in the War of the Rebellion. 31 vols. Washington, D.C.: Government Printing Office, 1894–1927.

Palladino, Anita, ed. *Diary of a Yankee Engineer: The Civil War Diary of John A. Westervelt, 1st New York Volunteer Engineer Corps.* New York: Fordham University Press, 1997.

Palmer, Beverly Wilson, ed. *The Selected Letters of Charles Sumner.* 2 vols. Boston, Mass.: Northeastern University Press, 1990.

"Papers of Hon. John A. Campbell — 1816–1865." *Southern Historical Society Papers* 42, no. 4 (September, 1917), 3–81.

Patrick, Jeffrey L., and Robert J. Willey, eds. *Fighting for Liberty and Right: The Civil War Diary of William Bluffton Miller, First Sergeant, Company K, Seventy-fifth Indiana Volunteer Infantry.* Knoxville: University of Tennessee Press, 2005.

Pearce, T. H., ed. *Diary of Captain Henry A. Chambers.* Wendell, N.C.: Broadfoot's Bookmark, 1983.

Pease, Theodore Calvin, and James G. Randall, eds. *The Diary of Orville Hickman Browning.* 2 vols. Springfield: Illinois State Historical Library, 1925 and 1933.

Peck, Theodore, comp. *Revised Roster of Vermont Volunteers and List of Vermonters Who Served in the Army and Navy of the United States during the War of the Rebellion, 1861–66.* Montpelier, Vt.: Watchman Publishing, 1892.

Pickenpaugh, Roger. *Captives in Gray: The Civil War Prisons of the Union.* Tuscaloosa: University of Alabama Press, 2009.

Pitman, Benn, ed. *The Trials for Treason at Indianapolis, Disclosing the Plans for Establishing a North-Western Confederacy.* Cincinnati, Ohio: Moore, Wilstach & Baldwin, 1865.

Potter, Jerry O. *The* Sultana *Tragedy: America's Greatest Maritime Disaster.* Gretna, La.: Pelican Publishing, 1992.

"Proceedings of the Second Confederate Congress: Second Session in Part." *Southern Historical Society Papers* 52 (1959), 1–500.

Quaife, Milo M., ed. *From the Cannon's Mouth: The Civil War Letters of General Alpheus S. Williams.* Detroit, Mich.: Wayne State University Press, 1959.

Rable, George C. *But There Was No Peace: The Role of Violence in the Politics of Reconstruction.* Athens: University of Georgia Press, 1984.

Racine, Philip N., ed. *Unspoiled Heart: The Journal of Charles Mattocks of the 17th Maine.* Knoxville: University of Tennessee Press, 1994.

Ray, J[ean] P. *The Diary of a Dead Man.* [Conshohocken, Pa.]: Acorn Press, 1979.

Reid-Green, Marcia, ed. *Letters Home: Henry Matrau of the Iron Brigade.* Lincoln: University of Nebraska Press, 1993.

Renda, Lex. *Running on the Record: Civil War–Era Politics in New Hampshire.* Charlottesville: University of Virginia Press, 1997.

Report of the Adjutant General of the State of Maine for the Years 1864 and 1865. Augusta: Stevens and Sayward, 1866.

Report of the Committee on the Conduct of the War of the Attack on Petersburg, on the 30th Day of July, 1864. Washington, D.C.: Government Printing Office, 1865.

Report of the Joint Committee on the Conduct of the War. 3 vols. Washington, D.C.: Government Printing Office, 1863.

Report of the Joint Committee on the Conduct of the War at the Second Session Thirty-Eighth Congress. 3 vols. in 1. Washington, D.C.: Government Printing Office, 1865.

Report of the Joint Committee on Reconstruction at the First Session Thirty-Ninth Congress. Washington, D.C.: Government Printing Office, 1866.

Report of the Judge Advocate General on the "Order of American Knights" or "Sons of Liberty," a Western Conspiracy in Aid of the Southern Rebellion. Washington, D.C.: no pub., [1864].

Report of the Treasurer and Selectmen of the Town of Conway for the Fiscal Year Ending March 14, 1865. Concord, N.H.: William Butterfield, 1865.

Rhea, Gordon C. *The Battle of the Wilderness, May 5–6, 1864.* Baton Rouge: Louisiana University Press, 1994.

————. *The Battles for Spotsylvania Court House and the Road to Yellow Tavern, May 7–12, 1864.* Baton Rouge: Louisiana State University Press, 1997.

————. *To the North Anna River: Grant and Lee, May 13–25, 1864.* Baton Rouge: Louisiana State University Press, 2000.

Richardson, Heather Cox. *West from Appomattox: The Reconstruction of America after the Civil War.* New Haven, Conn.: Yale University Press, 2007.

Robertson, James I., Jr., ed. *The Civil War Letters of General Robert McAllister.* 1965. Reprint. Baton Rouge: Louisiana State University Press, 1998.

Robertson, William Glenn. *Back Door to Richmond: The Bermuda Hundred Campaign, April–June, 1864.* 1987. Reprint. Baton Rouge: Louisiana State University Press, 1991.

[Roe, Alfred S., ed.] *The Melvin Memorial.* Cambridge, Mass.: Riverside Press, 1910.

Rosenblatt, Emil, and Ruth Rosenblatt, eds. *Hard Marching Every Day: The Civil War Letters of Private Wilbur Fisk, 1861–1865.* Lawrence: University Press of Kansas, 1992.

Salecker, Gene Eric. *Disaster on the Mississippi: The* Sultana *Explosion, April 27, 1865.* Annapolis, Md.: Naval Institute Press, 1996.

Sandburg, Carl. *Lincoln Collector: The Story of Oliver R. Barrett's Great Private Collection.* New York: Bonanza Books, 1960.

Sauers, Richard A., ed. *The Civil War Journal of Colonel William J. Bolton, 51st Pennsylvania, April 20, 1861–August 2, 1865.* Conshohocken, Pa.: Combined Publishing, 2000.

Schiller, Herbert M. *The Bermuda Hundred Campaign.* Dayton, Ohio: Morningside Press, 1988.

Scott, Robert Garth, ed. *Forgotten Valor: The Memoirs, Journals, and Civil War Letters of Orlando B. Willcox.* Kent, Ohio: Kent State University Press, 1999.

Sears, Stephen W., ed. *The Civil War Papers of George B. McClellan.* New York: Ticknor and Fields, 1989.

————. *Controversies and Commanders: Dispatches from the Army of the Potomac.* Boston: Houghton Mifflin, 1999.

Shannon, Fred Albert, ed. *The Civil War Letters of Sergeant Onley Andrus.* Urbana: University of Illinois Press, 1947.

Sherman, William T. *Memoirs of Gen. W. T. Sherman.* 4th ed. 2 vols. in 1. New York: Charles L. Webster, 1891.

Simon, John Y., ed. *The Papers of Ulysses S. Grant.* 30 vols. Carbondale: Southern Illinois University Press, 1967–2008.

Simpson, Brooks D. *Let Us Have Peace: Ulysses S. Grant and the Politics of War and Reconstruction, 1861–1868.* Chapel Hill: University of North Carolina Press, 1991.

Simpson, Brooks D., and Jean V. Berlin, eds. *Sherman's Civil War: Selected Correspondence of William T. Sherman, 1860–1865.* Chapel Hill: University of North Carolina Press, 1999.

Skinner Fine Books and Manuscripts Auction Catalogue. Boston, October 30, 2005.

Smith, Lester W., ed. "The Andersonville Diary of Private Alfred Lyth." *Niagara Frontier* 8, no. 1 (Spring, 1961), 14, 19–24.

Sommers, Richard J. *Richmond Redeemed: The Siege at Petersburg*. Garden City, N.Y.: Doubleday, 1981.

Sparks, David S., ed. *Inside Lincoln's Army: The Diary of Marsena Rudolph Patrick, Provost Marshal General, Army of the Potomac*. New York: Thomas Yoseloff, 1964.

Stephens, Alexander H. *A Constitutional View of the Late War between the States: Its Causes, Character, Conduct, and Results*. Philadelphia: National Publishing Company, [1868–70].

Sumner, Merlin E., ed. *The Diary of Cyrus B. Comstock*. Dayton, Ohio: Morningside, 1987.

Supplement to the Official Records of the Union and Confederate Armies. 100 vols. Wilmington, N.C.: Broadfoot Publishing, 1994–99.

Sword, Wiley. *Embrace an Angry Wind: The Confederacy's Last Hurrah — Spring Hill, Franklin, and Nashville*. New York: HarperCollins, 1992.

Sylvester, Lorna Lutes, ed. "The Civil War Letters of Charles Harding Cox." *Indiana Magazine of History* 68, no. 3 (September, 1972), 181–239.

Taylor, Walter H. *Four Years with General Lee*. 1877. Reprint, with an introduction and notes by James I. Robertson Jr. Bloomington: Indiana University Press, 1962.

Thompson, Richard Means, and Richard Wainwright, eds. *Confidential Correspondence of Gustavus Vasa Fox, Assistant Secretary of the Navy, 1861–1865*. 2 vols. New York: Naval Historical Society, 1918–1919.

Tilley, Nannie M., ed. *Federals on the Frontier: The Diary of Benjamin F. McIntyre, 1862–1864*. Austin: University of Texas Press, 1963.

Tower, R. Lockwood, ed. *Lee's Adjutant: The Wartime Letters of Colonel Walter Herron Taylor, 1862–1865*. Columbia: University of South Carolina Press, 1995.

Towne, Stephen E., ed. *A Fierce, Wild Joy: The Civil War Letters of Colonel Edward J. Wood, 48th Indiana Volunteer Infantry Regiment*. Knoxville: University of Tennessee Press, 2007.

Trefousse, Hans L. *Reconstruction: America's First Effort at Racial Democracy*. New York: Van Nostrand Reinhold, 1971.

———. *Thaddeus Stevens: Nineteenth-Century Egalitarian*. 1997. Reprint. Mechanicsburg, Pa.: Stackpole Books, 2001.

Trial of Henry Wirz. House Executive Document 23, 40th Congress, 2nd session.

Trimble, Richard M., ed. *Brothers 'Til Death: The Civil War Letters of William, Thomas, and Maggie Jones, 1861–1865*. Macon, Ga.: Mercer University Press, 2000.

Turner, Richard, and Vernon Turner, comps. *Letters of the Samuel Cook Turner Family, 1859–1889*. N.p.: privately published, 1995.

U.S. Congress. *Congressional Globe*. 38th and 39th Congresses.

Van der Linden, Frank. *The Dark Intrigue: The True Story of a Civil War Conspiracy*. Golden, Colo.: Fulcrum Publishing, 2007.

Wainwright, Nicholas B., ed. *A Philadelphia Perspective: The Diary of Sidney George Fisher, Covering the Years 1834–1871*. Philadelphia: Historical Society of Pennsylvania, 1967.

Wallner, Peter A. *Franklin Pierce: Martyr for the Union*. Concord, N.H.: Plaidswede Publishing, 2007.

Walton, William, ed. *A Civil War Courtship: The Letters of Edwin Weller from Antietam to Atlanta*. Garden City, N.Y.: Doubleday, 1980.

War of the Rebellion: A Compilation of the Official Records of the Union and Confederate Armies. 128 vols. Washington, D.C.: Government Printing Office, 1880–1901.

Warren, Stanley, ed. *The Effects of War: Letters of Joseph S. Rogers*. Warner, N.H.: Warner Historical Society, 2008.

Watson, Ronald, ed. *From Ashby to Andersonville: The Civil War Diary and Reminiscences of George A. Hitchcock, Private, Company A, 21st Massachusetts Regiment, August 1861–January 1865*. Campbell, Calif.: Savas Publishing, 1997.

Waugh, John C. *Reelecting Lincoln: The Battle for the 1864 Presidency*. [Cambridge, Mass.]: Da Capo Press, 1997.

Weber, Jennifer L. *Copperheads: The Rise and Fall of Lincoln's Opponents in the North*. New York: Oxford University Press, 2006.

Weld, Stephen M. *War Diary and Letters of Stephen Minot Weld, 1861–1865*. Boston: Massachusetts Historical Society, 1979.

Wert, Jeffry D. *From Winchester to Cedar Creek: The Shenandoah Campaign of 1864*. New York: Simon & Schuster, 1987.

Wiggins, Sarah Woolfolk, ed. *The Journals of Josiah Gorgas, 1857–1878*. Tuscaloosa: University of Alabama Press, 1995.

Williams, Charles Richard, ed. *Diary and Letters of Rutherford Birchard Hayes, Nineteenth President of the United States*. 5 vols. Columbus: Ohio State Archaeological and Historical Society, 1914–26.

Wittenberg, Eric J. *Little Phil: A Reassessment of the Civil War Leadership of Gen. Philip H. Sheridan*. Washington, D.C.: Brassey's, 2002.

Wynne, Lewis N., and Robert A. Taylor, eds. *This War So Horrible: The Civil War Diary of Hiram Smith Williams, 40th Alabama Confederate Pioneer*. Tuscaloosa: University of Alabama Press, 1993.

Younger, Edward, ed. *Inside the Confederate Government: The Diary of Robert Garlick Hill Kean*. Baton Rouge: Louisiana University Press, 1973.

Newspapers

Advertiser and Eastern Townships Sentinel, Waterloo, Canada East
American Traveler, Boston, Mass.
Boston (Mass.) *Daily Advertiser*
Boston (Mass.) *Evening Transcript*
Boston (Mass.) *Herald*
Burlington (Vt.) *Free Press*
Charleston (S.C.) *Mercury*
Chicago Tribune
Cincinnati (Ohio) *Daily Commercial*
Daily Bulletin, Memphis, Tenn.

Daily Chronicle, Portsmouth, N.H.
Daily Gate City, Keokuk, Iowa
Daily Picayune, New Orleans, La.
Daily Times, Leavenworth, Kan.
Daily Virginian, Lynchburg
Dakotian, Yankton, Dakota Territory
Democratic Standard, Concord, N.H.
Detroit (Mich.) *Free Press*
Eastern Townships Gazette and Shefford County Advertiser, Granby, Canada East
Evening News, Louisville, Ky.
Kansas Daily Tribune, Lawrence
Keene (N.H.) *Sentinel*
Memphis (Tenn.) *Daily Avalanche*
New Hampshire Gazette, Portsmouth
New Hampshire Patriot, Concord
New Orleans (La.) *Daily Picayune*
New Orleans (La.) *Times*
New York Herald
New York Times
New York Tribune
New York World
North Missouri Courier, Hannibal
Oxford Democrat, Paris, Maine
Philadelphia (Pa.) *Weekly Times*
Portland (Maine) *Daily Press*
Prairie du Chien (Wis.) *Courier*
Raleigh (N.C.) *Standard*
Richmond (Va.) *Dispatch*
Richmond (Va.) *Examiner*
Richmond (Va.) *Sentinel*
Richmond (Va.) *Times*
Richmond (Va.) *Whig*
Saint Albans (Vt.) *Messenger*
Southern Recorder, Milledgeville, Ga.
Sumter Republican, Americus, Ga.
Union and Dakotian, Yankton, Dakota Territory
Washington (D.C.) *Star*
Westfield (N.Y.) *Republican*
Weekly Herald, Saint Joseph, Mo.

Miscellaneous

Joseph P. Brainerd gravestone inscription, Greenwood Cemetery, Saint Albans, Vt.

Sources and Acknowledgments

One of my most frustrating discoveries, as a boy obsessed with Civil War history, was that many famous wartime tales simply could not have been true. Worse yet, it seemed nearly impossible to distinguish between those that were true and those that were not. Once I reached the stage of following those stories to their original sources, it became clear that the most unreliable anecdotes were usually those that had been recorded farthest in time from the events they described. Letters, diaries, and documents from the target period have to be weighed for motive or misapprehension, but those same flaws grow more complicated and less easy to detect when an account is recorded after the passage of time, which adds the handicap of fading or distorted memory. For the purpose of historical interpretation, therefore, I began seeking increasingly larger proportions of contemporary sources, until eventually I developed a decided prejudice against anything written very long after the fact. That habit began producing interesting diversions from conventional interpretations, much as court testimony leads to surprising conclusions when even the most reliable hearsay is excluded. I usually no longer consider the recollections of witnesses except to compare accounts, to argue a point, or to describe crucial events that are recorded only retrospectively, and generally not even then without an additional leavening of skepticism.

My debts to the curators and assistants in manuscript repositories around the country are therefore very heavy, and so numerous that I could not devote enough space to the individual recognition they deserve. The greatest concentration is naturally in New England, where states are small and libraries plentiful, and I am particularly grateful to the following: Paul Carnahan and Marjorie Strong at the Vermont Historical Society; Jan Albers, director of the Sheldon Museum in Middlebury, Vermont; A. J. McDonald of the St. Albans Museum in St. Albans, Vermont; Jeff Marshall and Prudence Doherty, in Special Collections at the University of Vermont; Sarah Hartwell, of the Rauner Library at Dartmouth College; Bill Copeley and Peter Wallner, at the New Hampshire Historical Society; Bill Ross, of Milne Special Collections at the University of New Hampshire; Frank Mevers, recently retired as state archivist at the New Hampshire Division of Archives and Records Management, in Concord; Nick Noyes, Bill Barry, and Jamie Kingman Rice at the Maine Historical Society; Peter Drummey and several others at the Massachusetts Historical Society; Sean P. Casey at the Boston Public Library; Jackie Penny, Nigel Gully, and Elizabeth Pope, at the American Antiquarian Society, in Worcester; Karen Eberhart at the Rhode Island Historical Society; Phil Weimerskirch, at the Providence Public Library; Kathryn James and Cynthia Ostroff, of the Beinecke and Sterling libraries, at Yale University. A little farther afield, I am indebted to the very accommodating Ellen Schwanekamp, at the Chautauqua County Historical Society in Westfield, New York; Mary Huth, in Special Collections at the University of Rochester; Ann Sindelar of the Western Reserve Historical Society, in Cleveland; Gwen Mayer, at the Hudson Library and Historical Society in Hudson, Ohio; Nan Card, at the Rutherford B. Hayes Presidential Library in Fremont, Ohio; John E. Haas and Janice Tallman, at the Ohio Historical Society; Anne Shepherd, of the Cincinnati Historical Society; Betsy Caldwell and others of her colleagues at the Indiana Historical Society; Nelson Lankford, as well as the library staff, at the Virginia Historical Society; Steve Nielsen, Bridget White, Eric Mortenson, Tracey Baker, and Hampton Smith, at the Minnesota Historical Society; Andrea Faling, at the Nebraska Historical Society; Lin Fredericksen and Darrell Garwood, at the Kansas State Historical Society; Thomas Miller, of the Western Historical Manuscript Collection at the University of Missouri; Dennis Northcott, of the Missouri Historical Society; George Rugg, at Notre Dame; Brian Dunnigan, Barbara DeWolfe, Bethany Anderson, and Janet Bloom, of the Clements Library, as well as Malgosia Myc and Marilyn McNitt of the Bentley Historical Library, all at the University of Michigan; Thomas D. Hamm, at Earlham College; Kathryn Hodson, of Special Collections at the University of Iowa; Olga Tsapina and Juan Gomez, of the Huntington Library in San Marino, California; Kathy Lafferty, at the University of Kansas; Jeffrey Flannery, Bruce Kirby, Jennifer Brathovde, and Patrick Kerwin, in the manuscript reading room at the Library of Congress; and, as always, Richard Sommers and David Keough, as well as the late Art Bergeron, of the U.S. Army Military History Institute.

Several other historians have contributed generously to the source material for this book, as they did for several of those that preceded it. Stephen Sears, George Rable, and A. Wilson Greene regularly shared the results of their extensive research on overlapping subjects, besides passing on research tips they stumbled across incidentally, and each has occasionally given me the benefit of his assessments of various sources or interpretations.

Will Greene, now removed to the fringes of the Chattanooga battlefield from his longtime home on the Petersburg battlefield, applied his phenomenal knowledge of Civil War geography, characters, and military actions to my manuscript, rescuing me from endless embarrassing mistakes besides giving me priceless opinions on presentation and interpretation. Jeff Wieand, of Concord, Massachusetts, also scrutinized the entire manuscript with a practiced eye for actual or inadvertent inconsistency and logical flaws, some of which led to stylistic revision and some to substantive reevaluation. While Jeff did not choose the title of the book, or suggest the preface, he is directly responsible for both being much different from what they were.

A number of very competent, congenial, and accommodating folks at Houghton Mifflin (now Houghton Mifflin Harcourt) have guided the production of the four-volume series that this book completes. The late Harry Foster initiated the idea and escorted the first volume through all its editorial vicissitudes, while Will Vincent and Nicole Angeloro carried on for the following volumes, and Larry Cooper saw each volume safely through the final phases of publication. Freelance copyeditor Melissa Dobson applied the same reliable eye to all four manuscripts, leaving me with a much humbler impression of my presumed perfection as a proofreader, and Catherine Schneider has been a very patient, helpful, and painstaking cartographer.

Ellen Schwindt also read the manuscript, and gave me the perspective of the well-educated general reader. She reminded me that not everyone knows instinctively which uniform every character wore, or where each battlefield is located, or even who won or lost all the major engagements. She also often reminds me, without saying a word, how fortunate I am to have lured her to New Hampshire.

Index